# The German Settlements in Bessarabia

## A Study of the German Immigration to, Successful Settlement in, and Ultimate Abandonment of Bessarabia

Burkett W. Huey

TIPS Technical Publishing
Carrboro, NC

ISBN 978-1-890586-48-5 (print)
ISBN 978-1-890586-49-2 (ePub)
ISBN 978-1-890586-50-8 (mobi)

---

Library of Congress Cataloging-in-Publication Data
Names: Huey, Burkett, 1941- author.
Title: The German settlements in Bessarabia : a study of the German
   immigration to, successful settlement in, and ultimate abandonment of
   Bessarabia / Burkett Huey.
Description: Carrboro, NC : TIPS Technical Pub., [2014]
Identifiers: LCCN 2016018140 (print) | LCCN 2016018554 (ebook) | ISBN
   9781890586485 | ISBN 9781890586492 (ePub) | ISBN 9781890586508 (mobi)
Subjects: LCSH: Germans—Bessarabia (Moldova and Ukraine)—History. |
   Bessarabia (Moldova and Ukraine)—History. | Bessarabia (Moldova and
   Ukraine)—Ethnic relations. | Bessarabia (Moldova and Ukraine)—Emigration
   and immigration—History. | Germany—Emigration and immigration—History,
Classification: LCC DK509.35.G3 H84 2016 (print) | LCC DK509.35.G3 (ebook) |
   DDC 947.6/00431—dc23
LC record available at https://lccn.loc.gov/2016018140

---

TIPS Technical Publishing, Inc.
108 E. Main Street, Suite 4
Carrboro, NC 27510
www.technicalpublishing.com

Copy editing and indexing: J. K. Maxwell
Design and composition: Robert Kern
Proofreading: Sarah-Gray Lesley

Printed and bound in the United States of America

*For Bertha Raugust Huey who sparked my curiosity*

*and Mary Carroll Huey who encouraged its development*

# Contents

# List of Tables

# List of Illustrations

## Maps

## Photographs

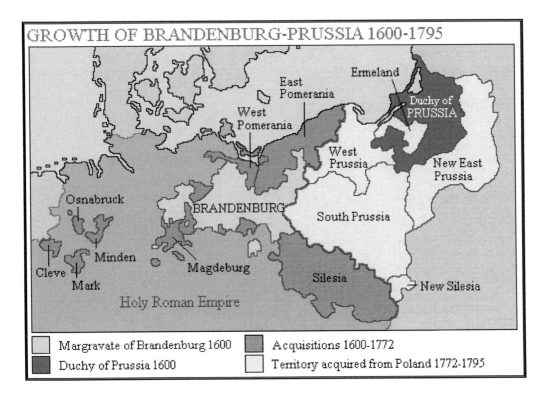

GROWTH OF BRANDENBURG-PRUSSIA 1600-1795

Ermeland

East Pomerania

West Pomerania

Duchy of PRUSSIA

West Prussia

New East Prussia

Osnabruck

BRANDENBURG

South Prussia

Minden

Cleve

Magdeburg

Mark

Silesia

New Silesia

Holy Roman Empire

Margravate of Brandenburg 1600

Acquisitions 1600-1772

Duchy of Prussia 1600

Territory acquired from Poland 1772-1795

**The Prussian provinces east of Brandenburg**

The German Immigration Routes to Bessarabia and South Russia from Prussia, Württemberg and the Rhineland, Part 1 (Courtesy of The American Historical Society of Germans from Russia)

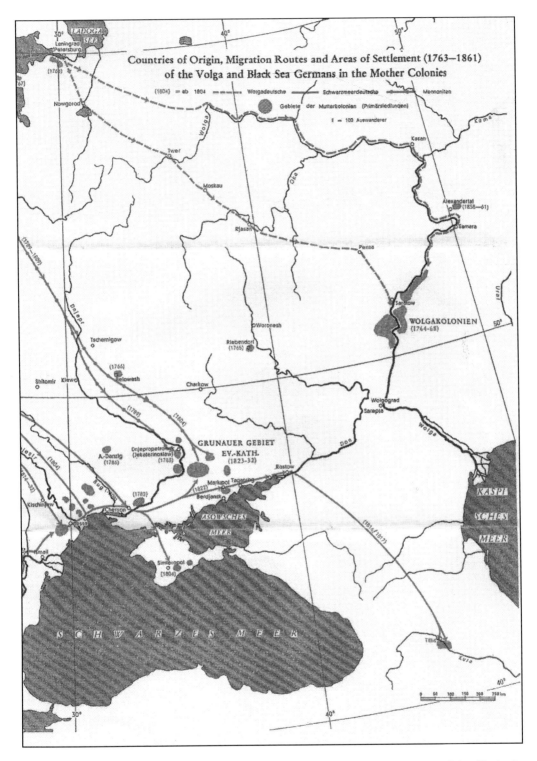

The German Immigration Routes to Bessarabia and South Russia from Prussia, Württemberg and the Rhineland, Part 2 (Courtesy of The American Historical Society of Germans from Russia)

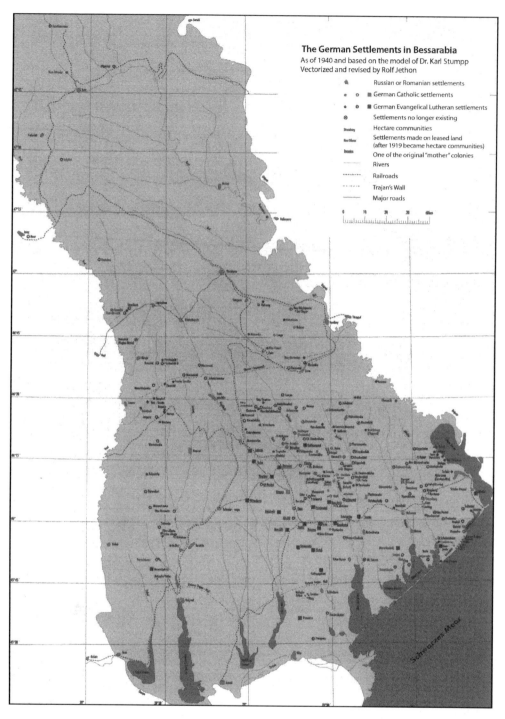

The German Settlements in Bessarabia (as of 1940 and based on the model of Dr. Karl Stumpp and vectorized by Rolf Jethon) (Courtesy of Rolf Jethon)

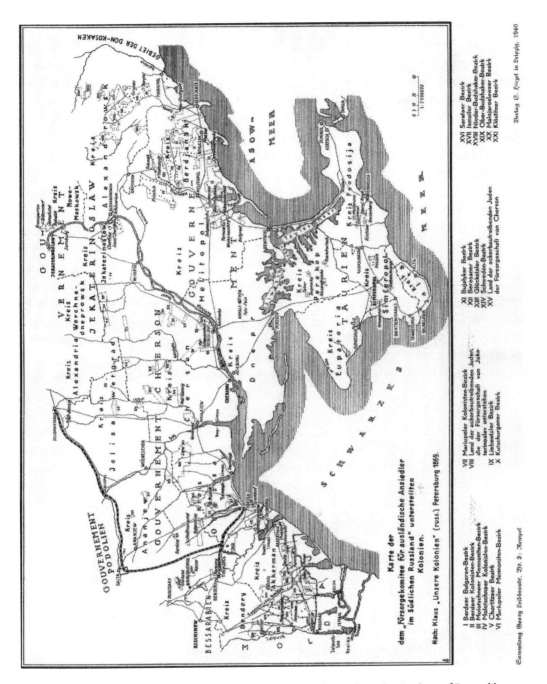

The 1869 Welfare Committee Map of the German Settlements in the South Russian Provinces of Bessarabia, Xerson, Tauride and Ekaterinoslav (Courtesy of The Germans from Russia Heritage Society)

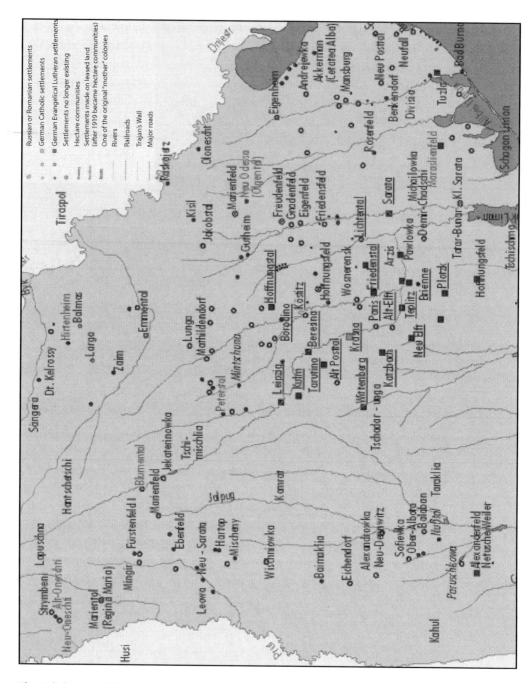

The Budjak Region of Bessarabia where the Majority of the German Settlements were Located
(Underlined settlement names indicate the original (1814-1841) colonies) (Courtesy of Rolf Jethon)

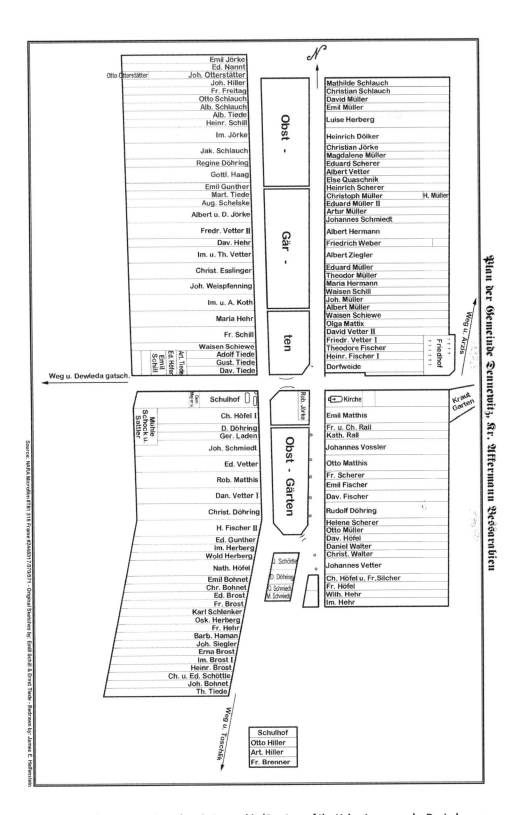

The Village Plan of the Dennewitz Colony in Bessarabia (Courtesy of the Heimatmuseum der Deutschen aus Bessarabien, Stuttgart)

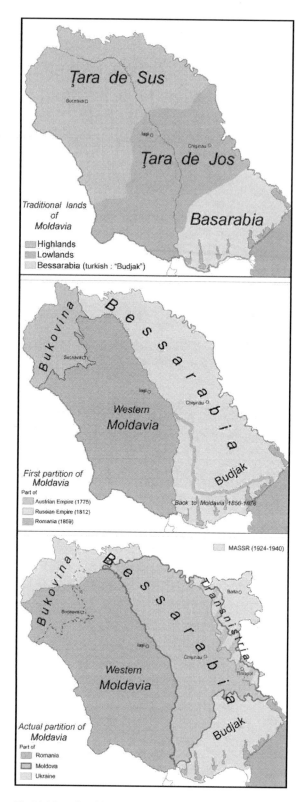

The Division of Moldavia

# Introduction

# Limited Sources Shape the Study of German Bessarabia

The Germans who settled in Bessarabia formed the last part of a large German peasant immigration to Imperial Russia. The Germans had been invited to settle underpopulated frontier areas of Imperial Russia. Such immigration started in the 1760s when Catherine the Great invited Germans to settle land along both sides of the Volga River near Saratov. In the period from 1790 to 1806, her son, Tsar Paul, and his son, Alexander I, invited large numbers of Germans to settle in southern Ukraine east of the Dniester River on land Russia had taken from the Ottoman Empire.

After 1806, Russia continued to seek control over more Ottoman territory beyond the Dniester River and even beyond the Danube estuary bordering the Black Sea coast. In May 1812, Tsar Alexander I concluded another peace with the Ottoman Empire. Under the terms of the Treaty of Bucharest, Imperial Russia obtained roughly 17,600 square miles (46,000 square kilometers) of additional territory that lay between the Dniester and Prut rivers running inland from the Black Sea coast to the base of the Carpathians. Historically, this area was the eastern half of the province of Moldavia, but to help secure its independent possession, Imperial Russia renamed this area Bessarabia. Following the defeat of Napoleon in 1814 and continuing up until the early 1830s, Russia continued to encourage the immigration of Germans. While the Southern Ukraine continued to be a destination for German immigrants, now a large number were settled in the newly acquired province of Bessarabia.

It is important to note that the Germans who settled in Bessarabia represent just a small portion of the German population that immigrated to Russia. Until the end of World War I, the German settlements in Bessarabia appear to have developed along roughly similar lines to those of German settlements elsewhere in Russia. While this study will argue that the Germans in Bessarabia were generally among the economically better off German populations in Russia and had the fewest numbers of landless poor, it would be hard to argue that, apart from having avoided the terrible consequences of Soviet life, their experiences in Russia were fundamentally different or special. What justifies a separate study of the Bessarabian Germans is that far more data has been preserved on this group of Germans than on any of the other German populations in Russia.

More records exist about the German settlements in Bessarabia because these Germans left en masse for Germany in 1940 and were able to take pieces of their history with them. They were able to do so because they left Bessarabia under the aegis of an agreement between the Soviet Union and Nazi-ruled Germany. The 1939 Molotov-Ribbentrop Pact allowed Germany to attack Poland and also permitted the Soviet Union to seek to annex former provinces of Imperial Russia that had become independent following the collapse of Imperial Russia in 1917–18. Bessarabia was one such province. In 1918, it became part of Romania. In June 1940, the Soviet Union attacked Romanian forces in Bessarabia, defeated them, and annexed Bessarabia. The Molotov-Ribbentrop Agreement permitted the German government to negotiate terms by which ethnic Germans in Bessarabia would be offered the opportunity to leave Bessarabia and resettle in Germany.

In contrast, Germans settled elsewhere in Russia had no such opportunity to leave and in doing so seek to preserve their lives, their communities, and their history. Instead, they were forced to endure the actions of the Soviet Union, which, in the interests of state power, starved them, confiscated their land, animals, and equipment, destroyed their communities and communal lives, and ultimately exiled them to Kazakhstan and Siberia. Their troubles were multiplied by the consequences of Germany's violent attack on the Soviet Union that led to the occupation of the Ukraine, which in the end caused many Germans there to flee as refugees. Though not living in the path of the fighting, the Volga Germans were also exiled to Siberia soon after Germany attacked the Soviet Union. Some Germans from the Ukraine were exiled as well in the early months of the war, but most Germans remained there under the occupation of the German army, to flee when the Wehrmacht began to retreat, or remain to be gathered in and exiled when Soviet control was reestablished. Even many of those who managed to reach Germany were retaken by Soviet authorities and shipped back to prison camps in Siberia as traitors. Whether forced into exile or fleeing as refugees, Germans from the Ukraine and Volga regions were not able keep control of many personal, community, or church records. The fate of those records is not known. Indeed, the same can be said of civil government records from the areas of Russia, the Ukraine, and Bessarabia where the Germans had formerly lived.

While far more is known about the Bessarabian Germans than about the other German populations who settled in Russia, it must also be noted that the available information on the Bessarabian Germans contains significant gaps and limitations.

Information about the Bessarabian Germans is quite rich in some areas, but sketchy or even totally missing in others. On the positive side, demographic information is particularly rich. This allows studies of population characteristics such as life spans, average ages at marriage, and family sizes to be particularly well grounded. Such demographic data also point to improving economic conditions and highlight the wide geographic backgrounds of the population and the mix of different regional German cultures in the colonial population. The available data are also quite strong concerning the founding of the different colonies in Bessarabia, their early economic development, and their struggles, successes, and failures. In contrast, there are very few data available concerning political and social issues within the settlements or on their relationships with the Imperial Russian government or, after World War I, with the Romanian government. Economic conditions in the second half of the nineteenth century, so important for understanding how the Bessarabian Germans could materially expand the number of their settlements or have the wherewithal to immigrate to North America, must often be intuited. There are few firsthand accounts from Bessarabian Germans. The available data are also skewed by the fact that there is far more material available on the villages of Kulm, Leipzig, Tarutino, and Sarata than on other Bessarabian villages.

It is to be hoped that potentially rich material on the German settlements in Bessarabia continues to be preserved in archives in different centers of authority of what was once Imperial Russia. It would appear that the Russian government regularly made economic studies of the colonies, kept track of civic, social, and political issues, gathered data on financial and food assets maintained in the German communities as well as on crime statistics, and after 1870, regularly considered the potential for disloyalty among its German population. Such archives might also contain detailed information on land sales and the means Germans found for funding these, and assessments of attitudes of emigrants leaving Russia, the numbers of the landless, and their potential for creating social unrest. As will be noted later in this chapter, a few scholars have had limited access to archival material that only whets the interest in having a better understanding of what has been preserved. Unfortunately, it is not possible to suggest even the general outlines of what archives might contain. The bitter resentment felt toward Germany in the Soviet Union following World War II did not encourage that government to permit access to materials about the German settlements in Russia. The breakup of the Soviet Union in 1990 has created new opportunities that have only slightly been explored. Post-Soviet Russia has let the uncertain and changing relations with the West govern its interest in opening state archives in St. Petersburg and Moscow. Some material has appeared from archives in Chisinau, now the capital of Moldova, once (as Kishinev) the provincial capital of Imperial Russian Bessarabia. There may be rich material in the district archives of Akkerman, now Bilhorod Dnistrovs'kyi, and Odessa in the Ukraine, and in the Romanian state archives in Bucharest.

A story must always follow its sources. In writing about the Bessarabian Germans, one is faced with both strengths in some areas and major limitations in others. This study will of necessity focus on those areas where existing data shed light. I hesitate to invite readers into a consideration of this background material, but in order to understand what can be said about the Bessarabian Germans and what cannot, it is necessary to have some perspective of the available sources. The goal of this chapter will be to give an overview of the major data sources on the Bessarabian Germans and thus of the topics that will be addressed in the body of this work.

In leaving Bessarabia in 1940, the Germans were allowed to take with them church documents and some of their records, photographs, and history. These records survived World War II and now form a major source for any study of German Bessarabia. Other records of German Bessarabia exist, some published in Imperial Russia during the nineteenth century, some by Germans in Romanian Bessarabia after World War I, and others collected by scholars and ethnographers in Germany interested in the German-speaking diaspora in Europe.[1] That there exists sufficient source material to consider even a limited historical study of German Bessarabia should be understood as the result of historical anomalies: that Bessarabia became part of Romania and not the Soviet Union in 1918, and that the Germans there were permitted to leave Bessarabia in 1940 when the Soviet Union gained control.

As noted above, the richest sources of data on German Bessarabia are demographic. When they left for Germany, the Bessarabians brought with them detailed church records of births, marriages, and deaths. These are in German. The richest material begins around 1833–35 and ends in 1885,[2] when the responsibility for maintaining such records was transferred to the local civic government district and *volost*[3] offices established under the reforms of Tsar Alexander II. The most complete records are those covering citizens living in one of the colonial villages established between 1814 and 1842 by the Imperial Russian government. These would be citizens living in the major Evangelical Lutheran parishes of Tarutino (1815), Alt Arzis (1818), Sarata (1830), Alt Elft[4] (1841), and Klöstitz (1843). Data from the new settlements founded after 1860 tend to be far less complete. Some of the new settlements, such as Eigenheim, founded in 1861, maintained records even before a church was built there. Perhaps other villages did as well, but their records do not appear to have been brought to Germany during the resettlement. As these records are from the Evangelical Lutheran parishes, its data do not include material from the Catholic villages, such as Krasna. These records of births, marriages, and deaths were organized by parishes of the Evangelical Lutheran church in Bessarabia.

When the Bessarabian Germans left Bessarabia in 1940, a copy of this population data collection was brought with them to Germany. Sometime during World War II, it was placed in the German state archives in Leipzig. Following the war,

---

1.  German nationals studying the diaspora of Germans settled outside of Germany could visit Romanian Bessarabia, and German speakers from Romanian Bessarabia could and did visit Germany. However, as the Soviet Union placed significant hurdles to travelers wishing to visit and all but barred external travel for its citizens, contact with the German communities in the Soviet Union before the start of World War II was significantly more limited.

2.  Demographic records for the period after the founding of the colony and up to 1833 do exist. However, as the best and most accessible collections of these data are currently the Mormon databases, they are organized by individual and so difficult to use for wider purposes.

3.  Following the abolition of serfdom in the Imperial Russian state in 1861, the term *volost*, which heretofore had a wide range of historical meanings referring to a designated area of land or district, was also used to describe the smallest civil governing unit. In transliterating Russian words from Cyrillic to Latin letters, this study will use the International Scholarly System format. Exceptions will be made in the case of Russian words that have achieved some currency in English: thus Moscow instead of Moskva, St. Petersburg instead of Sankt Peterburg, the Dniester River instead of the Dnestr River, and in the present example, volost instead of volost'.

4.  The official name of the Alt Elft settlement was Fere Champenenoise I (when Neu Elft split off in 1822, it became Fere Champenenoise II). However, as throughout its history the colony was commonly called Alt Elft by the Germans in Bessarabia, that name will be used here.

the Leipzig archives came under the control of the government of East Germany (DDR); access to these archives was not generally available to scholars from the West. After the collapse of DDR in 1989, Mormon researchers photographed these records and brought them into the public domain. In 1998, a group of North American descendants of Germans from Russia created the Odessa Digital Library. Among the records put online by the Odessa Digital Library (hereafter referred to as the Odessa3 Collection) is an edited variant of the Bessarabian church records taken from the Mormon microfilms that further organizes these data by decade with names listed alphabetically into separate birth, marriage, and death records.[5]

There are many gaps in these records. In each of the parish listings there are several gaps of roughly a year for which no data appear and there seem to be no records from any parish for 1880.[6] Genealogical data put together by some Bessarabian German families show that even in the periods where parish records were being actively kept, there are births, deaths, and marriages that do not appear in the Odessa3 Collection. These family records suggest that perhaps the most frequently missing category of data in the parish records are deaths of children who lived less than a year. There is a wide variation in the actual data maintained. Depending, evidently, on the diligence of the record keeper, death records, for example, may or may not have the date of birth, the place of birth, or the maiden name of a married woman. The handwritten records are not always easy or even possible to read, so mistakes in interpretation are always possible. However, in order to see the actual written record, one must, in a cumbersome fashion, look up each record individually.

Yet despite the missing pieces, the Odessa3 Collection forms the most accessible and accurate compilation of demographic data from the German communities in Bessarabia. Moreover, it provides an almost unique data source for a large population of nineteenth-century German farmers. The organization of data by surname grouped by decade makes more general studies of population trends practical. It is possible, as a result, to use these data to create credible demographic and cultural studies concerning the nineteenth-century Bessarabian Germans on life spans, family sizes, average ages at marriage, ages at the births of children, frequency of marriage, family marital connections, and the changing naming patterns for children.

A second important demographic source on German Bessarabia is Arthur Flegel's *Extended Relationships of the Kulm, Leipzig, Tarutino Communities in Bessarabia, Russia.*[7] Flegel, an American descendent of Kulm and Leipzig colonists, published an extensive listing, organized by surname, of the residents of these three villages and their marital partners. His data frequently include forebears of these colonist families as well as descendants now living in the United States, Canada, and Germany. Flegel's collection is particularly good and detailed for the first three generations in

---

5. http://www.odessa3.org/collections/stpete/bess/.
6. In his introduction to the marriage data for the period 1835–39, Thomas A. Stangl provides a listing by parish of the different data gaps. Thus, for example, for marriages in Tarutino Parish: (1) all data before 1833; (2) 4 December 1841 to 12 December 1842; (3) 16 December 1843 to 28 December 1844; (4) 25 November 1848 to 27 November 1849; (5) 18 December 1864 to 22 January 1867; (6) late December 1871 to 28 December 1873; (7) 29 December 1879 to 29 December 1880; and (8) all after December 1885. Stangl further notes that some of the missing data are to be found in other parish and village records. Stangl, "Bessarabian Village Marriage Records, 183x" (N.p.: Odessa Digital Library, 1997), http://www.odessa3.org/collections/stpete/bess/link/bess183m.txt.
7. Arthur Flegel, *Extended Relationships of the Kulm, Leipzig, Tarutino Communities in Bessarabia, Russia*, Germans from Russia Heritage Collection (Fargo: North Dakota State University, 2005).

Bessarabia. It becomes more spotty after 1885, perhaps a reflection of the missing data in the parish sources. Flegel's data are generally more complete with regard to families who moved to North America than for those who remained in Bessarabia until 1940. Apart from church records, Flegel clearly has had access to a significant number of family records put together by the descendants of Kulm, Leipzig, and Tarutino settlers now living in North America. Flegel has clearly taken the trouble to go back to the individual village records and so provides detailed material from before 1835.

Flegel offers a different cut of the demographic data than is supplied in the Odessa3 Collection. The organization of data by family makes generational relationships easier to see and study. With Flegel's data it is also possible to see marital interconnections within village families as well as the growing frequency over time of marital connections with families outside the village. Flegel's collection of data on the first settlers of these villages is particularly important. The birth places of the first settlers and their children become an important source of information on both where the colonists were living before 1814 as well as data on family movements in this pre-Bessarabian period. Flegel's data on succeeding generations shed light on the increasingly crowded conditions in these villages, which, it will be argued, form a major rationale for both the creation of new German villages in Bessarabia and the emigration of Germans from Bessarabia to North America. As Flegel's data also include material on new families who moved into these villages after their founding, his data provide information on the frequency of incomers and the places from which they came. Thus, while the basis of Flegel's data is genealogical, his focus on collecting the total population provides information on the history of these villages, their demographic growth and interconnections, and their physical and economic health.

Flegel's study, though, is not without limitations. It would appear that his basic source was the Mormon films of the parish records discussed above. The Odessa3 compilation of these records, however, contains numbers of people from Tarutino, Kulm, and Leipzig who are not included in Flegel's research, as well as information on marriages, births, and deaths occurring within families about whom Flegel provides other information. Flegel evidently did not see the materials in the collection of accounts of village life published as the "1990 Kulm Heimatskalender," which includes a census listing of the first settlers of Kulm, collected in September 1815. Data from the 1835, 1850, and 1858 Welfare Committee village censuses are also missing from Flegel's study, but these may have come into the public domain after Flegel had completed his data collection.[8] Nonetheless, Flegel's extensive compila-

8.  Referred to throughout this study as the Welfare Committee, the full title of this agency of the Imperial Russian government was the Welfare Committee for Foreign Inhabitants in the Southern Region of Russia; in Russian, the *Popečitel'nij komitet ob inostrannyx poselencax južnogo kraja Rossija*, and in German, as many of its officials were German-speaking, the *Fürsorgekomitee der Ausländischen Ansiedler in Süd Rußland*. It was established in 1818 as a result of P. D. Kiselev's study. Following his recommendations (see discussion of this in chapter IV), it was created as a branch of the Ministry of the Interior in St. Petersburg, with powers independent of the provincial governors and their administrations. It replaced earlier less successful state efforts to administer the government's relations with the immigrant colonies. Its function was initially to facilitate the successful establishment of German (and some Bulgarian) colonies in South Russia and Bessarabia. It later became the official body through which the Imperial Russian government sought to nurture and improve those colonies, to gather data measuring the success of its investment in them, and to regulate them by implementing laws and regulations. The Welfare Committee also collected taxes from the colonies. For most of its existence, the Welfare Committee was headquartered in Odessa and maintained district offices throughout Bessarabia and South Russia.

tion provides unique, detailed, multigenerational pictures of families from these three villages. His data will be used extensively in this work and will likely encourage other studies. Particularly helpful, too, are Flegel's footnotes offering data on sources, dates, places of prior and further family movements, and variant spellings.

As Flegel's data will be an important source for the present study, it should be noted as well that, clearly, it is limited to data from just these three villages. In the absence of data from other Bessarabian German villages, data from Kulm, Leipzig, and Tarutino will be used tentatively to suggest wider patterns and conditions. At present, it cannot be known how accurate such generalizations might be, but caution is prudent. While recognizing the value of having extensive data from Kulm, Leipzig, and Tarutino, it is necessary to point out that this is also a limiting factor.

Ute Schmidt has published the only detailed study of German Bessarabia.[9] Her book provides a general overview of many important topics concerning German Bessarabia: the special geography of Bessarabia, when and how the Germans emigrated there, how they adapted to that land and thrived, their social and civic organizations, the increasing pressure to become more Russian and then after 1918, more Romanian, and finally their abrupt departure in 1940. The great strength of her study is the portrayal of cultural life in the German settlements. Her sections on religious life and education particularly stand out. Her study is especially enhanced by a wonderful collection of photographs, paintings, sketches, and illustrations that give particular richness to her evocation of the life within the German villages. As with any description of German Bessarabia, the limitations of the available data also have impact: material describing conditions in one village has to stand for a broader sway, and much of her material and focus is on conditions in the twentieth century where her richest data come from. In general, her interests are broadly descriptive rather than analytical and are less focused on economic, demographic, and political conditions than on cultural history. A consideration of sources on German Bessarabia in Russian is generally missing. Overall, *Bessarabia: German Colonists on the Black Sea*, is a well-organized study that covers the full historical period of German settlement in Bessarabia and has become a critical source for all future studies.

There also exist four important general histories of the German colonies in Imperial Russia that investigate their development, growth, and fates. None focus extensively on Bessarabia, or develop issues related specifically to the Bessarabian colonies. These general histories are works by Adam Giesinger, Ingeborg Fleischhauer, Detlef Brandes, and Lev V. Malinovskij.[10] Each addresses major issues in the history of the German colonies: the rationale behind the Russian government's efforts to invite Germans to settle in Russia; the difficulties in establishing the colonies (often on land never extensively cultivated before); the change over time in the relations

---

9. Ute Schmidt, *Bessarabia: German Colonists on the Black Sea*, trans. James T. Gessele (Fargo: GRHC & North Dakota State University Libraries, 2011). This book was originally published in German as *Bessarabien: Deutsche Kolonisten am Schwarzen Meer* (Potsdam, Ger.: Deutsches Kulturforum östliches Europa, 2008).

10. Adam Giesinger, *From Catherine to Khrushchev: The Story of Russia's Germans* (Winnipeg, Man.: Marian Press, 1974); Ingeborg Fleischhauer, *Die Deutschen im Zarenreich: Zwei Jahrhunderte deutsch-russische Kulturgemeinschaft* (Stuttgart, Ger.: Deutsche Verlags-Anstalt, 1986); Lev V. Malinovskij, *Social'naja i xozjajstvennaja istorija nemeckix kolonistov v južnoj Rossii (1762-1917)* (Barnaul, Rus.: IPP Altaj, 2010); and Detlef Brandes, *Von den Zaren Adoptiert: Die Deutschen Kolonisten und die Balkansiedler in Neurußland und Bessarabien 1751-1914* (Munich: R. Oldenbourg, 1993).

between the colonies and the Russian government and the changes in attitudes of Russians towards Germans living in their midst; the causes for the economic growth; the comparative general prosperity reached in the colonies in the nineteenth century; and the destruction of the German settlements in Soviet times. Each gives special weight to different issues. All four use some primary source materials, but the works by Brandes and Malinovskij are particularly important as they bring to light materials from Imperial Russian archives, from German newspapers in Imperial Russia, and from contemporary and near-contemporary studies of the German colonies made in the nineteenth and early twentieth centuries and published in Russian and German. By drawing attention to issues that were similarly experienced across all the German settlements in Russia, these studies give a much broader context to many events in Bessarabia.

Giesinger covers a broader time period, from the establishment of the Volga colonies in the mid-eighteenth century to the tribulations of the exiled Soviet Germans in Central Asia in the 1970s. His primary focuses are on the largest groups of settlements: the Volga Germans and the numerous Mennonite colonies in South Russia. Giesinger has a thorough background in the many German-language sources and brings a balanced overview of the extensive primary and secondary data available in the 1970s. He seems less familiar with Russian sources, and his conclusions sometimes reflect this. For example, in his treatment of the important decrees of Alexander II of 1871 and 1874, which fundamentally changed the relationship of the German colonies with the Russian state, he merely repeats the traditions and viewpoints of the colonists (that the decrees broke promises), without considering Russian motivations or seeking to weigh the competing interests involved or their potential effects on the German communities.

Fleischhauer's focus is mainly on issues concerning the Germans settled in Russia from the late nineteenth century onwards. She briefly covers the founding of the German settlements, and recognizes that the widely separated German communities in Russia developed under differing influences and circumstances. Fleischhauer makes extensive use of Russian sources, notably newspaper reports and captured government archives, several of which are primary sources not widely known.[11] A particular strength of Fleischhauer's study is the attention she pays to relations between the German communities and the Imperial Russian government and the changing attitudes of Russian popular opinion toward the German communities. Fleischhauer covers fewer topics than Giesinger but compensates for this by the accretion of detail from her sources. Fleischhauer is a major source of information about the studies conducted by the Russian government during the late 1860s that were concerned with the German settlements and led directly to Tsar Alexander II's Decree of 1871. Fleischhauer's focus is primarily on ordering the material she has found around specific topics, and she generally shies away from drawing conclusions or presenting arguments or interpretations.

Malinovskij's work focuses on social and economic questions in the German colonies of South Russia in the period from the mid-nineteenth century up to the end of World War I. While he covers in broad perspective the major issues

---

11. Ingeborg Fleischhauer was part of the group of researchers who gathered village data for Stumpp in the German-occupied Ukraine during World War II. Several of her sources appear to be documents seen or confiscated by German authorities during that occupation.

concerning the German colonies in the Volga region, South Russia, and, to a lesser extent, Bessarabia, he pays closest attention to the Mennonite colonies in South Russia. Malinovskij uses a Marxist historical framework and so searches for signs that indicate the movement of the Germans in Russia from the stage of feudal agricultural holdings to bourgeois capitalist endeavors. For those reaching the latter stage, he hunts among groups of the poor and landless for emerging conflicts with the well-to-do farmers that would herald the expected transition out of capitalism. Given this focus, his study is particularly rich in highlighting the significant growth in the number of poor and landless Germans, whom he finds especially numerous among the Mennonites, and the increasing employment of the landless as temporary wage workers for richer farmers. Malinovskij also focuses on the moral issues raised by the widespread differentiation in wealth. As a result, though Malinovskij notes the great growth in prosperity that was achieved by most Germans living outside of the Mennonite districts, he offers little perspective on how this occurred or what consequences (apart from an increased number of landless citizens) it brought to the German settlements or social developments within these communities. This focus leads him to exaggerate poverty as almost the sole cause for the founding of daughter colonies and emigration. Malinovskij's frequent citation from archival materials, however, is an exciting reminder that these may contain rich, yet-to-be-studied materials, particularly with regard to the relations between the Imperial Russian government and the colonies. Malinovskij's work is also a reminder of the potential existence of archival collections of German-language newspapers published in Imperial Russia that may shed better light on economic, social, and political conditions within the German settlements.

Detlef Brandes's book on the German colonies in New Russia and Bessarabia is the most detailed and the most important of these general studies. His study is organized not chronologically, like the others, but by topics such as the arrival of the colonists in Russia, the economic development of the colonies, and the development of daughter colonies. He focuses not just on the German colonies but also on the colonies the Imperial Russian government established for Bulgarians and Gaugaz[12] in South Russia and Bessarabia. The great strength of his study is the great amount of pertinent data he has collected from pre-Revolutionary sources in Russia: from archives of the Imperial Russian ministries, from German-language newspapers from Odessa, and especially from many studies of the colonies, not well known heretofore, that were written in Russia mostly before World War I. A particularly important source for Brandes are the ministry archives in St. Petersburg that collected materials sent in by officials from South Russia and Bessarabia. Brandes and Malinovskij are the only historians of the Germans in Russia who have had the chance to work with material from these archives. Brandes appears to have been given much greater access to these materials. As a result, his book is a virtual treasure chest of information. Any study of the German colonies in Bessarabia and South Russia going forward will need to use and consider his picture of colonial conditions.

---

12. The Gaugaz are a Turkic-speaking Orthodox Christian people who lived in the eastern Balkans. Like the Bulgarians, they suffered hardships under Ottoman rule and so welcomed the invitation of Imperial Russia to settle in Bessarabia. Their colonies established in southwestern Bessarabia were established contemporaneously with those of the Germans.

Brandes, for the most part, lets the data he has collected speak for itself. The assumption behind this technique is that such data generally describe conditions existing in the German colonies and typify both the cast of other data seen but not used and the presumed features of data not yet accessed. The downside of this technique is that Brandes does not discuss the meanings of the similarities, differences, or complexities in the data he presents, nor does he address their causes or consequences.

There is another earlier general study that considers the German colonies in Russia. In 1843, Tsar Nicholas I invited August von Haxthausen, a German political economist and ethnographer, to travel through Russia. Haxthausen published an account of that journey and a commentary on the economic standing, and the dress, housing, and customs he found in the many villages and cities he visited.[13] Haxthausen's work contains a section on the Volga Germans and a longer one devoted to the Germans, especially the Mennonites, in South Russia. Haxthausen offers an interesting and educated commentary on the general economic health of the German villages and comparisons with neighboring Russian settlements. Haxthausen's study does not include material specific to German Bessarabia, which Haxthausen did not visit.

In considering the source material on German Bessarabia beyond genealogical data and the general studies of German colonies throughout Imperial Russia, one is struck as much by what is missing as by what exists. Few of the sources are firsthand accounts made by the Bessarabian German colonists themselves. The 1848 village histories, the Mutschall history of Tarutino, and the general study of Bessarabian villages that Albert Kern created stand out. Though family genealogies are increasingly appearing, some produced with a high degree of care and detail,[14] many are flawed by the use of assumed and suspect relationships.

The conduct of government within the German villages is another area for which there is very limited information. There is little that can be said about local politics, the varying or similar approaches to challenges or problems taken by different villages, what were the notable successes and failures in village administration, who were local leaders and what did they accomplish, or what social problems were faced or not faced. Similarly, it is not possible to trace the work of the Welfare Committee with the different German villages or its relationship with the two St. Petersburg ministries to which it reported. Archival material quoted by Brandes and Malinovskij gives glimpses into the relationship of the German villages with the

13. August von Haxthausen, *Studien über die inner Zustände, das Volksleben und insbesondere die ländliche Einrichtungen Rußlands*. Haxthausen's study was translated into English by Robert Faire as *The Russian Empire, Its People, Institutions and Resources*. Haxthausen, *The Russian Empire, Its People, Institutions and Resources*, trans. Robert Faire (London: Chapman and Hall, 1856).
14. Armin Zimmerman provides detailed information in German and English on several Bessarabian German families following connections of the Banko, Böttcher, Moldenhauer, and Mössner families, as well as a detailed listing of early settlers in fifteen Bessarabian German villages, which he has culled from the Odessa3 Digital Library and Flegel and posted at http://www.armin-zimmermann.eu/Bessarabien/index_englisch.html. Manfred Böhm has posted data in German on several Württemberg families who immigrated to the German villages of Alt Posttal, Borodino, Kulm, and Wittenberg in Bessarabia. His website, http://www2.genealogy.net/privat/boehm.m/index.html, however, has recently been pulled down. Doug Graumann has put together an extensive genealogy of the Graumanns of Kulm, Leipzig, and Tarutino, and the families they married into and posted this at http://wc.rootsweb.ancestry.com/cgibin/igm.cgi?op=show&db=dsgwest&recno=274.

Russian government, but no historian has had the detailed access to these materials that would permit even a limited study of these questions.

In contrast, there fortunately exist some data on the economic history of German Bessarabia. Three nineteenth-century economic surveys of the Bessarabian German colonies are known. These three surveys were made by the Welfare Committee and likely form part of repeated, possibly regular, studies the Welfare Committee made in its efforts to assess how well the Imperial Russian government's investment in these colonies was progressing. The surveys seek to delineate the economic state of the German colonies by counting their various assets. The surveys go down to the level of counting the numbers of animals, fruit trees, and grape vines. They note the different crops grown and their yields and provide village population levels. The three surveys were all made before 1860—that is, before the German settlements reached a mature economic footing. The light they cast is therefore on the early economic development of the German villages rather than on conditions when the villages were in their economic prime. While parts of several survey results are known, the reports and analyses written by the Welfare Committee for Ministry of Internal Affairs and the Ministry of State Domains in St. Petersburg are not.

While a proper and thorough history of German Bessarabia is currently out of reach, the many source materials on disparate aspects of German Bessarabia make it possible to patch together pictures, some detailed and some distant, that show portions of that history. This is not a history then, but steps toward one. If archives in Moldova, Russia, or the Ukraine do contain records of civil, tax, judicial, religious, and administrative affairs, or if memoirs or letters from the Bessarabian Germans come to light, then a better history can be written. Most of the existing sources on German Bessarabia focus on either limited time periods or specific narrow features of the settlements and their development. Given that the topics taken up in this study are derived from these sources, it is useful to look at the sources from this perspective.

## Data on the colonists who founded the first settlements in German Bessarabia
### Ethnographic work of Karl Stumpp

Karl Stumpp (1896–1982) produced a pioneering study of the Germans who came to South Russia and Bessarabia.[15] The chief focus of Stumpp's research was to identify the German colonists who established the first German settlements in Bessarabia and South Russia. Stumpp was particularly interested in tracing these colonists back to the villages in the German-speaking heartland from which they had emigrated. Working from what were disparate and often independent village sources, he put together detailed village-by-village lists of the people he presumed to be the original settlers. Stumpp also used this data to create a series of useful maps that locate the villages in Prussian Poland, Württemberg, Baden, Hesse, the Pfalz, and Alsace from which immigrants to Bessarabia and South Russia came. Of particular value is his identification of many of the locations of the German peasant communities

---

15. Karl Stumpp, *Die Auswanderung aus Deutschland nach Rußland in den Jahren 1763 bis 1862* (Tübingen: self-published, n.d.), translated into English: Stumpp, *The Emigration from Germany to Russia in the Years 1763 to 1862*, trans. J. S. Height (Lincoln, NE: American Historical Society of Germans from Russia, 1982).

in Prussian Poland. Such settlement locations have become harder to find, given the effort after World War II to sweep away all traces of the German presence in what was once Prussian Poland. Stumpp's lists of early colonists in Bessarabian settlements are not complete, as not all known immigrants are included, nor are they reliably accurate, as his lists mix together first-comers, their children born in Bessarabia, and later arrivals. Stumpp appears not to have been able to access the Bessarabian church records kept after World War II in the state archive in Leipzig, East Germany, which became available in the West only after 1989 and the fall of the DDR. The major strength of Stumpp's work lies in creating, from massively disparate sources, a reasonably accurate picture of the early colonists. His work in identifying the origins of the immigrants to Russia is particularly valuable. It is strongest in dealing with immigrants to Russia from Württemberg and the upper Rhineland, where Stumpp was able to aggregate data to show numbers of immigrants from specific villages.

Stumpp's life and work highlight sad and painful ironies implicit in any consideration of the German colonies in Russia: important material on the colonies exists in the public domain now because of the interest and support of the Nazi government in Germany, or because of its wartime occupation of Russia. With regard to German Bessarabia, a historical study is largely possible because Nazi Germany and the Soviet Union colluded to divide up spheres of interest in Eastern Europe. One small result of that collusion was the 1940 resettlement in Germany of the Bessarabian Germans, during which they brought to Germany some pieces of their history. Before World War II, Stumpp's career and intellectual interest in ethnography led him to associate himself with groups supported by and working in the interests of the Nazi government in Germany and its "racial" programs. During the war, Stumpp worked in the occupied Ukraine directing a research group that investigated the preservation of the German language and customs in the former German colonies there. This has led some to discredit his work on the basis that anything touched by the aims and interests of the Nazi German government should be seen as tainted and perhaps invalid.

Stumpp was a native of the German colony Alexanderhilf in South Russia near the border of Bessarabia. Very much a rarity among South Russian or Bessarabian Germans, he was educated at the university at Tübingen in Germany. After World War I, he came to Bessarabia in the early 1920s to teach high school in Tarutino. He returned to Germany in the 1930s to work with Dr. Georg Liebbrandt in the Institute for Germans in Foreign Lands, the Deutsches Ausland-Institut. This institute, referred to hereafter by its initials DAI, was made up of ethnographers, historians, and irredentists interested in the culture and history of German settlements outside of Germany in Eastern Europe. The institute sought to help those communities maintain their Germanness ("Deutschtum") and to increase their ties with Germany and its culture. The DAI, though not founded by the Nazi party, was increasingly funded by the Nazi government with whom it shared several interests, including that of bringing together the German diaspora in Europe.

Between July 1941 and March 1943, Stumpp was put in charge of an office in the occupied Soviet Ukraine, tasked with reporting on the degree to which citizens of villages, which had once been the German colonies of Imperial South Russia, had preserved German language and culture. This appears to be a task similar to one that the German army performed in Bessarabia in 1940 when signing up Bessarabian

Germans for resettlement. Stumpp, based in Dnepropetrovsk, was in charge of a group of researchers who visited the different German villages and then wrote reports about them.[16] It is not clear the degree to which Stumpp himself visited these villages. Stumpp's clear interest and background in the study of the ethnography give his work in the occupied Ukraine a certain rationale. On the other hand, since the German government's purpose for these investigations was to determine which citizens were to be considered Germans and thus to receive preferential, possibly life-saving, treatment, Stumpp's work has darker overtones connected to German atrocities committed in the occupied Ukraine. The investigation reports produced by the researchers working under Stumpp's command were created in conjunction with the work of the "Sonderkommando" military/police detachments. These special military units, sometimes using the village reports, sometimes accompanying the interviewers creating them, would execute Jews and exile Ukrainians and Russians found living in the German villages. As a senior civilian official of the Nazi government working in the occupied Ukraine, Stumpp should be presumed knowledgeable of the actions and intents of that government directed toward other ethnic populations.[17]

Stumpp's personal opinions, expressed in DAI documents from the 1930s and early 1940s, reflect anti-Semitic views.[18] His wartime activities in the occupied Ukraine darken his personal reputation and cloak his ethnographic data gathering in the colors of supporting and perhaps executing policies behind Nazi "racial" theories. Given that, following the war, Stumpp never apologized nor publically expressed sorrow or regret for the results of his actions, Samuel Sinner is right to criticize the Russian-German cause organizations both in Germany and North America for the unalloyed praise offered to Stumpp. Sinner, however, is wrong, I believe, in wishing to discard Stumpp's work because of Stumpp's personal moral failings and the prejudiced views of German ethnic superiority that appear in his work. The value of Stumpp's work rests on the

---

16. Adam Giesinger is quoted in Judith Rempel's report, saying that "from this base men went out to… German villages…and, with aid of local people, particularly teachers and village officials, filled out the prescribed questionnaires" (Judith Rempel, "Dorfberichte – Village Reports," lines 24–27, at http://www.odessa3.org/collections/war/reports/link/villrpt.txt). The questionnaires collected data on current village occupants, noting language capabilities, origins in Germany, and language proficiencies, as well as some genealogical records. The reports also focus on issues of the "racial" mixture and purity of the villagers encountered, meaning ethnic or linguistic German "purity."

17. Eric Schmaltz and Samuel Sinner have published an article in which they draw attention to the point that Stumpp "possessed clear evidence about what was going on" in the occupied Ukraine (Schmaltz and Sinner, "The Nazi Ethnographic Research of Georg Leibbrant and Karl Stumpp in Ukraine, and Its North American Legacy," in *German Scholars and Ethnic Cleansing*, ed. Ingo Haar and Michael Fahlbusch, 51–81 [New York: Berghahn Books, 2005], 60). They assert that he was aware of the mass killings of Jews and knew that the village reports collected by his staff were used by SS groups in killings that were reprisals against Soviet ill-treatment of German villages, and killings of residents of German villages who were deemed "insufficiently German." Samuel Sinner painted a far more damning portrait in a paper, "New Archival Discoveries on Wannsee Conference Participant Georg Leibbrant and 'SS-Mann' Karl Stumpp," presented at the German Studies Association Conference in New Orleans, LA, 20 September 2003. This paper had been available online at http://www.samuelzinner.com/uploads/9/1/5/0/9150250/leibrandt2012.pdf but it has now been taken down. Sinner notes Stumpp's anti-Semitic remarks published in 1939 and states that "Stumpp was well informed of the SS Killing activities" (6), charging that the village reports done by the group reporting to Stumpp "plainly state that various persons were shot on the spot (erschossen)." Sinner is here quoting from Meir Buchsweiler's *Volksdeutsche in der Ukraine am Vorabend und Beginn des Zweiten Weltkriegs—ein Fall doppelter Loyalität* (Gerlingen, Ger.: Bleicher, 1984), 368–69. Sinner is particularly outraged that Stumpp was never punished for his work, and that he did not apologize after the war for his actions.

18. In his article "Zur 125-Jahr-Feier des Deutschtums in Bessarabien" [*Deutsche Post aus dem Osten* no. 12 (1939): 18], Stumpp notes the value of remaining "pure" of Jewish blood (quoted in Sinner, "New Archival Discoveries," 4).

gathering and organization of data concerning the early German settlers in Bessarabia and South Russia, not on his opinions.[19] Stumpp's lists of individuals and families thought to be the original settlers of the German colonies in Bessarabia appear to have been developed from sources that he saw in Bessarabia—that is, from sources he saw before 1940. Stumpp does not appear to have been aware of early census counts made of the German colonies, such as those for Kulm from 1815 discussed below. Rather, he seems to have gone through the early death records from the first colonies and painstakingly put together lists of people thought to be the original settlers. For Bessarabia, Stumpp lists the names of the early colonists by settlement and includes a synopsis of the places from which these colonists came, as well as total numbers of the first settlers who founded each colony. Stumpp appears to have read the 1848 village histories that were collected and published in Germany in the 1920s and 1930s. As noted above, Stumpp's lists of first settlers in the Bessarabian colonies are incomplete and mix children of the first settlers and some later arrivals with the first settlers themselves. As a result, the number of founding settlers listed in the 1848 village histories never matches the number of first settlers in Stumpp's listings. Stumpp also attempted to group together individuals who have the same surname, but as his purpose was not to develop family genealogies, his assumptions that people are related are not always correct and so should be approached with caution. Nevertheless, starting from what was a chaos of data, Stumpp had a clear and extremely useful goal: to give a general picture of the names and origins of the first settlers to come to South Russia and Bessarabia. If he did not perfectly achieve that, his important study is one foundation upon which many later studies were built. The following chapter in this study, which seeks to show some of the complexity that lies behind the Germanness of the first settlers in Bessarabia, starts from Stumpp's work.

### 1815 Kulm census

Among the materials taken to Germany in 1940 during the resettlement by citizens of Kulm, Bessarabia, was a copy of a census made September 1, 1815 (O.S.),[20] a year after the colony was founded.[21] This census was surely made at the request of Russian officials. The 1815 Kulm census provides a list of the names of the immigrants, their ages as of September 1, 1815, and in several cases, the places from which they had emigrated.

19. Sinner, I believe, is also wrong to imply that the great interest in genealogical research by Russian-German cause organizations in Germany and North America after World War II indicates that such groups shared Stumpp's and Leibbrant's opinions on German ethnic superiority or their negative views of the qualities, abilities, and rights of other ethnic groups.

20. All dates prior to 1918 from Russian sources, including dates from the German colonies in Bessarabia, are based on the ancient Julian calendar. Dates using the current standard calendar, the Gregorian, are later than those of the Julian by the calculation noted below. The Gregorian calendar, named for Pope Gregory, was mandated in Catholic countries from 1582. The calendar change occurred because the older Julian calendar year, in use from Roman times, was slightly longer than the actual solar year with the result that the Easter calculation could no longer be traditionally made as the first Sunday after the full moon after the vernal equinox. Protestant Germany adopted the Gregorian calendar in 1698, Great Britain (and British America) in 1752, but Russia changed only after the Russian Revolution in 1918. In the nineteenth century, the Julian calendar had become twelve days behind (by the twenty-first century, fourteen days ahead) so that September 1, 1815 Julian, for example, would be September 13, 1815 Gregorian. Hereafter, and following general practice, dates cited from pre-1918 Russian sources will be noted O.S., meaning Old Style, to highlight that the date uses the Julian calendar.

21. Published in the "1990 Kulm Heimatskalender 1990" and included by Dale Wahl in his "Bessarabian Surname Origins Index" (N.p.: Odessa Digital Library, 1999), http://www.odessa3.org/collections/refs/link/bessorgn.txt.

The census is incomplete, as not everyone known to be in Kulm in 1815 is listed, and though children of settling families are often listed, wives are not. Even if incomplete, the Kulm census, as the only currently extant census of the early German colonies in Bessarabia, offers an important and interesting look at the wide spectrum of different situations among the early colonists ranging from families with adult and married children to the newly married to many single young men and women and even to children apparently coming on their own or finding themselves orphaned along the way.

It would be surprising if the Russian government had not requested and made similar censuses for other of the early German colonies: Krasna (1814), Borodino (1814), Tarutino (1814), Klöstitz (1815), Leipzig (1815), Wittenberg/Alt Posttal (1815), Alt Arzis (1816), Alt Elft (1816), Beresina (1816), Brienne (1816), Paris (1816), and Teplitz (1817). While this 1815 Kulm census offers an early and interesting look at one group of colonists, conclusions about its data cannot be taken far.

## Sources that focus on the early and middle life of the Bessarabian colonies

### 1848 village histories

State Councilor Eduard von Hahn, then the head of the Welfare Committee, sent out a circular letter dated January 8, 1848 (O.S.) that was expected to reach the mayors and school teachers in the over two hundred German villages in Bessarabia and South Russia.[22] In it, von Hahn asked each village to create an account of its founding and early development. Though the total number of villages that produced such histories is not known, most villages produced a history. Some were published before 1854 in the Odessa German-language newspaper *Unterhaltungsblatt für deutsche Ansiedler im südlichen Rußland*. Out of a potential total of 203, 190 such village histories were collected and published in Germany between 1905 and 1941.[23] The Odessa3 Collection includes English translations of village histories for twenty-two of the twenty-six German colonies in existence in Bessarabia in 1848.

The village histories typically make brief comments on the date the colony was founded, the origins of the first settlers, the nature and quality of soil conditions, descriptions of the village siting in the empty steppe, difficulties experienced in the first years of the colony, such as insect attacks on crops and cholera infestations, and finally the achievement of some prosperity and the consequences this brought. These histories are almost the only firsthand descriptions of the early life of the German colonies in Bessarabia.[24]

---

22. Tsar Peter the Great established a table of ranks that created a fixed hierarchy of equivalencies between civil service and military positions. This ranking system remained in place from Peter's time at the beginning of the eighteenth century until 1917. The civil rank of state councilor was the fifth highest, standing above the rank of colonel in the army and below that of major general.

23. Dale Wahl, "Introduction to the Village History Project" (N.p.: Odessa Digital Library, 1996), http://www.odessa3.org/collections/history/link/1848hist.txt. Wahl lists two volumes published by Konrad Keller in Russia, the first in 1905 and the second in 1914; 59 village histories published by Georg Leibbrandt and Josef Malinowsky in 1927 and 1928 in Germany; and Margarete Woltner's collection of 114 of the village histories, published in 1941. Not included in the Odessa Digital Library collection are the histories for Katzbach, Krasna, Schabo, and Tartar Bunar. The latter, founded only in 1845, may not have produced a history.

24. Among the rare first-person descriptions of life in the German colonies in Bessarabia that date from the early period of German settlement is a letter written in January 1841 by a husband and wife newly settled in the colony of Plotzk to relations and friends in their former home of Murr, Württemberg. Emanuel Schlecter, "A Letter Written by a Family who Migrated from Murr, Württemberg to Bessarabia in 1840," trans. Oliver Mogck, *Heritage Review* 38, no. 2 (June 2008): 16–20.

## Welfare Committee studies of economic progress in the German colonies in South Russia

### 1825–26 Welfare Committee study

In 1825–26, the Welfare Committee conducted a detailed survey of the population and economic holdings of the German colonies in the Imperial Russian provinces of Ekaterinoslav, Xerson, and Bessarabia. The Bessarabian data are based on nineteen settlements.[25] Sarata and Schabo, though part of the nineteen, are treated separately from the rest of the Bessarabian colonies, likely reflecting their special origins. The population survey is not a census, as no names are provided. Rather, it is a population count that breaks out the total numbers of males and females in each village, and indicates the number of families and the number of births, deaths, and marriages that occurred in 1825. In collecting economic data, counts are provided by village for animals kept (cattle, horses, pigs), farm equipment, fruit trees, grape vines and "forest" trees planted, and the yields returned of various grains, potatoes, and vegetables. This exhaustive survey, taken eight to eleven years after the founding of the German settlements, is the most detailed picture of the economic health of the German colonies in Bessarabia from any period.[26]

### The 1841 Welfare Committee study

In his 1869 study of colonies established for foreigners in Russia, Aleksandr Klaus included a summary page showing data collected by the Welfare Committee in 1841 that gathered roughly similar information as that collected in 1825–26.[27] This summary, however, does not show figures for individual villages. Instead, it combines the figures for the twenty-four Bessarabian German colonies then extant into four separate groups.[28] This permits only a general comparison of progress and change from 1825 to 1826. Klaus also includes data from the 1841 survey concerning German colonies in the Xerson, Tauride, and Ekaterinoslav provinces of South Russia. As a result, comparisons can be made between the data for German colonies in these areas with data from the colonies in Bessarabia. The summary page Klaus prints also includes data on Bulgarian colonies established by the Russian government in Bessarabia,[29] which

---

25. The nineteen settlements are: Kulm, Malojaroslavec I (Wittenberg), Malojaroslavec II (Alt Posttal), Tarutino, Krasna, Katzbach, Fere-Champenoise I (Alt Elft), Fere-Champenoise II (Neu Elft), Teplitz, Leipzig, Borodino, Klöstitz, Beresina, Paris, Alt Arzis, Neu Arzis, Brienne, Sarata, and Schabo.

26. The survey tables were contained in and formed the basis of Hans Rempel's study, *Deutsche Baurnleistung am Schwarzen Meer, Bevolkerung und Wirtschaft* (Leipzig: S. Hirzel, 1940). The survey tables are included in the Odessa Digital Library collection (http://odessa3.org/collections/towns/link/bsfarm.txt). The material on Bessarabia is contained in Tables 16–37.

27. This appears as Appendix VII in Aleksandr A. Klaus's book, *Naši kolonii: opyty i materially po istorii i statistike inostrannoj kolonizacii v Rossii* (St. Petersburg: V. V. Nusvalt, 1869).

28. The four groups are: (1) the Malojaroslavec Group, which from other data in Klaus appears to comprise Wittenberg, Alt Posttal, Kulm, Tarutino, Krasna, Katzbach, Alt Elft, Neu Elft, Teplitz, and Dennewitz; (2) the Kljastickij group comprising Klöstitz, Leipzig, Beresina, Borodino, Paris, Alt Arzis, Neu Arzis, Brienne, Friedenstal, and Hoffnungstal; (3) the Sarata Group comprising Sarata, Gnadental, and Lichtental; and (4) Schabo.

29. After the Imperial Russian government took control of Bessarabia in 1812, Bessarabia became a haven for groups of Orthodox Christian Bulgarians, Gaugaz, Serbs, and Albanians living south of the Danube estuary in lands still controlled by the Ottoman Turks. Ottoman law and Islamic custom allowed such Christians to retain their religion, but at the cost of prejudicial treatment and second-class citizenship. The Bulgarians and others fled to Bessarabia with the knowledge that they would be free from religious discrimination and in hopes that they might improve their economic standing. The Russian government provided them, as coreligionists, grants of unpopulated land in the steppes, making them often the neighbors to the German colonies founded there.

permits some comparisons to be made between them and the neighboring German settlements. The 1841 survey includes an additional section of data not included in the 1825–26 survey: counts of various crimes and misdemeanors prosecuted in the different local jurisdictions, which offer a distant picture of social problems in the colonies. The main text of the Klaus study deals with the state of health reached in the early 1860s by the German and Bulgarian colonies established in Imperial Russia. His focus is chiefly on the German Volga and Mennonite colonies and the large Bulgarian colonies in Bessarabia and Xerson. Apart from noting some points of comparison with the Bulgarian colonies in Bessarabia and the economic and sociological data contained in his appendix charts, he offers very little material focused specifically on the German settlements in Bessarabia.

## Other collections of economic data

Malinovskij and Brandes offer, as part of their consideration of economic conditions in the German colonies in Bessarabia and South Russia, selections of other Welfare Committee economic studies. Each quotes different aspects of a study carried out in 1857–58. There appear to have been regular Welfare Committee studies conducted between the 1830s and 1870s, and Malinovskij and Brandes provide different pieces of several of these in their works. Both also cite economic data collected after 1880 when the Welfare Committee no longer existed. Typically, the attention of Malinovskij and Brandes is focused on economic activities in the German colonies considered at the level of results for whole provinces. Occasionally, they will break down the provincial data to the level of Welfare Committee districts, which for Bessarabia were Klöstitz, Malojaroslavec (Alt Posttal), Sarata, and Schabo. However, except for a few examples with volost data from Bessarabia, they never provide information at the level of individual settlements. Even so, putting together the data quoted by Malinovskij and Brandes with the deeper materials available from 1825 and 1841 greatly raises the quality of economic data on Bessarabia, making it possible to provide better answers and suppositions in this area. Flegel provides detailed data on Leipzig citizens that clearly originates from the 1857-58 Welfare Committee study. By fortunate coincidence, pieces of that data collection must have been included with the church records he studied. Data are provided on 218 households that are located on properties numbered from 4 to 128. Counts of animals, wagons, shade and fruit trees, and grape vines are provided. In addition, these data include information on personal annual earnings, cash holdings, earnings derived from trades and mill ownership, and the costs of land leasing. In a unique way, this brings part of the Welfare Committee economic studies down to a personal level. Leipzig at this time was in a period of growing prosperity and had already begun to show varying levels of wealth that had developed among different families of the village, including the early emergence of a landless class of citizens. These data are as close as we can get now to a picture of economic development in a mature Bessarabian German village for any period after 1850.

Fortunate as we are to have detailed economic data from several different periods in the development of the German settlements in Bessarabia, the information available is still not sufficient to study economic issues in German Bessarabia with the thoroughness and detail expected from an economic history. There are no data available from any other period that even comes close to the level of detail available from the 1825 study. After 1825, it is not possible to compare results regularly in time on a village-by-village, district, or even provincial basis. We must therefore intuit the adaptations of the German colonies to their new environment and the changes in economic focus, as well as the changes in internal and external economic environments. We can deduce that by the 1860s, the German colonies had found and mastered crops and animals that prospered in local conditions and had found markets at which to sell these goods. This is implied by the fact that by the 1860s, the Bessarabian German colonies had reached sufficient levels of communal wealth that most colonies were able to undertake major civic building projects, such as putting up new churches, schools, and administrative offices.

We can similarly deduce from genealogical data that by the 1860s, Germans in Bessarabia had begun to accumulate sufficient capital or attain access to capital that permitted them to found new villages in Bessarabia and to emigrate from that province to found new settlements elsewhere. Genealogical data tell us that by the 1860s, conditions were becoming crowded in the German colonies. Subdivision of the original allotments was prohibited, so households were frequently made up of several sibling families living together to manage an inherited farmstead. In response to the crowding, beginning in the 1860s and 1870s, Bessarabian Germans begin to enter the land market. From this time until the start of World War I, they established new settlements on leased and purchased land in Bessarabia. They also emigrated from Bessarabia to start new settlements elsewhere in Imperial Russia, in Dobrudscha across the Danube in Romania, and in great numbers in North America. Such moves also imply some accumulated wealth and speak, though not with precision, to the fact that the Bessarabian Germans had access to capital from family savings, loans from neighbors, village orphan and fire funds, and ultimately from mortgages from Russian banks. We know this from individual examples but not from accumulated detail that would show the most popular paths, trends, costs, requirements, or who was most and least likely to benefit.

## The 1835, 1850, and 1858–59 censuses of German colonies in Bessarabia

After the breakup of the Soviet Union and the formation in 1991 of the independent country of Moldova out of the former Soviet republic of Moldavia, some census records from the Imperial Russian province of Bessarabia became available.[30] These had been kept in archives in Chisinau, the capital of Moldova, which, as Kishinev,

---

30. These censuses were published between 2003 and 2005 jointly by the Germans from Russia Historical Society (GRHS) and the Heimatmuseum der Deutschen aus Bessarabien. The strong presumption is that these censuses were made at the request of the Welfare Committee. The 1835 census was likely made in conjunction with the commencement of taxation of the German colonists and the onset of the repayment by the colonists of the costs the Russian government bore in bringing the colonists to Bessarabia. For example, at the end of the 1835 Kulm and Katzbach censuses is a list of individuals who as a result of age or senility were not in a position to pay their taxes. The Russian government had postponed the collection of taxes and the repayment of settlements costs for twenty years in order to help the German colonies establish themselves on a firm economic footing. Censuses from 1835 exist for Alt Elft, Friedenstal, Katzbach, Klöstitz, Kulm, Leipzig, Neu Arzis, Neu Elft, Paris, and Schabo. There are censuses from 1850 for eight of these ten plus Alt Arzis, Alt Posttal, Beresina, Borodino, Brienne, Dennewitz, Gnadental, Hoffnungstal, Krasna, Lichtental, Plotzk, Sarata, Tarutino, Teplitz, and Wittenberg (Katzbach and Neu Elft have an 1835 but not an 1850 census). There are 1859 census reports for Brienne, Friedenstal, Gnadental, Klöstitz, Kulm, Leipzig, and Neu Elft.

had been the provincial capital of Imperial Russian Bessarabia. The census records were clearly made under the authority of the Welfare Committee and are of ten German colonies in 1835, twenty-three colonies in 1850, and seven in 1858-59. These are true censuses that list the names and ages of the inhabitants and their children. The basic unit of data collection is a family unit rather than a household, so it isn't generally clear whether consecutively listed families are living together and working the same farmstead, or living on neighboring farmsteads.

The existence of the 1815 Kulm census together with censuses from that village for 1835, 1850, and 1859 make it possible to show changes occurring in the early life of the colony. This is another instance of the fact that while studies of German Bessarabia may benefit from the good data existing from one village, such circumstances also carry limitations.

## Sources that focus on the German colonies in Bessarabia in the twentieth century

### Albert Kern's *Homeland Book of the Bessarabian Germans*

Following the resettlement and World War II, Albert Kern, then living in Germany, put together a book that offers short historical and cultural descriptions of 172 Bessarabian German villages as well as brief histories of the different Evangelical Lutheran parishes in Bessarabia and histories of the different schools, academies, and hospitals the Germans founded there.[31] Kern, born in Alt Arzis in 1899, was the pastor of the large church at Tarutino at the time of the resettlement in 1940. While Kern uses the 1848 village histories for accounts of the founding of the early villages and has had some access to printed materials from the nineteenth century, the bulk of his work appears to have been built from exhaustive oral research with members of the different villages themselves. His book offers a wealth of detail on community life: the churches, schools, and administrative buildings constructed, commercial businesses established and their successes and troubles, religious life, hardships faced during and after World War I, and the formation by the Romanians of new settlements for the landless as well as the adjustment issues encountered after 1918 in moving to Romanian administration.

Kern's data are particularly important in developing an understanding of the process by which land for new settlements was purchased after the 1860s. He has collected some data on sellers, prices paid, and the number of purchasing families, which allows a calculation in some cases of per family costs. He makes it clear that land purchases were commonly made by family members from different villages thus fostering the continued mixing of colonist families and so explaining the growing dominance of South German speech. Kern also makes clear the important role Gottfried Schulz played in establishing new German settlements on purchased land in Bessarabia. Schulz was able to finance the purchase of large plots of land and then resell them subdivided into separate farmsteads. This allowed those who bought from him to be financially responsible for a far more limited obligation: the single farmstead they bought. Also important to the general economic development of

---

31. Originally published in German as *Heimatbuch der Bessarabiendeutschen*, 2 vols. (Hanover, Ger.: Hilfskomitee der evangelisch-lutherischen Kirche aus Bessarabien, 1976). The translated edition: Kern, *Homeland Book of the Bessarabian Germans*, 2 vols., trans. Ilona Richey, Germans from Russia Heritage Collection (Fargo: North Dakota State University, 1998).

German Bessarabia is that Schulz was one of the first to learn how to access capital from Russian banks for land purchases, and appears to have helped others use this path as access to capital.

Kern is also a critical source in developing pictures of the many new agricultural villages formed in the twentieth century. Those formed before World War I were the hardest hit by the economic losses brought by war, and those formed after the war were typically the poorest among all the German settlements. Kern's accounts also show the growing gap that was developing in the twentieth century between the old and new villages. The former remained generally the wealthiest agriculturally and were also places where commercial interests were playing increasingly important roles.

Kern's book also includes a list of Bessarabian German war casualties from service in the Russian army in World War I and in the German army in World War II, and the twenty-one articles comprising the resettlement agreement reached in Moscow September 3, 1940.

### Heimatbuch der Gemeinde Kulm

After the end of World War II and their dispersion throughout Germany, the former residents of Kulm put together a book describing vignettes of communal life and customs, details of the religious life and the local administration and its structure, sketches of important individuals, and through these illustrations, a kind of history of their Bessarabian village.[32] While the Kulm Heimatbuch reports on early events in the village from its founding in 1815, through the building of the large church between 1865 and 1868, to the introduction of Russian-language schooling in the 1880s, most of the accounts touch on events within living memory of the different compilers and so date to the early twentieth century. These include accounts of village customs, the different trades practiced, school and church life, and even games played. In the absence of similar materials from other German villages in Bessarabia, data from Kulm will be frequently cited under the supposition that occurrences in Kulm can be presumed generally typical in German Bessarabia. This presumption is exaggerated, as we simply do not know how similar or different customs in Kulm were to those present in the rest of German Bessarabia.

### Wilhelm Mutschall's History of the Community of Tarutino from 1814 to 1934

Mutschall wrote this study in 1934 as part of the commemoration of the 120-year anniversary of the founding of Tarutino.[33] Mutschall (1851–1936), a retired school teacher, put together this study having looked at village and church records as well as gathered stories and accounts about the village's past. His history is one of the

---

32. The "Heimatbuch der Gemeinde Kulm" evidently grew out of reunion of villagers held in Kornwestheim Baden-Württemberg in 1965 celebrating the 150th anniversary of the founding of Kulm. A translated version of the original German copy was published serially in *Heritage Review* 13, no. 4 (December 1983): 3–23; 14, no. 2 (May 1984): 19–36; 14, no. 3 (September 1984): 52–60; 14, no. 4 (November 1984): 33–48; 15, no. 2 (April 1985): 30–43; and 15, no. 3 (September 1985): 23–35.

33. Wilhelm Mutschall, *Geschichte der Gemeinde Tarutino von 1814 bis 1934* (Hannover, DE: Hilfskomitee u. Landsmannschaft d. Bessarabiendeutschen, 1966). A translation is appearing serially in *Heritage Review* 42, no. 4 (December 2012); 43, no. 1 (March 2013); 43, no. 2 (June 2013); 43, no. 4 (December 2013); 44, no. 1 (March 2014); 44, no. 2 (June 2014); 44, no. 3 (September 2014); 45, no. 1 (March 2015); and 45, no. 2 (June 2015).

few accounts in existence of Bessarabian Germans writing about their history and experience and as such its greatest value is in the many details it provides. His review, for example, of the difficulties Tarutino's first pastors experienced provides a unique picture of the slowly civilizing colony. Written chiefly for a local audience, however, he passes rapidly and in broad, general strokes through Tarutino's past. Emphasis is given to colorful events such as the Russian official Mendelsohn's harsh treatment of the early Tarutino colonists, or the local village officials making house-by-house inspections. This approach creates important limitations. There is little offered on the process of change or on how or whether the village overcame impediments. It is assumed as well that his audience will know and so not need to be told details about how things worked in the village, such as what could be bought or sold. As a commemorative piece, it was also apparently assumed that it would not be appropriate to touch on conflicts of opinion or failures. Yet when there are so few firsthand pictures of German Bessarabia, virtually every fact he offers informs and provides important contexts.

### Ute Schmidt's *Die Deutschen aus Bessarabien*

The major focus of Ute Schmidt's first book on Bessarabian Germans is to record the process by which these Germans were reintegrated into German society following their resettlement in Germany in 1940.[34] Schmidt has collected several oral statements made by Germans from Bessarabia providing detail about their experiences following the resettlement. Common topics covered include the tribulations many experienced in the last days and immediate aftermath of World War II, the difficulties encountered in adjusting to life and employment in Germany following the war, and new opportunities achieved. The first chapters of Schmidt's book do offer general pictures of the geography and climate of Bessarabia, population statistics, and some general treatments of themes such as the growth in economic prosperity. However, the real strength of this study lies in the discussion of contacts between Germany and Bessarabian Germans in the 1930s, and the recording of first-person accounts of the resettlement in Poland and later the escape from Poland to Germany in the last months of the war.

## The resettlement

Sources dealing with the resettlement of the German population of Bessarabia in 1940 are unusually rich. Officials of the German government and army made records of their negotiations with the Soviet Union and the resulting process of communicating with and evacuating the nearly ninety thousand Germans who had been living in Bessarabia. These records, preserved in German archives during World War II, were captured by the US Army and brought to the United States after the war. Apart from details on how the resettlement was structured and carried out, these records include observations made by German officials on the history of specific villages and the current economic activities within them. The German officials also made notes on the degree to which different villages had maintained the German language and German customs, whether the village ought to be kept together as a

---

34. Ute Schmidt, *Die Deutschen aus Bessarabien: Eine Minderheit aus Südosteurope (1814 bis heute)* (Köln, Ger.: Böhlau, 2004).

unit or split up in the resettlement, and highlighted individuals they thought troublesome. The most important sources on the resettlement are:

### DAI material

As noted earlier in this chapter, the DAI, founded in Stuttgart in 1917, was established with the goal of studying the conditions and achievements of German settlements outside Germany, as well as bringing those settlements into closer connection with Germany. In 1939, now working in close connection with the German government, the DAI became involved in that government's preparations for a potential resettlement into Germany of Germans living in Bessarabia. One preparatory study made by the DAI was a 1939 survey of who made up the educated people living in German Bessarabia—that is, teachers, pastors, lawyers, doctors, and architects. A second study provided population counts of Germans in the different Bessarabian villages, including counts by village of farmers who owned and who leased land. The DAI material also included several short sketches written by Stumpp before 1940 that described both the older Bessarabian German settlements and the new villages created by the Romanians for the landless. In July 1940, following the Soviet occupation of Bessarabia, the DAI sought to communicate to Germans living in Bessarabia possible outcomes for them. They drafted letters to circulate among the German villages. These letters sought to raise hopes of resettlement in Germany, as well as to create fears among Germans thinking of remaining in Bessarabia by reporting alleged atrocities committed against Germans by Jews.[35]

### Specific resettlement documents

Among these documents are some of the minutes of the meetings held between German and Soviet military and civilian authorities negotiating resettlement procedures held in Tarutino, Bessarabia, which date from September to November 1940, and highlight negotiating positions and aims.[36] German army records are preserved, offering data on the number of German refugees resettled in Germany from Bessarabia, Dobrudscha, and Bukovina in the fall of 1940, transportation routes used to take the refugees to the Danube ports, and horses and wagons used for this process.[37] Allen Konrad has translated a series of documents and charts made by German army personnel that offer first-person observation reports of the evacuation,

35. The state of friendship then extant (1939–40) between Nazi Germany and the Soviet Union was no doubt a major reason that the circulars did not raise the far more realistic fears concerning Soviet intentions of seizing all privately held farm land to create collective farms. While the depiction of Jews as harassing Germans in Bessarabia certainly reflects attitudes and prejudices of the Nazi German government and members of the DAI, given the lack of information about general community attitudes among Germans in Bessarabia, it should not be assumed that it was directed toward known fears or prejudices there. By 1940, there were numbers of Jews living and working in the larger Bessarabian German villages; Tarutino, in particular, had a large Jewish population. Relations between Germans and Jews appear generally positive. Tarutino Germans, for example, had gone to lengths to circumvent efforts by the Imperial Russian government to limit the number of Jewish residents. Many DAI documents have been photocopied and held in the library of the Germans from Russia Historical Society. A number of these have been translated and put online by the Odessa3 Collection at www.odessa3.org/collections/war/dai/.
36. Allen Konrad and Helmut Straeuli, trans., "DAI Film T81-317 Bessarabian Resettlement Minutes" (N.p.: Odessa Digital Library, 2004), www.odessa3.org/collections/war/dai/link/dai317e.txt.
37. Allen Konrad, trans., "Evacuation from Bessarabia and Bukovina, 1940" (N.p.: Odessa Digital Library, 2002), www.odessa3.org/collections/war/link/evac317.txt.

notes on routes used, and distances. These also include ship transport figures for taking the refugees up the Danube to Germany that give rich detail on the process of evacuation.[38] Finally, German officials who visited the different Bessarabian German villages during the resettlement process made brief notes about the village populations, professions, the distant family origins in Germany, dialects of German generally spoken, and the extent of ethnic—that is, German—consciousness.[39]

An interesting collection of photographs of the resettlement taken by a Japanese photographer, Akira Takiguchi, has recently (2004) become available. Takiguchi accompanied the German commission to Bessarabia in 1940 and took photographs evidently intended to document Germany's actions during the resettlement in a positive light. These include pictures of meetings and the packing of wagons in Bessarabia, the trek to the Danube, and river travel to Germany.[40]

When the refugees were brought to relocation centers in Germany, they were asked to fill out family questionnaires, which provided for the German authorities both a census of the population taken in, and, given the Government's skewed focus on ethnicity, some background on the Germanness of those arriving.[41] The questionnaires provide data on names and birthdates of the arriving families and frequently give details about their parents and in some cases grandparents. Refugees, likely aware at least to some degree of the importance of establishing their Germanness for the German government, would often add comments about remembered ancestors and their family origins in Germany. Filmed copies of many of the questionnaires have been preserved in the German government archives in Koblenz.

The questionnaires provide twentieth-century genealogical data for numerous German families in Bessarabia and Dobrudscha. For some families, the data go back far enough to reconnect with the information preserved in the church parish records, which stop around 1885, thus providing a more or less complete track from the first generation to arrive in Bessarabia to resettlement. The material in the questionnaires is the main source for continuing demographic studies of the German Bessarabian population beyond the nineteenth century. This material is also important for establishing the continued mobility of the Germans within Bessarabia. It highlights the pattern of children, particularly the younger children in a family, leaving their birth villages to settle in new villages elsewhere in Bessarabia. Immigration to North America stopped with the beginning of World War I. After the war, Brazil made several efforts to attract settlers and succeeded in drawing small numbers, particularly in the 1920s. There was also a small emigration from German Bessarabia back to Germany, but emigration after World War

38. Ibid.

39. E. Wise, "DAI Film - T81-316 Bessarabian Village Reports" (N.p.: Odessa Digital Library, 2000), www.odessa3.org/collections/war/reports/link/dai316.txt; and Horst Gutsche, "Bessarabian Village Reports, DAI T81 316" (N.p.: Odessa Digital Library, 2002), www.odessa3.org/collections/war/reports/link/suppl.txt.

40. Akira Takiguchi and Axel Hindemith, *Heimkehr der Bessarabiendeutschen: Farbfotos vom Herbst 1940* (Tokyo: Selfpublished, 2004), http://www.history.jp/wehrmacht/heimkehronline.pdf. Ute Schmidt's book *Bessarabia: German Colonists on the Black Sea* contains several of these photographs.

41. Copies of the questionnaires are in the library of GRHS in Bismarck, North Dakota, and data from these films were put on the web by Dale Wahl in 1997–98 at www.odessa3.org/collections/bess/koblenz.

l appears, from the questionnaires, to never again have reached the large numbers seen in the thirty years before the war.

## Materials on the life of German peasants in Prussia and Württemberg in the eighteenth century

It is very difficult to connect German Bessarabian immigrants with the specific circumstances of their lives on leased land in Prussia or on free holdings in Württemberg. Most immigrants from Prussia came from territories now part of Poland that underwent significant political and social changes during and after World War II. Following the end of the war, German citizens of East Prussia, Pomerania, Neumark Brandenburg, and Posen were forcefully encouraged to move west beyond the Oder-Neisse line. The Soviet Union took the eastern third of pre-war Poland, causing Poles living there to move west. Poland's government then sought to settle these Poles in areas where German speakers had lived before the war. The fate of eighteenth-century estate records from Prussian and Polish estates in what were the Prussian and Imperial German provinces of Pomerania, West and East Prussia, and Posen, or of church records from the Evangelical Lutheran parishes in these provinces, is not fully clear. Many estate records were burned in the destruction of estates that accompanied the passage of the Red Army, though some appear to have survived. Polish historians of eighteenth-century peasant conditions have generally ignored German peasant experience on estates in Poland. Parish records from German churches appear from genealogical studies to have had a better chance of survival, but likely, because of the difficulty of access, have not yet been much pursued by those interested in the pre-Bessarabian life of German families. The efforts of the Polish government to wipe away traces of the former German presence in what was Prussian Poland have made it more difficult to find German settlements. Polish authorities have been sensitive about searches for and expressions of interest in documents relating to a German past in this region. Such sensitivities, likely relating to fears of German interest in recapturing lost lands, have increased the difficulties of research.

Understanding eighteenth-century German peasant life in Prussia is significantly helped by the work of William Hagen, who studied the eighteenth- and nineteenth-century estate records of the von Kleist family holdings in the Bluthen Parish, near Stavenow in Brandenburg.[42] Because these records found their way to archives between the world wars, they escaped the general destruction of Prussian estate records in Germany. Hagen's work offers a data-rich picture of the harsh conditions of peasant life in Brandenburg and the narrow window for economic success peasants had as their tenure rights for use of land depended on providing both labor on the landowner's land and payments in produce or cash for the land they cultivated in their own right. Though his conclusions are in line with the general shape of the portrait German historians have drawn about the conditions of peasant life in Prussia, Hagen's work does contradict one view argued by many German historians who saw peasants as helpless and unable to resist the harsh demands

---

42. William W. Hagen, *Ordinary Prussians: Brandenburg Junkers and Villagers, 1500–1840* (New York: Cambridge University Press, 2002); and his article "Village Life in East Elbian Germany and Poland 1400–1800," in *The Peasantries of Europe from the 14th to the 18th Centuries*, ed. Tom Scott (Harlow, UK: Addison Wesley Longman Higher Education, 1998), 174–75.

of their noble landlords. Hagen also provides from the Bluthen records one of the few detailed demographic pictures of eighteenth- and nineteenth-century Prussian peasant average lifespans and marriage rates. Hagen also provides detailed pictures of the tenure relationships under which peasants held land and the marriage and inheritance customs of Prussian peasants. The detail Hagen has provided gives some comfort to scholars extending the relevance of the peasant conditions he described to conditions further east in West Prussia and Posen, where many of the Bessarabian German immigrants lived prior to their immigration to Russia. Hagen's specific demographic and economic data also form useful points of comparison with data from German Bessarabia, which at times show that significant differences have emerged between the two German peasant communities.

Many of the German immigrants who came to Bessarabia from Prussian Poland were from families who had immigrated to Poland from German territories in the upper Rhineland. Such immigration to Prussian Poland occurred in the period from 1790 to 1805. Responding to Prussian interest in drawing settlers from elsewhere in the German-speaking lands, the immigrants took up tenures on land that had come under the control of the Prussian crown as a result of the second and third partitions of Poland (1793, 1795). Most of these immigrants came from Württemberg but there were also numerous families who came from Baden, the Pfalz, Hesse, and Alsace. The custom of partible inheritances in this region led to increasingly smaller freeholds. When bad weather, increased taxation, or the falling prices of crafts created difficult economic conditions for such small freeholders, emigration became a common answer. Emigration, particularly from Württemberg and Baden, also appears to have been driven by religious controversy. The Evangelical Lutheran Church attracted many peasant adherents wanting a more emotional relationship to religion that gave prominence to an individual's devotional life. When conflicts erupted between the Evangelical Lutherans and the more orthodox Lutheran clergy who dominated the local church hierarchy, Evangelical Lutheran adherents became worried and started to think of emigration. From the late seventeenth to the mid-nineteenth century, many peasants and poor townsfolk in the upper Rhineland came to the conclusion that emigration was the necessary answer. The destination opportunities were many: Pennsylvania, Hungary, Serbia, Prussian Poland, and Russia.

The causes and patterns of this emigration have been well examined.[43] However, studies comparable to what Hagen has done on eighteenth- and nineteenth-century Prussian villages that also consider changes and continuities over extended periods of time on landholdings, customary life, and the demographic patterns within specific villages in Württemberg are hard to find. It is clear in general, however, that peasants leaving the Rhineland for Prussian Poland and then subsequently for Russia significantly increased the size of their family landholdings but did so at the cost of working in far more primitive conditions and, in Prussian Poland, owing a significant portion of the harvest yield as payment for their leases.

Stumpp, as noted earlier, has done extensive work in tracing back the family origins of Bessarabian immigrants to their villages in Württemberg, Baden, the Pfalz, Hesse, and Alsace. This provides a very useful picture of the areas from which emigration was concentrated, but Stumpp's work does not touch on the timing or

---

43. Mack Walker, *Germany and the Emigration 1816–1885* (Cambridge, MA: Harvard University Press, 1964).

patterns of the emigrations from the upper Rhineland. Stumpp has created a very useful map of villages in Prussian Poland from which both Rhineland and Prussian peasant families left for Bessarabia. With regard to the settlements Rhinelanders created in Prussian Poland, Erich Weise has provided solid work on the locations, and the changing conditions under which these settlements existed in Prussia.[44] As Weise's study is particularly focused on conditions in these settlements after 1815, his book is less helpful to those wanting a better understanding of the difficulties of establishing the new settlements in Prussia and relations with landlords prior to 1815, which would add to an understanding of the reasons numbers of Rhinelanders elected to leave for Bessarabia.

While it is possible to describe the conditions of peasant life in Prussian Poland and Württemberg in the period prior to the immigration to Bessarabia and so arrive at an understanding of potential causes why the immigrants elected to move, it is not possible to do this by taking into consideration the actual stated rationale that drove any individual family to making this decision. While many of the immigrants had the rudiments of literacy, frequent letter writing, much less the creation of memoirs, was not a part of their culture. As a result, it is not surprising that written accounts do not appear to exist. Nonetheless, the several studies of peasant life in Prussia made by German historians do enable one to form a clear picture of conditions in Prussia and the Rhineland prior to the immigration to Bessarabia and so to create reasonable presumptions as to why people would elect to leave for Russia. Once having arrived in Bessarabia, there appear to have been no efforts made to return, even though some were appalled at the primitive and desolate conditions they found. Indeed, one theme of the present study will be that after the early hardships were overcome in Bessarabia, the immigrants were in far better shape economically than they ever had been in Prussia or the Rhineland.

In considering the sources and data available on the Bessarabian Germans, what is most striking is both the wide range of material and the enormous gaps. It is this fact that leads me to conclude that at present, it is not possible to write a study describing itself as a history of German Bessarabia. There are just a few areas where research stands on firm ground and meaningful conclusions can be drawn. Such areas include economic conditions in the colonies up to 1841, demographic studies of the colonists in the mid-nineteenth century up to 1885, and the why and how of the 1940 resettlement to Germany. There are additional areas where a reasonable amount of background detail exists so that tentative but reasonable positions and conclusions may be drawn. These include the identities of first colonist families, a reasonable supposition about why they left Prussian Poland and Württemberg, what crops were grown and animals raised in Bessarabia and where these were marketed, how the first colonies were established, and what difficulties colonists went through to establish them. Similarly, there are data concerning why the Russian government, in the late 1860s, came to the conclusion that it was in Russia's interest to end the special privileges given the German colonies. The German colonists responded in several different ways to the government's change in policy toward them. One was to leave Russia altogether, and we can follow some of those emigration patterns from Bessarabia to North America. It is possible, also, to form reasonable conclusions about how the Germans in Bessarabia went about

44. Erich Weise, *Die Schwabensiedlungen im Posener Kammerdepartement 1799-1804* (Würtzburg, Ger.: Holzner-Verlag, 1961).

purchasing land to found new settlements and something of the costs they paid and thus something of the assets families had at their disposal. While we have little data on how the Germans remaining in Russia reacted, we can see the development after 1870 of negative attitudes toward them in the popular press concerning, in particular, German land purchases or German resistance to assimilation. Finally, while little hard data exist, there is much secondary information that points to the economic collapse that World War I brought to Bessarabia, as well as how the German communities partially rebuilt that economy in the 1920s and 1930s.

There are many other areas where only some information is known. Here, one is grateful for glimpses that are offered and the tentative hypotheses possible. These areas include the development of commercial businesses from the late nineteenth century up until 1940, social customs in the German villages, educational, religious, and cultural life, relations with and attitudes toward the neighboring non-German settlements, technological improvements, and changes that took place in the role women played in the social and economic life of German Bessarabia.

Unfortunately, there are also many areas about which very little or nothing is known. There are almost no accounts from any period offering individual perspectives, successes, failures, hopes, and fears. There is very little concerning the civic and political lives of the villages. It is not possible to determine in what areas the German colonies could or did act independently during the period before 1870 when they were administered by the Welfare Committee, or in what areas and how they were dependent on the Welfare Committee. We know little of the Welfare Committee's relationships with individual villages over time, when and how it acted usefully or when its actions impeded progress, or what happened when conflicts between individual villages and the Welfare Committee erupted and how these played out. There are few data on how the German communities adapted to Russian administration after 1870 and to what extent they participated in wider roles within the Imperial Russian state, what the relationships between the Germans and the judicial system were like, or the community effects of men returning from service in the Russian army. We know very little about community leaders and their opinions or achievements. We similarly know almost nothing about the most central questions concerning the Germans in Russia: the changing attitudes among the colonists toward Russia and toward assimilation. We also know very little about the other side of this question: As pressures to assimilate grew, what did Bessarabian Germans consider the most valuable parts of their culture, what they did they think most important to defend and then what did they do? Becoming part of Romania in 1918 brought up these same questions, but within a Romanian political, cultural, and linguistic framework.

While major gaps exist, what is known now is not inconsequential or unimportant, as Ute Schmidt has demonstrated. The material that is currently available certainly makes possible the creation of a study of parts of that history, and this is the goal of the present work. I have sought here to organize the available material topically and chronologically and to consider the implications such materials raise both in their own right and within the frameworks created by the better-grounded studies of eighteenth-century German peasant life, and of nineteenth- and twentieth-century economic, social, and political conditions and changes within Imperial Russia and post–World War I Romania.

# Surnames and the Origins of the First German Settlers in Bessarabia

The most detailed source materials about the Germans who came to Bessarabia beginning in 1814 are church records of births, marriages, and deaths, which their descendants brought with them when they abandoned Bessarabia in 1940. In seeking to piece together a picture of the early settlers in Bessarabia, these records tell us two significant pieces of information: the surnames of the immigrants and where they were living in the period just before they came to Bessarabia. The next chapters will consider where these immigrants came from, the conditions they were living under before they came to Bessarabia, and what can be deduced about both their reasons for leaving and the attractions of Bessarabia. The present chapter will consider their surnames and what these tell us about the earlier origins of the Bessarabian immigrants.

The surnames of the Germans immigrating to Bessarabia suggest these immigrants were not a homogenous group linked by family, regional, or even linguistic ties, but rather displayed a wide variety of backgrounds and spoke quite different forms of the German language. These surnames link Bessarabian Germans to different parts of the changing ethnic and cultural landscape of Prussian Poland from which the great majority emigrated. This can be shown from a broad consideration of the surnames of settler families listed by Stumpp for the twenty-five Bessarabian German villages founded before 1840. Given the more complete data available about the first families to settle the villages of Kulm, Leipzig, and Tarutino, it is possible to go further and break out within these communities the prevalence of different family backgrounds and language histories.

The great majority of Bessarabian Germans did not have a surname of long standing. The ancient Germanic practice, still preserved in Iceland, was for a child to be given two names: a first name by which they would be called, such as Johann or Maria, and a second name to distinguish them from others bearing the same name. This second name was a patronymic, meaning that it connected them to their father. Thus children of a man named Martin would be Johann Martinssohn and Maria Martinstochter. From the early Middle Ages onward, patronymics were being displaced by a different form of identification, that of descriptive phrases. These were phrases denoting occupations, origins, or traits, so it might be Johann the Cooper, Johann from the Beechwood, or Johann the Tall One. In small communities with few connections to the wider world, this practice served well enough for all needs of identification.

Wealthier peasant families began to acquire more permanent names either as a means to distinguish land ownership or through their involvement in legal proceedings over property. For most peasant families though, permanent surnames were acquired out of the state's desire to record tax and military obligations. For many German-speaking peasants, fixed surnames were being acquired in the seventeenth century, though some of the Bessarabian immigrants, as will be noted below, appear not to have gained a surname until the end of the eighteenth century. By the time they immigrated to Bessarabia, all the Germans had acquired a surname. Spelling conventions for these surnames, though, were not yet fixed, reminding us that for many, names were often something said to others to identify oneself, not something associated with the fixed spelling of a written word. While the immigrants to Bessarabia from Prussian Poland, Saxony, Mecklenburg, Württemberg, Baden, and the upper Rhineland spoke different forms of West Germanic, they recognized the existence of communality in their languages. The surnames they carried were no doubt, in their eyes, names associated with forms of German and so were clearly different and to be distinguished from the surnames of Polish, Ukrainian, Russian, or Moldavian peasants they encountered.

Among themselves, German speakers in the eighteenth and nineteenth centuries typically identified themselves not as Germans but rather by their regional homelands, calling themselves Prussians, Saxons, Schwabians, Mecklenburgers, or Bavarians. Given that the common meanings and unities currently attached to the concept of being German are likely to be both broader and different from those felt by the Bessarabian immigrants, it would be useful to step back and define what will be meant by the term "German" in this study. Of the many potential meanings the word German might carry, I will seek in this study to limit it to describing people who were native speakers of one of the West Germanic languages. I have sought to avoid using the term German to describe other cultural distinctions such as customs, dress, and food. In the eighteenth and nineteenth centuries, these were far more likely to be determined and differentiated regionally, making such terms as Prussian, Bavarian, or Schwabian more apt.

From the late eighteenth century to almost the present time, it has been generally and popularly presumed that speakers of West Germanic were by and large the direct descendants of the historic Germanic tribes who in post-Roman times came to control, in separate pieces, most of what is now the modern state of Germany and parts of the Low Countries, Switzerland and eastern France. This concept has recently been significantly undercut by genetic studies of European populations. Comparisons of DNA between contemporary European peoples and the remains of people who lived in the same territories in prehistoric times suggest the long-term stability of population within Europe. In other words, it would appear that language areas have changed rather than population groups. As a result, it would strongly appear, for example, that much of the current population of the German Federal state of Baden Württemberg descend from the Celtic-speaking population who were living there in Roman times. Their antecedents were living there before the Celts came to dominate the area. Before the Celts came, they spoke another language or languages not known to us. New explanations for the spread of languages in prehistoric times hypothesize that small groups of politically unified and militarily powerful people who shared a language moved to new territories where, instead of killing off or driving away the people living there, as was previously supposed, the new arrivals simply dominated and that over time the subservient people adopted the language of the ruling group.

While from the perspective of the early nineteenth century, such a language change would have been a feature of the remote and unremembered past in Baden, Württemberg, and Bavaria, it was quite another story in Prussia east of the Oder River. There, language change was actively occurring up to and beyond the time the Bessarabian colonies were founded. Even further west of the Oder along the lower Elbe River, West Slavic Polabian was spoken until the mid-eighteenth century. East of the Oder, from the seventeenth century onward, German was becoming the first language for groups of peasants in Pomerania and West and East Prussia who earlier spoke the West Slavic Slovincian, Kashubian, and Polish languages[1] or the Baltic Prussian and Lithuanian languages.[2] The reverse process also occurred where German-speaking peasants in Silesia and Great Poland became Polish speakers.[3]

---

1. Up until the eighth century CE, West Slavic–speaking peoples dominated the northern plains of what is now Germany up to and including the lower reaches of the Elbe River. West of the Oder River, these would include the Obotrites, allies of Charlemagne against the Saxons, in modern Holstein, Hamburg, and northern Hanover; the Polabians along the Elbe River south to the Saale; the Veleti in modern Mecklenburg Vorpommern; and the Sorbians (also called Wends and Lusatians) south of Berlin. All of their descendants (except some of the Sorbians) now speak German. Some fifty thousand people in eastern Germany currently speak Sorbian. East of the Oder River, most of the known West Slavic languages continue as living languages. Only Slovincian, whose speakers formed a distinct group well into the nineteenth century in most of what is now western Pomerania, disappeared into German, closely related Kashubian, or more distant Polish. East of the Slovincians were the Kashubians who lived in the western delta region of the Vistula River and the forested lake lands southeast. Kashubian is still spoken in Poland, though many speakers adopted German in the nineteenth century. South of the Notec (German Netze) River, Polish was the dominant West Slavic language.

2. The Prussian-speaking people lived east of the Vistula River delta. Their language, often called Old Prussian to reduce confusion with the German dialects of Low and High Prussian spoken in this region later, belongs to the Baltic language group of Indo-European, along with Lithuanian and Latvian. The Prussian language became extinct by the early eighteenth century, with former speakers mainly adopting German as their spoken language. In the northern two-thirds of East Prussia, German also made many inroads replacing forms of Lithuanian, though here the Baltic language was more resistant to change.

3. Language changes in this direction are apparent in Polish surnames of German origin such as Szulc, Szmit, and Sznajder among several others.

This linguistic issue is of interest in the study of the German speakers who emigrated from Prussia to Bessarabia in the early nineteenth century, because the onomastic study that follows suggests that there was a substantial minority among the Bessarabian Germans with surnames that derive from West Slavic or Baltic roots. It is likely that such families had adopted German as their language only within the prior one hundred to two hundred years. This is suggested by the fact that Prussian peasants tended to acquire fixed surnames only after the late seventeenth century when the fiscal apparatus of the Prussian state grew sufficiently organized to be able to record extensive tax payments and demand that surnames become fixed. In Prussian Poland, this generally occurred in the late eighteenth century only after the Prussian state had acquired large portions of Poland in the partitions. The fact that surnames retained Slavic and Baltic words indicates some memory of a prior language use when the surnames became fixed. The same issues are raised with another segment of the Bessarabia colonists who have surnames with North Germanic origins and so point to a similar linguistic transition. The wide linguistic diversity in the surname origins of the Bessarabian colonists is thus not just the frequently cited distinction between Low German–speaking Prussians and High German–speaking Schwabians,[4] but within each of these groups as well. This in turn suggests that among the first-generation of colonists, there existed a wider diversity in cultural habits than has been commonly presumed.

It is important to remember, too, that the great majority of the Bessarabian colonists came from Prussian Poland, where, for the German-speaking world, there was an unusual mix of people of different territorial backgrounds, people speaking different forms of German, and people who spoke languages other than German. This mix of peoples in Prussian Poland inevitably highlighted differences and so likely caused families to hold more tightly to their own peculiarities, their received family customs, and received forms of language. This was certainly the habit of the first-generation immigrant groups who were mixed together in North American cities. This suggests that at the time of their immigration to Bessarabia, the many differences existing among the colonists stood out for them as much as their similarities.

In contrast, descriptions of the Bessarabian Germans written by their twentieth-century descendants often portray them as a close-knit group sharing very similar customs and language. It is commonly noted that originally there were two separate linguistic and cultural groups among them, Prussians and Schwabians, who over time merged together. I believe this to be a perspective of the fourth, fifth, and sixth generations reflecting that over time and in their isolated situation in Russia, differences were smoothed and a generally common culture had developed. This chapter will argue from a study of the surnames of the Bessarabian Germans that at the

4. High German is a term that describes dialects spoken in central and southern Germany south of the Benrath and Speyer lines that mark major consonant shifts that occurred in West Germanic. The Benrath Line, running east–west, generally parallel to the southern border of the Netherlands, marks the distinction between the pronunciation "machen" (Middle and High German to the south) and "maken" (Low German to the north). The Speyer Line, which runs generally along the Main River, marks the distinction between "appel" as pronounced to the north and "apfel" to the south. The German term "Hochdeutsch," High German, is also used now to describe current standard German, which is not the meaning intended here. Forms of German spoken to the north of these linguistic markers are called Low German, "Niederdeutsch," or often "Plattdeutsch." If the distinction between language and dialect is defined as comprehensibility, then Low and High German could be considered separate languages spoken in separate areas in the German-speaking world.

time of their arrival in Bessarabia, the immigrants had far more widely differentiated backgrounds and likely customs than has generally been supposed. Such a view is supported also by data discussed later in chapter III that indicate that the colonists were composed of many separate but small family groups drawn from a wide variety of villages. They came to Bessarabia not as villagers moving together, but as disparate families, sometimes as large family groups of several adults, but generally as separate families whose pre-immigration acquaintance was slight, if it existed at all. It is supported further by data discussed in chapter VII which indicate that in marriages occurring in the first years after the colonists had reached Bessarabia, marriage partners were typically chosen from families with similar backgrounds, often from those who had emigrated from villages in same general region in Prussian Poland.

German-speaking lands of the eighteenth century were divided into a large number of jealously independent mid-sized and small principalities. The few larger states—Prussia, Saxony, Bavaria, Austria, and Württemberg—were not powerful enough to dominate their many smaller neighbors. The long-term division of the German-speaking lands into many political entities encouraged the development of regional forms of German to gain social and literary standing. As a result, German surnames often reflect the regional forms of spoken German where families were living when they acquired a surname. In considering the regional spread of these surnames among the Bessarabian immigrants, what stands out is just how varied they were, how many different regions of the German-speaking world they came from. Although the majority of the Germans who came to Bessarabia emigrated from Prussian Poland, this fact does not undercut the argument of diversity. The German population in Prussian Poland was unusually diverse. As Prussia gained control of Pomerania and later Royal Prussia and Great Poland in the three partitions of the Polish Kingdom, it sought immigrants widely within the German-speaking world. Prussia's intentions in the settlement of German peasants in these territories were to increase the population, improve the agricultural economy, and to build a more supportive German (versus Polish) presence within them.[5]

## Many German immigrants to Bessarabia have family backgrounds in Württemberg and Baden with their surnames suggesting a variety of origins

While some of these immigrants came directly to Bessarabia from southern Germany, the majority of immigrants with a Württemberg or Baden background came to Bessarabia from Prussian Poland, where they had settled in the period from 1790 to 1806. Whether coming directly from southwestern Germany or Prussian Poland, these immigrants spoke variants of High German. The family origins of Bessarabian Germans in southwestern Germany can often be identified through their surnames, which have High German sound changes, are based on terms used in southern Germany, refer to places in southern Germany, or have prefixes or suffixes typically used there. In some cases, these tie families to origins in Württemberg.

---

5.  In the reigning concepts of late eighteenth-century political economy, population size was seen as directly proportional to political power. Increasing the population within a state by attracting immigrants from without to under populated areas was understood to be an important tool within the control of states to increase state power. See Ulrich Adam, *The Political Economy of J. H. G. Justi* (New York: Peter Lang, 2006) on the Cameralist views of von Justi, who had great influence in Prussia and on Friedrich the Great.

For example, the Schöttle family of Wittenberg, Bessarabia, who came there from Plotzk in Prussian Poland, has a surname derived from a Middle High German word for curds. The suffix -le in their surname, however, gives it a form found almost exclusively in Württemberg. The form of German spoken in Württemberg and the neighboring region of eastern Bavaria is called Schwabian and many surnames in this area end in the suffixes -le, -el, -ehl, or -lin.[6] The Gäckle family, who emigrated to Alt Posttal, has a surname clearly indicating a Schwabian origin as it is derived from a Schwabian word for someone who is known for joking. The Eberle surname of another Wittenberg family is derived from a Schwabian short form of the name Eberhard which might be Eberl in Bavaria or Eberlein in Central Germany. The Kisse family of Leipzig has a surname tied to Baden rather than Württemberg. The surname is found almost exclusively in Baden and is derived from the Middle High German word *kis* meaning "gravel" and was likely a place name for those who lived on gravelly land.

Other surnames carrying linkages to specific places in southern Germany include the Baier or Bayer family of Alt Arzis, whose surname suggests they came from Bavaria, and the Bäsler family of Leipzig, whose surname suggests they came from the city of Basle in Switzerland. The Höger family of Borodino and Tarutino has a surname that is specific to Bavaria, as it is derived from the Bavarian form of the occupational term Heger, describing a forest warden. The Kneppfle family from Tarutino has a surname that mixes Bavarian and Schwabian elements with the "–le" suffix tied to a Bavarian word for button making, perhaps suggesting an origin in Bavarian Schwabia east of Württemberg.

Many Bessarabian German surnames that are clearly from southern or south-western Germany are not specific to individual areas. The Binder family of Teplitz, for example, has a surname derived from the common occupational term used in southern Germany for a cooper, where as a family name with that trade whose origins lay in the northern German speech areas would be called Böttcher, like the families of that name from Kulm, Tarutino, and Leipzig. The southern German origin of the Funk family of Alt Elft and Tarutino is indicated by fact that their surname is derived from the High German word for "spark," indicating work as a smith. Similarly, the Flegel family of Kulm has a surname derived from the central and southern German word used to describe someone who threshes grain with flails. Other Bessarabian German surnames with a clear but unspecific southern German origin are: Kuhn, a High German short form of the given name Kunrat (Konrad); Kurz, a High German term for a short person; Lobe, derived from the High German given name Leb/Lebe describing someone with a fierce ("lion like" from *löwe*) personality; Schäfer from the High German word for shepherd; Schütze, from the southern German occupational term for a forest ranger or field guard (the northern German word and surname would be Schütte); and Selcho, derived from southern German terms for someone who smokes meat or works as a pork butcher.

---

6. The word Schwabian is derived from the name of the Germanic Suebi tribe who, moving from the region of the lower Elbe River, came to dominate what is now southwestern Germany in the post-Roman period. A sign of the continuing prevalence of a Schwabian German identity is the motto often seen in the state of Baden Württemberg: *Wir können alles außer Hochdeutsch* (We can do anything except speak standard German).

## Differing north German origins are also suggested by family surnames

In a similar fashion, families with origins in northern Germany and Prussia are distinguished by surnames that are based on Low German words or occupational or descriptive terms used exclusively in the north. In some cases these surnames, like some from the south, can be linked to specific regions. The Lasson family from Leipzig and the Jesse family from Leipzig and Brienne have surnames formed from the Scandinavian (and probably Danish) first names Lars and Jens, suggesting family origins in Schleswig or further north. The surname of the Frieß or Friesz family from Tarutino identifies them as Frisian and ties them to the far northeast corner of Germany. Johann Hey, appearing only in the 1815 Kulm census, and the Jabs family of Leipzig also have surnames derived from Frisian personal names. Several families have surnames that suggest Saxon origins such as: the Gellert family from Kulm, whose surname is derived from the Saxon word meaning "to cry out"; the Henneberg family, also from Kulm, whose surname is derived from a place name in Thuringia; and the Teschner family from Kulm and later Borodino who has an occupational surname that was quite common in Saxony describing someone who was a pocket maker. The Pommeranke family from Paris, Bessarabia, has a surname that describes them as Pomeranian. The Flato families from Kulm and Klöstitz have a surname derived from the place name Flatow, which is found in Vorpommern, Mecklenburg, and Brandenburg. Like the surnames Frieß, Baier, and Bäsler, Pommeranke and Flato were not likely acquired until after the families had left the areas after which they were named.

As with surnames denoting a southern German ancestry, there are many northern German surnames that, while they do not point to specific locations, are clearly northern German, because they are derived from Low German words, or from occupational terms or descriptive words used exclusively in the north. The Pahl family from Leipzig, for example, has a surname derived from the Low German word for stick, where a family with a central or southern German origin would be named Pfahl. Another example would be the different families from Klöstitz, Paris, and Alt Elft with the surname Schröder, a Low German occupational name for a tailor, which in southern Germany would be Schneider. Similarly, the Pelz family from Leipzig has a surname based on the northern German term for a furrier, which would have been Kürschner had they come from the south. The Teig/Teige family, also from Leipzig, has a surname based on the common northern German term for a brick- or tilemaker, which would have been Zeigler had they come from southern Germany. The origin of surname of Schiewe family of Tarutino is the Low German term especially found in Pomerania for a slater or roofer.

There are a large number of surnames among the Bessarabian Germans that indicate northern origins of the family, as they are derived from Low German forms of popular first names. Among these are the surnames Arndt, Bunk, Fredrich, Hentz, Lemke, Lütke, Mertins, and Röhl, which are Low German forms of the first names Arnold, Buno, Friedrich, Heinz, Lambert, Lütold, Martin(s), and Rodolf (Rudolf) respectively.

## Names with Slavic linguistic roots form a distinctive subgroup among the colonists with northern German origins

Surnames with Slavic linguistic roots are particularly common for families whose origins lay in Prussia, especially east of the Oder River. The most common form of surnames with Slavic roots among the Bessarabian Germans are surnames derived from Slavic personal names such as: Ganske and Janke from Jan, Jeske or Jeschke from Jeszek, Kupke from Kuba (the short form of Jakub), Manske and Schimke from Szimon, Priebe from Pribislav, Prenzel from Premislav, Radach from Radoslav, Retzlaff from Ratislav, Tezlaff and Uttech from Tech, and Wutzke from Woitzek. The diminutive suffix -ke is a frequent motor for Slavic name formation. There is also a presumptive West Slavic linguistic background for surnames ending in -ak, -ach, or -ek. Such suffixes are used in Slavic languages to typify or characterize a person by a descriptive adjective or noun. Thus the surname Banek/Banik of a Tarutino family is derived from the Slavic word for baths or bath house, and the surname Worak/Worach of a Kulm family is derived from the West Slavic word for plowing. Some surnames with the suffix -ke may be combinations of German and Slavic linguistic roots, such as Uttke from the old German name Ude, Reinke from the Frisian name Reinker, and Rutschke from Rutsch, a short form of Rudolf in both German and Slavic.

A second group of surnames of the Bessarabian Germans with clear Slavic roots are those formed as descriptive names using Slavic words. Among these are the surnames of the Kulm family Bobermin, derived from the Slavic word *bober* or "beaver"; Guse, another Kulm family, derived from *guz* meaning thick or *guzka* meaning "butt" (of humans or animals); the surname Milbradt of a Tarutino family derived from the Slavic words *mily brat* or "dear brother"; Quaschnik of a Leipzig and Kulm family derived from the Slavic word *kvaszny* or "sour"; and the surname Zappel of a Borodino family that is derived from the word *czapla* or "heron."

Where surnames are based on a Slavic personal name or on a descriptive Slavic word, the surname carries a reasonable presumption that the family had been speakers of a West Slavic language at a time close to when they acquired their surname. This is not to say the family carried this memory when they immigrated to Bessarabia, although it does suggest the existence of a cultural background different from that of people whose family origins were in lands further west. Other names that suggest a family's Slavic linguistic background are Kujat, the West Slavic term for someone from Kujavia, the region along the west bank of the Vistula River south of Bromberg (Polish Bydgoszcz); Pätzer, from a place name in Bohemia; Pohl, from the word for Pole or Polish; and Wendland, for someone from the West Slavic-speaking Wendish (Sorbian) area southeast of Berlin.

Several Bessarabian Germans have surnames ending in the suffix -sky or -ski, a common West Slavic name formation associating a person with a place. Examples would be the names Borofsky/Boroske, Farowsky, Manske, Tornasky, and Tschikorsky. While this might suggest a Slavic linguistic background for the family, it could also result from the fact that the family acquired their surname from the name of the estate in Prussian Poland on which they were holding land in tenancy when, likely, the Prussian tax authorities recorded and so fixed their surname.

This latter situation would clearly appear to be the case for the family of Johann Kubatsky or Kubatzki who moved in the 1820s from the village of Worms in the Beresan District, north of Odessa in South Russia, to Tarutino in Bessarabia. His father had immigrated to Rohrbach, a neighboring village to Worms, in 1814, from Wisgren in Prussia, where Johann was born in 1794. The family originally was from Dettenhausen near Tübingen in Württemberg. The surname Kubatsky/Kubatzki, though, is created from Polish linguistic roots. Kuba is the Polish diminutive of the name Jakub and the suffix -*ski* creates a surname from a place name associated with the name Kuba. The family could not have had such a surname in Württemberg, so it is likely the result that they either had no formal surname when they immigrated to Prussian Poland, or became detached from a former surname during this move. The surname Kubatsky was surely acquired in Prussian Poland.[7]

## A few surnames of families from northern Germany indicate a Baltic linguistic heritage

Yet another linguistic and cultural background is suggested by Bessarabian German surnames derived from Baltic Prussian or Lithuanian words. The Baltic languages (Old Prussian, Lithuanian, and Latvian) form a separate linguistic group within the Indo-European language family, like Romance, German, or Slavic. Surnames with Baltic linguistic roots suggest family origins in lands lying east of the lower Vistula River where Prussian was spoken until the mid-eighteenth century or farther east in East Prussia where Lithuanian was (and remains) the speech of many peasants. Among the Bessarabian Germans, there are far fewer names showing a Baltic linguistic ancestry than a West Slavic one, but they do exist. Among these would be: the Kalmus family from Kulm, whose surname is derived from the Baltic word for the gladiolus flower; the Klukas families from Katzbach and Alt Arzis, whose surname is derived from the verb *klukis* meaning "to chatter"; and the Raugust/Raugusch family from Kulm, whose surname is derived from the old Prussian verb *raugti* meaning "to ferment or leaven" and so suggests an occupational name tied to the making of beer, bread, or cheese.

## The variety of linguistic and geographic origins for the surnames of German colonists in Bessarabia suggests a broad mixture of different cultural backgrounds

The surnames of the German colonists reflect origins in all corners of the German-speaking world, from Friesia and Schleswig in the north and northwest to Bavaria in the south, and from Slavic and Baltic regions in the northeast to Baden and Württemberg in the southwest. This suggests that the village cultures initially created in Bessarabia were a mixture of the many different patterns brought by the immigrants. This emphasizes too that cultures established by the Germans in Bessarabian villages, like the different cultures German immigrants established throughout the United States, Canada, Brazil, and Argentina, are fundamentally different from the long-standing village cultures in Germany itself. The latter were

---

7. Flegel, *Extended Relationships*, 401. Flegel's source for Wisgren is evidently the Tarutino church death record or possibly from Stumpp who saw that record (Stumpp, *Emigration from Germany to Russia*, 345). Stumpp lists Johann as "Kubalsky" (Stumpp does give Johann's father, also a Johann, the surname Kubatzki).

created from the long-term social and legal adjustments made by relatively stable population groups. With the former, the customary ways of different groups of German speakers were mixed so that a jumble of customs, habits, foods, methods of organization, farming, and husbandry might initially be observed before a new common culture developed over time.

It is true that not all of the early German settlements in Bessarabia mixed people with widely different backgrounds. Some of the original villages were composed of immigrants who likely shared much in common. Thus, the inhabitants of Wittenberg and Alt Posttal, which was spun off from it, were mainly Württembergers and other upper Rhinelanders who had immigrated to Prussian Poland after 1790. The inhabitants of Teplitz, Lichtental, and Plotzk had come directly from Württemberg, and those in Sarata from Bavaria, while in contrast, the inhabitants of Kulm, Leipzig, Tarutino, and Brienne were mainly northern Germans from Prussia and its neighbors. Nevertheless, as the breakdown of the early inhabitants of Kulm, Leipzig, and Tarutino will show, there was a good deal of diversity even in villages with strong majorities. Other villages, such as Alt Elft, Arzis, Beresina, Borodino, Friedenstal, Katzbach, Klöstitz, and Paris, were mixtures from the beginning. Stumpp, in his description of the 115 early families to settle Borodino, for example, indicates that 73 were from southwestern Germany (64 from Württemberg and the remainder from Baden), 22 from Mecklenburg, 18 from Prussia, and 2 from Saxony.[8] As newcomers became settled in the villages and as marriages took place between individuals with different backgrounds both within and crossing village boundaries, a general mixing of people with different sorts of German backgrounds occurred.

## It is possible to probe more deeply into the backgrounds of the first citizens of Kulm, Leipzig, and Tarutino through a study of surnames

Surnames provide a better look at family backgrounds and origins than does the immigrant birth location information, which is often only one generation deep. Almost all of the immigrants to these villages came from Prussian Poland, but the great majority had family origins elsewhere. Sometimes there are genealogical data available that offer insight into family origins before the relocation to Prussian Poland, and I have used these in developing the charts below. However, for many families from these three villages, the linguistic backgrounds of their surnames provide the only means to see at least dimly beyond the limitations of birth location data.

Data concerning the early settlers of Kulm, Leipzig, and Tarutino come from several sources. For Kulm, there exists an early census from 1815, the second year of the colony's existence.[9] Data for the early Leipzig and Tarutino citizens as well as for several Kulm citizens missed in the 1815 census are available from Flegel's *Extended Relationships* study, which is organized by families and is primarily based on information from the village death and birth records that were maintained contemporaneously in Bessarabian church parishes.[10] Finally, Stumpp, who had access to these parish sources, provides a list of presumed early settlers for these three villages as part of his efforts in gathering similar data for each of the twenty-five Bessarabian

---

8. Stumpp, *Emigration from Germany to Russia*, 512.
9. Wahl, "Bessarabian Surname Origins."
10. Flegel, *Extended Relationships*.

German settlements founded before 1841.[11] Stumpp's listings, however, are less useful in that they mix early settlers with later arrivals and, perhaps as a result of having access to only limited records, miss many of the people that Flegel shows were resident in Kulm, Leipzig, and Tarutino in their first years of existence. The origins of the Kulm, Leipzig, and Tarutino first settlers, as indicated by birth data and other genealogical information, are listed in table 1–1.

The settlers of all three villages are dominated by those coming from Prussia. Tarutino is slightly more diverse, with 14.3 percent of its settlers coming from Württemberg. When the linguistic origins of the settlers' surnames are considered, the impression of diversity of the populations in each of the villages is increased.

Looking at the linguistic origins of the surnames of the three villages (see table 1–2), the predominance of northern German origins is reduced, though northern Germans still form a majority. Combining the figures from the three villages, slightly over half (178 or 50.8 percent) have surnames formed from Low German words, from terms used exclusively in northern Germany, or are built from Slavic or Baltic linguistic roots. Surnames that show a central or southern German origin make up a material portion of these villages, varying between a fifth and a quarter of the total. A quarter of the surnames (90 or 25.7 percent) cannot be placed linguistically, as they are found throughout the German-speaking territories. These

**TABLE 1–1.   Origins of the first settlers of Kulm, Leipzig, and Tarutino**

| | Kulm | | Leipzig | | Tarutino | |
|---|---|---|---|---|---|---|
| | Number | Percent | Number | Percent | Number | Percent |
| Prussian Poland[a] | 62 | 63.2% | 54 | 54.0% | 57 | 38.8% |
| West Prussia | 10 | 10.2% | 3 | 3.0% | 11 | 7.5% |
| Pomerania | — | — | 3 | 3.0% | 9 | 6.1% |
| Silesia | 3 | 3.1% | 1 | 1.0% | — | — |
| Brandenburg[b] | 9 | 9.2% | 10 | 10.0% | 5 | 3.4% |
| Prussia[c] | 3 | 3.1% | 11 | 11.0% | 18 | 12.2% |
| Mecklenburg[d] | 2 | 2.0% | 3 | 3.0% | 22 | 15.0% |
| Total Prussia | 89 | 90.8% | 85 | 85.0% | 122 | 83.0% |
| Saxony | — | — | 5 | 5.0% | 1 | 0.7% |
| Württemberg | 8 | 8.2% | 8 | 8.0% | 21 | 14.3% |
| Other German Areas[e] | 1 | 1.0% | 2 | 2.0% | 3 | 2.0% |
| Total Non-Prussian | — | 9.2% | 15 | 15.0% | 25 | 17.0% |
| **Total** | 98 | — | 100 | — | 147 | — |

a. I include here origins listed as "Prussian Poland" and "Poland." For the most part, these refer to villages in South Prussia and New East Prussia.

b. This includes villages in Neumark Brandenburg east of the Oder River.

c. This includes origins listed only as "Prussia" without a province or region as well as places noted as being in Prussia that appear not to be in Prussian Poland.

d. The two principalities (after 1815, duchies) of Mecklenburg-Schwerin and Mecklenburg-Strelitz were politically independent of Prussia until 1870. However, surrounded by Prussia, Mecklenburgers historically shared with Prussians very similar linguistic and cultural patterns, and as a result I have grouped the immigrants from Mecklenburg with those from Prussia.

e. These are comprised of one person from each of the following regions: Alsace, Bavaria, Bohemia, Austrian Galicia, Hesse, and the Pfalz.

11. Stumpp, *Emigration from Germany to Russia*, 502–63.

TABLE 1–2. **Linguistic features of the names of the first settlers also point to geographical and cultural origins**

| | Kulm | | Leipzig | | Tarutino | |
|---|---|---|---|---|---|---|
| | Number | Percentage | Number | Percentage | Number | Percentage |
| North German | | | | | | |
| Low German | 22 | 20.6% | 22 | 22.0% | 19 | 13.3% |
| North Origin | 17 | 15.9% | 14 | 14.0% | 18 | 12.6% |
| Slavic | 16 | 15.0% | 20 | 20.0% | 26 | 18.2% |
| Baltic | 2 | 1.9% | — | — | 2 | 1.4% |
| Total North | 57 | 53.4% | 56 | 56.0% | 65 | 45.5% |
| High German | 16 | 15.0% | 13 | 13.0% | 22 | 15.4% |
| South German | 7 | 6.5% | 8 | 8.0% | 16 | 11.2% |
| Total | 23 | 21.5% | 21 | 21.0% | 38 | 26.6% |
| No Clear Origin | 27 | 25.2% | 23 | 23.0% | 40 | 28.0% |
| **Grand Total** | 107 | | 100 | | 143 | |

are frequently surnames derived from personal names such as Franz, Isaak, Marks, or Martin; common occupational names such as Fischer (fisher), Müller (miller), Schultz (village head), or Vogel (bird catcher); descriptive place names such as Bock (buck, often a house sign), Rondthaler (round valley), or Somerfeld (summer field).

Kulm and Leipzig have the greatest number of northern German surnames, but even in these villages the figures do not reach 60 percent. As the early population of both Kulm and Leipzig included over 20 percent with surnames indicating central or southern German origins, this suggests both had a healthy diversity of linguistic and cultural backgrounds. It is also worth noting that while each of these three villages have northern German majorities, composed often of families with origins east of the Oder river or from Brandenburg, there are many other origins within this northern German population. The surname of Martin Friesz of Tarutino, as noted earlier, identifies his background as Frisian. Friesz was born in 1789 in or near Marienburg in West Prussia in the estuary of the Vistula River.[12] Marienburg lies in an area that from the early seventeenth century drew many Netherlanders and Frisians, particularly Mennonites, who were skilled at draining and creating rich farmland out of the wetlands. The Hiller family of Tarutino, the Kliem family of Kulm and the Hennig, and Rauhut families of Leipzig all have surnames that suggest family origins in Silesia. The Busse family of Kulm have a surname that points to a background in Westphalia, the Sperling family of Kulm one that suggests Saxony, and the Lack family of Leipzig one that is frequently found in the wetlands south of Hamburg. Fifteen percent of the Tarutino families have backgrounds in Mecklenburg, a region west of the Oder River surrounded by Prussia. Mecklenburg's peasant population contained many families who had been speakers of West Slavic dialects but had become German speakers by at least the mid-seventeenth century.

Also striking among the northern German population in these three villages is the material number of surnames that indicate families with a Slavic language background. Kulm has the smallest number at 16 percent, and Tarutino the largest with slightly over a quarter (26 percent). Not surprisingly, where a place of origin can

---

12. Flegel, *Extended Relationships*, 192.

be identified, all but one of the settlers with surnames having Slavic roots came to Bessarabia from villages east of the Oder River in Prussia. There are additionally four families, two in Kulm and two in Tarutino, with surnames derived from Baltic languages.

It cannot be known now whether any of the families with surnames that have Slavic or Baltic linguistic roots retained any memory of their family's linguistic past at the time of their immigration to Bessarabia. As cultural habits are notably slow to change, it is probable that some portion of their former pre-German cultural habits survived within the German linguistic setting they adopted and were taken with them to Bessarabia.

The surnames of the Kulm, Leipzig, and Tarutino settlers also underline the general peasant backgrounds of the colonists. Most German and West Slavic peasant surnames were created from one of four name formation patterns: (1) personal names often put in shortened forms and showing features peculiar to the linguistic area the family came from, (2) personal descriptive characteristics, which also tended to use local and colloquial forms, (3) occupational words, and (4) place names. All of the 350 Kulm, Leipzig, and Tarutino surnames are derived from one of these four patterns, with personal names being the largest and representing roughly a third of the names (see table 1–3).

A large number of the surnames from these villages are based on regional speech forms. Among surnames formed from the 114 personal names, for example, 73.7 percent of the surnames in that category are derived from regionally specific forms of personal names, such as the surname of the Leipzig family Mertins, which is based on a Low German form of the name Martin. The regional diversity reflected in the surnames of these colonists suggests an equivalent diversity in cultural backgrounds.

If the surnames of the colonists reflect a wide diversity in family backgrounds, there were also important shared features in these backgrounds. What many of them held in common was that their families had moved from elsewhere to take up land tenures in Prussia, especially in Prussia's newly acquired territories in what, before 1772, had been the Kingdom of Poland. They shared family backgrounds of movement, of pulling up stakes, of taking risks with the goal of establishing themselves in a better place, and the experience, for better or worse, of surviving that movement. These will be themes of the following two chapters. Here I want to put forward the idea that the wide diversity existing in their surname origins suggests that the most common feature uniting them wasn't their language or culture but rather their recent similar experiences of immigration and the confidence that came from having survived those experiences.

TABLE 1–3. **Surname patterns of the first settlers of Kulm, Leipzig, and Tarutino**

|  | Number | Percentage |
| --- | --- | --- |
| Personal Names | 114 | 32.6% |
| **Personal Descriptions** | 89 | 25.6% |
| Occupational Names | 81 | 23.1% |
| Place Names | 66 | 18.8% |
| **Total** | 350 |  |

# The Economic Situation of German Peasants in Eighteenth-Century Prussia, Württemberg, and the Upper Rhineland

The great majority of the first wave of Germans to come to Bessarabia came there from Prussian Poland—that is, those parts of Poland that Prussia had absorbed as its part of the Three Partitions of Poland (1772, 1793, and 1795). The great majority of these German-speaking peasant farmers, however, were not long-term residents of Prussian Poland. Their emigration from Prussian Poland to Bessarabia was thus not their first experience in pulling up stakes and seeking better circumstances. Somewhat under half of those who left Prussian Poland for Bessarabia had come from other Prussian territories such as Brandenburg, Neumark Brandenburg, Pomerania, Silesia, and East Prussia, or neighboring Mecklenburg and Saxony. Most of these had come to Poland during the eighteenth century, though some had arrived as early as 1650. Many other Bessarabian Germans were originally from the upper Rhineland, especially from Württemberg and Baden, and immigrated to Prussian Poland after 1790.

German peasants were motivated to immigrate to Prussian Poland and to take leases from German and Polish landowners to escape a variety of problems: high rents and taxes, small family holdings, and the destruction and disease that accompanied living in war zones, as well as conflicts within the Lutheran Church.

Prussian Poland was largely made up of two regions of the pre-partition Polish Commonwealth (Rzeczpospolita Polska): Royal Prussia[1] (Prusy Królewskie) and Great Poland (Wielkopolska). Royal Prussia was situated in the lower Vistula River valley running north from Thorn (Polish Toruń) to Danzig. It became a distinct region after 1466 when the German and Polish gentry and towns in this region, combining against the Teutonic Order's rule, attached themselves to the Polish Kingdom. The remaining part of Prussia, called Ducal Prussia and centered in East Prussia and Pomerania, became, with Brandenburg, the core from which the Kingdom in Prussia emerged in the eighteenth century. German-speaking nobility and peasant colonists had settled Royal Prussia in the twelfth and thirteenth centuries. German townsmen began to appear in Royal Prussia at the end of the thirteenth century. In the mid-sixteenth century, many Mennonites fleeing persecution in the Netherlands settled in the Vistula delta region. In the Netherlands, they had become skilled in draining the wetlands and swamps to create a rich farmland. Their success led the now generally Polish-speaking gentry[2] to invite more German peasants to settle by clearing woodlands and draining the lowlands upstream from the Vistula delta in areas not already settled by Polish peasants. German weavers were drawn to towns in Royal Prussia, creating a profitable textile industry. Royal Prussia was taken from Poland in the first partition of 1772 and formed the basis thereafter of the Prussian province of West Prussia.

Great Poland, located to the south of Royal Prussia, was an area extending from Poznan (Polish Poznań, German Posen), the capital of Great Poland, east to the ancient town Kalisz (German Kalisch). Though Great Poland had a far smaller population of German speakers, it did have in its western regions an extensive German medieval settlement, some of which continued to be German-speaking in the eighteenth century. Beginning in the late seventeenth century, the Polish gentry here too began inviting German peasants to clear land that would then be leased to them. The high tide of such German immigration to Great Poland was in the eighteenth century and generally followed the pattern established earlier in Royal Prussia. Beginning in the late 1780s, numbers of German peasants from Württemberg and the Rhineland were drawn to Great Poland and took leases on land extending east from Kalisz and Konin toward Warsaw. Immigration to Great Poland increased

---

1. The Polish term Royal Prussia was called "royal" as it was nominally ruled by the King of Poland in contrast to the initially smaller state ruled at first by the Teutonic Knights and later by the Hohenzollern dukes who, after 1701, were permitted to call themselves kings "in" but not "of" Prussia. Royal Prussia was made up of Pomerellen as well as the districts of Elbing (Polish Elbląg), Marienburg (Polish Malbork), Kulm, and Warmia. See Map 1 in Karin Friedrich, *The Other Prussia: Royal Prussia, Poland and Liberty, 1569-1772* (New York: Cambridge University Press, 2000). The population of Royal Prussia included the descendants of the Baltic Prussian-speaking people who, by the eighteenth century, generally spoke German or Kashubian, as well as many German speakers who had moved there from the west from the twelfth century onward as nobles, townsfolk, and peasants, and Polish and Kashubian speakers who had moved there from the south and the western Baltic coastlands.

2. Hagen, quoting Ilse Rhode's *Das Nationalitätenverhältnis in West Preussen und Posen zur Zeit der Polnischen Teilungen*, notes that by 1772, "German noble surnames were great exceptions." William H. Hagen, *Germans, Poles, and Jews: The Nationality Conflict in the Prussian East, 1772-1914* (Chicago: University of Chicago Press, 1980), 4.

significantly after 1793, when Prussia took control of this jurisdiction in the Second Partition of Poland and reconstituted it as the province of South Prussia. When Prussia regained de jure control of most of this territory after the Napoleonic Wars in 1815, Great Poland became the Posen Province of Prussia.

Prior to Prussia's absorption of Royal Prussia and Great Poland, the Polish gentry in these areas had strong reasons for inviting German peasants to clear and settle on land they controlled. In the first place, there was much open land to settle. Poland, before the partitions in the eighteenth century, had an average population density of 39 persons per square mile. Prussia, then equally dominated by agricultural estates, had an average density of 75 people, and France, also still predominately rural, had an average density of 128 people.[3] The Polish peasant population in the eighteenth century remained generally flat. This occurred in part because the conditions under which the Polish peasantry existed were very harsh: they worked as virtual serfs tilling the gentry's land, with the majority having only garden plots for themselves. Hagen notes declining grain exports and seed-yield ratios from Polish estates from the mid-seventeenth to the mid-eighteenth century,[4] which implies both that the Polish peasant population remained relatively flat, and that the Polish gentry estate owners had reached a limit in what they could economically derive from the existing land and forced labor system. Another major factor lying behind both the lack of growth among the Polish peasant population and the growing interest of Polish gentry landlords in attracting settlement by German peasants was the fact that estates in both Royal Prussia and the northern parts of Great Poland suffered significant crop destruction and animal confiscations during the Swedish Invasion (1655–60) and the Second Great Northern War (1700–21). This led not just to peasant hardships and even deaths, but to long-term poverty that limited family size. For some Polish peasants, the troubles led to emigration from the area. The result for estate owners was a decrease in income which, with the existing serf-based economy, could only be improved slowly.

To maintain or increase their income, the gentry had to clear unused woodlands and swamps, and so turn more of their land to profitable use. German peasants from Prussia were sought for this task as they had done this already in Brandenburg, Pomerania, and East Prussia. To attract them, however, the Polish gentry had to offer positive terms, and they did. Generally, German peasants were offered leases on plots of 30–80 acres of land that they would first have to clear. Leasing costs appear to have been a little better than the terms these peasants had from the Prussian gentry, as discussed below, but the leased plots were larger. The German peasants, who were almost all Protestant, could build churches, practice their religion, and school their children in German. The Germans, unlike Polish peasants, were also offered hereditary rights to retain their land leases. Given the efforts of the Catholic Church in Poland at this time to eradicate the practice of the Protestant religion among the long-settled German townsfolk in Royal Prussia and Great Poland,[5] offering

---

3. Ibid., 9.
4. Ibid.
5. Conflicts frequently occurred between Catholics and Protestants in seventeenth- and eighteenth-century Royal Prussian towns where there were material populations of Protestants, most but not all of them German. The most notorious example such conflict was the so-called "Thorner Blutgericht" ("Bloody Court of Thorn") of 1724, when the Protestant mayor and nine other officials were blamed for neglect of duty following a riot between Catholic and Protestant students. A trial was held in Warsaw and a military detachment then came to Thorn and executed the accused.

freedom of religion to the incoming German peasants was surely a sign that the Polish gentry perceived material economic advantages to be gained by attracting German peasants. It is also clear that the Polish gentry did not ask the Polish peasantry to make such land clearances. Perhaps the landowners felt Polish peasants hadn't the skills and knowledge required, or perhaps Polish peasants had stubbornly refused to leave the meadowlands they historically preferred. Perhaps the Polish gentry realized that to incent their peasantry to clear and settle new lands, they would have to offer better terms to them, and that in doing so, they would disturb and undercut the serf labor economy into which they had forced much of their peasantry and so create social unrest.

One example of terms offered by Polish noble landlords to attract German peasants to establish farms on their land is the contract offered by the Zamojski family to one hundred German Catholic peasants. This contract, preserved in the State Archives of Lublin, is from 1785 and forms an offer to rent land to German peasant families.[6] The land offered was quite likely the marshy area bordering the Łabunka River north of the town of Zamość. The German settlers founded there a village, still called Sitaniec-Kolonia, from which came many of the first families to settle the Krasna colony in Bessarabia in 1813–14.[7] The offer included some 25 acres of land, material to build houses, as well as animals, wagons, and tools.[8] After three years, the settlers would be liable for both taxes and eight days of work annually that would benefit the noble owner's interests. The offer of money and materials to come to an area well southeast of Warsaw and far from other areas of German peasant settlement suggests the Zamojski offer was directed at relatively poor German peasants and would not have been as generous in terms of rent and mandatory work for the landlord as those offered to settlers in Royal Prussia and Great Poland. It was, however, far more generous than the terms offered to local Polish peasants.

After Prussia took control of Royal Prussia and Great Poland, the Prussian government further encouraged the immigration of German peasants. The Prussian state was very interested in populating crown lands with German peasants. After the partitions, Prussia transformed Polish crown land directly into Prussian crown land. In several cases, that meant forcing out members of the Polish gentry who claimed land rights to crown land without offering compensation. Also taken in as new Prussian crown land were the estates owned by the Catholic Church, though

6. Ted J. Becker, trans., "Zamosz (Poland) Settlement Contract of 28 February 1785," *Heritage Review* 41, no. 4 (2011): 31–35. The original contract in German is in the State Archives in Lublin (Archiwum Państwowe w Lublinie), and was issued on 28 February 1785 by J. Kolmannhuber, District Sergeant. Lublin was a district center in 1785. The original contract is noted as being filed in the then Provincial capital of Lemberg (Polish Lwów, now Ukrainian L'viv). The southern half of the Polish Province Lwów, including the area of Zamość, had been incorporated into Austria in the first Partition of Poland in 1772.

7. Sitaniec-Kolonia is the Schitonitz identified by Stumpp (*Emigration from Germany to Russia*, 528) and mentioned in many Krasna genealogies as one of two villages that sourced most of the first Krasna immigrants. The term *kolonia* (colony) attached to a Polish village name often implied a settlement established for German peasants having different terms and rights than nearby Polish villages.

8. The offer was for farmsteads of "30 koretz" of land. A *koretz, korzec* in Polish, is typically a unit of volume but was also used in eastern Poland as a unit of area of varying dimensions. The assumption made by Ted Becker, who translated the charter, of 0.88 acre is reasonably consistent with other eighteenth-century appearances of this measurement. The charter offered to provide two horses, oxen, and cows, and a single pregnant pig for each farmstead.

here the church was compensated by annually receiving a fixed percentage of the yield. Finally, Prussian crown land was increased in Prussian Poland by the purchase of estates from the Polish gentry.[9] Friedrich the Great ordered such purchases made when he became irritated at members of the Polish gentry in West Prussia who leased out all of their land and then moved to Warsaw so as to live outside of Prussia. Seeking to import German peasants onto the newly acquired crown land, Friedrich the Great, his successors, and the Prussian government were motivated by political and economic goals rather than nationalistic ones. This was not an effort of ethnic cleansing that expelled Poles to make room for Germans. Friedrich the Great would likely have preferred French and English peasants, as he considered them more skilled. "This [policy] depended less on language than on political allegiance and obedience, and on productive, thrifty and enlightened behavior in private life."[10] Prussia brought in Germans because they were available, because they were good agriculturalists, and because the government felt they would willingly accept the Prussian system.

By 1795, estimations of the number of German peasants living in West and South Prussia—that is, in the former provinces of Royal Russia and Great Poland—indicate that the Germans were the majority in one region and a substantial minority in others (see table 2–1). The data is from Prussian census information on religious adherence. However, because Germans were the only Protestants in the rural districts of these provinces, it is a good measure of the linguistic and cultural divide.[11]

By 1795, German peasants formed a majority in rural West Prussia, a territory that Prussia had controlled since 1772. Certainly the German majority here was helped by the existence of the large Mennonite population in the lower Vistula, but it also reflects the significant immigration of German peasants in the eighteenth century both before and after the Prussian takeover. The Netze District was the territory on both sides of the Netze (Polish Notec) River to the west of Bromberg (Polish Bydgoszcz). This area, historically attached to Great Poland, was taken over by Prussia in 1772 and combined with Royal Prussia to form West Prussia. When Prussia took control of Great Poland in 1793, the Netze District was reattached to South Prussia, the former Great Poland. German peasants start to appear in the Netze District in large numbers from the beginning of the eighteenth century onward and by 1795, formed 36 percent of the rural population. In South Prussia, where the German peasant population in 1795 was concentrated to the north and west of the city of Poznan, German speakers made up an estimated 20 percent of

TABLE 2–1.  **Numbers of Protestants and Catholics per Prussian region**

| Region | Protestants | Catholics |
| --- | --- | --- |
| West Prussia | 239,500 | 221,000 |
| The Netze District | 24,000 | 42,000 |
| South Prussia | 90,000 | 362,000 |

9.  Hagen, *Germans, Poles, and Jews*, 39.
10. Ibid., 44.
11. The figures are quoted in Hagen, *Germans, Poles, and Jews*, 15. Hagen describes these as estimations which he has taken from studies made by Ilse Rhode, *Das Nationalitätenverhältnis*, and Georg Dabinnus, *Die ländliche Bevölkerung Pommerellens im Jahre 1772 mit Einschluss des Danziger Gebiets im Jahre 1793* (Marburg, Ger.: n.p., 1953).

the rural population. The large influx of German peasants from Württemberg and the upper Rhineland to the area east of Kalisz in this province was only in its early stages in 1795.

The German peasants who immigrated to Prussian Poland and took leases to clear and settle land were called Hauländer, a word that was borrowed into Polish as *olędrzy*. Hagen sees this as a corruption of the word Hollander "recalling the Mennonite pioneers" who came in the sixteenth century.[12] The term, however, may also derive from the German word *Hau* meaning "cutting" or "felling" and so note that those who created fields and settlements did so by cutting down forested areas or swampy scrub land.

## German peasant tenants in Prussian Poland were obligated to provide both service and cash as lease payments under a system called Gutsheerschaft, which gave the nobility and the crown great powers as landowners

Although holding tenure under far better terms than Polish peasants, the German Hauländer in Prussian Poland lived under a demanding economic system. As in the rest of Prussia, all the arable land was owned by the crown or by the gentry and the peasants' title to use of the land was via lease. In Prussia, such leases were to be paid for by annual rents, partially in cash and partially in labor on the manor land. In addition, peasants paid taxes to the state. In Prussia, the sum of peasant cash rents and taxes in years of good harvests typically came to half of the value of the crops. In Poland, while German peasants owed cash rents and manorial farm labor as a cost of leases, taxes were distinctly lower than in Prussia. As German peasants coming to Poland were not subject to Polish military conscription, leasing lands in Poland before the partitions offered distinct advantages to German peasants over leases in Prussia.

In Western Europe, the growth of trade and industry enlarged towns and cities. As urban centers developed, so did an economy based on the exchange of money for increasingly attractive goods. Large landowners in Western Europe began to find themselves falling behind economically when they depended on the farm work of tenants or peasants performing feudal duties. Their answer was to drive away peasants and enclose their manors for sheep and cattle or to turn to paid agricultural work rather than halfheartedly performed labor obligations. Such changes were far slower to come farther east. Beyond the Elbe River, trade and industry remained minor features of the economy; towns were small and cities grew from the administrative needs of the principalities more so than from trade and commerce. From the late sixteenth through the eighteenth century, the economy east of the Elbe was dominated by large manor estates on which labor was performed by peasants as part of their costs for leasing plots of land. The gentry landowners were able to sell their grain profitably in country or in the growing market for grain shipped to Western Europe. Only toward the end of the eighteenth century were some Prussian landlords starting to see advantages in farming with paid labor instead of peasant duties.

---

12. Hagen, *Germans, Poles, and Jews*, 5.

In Prussia, the economic system that divided manor lands by leasing part to peasants with the stipulation that they work the land retained by the landowner as part of their lease payment was called Gutsheerschaft. The term comes from the noun *Gut*, or property, which in Prussia also came to mean a landlord's large manor estate. During the seventeenth century, similar large agricultural estates dependent on peasant labor in return for tenancies also appear in the northern regions of the Kingdom of Poland, especially in Royal Prussia and the western regions of Great Poland. In Poland, this system is called *system folwarczno pańszcznainy* (a system of manorialism with compulsory labor).[13]

In both Prussia and Poland during the sixteenth and seventeenth centuries, gentry landlords sought to enlarge their manor holdings. Financial hardships caused peasants owning land to lose title and pass into leaseholders. Gentry power also increased gentry holdings at the expense of peasant land by ending open-field systems and replacing them with areas of specific farms. Gentry control and authority grew as well. Gentry landlords sought, often successfully, to increase labor and cartage requirements as the price of tenancy. Landlords were also responsible for changing cultivation practices. The practice of three-field crop rotation, which left a section of fallow land with each season, was generally replaced (in Prussia at least) by a continuous-use system based on an increased use of fertilizer.

The Gutsheerschaft system grew up in Prussia and Poland in the sixteenth and seventeenth centuries out of the combination of two separate factors: an increase in the coercive powers of the nobility, which resulted from wars and the failure of a central authority to counterbalance local authority, and the growth of a significant grain trade with the increasingly urban Western Europe out of ports in the Baltic.[14] The Gutsheerschaft system describes not just the domination of landholding by the gentry but a system in which the gentry landowners acquired significant legal, political, social, and economic powers over their peasant leaseholders:

> *Manorial lordship was a much more powerful form of noble authority over subject villagers than a noble landlordism contenting itself with the levying of rents in cash or kind. Manorial lordship reduced the villages to appendages of the domanial economy. The manorial courts dominated the village communes, judging the individual villagers as economic subjects of the manor as well as in their private lives. Where personal serfdom prevailed, manorial lordship extended to full-scale control over the villagers' lands and farmsteads, and over their rights of marriage and inheritance as well.*[15]

## German peasant conditions in Prussian Poland

Peasants in Prussia and German peasants in Poland lived in villages with their fields, orchards, meadows, and woodlands surrounding the village. The open-field system,

---

13. Hagen, "Village Life," 157. Hagen quotes here from the work of the Polish historian Jan Rutkowski.
14. Ibid. Hagen is following arguments developed by Jan Rutkowski that it was the combination of these factors that produced such a manorial economic system. It did not appear with just an increase in seigneurial authority (as in Russia), nor did this manorial system come into existence with an increase in export opportunities where that occurred without an increase in the power of the nobles over local peasantry, such as in Sicily.
15. Ibid., 151.

prevalent in medieval times in Prussia, had been replaced by more unified household land allotments. Peasant society was divided into different levels based on the amount of land held by a household. At the top were fullholders, referred to as Bauer or Wirt in German, who in Brandenburg usually held two hides or Hufen of land, roughly 70–90 acres.[16] Fullholders in Poland held smaller amounts of land. Halfholders, Kossat, were the next level down, typically having less than half that amount. Then came smallholders or cottagers, Kätner or Gärtner, who had independent households but held only small amounts of land, often just garden land around their home, and worked nearly full time on the manor farm or for fullholders. Below the smallholders were unmarried hired laborers, male and female, who lived with and worked for full- or halfholders, often performing the labor services on the manorial farm required of the householder's lease. Farm laborers received room and board and cash, which, when saved, might provide the wherewithal for marriage and a leasehold of their own. Smallholders and farm laborers formed a clear majority of the peasant population in Prussia.[17] Days of labor on manor land in Prussia might range from the equivalent of one to two days per week to almost six, with the latter coming close to the system of serfdom under which most Polish peasants lived.[18]

Leaseholds were generally hereditary, which suited landlords as this encouraged land improvements and stability. Peasants preferred this arrangement as well for the security it provided. Landlords, however, were careful to ensure that an inheritance went to someone capable of maintaining the lease requirements; they did not offer new leases to families who did not demonstrate they had the means to support a lease.

In fullholder households, children would frequently remain in the parental home and, as they reached their mid-teens, would replace hired non-family help. After marriage, not all children left a fullholder's household: married children might remain if the economic viability of the leasehold demanded their labor. At a parent's death or decision to give up the leasehold and retire to a cottage on the tenancy, one child would inherit the tenancy (usually needing the landlord's blessing) and other children would take their inheritance shares of the value of the household to purchase another leasehold or remain and retain their share if other leaseholds were not available or exceeded their financial capabilities.

---

16. Hagen, *Ordinary Prussians*, 192. Landholding for fullholders in Hagen's study varied between those in the village of Blüthen, who averaged 29.0 ha of arable, 0.9 ha of meadow, and another 5 ha of pasture and woods, having a total lease holding of 34.9 ha or 86.2 acres, and those fullholders in the village of Glövzin who averaged 24.5 ha of arable, 0.9 ha of meadow, and 7 ha of pasture and woods for a total of 32.4 ha or 80.1 acres.

17. Edgar Melton estimates that in the mid-eighteenth century such landless and semi-landless farm workers may have accounted for as much as two-thirds of the peasant population in Prussia. Melton, "The Transformation of Rural Economy in East Elbian Prussia," in *The Rise of Prussia 1700-1830*, ed. Philip Dwyer (New York: Longman, 2000), 120.

18. Prussian and German historians have argued for a distinction between the unlimited labor service required under German arrangements in some regions of Prussia (Gutsheerschaft) and serfdom as practiced in contemporary Russia. Under the former, the landlord received the services from peasant farmsteads who, at least among the fullholders, hired and at times boarded and partially fed farm laborers, who actually performed the required services, thus freeing the peasant to work on his own family's land. Sometimes these were the children of the peasants. This created in Prussia a class of peasants, better off than farm laborers, who didn't exist in Russia. In Russia, there was no middleman between lord and peasant—that is, the peasants themselves generally farmed the lord's land. Such a fine distinction would not be appropriate for Polish peasants in Poland. While they held leases for small plots of land, by the seventeenth century, the great part of their week was spent, like peasants in Russia, in labor on manor lands.

Marriage was by no means universal for peasants and those who married typically did so late. Hagen shows from the eighteenth-century Blüthen parish records in Brandenburg that perhaps a quarter of the population did not marry and the average age at marriage for men was over thirty-one and for women twenty-seven.[19] Later ages at marriage for peasants was the result of the fact that income was needed in order to attract a marriage partner and for the couple to support themselves once married. Income meant access to land either via inheritance, acquiring a lease, or from a family holding large enough to support a married child. In Prussia after the beginning of the eighteenth century, virtually all young men were obliged to do active military service in the Prussian army, after which they would have temporary reserve duty. While on reserve, however, they might work in their own household or find employment in another and so ultimately save sufficient capital for the time they might inherit, or, using their savings and their inheritance share from their parent's household, acquire a leasehold elsewhere.

During the eighteenth century, grain grown on manor estates was in increasingly high demand. Internally, the Prussian state sought larger grain supplies to feed its growing army, while the growth of cities and towns in Western Europe steadily built up the size of the external grain trade. As a cash-based economy began to spread east, crown and gentry landholders in Prussia and Prussian Poland sought ways to increase the income they derived from their manors.

Landowners in late eighteenth-century Prussian Poland sought increased income by changing traditional practices: They sought to lease fewer plots of land, to hire labor instead of gaining it via leasing arrangements, and, when they leased land, to place stronger holds on lessees.

Throughout the eighteenth century the cash needs of both the Prussian state and the Prussian gentry landlords steadily grew. Friedrich the Great fought two major wars and made Prussia a European power. Status symbols that reflected and defined the gentry's lifestyle were increasingly driven by the acquisition of clothing, furnishings, food, and drink that could not be produced on manor estates and had to be purchased with cash. Both the Prussian state and the Prussian nobility were primarily dependent on agriculture for income. Both attempted similar means to grow their income. Increasingly, they became interested in commuting the labor services owed by peasant leaseholders on crown and gentry manor land into cash payments.

Landlords came to realize that the required labor, though performed without cost to them, was often performed halfheartedly and without the same care and attention the peasants provided to their own land. Cash received in lieu of unwilling labor could be used to purchase labor that had greater incentive to perform well. Landlords also came to realize that they earned more from the sale of crops grown on manor land than from the payments made to them by lessees. Because the most

---

19. Hagen, "Village Life," 180–81; and Hagen, *Ordinary Prussians*, 270–73. Hagen notes that the average age at marriage for fullholders was lower—around twenty-six for men and twenty-four for women, given their economic position and the direct relationship between material well-being and the ability to marry. High average ages at marriage were not just a feature of Prussian peasant life: Wolfgang Kaschuba notes that the average age for men in Kiebingen in Württemberg dipped below thirty only after 1875. See Kaschuba, "Peasants and Others: The Historical Contours of Village Class Society" in *The German Peasantry: Conflict and Community in Rural Society from the 18th to the 20th Centuries*, ed. R. Evans and W. Lee (New York: St. Martin's Press, 1986), 251.

common grain grown in Prussia, rye, produced low yields, typically 4–6 to 1, there were clear limits to productivity increases. Landowners came to realize that they would increase their income if they increased the amount of grain produced on manor land. To increase the size of manor holdings, landlords sought to decrease the amount of land that was leased. Leases for halfholders and especially cottagers were not renewed on the deaths of tenants. While not yet widely prevalent, practice was starting to tilt toward peasants becoming farm laborers paid in cash for their full-time work on manor land. Though such peasants kept a garden and an animal or two, a material portion of their food supply was now purchased. Regarding peasant fullholders, the most efficient peasant tenants, crown and gentry strategy toward the end of the eighteenth century was to tighten their hold on such peasants both by adding terms to lease arrangements that made it more difficult for peasants to leave, and by continually seeking to increase leasing costs.

Gentry efforts in Prussia in the eighteenth century to increase their leverage over peasants leasing land or supplying labor on their manors, however, were undercut by two other factors: the effects of warfare, which destroyed farms and crops, and killed peasants or caused them to flee, and the Prussian acquisition of large parts of Poland that caused the Prussian government to seek to place German peasants on the newly acquired crown land there. In Prussia, the Second Northern War, which ended in 1721, and the Seven Years' War, which ended in 1765 brought, great personal and economic hardship. As a result of the Seven Years' War, Prussia was estimated to have lost perhaps 10 percent of its population, with the heaviest losses occurring in Pomerania and East Prussia.[20] The combination of fewer families to continue or to take up tenancies and the difficulties of sustaining life under the existing tenant agreements led to significant changes in the labor market. The labor shortage pressed landlords to seek to attract new tenants who might fill vacant land and encouraged peasants to attempt to gain release from burdensome lease agreements. However, hereditary leaseholds, called Erbpacht,[21] were not easily broken in Prussia. Landlords would allow leaseholders to break a lease for better opportunities, though this usually required that a payment be made to buy out open obligations and that the landlord find a suitable new leaseholder. This was an expensive proposition and not often encountered.[22] Leaseholders who couldn't make ends meet or hoped to find a better opportunity elsewhere at times just left, abandoning their leases, but this course meant taking minimal seed stock and animals. Runaways were aggressively pursued, so this course bore great risks. Even when the new landlord provided a Hofwehr of seed, basic animals, and tools, these were not likely to be first-rate, and so those who left without agreement would often restart in a position further down the economic scale.

---

20. East Prussia is estimated to have suffered a population loss of ninety thousand people and Pomerania a loss of seventy thousand. As Friedrich the Great directly equated population size and state power, following the war he caused Prussia to make significant efforts to attract new settlement to Prussia east of the Elbe. See H. M. Scott, "1763–1786: The Second Reign of Frederick the Great?" in Dwyer, *Rise of Prussia*, 193.

21. From *Erbe*, which, as a neuter noun, means "an inheritance," and as a masculine noun, means "an heir."

22. Hagen, in his detailed accounting of eighteenth-century Stavenow Brandenburg leaseholders, does cite an instance where a neighboring landowner allowed a Joachim Müller to leave the latter's smallholding to take a lease in Stavenow from childless relatives, noting he did this "unwillingly, in view of [Müller's] loyalty and industriousness," but did it asking only that the Stavenow holdings of the von Kleists return the kindness. Hagen, *Ordinary Prussians*, 152.

Where Prussian landlords sought to tighten hereditary tenancies by making them more burdensome and harder to leave, their efforts were mitigated by the growing availability of land for lease in Poland. Even before the partitions, Polish landlords sought to attract German peasants by offering them better terms for leases than existed in Prussia. German peasants put a high value on leases that were hereditary, as such leases offered assurances that land and the improvements made on it might be kept within a family's possession. Recognizing this, Polish landlords offered incoming German peasants hereditary rights to the equivalent of a full-hold lease. Such leases were a significant change in local custom and represented a major reduction in landlord rights. The fact that they were offered is an indication of the great value Polish gentry landlords put on attracting German peasants. The customary leaseholding rights of Polish peasants living on the same manor were, in contrast, indeterminate by nature, referred to in Polish as *dzierzana bezterminowa*, which meant they were hereditary by custom but not by law and as a result the landlord could deny rights to a peasant's land at will.[23]

The Prussian crown as well as German and Polish landlords in Prussian Poland also offered temporary leases, called Zeitpacht, as a means to lure prospective peasant tenants. In Prussia, such leases were relatively rare and had generally been offered only to well-to-do peasants who possessed their own livestock and so were considered able to take on fullholder responsibilities. After the partitions in Prussian Poland, temporary leases were viewed by both landowners and prospective tenants in a different light. Offers of fullholder-sized leases clearly were attractive to peasants from elsewhere in Prussia and from Württemberg and the Rhineland, but the attraction must have been counterweighed by fears and concerns. These might have centered on the need to clear or drain the land, the large or majority Polish Catholic population already living there, or even the permanence of Prussia's hold on the territory. Temporary leases of four to six years, despite the risks, would not lock a peasant family in to a bad situation. It was certainly the hope of the Prussian bureaucracy who initiated the temporary leases and the Polish and German gentry landowners who followed suit with these leases that the incoming German peasants would stay and the leases would ultimately become hereditary. Prussia had some history with this practice, as the government of Friedrich Wilhelm I had offered six-year leases on crown land in East Prussia to the Austrian Lutheran refugees from Salzburg in 1731–34. This generally worked out well for the Prussian government, as the leases had, over time, become hereditary and the government was able to raise rents.[24]

## Numbers of German-speaking peasants moved to Prussian Poland after the partitions, and after 1790, many of these came from Württemberg and Baden

Prussian peasants who immigrated to the new Prussian territories in Poland appear frequently to have been the younger sons of leaseholders. They were not likely to have been peasants who had purchased their way out of hereditary leases. While buyouts occurred, they were not common. It would be even less likely that such

---

23. Hagen, "Village Life," 158.
24. Emil Daniels, "Prussia under Frederick William I," in the *Cambridge Modern History*, ed. A. W. Ward, G. W. Prothero, and Stanley Leathes, vol. 6, *18th Century* (Cambridge, Eng.: Cambridge University Press, 1909), 218.

Prussian peasants were runaways who had abandoned leases. While the Prussian government was eager to bring in German-speaking peasants to settle West and South Prussia after they were acquired in the partitions, they did not wish to do so at the expense of the crown or of the nobility in other parts of the kingdom. Peasants who had abandoned their holdings were, as Hagen reports for Stavenow in Brandenburg, aggressively sought, frequently caught, and brought back in chains. If they escaped capture, they were most likely to seek to establish themselves outside of Prussia or in towns where their past could be obscured.[25]

Before 1790, most of the German peasants who settled in Prussian Poland came there from other parts of Prussia. Not surprisingly, regions neighboring Prussian Poland such as Pomerania, Neumark Brandenburg, and Silesia supplied many of these immigrants, but records indicate that some came from farther away in Brandenburg or the independent Kingdom of Saxony and the princedoms of Mecklenburg. Losses of crops, seed stock, and animals caused by government requisitions and the passages of armies during the Seven Years' War initiated a period of widespread population movement among the Prussian peasantry. Efforts to escape the fighting or to start anew appear to have been two major causes for peasants to have moved to take leases on land in Poland. For others, the opportunity to lease a fullhold, to have a lease in one's own right when another sibling was to take the family leasehold, or, before the Prussian takeover, the opportunity to avoid conscription in the Prussian army may have been the motivating rationale.

Beginning in the late 1780s and starting in force in the mid-1790s, another group of peasants became an important focus of the Prussian government's effort to increase the immigration of German peasants into Prussian Poland. These were peasants from Württemberg especially, but also from other upper Rhineland states such as Baden, Alsace, Hesse, and the Bavarian-controlled Pfalz. Early portions of this group were drawn by offers from the Polish gentry, but most came after 1793 when Prussia took over the province of Great Poland in the Second Partition of Poland, creating South Prussia, and after the Third Partition in 1796, when Prussia created New East Prussia. Brandes quotes estimates that suggest that after 1800, Friedrich Wilhelm III settled 13,600 people in these two new Prussian provinces, with most coming from Württemberg.[26] Many of these new settlements were located on land around the city of Łodz and eastwards toward Warsaw. This immigration to Prussian Poland from Württemberg and the Rhineland stopped in 1806, when warfare erupted between Prussia and France.

The area along and inland from the upper Rhine River had a German-speaking majority from shortly after the end of the Roman era. By the medieval period the area had been divided into a welter of small states and semi-independent towns intermixed with church lands and the holdings of larger and more powerful prince-doms. The Duchy of Württemberg and the Margraviate of Baden were, in the eigh-teenth century, the largest and most powerful states. Protestant peasants were also attracted to Prussian Poland from Alsace across the Rhine as Catholic France had

25. Hagen, *Ordinary Prussians*, 110, 480–82. Stavenow's proximity to independent Mecklenburg meant that runaways could find some refuge there. Towns were frequently a goal for those abandoning lease obligations, as the proverb from earlier feudal times still rang true in the eighteenth and early nineteenth centuries: *Städtluft macht frei*, or "City air brings freedom."
26. Brandes, *Von den Zaren Adoptiert*, 88.

acquired most of this territory in 1648 in the Treaty of Westphalia, which ended the Thirty Years' War. That same treaty placed generally Protestant Pfalz under the control of the Catholic Duchy of Bavaria, creating reasons for Protestant peasants there to seek other lands where they might freely practice their religion.

In the eighteenth century, peasants in the upper Rhineland generally lived on land they held by rights of freehold. However, from early medieval times, many peasants had been compelled, in exchange for their security, to perform services on the lands held by the nobility or church. By the eighteenth century, such services were frequently transmitted into payments in cash or kind. Such payments, together with the taxes levied by the states for government organization and for the upkeep of princely lifestyles, constituted a major burden for peasants even in good years. In the late fifteenth and early sixteenth centuries, such a burden led to unsuccessful peasant revolts. The burden of taxes eased slightly after the Thirty Years' War in the mid-seventeenth century, as, with the significant property destruction and loss of life, noble landlords eased their requirements as they sought to retain peasants. The end of the Thirty Years' War began a period of peace and growing prosperity and with that, an increase of population. As population grew, however, the size of peasant freeholds decreased. The traditional practice among peasants was to divide their freeholds among their children as inheritance shares, creating, over time, smaller and smaller plots of arable land for families. During the eighteenth century, increasingly small family landholdings coupled with steady increases in taxes brought many families into dangerous circumstances. Fewer and fewer peasants could feed their families from the produce of their own lands and thus were forced to find means outside of agriculture to produce income in order to buy food as well as pay taxes. Cottage crafts of weaving cloth and straw, and making tools and handicrafts such as clocks out of wood grew in importance. It was typical also for families to hire out their children to other families with larger plots of land or to the estates of the nobility to create additional sources of income.

The economist Friedrich List, studying the emigration from his native Württemberg in the early nineteenth century, described a situation that was equally true of the mid- to late eighteenth century. To List, every economic improvement in agriculture, such as the cultivation of potatoes and the use of improved fertilizers and fodders, encouraged the growth in the number of marginal landholdings by making peasants feel they might be able to survive on smaller and smaller plots. List saw this as building what he called a "dwarf economy" (Zwergwirtschaft), by which he meant increasingly marginal landholdings supported by some sort of craft or trade.[27] The broad spread of such a dwarf economy meant that in good years, families felt they could enjoy a life that was based on a mix of agriculture and trade, and the peasant population grew. However, in the regular occurrence of bad grain harvests and bad years for grapes—as wine was a major cash crop particularly in Württemberg and Baden—peasants were reduced to states of near or actual starvation, and emigration became a frequent solution.

The effects of the dwarf economy also created the potential for significant economic dislocations. Land hunger drove upland villages to push fields farther into more marginal land deeper in regions like the Black Forest that produced lower

---

27. Friedrich List, *Die Ackerverfassung, die Zwergwirtschaft und de Auswanderung in Schriften, Reden, Briefe* (Berlin: R. Hobbing, 1928), 447–48.

yields for harder work. With many eager to increase their landholdings, the price of land rose, but land prices were not commensurate with the income that might be derived from the purchased acres. Stated differently, as the costs for margin-ally productive land increased, the value of labor decreased. With the continuing increases in that part of the population who could survive only by purchasing addi-tional grain and foodstuffs in the local markets, the prices of grain steadily increased. This drove more families into producing crafts or seeking to sell their labor, and so reduced the prices of those crafts and the earnings that their labor would yield. As pressures within this non-virtuous circle increased, it became harder and harder for peasant families on the economic margins to sustain life.

The pressures on families straining to make ends meet increased when local rulers increased taxes. Over time, the dukes of Württemberg and the margraves of Baden, threatened first by royal and later by republican France, raised taxes to increase and equip their military. Hard-pressed by France in the last decade of the eighteenth century and first decade of the nineteenth century, Württemberg joined France in military expeditions in Germany against Austria and Prussia. Taxes also rose throughout the eighteenth century, as there was a steady but significant rise in the costs of display in dress, jewelry, and household, fundamental markers of the lifestyle of the nobility. As was noted with regard to the nobility in Prussia, the nobility in the upper Rhineland could not make such desired items on their estates; they had to be purchased. To maintain the symbols of their noble status, the rulers of principalities large and small, as well as nobles living on the proceeds of their estates, sought to wring greater payments from citizens via taxes or from payments in lieu of service. With larger numbers of the population living closer to the margin of poverty, such increases in taxes and payments increased the likelihood that in bad years many peasants and poorer townspeople in this region would think of emigration as a way out of their troubles.

As a result, from the early eighteenth century onward, the upper Rhineland, and in particular Württemberg and Baden, regularly saw large numbers of people turn that possibility into action and leave. The legal requirement to emigrate at that time included the obligations to purchase with a lump sum payment exemption from the family's service payments, as well as to pay state and parish taxes. Many quietly left, abandoning their small plots of land, which then escheated to the state. Hans Fenske has estimated that in the eighteenth century, over 500,000 adults migrated from the Rhineland principalities to Eastern Europe with Prussia, Russia, and Hungary as primary destinations.[28] Mark Häberlein has estimated that another 100,000 to 125,000 Rhinelanders and German-speakers from Switzerland left for North America in the eighteenth century, most arriving between 1720–75 and settling in Pennsylvania west of Philadelphia.[29]

In addition to the economic factors that led families and individuals to leave Rhineland Germany, some immigrants from Württemberg and Baden to Prussia in the period from 1792 to 1806 were motivated at least in part by religious reasons.

---

28. Hans Fenske, "International Migration: Germany in the 18th Century," *Central European History* 13 (1980): 337–38. These figures are also used in Mark Häberlein, "German Communities in 18th Century Europe and North America" in *European Migrants, Diasporas and Indigenous Ethnic Minorities*, ed. Matjaž Klemenčič and Mary N. Harris, 19–34 (Pisa: PLUS-University Press, 2009).

29. Häberlein, "German Communities," 28.

The Protestant Church in Württemberg and Baden, as well as in the many smaller sovereign entities in that region, was dominated throughout the eighteenth century by the "orthodox" Lutheran clergy who tended to emphasize a rational, intellectual, and even scholastic approach to religious belief. In the mid-seventeenth century, an opposing view of Lutheranism had grown out of the teachings of Phillipp Spener and August Francke. These pastors stressed a more emotional relationship to religion that gave prominence to an individual's devotional life, enriched often by Bible reading in small communal groups. Spener's ideas in particular created a religious movement called Pietism that won adherents throughout the German-speaking lands and was especially popular among peasants in Württemberg and Baden. In the eighteenth century, such views coalesced to form a parallel branch of the Lutheran church whose adherents called themselves Evangelical Lutherans. Prussia's Hohenzollern rulers from the time of Friedrich Wilhelm I (1713–40) gave tolerance and ultimately preference to the Evangelical Lutherans. Thus, when, in the 1780s, a religious revival in the upper Rhineland raised again conflicts between the Evangelical Lutherans and the leadership of the Lutheran church in Württemberg and Baden, the Prussian offer of settlement possibilities in Prussian Poland came with the additional sweetener that here Evangelical Lutherans could worship with the full blessings of the state.

Evangelical Lutherans would, in fact, become the dominant form of Lutheranism in Prussian Poland. It is impossible from our vantage point to determine to what degree religion was a major factor in bringing people from Württemberg and Baden to Prussian Poland. There is little in the way of first-hand commentary from the Rhineland emigrants explaining their rationale. Civil servants in Württemberg in a similar period of heavy emigration during the second decade of the nineteenth century concluded that religion was far less of a factor in causing emigration than economics.[30] In contrast, where descendants of these Rhineland emigrants comment on the causes leading their ancestors to move to Prussia, religion is prominently mentioned.[31]

Apart from the issues of smallholdings, with their precarious economic consequences and religious concerns, emigrants leaving Württemberg and Baden for Prussia in the period from 1790 to 1806 may also have been influenced by the negative economic effects of the French Revolution in the Rhineland. The French army invaded both states in the early 1790s and though the prior rulers remained in power, the region underwent major changes as a result of French influence and pressure. An important French aim was to destroy whatever power Austria had accrued via its leadership and control of the Holy Roman Empire. The French army's presence caused the structure and connections of the Holy Roman Empire to crumble and dissolve in the Rhineland. Lands on the east bank of the Rhine were absorbed temporarily into France. In compensation for lands lost there, the Duke of Württemberg and the Margrave of Baden were encouraged to take over several of the the myriad petty states, free cities, and ecclesiastical territories existing on their borders. As a result of territorial seizures in the period from 1796 to 1812, Württemberg more than doubled in size. The Duke of Württemberg became a king and the Margrave of Baden a grand duke. Württemberg and Baden were now allies of France and expected to

---

30. Walker, *Germany and the Emigration*, 51–52.
31. Among many examples, see Stumpp, *Emigration from Germany to Russia*, 27.

meet French demands for soldiers and financial support for the French army. To support the French demands as well as to equip their courts with luxuries attendant to their increase in status, the governments of Württemberg and Baden raised taxes and sought to be more efficient and diligent in collecting them. The result was to increase the likelihood that peasants and the poorer townsmen struggling to make ends meet would be driven to emigrate. While Prussia's offer of larger plots of land to rent was a strong pull, the economic difficulties brought by the French Revolution in the period from 1790 to 1806 were perhaps an even stronger push.[32]

Prussian Poland was a very different place from the Rhineland. It isn't clear the degree to which Württembergers and Rhinelanders electing to immigrate to Prussian Poland realized that some of the conditions there might raise problems and concerns for them. Crops were different and the means and market for the trades used to supplement agricultural income were far less developed. While land allotments in Prussian Poland were far larger than those left behind and so resolved the basic issue of finding sufficient means for family support, the land was not to be owned by the immigrants but leased. Both the Prussian crown and gentry landowners regularly and successfully sought to increase leasing costs after the immigrants arrived and settled. This created uncertainty for peasants in anticipating how much of a crop was needed to meet obligations. Another problem faced by German peasants who immigrated to Prussian Poland was the build up of debt. Landowners often offered peasant lessees easy access to credit with the purpose of building an amount of debt sufficient to tie lessees firmly to their estates.

Prussia, in addition, was far more organized a state than the different political and taxing entities in Württemberg and the Rhineland. Prussia was very efficient in creating its tax rolls and in using these to collect taxes; it was harder there to escape the state and its demands. Conscription into the Prussian army was another issue. All peasants living in Prussia were subject to conscription, whereas in Württemberg military forces were hired. In the first decade of the nineteenth century, Prussia steadily built up its already large army as concerns about France rose. It is not unlikely that peasants living in Prussia developed some aversion to the idea of conscription as the numbers taken increased. Finally, unlike Württemberg and the Rhineland, Germans in Prussian Poland were living in the midst of large number of Poles who did not share their language, customs, or religion. Hagen describes the rural eighteenth-century German Hauländer communities as an archipelago of fragmented, sometimes isolated settlements.[33]

At the end of the eighteenth and beginning of the nineteenth century, the governments of Prussia, Württemberg, and Baden viewed emigration in strict cameral economic terms as a loss of state resources and so something that should be opposed. This is not the place, however, to consider in any detail the attitudes and policies of the several German states with regard to emigrants leaving their jurisdictions.[34] Emigration was not considered an issue by the Prussian government, as Prussia

---

32. My focus here is a discussion of the different factors motivating Württembergers and other upper Rhinelanders to elect to immigrate to Prussian Poland in the period from 1790 to 1806. In chapter III, I will address the sometimes similar, sometimes different motivations of Württembergers who emigrated directly from southwest Germany to Bessarabia in 1816–17 and 1830–40.

33. Hagen, *Germans, Poles, and Jews*, 17–20.

34. This issue is well covered in English in Mack Walker's excellent study: *Germany and the Emigration*, 22–24 and 51–52.

experienced a net inflow of surplus immigration through 1844. In Württemberg and Baden, which continued to see a material outflow, the governments felt powerless to prevent emigration, though from time to time, local officials sought to increase hurdles. There was, at this time, little of the later mid-nineteenth-century liberal view that emigration was a natural result of overcrowding and indeed helped the poor to better lives as well as helping those remaining by removing the poor.

### The first German settlers in Bessarabia were frequently families and individuals who had in the recent past moved to and established themselves in Prussian Poland

Most of the first German colonists in Bessarabia belonged to one of the two groups that have been discussed above: peasant immigrants to Prussian Poland coming from elsewhere in Prussia and northern Germany who settled there in the period 1720–1806, and Württembergers and upper Rhinelanders who came to Prussian Poland mainly between 1792 and 1806.[35] The family histories of these Bessarabian German immigrants suggest that virtually all had come to Prussian Poland from somewhere else, that none of them were long-term natives of the area that became Prussian Poland. For many of the Bessarabian German families, relocation to Prussian Poland occurred within living memory, often within the experience of the Bessarabian immigrant him- or herself. The next chapter will consider this as a potential factor in assessing the risk and making the decision to immigrate to Bessarabia; here I raise it as forming a common experience shared by most of the German peasants who immigrated to Prussian Poland.

Once settled in Prussian Poland, whether taking temporary or hereditary leases, the family histories suggest most families remained in the same village they first came to and so, presumably, retained the same leaseholding. This is the impression given by the extensive genealogical data collected by Flegel on the German settlers who, upon leaving Prussian Poland, founded the villages of Kulm, Leipzig, and Tarutino in Russian Bessarabia in 1814–16. Such is the case, for example, of Johann Rath, who was born in 1764 in Pfalzgrafenweile, Württemberg. By 1799, he immigrated to Lissewa (Polish Lisewo) in South Prussia, where he lived and raised a family before emigrating to Kulm in 1814.[36] Similarly, Christian Schimke, who was born near Fürstenfelde (now Boleszkowice) in Neumark Brandenburg, Prussia, in 1753, was settled by 1783 in Trikowo (Wielka Trzcianka) east of the Vistula River in an area that became the short-lived Prussian province of New East Prussia after the Third Partition of Poland. He remained there until 1814, when he took his family to Kulm.[37] Michael Kannewischer, who was born in 1772 near Landsberg in Neumark Brandenburg,

---

35. The founders of the colony of Teplitz, Bessarabia, settled in 1817, form an exception to this rule. As will be noted in the next two chapters, the first Teplitz settlers had come to Russia directly from Württemberg and were on their way to establish themselves in the Russian Caucasus. When many of the party were sickened with typhoid fever or possibly the plague on their arrival in Bessarabia, this caused the party to conclude they could go no further and so they settled in Bessarabia.

36. Flegel, *Extended Relationships*, 554, 556. Pfalzgrafenweile lies between Freudenstadt and Altensteig on the edge of the Black Forest. Lissewa is on the west bank of the Prosna River near its junction with the Warta.

37. Ibid., 624. New East Prussia, Neuostpreußen, was created from land taken by Prussia in the Third Partition of Poland in 1795, and was located east of the Vistula River lying underneath East Prussia as far as the Nieman River. It became part of Russia after 1815. Wielka Trzcianka was inland from the Vistula River from Dobrzyn and Chalin.

Prussia, was, by 1808, settled in Sulzfeld, South Prussia, from which, in 1814, he immigrated to Tarutino.[38]

Some families, once settled in Prussian Poland, did change leaseholds. Judging again from Flegel's data on settlers in Kulm, Leipzig, and Tarutino, the numbers of those who lived in more than one place in Prussian Poland before immigrating to Bessarabia were small: less than 5 percent of the families who emigrated. The nature of the moves such families made, however, could vary significantly. Adolf Götz, a Borodino immigrant born in Anklam Pomerania, Prussia, had taken a lease in Jaschnitz, West Prussia (Polish Jeżewnica), where he was living in 1805. By 1809, he had moved some 15 miles farther north to the settlement of Wilhelmswalde, West Prussia (Polish Brzeźno), from which he immigrated to Bessarabia.[39] Christoph Kleist and Anton Lobe made somewhat longer moves in Prussian Poland. Kleist, a Tarutino immigrant, in 1791 had a tenancy near Pleschen (Polish Pleszew), then still part of the Kingdom of Poland. By 1797, he had another one some 50 miles north near Schlesin (Polish Ślesin) when the area was incorporated into South Prussia after the Second Partition of Poland.[40] Anton Lobe, a Kulm immigrant, was born in Erdmannsweiler, Württemberg, and in the period from 1786 to 1804, was a leaseholder near Kochanow in what became South Prussia. By 1806, though, he had taken land near another German settlement around Semlin, some 75 miles further west.[41]

Long moves over significant distances in Prussian Poland were extremely rare but did occur. Michael Steuk represents such an outlier. He was born in 1767 in "Utznendorf" (likely Uschneudorf) in the Netze District in the province of Great Poland, and was one of the original settlers in Tarutino in 1814. Up until at least 1796, he was living near Schönlanke (Polish Trzcianka), some 10 miles west of Uschneudorf. By 1796, he had established his family some 250 miles further east in Königshuld (Polish Paproc Duże) in New East Prussia, and by at least 1811, he and his family were living in "Jalkov" (likely the Jarantow Kolonie), which at that point was in the Duchy of Warsaw roughly 225 miles to the west.[42]

---

38. Ibid., 343, 345. Sulzfeld neighbors the city of Łodz on the northeast. The province of Neumark Brandenburg noted in several examples here was a portion of the Margraviate (later, the Duchy of Brandenburg) located on the east side of the Oder River. Control over this region was fought over by the Margrave of Brandenburg and the King of Poland during the fifteenth century. For much of the sixteenth century it was controlled by members of the margrave's family, passing ultimately to Hohenzollern Margrave Johann Georg by the end of that century. With a large German-speaking population from the mid-seventeenth century onwards, it remained part of Prussia and later Germany until 1945.

39. Ibid., 215. The dates here and those used in the remainder of this paragraph are established by the births of children. Anklam is in Vorpommern west of the Oder; Jaschnitz is the village of Jeżewnica west of Neuenburg on the Vistula; and Wilhelmswalde is the village of Brzeźno northeast of Skórcz.

40. Ibid., 362. Pleschen is 20 miles northwest of the town of Kalisch (Polish: Kalisz) near which Kleist was born; Schlesin is about 10 miles north of Konin.

41. Ibid., 435. The German section of the Polish village of Kochanów was called Erdmannsweiler, as several families from that village in Württemberg settled there. It lies along the Rawka River midway between Łodz and Rawa. Semlin (Wola Sypinska) was reclaimed farm land along a tributary of the Sadkowka River some 20 miles north of Sieradz.

42. Ibid., 694–95. Uschneudorf (Polish Nowa Wies Ujska) is located about a mile south of Usch (Polish Ujście) and, like Schönlanke, was part of the Kingdom of Poland until the First Partition of Poland in 1772. Königshuld (probably the settlement of Groß Königshuld located about 15 miles southwest of Zambrów) was in territory absorbed into Prussia in the third and last partition of Poland in 1795, suggesting that Steuk's presence there in 1796 followed Prussia's takeover. Flegel's information on Jalkov comes from Bessarabian death records, which locate the village near "Stawispin, Kalisch." This clearly refers to the town of Stawiszyn 9 miles north of Kalisch (Polish: Kalisz).

Moves of any distance would require some cash reserves to cover the transportation costs of moving the household belongings as well as to handle the taxes and tenancy fees that would come due if relocation took place before earnings from the land that year were available. On some leases in Prussian Poland, peasants owned or were given tools and livestock and so were free to take these when leaving. In other situations, cash may have been needed to purchase livestock and seed at the new locality. It is true that in attracting new tenants landlords sometimes offered a basic grant of farm equipment, tools, furniture, seed, and livestock, the Hofwehr or "iron stock."[43] Such an iron stock grant was part of the tenancy and would remain the property of the landlord, but was offered to help the new tenants get their feet on the ground. Where such help was a necessary inducement, landlords, however, would only offer it to help tenants whom they believed could support themselves in short order—that is, pay the tenancy fees and taxes, perform the required manor labor, and survive without the need of further help. Landlords would thus look to a peasant's past experience and their material wealth as a sign of their potential. Landless or semi-landless peasants typically found it difficult to save sufficient cash to take over leases for large land allotments or to attract the interest of distant landlords unless by inheritance or marriage they had materially improved their financial position.

## While moving to Prussian Poland likely brought greater holdings of land to German peasants, it also made them subject to the demands of the Prussian state and subject to its fate

Prussia continued to attract immigrants to its new territories in Prussian Poland until 1806, when politics and war intervened. Napoleon, concerned about France's old enemy Austria and desiring to neutralize support for Austria, pushed hard on the larger German states to join France in fighting Austria. Prussia wanted to stay out of the conflict and indeed was happy to see Austria, its rival, under pressure. The price of that neutrality, however, kept rising, and by 1805, with Austria defeated, Prussia found itself alone and finally forced to enter the fight against France. We will take up the details and consequences of Prussia's actions in the next chapter as part of considering what led Germans in Prussian Poland in 1813 to take up Russia's offer to settle in Bessarabia. Here, in a discussion of peasant movement to Prussian Poland, it is important only to note that when Prussia became a combatant against France in the summer of 1806, peasant emigration from Württemberg, Baden, and the Rhineland, and from elsewhere in Prussia into Prussian Poland stopped. As the possibility of conflict with France grew, the Prussian government ceased efforts to encourage immigration. Surely for their part, fears concerning the presence of foraging and marauding troops, much less fighting itself, led peasants to postpone any thoughts of moving to Prussian Poland. Immigration, however, appeared to be steady well into 1805.[44]

Having settled in Prussian Poland, whether coming from elsewhere in Prussia or from Württemberg and the Rhineland, peasant immigrants likely hoped for stability

---

43. Hagen uses the term *Hofwer*, which he translates as "iron stock," to describe a basic collection of farming implements that a landowner might offer an incoming tenant. Hagen, "Village Life," 173.

44. H. M. Scott, "Prussia's Emergence as a European Great Power, 1740-1763" in Dwyer, *Rise of Prussia*, 156.

and the opportunity to feed their families adequately and build up the economic capabilities of their leaseholds. With leaseholds in Prussian Poland typically of the large fullholder acreage, it may have been that for many immigrants to Prussian Poland, particularly those from southwestern Germany, their leaseholdings were substantially larger than the land they had worked before. Weighing against the larger allotments and as a hurdle to establishing their leaseholds in Prussian Poland on a positive footing was the fact that for many German immigrants, a first task was to establish viable farm and pasture land. The easily tilled meadowlands were not available, as Polish peasants were long-established settlers there. The German peasants were allotted unoccupied wetlands, woodlands, and uplands, which they had to turn to agricultural ends. Fortunately, most came with the skills to do this, which was a major reason their immigration was sought.

After Prussia established its control over this territory following each of the three partitions of Poland, the needs of the Prussian state became a significant and additional challenge for German peasants who had settled there earlier and for peasants seeking to establish themselves there after the partitions. Prussia placed heavy demands on its peasant population both in terms of taxes and its needs for manpower to fill its army's ranks. Prussia was a small country with big-country aspirations. It had a population of only 2.5 million in 1740 at the beginning of Friedrich the Great's reign and grew to 5.8 million in 1786, with the acquisitions of Silesia and Royal Prussia. In comparison, France, in 1786, had a population of about 28 million citizens. Prussia was not particularly well-endowed with material or economic resources. The most prosperous sections of Prussia were the small counties of Mark, Cleves, and Ravensburg on the border of the Netherlands, not the far larger and more populous territory east of the Elbe. But for Silesia, eighteenth-century Prussia was relatively untouched by the industrial revolution. It lacked a financial market to sell or buy government debt, and it relied on the tariff-protected production and sale of agricultural products, particularly grain to Great Britain, as its economic engine.

Prussia's political strengths in the eighteenth century rested firstly on its large and well-trained army, supported by an unusually well-organized state administration and an efficient tax collection system. Prussia maintained an army of major power importance. Drawing on a well-organized conscription system taking young men from each district (Kreis) within the country as well as hiring recruits from elsewhere in the German-speaking lands, Friedrich the Great built up the army to nearly two hundred thousand men. Friedrich made his state "a first-class power on third-class resources."[45] Many of those resources were supplied by the Prussian peasantry. While many members of the Prussian army were recruited outside of Prussia with the help of funds from Great Britain, a material portion, over 40 percent for the army in 1786,[46] was built up internally via conscription. At the end of the eighteenth century, the majority of Prussian peasant families had a son or a relative currently serving in or discharged from the Prussian army.

The costs of maintaining such a large army took up a substantial portion of the annual income of the Prussian crown. During the time of Friedrich the Great's father, Friedrich Wilhelm I, the army expenses came to 70 percent of royal income.

---

45. Scott, "Second Reign of Frederick the Great?" 186.
46. Ibid., 188.

"Between 1740 and 1756 [the cost of the army] rose to 83 per cent and, during the Seven Years War, it would reach 87 per cent."[47] Despite outside help from Great Britain, a significant part of the cost of maintaining the growing Prussian army was paid for via internal taxation or fees from crown estates. Much of the weight of taxation fell on the peasantry. The nobility paid little in taxes until the nineteenth century, and Prussian towns up until 1766 only paid generally small, traditional, and self-regulated taxes. In 1766, the indirect and much-hated "Régie" consumption tax was imposed on the towns, but, as they generally remained both small in size and small as a proportion of the total population, the towns were not major tax contributors.[48] The peasants were expected to make regular cash payments out of income they received from the sale of grain grown on their leaseholds or from the sale of their own animals. Such tax payments were in addition to the leasing costs in cash and labor obligations owed to the noble or crown who owned the land they leased.

As noted earlier, Hagen's study of the Stavenow estate in Brandenburg suggests that in good years, the largest peasant leaseholders, the fullholders, had "royal and seigneurial exactions" equal to nearly half of the rye (27 of 60 bushels) they produced.[49] In years of good weather when the country was not at war, all was well, but no peasants became rich or bumped up against the boundaries of the tiny Prussian middle class. In average years, even fullholders occasionally struggled to make ends meet. In bad years when there were large crop failures or when crops were ruined or confiscated by passing troops, both tax and tenant fees could not be fully collected and malnutrition preceded starvation. The organizational capability of the Prussian state, the sophistication of its tax records, allowed the state, with its "third-class resources," to support its great ambitions. For the Prussian peasantry, however, the ambitions and sophistication of the state and the efforts of gentry landlords to improve manor returns at the expense of the peasantry put increasing pressures on the agricultural margins they needed to support and sustain their livelihoods.

Living standards for the peasantry did increase during the eighteenth century, but the improvements were far more substantial among the gentry. While German peasants in Prussian Poland were not considered personal property, as occurred with Polish peasants whose Polish landlords sold their labor to others, landlords did not consider themselves and the German peasants leasing their land as bound together in a mutually beneficial agricultural enterprise. Rather, landlords tended to view the peasants as a somewhat lower form of humanity whom they were justified in pushing into desperate straits to extract the maximum gain. Such attitudes were reinforced by the significant differences in dress, deportment, and cleanliness that separated the gentry from the peasants, as well as the often striking differences in physical appearances, as the gentry (with a better diet richer in protein) were often materially taller, heavier, and healthier.

---

47. Scott, "Prussia's Emergence," 165.

48. The Regie was the name given to a series of excise taxes and tolls introduced by Frederick the Great. Such taxes were seen as injurious to local trades and were very unpopular. Scott notes that "it aroused considerable opposition" ("Second Reign of Frederick the Great?" 197). Karin Friedrich notes that coming after the end of the Seven Years' War, "the Regie further undermined the opportunity of urban crafts to recover their productivity." Friedrich, *Brandenburg-Prussia, 1466–1806: The Rise of a Composite State* (Basingstoke, Eng.: Palgrave Macmillan, 2012).

49. Hagan, *Ordinary Prussians*, 211. Hagan's estimate is based on an average household size of four adults, one retiree, and two children.

Until 1807, German peasants who had immigrated to Prussian Poland appear to have been somewhat better off on the whole than peasants elsewhere in Prussia. Average leasehold size was of the fullholder size and so larger than elsewhere. Though subject to a combination of lease payments and increasing tax liabilities, leasing costs, at least, tended to be lower in Prussian Poland than in other parts of Prussia, in part in recognition of the fact that the German peasants had had to create agricultural property from land that had not been previously tilled. Though the crown and gentry landlords in Prussian Poland were seeking to increase the costs of leasing land, this trend had started later and so was developing more slowly than in the rest of Prussia.

After war broke out with France in 1807, however, the situation for peasants in Prussian Poland changed radically and quite diminished many of the positives that German immigrants had found in moving there. The Prussian army was totally defeated and Berlin was occupied by the French. Prussia itself underwent a near-death experience. The French broke apart the Prussian state and created from Prussian and Austrian Poland the Duchy of Warsaw, an apparent re-creation of the vanished Kingdom of Poland but dominated by French interests and needs. The Polish Catholic Church now sought to regain lands lost to the Prussian crown in the partitions, leasing terms were no longer certain, and the French were demanding huge tribute payments, which under Polish custom, were to be paid by exactions on the peasants. In the summer of 1812, the huge French army requisitioned animals and grain reserves as it prepared for a massive attack on Russia. In the winter of 1812–13, the remnants of that defeated army passed through Prussian Poland, taking what they could. It was following this frightening and economically destructive period that the victorious Imperial Russian state offered German peasants in Prussian Poland the opportunity to settle lands in newly acquired Bessarabia far away near the shores of the Black Sea.

# III

# The German Emigration to Bessarabia, 1814–47

Bessarabia, as the name for a distinct territorial and political identity, is not of ancient lineage. It only dates from the end of the eighteenth century. It was used to describe land areas of varying size west of the lower Dniester River then under contest between Russia and the Ottoman Empire. When Imperial Russia in 1812 gained legal control over a part of this territory, the land running inland from the Black Sea between the Dniester and the Prut rivers, it gave the name Bessarabia to designate specifically this new acquisition.

Russia's acquisition of Bessarabia was just one episode in its long conflict with the Ottoman Empire, through which Imperial Russia gained control of what is now the southern half of the Ukraine. Russia, from the time of Peter the Great (1682–1725), had been steadily pushing its frontiers southward toward and then along the Black Sea coast. Russia's army and navy had waged notably successful campaigns during the reign of Catherine the Great (1762–96). In 1774, following victories over the Ottoman army and the destruction of its fleet, Russia gained control of the Crimea. After more fighting in 1792, the Treaty of Jassy confirmed Russia's hold on the Crimea and gave them the large Ottoman province of Yedisan, land between the Bug and Dniester rivers that became the Imperial Russian province of Xerson. Catherine's grandson Tsar Alexander I reopened this conflict, and, in campaigns lasting from 1806 to 1810, the Russian army crossed the Dniester frontier and, pushing along the sea coast, went far beyond the Prut River to occupy Bucharest and even areas south of the Danube. Russia combined several different aims in these wars: a strategic goal of gaining control of the north shore of the Black Sea, a military goal of acquiring a warmwater port for its navy, and a religious goal of protecting the Orthodox population that had been living in this area under Turkish domination. Perhaps, too, Russia had a romantic, historical goal of seeking to gain control of territory that had once belonged to Russia's forebear, the Russo-Swedish state Kievan Rus that had ruled over this area from the tenth through the twelfth centuries.

In the spring of 1812, with a large Russian army still in Romania, Alexander was facing significant problems. Napoleon was massing his huge army in Poland and giving every indication that he was preparing to launch an attack on Russia. Wanting to unite his forces by bringing the army in Romania back to central Russia, Alexander prudently decided to end his war with the Ottoman Empire. In the Peace of Bucharest, signed on May 28, 1812 (O.S.), Russia agreed to stop the fighting and to withdraw from some of the territory it had conquered, but in recompense, the Ottoman Empire was forced to cede to Russia another large block of territory. As a result of this treaty, the area between the Dniester River on the east, the Prut River on the west, the Danube and the Black Sea on the south, and the Podolian foothills of the Carpathians on the north became part of Imperial Russia. This territory of some 17,600 square miles had been traditionally part of a region called Moldavia, named after the Molda/Moldova River flowing out of the Carpathians. The regional name has also historically described the largest population group living there who speak a Romance language with close ties to Romanian.[1]

In giving the name Bessarabia to this new province acquired from the Ottomans, the Russian intention appears to have been to create a clear distinction from the larger section of Moldavia across the Prut to the west, which remained legally under the jurisdiction of the Ottoman Empire. The term Bessarabia had been used to describe the southern steppeland portion of this area, as is attested by an Austrian map of 1770.[2] The Russians, in their 1806–12 campaign against the Ottoman Turks, however, were already using the term Bessarabia to describe in very general terms the territory between the Dniester and the Prut rivers.[3] Given that one of Russia's justifications for taking this territory was to protect the Moldavian, Bulgarian, and other Christian Orthodox peoples living here, the use of the term Bessarabia may also have been an attempt to hark back to a Christian past. The name Bessarabia comes from the surname of the noble Romanian Basarab family which is derived from Basarab I, the fourteenth-century Christian ruler of Wallachia, the region that now forms the central and western parts of Romania north of the Danube.[4] The Basarab family had

1.  Whether Moldavian is a separate language from Romanian or a dialect of Romanian is very much a political question. When the Soviet Union took over Bessarabia in 1940, it called the area Moldavia and the language spoken there Moldavian in an attempt to thwart efforts by Romania to reclaim this area. Following the breakup of the Soviet Union in 1991, the new country of Moldova has decided to remain independent of Romania and sought to continue to assert differences. Unlike Romanian, Moldova uses the Cyrillic alphabet for written Moldavian and has based its formal language on dialects linguistically (and geographically) most distant from Romanian.

2.  Franz Johann Joseph von Reilly, "Die Otschakowische Tartarey oder Westliches Nogaj, auch Jedisan," http://en.wikipedia.org/wiki/File:Yedisan.jpg.

3.  George Jewsbury, *The Russian Annexation of Bessarabia: 1774–1828* (New York: Columbia University Press, 1976), 48–49.

4.  The name Basarab is not linguistically Romanian in origin, however. It is most likely Cuman and comes from the words *basar* meaning "to rule" and *aba* meaning "father." The Cumans or Polovetsians were a Turkish-speaking tribe who, following the grass steppe road from Asia, controlled in the tenth and eleventh centuries large parts of South Russia west of the Dniester River to present-day Wallachia. Beaten by the Kievan Rus in the twelfth century and by the Mongols in 1236, they took refuge in Hungary and later Bulgaria, becoming generally Christian. One of the more noted princes from the Basarab family was Vlad Tepes, referred to in legend as Vlad the Impaler. Bram Stoker in the nineteenth century created the Dracula story in part from the legends about Vlad Tepes.

allegedly controlled this southern steppeland section of the Russian province before the Ottoman authority was established in the fifteenth century.

The southern third of the new Russian province of Bessarabia was generally unin-habited steppeland. It was here that the Russian government wished to plant the German colonies. Under the Ottomans from the fifteenth century until 1812, this steppeland had been called the Budjak, a term derived from the Turkish word *bucak,* meaning "corner" or "triangle."[5] While this term described the shape of this piece of land that curved southwest from the estuary of the Dniester to that of the Danube, giving it an individual name obscures the fact that it is but one small part of a vast geographical formation. The steppe was a rolling, treeless, grassy plain as much as 200 miles wide that stretched several thousand miles from Asia south of the Ural Mountains to the Pannonian Plain in central modern-day Hungary. The steppe had been a home to nomadic peoples after the domestication of the horse as well as a highway for such peoples in Asia to move west and into Europe. By this route in the prehistoric period, members of the different Indo-European-speaking tribes started moving from Asia toward Europe beginning around 4000 BCE. When the steppelands north of the Black Sea coast first appear in written history, what attracted attention was their function as a homeland for nomads and as a highway for the movement of peoples. In the seventh century BCE, the Greeks, having estab-lished trading colonies along the Black Sea shoreline, developed contacts with the warlike Scythians living in the steppe inland from the Greek settlements. Herodotus visited the area in the fifth century BCE and noted both the beautiful gold work and cruel customs of the Scythians. By the second century BCE, the Scythians had moved west and north, pushed by another Indo-European-speaking tribe, the Sarmatians. The Sarmatians, like the Scythians before them, were a nomadic people who regularly raided the coastal towns. By the end of the Roman era in the fourth century CE though, stronger Finno-Ugric-speaking nomadic tribes began to appear from further east and drove the Sarmatians west into present day Romania and Hungary. From the fourth century to the thirteenth century, a steady stream of different peoples passed along all or parts of this grassland highway, many going all the way to Pannonia in Hungary: the Goths coming from northern Europe, the Turkic-speaking Huns from Asia, the apparently Turkic-speaking Avar confed-eracy following the Huns, the Turkic-speaking Bulgars, the Finno-Ugric-speaking Magyars, the Slavic-speaking tribes who settled the Balkans, the Turkic-speaking Pechenegs, Cumans, and Polovicians, and finally the Mongolic-speaking Tartars. The Tartars were pushed westward and then conquered by the Mongols, the most organized of all the nomadic groups, whom the Tartars then joined in the thirteenth century in making attacks on Western Europe.

The procession of peoples was accompanied by a steady improvement in the tech-niques of conducting warfare on horses. The steppe throughout this period was a dangerous place to be if you were not mobile. The regular passage of mounted and warlike nomads also meant that the steppe area could not harbor any permanent settlements until after the fourteenth century. The Mongols and their Tartar and

5. According to Max Vasmer, the term came into Russian usage in the eighteenth century. Vasmer derives the term from the Crimean Tartar and Turkish word *budjak,* meaning "corner." The same term was taken up in Romanian as "Bugéc" or "Bugég" to refer to the Bessarabian steppeland. Max Vasmer, *Etimologičeskij slovar' russkogo jazyka,* vol. 1, *A–D* (Moscow: Progress, 1964), 229–30.

Cuman allies were finally beaten back by forces generally led by Hungarians, who in the fourteenth century ended the control the nomadic peoples held over lands west and north of the Danube and much reduced their control of the steppelands in what was to become Bessarabia. From the fourteenth century onward, the Bessarabian steppe supported some small permanent settlements of Tartars and later Moldavians, with larger numbers of nomadic Tartars also continuing to live on the steppe. Even after the fourteenth century, the population in the Budjak remained light as memories of the defenselessness of settlements continued to be influential.

Further inland from the steppe region in the wooded foothills that rolled northward into the Carpathian Mountains, the land was far more conducive to settlement. This area had sustained, from prehistoric times, farming communities that supported a small nobility that was engaged in frequent warfare. With the constant danger from the nomads to the south, towns and the trading occupations these upland settlements supported remained sparse until well after the fifteenth century, when the power of the nomadic tribes on the steppe had waned. Throughout the medieval period, the great majority of the population in this upland area referred to themselves as the Romani and were called the Vlachs by their neighbors. These people were the linguistic descendants of the citizens of the Roman province of Dacia and are the ancestors of the present-day Romanians and Moldavians.

In medieval and early modern times, there was no cohesive state that joined the different Romani noble families and their territories. The northeastern region where the Romani lived came to be called Moldavia by at least the fourteenth century, and the term, up until the beginning of the nineteenth century, described an area stretching from the Carpathian Mountains and Transylvania to the Dniester River. The Russian province of Bessarabia and its smaller descendant, the current country of Moldova, thus, only occupy less than half of the historic region that was called Moldavia.

In the twelfth through the fourteenth centuries, the most powerful local rulers in Moldavia allied themselves alternatively with Hungary and Poland-Lithuania, paying tribute in efforts to maintain local autonomy. By the late fifteenth century, the Ottoman Empire had moved close enough to demand tribute from Moldavian nobles, though local princes retained their authority and continued their warfare against each other. Moldavia remained a lightly populated area that supplied grain and animals to the Ottoman Empire. Direct Ottoman control was gradually imposed beginning in the sixteenth century in response first to Polish and then, in the seventeenth century, to Russian interest in this area. Ottoman rule increased the tribute requirements and delegated power to a series of nonnative overlords who held office for limited periods of time. The overlords focused on enriching themselves and producing the required tribute for Istanbul. Corruption, the severe demands on the peasantry, and the lack of interest in local improvements made Moldavia one of the most benighted, cruelly ruled areas of Europe.[6] Many in the local gentry in Moldavia in the eighteenth century began to look to Russia as a means to end the control of the Ottoman Turks, and, when the Russians invaded in 1806, allied themselves with them.

---

6. George Jewsbury makes this point in some detail (*Russian Annexation of Bessarabia*, 7–29). He quotes William Wilkenson, the British Consul in Bucharest in the first decade of the nineteenth century, noting, "There does not perhaps exist a people labouring under a greater degree of oppression from the effects of despotic power and more heavily burthened with impositions and taxes than the peasantry of Moldavia and Wallachia" (14).

## The Russians gained part of Moldavia by treaty, named the part they controlled Bessarabia, and brought in settlers they thought would help secure their control

The Treaty of Bucharest of May 1812 gave Imperial Russia legal control of the land between the Prut and Dniester rivers. The Russian government renamed this territory Bessarabia. Bessarabia consisted of two distinct geographic parts: the Budjak steppeland running 150 to 200 miles inland from the Black Sea coast, and Moldavia, the hilly and forested piedmont area beyond the Budjak in which the Romanian-speaking Moldavians predominated.[7] Small villages were the norm in Bessarabia. There were three larger towns: Kishinev (Chisinau in Romanian), which became Bessarabia's capital, the border fortress of Bender (Tighina in Romanian), and the ancient Phoenician and later Greek colony of Akkerman (present day Bilhorod Dnistrovs'kyi) established along the estuary of the Dniester River. In attracting German colonists in 1814, the Russian government was seeking to settle the first of these regions, the relatively unpopulated steppeland area of the Budjak.

The Budjak steppe region, where the German colonies were established, was even more lightly populated in 1814 than it had been in 1800. This was because during the period from 1808 to 1812, even before they had gained legal control of the area, Russia forced most of the Tartars (then the largest linguistic group living in the steppe) to move to the Crimea. The Russian motivation was to separate them from the Ottoman Turks, their coreligionists, and so increase the security of the Russian possession of Bessarabia. Writing in the 1860s, Aleksandr A. Klaus, a Russian official of Volga German ancestry, who made a study of the German colonies in South Russia, callously described the area in 1812 as "abandoned" by the Tartars, a vast steppeland with very few settlements: "Bessarabija byla soveršenno ostavljena tatarami i predstavljala odne obširnye stepi, s ves'ma redkim osedlym naseleniem."[8] Only a few geographical names remained to indicate their long presence here.[9] The Budjak also contained a few settled and nomadic Moldavians who raised horses, sheep, and cattle. The Moldavian villages often had vineyards that did well in the alkaline soils, and from the Moldavians, the new German colonists learned how to adapt the experience the Germans had with vineyards to new climate conditions and grape varieties. Klaus also reports a number of Orthodox Bulgarians and Gaugaz,[10] refugees from the Ottoman Turks, who had been allowed to create settlements in

---

7.  When Bessarabia was under the control of the Ottoman Turks, it had been divided into three administrative sections: the Budjak, the area around the Turkish forts (Akkerman, Bender, Ismail, Khotin, and Kilia), and Transpruth Moldavia (Jewsbury, *Russian Annexation of Bessarabia*, 48–49, 56–57).

8.  Klaus, *Naši kolonii*, 304. It is estimated the Russians moved five thousand Tartar nomads to the Crimea (see Schmidt, *Die Deutschen aus Bessarabien*, 38; and Jewsbury, *Russian Annexation of Bessarabia*, 49). Following the Soviet recapture of the Crimea in 1944, Stalin forcibly exiled the Tartars living in the Crimea to Asia as punishment for their alleged support of the Germans during World War II.

9.  Some were retained in names of German settlements founded in the late nineteenth and early twentieth centuries, such as Basyrjamka, which comes from the Turkic Tartar word for salt hole. Kulm was first named Madar from the Turkic Cuman word meaning "a place where water is found."

10. The Bulgarians are a South Slavic-speaking people whose language came from Slavic tribes who invaded the southeast Balkans in the post-Roman period. Their name, however, comes from the Turkic-speaking Bulgars who took control of Moesia in the seventh century. The Gaugaz are an Oghuz Turkic-speaking people who became Orthodox Christians and had villages stretching from coastal Bulgaria and Romania to the edges of the Budjak in Bessarabia.

Bessarabia in the period from 1806 to 1812 when Russia had already gained de facto control of the area. There may have been at this time a few villages of Russian- or Ukrainian-speaking Slavs in the Bessarabian steppe, as the steppelands throughout South Russia had been places of refuge for Ukrainian and Russian peasants escaping serfdom for several hundred years.

From the time of Tsarina Catherine the Great (1762–96), Russia had a developed national policy of inviting peasants from Western Europe, particularly Germans, to settle territories in Russia beyond the borders of Slavic settlement. In the period from 1763 to 1769, the Russian government had invited German peasants from Bavaria and the upper Rhineland, stretching from Baden to the Pfalz, to settle on lands along the middle Volga. In the period from 1787 to 1797, Mennonites from the Vistula River estuary in West Prussia were invited and came to the lower Dnieper River valley. In the period from 1803 to 1809, numbers of Germans from the upper Rhineland and especially Württemberg came to settle the Xerson Province of South Russia east of the Dniester River.[11]

The Imperial Russian government had several goals in mind in carrying out this policy. One was following the cameral economic thought to increase Russia's intrinsic national wealth and state power by increasing the size of its population.[12] Russia, though significantly larger in area than any other state in Europe, had a population in 1812 roughly the same as that of France.[13] A second goal was to settle underpopulated border areas (thereby establishing more definite Russian suzerainty), as well as to increase the hurdles for recapture of these areas by their former owners. This was particularly true for Bessarabia and the Caucasus. A third goal was to create a buffer zone protecting areas of Russian settlement from potentially troublesome non-Slavic tribes. This is particularly true for the Volga region and the Caucasus. A fourth goal was to settle free populations only in these border regions, so as to not destabilize the existing system of serfdom that was the norm throughout the Russian heartland, under which Russian and Ukrainian peasants were the property of the estates on which they were born. The border regions to the south and beyond the Russian frontier had long been a refuge for runaways, some of whom formed the Cossack bands. It was feared that if large numbers of serfs were invited to settle these lands, the temptation to escape would be hard to check, and if serfs were given freedom as an incentive to move and create new settlements, this would prove troublesome in the regions they had left behind. Yet another goal of the Russian

---

11. In noting here the existence of German peasant immigration to Russia prior to the arrival of the first Germans in Bessarabia in 1814, it is important to remember that German immigration to other parts of Imperial Russia continued contemporaneously with that to Bessarabia. In the period from 1818 to 1842, large numbers of Germans from the upper Rhineland and Prussian Poland continued to settle in Xerson Province east of the Dniester River and the Ekaterinoslav Province further east toward the Dnieper. In 1816–18, a group of some six thousand Germans, mainly from Württemberg, came to the South Caucasus to create villages in territory Tsar Alexander I's army had taken from Persian control.

12. Cameral, from the German *Kammer* ("chamber"), describes theories popular in the eighteenth and nineteenth centuries advocating a more efficient management of state properties. These theories favored such endeavors as increasing the population of the state, improving its useful land area by draining swamps and marshes, and improving farming techniques.

13. In 1810, Russia had an estimated population of 41,300,000 vs. 38,000,000 in France, 19,000,000 in the Austro-Hungarian Empire, just under 18,000,000 in the United Kingdom, and roughly 5,000,000 in Prussia. "World Population: Major Countries 1810," The Napoleon Series, last modified 2005, http://www.napoleon-series.org/research/abstract/population/population/world/c_world3.html.

government in inviting German peasants to settle was to introduce improved levels of agricultural and animal husbandry into Russia. The higher yields of grain, which the foreign peasants were thought able to produce, would increase the grain supply and decrease the chances of famines that had regularly occurred in Russia's past. It was hoped, too, that the native peasantry exposed to other and better methods would adopt them with positive results. Not surprisingly, given the normally slim margins of their existence, the Russian/Ukrainian peasantry was very resistant to any inducements to change.

## In its efforts to settle Bessarabia, the Russian government continued its practice of seeking to attract Germans peasants

On November 29, 1813 (O.S.), Tsar Alexander I issued a decree offering favorable terms to German peasants willing to immigrate and establish settlements in Bessarabia. The terms offered were generally similar to those used in the period from 1801 to 1809 to attract German peasant settlement further east of the Dniester River on the steppelands of the Ukraine above Odessa. The terms offered in 1813 did, though, incorporate a change in focus made midway during the effort to bring Germans to South Russia. In 1804, the Russian government had become apprehensive that the enthusiastic response by Germans peasants included numbers of poor townsmen with little experience in agriculture and small or no financial savings to see them through the difficulties of establishing themselves in Russia. In response, Count Viktor Pavlovič Kočubej, Minister of the Interior, issued a directive specifying that only experienced farmers and tradesmen with property of at least 200 Florins should be accepted.[14] The formal terms offered to Bessarabian settlers in 1813 included the minimum standards of the Kočubej directive.

The Russian offer of 1813 to Germans also included a number of new points of emphasis as well as one important change in Russian policy. The decree, which Alexander I signed in 1813, was directed to German peasants living in what had been Prussian Poland before Napoleon's war with Prussia and later attack on Russia. In focusing on just these peasants, the Russian government was hoping to reduce the problems of establishing the new colonies. The tsar's decree noted that the experiences these peasants had when immigrating to Prussian Poland and establishing new settlements there were similar to the challenges they would have in immigrating to Bessarabia.[15] The 1813 decree also took into account new thinking about the economic possibilities of these southern lands taken from the Ottomans. Having now a better grasp of the agricultural possibilities of the new territories, including a sense of what the Ottomans had sought to encourage, the November 1813 decree indicated that a priority would be given to those with skills in "agriculture, horticulture, wine growing, and silk culture."[16]

The one change in Russian policy in the terms offered to the Germans willing to settle in Bessarabia was that such settlers would be prohibited from subdividing the property given them, including subdivision among heirs as part of an inheritance

14. Giesinger, *From Catherine to Khrushchev*, 34. Malinovskij also stresses the Russian government's increased concerns after 1801 to make a more careful selection of colonists (*Social'naja i xozjajstvennaja istorija*, 24).

15. Fleischhauer, *Die Deutschen im Zarenreich*, 117.

16. Shirley Fischer Arends, *The Central Dakota Germans: Their History, Language and Culture* (Washington, DC: Georgetown University Press, 1989), 26.

settlement. The Russian government was beginning to develop concerns about the growth of landless peasants and poverty in some of the German colonies on the Volga and in South Russia. The government saw partible inheritance as a major cause of such trends. German peasant tradition was to divide a family's property equally among heirs. As the intention of the Russian Government was not to offer additional property to the immigrants, permitting the division of land via inheritance settlements or sales would inevitably lead to smaller and smaller land allocations for families. It is not clear whether the government drew this conclusion solely from observing developments within Russia, or was influenced by the advice of its representatives and agents in Württemberg from where it had drawn many immigrants to South Russia before 1812 and where partible inheritance leading to insufficient property allocations was generally seen to be a primary cause of poverty and the resulting emigration.

The Russian government had concluded that to attract colonists, it would need to offer inducements. That inducements were offered was a sign the government understood that there might be legitimate worries about immigrating to Russia's borderlands won in warfare with the Ottoman Turks. Perhaps, in addition, the Russian government calculated that inducements might attract a better quality, more prosperous group of peasants.

The terms offered to Germans in Prussian Poland were in fact attractive and generous. As the list below highlights, the Russian terms focused on areas thought to be important to potential colonists. The offer to Germans, however, was not without attention to Russia's own self-interest. The land to be settled was empty, uncultivated and, having been won by military victory, was offered at no further cost to Russia. In areas of the offer that required current Russian government expenditures, costs would be recouped by later payments from the settled colonists. These, however, would be treated generously as interest-free loans.

To find potential immigrants, the Russian government hired agents who, in the winter of 1813–14, visited German villages in Poland under Prussian and Russian control. These agents were empowered to make the following offer to those willing to settle in Bessarabia:

- The German colonists would be given large family plots of unsettled land which had significant but undeveloped agricultural potential. Each family was to be allotted 60 desjatina of land, or about 162 acres or 65 hectares, which they would hold with rights of inheritance and transferability but could not subdivide.[17] The colonists would not individually own their plots—all land was owned by the community. Thus any sales or changes in title would need community approval.[18] Land grants of 60 desjatina per family were standard also for German peasants coming to South Russia in the first decade of the nineteenth century,[19] but were at the larger end of land grants made to Mennonites coming to South Russia at the end of the eighteenth century. Land grants of 60 desjatina were also roughly

---

17. The Russian land measure desjatina is equal to 1.093 hectare or 2.7 acres.

18. Wilhelm Mutschall, "History of the Community of Tarutino from 1814 to 1934," *Heritage Review* 44, no. 3 (2014): 16.

19. Fleischhauer, *Die Deutschen im Zarenreich*, 165. Perhaps the appearance of problems with poverty among earlier colonists resulted in the consistently large land grants in Bessarabia. The grant of 60 desjatina of land to the Germans also contrasts with grants of 30 desjatina per family given to Russian crown peasants in 1824–25 to encourage them to move from crown lands in South Russia to steppeland near Akkerman in Bessarabia (Jewsbury, *Russian Annexation of Bessarabia*, 69).

twice the size of a fullholder's leased tenure in Brandenburg.[20] As it was beyond reason for peasants in Prussian Poland to hope they might own the land they farmed, the Russian government likely hoped this would be a central attraction.

- Colonists would have the right to practice their religion, including the right to build churches and religious schools and to employ pastors and teachers.

- Colonists would have the right to maintain their use of the German language in churches, schools, and dealing with the government.

- Colonial villages in Bessarabia would have local self-government. Village officials would be elected by the landholding male colonists of the settlement and so the Germans would maintain in Russia their customary civil rights and social practices.

- Colonists would be exempted from requirements for civil or military service, as well as from the duty to provide quartering for the military should troops be sent to Bessarabia. The military service demanded of Russian peasants in 1814 was a twenty-year commitment to active duty, a virtual adult lifetime. This right was highly prized by the colonists and they felt much aggrieved when the Russian government took it back in 1874.[21] As these German peasants had been subject to military conscription as Prussian citizens and were not known to have protested this issue in Prussia, it is not obvious why the Russian government had included this right in the terms. It likely was a carryover from the terms offered earlier to the German-speaking Mennonites, for whom the promise of freedom from military service had proved very important in attracting them to Russia. Possibly, this right continued to be offered to non-Mennonite German colonists thereafter with the thought that it would be attractive and that conscription would be a distraction in establishing the colonies, where the focus was to be on economic development.

- Colonists would also be supplied with food once they crossed into Russia and food supplies would be continued until they were able to plant and harvest crops after their arrival. The colonists would also be supplied with seed, tools, and building materials in Bessarabia to establish their farms and to build homes to live in. The costs the Russian government absorbed in supplying food, seed, and tools would be treated as an interest-free loan to the colonists. This loan would be paid back in installments that would begin ten years after their arrival in Bessarabia—that is, well after (it was hoped) the colonies had been established on firm economic ground.

- Colonists would not be liable for state taxes or other financial levies for ten years in order to help them establish themselves in Bessarabia. Russian taxes, though they varied considerably during the relationship of the German colonies with Imperial Russia, were materially lower than those paid by peasants in Prussia.

---

20. Hagen (*Ordinary Prussians*, 162) provides one of the few assessments of average peasant landholdings based on extensive data. On the Stavenow manors of the von Kleists in Brandenburg, Hagen reports fullholders generally having tenure to 2 hides ("hufen") of land, roughly 85 acres. Average fullholder land tenures only amount to 31.5 desjatina, about half of what colonists were offered to come to Bessarabia.

21. As will be discussed in some detail later, there appear to be differences in understanding on this right. German colonist sources saw this freedom from military service as "forever exempted" (Daniel Wölfle, "Establishment of the Village of Kulm" in "Heimatbuch der Gemeinde Kulm," *Heritage Review* 13, no. 4 [1983]: 3; and Schmidt, *Die Deutschen aus Bessarabien*, 13, who describes this as "die unbefristete Befreiung vom Militärdinst"). In contrast, Russian sources, even before 1871, make no mention of "forever" or *unbefristete* ("unlimited"). Klaus, writing in the 1860s (*Naši kolonii*, 317), only mentions a general "freedom from military and civil service" ("svoboda ot voinskoj i graždanskoj služby"). The fact that the tsars never placed limits on their right to change laws or regulations may not have been fully understood by potential immigrants.

## The first nineteen German colonies were established in Bessarabia in the period from 1814 to 1825

The great majority of the settlers of these nineteen colonies were Germans coming from Prussian Poland.[22] As we have seen in the prior two chapters, these were German peasants who were immigrants to Prussian Poland coming there to lease land, often after Prussia's acquisition of this territory in the Three Partitions of Poland. Their origins lie in different parts of the German-speaking world: some were from Prussia and other parts of northern and central Germany, and others from Württemberg, Baden, and the upper Rhineland. Three of these nineteen colonies, however, were founded by immigrant groups coming to Bessarabia directly from Western Europe: one from Württemberg (Teplitz), a second from Bavaria and Württemberg (Sarata), and a third (Schabo) generally from Switzerland.

A study of Bessarabia dating from the 1820s, based no doubt on census data collected by the Welfare Committee, offers the breakdown of the different regional backgrounds of the first Bessarabian German colonists seen in table 3–1.[23]

This establishes that the vast majority (91.2%) of the German colonists who had reached Bessarabia by the 1820s had family origins in Prussia, including Prussian Poland or Württemberg. Given the likelihood that the figures quoted are based on self reporting, there is a reasonable chance that the top two categories, those coming to Bessarabia from Prussian Poland and Württemberg, are not mutually exclusive. With the exception of the Teplitz and Sarata colonists, there were not many German colonists in Bessarabia who came there directly from Württemberg. Instead, most of those with ultimate origins in Württemberg came to Bessarabia after having first immigrated to Prussian Poland sometime after 1790. Thus, it

TABLE 3–1.  **Regional backgrounds of the first Bessarabian German colonists**

| Region | Number of colonists | Percentage Bessarabian pop. |
|---|---|---|
| Prussian Poland | 3,198 | 34.2% |
| Württemberg | 3,143 | 33.6% |
| Prussia | 2,188 | 23.4% |
| Bavaria | 378 | 4.0% |
| Mecklenburg | 225 | 2.4% |
| Switzerland | 73 | 0.8% |
| Saxony | 68 | 0.7% |
| France | 52 | 0.6% |
| Austria | 18 | 0.19% |
| Hungary | 17 | 0.18% |
| Baden | 3 | 0.03% |
| **Total** | 9,363 | |

---

22. Three of the nineteen settlements were spin-offs. To permit colonists with land far from the settlement site to live closer to the land they worked, the Welfare Committee permitted three colonies to subdivide and create a new village site within their original land grants. In this way, Alt Posttal was formed from part of the Wittenberg settlement in 1823, Neu Arzis from the Arzis settlement in 1825, and Neu Elft formed from Elft (hereafter Alt Elft) also in 1825.

23. Brandes, *Von den Zaren Adoptiert*, 90. Brandes's source is a statistical description of Bessarabia published in Russian in 1899 which was based on data from 1822 to 1828.

would appear reasonable to presume that numbers of those who are listed as coming from Prussian Poland had Württemberg origins and many of those listed as coming from Württemberg did so after spending time in Prussian Poland. Judging, too, from the extensive data on the first colonists to settle Kulm, Leipzig, and Tarutino discussed in the following chapter, it would also seem likely that those included among the group coming from Prussian Poland included numbers of people with recent backgrounds in Mecklenburg and Saxony that would raise the totals for those categories.

The first three German colonies, Krasna, Borodino, and Tarutino, were founded in 1814, with the Krasna settlers first to arrive in the fall of 1813. Four colonies, Klöstitz, Kulm, Leipzig, and Wittenberg, were founded the following year and a half, and five more, Arzis, Beresina, Brienne, Elft, and Paris in 1816. In 1817, a group of Württembergers, bound for the newly conquered Russian Caucasus, were overcome with sickness just as they crossed into Bessarabia after having traveled down the Danube. The surviving elements of this group, unable to proceed much further, were allowed to remain in Bessarabia and they established the colony of Teplitz. In 1821, Katzbach was founded with new immigrants from Prussian Poland, and the tiny colony of Schabo was founded in the former Turkish vineyards along the estuary of the Dniester with immigrants from Switzerland. In 1822, a group of religious separatists from Bavaria and Württemberg founded the colony of Sarata.

## What attracted the German peasant immigrants to Bessarabia?

There is no direct evidence from the first generation of colonists on their reasons for leaving Prussian Poland or Württemberg, Bavaria, and Switzerland. If the early German colonists wrote letters to relations and friends who remained behind, these have not survived or reached the public record. Nor are there written memoirs by the colonists describing why they elected to leave behind situations they had established or inherited. As a result, it is not possible to know how individual families sorted out their worries and hopes and made their decisions. To pull up stakes and move many hundreds of miles to an alien country commonly thought far more primitive than any of the German lands had to be a difficult decision. It would have been all the more so as Bessarabia was territory the Russians had just taken from the Turks. Who could be sure that Russia would continue to hold it?

Some references to the factors influencing the immigrants appear in the short village histories that many of the Bessarabian villages put together in 1848. This was still within living memory but over thirty years after the settlements were established. There are also traces of the influences and hopes, though often not clear ones, appearing in the Kulm Heimatbuch, put together by Bessarabian refugees in Germany after World War II, as well as in traditions carried by nineteenth-century immigrants to North America. While such sources are helpful in identifying factors that supported decisions to emigrate, they are distant and hardly contemporary. Most highlight a generally similar bundle of financial losses that led German peasants, especially in Prussian Poland, to consider positively the Russian offer to establish colonies in Bessarabia:

- The heavy tax burden in Prussian Poland, presumably including the French tribute demands in the time of the Duchy of Warsaw,

- The loss of crops, livestock, and income caused by the quartering and passage of troops that followed Napoleon's victory over Prussia in 1806–7, and

- The buildup and passage of Napoleon's huge army invading Imperial Russia in 1812 and its passage in return and defeat in the winter of 1813.

In the first decade of the nineteenth century, Prussia's King Friedrich Wilhelm III had two major political goals as Napoleon sought to use French strength to rearrange radically power relationships in Central Europe. Friedrich Wilhelm sought to keep Prussia out of the Napoleonic Wars and to maintain Prussia's position as a near major European power. These proved difficult goals to achieve, particularly as Russia and Austria had limited interests in helping Prussia succeed. In 1806, following Austria's major defeat at Austerlitz (December 2, 1805), Prussia was obliged to become a client and ally of France. However, as French demands increased and included the demand to close Prussia's Baltic seaports to grain shipments to Britain, the major external source of Prussian state income, Prussia found itself in an impossible and isolated position. Deciding at last to fight France, Prussia was forced to face Napoleon without allies. The result was the catastrophic defeats at Auerstedt and Jena in October 1806, which led to the French occupation of Brandenburg and Berlin. The Prussian King and government fled to Memel at the far corner of East Prussia.

The consequences of these defeats for Prussia were painful. On July 7, 1807, Napoleon and Tsar Alexander I of Russia met on a barge in the Niemen River to discuss a settlement. Prussia's King Friedrich Wilhelm III was treated as someone of little consequence and had to await the results of the negotiations on the bank of the river. On July 9th, Prussia was obliged to agree without changes to the terms of the Franco-Russian Peace of Tilsit. This treaty had several major impacts on Prussia:

- Prussia would lose about half its territory, including nearly half of its population. Most of Prussia's gains from the Three Partitions of Poland now became the Duchy of Warsaw. While this new state was provided with a king, Friedrich Augustus I of Saxony, and a bicameral legislature, it was in fact a satellite state totally controlled by France, though much local power was given to the Polish gentry and church.

- Prussia would have to pay a war indemnity to France. The amount was not specified in the Peace of Tilsit but later was set at 120 million francs. This is estimated to be perhaps sixteen times the prewar revenue of the Prussian government.[24] The French, realizing in 1808 that impoverished and truncated Prussia would not be able to pay the indemnity forced on it, compelled the Duchy of Warsaw to purchase much of the Prussian debt in what amounted to a nineteenth-century version of a structured settlement.[25]

- While the French army remained camped in Prussia and the Duchy of Warsaw, it was to have full rights of quartering of troops and the

---

24. P. G. Dwyer, "Prussia during the French Revolutionary and Napoleonic Wars, 1786-1815" in Dwyer, *Rise of Prussia*, 252.

25. The outstanding debt, estimated in 1808 to be 43 million gold francs, was settled at a discount of under 50% at 21 million francs. The Duchy made payments to France for four years, but Prussia, without resources or even central control over much of its territory, did not.

requisition of food to feed itself and of animals and fodder to support the army's needs.[26]

- The treaty closed the ports of Danzig, Thorn, and Königsberg to grain trade with Great Britain. This cut off Prussia's major source of foreign exchange and a major source of income for the Prussian gentry and peasants. It similarly cut off the British market for grain produced by gentry manors and German and Polish peasants in the Duchy of Warsaw.

German peasants in the former Prussian Poland saw many negative consequences resulting from the Peace of Tilsit and its aftermath. In West Prussia, which but for the Netze District remained part of Prussia, taxes significantly increased to collect funds for the indemnity owed to France that appear mainly to have been used to support what was left of the Prussian state. In South and New East Prussia, which collectively formed the initial size of the Duchy of Warsaw,[27] extra taxes were levied by the new Polish French government to pay the portion of the Prussian debt to France that the Duchy had taken on. Not surprisingly, Polish landlords, now with a supportive government in Warsaw, sought to right old wrongs created by Prussian treatment after the partitions. Old claims to land were resurrected and former rights against peasants and towns were asserted. The Catholic Church, which had not been favored under the Prussian administration, now sought to reclaim its former rights to land and income that had gone to the Prussian crown.[28] Occasionally, the Catholic Church sought to claim tenancy payments in arrears from German peasants who had paid these to the Prussian crown. The grain market, which had rested on foreign trade, virtually collapsed, causing grain prices to drop, which increased the burden of making tax and lease payments. Perhaps the heaviest burden borne by German peasants in West Prussia and the Duchy of Warsaw were the demands of quartering, feeding, and supplying the huge French invasion force for Russia in 1811–12. Though of shorter durations, the disastrous winter retreat of the starving French army in early 1813 and the accompanying advance of the Russian army in pursuit imposed additional significant burdens. Both armies needed to live off the land and both used road systems that ran through the heart of the heaviest area of German settlements.

Several of the 1848 Bessarabian village histories note the troubles and depredations caused by the Napoleonic Wars as a primary factor which led their citizens to

---

26. Dwyer, "Prussia," 253–54. In February 1812, recognizing Russia would not offer meaningful help against the French, Prussia entered into a humiliating treaty with France under which it would supply twenty thousand troops as well as take on the responsibility of quartering and supplying the huge French invasion force that would be put together later that spring.
27. In 1809, France added the Austrian province of West Galicia, Austria's portion of the Third Partition of Poland, to the Duchy of Warsaw following a further defeat of the Austrians by the French.
28. To understand the motivations of the Catholic Church at this time, it should be remembered that in the regions of Poland that Prussia had taken control of following the partitions, the church had suffered major setbacks in income. Karin Friedrich notes, for example, that as result of the First Partition of 1772, the Catholic Church in what became West Prussia "lost over two-thirds of its pre-1772 income." Friedrich, *Brandenburg-Prussia*, 107.

leave Prussian Poland for Bessarabia.[29] The village history for Borodino, for example, notes that the offer to resettle in Bessarabia was attractive because the colonists had "endured a great deal of suffering and incurred substantial losses in their former settlements, largely because of the military operations and the frequent billeting of local and foreign troops during…the French campaigns."[30] The Alt Posttal village history refers to the "devastating military expeditions of the French."[31] The Klöstitz village history comments on "suffering oppression for years by warlike conditions and…loss of property."[32] The Wittenberg village history notes the Germans agreed to emigrate from Poland "because of revolutionary unrest in Poland in…1810 and 1811 and the maneuvering of French troops on their way to Russia in 1812."[33] The Kulm Heimatbuch, put together in Germany in the 1960s by some of the 1940 Kulm refugees and their descendants, also remembers the effects of the Napoleonic Wars: "Through the advance and retreat of Napoleon's army, the population had almost all of their possessions robbed."[34]

Several of the 1848 village histories note a second cause for the emigration of Germans from Prussian Poland to Bessarabia: persecution the Germans suffered from Polish landlords and the Polish Catholic Church as these landlords and the church sought to use the greater powers they had under the Duchy of Warsaw to regain rights lost under Prussian government administration. After referring to the military depredations, the Alt Posttal village history notes the following: "There was religious persecution by the Catholic Church, which resulted in the loss of most of their newly gained properties, and many other hardships inflicted by the Polish subjects."[35]

The Kulm Heimatbuch describes similar issues but separates them into distinctly different causes: "In Poland…our ancestors…suffered under the tyranny of Polish

---

29. As noted in the introduction, the 1848 village histories were documents created by the German villages in Bessarabia and South Russia following a request by Friedrich von Hahn, then President of the Welfare Committee of Foreign Settlers in South Russia. Von Hahn's letter of January 1848 went out to mayors and school teachers of the 203 German villages in the Black Sea region, enjoining them to write an account of the founding and development of their colony. This was evidently in an effort to show how far the colonies had progressed. This request produced a number of histories. Some were printed in the 1850s in an Odessa German-language newspaper. In the period from 1904 to 1941, 173 were collected and published in different editions in Germany (the most complete being the 1941 edition by Margarete Woltner containing 114). The Odessa3 collection contains translations of 53 of these, including 22 from the Bessarabian villages.

30. The reference to "local" troops is to Prussian military units required by Prussia's agreement with the French to join the campaign against the Russians. Eckert, "Borodino – 1848 Village History," trans. J. R. Hubert (N.p.: Odessa Digital Library, 1999), http://www.odessa3.org/collections/history/link/borodino.txt.

31. Wilhelm Kludt, "Alt Posttal – 1848 Village History," trans. Elvire Necker-Eberhardt (N.p.: Odessa Digital Library, 2000), http://www.odessa3.org/collections/history/link/altpost.txt.

32. G. Schaeff, "Kloestitz – 1848 Village History," trans. Elli Wise (N.p.: Odessa Digital Library, 1997), http://www.odessa3.org/collections/history/link/kloes.txt.

33. Johann G. Kurz, "Wittenberg – 1848 Village History," trans. Elli Wise (N.p.: Odessa Digital Library, 1996), http://www.odessa3.org/collections/history/link/wittenbg.txt. The reference in the Wittenberg history to "revolutionary unrest" is unclear but may refer to actions of Poles who hoped that by ardent support of France the Duchy would ultimately become an independent Polish state, or may refer in general to the revolutionary times when boundaries suddenly moved and old states like Prussia and Austria were crushed and new states such as the Duchy came into being. The Neu Elft village history also refers to the reasons for emigration as people being "troubled by revolutions and wartime unrests." I. Kurz, "Neu Elft – 1848 Village History," trans. Roswita Niessner (N.p.: Odessa Digital Library, 1996), http://www.odessa3.org/collections/history/link/neuelft.txt.

34. Wölfle, "The Establishment of the Village of Kulm," 3.

35. Kludt, "Alt Posttal – 1848 Village History."

landlords. The very powerful Catholic Church in Poland constantly oppressed them in their confessional life."[36]

The complaint in the Alt Posttal village history likely refers to efforts of the Catholic Church in Poland during the period of the Duchy of Warsaw to recover land that Prussia had claimed as crown land after the partitions. The "newly gained properties" threatened with loss mentioned in the Alt Posttal history were the lands settled in South Prussia in the recent past by the Württembergers and Rhinelanders who formed the majority population in Alt Posttal. The Alt Posttal History also implies that the Catholic Church may have wanted to replace the German Protestant tenants with other—that is, Catholic—tenants. The passage in the Heimatbuch refers, however, to other interests and actions of the Catholic Church. After the return to quasi-Polish rule in the period of the Duchy of Warsaw, the Catholic Church in some areas of Poland attempted to reimpose its hegemony in religious affairs. This included the payment of tithe obligations from peasants of all religions and may have included attempts to restrict the meetings of non-Catholic denominations. Both passages also appear to make references to the attempts of Polish landlords to increase lease obligations using the change in jurisdiction as a means to restate leasing terms. A memory of this also appears in Mutschall's history of Tarutino. In discussing the miseries of the Germans in Poland, Mutschall notes "the oppressive lease agreements signed with the Polish nobility."[37]

Bad weather causing crop failures in the first decades of the nineteenth century was another factor that was noted for creating peasant hardship and encouraging thoughts of emigration. The first decade of the nineteenth century had several years of wet and chilly summers producing low yields at harvest. Low yields worsened the effect of the exactions of the French and allied troops and lowered the margins for sustainable life. The winter of 1813–14 was particularly cold and long. While such weather, particularly coming during the decision period, might have been influential for the first wave of colonists in 1814, weather problems, particularly cool and wet summers, were definitely influential for those electing to immigrate to Bessarabia later. The huge eruption of the Mt. Tambora volcano on the Indonesian island of Sumbawa occurring between April and July of 1815 produced difficult conditions around the world. The summer of 1816 in northern Europe was extremely rainy and cold, producing poor (and in some cases no) grain harvests. As a result of the ash cloud from the Mt. Tambora volcano, 1816 is often mentioned as the "year without a summer." Commentaries on emigration from Württemberg in the second decade of the nineteenth century mention the terrible summer of 1816, but stress several years of bad harvests as the major causal factors.[38]

Written at some distance from the period in question, the references in these accounts to the hardships and worries that spurred Germans to leave Prussian Poland do not mention other concerns that might well have been motivations for emigration. These include the fact that decisions had to be made before the Congress

---

36. Wölfle, "The Establishment of the Village of Kulm," 3.
37. Wilhelm Mutschall, "History of the Community of Tarutino from 1814 to 1934," *Heritage Review* 42, no. 4 (2012): 5.
38. Mack Walker notes that "high food prices and famine in 1816 and 1817 were not caused by a single bad harvest; 1816 was the climax of a series of bad years" (*Germany and the Emigration*, 4). I. Baumann stresses the poor harvests of 1809–16 as a major factor behind the emigration. Baumann, "The Reasons for the Emigration of Our Forefathers," *Heritage Review* 14, no. 3 (1984): 46–50.

of Vienna announced the disposition of lands that had made up Prussian Poland. Would the victorious powers leave the Duchy of Warsaw in place, with all the associated dangers that would mean for German Protestant peasants living there? Would South Prussia be returned to Prussia, bringing the likelihood of significant tax increases to repair the empty coffers of the Prussian government? What would be the actions now of the gentry landlords, who also had suffered considerable financial losses? Would peasants be forced to restate leasing rights to retain their land? With Russian troops in control of much of Poland, would the victorious powers give control of this territory to Russia, and if so, what would that mean for the rights of German peasants there?[39]

In contrast to the several statements that refer to the economic tribulations of peasants in Prussia during wartime as encouraging thoughts of accepting Russia's offer to come to Bessarabia, there is very little mention about why the Russian offer seemed attractive or what features were found particularly so. The 1848 village histories for Beresina and Wittenberg do refer to special "privileges" and the Neu Elft village history comments on "promises of land and support," but none of the three offer any detail.[40] The Alt Posttal village history is the only one to list features of the Russian offer. Not all parts of the Russian offer are noted here and there can be no certainty as to whether the order of listing relates in any way to deemed value or importance. Alt Posttal remembers first the "freedom from all taxes and land obligations."[41] This is followed by: (a) the payment of 270 rubles per family to get established, (b) the 60 desjatina of land given to each family, (c) 5 kopeks paid per person per day for food that was paid from the date of arrival in Russia to the first grain harvest, (d) freedom from military conscription and in general from obligations to quarter troops, and (e) permission to build churches, employ pastors, and observe their own religious customs.[42] The treatment of the Russian terms in the Alt Posttal history appears to be an effort to give substance to the idea that the colonists "joyfully" left Prussian Poland for Bessarabia. The combination of their very difficult circumstances with the strong attractions of the Russian offer seemed miraculous—the Germans "looked joyfully to the heavens when the high crown of Russia opened the door to emigration."[43] A similar tone appears in the Kulm Heimatbuch. Tsar Alexander's offer coming "at a time of economic oppression" when conditions looked bleak was considered "an instrument of God," a miraculous intervention to succor and support the suffering Germans.[44]

In spite of the lack of references to attributes of the Russian offer that "pulled" immigrants, the positive inducements were an important reason settlers agreed to make the long journey to an unknown and unpopulated land. Bessarabia was far away: roughly 700 miles from Bromberg in Prussian Poland as the crow flies, but the distance to travel by river and road was at least double that. Return to Prussia

---

39. Though Russia was in real control of Poland from the spring of 1813 on, the terms of the Congress of Vienna were not finally settled and published until 1815. The first wave of German immigrants to Bessarabia from this area of Poland had to make their decision during the winter of 1813–14—well before whatever changes were in store for Prussian Poland had been agreed to and the decisions of the victorious powers stated publically.

40. Kurz, "Neu Elft – 1848 Village History."

41. Kludt, "Alt Posttal – 1848 Village History."

42. Ibid.

43. Ibid.

44. Wölfle, "The Establishment of the Village of Kulm," 3.

would likely be very difficult, if not impossible. Colonists would be leaving behind families, support systems, familiar cultural and economic systems—if not their native ground, at least very familiar circumstances. Bessarabia, on the other hand, had just been wrested from the control of the Turks who had, in European imaginations, a very negative and cruel reputation; perhaps the Turks would return.

Shirley Fischer Arends, in her book on the German Russians who settled in the Dakotas, gives stress to one of the attractions of the Russian offer as particularly important for drawing Germans from Prussia: the German peasants wished to own the land they farmed.[45] Arends does not state the basis she has for drawing this conclusion. Nonetheless, she describes what was in fact a significant benefit. It would have both provided immigrants the opportunity to increase the financial benefits of their labor by eliminating lease payments and given them a fixed asset in real property. To German peasants, such an opportunity would have seemed extremely remote and almost beyond all possibility of occurring in Prussia, where peasant ownership of land was rare.

Another factor that may have influenced Germans to accept the offer was that Russia had made similar offers earlier to other Germans and such offers had resulted in successful German settlements being established in South Russia. In the period from 1789 to 1809, numbers of Germans, notably from Württemberg and the upper Rhineland as well as German- and Frisian-speaking Mennonites from the Vistula River delta, had established colonial settlements in the Xerson and Ekaterinoslav provinces on the steppelands between the Dniester and Dnieper rivers east of what was to become Bessarabia.[46] It is difficult to know the degree to which the early German settlers in Bessarabia might have known about the German settlements already founded in South Russia. Given the limited written culture that existed at this time among German peasants in Prussian Poland, it would seem unlikely that letters were exchanged between Prussian Poland and South Russia asking for advice. It may be that some information was passed through channels in the Evangelical Lutheran Church, or more simply that Germans living in Prussian Poland were aware of the existence of the earlier German settlements in Russia and the fact that nothing catastrophic had happened there. It would seem likely that the continued existence of such German colonies in South Russia gave some confidence and hope to those electing to go to Bessarabia that Russian promises were not ephemeral, that the risks were tolerable, and that their new settlements might succeed.

Religion, or rather the right to practice one's religious beliefs without hindrance from the state, was another positive reason some immigrants elected to come to Bessarabia. This would appear a rationale for the Roman Catholics originally from Bavaria, Franconia, and the Pfalz, who leased lands in South Prussia in the period from 1800 to 1803 and then founded the colony of Krasna, Bessarabia, in 1814. While under Prussian administration, they may have received preference as German speakers, but as Catholics they were likely to have been treated as less than first-class

45. Fischer Arends, *Central Dakota Germans*, 25.
46. German Mennonites had immigrated to Royal Prussia and particularly the former marshlands of the Vistula River delta in the sixteenth century, where they had been particularly successful in establishing productive farmland. When Prussia acquired this territory in the First Partition of Poland (1772), Mennonites became interested in leaving when Prussia started to ask for extra fees as a tax on Mennonites to maintain their pacifist beliefs and not be liable for conscription to serve in the Prussian army.

citizens. In the period of the Duchy of Warsaw, preferences were reversed and Catholics were treated most favorably. Following the partitions, the Polish Catholic church, however, had taken on the role of preserving the Polish language and Polish folk culture as well as keeping alive hopes for the return of an independent Polish national government. It is likely that during the period of the Duchy, the German Catholics were feeling some pressure to use Polish in church and in religious education. Under Russian rule, beginning in 1813, they, like the German Protestants, may have had concerns about their religious freedom in Russian Poland.

## Both religious and economic reasons lie behind the immigration from Württemberg, Baden, and Bavaria to Bessarabia

Religious motives played a particularly important role also in the founding of the Sarata colony in 1822 and possibly the immigration of Württembergers who founded Teplitz in 1817. In the upper Rhineland, the collapse of French power after 1814 was accompanied by religious revivals. Pietist views stressing the positive values of more emotional, personal, and less formal religious practices were once again popular. Civil authorities in the small West German states tended to offer support to religious revivals because they saw these as building conservative attitudes that were antithetical to the ideals propagated by the French Revolution. In the region just to the east of Württemberg, the so-called Schwabian Bavaria, Father Ignatz Lindl in the second decade of the nineteenth century built up a following in Catholic parishes.[47] He preached spiritualistic views that had much in common with the concepts and practices of the Protestant Pietists. These included the importance and value of joint Bible reading, discussion, and prayer, and the view that members of the lay community touched by the spirit of God could interpret the Bible. The Catholic Church did not consider this approved doctrine and removed Lindl from his parish and forbade his preaching. Lindl then moved to St. Petersburg, Russia, where he persuaded the Russian government to give him a grant of land in Bessarabia to which he would attract his German followers and found an agricultural community. Lindl had maintained written contact with his followers in Bavaria and wrote letters urging followers from Bavaria and Württemberg to join him in Bessarabia to found the colony of Sarata and create there "an apostolic brotherhood based on the principles of community property."[48] The Russian authorities had evidently taken Lindl initially to be similar in views to the Protestant Pietists with whom they were familiar. When they learned of Lindl's ideas of communal property and his messianic goals and inflated self view, they considered him dangerous and in 1823, expelled him from Russia. Groups of his followers, however, did come to Russia in 1821–22 and, as the following chapter will discuss, founded the colony of Sarata, where they chose

47. Schwabian Bavaria refers to an area northeast of Ulm in Bavaria where Alemannic German (Schwabian) rather than Bavarian is generally spoken. This was a relatively recent addition to Bavarian territory. Bavaria acquired this territory in 1803 as the result of an agreement reached by the Imperial diet of the Holy Roman Empire, the "Reichsdeputationshauptschluss" (the Imperial Deputation's Principal Conclusion), whereby Bavaria and a few other major principalities were compensated for territories lost to France west of the Rhine by being given free rein to take over by force small neighboring principalities and church territories.

48. Arnulf Baumann, "Background to Ignaz Lindl's Expulsion from Sarata Bessarabia in the Context of Russia's Political and Religious History," trans. J. Gessele, *Heritage Review* 36, no. 1 (2006): 37. This issue of *Heritage Review* also published a translation of Florian Mayr's article that describes the growth and development of Lindl's spiritualist preaching in Bavaria (Mayr, "Gundremmingen and the Followers of Lindl," *Heritage Review* 36, no. 1 [2006]: 13–24).

to adopt private rather than communal property rights and became Evangelical Lutherans.

Religious beliefs may also have been a factor in drawing the colonists who founded Teplitz in 1817 from Württemberg to Russia. In the period from 1815 to 1818 in Württemberg, the Pietist Baroness Julie von Krüdener had stirred up interest in immigration to Russia by popularizing the idea in speeches and religious tracts that Tsar Alexander I was sympathetic to Pietism. Alexander was often portrayed at this time as the savior of Europe, freeing the continent not just from Napoleon and French political power but also from French secularism. Krüdener emphasized that Alexander was blessed with a large but underpopulated land and would welcome Pietists from Württemberg. One historian of the emigration of Germans from Württemberg to the Russian Caucasus, the original destination of the Teplitz group, has concluded that religious motives were behind the decisions that many made.[49]

While it is true that Pietist practices underwent a revival in Württemberg after the defeat of the French, and that the desire to practice such views in peace was one factor motivating immigration, it is difficult to deny the overwhelming importance of economic issues in spurring emigration from Württemberg and the Rhineland at this time. As noted earlier, the second decade of the nineteenth century was marked in Germany by a series of poor harvests, culminating in the unusually bad year of 1816. Economic conditions were worsened further in this period by the fact that with the end of the French-inspired blockade of Great Britain, inexpensive British manufactured cloth again became readily available. This hurt the local weaving trade and consequently, hurt peasant landowners who had been able to survive on small plots by finding a second income in this trade.

Giesinger, Fleischhauer, and Stumpp argue that both economic and religious factors lie behind the Württembergers' choice to emigrate in the period from 1816 to 1817.[50] Without offering comparative weights, they each note that both the hunger resulting from poor harvests and the desire to practice one's religion unhindered were important. Mack Walker, however, argues strongly for the primacy of economic factors. To the argument that Pietist concerns such as those raised by Krüdener were significant in the immigration to Russia, he notes that the great majority of emigrants from Württemberg went to the United States, not Russia. To the argument that "most historians have distinguished the eastward movement by assigning it a religious motive," he replies that "only a small minority of the Auswanderer themselves declared such a motive."[51] Walker then refers to Paul Hoffmann's study of German colonies in the Caucasus and notes that of the "approximately 6,000 Württembergers who went all the way to Transcaucasia in 1816–17, not more than 250 were really Separatists."[52] Walker also quotes a thoughtful memorandum written at this time by an official in the Württemberg district of Sulz who tried to talk people

49. Paul Hoffmann, *Die deutschen Kolonien in Transkaukasien* (Berlin: Verlag von D. Reimer, 1905). See also Walker, *Germany and the Emigration*, 10–12. Walker further notes that in the period from 1815 to 1816, the Imperial Russian consul in Stuttgart was offering passage to Russia for those wishing to take up land in Transcaucasia.

50. Giesinger, *From Catherine to Khrushchev*, 38; Fleischhauer, *Die Deutschen im Zarenreich*, 168; and Stumpp, who offers more detail (*Emigration from Germany to Russia*, 26–28).

51. Walker, *Germany and the Emigration*, 14–15.

52. Ibid.

out of leaving and in doing so sought to understand their rationale for emigrating. In considering their rationale, the official concludes that

> *the only reason for their emigration lies in their declining hope of being able to get along respectably in their Fatherland—and I too am convinced that reasons for so universal an Auswanderung mania lie not in an attraction from the outside, but in a certain despair of the possibility of a future in the Fatherland.*[53]

The Sulz region, though, was not one where Pietist Separatists were numerous. The memorandum quoted above also notes that "there are no Separatists here."[54] As a result, this may not be a good argument for the absence of religious motivations. While Walker's basic argument, that economic causes formed a dominating rationale for emigration, is well taken, Walker goes too far, I feel, in appearing to exclude or significantly minimize other causes. With almost no firsthand information from the emigrants themselves, we are far removed from understanding actual causation. For example, Walker's assertion that no more than 250 of the 6,000 Württembergers going to the Caucasus were "really" Separatists refers only to the fact that some groups of emigrants so distinguished themselves. This does not establish that emigrants who did not refer to themselves as Separatists were not motivated by religion in deciding to leave Württemberg. Even Walker's clinching argument that emigration from Württemberg came to a stop once the good harvest of 1817 was taken in isn't conclusive that economic factors, to the exclusion of virtually all others, were responsible for the emigration. It does strongly suggest that economic conditions were critical and the good harvest provided an important respite. Emigration, however, did not stop after 1817. The real point is that we are too far removed from those who emigrated to know what factors they considered and what weights they put on different factors. From our distance, the economic evidence does look overwhelming, but we do know that Pietist beliefs had many adherents in Württemberg, that they were influential in encouraging the immigration to Prussian Poland earlier, and were clearly important in bringing Lindl's followers from Bavaria and Württemberg to Sarata. Giesinger notes a group of forty families who left Württemberg in September 1816 to go to the Caucasus who were led by men who had been imprisoned for their Separatist views, as well as other Germans from Württemberg with more Chiliast views "going eastward 'to meet the Lord'."[55] Clearly, at least some emigrants were highly motivated by religious reasons; and thus, Walker's argument overreaches when he explains religious motivation as an inconsequential factor. The degree to which religious or other motivations existed among the economic pressures, though, is impossible to measure at this distance.

## Four additional German colonies were established in Bessarabia in the 1830s

Gnadental (1830–33), Friedenstal (1834), Lichtental (1834 and 1838–40), and Plotzk (1839–40) were populated with immigrants who came directly to Bessarabia from

---

53. Ibid., 22.
54. Ibid.
55. Giesinger, *From Catherine to Khrushchev*, 39–41.

Württemberg and the upper Rhineland or whose families originated in that region.[56] Emigration from Württemberg and the upper Rhineland during this later period continues to reflect the economic themes noted earlier: shared inheritances created smaller family allotments of land, additional sources of income became increasingly important, and bad harvest years or changing economic circumstances created issues of survival and so increased the pressure to emigrate. Several aspects of the emigration that occurred during the period from 1830 to 1845, though, make it look different from that which occurred earlier. Where in 1814–16, weaving as a second income was the only trade under pressure from the opening of the Rhine to imports from Great Britain, a number of other trades that had been taken up to supplement farm income now also came under attack. The industrial revolution that had taken place in Great Britain allowed it to produce finished goods so cheaply and efficiently that British imports undersold local craft work. Now not just weavers but carpenters, blacksmiths, and masons were having difficulty competing. A second difference noted by contemporary observers differentiating emigration that occurred after 1830 was that it now seemed to take less pressure to induce thoughts of emigration. Families emigrating after 1830 increasingly responded to "declining standards for themselves and their children, rather than absolute lows."[57] A third change in emigration from Württemberg and the Rhineland after 1830 was that town dwellers were now increasingly among the emigrants. Artisans and apprentices working in towns were now finding it harder to support themselves not just because of imports from British manufactures but because of the Zollverein, the German customs union that had gone into effect in 1818. The removal of local tariffs increased the value of efficient production. Factories became more of a feature in German-speaking lands when the perceived potential of trade began to appear greater than the hurdle of startup costs. Increased trade and manufacturing had the effect of creating a surplus of artisans. In consequence, as Walker has observed, emigration in this period "probably included a higher proportion of prosperous, skilled, and educated people than of any other time."[58]

In the 1820s, the Welfare Committee began to raise concerns that the basic skill level for accepting immigrants needed to be higher. As will be discussed in later chapters, some of the German communities in South Russia were doing poorly and had started to create a landless underclass because the combination of low skill levels and insufficient initial funds led some to fail and become workers dependent on their neighbors. As a result, the Russian government became particularly intent from the 1820s on to pressure agents to consider accepting only those people with demonstrated skills and some personal funds. Whether they came from Württemberg or Poland, it is likely that the immigrants to the Bessarabian colonies founded after 1830 were held to higher standards. It is interesting to note that the emigration data presented by Walker

---

56. Plotzk and especially Friedenstal also had numbers of German colonists who came there from Poland, thus replicating the pattern in many of the first Bessarabian German colonies with a mixture of Germans from the north and Germans from the Rhineland. There were two additional German colonies established in Bessarabia during this period: Dennewitz. founded in 1834 with settlers coming from well-established families in earlier Bessarabian settlements, especially Alt Posttal, Kulm, Tarutino, and Wittenberg; and the colony of Hoffnungstal, which was founded in the period from 1842 to 1847 with settlers coming from some of the overcrowded settlements in South Russia whose families had come to South Russia originally from Württemberg, often before 1806.

57. Walker, *Germany and the Emigration*, 51–52.

58. Ibid.

suggests that conditions in the Rhineland at this time were creating greater numbers of emigrants with some financial reserves and town-based skills.

There is no direct evidence confirming greater skills or greater personal means as traits of the colonists founding the post-1830 settlements in Bessarabia, although there is some indirect support. The 1848 village history for Gnadental notes that settlers brought with them, on average, assets of 700 rubles, and the village history for Lichtental gives average assets of the arriving colonists as 600 rubles.[59] This suggests the new colonists brought with them some supporting assets and contrasts with the reports in the village histories of Leipzig and Sarata that colonists coming there over a decade earlier were poor. It is not possible to conclude from this, however, that the German colonists arriving after 1830 were generally better off than earlier groups of colonists. The Kulm and Wittenberg histories indicate colonists arrived in 1814–15 with assets ranging from 400–1,000 silver rubles in Kulm and from 200–1,000 rubles in Wittenberg, which suggests a variety of supporting assets among earlier colonists.[60]

The *Heritage Review* in 2008 published two letters written in early 1841 to family members in Murr, Württemberg. The letters were written by a husband and wife, Friedericka (Koch) and Friedrich Schlechter, who had recently settled in Plotzk Bessarabia. Their ability to compose and write attests to their education, which their letter suggests was not common in their new settlement with its majority of German immigrants coming from Poland. This implies that by the 1840s standards of education for peasants in Württemberg may have been higher than those for German peasants in Russian Poland or even German Bessarabia.

These letters also offer almost the only first-person commentary on the rationale for giving up a much missed life in Württemberg and coming to Russia. Both indicate that the ability to improve living standards was critical. Friedericka Schlechter quotes a relation of her Württemberg friends saying that "if your means are such that you have enough for a livelihood, one is better off to stay in Germany," and notes later that although she doesn't like it in Bessarabia, "one thing that is better here is the fact that there is more to eat." Friedrich Schlechter summarizes his decision as "a father needs to make decisions concerning nourishment for his family…a decision has to be made one way or the other: should we risk all, go to Russia and hope for a better standard of living."[61]

We have been considering to this point the motivations that led Imperial Russia to offer attractive terms to Germans in Prussian Poland to immigrate to Bessarabia,

---

59. Jacob Koch, "Gnadenthal – 1848 Village History," trans. Elli Wise, (N.p.: Odessa Digital Library, 1996), http://www.odessa3.org/collections/history/link/gnadntal.txt; and Hahn, "Lichtental – 1848 Village History," trans. Adam Geisinger (N.p.: Odessa Digital Library, 1996), nd. http://www.odessa3.org/collections/history/link/lichtent.txt.

60. In contrast, Malinovskij, emphasizing that the Germans immigrating to South Russia were escaping the consequences of war, devastating hunger, failed crops, and higher taxes ("vojna, opustošenie golod, neurožaj, ucilenie nalogovogo bremeni"), stresses the general poverty of the immigrants (*Social'naja i xozjajstvennaja istorija*, 34–35). Malinovskij's efforts to build a case for what he portrays as the overwhelming poverty of the German colonists in South Russia leads him often to overlook signs to the contrary and so to miss, in the present point, the far more mixed economic standing of the arriving colonists.

61. Schlechter, "A Letter," 16–20. Stumpp lists Friedrich Schlechter as coming from nearby Murrhardt Württemberg (*Emigration from Germany to Russia*, 543), though the 1940–41 Koblenz questionnaires filled out by his descendants remember it as Murr. E. Wise, "Sofiental Bessarabia – a Koblenz Extraction" (N.p.: Odessa Digital Library, 2003), http://odessa3.org/collections/bess/koblenz/link/sofiental.txt.

as well as the reasons and rationale that led these Germans to accept this offer. In reviewing the apparent motivations of both sides, it is clear that they are quite different. This was clearly a marriage of convenience. The Russian government was not concerned about the plight of the Germans in Prussian Poland, nor was it thinking about creating a German cultural or linguistic world in Bessarabia. Russia wanted to populate the empty steppe with Christian peasants who would help it lay stronger claim to the territory, not trouble political stability within Russia, and would bring better agricultural techniques. The Germans coming to Bessarabia were not motivated by Russia's strategic goals and interests. They wanted more land, land sufficient to feed their families and create a surplus. They wanted to be able to own that land and so not have to pay tenancy costs in cash and labor. As often happens, great differences can occur between hopes and promises on the one hand and actual experience on the other. While the basic features of the Russian offer were honored and delivered to the German immigrants, there were also unhappy surprises and difficulties, as the next chapters will discuss. Perhaps, too, those who made the choice to immigrate to Bessarabia imagined that with other Germans like themselves they would form, in this far away, nearly unpopulated land, a semi-independent, German-speaking, agricultural world. This was not to prove the case and the immigration to Bessarabia, like that to North America, would, as we will see, ultimately raise questions of language, assimilation, and loyalty.

# IV

# The Founding of the German Colonies in Bessarabia

Beginning in the summer and fall of 1813 and continuing into the winter and spring of 1814, the Imperial Russian government dispatched agents to visit German villages in Poland. The agents were to talk up the attractive terms to be offered those willing to immigrate to Russia and settle in the newly acquired province of Bessarabia. The agents were then to sign up those willing to accept this offer and organize them into travel parties. We can infer these facts from the accounts of the different 1848 village histories for the Bessarabian colonies.

In 1813, civil authority had almost dissolved in the former Prussian Poland. Following the disastrous retreat of Napoleon's army from Russia in the winter of 1812–13, the French-dominated Duchy of Warsaw no longer existed. To the extent that any civil authority existed above the community level, it was supplied by the Russian army and Russian civilian authorities who had taken general control of the former duchy in the expectation, partially fulfilled, that Russia would acquire this area in the ultimate peace negotiations. Even in West Prussia, which had remained part of Prussia and had not become part of the Duchy of Warsaw, the severely weakened Prussian state maintained only nominal control in 1813 through early 1814. Thus, it would appear that, in 1813, agents of the Russian government could move about freely in the areas where the German villages were located. In stating that "because of unique circumstances, the Russian government sent a friendly invitation to move to Russia and settle there," the Wittenberg village history is certainly referring to the devastating aftermath of Napoleon's failed invasion.[1] Another aspect

---

1. J. G. Kurz, "Wittenberg – 1848 Village History," trans. E. Wise (N.p.: Odessa Digital Library, 1996), http://www.odessa3.org/collections/history/link/wittenbg.txt. All references to village histories in this chapter refer to the collection of translated Bessarabian village histories from 1848 that are contained in the Odessa3 Collection: http://www.odessa3.org/collections/history.

of these "unique circumstances" was the fact that agents of the Russian government were able act without Prussian permission or constraint in areas that, before 1807, had been parts of Prussian Poland.

Five of the 1848 Bessarabian village histories mention a Russian agent whom they call "Commissioner Krüger." The Wittenberg village history notes that in 1814, he "came to Poland himself to hand out the necessary passes"[2] for those accepting the offer to immigrate to Russia. The Borodino history comments that colonists destined for that village "started out on their journey to Bessarabia under the leadership of Commissioner Krüger,"[3] and the Klöstitz history calls attention to the fact that "under the leadership of Commissioner Krüger many groups were leaving."[4] As Krüger was providing the necessary documentation for travel, had apparently come to Poland from Russia, and had been provided with a title, we may infer that he was a Russian citizen of German ancestry acting as an agent of the Russian government. Krüger, in addition to providing prospective immigrants with the documentation and passes necessary to enter Russia, appears to have had a general responsibility of organizing travel groups, establishing departure points, and setting dates for departures that were to occur from the spring through the fall of 1814. This is apparently the meaning of the phrase "under the leadership of Commissioner Krüger" used in the Beresina, Borodino, Brienne, and Klöstitz village histories.[5]

Another named Russian official, Baron von Wittenheim, is mentioned in the Arzis village history as the leader of the first group of Arzis colonists who left Poland for Bessarabia in 1814.[6] This group, generally coming from settlements around the city of Marienwerder (Polish Grudziadz) in West Prussia, left for Bessarabia from Thorn (Polish Torun), which in 1814 was occupied by Russia. The presumption is that von Wittenheim, as a Russian official in Thorn, issued documents to the immigrants and possibly provided funds for their journey. The Beresina village history records that instructions and presumably immigration documents were provided by the Russian Governor "Lansque" and Governor General "Woiwutzki,"[7] with the subsequent travel arrangements then made by Commissioner Krüger.

---

2. Ibid.
3. Eckert, "Borodino – 1848 Village History."
4. Schaeff, "Kloestitz – 1848 Village History."
5. The phrasing in the Brienne village history, however, does raise the possibility that Krüger traveled with these villagers: "The 84 families of settlers emigrated as an independent group and arrived in Russia under the leadership of Commissioner Krüger." C. Minderlin, "Brienne – 1848 Village History," trans. E. Necker Eberhardt (N.p.: Odessa Digital Library, 2000), http://www.odessa3.org/collections/history/link/brienne.txt. Krüger's leadership role for parties of settlers destined for other villages and the frequent notation of other settler travel guides suggest that Krüger had a general organizational responsibility for many groups.
6. The von Wittenheims were a German-speaking, noble family whose estates were in the province of Courland in Russian-held Latvia. The official noted in the Arzis history is possibly the later author of books on canals and railroads in nineteenth-century Russia, Otto von Wittenheim, then early in his career in Russian state service. While the paragraph in the Arzis history referring to Baron von Wittenheim starts with the date 1816, this refers to the date the village settlement began in Bessarabia; von Wittenheim's help would have occurred in 1814 before the group left Poland.
7. Although Napoleon rapidly retreated west from Poland in early 1813, he subsequently began raising a new army. With growing concerns about Napoleon's strength and intentions, the Russian army occupying the former Duchy of Warsaw did not establish a formal civilian government at this time, but rather ruled by martial law. "Lansque" may be the General Sergej Lanskoj who commanded a division of Russian troops in Poland in the winter of 1813–14. General "Woiwutzki," probably Vojevudzki, I have not been able to identify.

Krüger and these other named officials do not appear to be the agents who disseminated the news of the Russian offer among the many German villages in Poland. As the German settlements in Poland from which colonists came were scattered over a broad area, it is likely that the Russian government paid several German-speaking agents to visit such villages where they would have described the offer and answered questions. These visits appear to have begun in 1813 and continued at least into the late summer of 1814. Agents would likely not have remained in small German settlements for a long time and may well have come through once to make the offer and then again later to sign up those willing to take it. Where there were several German villages clustered near each other and prospects of finding immigrants were greater, such agents may have made several visits, with the Germans there committing to decisions at different times.

Judging from Stumpp, Flegel, and the 1815 census data from Kulm, it would appear that, in some cases, families, friends, and acquaintances from the same village in Poland agreed to emigrate together and so were assigned to the same travel party and came to settle in the same village in Bessarabia. For example, the three family groups who came from Zachersberg (a suburb of Bromberg, West Prussia) all went to Kulm, as did the two families from Schachorowna (Szaradowo) west of Schubin in West Prussia.[8] The four individuals and families who emigrated from near Politz (Polish Police, south of Koło) all went to Tarutino. Similarly, the three families who left the village of Rogasen (Polish Rogożno), northeast of Obornik, all went to Leipzig, Bessarabia.[9] Where people from the same village in Poland ended up in different settlements in Bessarabia, the presumption is that they did not sign up at the same time and so were not assigned together. There are, for example, German colonists in Kulm, Leipzig, Klöstitz, Beresina, and Paris from the Lentschütz area (Polish Ł e̜ czyca, north of Łodz), and colonists in Kulm, Leipzig, Klöstitz, Arzis, and Paris from the region of Thorn.[10]

## For most colonists, the long immigration journey was from Prussian Poland to Bessarabia

To begin their journey to Bessarabia, colonists appear to have gathered with their belongings, carts, and animals at predetermined points in Poland. The Alt Arzis

---

8. The three Zachersberg families were those of Gottfried Baner, Jacob Fledrich (probably Fredrich), and Michael Zahn. The two families from Schachorowna were those of Karl Knol and Gottlieb Leischner. Data is from the 1815 census of Kulm.

9. The four individuals and families from near Politz were Christian Brüge, Christian Esslinger, and Heinrich Wonnenberg from Politz, and Gottlieb Milbradt from Skąpe across the Warta River. The three from Rogasen were the Gottlieb Müller, Luise Pretzlau, and Joseph Schweitz(er) families (Stumpp, *Emigration from Germany to Russia*, 549, 551, 552, 534). In one of Stumpp's rare errors in his map of German settlements in Prussian Poland from which colonists emigrated to Bessarabia ("Orte, aus denen im Jahre 1814 Auswanderungen nach Rußland, insbesondere nach Bessarabien stattgefunden haben"), he places Politz due east of Koło, whereas the two villages of Politz (Police-Mostowe and Police-Srednie) are on the west bank floodplain of the Warta River, perhaps four miles south of Koło.

10. Perhaps the fact that decisions to emigrate were made at different times explains why members of the Lemke/Lemptke family from Schöndorf, a suburb of Bromberg, ended up in separate villages in Bessarabia, with some in Kulm and others in Leipzig. This would also explain how families from Lentschütz came to Kulm (Bech/Biech), Leipzig (Hanneman, Kranich), Klöstitz (Bauch, Kelm, Falenberg, Kuck, Küst, Neitz, and Schmollinger), Beresina (Wössner), and Paris (Bech, Kelm). Similarly, families from Thorn went to Kulm (Erdman, Schimke, Winter), Leipzig (Burkhardt, Lemke, Lütke), Klöstitz (Engel, Hoffman, Kelm, Krämer, Mauch, Steinhülb), Arzis (Franz), and Paris (Kelm).

village history notes that eighty-two colonist families headed to that village left from Thorn in 1814 and another forty-one left in 1815 from "Canin" (Konin is meant) in Great Poland. The Brienne colonists apparently gathered and left from the city of Bromberg (Polish Bydgoszcz) downstream from Thorn. Flegel notes, though without offering a source, that colonists bound ultimately for Kulm left from Pabianitz (Polish Pabianice) near the city of Łodz.[11]

The impression given by the village histories is that with the exception of the Brienne and Teplitz settlers, who came as a single group, the German immigrants traveled to Bessarabia in many small, independent groups. The travel parties formed in Poland and were kept together on arrival in Bessarabia even when it was not possible to settle them immediately on land there. As a result, they formed the building blocks from which Russian officials put together village populations. The Leipzig village history suggests that three groups formed the basis of that settlement. Several colonies note in their histories that travel groups were led by colonists. Leipzig's three groups, for example, were led by Martin Friesz, Friedrich Riesz, and Peter Steinke. The Alt Posttal history, describing the foundation of Wittenberg,[12] notes that a settler group left Poland "under the leadership of the colonists Bernhard Bohnet and his assistant Martin Vossler."[13] The Kulm history mentions that "most of the immigrants to the colony arrived by train under the leadership of Gottfried Radach."[14] Mutschall's Tarutino history notes that colonist families met at designated assembly points where they were provided with passports and organized into traveling groups. For the Tarutino traveling groups, a Russian official was assigned as a guide, and someone within the group was selected (or possibly elected) as a "traveling mayor."[15] The Wittenberg history also notes a role being played by a "Russian official," but the duties of this official are not clear and whether he is accompanying the travel group is not specified. Where a village history names a colonist as the travel group leader, as noted with Alt Posttal above, this person may be the same "traveling mayor" selected from the group as described by Mutschall. Not all travel groups, however, had leaders. The Alt Elft and Paris histories both note that groups bound for these sites came without leaders. The Alt Elft history adds that they only had "written documents which permitted them to receive travel money and lodging."[16]

Travel by German peasants to Bessarabia began in the fall of 1813, when ninety families destined to found the Krasna colony reached Kishinev, Bessarabia, and spent

---

11. Flegel, *Extended Relationships*, 10.

12. Alt Posttal, it will be remembered, was carved out of the village of Wittenberg in 1823.

13. The Alt Posttal history states that the party led by Bohnet was 138 families, by implication the whole community of Wittenberg/Alt Posttal. Kludt, "Alt Posttal – 1848 Village History." In the Wittenberg account, the 138 families are noted as including 16 Prussian families who likely came separately from the Bohnet party to Bessarabia (Kurz, "Wittenberg"). The Wittenberg account also notes that the combined early village (that is, including the Alt Posttal half) was pulled together from several temporary resting points in Moldavian villages in Bessarabia. This would suggest that the Bohnet-led party was but one of several to create the population of Wittenberg.

14. C. Straub, "Kulm – 1848 Village History," trans. L. R. Ketterling (N.p.: Odessa Digital Library, 1997), http://www.odessa3.org/collections/history/link/kulm.txt. The German word Zug is used here to describe a group of wagons as well as people on foot all traveling together. There was, of course, no railroad line to Bessarabia in 1814.

15. Mutschall named Gottfried Scheuchner, the head of one of the colonist families, as the traveling mayor and implies that he was selected by the colonists themselves: "The founders of Tarutino had Gottfried Scheuchner as their traveling mayor." Wilhelm Mutschall, "History of the Community of Tarutino from 1814 to 1934," *Heritage Review* 43, no. 1 (2013): 6.

16. D. Mayer, "Alt Elft – 1848 Village History," trans. R. Niessner (N.p.: Odessa Digital Library, 1996), http://www.odessa3.org/collections/history/link/altelft.txt.

the winter of 1813–14 there. These first German arrivals in Bessarabia were Catholics from the villages of Orschokow south of Warsaw and Schitonitz near Zamość in the pre–Duchy of Warsaw Lublin district of Austrian Poland.[17] They were the first group to travel, perhaps because their starting point was the farthest east and thus closer to the formal Russian state border. The Neu Elft history indicates that the immigrants who settled Alt Elft left Poland in the spring of 1814. The Klöstitz history indicates colonists left Poland in the summer of 1814 and arrived in Bessarabia in September of that year. Alt Posttal's history is the only one to give departure and arrival dates when it states that at least some of Wittenberg's colonists left Poland in September of 1814 and arrived in Bessarabia in November. The dates provided in a few of the village histories suggest that Russian authorities in Poland staggered departures for Bessarabia. This may have been in an effort not to overwhelm what proved to be the very meager assistance available along the way for the immigrants, and to enable officials in Bessarabia adequate time to settle the arrivals in temporary housing. The village histories do make it clear that most of the Germans who settled in the colonies of Arzis, Alt/Neu Elft, Wittenberg/Alt Posttal, Beresina, Borodino, Brienne, Klöstitz, Kulm, Leipzig, Paris, and Tarutino left Poland and reached Bessarabia sometime in 1814.

The most common route from Poland to Bessarabia began with river transport. Colonists would travel on the Vistula River upstream or downstream, depending on their starting point in Poland, to the mouth of the Bug River. There they would transfer to barges going upstream on the Bug that would carry them at least past Brest on the Russian east bank. The Alt Posttal village history mentions that one group destined for Wittenberg entered Russia at "Uschtschluk"—that is, they crossed into Russia proper from the theoretically semi-independent Russian Poland. Uschtschluk is the river port Ustilug on the upper Bug River. From this point the upper Bug River enters Austrian territory, which the Russian government would have wished to avoid. Instead, from Ustilug or Brest, the German immigrants would have left the river and headed east and then southeast into Russia, following trading roads through Luck and Proskurov (present day Xmel'nickij) to Mogilev on the upper Dniester River and Soroki (now Soroca) on the Dniester in Bessarabia.[18]

From Soroki, they would then have followed the military road south to Kishinev, the new capital of Bessarabia, and possibly further east to Bender. This was a journey of at least 750 miles from Warsaw, Poland. The length of the journey was extended by following a route that took the German immigrants east into Russia sooner rather than the more direct route that would have offered a longer transport by boat, but would have required long travel within Austrian Poland. This latter route went southeast upstream on the Vistula and San Rivers from Warsaw to reach Lemburg (L'viv) in Austrian Galicia. For the Russian authorities, the longer eastern route meant that more of the trip occurred within Russia, where supplies and protection could be provided for the traveling groups. Some of the colonists rode in wagons

---

17. The 1785 Zamojski charter (see discussion above in chapter II), in which the names of several of the first Krasna colonists are cited, strongly suggests that Schitonitz was the village of Sitaniec-Kolonia just north of Zamość. While Orschokowin has not been definitively identified, a reasonable case may be made for associating it with the village of Orzekowo near Jasieniec southeast of Grojec (some 45 miles southwest of Warsaw) where a number of German colonies, including ones made up predominantly of Catholic Germans, were established in the first decade of the nineteenth century.

18. The Neu Elft village history reports that a group destined for that village arrived in "Sorokoi" in August 1814, having left Poland that spring. Kurz, "Neu Elft – 1848 Village History."

with their goods, some rode horses, and some apparently walked for much of the distance following the end of river transport.

## Colonists who came to Bessarabia from Württemberg and Bavaria between 1817 and 1825 or in the 1830s and early 1840s had an even longer passage

While Germans immigrating directly from Württemberg and Bavaria to Bessarabia have not left us descriptions of their travel, we do have a decent idea of the routes they likely took. There exist two accounts written by Germans who, in the period 1817–20, traveled from Württemberg and Bavarian Swabia to Odessa. Each account describes a different route, but the two routes taken were likely the routes taken by all the Germans coming to Bessarabia from Württemberg or Bavaria. One account is that of Friedrich Schwartz, who traveled from Kupferzell near Schwäbisch Hall in Württemberg to Odessa in 1817; the second account is by Jacob Mayr, who traveled to Odessa from Lauingen on the Danube (downstream from Ulm in Bavarian Swabia) in 1820.[19] Stumpp has mapped the two routes for comparison. Both parties began by traveling by boat to Vienna on the Danube. There, Mayr went over land north into Austrian Poland and then east into Austrian Galicia to enter Russia at Radzivilov (now Radyvyliv in the Ukraine) opposite Brody, where his route joined the same overland route south taken by the Bessarabian colonists coming from Poland.[20] This journey to Odessa took Mayr 82 days. Schwartz, traveling by river transport, needed only 67 days to go from Alpeck near Ulm to Ismail on the Danube estuary in southern Bessarabia. However, Schwartz's party was held up in quarantine in Ismail, likely by cholera, and as a result, his full journey from Kupferzell to Odessa took 133 days. The Teplitz colonists, also traveling in 1817, took the same Danube route from Württemberg. They were intending to settle in the Russian Caucasus but were stopped in southern Bessarabia by an outbreak of typhoid fever or possibly the plague in their party and, weakened by this, elected to remain and settle in Bessarabia.[21] In Stumpp's comment on the Bessarabian colony of Schabo, he gives a brief routing for the colonists coming from the French-speaking cantons of Switzerland in 1822, which appears similar to the route taken by Mayr.[22]

## Many village histories comment on the poverty of the arriving immigrants

The 1848 village histories offer various reasons for such poverty. In some cases the colonists were poor to begin with. The Tarutino history notes, for example, that "most of them were poor and some of them only came with what they wore." The

---

19. Stumpp, *Emigration from Germany to Russia*, 40.
20. At Jampol' on the Dniester, Mayr did not cross to Soroki in Bessarabia, as colonists bound for Bessarabia would have, but remained on the eastern bank of the river as he headed for Odessa.
21. Kern describes the sickness that felled the immigrants who became the Teplitz colonists as "typhoid and fever" (*Homeland Book*, 93). Schmidt provides a detailed account of Swiss immigrants held in quarantine in late September 1817 at the Bessarabian border on the Danube, in which the illness creating the quarantine is referred to as the plague. As the immigrants who settled Teplitz appear to have been released from their quarantine at the Bessarabian border in August 1817, this would argue for identifying the plague as the cause of their sickness too (Schmidt, *Bessarabia: German Colonists*, 62–65).
22. Stumpp, *Emigration from Germany to Russia*, 548. Stumpp notes: "Weg: Österreich—Ungarn—Karpaten—Bukovina."

Alt Posttal history notes that a portion of the Wittenberg settlers were so poor "they had to make [the] journey on foot," and the Borodino history implies a general state of poverty among its first inhabitants by noting that "their resources were so meager that only a few families owned a team of horses and a wagon."[23]

Other histories, though, state that the reason some immigrants were poor when they arrived in Bessarabia was that even though they began their journey to Bessarabia with funds, they were forced to spend these along the way to support themselves. Though the Russian government had promised a travel subsidy, the actual provisions were at times insufficient, spoiled, or not supplied. Those who spent through the funds they had brought had to sell belongings or even sell their labor to finish the journey. The Alt Elft village history, for example, notes that "it is easy to understand that on this long journey, even though they received travel money, they used up most of their resources. [They] sold off their possessions and with all their money gone, arrived at their destination with their earthly goods exhausted."[24] The Paris history makes the same point: "Although [the colonists] received some travel money, the long journey reduced most of the settlers to want and poverty."[25] The Leipzig history makes this point, too, when it comments that "the people from Poland used their financial means for the journey." However, this history goes on to say that many of the new colonists were poor to begin with: "Many came without horses or a wagon and were supported by others."[26]

Not all the colonists were without means when they arrived in Bessarabia. The colonists that settled Kulm are reported in their 1848 history as arriving with "various possessions, property which included horses and wagons" and between 400 and 1,000 rubles silver per family in cash.[27] The Wittenberg history offers a much more vague indication of the financial status of the arriving settlers when it breaks the holdings of the families into general categories: "At the least a few had 20 to 100 ruble, some had 100 to 200 ruble, and the rest had 200 to 1000 ruble (silver)."[28] The Neu Elft history describes more limited assets, noting that holdings were "generally modest, approximately 10–200 silver rubles per family."[29] Finally, the Neu Arzis and

---

23. Kludt, "Alt Posttal – 1848 Village History"; and Eckert, "Borodino – 1848 Village History."
24. Mayer, "Alt Elft – 1848 Village History."
25. A. Dieno, "Paris – 1848 Village History," trans. R. Niessner (N.p.: Odessa Digital Library, 1996), http://www.odessa3.org/collections/history/link/paris.txt.
26. A. Trautmann, "Leipzig – 1848 Village History," trans. L. R. Ketterling (N.p.: Odessa Digital Library, 1997), http://www.odessa3.org/collections/history/link/leipzig.txt.
27. Straub, "Kulm – 1848 Village History."
28. Kurz, "Wittenberg – 1848 Village History." The author of the Wittenberg history appears to have used "ruble" as both the singular and plural forms of the noun.
29. Kurz, "Neu Elft – 1848 Village History." The Russian currency was and continues to be the ruble (*rubl'* in Russian), a unit that is subdivided into 100 kopecks. For the eighteenth and nineteenth centuries it is very difficult to assign meaningful values to ruble-denominated sums other than for goods purchased internally within Russia. Only in 1897 did Imperial Russia adopt a fixed gold-based standard for the ruble and so make economic comparisons with Western currencies possible. Before 1897, there were no clear exchange rates with Western currencies, and moreover, Russian coinage was regularly debased or improved at the varying whims and needs of the government. The value of any lot of silver coins would thus depend on the amount of actual silver in them. Paper rubles were also issued regularly but were valued at a lower rate than the equivalent sum in silver coins. The official exchange rate between paper and silver rubles in 1836 was 3.58 to 1, as reported in the newspaper the *Sanktpetersburgische Handelszeitung*, 8 January 1836 (O.S.). The Leipzig history, for example, gives a similar valuation in 1848, when it notes that the per-colonist debt of 1,114 paper rubles was the equivalent of 318.285 silver rubles, a valuation difference of 3.5 to 1. With silver ruble coins of many differing silver contents in existence throughout the nineteenth century, different "silver" coins would have different values vis-à-vis paper currency.

Brienne histories note in passing that many colonists arrived with some money left over from their journey.

## When the German immigrants reached Bessarabia from Poland, most found that the Russian officials there weren't yet prepared to assign them land and settle them

Upon reaching Bessarabia, the great majority of Germans were quartered in the homes of Moldavians in villages north of the steppeland where they were to settle. It isn't clear whether Russian officials had completed surveying the potential village sites for the Germans in the Bessarabian steppeland. It is clear that some village sites had been selected, and it is also clear that Russian officials had not fully settled title issues with Moldavians and Bulgarians who had leased some of the intended settlement sites for grazing. With many Germans arriving in Bessarabia past the growing season in the late summer and fall of 1814, Russian officials may have felt it would be better for the colonists to be quartered over the winter, as there was generally no housing available on the sites where villages were to be created. The Russian officials may also have felt that quartering the arriving colonists would simplify issues of providing food.

The first Germans colonists arrived in Bessarabia in the fall of 1813 and were quartered in Moldavian villages near Kishinev over the winter. In the spring of 1814, they were brought south to the west bank of the Kogil'nik River,[30] just beyond its confluence with the Ančokrak River, and here these ninety families, mainly of Catholic faith and so generally unique among the early Bessarabian Germans, established the colony of Krasna. Other groups of Germans arrived in Bessarabia from Poland in the early summer of 1814. Some were to be settled on the east bank of the Saka River about 10 miles northeast of Krasna as the Borodino colony. When they arrived, however, Moldavian families were still living on the site, and the one hundred German families were temporarily "provided with living quarters for 13 weeks in the surrounding Moldavian villages." The Borodino families were able to occupy their village site in the fall of 1814 and spent the winter in "hastily constructed huts of wickerwork and clay."[31] The only other group of Germans to be placed on their village site in 1814 was the first portion of the Tarutino settlers. Upon their arrival in southern Bessarabia, they appear to have been taken directly to the site intended for their village just upstream on the Ančokrak River from Krasna. Given that the 1848 Tarutino Village History names Borodino as the "earlier founded colony,"[32]

---

30. The Kogil'nik is the Russian name for the river, though the Germans tended to refer to this river as the Kugelnik. For the names of rivers and other natural land features in Bessarabia, I have used the 1907 Lev S. Berg map "Etnografičeskaja karta sel'skogo naselenija Bessarabii" ['The ethnographic map of the rural population of Bessarabia'], commons.wikimedia.org, http://commons.wikimedia. org/wiki/File:Lev_S._Berg_-_Ethnographic_map_of_Bessarabia.jpg). This map, prepared by Berg from data supplied by V. N. Butovič and others, provides the most complete geographical portrait of Bessarabia during the Imperial Russian period. I have used this to maintain a single standard for geographic terminology. As a result, spellings will frequently differ from the variety of spellings found in German, English, and American sources. The German variants often seem based on a transliteration of the spoken German form rather than on any cartographic study.

31. Eckert, "Borodino – 1848 Village History."

32. The 1848 Leipzig village history, however, offers a different perspective, saying "Tarutino was the first established colony and Borodino was the second." This, of course, overlooks the clear primacy of the Krasna colony and emphasizes the fact that religious differences in German Bessarabia kept people and traditions separate. The Borodino history does not comment on this question. Trautmann, "Leipzig – 1848 Village History."

it may be that the Tarutino settlers first reached their village site in the late fall of 1814. They, too, found the site occupied by ten Moldavian families who had leased the land and were living as nomads grazing their herds. With the arrival of the Germans, the Moldavians left or were ordered away, and the Germans took over and spent the winter in "crude huts made of shrubbery and clay."[33] The fact that the huts there "provided shelter for 100 families," far more than the apparent needs of the ten Moldavian families, might be an indication that Russian authorities had provided some additional building materials in anticipation of the arrival of the Germans.[34]

The Alt Posttal history indicates that the immigrants intended to settle Wittenberg were living in Moldavian villages near Kishinev and Bender from November 1814 to June 1815. This may be the region in which most of the arriving German colonists were temporarily placed. In the spring of 1815, 508 families were gathered and taken to four separate village sites to found Klöstitz (134 families), Kulm (108 families), Leipzig (128 families), and Wittenberg (138 families). An additional 571 colonist families who had arrived in Bessarabia in 1814 had to remain for another year in Moldavian villages and weren't settled on the sites of their villages until the spring of 1816. These were the colonies of Arzis (82 families), Alt Elft (125 families), Beresina (139 families, later reduced to 137), Brienne (84 families), and Paris (141 families). The Arzis history remembers the unhappiness of the extra year's wait, noting that if the immigrants had been able to go "directly to their settlement place, things would have been much better," and complaining that while quartered among the Moldavians, the Germans fed "themselves miserably with meager rations and money."[35] Other Arzis sources report that during this two-year wait to be settled on the land designated for their village in Bessarabia, the Arzis colonists had to support themselves by hiring themselves out as day laborers.[36] While most of the Germans who were quartered in Moldavian villages appear to have been living in the area between Kishinev and Bender just to the north of the steppeland, those destined for Alt Elft were kept far to the north near Soroki, along the Dniester River just inside the Bessarabian border.[37] These Germans may have been halted in Soroki because conditions further south were becoming too crowded.

## Before colonists could be settled, land surveys were made to set the distances between settlements and then to measure the land area for each settlement

The process of settlement began with an official taking colonists out to the site where their new villages were to be created. Three of the village histories mention a Russian official named Müller who helped them establish their villages. Müller, who

---

33. D. Martin, "Tarutino – 1848 Village History," trans. E. Wise (N.p.: Odessa Digital Library, 1996), http://www.odessa3.org/collections/history/link/tarutino.txt.

34. Ibid.

35. Neumann, "Alt-Arcis – Village History," trans. E. Necker-Eberhardt (N.p.: Odessa Digital Library, 2000), http://www.odessa3.org/collections/history/link/altarc.txt.

36. Malinovskij, *Social'naja i xozjajstvennaja istorija*, 40.

37. No other village history mentions staying as far away from their future village site as Alt Elft. The Alt Posttal history mentions staying in villages near Kishinev, and the Bender and Paris villages simply stayed along the Dniester River, presumably in the settled area near Bender. The Arzis and Brienne histories mention staying with the inhabitants of "Moldau." I believe Dr. Elvire Necker-Eberhardt, the translator of the Brienne history, is correct in interpreting "Moldau" as a general reference to Moldavian villages.

is often given the title president (or in the Alt Elft history, director), was presumably a German speaker and was based in Tarutino at least in the period from 1816 to 1817. Müller had the responsibility of showing groups of new colonists where their new settlements were to be located. The Paris village history mentions that "President Müller of the Tarutino office showed them the places where they were to inhabit."[38] Using similar wording, the Alt Elft history notes that "Director Müller showed them the places where they could live."[39] What is meant in these passages, as well as in a similar one in the Neu Arzis history, is that Müller took them to the site where their village was to be created and in some way, either by walking the bounds or by using a map, survey, or other markers, indicated what was to be the land area of the new colony. The Arzis history suggests, in addition, that the site had been surveyed: "The steppe where the immigrants were to settle was designated by President Müller and was already laid out for 123 families, 60 desjatina per family."[40]

Given the issues of the Kulm village siting, discussed below, it is likely that surveyors had determined where the village buildings ought to be placed in the land area given to each colony. Müller would not have been an official of the Welfare Committee,[41] but was clearly a person of civil authority. References in the Brienne and Leipzig histories indicate Müller was responsible for establishing, likely in 1817, the first official names for these villages.

Müller is also mentioned in a different light in the Neu Elft history. There he is pictured, much like Commissioner Krüger in other histories, as a Russian official who came to Poland and then personally led the Elft immigrants from Poland to Bessarabia: "In the spring of 1814, under the guidance of a Russian official, president Müller, they left Poland and arrived in Moldavia near the city of Sorokoi in August of the same year."[42]

It is possible that the meaning here is that Müller, like Krüger, organized or even led travel parties to Bessarabia. Such an interpretation, though, is weakened by the fact that the Alt Elft history, in describing the same journey by the same people (the Alt and Neu Elft colonists lived together in a single village until 1825), mentions that "the immigrants had no leaders on their journey" to Bessarabia. Some doubt on Müller's presence in Poland is also cast by the fact that, unlike Krüger, no other histories mention Müller issuing documents or organizing travel parties in Poland. Perhaps the Neu Elft passage reflects that Müller met the Elft party en route or in Soroki and was responsible for quartering them there. As with many other aspects of the history of the German colonies in Bessarabia, one hopes that archival material exists in Moldova, the Ukraine, or Russia that would reveal Müller's identity and clarify the role he and others played in helping the colonies become established.

Except for Kulm, the early German villages in Bessarabia were all sited in the meadowlands or on the bluffs that bordered the banks of rivers. The village fields occupied part of these floodplain meadows and climbed the hills rising from the

---

38. Dieno, "Paris – 1848 Village History."
39. Mayer, "Alt Elft – 1848 Village History."
40. Neumann, "Alt-Arcis – 1848 Village History." State *desjatina* (Russian *kazënnaja desjatina*) are equal to 1.0925 hectare, 10,925 m², 117,600 ft², or roughly 2.7 acres.
41. The overall management structure and the specific responsibilities given to individual Russian officials charged with establishing the German colonies in Bessarabia have not been well established for the period before 1818, when the Welfare Committee was created.
42. Kurz, "Neu Elft – 1848 Village History."

valley floors. The geography of the Budjak steppeland is dominated by a series of small south-flowing rivers that drain into the Black Sea. Twelve of the thirteen colonies founded before 1820 were placed along the Kogil'nik River and its tributaries, the Ančokrak and Saka/Čaga.[43] Nine colonies are located along the Kogil'nik itself as it makes an L-shaped journey south from Leipzig, the most northerly sited early German colony, passing Kulm, Beresina, Krasna, Paris, Alt Elft, and Teplitz to reach Brienne and Alt Arzis on opposite banks. Tarutino, south of Kulm, is on the Ančokrak, which joins the Kogil'nik just above Krasna. Borodino, east of Leipzig, is on the Saka, which joins the Čaga at Klöstitz, which then flows south to join the Kogil'nik at Alt Arzis. Wittenberg, located just to the west of Krasna, is on another river system, the Kirgiz Kitaj. The Russian government appears to have presumed that the rivers would form the major water supply for the colonies, though, as will be discussed in the following two chapters, the German colonists considered wells and springs better and more reliable sources. In all cases, the German colonies in Bessarabia were to be peasant villages of the common European village style: houses were clustered together in villages, rather than separately sited on a family's land. Each house had a plot for gardens and orchards attached to it, with the bulk of a family's land used for growing crops and raising animals in the broad area surrounding the village.

The Kulm village history records that after viewing the village site proposed by the Russians on the west bank of the Kogil'nik in a valley downstream from Leipzig, the "village leaders" wished to move the village settlement location from the valley floor to the ridgetop above the river. The Kulm history remembers various reasons for this desire to relocate: the fear of "unhealthy air" trapped in the river valley fog, concern that grasses wouldn't grow with the village located in the same meadowland, or the thought that it might be dangerous bringing loaded wagons downhill to the village from the fields above. The Russian authorities, perhaps Müller though he is not mentioned, agreed that if water could be found on the ridgetop, the village might be resited there. Water was found in several springs by a delegation of twelve village men sent to search, so Kulm was built there and not in the valley.

As noted earlier, problems with the location of the village in relation to its fields came up quickly in the settlements of Wittenberg, Elft, and Arzis. Placing the site of the colonial villages on the banks of rivers and streams meant that for such colonies, the village site was not in the center of the land area that had been assigned to it. In these three villages, the fields located at the far edge of the colony's land were too distant from the village settlement for comfortable use: some fields were 12 *versts* from the Wittenberg settlement, and 10 from Elft and Arzis.[44] The Wittenberg history says this distance made it difficult to "make full use" of their land.[45] The Alt Elft history comments that the "settlers lost much time going back and forth,"

43. The Saka River appears as the Saok or Sorok in German sources, and the Čaga is often spelled as the Tschaga. Wittenberg's Kirgiz Kitaj stream, noted later in this paragraph, appears as the Kirgis Kitai in German sources.
44. The prerevolution Russian standard measurement of distance was the *verst* (Russian *versta*). As the majority of Russian numbers govern the genitive plural, this form, "verst," has become the standard treatment in English. The verst is roughly 3,500 feet, so that there are roughly 1.5 versts to a mile, and at 1,066 meters, a verst is slightly longer than a kilometer.
45. Kurz, "Wittenberg – 1848 Village History."

and the Alt Posttal history mentions that efforts to equalize the hardship by giving colonists narrow strips of land that extended from one village boundary to another "restricted [farms] to too narrow a space."[46] In 1823, the Welfare Committee agreed to let the Wittenberg colony divide its land in half, and Alt Posttal was founded in its northeastern section where the post road from Ismail crossed the head of the Kirgiz River some 5 versts southwest of Tarutino. Similarly, in 1825, Neu Elft was founded in the southern reaches of that colony's lands at the head of the Allijaga valley, splitting Elft into Alt and Neu Elft. In the same year, Neu Arzis was created with a third of the Arzis population on the far northeastern edge of the Arzis land allotment.[47]

In establishing the new German colonies in Bessarabia, the Russian government officials appear to have initially set a standard distance of separation at 10 versts (6.67 miles) between the different German settlements. This was the distance from Kulm to the neighboring Leipzig colony to the north in the Kogil'nik valley, and to the Tarutino colony on the ridge road to the south. The Catholic colony of Krasna was 10 versts south of Tarutino, Alt Elft was 10 versts south of Krasna, and Brienne was 10 versts beyond Alt Elft. Where a colony was set in another river valley or on the opposite side of a river, the 10-verst rule was broken. Thus, Berezina, across three ranges of hills from Tarutino and in a separate river valley, was only 5 versts distant by road. Borodino was only 7 versts from Klöstitz, but the two colonies lay on opposite sides of the Saka River. Paris was placed about 2 versts north of Alt Elft but was on the opposite west bank of the Kogil'nik, and Brienne was directly opposite Arzis but separated by the Kogil'nik and its junction with the Čaga River. When Russian authorities decided to settle the disease-weakened Teplitz Germans in Bessarabia in 1817, they placed the colony at the bend of the Kogil'nik about 6 versts from Alt Elft and 7 from Brienne. Clearly wanting to fit the Teplitz colonists in among the other German groups, the Russian authorities, with some experience now in establishing the colonies, may have become less concerned about maintaining set distances between them. Similarly, for colonies founded in Bessarabia after 1817, there appears to be fewer concerns about distance. Gnadental (founded in 1830)[48] was about 6 versts east of Arzis with both villages on the north side of Kogil'nik, Friedenstal (founded in 1834) was about 8 versts upstream from Arzis on the Čaga, and Lichtental (founded in 1834) was located 6 versts to the east of Neu Arzis, though in a different valley.[49]

---

46. Mayer, "Alt Elft – 1848 Village History"; and Kludt, "Alt Posttal – 1848 Village History."

47. The Alt Elft history notes that the request to split the village was made and approved in 1823, which would suggest that the Welfare Committee considered this request simultaneously with that of Wittenberg and possibly Arzis. The Neu Elft history notes that this village was established in 1825, meaning, likely, this is the year when people moved. The Alt Arzis history mentions that Neu Arzis citizens moved away in 1824, which could suggest an 1823 approval also. The Neu Arzis history, however, dates the founding of this colony to 1825.

48. Kern reports (*Homeland Book*, 107) that the Welfare Committee approved the founding of the colony on May 14, 1829 (O.S.).

49. In 1830, the Welfare Committee, which was also responsible for the oversight of colonies of Eastern Orthodox Bulgarians in Bessarabia and South Russia, established an additional colony for Bulgarians, called Devlet Agač, some 4 versts south of Neu Elft (1825); however, the two colonies were located on opposite banks of the Allijaga River. Devlet Agač was also about 7 versts northwest of the German colony of Dennewitz, which was founded four years later in 1834.

## The Russian government's intention of offering 60 desjatina of land to each German family largely determined the number of families that would be settled in each colony

Before Germans could be taken to the sites of the new colonies, Russian surveyors measured the boundaries and determined the land area size of each. This figure divided by 60 gave the Welfare Committee authorities the number of families that might be settled in it. It should be noted, though, that while the intention of the Russian government was to make grants of 60 desjatina per family, this was a theoretical number. The actual grants were roughly in the range of 60 desjatina per family but varied slightly among the different colonies. It would appear that a factor creating the delay that kept many Germans in Moldavian villages an extra year (until 1816) was the need to measure out land areas for additional colonies sufficient to settle the actual number of families that had reached Bessarabia in 1814.

Records in the keeping of the Imperial Russian Ministry of State Domains on German Bessarabia published by Klaus provide a comparison of the original allotments and intended family populations of the first German colonies in Bessarabia (see table 4–1).[50]

The number of families per colony listed in this report is apparently the number the Russian government intended to settle rather than the actual number that were settled. This is implied by comparing the number of families listed in the ministry's report with number of founding families given in the 1848 village histories and in Stumpp, which is the figure given in parentheses in the No. of Families column.

TABLE 4–1.    **Original allotments and intended family populations of first colonies**

| Colony | Founded | No. of Families | Area (desjatina) | Per-family Avg. |
|---|---|---|---|---|
| Krasna | 1814 | 112 | 6,736.6 | 60.15 |
| Borodino | 1814 | 111 (115) | 6,698.0 | 60.34 |
| Tarutino | 1814 | 133 (136) | 7,980.8 | 60.00 |
| Kulm | 1815 | 106 (108) | 6,358.9 | 60.00 |
| Klöstitz | 1815 | 134 (134) | 8,030.8 | 59.93 |
| Leipzig | 1815 | 126 (128) | 7,434.5 | 59.0 |
| Wittenberg | 1815 | 134 (138) | 8,138.0 | 60.73 |
| Arzis | 1816 | 121 (123) | 7,298.8 | 60.32 |
| Beresina | 1816 | 135 (139) | 8,097.0 | 59.98 |
| Brienne | 1816 | 83 (84) | 4,984.6 | 60.05 |
| Elft | 1816 | 126 (125) | 7,652.6 | 60.73 |
| Paris | 1816 | 120 (121) | 7,202.5 | 60.00 |
| Teplitz | 1817 | 101 (98) | 5,866.1 | 58.08 |
| Sarata | 1821 | 101 (60) | 6,060.0 | 60.00 |
| Schabo | 1821 | 60 | 3,926.0 | 60.4 |
| Katzbach | 1821 | 64 (28) | 3,889.0 | 60.78 |

---

50. The figures are from Appendix II in Klaus (*Naši kolonii*, 22, 25–26), titled "Vedomost' o kolonijax inostrannyx poselencev, osnovannyx na zemljax po nadely ot kazny i sostojaščix v vedenii Ministerstva Gosudarstvennyx Imuščestv" (A listing of the colonies of foreign settlers founded on lands [granted] by allotment from the state and [which] are under the jurisdiction of the Ministry of State Domains). The land areas are given in state desjatina (Russian *kazënnaja desjatina*).

The Per-family Average column indicates the average land allotment based on the number of families that actually settled in the village, not on the theoretical number planned for the village. Of the thirteen village histories that report the number of founding families, only the Klöstitz history reports the same number as the ministry report. Nine of the twelve that show differences report a founding population of families slightly larger than the intended number. The village histories indicate that the extra families were accommodated within the surveyed village allotments, thus reducing the planned family holding shown above by slightly over 1 desjatina per family on average. The Kulm village history reports, for example, that 108 families settled on 6,358 desjatina, which resulted in an average holding of 58.9 desjatina per family instead of 60.0, and the Leipzig history reports 128 families on 7,434 desjatina, or 58.1 per family versus 59.0.[51] The Russian authorities, faced with slightly more German colonists in hand than they planned for in the intended assignments, fit in the additional families, likely with the presumption that the net effect would be small enough not to agitate. Not all colonial villages had more families than the intended allotments: Teplitz (1817), Katzbach (1821), and Sarata (1821) had fewer families and so ended up with average allotments greater than 60 desjatina. In the case of Teplitz, this appears to be the result of families not surviving the epidemic that caused them to settle in Bessarabia. With regard to Katzbach, the undercount was only temporary. Stumpp suggests that the colony was founded by 28 families who had come from Poland in 1821 and that over time other families, including 27 from other colonies in German Bessarabia, were additionally settled there so that by 1837 the total had risen to 65, one more than the full intended allotment.[52] The Brienne village history refers to family allotments in that colony of 50 desjatina, which surely must be in error. The 84 founding families have a per-family average of 60 desjatina using the ministry's figures for the size of the village.[53]

---

51. The 1848 village histories for Kulm, Leipzig, and Wittenberg report the colony land size, as the sum of two measurements: so many desjatina plus a secondary total of faden, this latter always being a fraction of 1 desjatina. Thus the total land allotment for Kulm is reported to be 6,358 desjatina and 2,302 [square] faden. The term *faden* is Austrian and South German, the linguistic equivalent of the English fathom, and represents a common measurement that in German-speaking lands could vary between 4.5 feet and 8.1 feet. The actual measurement reported in these village histories, though, is not faden but the Russian equivalent of the fathom, the *sažen'*, which measured 1.136 meters or 6.9 feet. The ministry's report notes that Kulm's area was 6,358.9 desjatina, which would be equal to the 6,358 desjatina and 2,302 square sažen' reported in the village history. Flegel (*Extended Relationships*, 11) reports Kulm's land area to be 7,057 desjatina, which he takes in error from Kern (*Homeland Book*, 135), who reports a total land area for the village of 7,057 hectares. Kern's hectare figure is about 100 desjatina over Kulm's original allotment. Mutschall's total of the original land area of Tarutino as 8,305 desjatina is so much larger than the figure in the Tarutino Village History as to suggest it dates from a later period in Tarutino's history. Mutschall, "Community of Tarutino," *Heritage Review* 42, no. 4: 8.

52. Stumpp, *Emigration from Germany to Russia*, 524. Stumpp reports: "1821 ließen sich 28 Fam. aus Polen nieder. 1828 kamen 8 Fam. aus Alt Posttal und Kulm/Bess.; 1825 kamen 19 Fam. aus Krasna/Bess…; 1837 wieder 7 Fam. aus Polen, eine aus Baden und 2 aus Württemberg." ("In 1821 28 families from Poland settled, [then in] 1828 came 8 familes from Alt Posttal and Kulm; [in] 1825 came 19 families from Krasna Bess[arabia]…; [in] 1837 again 7 families from Poland, one from Baden and 2 from Württemberg") The 1828 date for the additional families from Alt Posttal and Kulm is out of sequence and so may be a misprint.

53. Kern reports the size of Brienne in the twentieth century to be 5,560 hectares, which is 5,089 desjtina, 100 desjatina over the original allotment listed in the ministry report, giving further support to the conclusion that the average family holding for the founding colonists in Brienne was around 60 desjatina (*Homeland Book*, 83).

## While the number of families settling in each of the German villages is known, the population counts for each village are far less exact

It is a difficult task to move from the number of families settling a village to figures for each colony's initial total population. Different sources report different population numbers without attempts to reconcile. Kulm, with a variety of different estimates of early population totals, provides a good example to consider this issue. The Kulm village history reports that there were 108 families forming the original settler group: "Originally there were 80 families that settled in the colony who came together from Poland, later 28 Wuerttenbergers from other established colonies settled in Culm [Kulm] to bring the total to 108 families."[54]

Stumpp picks up the total of 108 families from the Kulm village history and repeats much of the passage quoted above in his introduction to a listing of the names of the early Kulm settlers. Yet in the list that follows in Stumpp of individual families and their origins, there are 178 families with over 130 different family names. Flegel, in his introduction, describes a somewhat larger settlement group in Kulm that is comprised of 124 families: 80 families from Prussian Poland, 34 (instead of the village history's 28) families who came from other communities in Bessarabia, and an additional 10 families "from previously established communities near Odessa."[55] For the founding population of Kulm, Flegel gives a count of 520 people in all, of whom 270 were male and 250 were female.[56] Flegel does not provide an explanation for the differences between his counts of the number of families and people settling in Kulm and those appearing in Stumpp and the 1848 Kulm village history. The time focus of Flegel's counts may be one cause. It would appear that Flegel was aiming for counts when Kulm was fully settled and all the farmsteads were taken. That would be not Kulm in 1815, but sometime in the next year or two, although still clearly before 1825. As will be discussed in the following chapter, the Welfare Committee made an economic census of the German colonies in Bessarabia that counted the Kulm population then as 694 people.[57]

The September 1, 1815 (O.S.) census gives a unique view of Kulm just months after the colony was founded, clearly in a period before the full and final settling-in process was completed. This census gives the names of 285 individuals bearing 102 different surnames, the places from which many of them immigrated, and their ages as of September 1st. The census does not capture the complete population then in Kulm. Comparisons of the census with other sources, particularly the 1835 Kulm Census and Stumpp's and Flegel's listings, show that the 1815 census leaves out many adults known to be part of family parties and many children who accompanied their parents to Kulm. In terms of numbers, the largest group of missing individuals is children in families where the census lists only the father. The most significant missing piece among the adults is the near-total absence of the wives of married male immigrants. Dorothy and Jacob Krüger are the only married couple where a

---

54. Straub, "Kulm – 1848 Village History."

55. Flegel, *Extended Relationships*, 10.

56. Ibid.

57. Hans Rempel, *German Farming Achievements in the Black Sea Region, Population and Economy, 1825*, trans. Roland Wagner (N.p.: Odessa Digital Library, 2002), Table 16, http://www.odessa3.org/collections/towns/link/bsfarm.txt.

wife is listed along with her husband in the census.[58] While the census appears to include most adult males known to be in Kulm in 1815, it does miss some: the census lists Johann Lengner (Längner) but not his brother Christoph.[59] The impression left is that perhaps there are as many as 120–200 additional people then in Kulm who were not counted.

The September 1815 census of Kulm presents a variety of different situations among the immigrants. Of the 102 surnames, at least 70 refer to family groups and 21 to young single men and women coming to Kulm either alone or with unmarried siblings. For the remaining 11 surnames, there isn't sufficient information in the several sources on Kulm to determine whether in 1815 these men, generally in their early thirties, were married at that time or not.[60]

Not surprisingly, the largest cohort in the 1815 census is made up of married couples with children, in several cases, adult children. A. A. Klaus, among others, has suggested that the Russian agents in Poland charged with recruiting and organizing the German peasants for immigration to Bessarabia had been instructed to take only well-established and experienced peasant farmers. This was a reaction to problems that had occurred in a number of the South Russian German colonies settled a decade earlier where poorer and inexperienced settlers, including some former townspeople, needed extensive help to get themselves on their feet in Russia. As marriage among peasants in eighteenth-century Germany required the accumulation of both capital and farming experience, marriage itself represented a sign of some success in life. Having the labor of children to help was another major factor in a peasant family's success. With about two-thirds of the early Kulm immigrants made up of families, the agents for Russia appear to have been following established patterns of success.

In spite of the preponderance of family groups among the 1815 count of Kulm settlers, there is a strikingly large number of single young men and women. Of the 102 surnames, at least 21 appear to have been young and unmarried. Some, like the brothers Ludwig and Friedrich Mewes (Möwes) and Christian and Karl Selcho, were young men in their twenties intending to create a farmstead together. Working together, they were old and strong enough to be assumed able to manage a farm successfully, and by doing this together, they hedged risks. In contrast, there are four groups of siblings all under age twenty who would appear to pose much higher risks. The three Priess brothers (ages sixteen, eleven, and nine) seem quite young to have been accepted for immigration on their own. Even more questionable are the Linse siblings led by eighteen-year-old Gottfried with two younger sisters.[61] While it is

---

58. Dorothy Krüger, who the census indicates was thirty-six years old on September 1, 1815 (O.S.), would thus have been born between 1778 and 1779. Flegel lists her as Jacob's wife and her birthdate as 1779 (*Extended Relationships*, 398).

59. Flegel, *Extended Relationships*, 416. The two brothers, their wives, and children came from Freidorf in Silesia. Stumpp lists both brothers but lists Christoph as Christian (*Emigration from Germany to Russia*, 351, 530). It is clear that spelling conventions for surnames were still quite variable for those compiling the 1815 Kulm census; surnames were written down as the scribe heard them pronounced. In citing names from the census in the text that follows, the surname as spelled in the census is provided followed in parentheses by the form the surname ultimately took.

60. Mutschall reports that in Tarutino, single individuals "did not have a right to a parcel of land; only fathers with families." Mutschall, "Community of Tarutino," *Heritage Review* 42, no. 4: 8. This does not appear to have been the practice in Kulm.

61. Only Gottfried Linse is listed in the Kulm 1815 Census. Stumpp, however, supplies the names and birth years of his younger sisters, Anna (1803) and Rosine (1807) and implies they accompanied him. Stumpp, *Emigration from Germany to Russia*, 530. Flegel does not include them in his study.

possible these were orphans whose parents died on the way to Bessarabia, it is also possible that the census for some reason did not pick up their parents. This appears to be the situation for the three Roloff brothers (ages eighteen, twelve, and nine) who appear apparently on their own in the 1815 census but who Flegel indicates were part of a family group headed by their father, Johann Roloff, who came to Kulm in 1815.[62] Similarly, the three Schöller siblings listed in the 1815 census as led by sixteen-year-old Louise appear to be the children of the Johann Schüler, who in the 1835 Kulm census is a widower living on his own.[63] There are some children who appear in the census without supportive siblings or evident parents: Mathaeus Schäfer, age thirteen; Jacob Fledrich (Fredrich), age fifteen; and Christine Breudt, age fifteen. Clearly too young to start a farmstead on their own, these children, if truly without parents, would probably have come to Bessarabia with the intention of working for other families. Ludwig Gulke, age eight, appears to be a slightly different case. He likely immigrated to Leipzig with other family members, but appears in the 1815 Kulm census because it was considered expedient to hire his labor out while the rest of his family group were establishing themselves in nearby Leipzig.[64]

Among the new residents listed in the 1815 census of Kulm are seven women, some with young children and others accompanying children who were now married adults with families of their own. They are all, apparently, widowed heads of household. Some, like Elisabeth Raugusch (Raugust), age sixty-eight, with two married sons in their thirties, Katharina Leischner, age fifty-six, with one twenty-seven-year-old married son, and Anna Flegel, age fifty-two, with one twenty-nine-year-old married son and two unmarried sons ages twenty-six and nineteen, appear have relinquished family leadership to their adult sons. They came to Bessarabia with their surviving family because there was likely no other choice. Others, like Luise Marks, age thirty-seven, who appears in the census with two sons (possibly stepsons) in their early twenties and another fourteen-year-old son, are more clearly heads of household. Luise Marks apparently began the journey to Bessarabia in 1814 with a husband, but by 1815 and newly arrived in Bessarabia, she had become a widow.[65] There is no trace of a husband present in Bessarabia with Elisabeth Wirs (Wirsch), age thirty-three, or with Rosine Kalmus, age thirty, and the census does not list any dependent children with them. Other records, however, indicate that they came to Kulm with young children and by

62. Flegel, *Extended Relationships*, 589.
63. Louise's younger brother Martin, who appears in the 1815 census as an eleven year old, is deceased by 1835. His son Johann, though, is listed in the 1835 census as the "son of the late Martin Schüler" living with his mother and stepfather. Flegel lists the family as Schieler/Schueler. He places Louise and Martin together as siblings but separates them from Johann, who was likely born in 1802, according to the 1815 census. Johann is probably the Johann listed as person #5 within Flegel's Schueler group. Flegel, *Extended Relationships*, 644.
64. Ludwig Gulke appears to be the brother of Martin Gulke; both were relations of Juliana Gulke Lang and Eva Gulke Lang, who were establishing themselves in the neighboring settlement of Leipzig. Jacob Fledrich (Fredrich) could be the fourteen-year-old son of the Tarutino colonist Jacob Fredrich, who is listed in Flegel as born in 1801 (*Extended Relationships*, 183).
65. Stumpp, in his general collection of the names of early immigrants to Russia, lists Johann Marks as going to Kulm in 1814 (*Emigration from Germany to Russia*, 366), but in his listing of the early Kulm residents only has Luise and two sons (530). Flegel (*Extended Relationships*, 452) lists Johann Marks, suggesting only that he died "after 1814." Concerning the oldest son, Michael, who is listed as age twenty-two in the 1815 census and age forty in the 1835 Kulm census, Flegel seems on good ground when he notes the age difference between Luise and son Michael and concludes he is "probably a stepchild of Luise."

1835 succeeded in establishing farmsteads.[66] Of the seven women, all but Rosine Sanftleben succeeded in establishing ongoing farmsteads.[67] As with the case of the young single men, the fact that there were women who were heads of households reminds us of the fact that for some households, it is likely that communal efforts of neighbors and fellow villagers were necessary to provide the labor required to create arable fields and to put up houses and farm buildings and so formed an important part of the process of establishing the colonies.

Considering each of the 102 separate surnames in the 1815 Kulm census as a different immigrant group, the average age for a head of household or single immigrant is 36.4 years.[68] Considered as a pattern, however, the ages are not heavily bunched together in the thirties, but are spread out along a wide range from age eight to age sixty-five. A quarter of the group (25 of the immigrants) were men and women under the age of thirty, with 6 boys and girls younger than age twenty, and another 13 young men between twenty and twenty-five. At the other end of the spectrum, 35 of the leaders of immigrant parties were over the age of forty, with 14 members of this cohort over the age of fifty.

The 21 members of the Müller family from Neudorf an den Obra in South Prussia formed the largest family group in the 1815 Kulm census.[69] They were led by sixty-six-year-old Christoph Müller and his three adult married sons, Gottlieb (age fifty), Johann (age forty-one), and Christian (age thirty-six). The 1835 census of Kulm shows the children of this family occupying at least three separate farmsteads. Twenty-four Kulm families appearing in the 1815 census will, in the 1835 census, occupy two or three farmsteads each. As the following chapter will take up in more detail, having several adult hands and skills to draw on would be an important asset in establishing successful farmsteads in Bessarabia.

---

66. Stumpp, in his listing of early Kulm residents, has Elisabeth Wirsch at the same age as the Elisabeth Wirs of the 1815 census (*Emigration from Germany to Russia*, 531). Stumpp also adds children: Justine (born 1800) and Wilhelm (born 1802). The 1835 census of Kulm includes Wilhelm and a brother Johann, both of whom ought to have been in the 1815 census. The Dorothea Wirsch, age fifty-four, listed in the 1835 census as among the older unmarried population is very likely the Elisabeth Wirs of the 1815 census (then age thirty-three). Johann Wirsch's age in the 1835 census (twenty-two) suggests that Elisabeth/Dorothea Wirsch's husband may well have been alive when the family was accepted by the Russian agent as an immigrant family. Flegel's listing on Rosine Kalmus indicates children born in 1810 and perhaps 1812 who later have histories in Kulm (*Extended Relationships*, 343). Rosine Kalmus's son, Matthias, died in February 1832 during the cholera epidemic in Kulm, and her daughter Anna and Anna's husband Jacob Henke took full ownership of the farmstead Rosine had started. As with Elisabeth/Dorothea Wirsch, this indicates the existence of a husband in Prussian Poland close to the time of emigration. The missing Wirsch and Kalmus children in the 1815 census is another reminder of its limitations.

67. Stumpp, in his general list of immigrants to Russia, includes Rosine Sanftleben and a younger daughter or possibly sister, Maria Sanftleben, who would have been twenty-three in 1815 (*Emigration from Germany to Russia*, 414). In his general listing, Stumpp indicates they went to Leipzig. He does not include them, though, in his separate listing of early Leipzig immigrants. The Sanftlebens do not appear in Flegel.

68. In calculating the average age, I have excluded older fathers where a middle-aged child was likely the head of household. In this way I counted Johann Kothe, age thirty-four, rather than his father Gottfried, age seventy-six.

69. The 1815 census records that they came from "Neudorf Prussia." Death records from Bessarabia have led Flegel and several other genealogists to identify this as Neudorf a/d Oder. As such a village does not appear on eighteenth- and nineteenth-century maps of Prussia or Poland, I believe this to be a misreading of the similar-looking Neudorf a/d Obra. The Obra River is a tributary of the Warta, and Neudorf a/d Obra lies at the beginning of a broadening of the river called the Bentschener See to the southwest of Tomischel in an area absorbed into Prussia in the Second Partition of Poland of 1793. There were several German settlements in this region that date from the early eighteenth century and provided immigrants to Bessarabia.

The 1815 Kulm census describes a population that wasn't yet finally settled. In comparing the 1815 Kulm census with the far more detailed one of 1835, there are twenty-seven family surnames, over a quarter of the total from 1815, that are no longer associated with Kulm. Twelve of these are shown to be individuals or families who moved to other settlements in German Bessarabia, most of them to nearby colonies. For example, five families moved to Leipzig, two to Tarutino, and another two to Borodino For the other individuals, their fate is unknown: some may have died trying to establish themselves in Kulm, while others may have succeeded in moving.

Finally, the 1815 Kulm census provides for many immigrants the name of the village they had left behind to come to Bessarabia. All of Kulm's population in 1815 came from what had been Prussian Poland before 1807, with a large majority that can be traced beyond that to earlier family origins in Prussia, Mecklenburg, and other states in northern Germany. Places from which Kulm's population had emigrated are provided for 75 out of the 102 surnames. Places of origin are not concentrated in a few areas but are widely spread over a large area in Prussian Poland. The heaviest concentration, sixteen families and individuals, comes from the area around Łodz, with seven families alone coming from Pabianitz (Polish Pabianice) southwest of Łodz, representing the largest number from any one settlement. Other areas with high numbers are villages near Tomischel (Polish Tomiśl), west of Poznan, and Grojec, south of Warsaw, with five families each, and Landsberg (Polish Gorzów Wielkopolski), the Bromberg suburb Zachersburg, and the village of Borosowa on the Vistula, with three families each. What is striking about the listing of places of origin is that nearly two-thirds, forty-nine of the seventy-five families and individuals with identifiable places of origin, immigrated to Kulm with another family or individual from the same village.

## The German villages in Bessarabia were established on the empty steppe

When the Germans were taken to the locations where their villages were to be placed on the Bessarabian steppe, there seems to have been almost universal shock that there was nothing there but rolling grasslands. Almost all the 1848 village histories mention the overwhelming impression of the empty steppeland dominating the scene. The Alt Arzis history says that "it was totally empty and desolate"; the Alt Posttal history remembers there was "nothing except steppeland covered with high grass."[70] The fact that almost every history mentions that there were no houses at the village site may carry the thought that some kind of shelter had been expected. The first Tarutino settlers, as noted earlier, did find "crude huts made of shrubbery and clay available to them," but this was unique.[71] The Wittenberg commentary remembers the surprise that at arriving at the village site, there were no signs of either settled life or the conveniences that earlier habitation would have created: "There were no houses or shelter to be found by the immigrants and there was no trace of woods, gardens or vineyards."[72]

Several village histories mention that the site of their village had been used before by Moldavians and Bulgarians as pasture for cattle, sheep, or horses. To the

---

70. Neumann, "Alt-Arcis – 1848 Village History"; and Kludt, "Alt Posttal – 1848 Village History."
71. Martin, "Tarutino – 1848 Village History."
72. Kurz, "Wittenberg – 1848 Village History."

writers of the Beresina history, this was the reason there were no finished houses at the village site. In the memories of several villages, such as Tarutino, Leipzig, and Teplitz, herdsmen occupied the village site when the Germans arrived. The Wittenberg village history reports that two Bulgarians held legal title via a lease to the village land. This prior right evidently did not raise difficulties, though those writing the history remembered the names of the Bulgarians. Such was not the case in Arzis, however, where a Bulgarian named Karestoy held lease. Initially, at least, he prevented the Germans from using half the arable land. Eight years of legal action ensued before Karestoy was forced to give up his lease, and during that period the Arzis settlers had to pay rent.[73]

The first task on arrival at the village sites was to build temporary housing. These first dwellings were evidently often dugouts built partially underground. Malinovskij refers to them as such (*zemljanki*) and quotes one observer who describes these sardonically as "graves for the living" (*mogily dlja živyx*).[74] In the Paris history, these structures are described as "tent-like huts which [the colonists] covered with grass and reeds in which they lived until the fall."[75] The Alt Elft history also notes huts "covered with grass and reeds."[76] The Klöstitz history refers to "huts made of cane in which [the colonists] lived in for more than a year."[77]

The Russian government promised help in building more permanent houses and farm structures. The Leipzig history notes building supplies were delivered in their first year, 1815, and "the settlers built compressed clay/loam houses."[78] Beresina reports that they had to live in earthen huts until 1816 when the government supplied them with wood and reeds. The Alt Posttal history describing early Wittenberg portrays the first structures there as built from "shrubs"; the Wittenberg history refers to these same structures as "woven houses." Later, the government supplied Wittenberg settlers with perhaps the most complete building supplies of any of the colonies, which allowed the colonists to construct wattle and daub housing: "The settlers received the necessary brushwood, 4 corner posts and 2 faden of reeds for roof construction. They received the necessary doors and windows, 1 plank for the construction of a bench and 15 rubles B.A. (bank assignation) for building costs."[79]

The Beresina history notes that its colonists received 12 rubles (50 B.A.) to defray building costs and that building went quickly, as the colony received in addition some help from Russian soldiers, who built a number of their houses. Similarly, the eighty-four families settling Brienne each received 20 "Holland Dukaten" to cover

---

73. Kern notes that the citizens of Beresina had a similar issue (*Homeland Book*, 122). Their original grant of land retained some "user's rights" which were not removed until 1871. To gain full title, they were to pay annual small portions of the total per-family cost of 4,804.49 rubles with a schedule of payments that was to last from 1888 until 1930. Payments were evidently made until the end of World War I.

74. Malinovskij, *Social'naja i xozjajstvennaja istorija*, 40. Malinovskij is quoting here comments made by Christian Züge published in 1802 on German settlements in South Russia, not Bessarabia, but the description is apt for Bessarabia as well.

75. Dieno, "Paris – 1848 Village History."

76. Mayer, "Alt Elft – 1848 Village History."

77. Schaeff, "Kloestitz – 1848 Village History."

78. Trautmann, "Leipzig – 1848 Village History."

79. Kludt, "Alt Posttal – 1848 Village History". The "15 rubles (B.A.)" were the paper rubles noted in several of the village histories. They were government-issued promissory notes used as a substitute for cash and which had varying relationships in value with silver rubles. Also, in reference to the "2 faden" of reeds, the actual measurement here is the Russian *sažen'* (see footnote 51 above).

"housing, a plow and a wooden wagon."[80] Arzis colonists received only 10 rubles per family, "as well as some stakes, shrubs and beams."[81] The Paris colonists also received only 10 rubles for building, and worse, found that the lumber for building had been left long before their arrival and so was in "bad condition" from the rain and heat.[82] While Alt Elft mentions no funds, it also reports finding lumber "in very bad condition from long exposure to the rain and heat."[83] As the Paris and Alt Elft histories refer to huts of grass and reeds and then of clay, the provided building materials may have been generally unusable. The Teplitz colonists, still weak with illness, were put on their village site in quarantine, with each family given 100 rubles in silver coins to purchase materials to build houses and establish farms.

The Russian government made efforts to supply farming and household equipment and seed grain, as well as food supplies. Several histories reported that food was delivered monthly to villages until the first harvest came in. The Leipzig history provides a detailed listing of what the colonists received to establish their farmsteads: "Each family got a pair of oxen including a yoke, a cow, a wooden Moldavian wagon, a plow, a harrow, a spade, a hoe, 2 scythes, a hammer."[84]

The Paris, Wittenberg, Kulm, Elft, Borodino, Klöstitz, and Tarutino histories report essentially similar outlays for farm and household equipment. Beresina families instead received 135 paper rubles so that they might purchase these items, and the Brienne settlers were to cover such with their Holland ducats. The Arzis history notes that some colonists bought a cow and a horse with their own funds but that "these then did not receive crown money for inventory."[85] This implies that colonists there, like those in Beresina and Brienne, were given the funds to purchase farm implements rather than the implements themselves. The Neu Arzis history, covering the same settlement, notes that some colonists received a wagon and a plow and speaks of the "remaining possessions" being purchased from funds the colonists brought with them.

Beyond farm and household supplies, the Russian government provided food supplies and seed to the colonists, as the Kulm history carefully lists: "Every month they received a pud of rye flour and an oka of salt. Each family received 2 tschk wheat, 1 tschk oats and 1 tschk potatoes which provided seed for the 1816 planting."[86]

---

80. The Holland Ducat, typically a gold coin, was in the eighteenth and nineteenth centuries a frequent coin of international commerce throughout Europe. Its popularity led several countries to profit from minting their own versions, including Russia, where both gold and silver ducats were minted. Minderlin, "Brienne – 1848 Village History."

81. Neumann, "Alt-Arcis – 1848 Village History." In contrast, the Neu Arzis history describing the same situation for the same group of people has a different memory. It reports that colonists in Arzis received "20 Dutch Dukaten" to cover building and other expenses of getting established, and mentions in addition that "a few settlers also received a wooden wagon and a plow." C. Ziemann, "Neu Arcis – 1848 Village History," trans. E. Wise (N.p.: Odessa Digital Library, 1996), http://www.odessa3.org/collections/history/link/neuarci.txt.

82. Dieno, "Paris – 1848 Village History."

83. Mayer, "Alt Elft – 1848 Village History."

84. Trautmann, "Leipzig – 1848 Village History."

85. Neumann, "Alt-Arcis – 1848 Village History."

86. Straub, "Kulm – 1848 Village History." A *pud* is an ancient Russian measurement of weight that is equal to 16.381 kilograms or 36.11 pounds. An *oka* is a unit of weight used throughout the Ottoman Empire and in lands, such as Bessarabia, that were formerly part of the Ottoman Empire. When used as a measure of weight in the Ottoman Empire, it was typically 1.28 kilograms or 2.8 pounds (US). Vladimir I. Dal' in his dictionary (*Tolkovyj slovar'*, vol. 2, *I–O* [St. Petersberg: M.O. Vol'f, 1881], 686) spells the word in Russian usage as *oko* and defines it as a Tartar measure of weight equal to 3 *funt*. The funt, or pound, was 409.5 grams, making a Russian oko slightly lighter than the Ottoman unit at 1.228 kilograms. *Tschk* is an abbreviation of the term četverik. A *četverik* is a Russian measure of volume equal to 26.239 liters, 27.726 quarts (US), or 0.7438 Winchester bushels. Used for grain, a *četverik* is also a unit of weight equal to one-eighth of a četvert', or 0.4375 pud, or 15.8 pounds.

The Wittenberg history mentions colonists there received monthly a pud of flour and "some grits" to survive on until the first harvest plus four četverik of wheat and another four of potatoes for planting.[87] Alt Elft reports receiving a roughly similar amount of seed as Kulm, though it calls this allotment "small." Food provisions, as noted in many of the village histories, were to continue until the first harvest came in. For Kulm and Wittenberg, this would have been, at the earliest, the fall of 1815. However, food may have continued to be supplied for much longer than the first harvest. The Kulm Heimatbuch, after repeating the same food provisions as noted in the village history, adds that the Russian government continued to supply the flour and grits monthly through June 1817.[88] The Klöstitz colony, founded in 1815, reports receiving food supplies for two full years.

To provide the building, farming, and food supplies to the German colonists, the Russian government contracted out supply services to merchants in Bessarabia or nearby Odessa. As was common practice in Russia throughout the nineteenth century, such suppliers bid low to receive the contract and then made their money through delivering the least costly goods they could find, which might include goods of low quality or goods that were old or spoiled. Another means of finding profit was by delivering less than the promised amounts. The Alt Posttal history complains that the good intentions of the Russian government were undermined by "the greed of suppliers, especially by a man named Pollnor."[89] Some goods that were supplied came "half spoiled";[90] the daily food allowance of 5 kopecks provided in addition to the grain and grits was not fully paid. In listing the troubles early colonists faced, the Neu Elft history notes that because the colonists didn't know Russian and weren't familiar with local customs, they "often were cheated and robbed."[91] The Tarutino history makes the strongest statement on this point, complaining that "ruthless lower officials shortened the supplies and delivered bad or spoiled goods."[92] Malinovskij quotes a report, evidently sent back to a ministry in St. Petersburg from Bessarabia at this time, that notes that local government officials as well as contractors "were more inclined to look after their own interests rather than those of the state" ("bolee nabljudali svoju pol'zu, neželi kazennuju").[93]

Shortchanging may have been the cause of the differences between the cash building allowances (noted earlier) that were offered to the colonists of Wittenberg (15 rubles), Beresina (12.5 rubles), Brienne (10 rubles), Arzis (10 rubles), and Paris (10 rubles). This may also explain the differences in the seed allotments given to

---

87. Kurz, "Wittenberg – 1848 Village History."

88. Wölfle, "The Establishment of the Village of Kulm," 4.

89. Kludt, "Alt-Posttal – 1848 Village History." This same supplier appears more positively in the Beresina history. There identified as "Polno, a supplier," he is described neutrally as providing the wood and reed cane used for the early houses. Foerster, "Beresina – 1848 Village History," trans. E. Necker-Eberhardt (N.p.: Odessa Digital Library, 2000), http://www.odessa3.org/collections/history/link/beresina.txt.

90. Mutschall's Tarutino history reports that "often flour arrived late and was also wet because of the rain and had formed hard clumps so that one had to chop it…with an ax." Mutschall, "History of the Community of Tarutino from 1814 to 1934," Heritage Review 42, no. 1 (2012): 8.

91. Kurz, "Neu Elft – 1848 Village History."

92. Martin, "Tarutino – 1848 Village History."

93. Malinovskij, Social'naja i xozjajstvennaja istoriaja, 47. Malinovskij also notes examples of some disappointed German immigrants seeking to leave Russia and return to their earlier homes (52–53). Among these is an example from 1817 in the Kučurgan District of Xerson; however, I have found no such attempts occurring among the Bessarabian Germans.

colonists in Wittenberg and Kulm, though it would seem equally possible that these differences were the result of the kinds of seed stock that were available. Similarly, the decision to give funds to Beresina, Brienne, and Arzis colonists to purchase farm and household equipment may not be an indication of fraud but of the unavailability of the necessary implements.

## The German colonists were expected to repay the Russian government for the costs of bringing them to Russia and establishing them in their new villages

The Russian government treated the costs of bringing the Germans to Bessarabia, feeding them and providing housing materials, farm equipment and seed as a long-term interest-free loan. The colonists were to pay back this loan in annual installments beginning ten years after their arrival in Bessarabia. As will be discussed in the following chapter, ten years proved too short a time for the colonists to be sufficiently well-established, and the beginning of payment was postponed for another ten years until 1833.[94] The fact that an extension was granted should be taken to indicate that senior officials in the Russian government viewed the colonies as a state asset that, if treated well, would ultimately pay back positive returns.

Four of the histories report the total per family obligations for their village. These were to be paid the Russian government in ten annual installments, presumably in amounts of one-tenth of the total per year. The accounting that stands behind this would have reflected the prices of goods theoretically delivered rather than what had actually occurred. Given Russian state accounting practices, it is probable that the debt was computed as a total per village amount, and this total figure was then communicated to the village for it to divide up for payment as the villagers saw fit.[95] For example, the Sarata history indicates that each family was to pay a flat annual contribution of 14 rubles, with the remainder of the community debt apportioned according to the number of cattle each family had. The four villages that provided figures give a total per family obligation, which suggests that unlike Sarata, each family was expected to pay the same fixed annual amount. It would seem likely, however, that in these villages, the total community obligation was divided among the 60-desjatina family farmsteads then in existence (i.e., that were existing in 1833) rather than among the founding families or their descendants alone. The four villages reporting per-family obligations provide figures roughly in the neighborhood of a total per-family debt of 1,000 rubles (see table 4–2).

While Sarata used a means test to determine the actual family payment, an average family payment can be worked out from information in the village history.[96] This comes to 833.33 rubles, much like that of the colonies listed above. Fleischhauer,

---

94. As reported by both the Neu Elft and Wittenberg histories. Kurz, "Neu Elft – 1848 Village History"; and Kurz, "Wittenberg – 1848 Village History."

95. This was the practice of the Russian government and Russian landlords in assigning tax and feudal rent and labor burdens to Russian peasant villages.

96. The Sarata history notes: (a) that the Russian government "supported [the founding the settlement] with 50,000 rubles," and (b) the 60 families that [originally] settled here. If the cost was divided among the 101 families there when the colony was fully settled in the 1830s, the per-family average cost would come down to 495.05 rubles. M. Natterer, "Sarata – 1848 Village History," trans. E. Wise (N.p.: Odessa Digital Library, 1996), http://www.odessa3.org/collections/history/link/sarata.txt.

TABLE 4–2.  Per-family debt for Alt Posttal, Wittenberg, Neu Elft, and Tarutino

| Village | Per-family debt |
| --- | --- |
| Alt Posttal | 1,114 rubles |
| Wittenberg | 1,114 rubles |
| Neu Elft[a] | 953 rubles |
| Tarutino | 820 rubles |

a. Although not mentioned in the Alt Elft history, this was presumably the per-family debt owed by members of that community as well.

without attributing a source, asserts that the cost of bringing a German family to a colony in Russia was about 5,000 rubles.[97] Based on the data above, this figure appears exaggerated.

## The settlements were ultimately assigned names that commemorated Russian and Allied victories over Napoleon

The names given to the new German settlements in Bessarabia went through several iterations until 1817–19, when all were assigned names associated with Russian and Allied victories over Napoleon. In the earliest stage of naming, several of the colonies adopted names for themselves from place names used by the nomads who had been grazing cattle, horses, and sheep on the land assigned to the Germans. Kulm was called Madar after the Kuman Turkic words *ma*, meaning "water," and *dar*, meaning "place."[98] Many of these early village names were the names of the rivers along which the colonial settlements were located: Beresina was called Kugelnik, Borodino was Soak, Klöstitz was Tschaga,[99] Leipzig was Skinos,[100] and Tarutino was Anshakrak. In a second stage, the German colonies took on names that were based on a German form of the Christian names of Russian tsars or members of the Russian royal family. Kulm became Paulsberg ("Paul's mountain"), Tarutino was called Elisabeth, Leipzig was Catherinesruh ("Catherine's rest"), Elft was Michaelsruhm ("Michael's fame or glory"),[101] Brienne was Peterswunsch ("Peter's wish"), Borodino was Aleksandr, and Wittenberg was Mariental ("Marie's valley"), named after the Dowager Tsarina Maria.[102] The Russian authorities, on the other hand, appear to have prosaically referred to the colonies in their early stages by numbers: Tarutino was Colony #1, Elft was #11, Teplitz was #12, Arzis #14, and Brienne #15.

97. Fleischhauer, *Die Deutschen im Zarenreich*, 171.
98. Wölfle, "The Establishment of the Village of Kulm," 5. The 1901 Austro-Hungarian military map of Bessarabia (J. Meier and K. Radler, http://lazarus.elte.hu/hun/digkonyv/topo/200e/47-46.jpg) gives Madar in parentheses as an alternate name for the settlement.
99. The Klöstitz village history reports that the name Emaut was first used. Klaus lists many of these early names in Cyrillic after the formal name of the village in Appendix II of his work (*Naši kolonii*, 25–60). Several of these early names also appear on the Austro-Hungarian military map of 1901 (see footnote 92 above).
100. The Skinoza River joins the Kogil'nik at the north edge of Leipzig.
101. Mixail (Michael) Romanov (1586–1645) was the founder of the dynasty that ruled Russia until 1918.
102. The Dowager Tsarina Maria Fëdorovna, the second wife of Tsar Paul I, was born the Duchess Sophie Marie, the daughter of Friedrich II Eugen, Duke of Württemberg.

Sometime in the period between 1817 and 1819, as several histories relate, all the German colonies in Bessarabia were given new and generally permanent names.[103] The impetus for creating the new names appeared to have come from St. Petersburg, though local Russian authorities may have been responsible for picking the actual names. The Alt Elft history notes that its formal name, Fere Champenoise, came from the government, meaning likely the Welfare Committee. The Brienne history assigns responsibility to General "Bachmet"—that is, to General Aleksej Nikolaevič Baxmetev (1774–1841), who became military governor of Bessarabia in 1818. This would date at least Brienne's name change to no earlier than the summer of 1818. Wilhelm Mutschall, in his history of Tarutino, notes a tradition that the change in all colony names occurred after a visit of Tsar Alexander I to Bessarabia.[104] Tsar Alexander did pass through Bessarabia in April 1818, though he did not visit the area where the German villages were located. Mutschall's assertion also does not fit with the Tarutino village history, or with that of Leipzig, which both remember the name change occurring in 1817. While the name changes may well have sprung from a single decision, the village histories suggest they were put in place over a period of time.

The new names of the German colonies commemorated Russian and Allied victories over Napoleon. The colony of Borodino was named after the site of the most significant battle fought between the Russian army and Napoleon during the latter's invasion of Russia. The battle of Borodino occurred on September 7, 1812, some 80 miles east of Moscow. A combined seventy-five thousand casualties were suffered in a battle in which both sides claimed victory. Tarutino was one of the names given to a battle fought on October 18, 1812 between Russian forces under the command of General Bennigsen and French forces under the command of General Murat. Beresina was the name of a river where, during the retreat from Moscow, Napoleon suffered the loss of some twenty-five thousand troops while trying to cross under Russian fire in November 1812. Kulm's name came from the German form of the Bohemian village Chlumec in Saxony, near which a major battle was fought on August 30, 1813, in which the forces of French General Dominique Vandamme were trapped and defeated by a Russian force under General Ostermann-Tolstoy and a Prussian force led by General Kleist.[105] Teplitz was named for a Czech village, Teplice, where in August 1813, Tsar Alexander I signed a treaty with Emperor Francis I of Austria and King Friedrich Wilhelm III of Prussia that formed a triple alliance against Napoleon. Arzis was named after the battle fought at Arcis sur Aube, north of Troyes in France, where on March 20–21, 1814, Napoleon's army retreated from the Austrians under General Schwartzenberg.

---

103.  The Leipzig and Tarutino histories report the name change took place in 1817, while the Teplitz history says 1818, and the Brienne history says 1819. Trautmann, "Leipzig – 1848 Village History"; Martin, "Tarutino – 1848 Village History"; A. Kludt, "Teplitz – 1848 Village History," trans. R. Niessner (N.p.: Odessa Digital Library, 1996), http://www.odessa3.org/collections/history/link/teplitz.txt; Minderlin, "Brienne – 1848 Village History."

104.  Mutschall, "Community of Tarutino," *Heritage Review* 42, no. 4: 7.

105.  Chlumec, now in the Czech Republic, lies three miles northeast of Teplice, the source of the name for the Teplitz colony. Once part of Saxony, both are just across the present border with Germany near the old Altenberg road to Dresden. The name of the German Bessarabian colony Kulm thus has no relationship with the Polish town Chełmno (also called Kulm in German) from which a number of the German groups had left on their journey to Bessarabia.

Wittenberg and Elft also received names from battles fought in the Napoleonic wars that became their official names used in dealings with the Russian government. The colony of Wittenberg was renamed Malojaroslavec after the village in Russia where, on October 24, 1812, Russian troops prevented the retreating French army from taking a more southerly and less ravaged route. When this colony split in two in 1823, the original village, Wittenberg, was called Malojaroslavec I and the new village, Alt Posttal, was called Malojaroslavec II. Possibly because these village names differed only by the numeral, the Germans in Bessarabia came to use other names, Wittenberg and Alt Posttal, for them. Wittenberg's name, according to Kern, came from the pronunciation of Württemberg in the southern German speech of the village.[106] Alt Posttal was named for the old post road that ran through its center, which was the major road connecting the forts of Ismail on the Danube estuary and Akkerman on the Dniester. For apparently similar reasons the names Alt and Neu Elft were commonly used by the Germans instead of Fere Champenoise I and II. The name Fere Champenoise comes from a battle fought on March 25, 1814, outside a French town of this name just north of Arcis sur Aube where Prince Wilhelm of Württemberg and Prince Konstantin of Russia defeated a much larger French army.

### Problems that developed between the new German colonies and local Russian civic authorities led the Russian government in St. Petersburg to create a new agency independent of the provincial governments that would oversee affairs with all the German colonies in Russia

Given that the German settlers coming from Prussian Poland to Bessarabia would be facing clear hurdles in dealing with a new government, a different language, and unfamiliar business and social customs, the Russian government went to some lengths to try to smooth their transition to Russia. Not everything concerning the creation of the new colonies in Bessarabia, however, came off without problems. As noted earlier in this chapter, there were issues with suppliers shortchanging or not making deliveries of supporting funds, food, and farmstead implements. The colonists in Arzis had eight years of problems in gaining full access to the village's land from a Bulgarian who held an earlier title to part of them.

An even more serious situation developed from problems between the German colonists in Tarutino and Russian officials there in the first years of settlement. In the summer of 1815, a conflict developed between the German colonists in Tarutino and a Russian official located there named Mendelsohn. Mutschall, in his history of Tarutino, gives two separate versions of this conflict, both leading to the appearance of Russian troops and the arrest of Pastor Schnabel. In one version, conflict came when Mendelsohn rented pasture land to an outsider;[107] in the second Mendelsohn was unwilling to open a grain storehouse, at a time when food supplies were low

106. Kern, *Homeland Book*, 66.
107. Mutschall, "Community of Tarutino," *Heritage Review* 42, no. 4: 10. This is the version Schmidt tells in *Die Deutschen aus Bessarabien*, 54–55, and in more detail in *Bessarabia: German Colonists*, 91–92. Schmidt is relying on Johann Georg Kurz's 1857 overview of the German colonies in South Russia and Wilhelm Kludt's 1862 study of the German communities in Bessarabia.

before the harvest had come in.[108] In both versions, Mendelsohn, feeling threatened, fled to Kishinev, the provincial capital of Bessarabia. There he reported that
a revolt had occurred in Tarutino. This report created a major civil and military
issue. The Imperial Russian government was extremely sensitive to any disturbance
that suggested a peasant uprising, as memories lingered from the revolt led by the
Cossack Emelian Pugachev in 1773–74 in South Russia. The provincial governor,
Major General Harting, brought a detachment of troops down to Tarutino to quell
or at least make sure no "revolt" had or was to occur. He fired shots as warnings
against resistance and beat several colonists, perhaps killing one. He arrested the
spokesman for the colonists, Pastor Schnabel, and brought him back to Kishinev as
a prisoner.

Other views of this incident are possible. Brandes identifies Mendelsohn as a
*smotritel'* or supervisor, a person hired by the Russian government to provide, watch
over, and distribute the food and supplies promised to the colonists. Brandes, gave
credence to version two, the break-in of the grain storehouse, and felt that Pastor
Schnabel was simply disobeying the orders, not just of Mendelsohn but also of
another smotritel' named Prochnickij, not to touch the wood and grain under their
care.[109] Both Brandes and Mutschall also imply that bad feelings had developed
between the Tarutino colonists and the supervisors, as the supervisors, treating the
German colonists as they would have treated Russian peasants, quickly resorted to
blows when they saw something they didn't like, treatment the Germans would
have found demeaning.[110] Klaus makes perhaps an oblique reference to this incident
when he notes that although this was a time of peace, the foreign colonists suffered
"the same inconveniences [*neudobstva*] that exist in time of war."[111] Klaus here sees
the origin of the problem in the unfortunate selection of officials who unnecessarily
produced quarrels between "the foreigners and the native inhabitants."[112]

It ultimately became clear that no revolt had occurred in Tarutino, but it took
a year and a half and a hearing in court for Schnabel to be able to return freely
to Tarutino.[113] The incident in Tarutino appears to have been an important factor
leading the Russian government to conduct a review of its management of the

---

108. Mutschall, "Community of Tarutino," *Heritage Review* 43, no. 1: 5. In this version Germans from
 Tarutino, accompanied by Pastor Schnabel, broke into the storehouse. Brandes also provides
 details of this affair that I use in the discussion that follows in *Von den Zaren Adoptiert*, 185–86.
 Malinovskij briefly mentions the Tarutino revolt (*bunt*) in *Social'naja i xozjajstvennaja istoriaja*
 (54). Malinovskij notes that the description of this as a peasant revolt drew the attention of Soviet
 historians. The Tarutino village history makes no mention of these troubles, nor is it recalled in
 any of the other village histories, no doubt as these events would have been out of keeping with
 the positive story the village histories wished to tell about relations with the Russian government.
109. Brandes, *Von den Zaren Adoptiert*, 185.
110. Brandes, *Von den Zaren Adoptiert*, note 3; and Mutschall, "Community of Tarutino," *Heritage
 Review* 42, no. 4: 10.
111. Klaus, *Naši kolonii*, 305.
112. Ibid. Both phrases in quotes above also appear in Klaus as quotes. Klaus, who is writing in the
 1860s, appears to cite here and on the following page notes that were attached to a handwritten
 letter (*reskript*) sent by Tsar Alexander I to the governor-general in Bessarabia, possibly Harting
 himself, though the notes may be those of Kiselev.
113. Mutschall, "Community of Tarutino," *Heritage Review* 43, no. 1: 5. The cashiering of General
 Harting and Supervisor Mendelsohn occurred as a result of the reforms proposed by Kiselev,
 discussed in the text that follows. Schmidt's account of the results of this affair implies that
 the intervention of the Russian Orthodox metropolitan caused "the affair [to be] shifted to the
 capital of St. Petersburg" (*Bessarabia: German Colonists*, 92). I have found no record of the Russian
 Orthodox metropolitan intervening in this affair. Such an intervention would have been unusual.

German colonists. One of the government's first steps was to take responsibility for the affairs of the new German colonists in Bessarabia away from the provincial government under General Harting. In his place, the government brought in Count Pavel D. Kiselev, then a young general serving as chief of staff of the Second Army headquartered in Tul'čin just to the north of Bessarabia. Kiselev reestablished peace and continued the settlement of the new German colonies. Kiselev's major assignment, however, was to make a study of how the new German and Bulgarian colonies in Bessarabia and the older German colonies established in the Xerson and Ekaterinoslav provinces were being managed.[114] Kiselev found corruption and rot in abundance. His report to Tsar Alexander I notes that "everything there [in Bessarabia] is for sale" and that the senior officials "are obliged to steal more than the rest seeing that they have paid twenty or thirty thousand rubles apiece for their nominations."[115] Kiselev's report to the tsar suggests that the colonies be managed by a single organization that crossed provincial boundaries and was independent of the different provincial governments. Alexander I approved Kiselev's suggestions and issued an *ukaz* or formal decree on March 22, 1818 (O.S.).[116] This decree established the Welfare Committee, known formally as the Welfare Committee for Foreign Settlements on the Southern Borderlands of Russia,[117] as the sole agent of the Russian government responsible for the affairs of the German colonies in Bessarabia and South Russia.

The ukaz of Alexander I creating the Welfare Committee capped a period in which the Russian government had tried several different ways to manage the German colonies within its borders. The German colonies in the Volga region, though initially supervised from St. Petersburg, had, after 1782, been administered locally by the offices charged with overseeing the Russian crown peasantry.[118] By the time the Russian government was seeking to settle German peasants in South Russia in the 1790s, this supervisory arrangement was considered inadequate and possibly harmful to the development of the German colonies. As a result, in 1797, the Russian government created a special section in the Office of State Economy charged with overseeing the foreign colonies in South Russia and Bessarabia.[119] Oversight of the Volga colonies was transferred to this special section, and in 1800, a field office was established for South Russia in Ekaterinoslav on the Dnieper (now the Ukrainian city of Dnipropetrovs'k). This field office controlled the expenditure of state funds for establishing and maintaining the new colonies in South Russia, collected taxes

114. Fleischhauer, *Die Deutschen im Zarenreich*, 170–74.

115. Charles U. Clark, "Russia Organizes the Province," chap. 8 in *Bessarabia: Russia and Romania on the Black Sea* (New York: Dodd, Mead and Co., 1927), http://depts.washington.edu/cartah/text_archive/clark/mobile.html. Clark also indicates that because General Harting's administration was so noted for its sale of offices, his replacement as provincial governor of Bessarabia, General Alexei Bakhmetiev, was advised to send all of Harting's appointees out of Bessarabia.

116. An *ukaz*, which is sometimes rendered into English as *ukase*, was in Imperial Russia a formal decree issued by the tsar and having the force of law.

117. This translates the Russian title for the committee which is Popečitel'nyj komitet ob inostrannyx poselencax južnogo kraja Rossii. The Welfare Committee is also often referred to by the German translation, the Fürsorgekomitee der ausländischen Ansiedler in Südrussland.

118. I rely here and further in this paragraph on the overview provided by Hans Rempel: "Introduction" in *Deutsche Bauernleistung*, 2–5. Giesinger also covers this history more generally: *From Catherine to Khrushchev*, 51.

119. This was the "Ekspedicija Gosudarstvennago Xozjajstva, opekunstva inostrannyx i sel'skago domovodstva," the Special Department of the Office of State Economy for the Guardianship of Foreigners and their Villages.

from them, and compiled annual reports on the colonies. This field office, however, had no judicial authority and, with the significant growth in the number of colonies, was significantly understaffed for the work assigned. In 1802, with the accession of Alexander I to the throne, the special section and its field office were placed under the authority of the Ministry of the Interior. Sorting out the Tarutino "revolt" in Bessarabia highlighted several problems with the past arrangements for the German colonies: there was a need for broader authority than simply covering fiscal matters, there was a need for far more staff given the large number of new colonies and the extensive area in South Russia and Bessarabia where they were located, and there was a need for the organization overseeing the colonies to be led by someone of sufficiently high rank to have credibility both in St. Petersburg and with the provincial governors.

The Tsar's Decree of 1818 established an organization to be led by a senior official with the rank of privy counselor, the third highest in the table of ranks and equivalent to a lieutenant general in the army.[120] The head of the Welfare Committee was its president, and he was to be assisted by two advisors who managed a staff of eighteen. The purview of the Welfare Committee was not just the German colonies but also the colonies that were established in both Bessarabia and South Russia for Bulgarian Orthodox refugees escaping from Turkish rule. The first president of the Welfare Committee was General Ivan N. Inzov (1768–1845), who held this post from 1818 until his death in 1845.[121] The Welfare Committee was initially headquartered in the city of Xerson until 1819, when it moved upriver on the Dnieper to the city of Ekaterinoslav. Headquarters were later moved to Kishinev in 1822 and to Odessa in 1833. The Welfare Committee split its work into nine districts, each headed by a resident inspector. The German colonies in Bessarabia were supervised from the district office in Akkerman (now the Ukrainian city of Bilhorod Dnistrovs'kyi), the former Byzantine and Turkish fortress town located east of the colonies along the estuary of the Dnieper. Mutschall reports that the Welfare Committee district office placed an official in Tarutino to oversee the connection with the German colonies.[122] The Welfare Committee reported to the Ministry of the Interior until 1837, when Tsar Nicholas I transferred the reporting relationship of the Welfare Committee to the Ministry of State (i.e., Crown) Domains. This ministry was, in 1837, headed by Pavel D. Kiselev, whose relationship with the Welfare Committee now came full circle, as it was his report to Tsar Alexander I in 1817 that was instrumental in creating it.

Creating the Welfare Committee with powers independent of the provincial governments implies that the Russian government of 1818 placed great value on the colonies, especially the German colonies. The potential growth of those colonies into thriving agricultural centers with economic strengths on a par with similar thriving peasant centers in Western Europe was presumably a major source of that value. Though the attitude of the central Russian government to the German colonies in Imperial Russia was to change over time, it continued to have at its core

120. The rank in Russian is a "tajnyj sovetnik." For the Russian table of ranks, see note 22 of the introduction.
121. General Inzov was succeeded by Eugen von Hahn (1845–49), Friedrich Baron Rosen (1849–53), Pavel F. Baron Mestmarcher (1853–56), Vladimir Islavin (1856–58), and Alexander von Hamm (1858–66).
122. Mutschall, "Community of Tarutino," *Heritage Review* 42, no. 4: 11. The first holder of this office in Tarutino was Captain Ivan Kotovich.

the cameralist economic thought that the colonies represented important assets for Russia. Time and again when pressures rose on the Imperial government to limit the rights of the colonies by, for example, preventing them from acquiring additional land, the central government chose to ignore such pressures, preferring to let such assets thrive.

Once the troubles in Tarutino had been resolved, relations between the Bessarabian colonists and the Russian government in St. Petersburg and Kishinev became quiescent and distant. The Welfare Committee now became the face of the Russian government and took up an active role in helping the colonies become established and grow. It also served the colonies as the ultimate legal, judicial, administrative, and tax authority.

When the German colonists were settled in their new villages, what was probably front of mind for them was the strange, open, and unpopulated land and the enormous amount of work to be done. They needed to get crops in the ground, to build sheltering houses and barns, and to face up to the question of whether they could build here, in greater freedom, lives that provided more prosperity and safety than the ones they had left behind.

Like the villages the colonists had left behind in Prussian Poland and Württemberg, the German colonies in Bessarabia were nucleated settlements with fields surrounding the clustered farmsteads. Several of the 1848 village histories describe nearly identical settlement designs: two rows of houses facing each other across a wide street, each house with its narrow yard of one desjatina stretching out behind, land which ultimately was to contain stables, threshing areas, gardens, and orchards. The picture presented in the Alt Elft history would thus seem to be typical: "The colony is positioned lengthwise north to south in two rows."[123] The Alt Posttal, Brienne, Neu Elft, Paris, and Wittenberg histories and the Kulm Heimatbuch describe the same pattern. Maps of the settlements, as well as Google satellite views, suggest that Alt Elft, Arzis, Beresina, Borodino, Katzbach, Klöstitz, Leipzig, Tarutino, and Teplitz began in this fashion as well. Sarata, with its main street bisecting two north–south streets, and Krasna, with its central area off to the side of its long street, appear slightly different from the general pattern. As will be discussed in more detail later, such similarities resulted from the fact that the Russian authorities preferred this design rather than it being a concept the German colonists brought with them.

Having been shown where their settlement was to be placed and the boundaries of its surrounding land, and likely having gasped at the enormity of the task in front of them, the German colonists set to work to put up places to live and create farmsteads. The village histories, which are the best sources on the early life of the German colonies, indicate in unison that the process of building the colonies and creating self-sufficiency and then prosperity was slow and difficult. This will be the subject of the following chapter.

---

123.  Mayer, "Alt Elft – 1848 Village History."

# V

# The German Colonies in Bessarabia had to Overcome Many Difficulties to Establish Themselves on Firm Ground

Commentaries on establishing the German colonies in Bessarabia have frequently used a short maxim to describe the progression of the first generations there:

| Den Ersten der Tod | [For] *The first* [generation there is] *death* |
| Den Zweiten die Not | [For] *The second difficulties* [but] |
| Den Dritten das Brod[1] | *The third has bread* |

---

1. I have not found the origin of this maxim. It appears frequently in descriptions of the establishment of the Schwabian and Rhineland German settlements in the Banat and other Hapsburg lands in what is now Romania and Hungary, in depictions of the settlement of the North German fen and moor lands, and even in the accounts of the early years of German settlements in Ohio and Texas. See Schmidt, *Die Deutschen aus Bessarabien*, 46; Rick Heli, "Deutsche Genealogie: Donauschwaben im Banat" (N.p.: genealogienetz.de, 2000), www.genealogienetz.de/reg/ESE/dsban-d.html; Konrad Gerescher, "Das Portal der Ungarndeutschen" (lecture, University of Szeged, College of Teacher Training, Szeged, Hun., September 9, 2002), http://www.ungarndeutsche.de/de/cms/index. php?page=donauschwaben; and Rolf Geffken, *Die große Arbeit: Worpswede in Leben und Werk Rainer Maria Rilkes* (Bremen, Ger.: Falkenberg, 2014), 15.

In three generations, most of the German colonists in Bessarabia adapted successfully to very different conditions than those left behind in Prussian Poland or the Rhineland. Climate and soil conditions were new for them, which meant the colonists needed to master different agricultural crops and to raise different breeds of stock. There were markets for their surplus, but access to markets beyond those in their own villages was not as easy. In mastering new conditions, the colonists created settlements that (at least through 1914) were significantly more prosperous than those they had left behind. They were better fed and clothed, lived longer lives on average, and had far greater freedom and control over their lives than the peasants who had remained in the villages in Prussian Poland and Württemberg.

It wasn't easy to make this transition and not everyone did. The 1848 village histories report a difficult transition to Bessarabia with much suffering and many deaths in the first years of the settlements. Successful adaptation to conditions in Bessarabia varied significantly among the different German colonies and varied even within the same village. Some of the settlements had better land to work with or learned to adapt to the different conditions better and sooner. Within the same settlement, some worked harder, learned more quickly what crops, animals, and techniques could be successful, and so adapted within a few years of arrival; others struggled and found it difficult to grow crops, and, burdened with discouragement, took at least a generation to adapt. Moreover, new tests kept arising. Field pests such as locusts, gophers, and field mice threatened and destroyed crops. Regular outbreaks of rinderpest killed numbers of cattle.[2] The amount of rain turned out to be the most critical element in producing decent harvests, but the timing and annual amounts of rainfall varied. Those who learned how to deal successfully with the irregularity of rain and which crops handled droughts better were sooner on stable ground.

The early stages of settlement were very difficult for all of the colonies. The colonists were, for the most part, grain farmers accustomed to techniques honed in the wet clay soils of Poland or the lighter clay of the woodlands of southern Germany. The climate was different in Bessarabia. The steppeland had a continental climate of long, hot, and dry summers and short but cold winters with much snow.[3] Poland and especially Württemberg and the upper Rhineland had more rain and milder summers and winters. The soil conditions of the Bessarabian steppelands were also very different. The top layer of soil in the valleys was black dirt, often several feet thick, but it was heavily alkaline with high pH levels. Along the hillsides, the alkaline layer was thinner over layers of clay and sometimes sand. South of the German colonies in Bessarabia, the steppe rivers reached estuaries often blocked by dunes from full access to the Black Sea, and so spread out to form small, highly salty seas called lakes (*ozero*) when separated from the Black Sea by dunes, or bays (*liman*) when partially open to the sea. The hot summer sun regularly evaporated water from these estuary waters and winds blowing from the south over centuries deposited large amounts of salt crystals throughout the Bessarabian steppelands. Spring runoff then concentrated the alkali in the valleys.

All of the 1848 village histories comment on the alkaline soil the colonists found in their settlement sites. The description in the Klöstitz history is very typical, if more detailed:

---

2. Rinderpest is an infectious, viral disease of cattle that is highly fatal.
3. Schmidt, *Die Deutschen aus Bessarabien*, 39–41.

*The soil of the land assigned to the colony Kloestitz varies. In the higher elevations, the Fuss deep soil,[4] was black, containing some alkali and occasionally had underlying patches of white and reddish clay. The soil in the valleys is almost all alkali, mixed only with a little black dirt and sand.[5]*

The soil, even the valley soil, could be fertile and produced decent harvests when there was sufficient rain. The Alt Arzis history notes "when sufficient rain falls, the grain and grass thrive," but without it "the grass and crops turn yellow or are burned," and the Tarutino history states "during dry seasons…the harvests were rather meek."[6] For some colonies, such as Alt Arzis, Brienne, Leipzig, and Teplitz, the heavy concentrations of alkali in the valleys created patches of useless land. The Alt Arzis history, referring, like several other histories, to the alkali as saltpeter, notes that "both ends of the valley…consist of many layers of saltpeter covering many desjatines of useless land. No grass or any vegetation grows there."[7]

Just getting started was difficult. The steppeland had never been plowed and so was very hard to turn. The Paris and Alt Elft histories both note that "six to eight oxen were needed to pull the plow" and break the soil.[8] As each farmstead had been given only two oxen, the main point underlined, of course, is that the steppe soil was hard to plow, but another important point is also implied here: cooperation among the families founding settlements was required and apparently came naturally. The Alt Posttal history also comments on the difficulty of plowing the steppe soil for the first time. It notes that families in the early Wittenberg settlement were given steers instead of oxen for draft animals, and these were considered too weak and presumably too small to do much good with the plow. As a result, "three to four farmers had to be harnessed together in order to put a plow to work."[9] As the colonists were quite unfamiliar with the radically different alkaline soil of the steppeland, harvests in the first years were not good. The Tarutino history notes that colonists there, "unfamiliar with the characteristics of the soil, were unsuccessful in the way they farmed…many died in the first years and several became discouraged."[10] The Leipzig history also speaks of discouraged settlers who felt that "nothing grows here anyway."[11] The Neu Elft history remembers that in the first years harvests were so lean that "many families were forced to earn their bread working for Bulgarians or Moldavians" in nearby villages.[12]

---

4.  The German Fuss, a measurement of length, is slightly longer than the English foot at 12.44 inches or 31.3 centimeters.
5.  Schaeff, "Klöstitz – 1848 Village History."
6.  Neumann, "Alt-Arcis – 1848 Village History"; Martin, "Tarutino – 1848 Village History."
7.  Neumann, "Alt-Arcis – 1848 Village History."
8.  Mayer, "Alt Elft – 1848 Village History"; Dieno, "Paris – 1848 Village History." This is one of several similarities between these two histories. The comment noted on the following page that the village would have prospered more quickly if they had planted orchards and vineyards sooner is another similarity. The implication is that one or both of the authors saw a draft of the other's history before putting their history in final form. Both histories are dated in the first week of May 1848.
9.  Kludt, "Alt Posttal – 1848 Village History."
10. Martin, "Tarutino – 1848 Village History."
11. Trautmann, "Leipzig – 1848 Village History."
12. Kurz, "Neu Elft – 1848 Village History."

## To achieve a solid economic footing, the colonists needed to adapt to new soil and climate conditions that encouraged trying new crops and different breeds of animals

Learning what kinds of plants did well in this soil and climate and the techniques needed to help them thrive was the answer. Peasant farmers, however, were instinctively conservative and resistant to the introduction of new techniques. The high price of failure made the adoption of different crops and techniques extremely risky. Over time, the colonists came to learn that some plants did better than others in the alkaline soil. Grapevines, fruit trees, hard Turkey Red wheat, and potatoes all did well. Different communities noted different outcomes, though. Neu Elft mentions that the soil on hillsides suited the cultivation of grain and grass but not vineyards, while the Wittenberg history notes that "the soil in the hills was best suited for vineyards and grain crops."[13] In settlements such as Sarata and Wittenberg, settled by colonists who came from or had family backgrounds in Württemberg, vineyards were put in soon after the colonies were founded. In Sarata, the Württembergers earned "a lot of sly comments" from the beer-fancying Bavarians in the colony, who changed their tune when wine was produced, commenting that "a glass of wine should not be despised, especially when there is no beer."[14]

In Wittenberg, though colonists had put in grapevines in the first year, they tended them as they had in southern Germany and so cropped them too short, and as a result, the vines did not bear fruit. The Wittenberg history uses this as an example of the acclimatization process necessary for the German colonists to succeed in Bessarabia:

> Not aware about the conditions of land, nor familiar with the climate, they worked the fields, the vineyards and the gardens, the same as they had in their land of origin. They had to experience on their own, that they had to use the land differently to have success, especially with the vineyards.[15]

As colonies began to put in vineyards and fruit trees, their fortunes rose. Over time, the colonists would learn that fruit orchards and vineyards would do well in the steppe soil. Kern notes that "farmers…were skeptical about orchards and vineyards,"[16] but when little came from their attempts at growing grain, they tried and were successful with fruit. The Alt Posttal history mentions that in 1825, soon after the village was founded in 1823 after splitting off from Wittenberg, grapevines were planted in the hills on both sides of the new village. By 1828, the history notes the harvest was abundant, indicating that some lessons about viniculture in Bessarabia had been mastered. The Paris and Alt Elft colonists, generally coming from Prussia, were late in seeing the advantages in planting vineyards and both histories note the settlements would have prospered more quickly if they had planted orchards and vineyards sooner. The Klöstitz history gives the impression in its last paragraph that suggestions from the Welfare Committee urging the planting of vineyards had been taken to heart perhaps as late as the 1840s, and now—that is, in 1848—the vineyards

13. Kurz, "Wittenberg – 1848 Village History."
14. Natterer, "Sarata – 1848 Village History."
15. Kurz, "Wittenberg – 1848 Village History."
16. Kern, *Homeland Book*, 66.

formed the economic means that would hopefully "lift the individual as well as the community as a whole."[17]

By trial and error the colonies began to understand how improve their circumstances in this new environment. Such improvements may have been led, as the Leipzig history suggests, by single families who would attempt new approaches and whose successes would then be imitated by others. It would appear, however, that a major influence teaching the German colonists how to adapt came from their contact with and observation of the Moldavian, Bulgarian, Russian, and Ukrainian populations living near them. While the Germans considered these populations comparatively primitive and thought themselves harder workers and better farmers, the Moldavians and Bulgarians had long experience with the steppe climate and with the crops and animals that did best in the steppelands. The Moldavians and Bulgarians had developed native grapes and hybrids and were famous for their orchards. Russian and Ukrainian peasants had developed varieties of hard wheat that did better than other grains in the steppe soil and even produced reasonably well in seasons when rain was scarce. The first Moldavians and Bulgarians the Germans encountered in the steppelands were herders of cattle, sheep, and horses who were following traditions that archeology now shows to have stretched back to at least 6000 BCE. Local breeds of these animals were smaller in size than those the Germans had known. At first, the Germans looked down on local stock, but, as these dealt better with the hotter summers and colder winters, they came to see value in them. While the village histories do credit the Welfare Committee for its suggestions particularly on vineyards and fruit trees, the histories do not acknowledge the many things gained from observing the grains successfully grown and the animals successfully raised by the Moldavian, Bulgarian, Russian, and Ukrainian peasants living near the Germans.

The Tarutino history highlights three causes for the early difficulties of the colonists that summarize ideas appearing in several of the other histories. To Daniel Martin, the Tarutino historian, the causes were:

1. "Not knowing the language." The colonists could not communicate with other populations living nearby. This is as close as any of the histories come to implying that the colonists were hurt by barriers to learning about what worked in their new environment. What may also be meant here is the point made in the Neu Elft and Wittenberg histories that because the Germans didn't know the local languages, they were often victims of being lied to and cheated.

2. Being "unfamiliar with the characteristics of the soil" at first led to low yields and crop failures. As noted earlier, the Wittenberg history makes this point, commenting that success came when they "used the land differently."[18] In making a similar point, the Alt Arzis history notes that the colonists in that village were ill-prepared for the different conditions in Bessarabia, as they possessed "little understanding or foresight," implying that the farming knowledge they brought with them was not helpful in Bessarabian conditions.[19]

3. The colonists had trouble adjusting to the more extreme climate and to the lack of wood for use in housing and heat. To the Tarutino historian,

17. Schaeff, "Kloestitz – 1848 Village History."
18. Kurz, "Wittenberg – 1848 Village History."
19. Neumann, "Alt Arzis – 1848 Village History."

the colonists had come from "wooded areas" and so were unprepared to deal with the cold winters in Bessarabia where there was little wood to provide shelter and heat. This point is also picked up in the Sarata history where, in listing three reasons for the high number of deaths in the first years of the colony, it included the "bad living quarters" caused by insufficient wood to cover and heat the shelters that had been put up.[20] The Leipzig history makes a similar point when it notes that many died in the first two years of settlement "because they could not adapt to the climate or because of inadequate preparation for the living conditions."[21]

The availability of good water was a critical element for the colonies. Groundwater aided the growth of crops and was especially necessary to maintain livestock; it was, in the early years of the colonies, the main source of liquid for the colonists. Water conditions varied a good deal among the colonies. All had access to water from the rivers and streams next to which most of the German villages were set. These, however, were not always flowing. Snowmelt and rain were the major sources and these waterways often dried up in the hot summers. Many villages built dams to hold river water, and the ponds these formed were generally used as a source of water for animals. Water for human usage typically came from wells and springs. Kulm was greatly favored by the presence of several good springs at its hilltop site; for most of the German settlements, wells formed the major source of water for drinking and cooking. Alt Posttal, Alt Elft, and Neu Elft report wells on each farmstead with the former two reporting water in abundance and of good quality. Borodino and Plotzk had to go deep for water, finding it at 4–5 sažen' (27–35 feet) and 7 sažen' (48 feet), respectively. The depth they had to dig implies that fewer wells were dug and, as in Kulm, common community sources were maintained. Several of the village histories note that at least some of the water in their villages had been contaminated by alkaline salts leeching from the soil into the groundwater. The Katzbach history notes that wells dug on the right side of the Allijaga River were undrinkable; the Neu Elft history, when noting that each farmstead had a well, also adds that "most of them produce salty and bitter water [and] only a few have good drinking water."[22] The lack of good drinking water in Sarata was noted as one of the three major causes of sickness and death in that colony's first years.

## The first years in Bessarabia mixed periods of significant progress with others of major setbacks, as adapting to the new conditions was gradual

Despite the hardships, some villages made rapid progress. The Tarutino history notes the improvements from 1815 to 1818 where "even by poor farming, the harvests

---

20. The two other causes the Sarata history offers for the high mortality in the first years of that colony were: (1) Lack of food—the Sarata colony appears not to have had the promise from the Russian government of supplies of food until the first harvest; using their own funds, the colonists sent away to Kishinev for food supplies, which weren't altogether adequate to feed them, and (2) Lack of good drinking water as the alkaline salts had here penetrated much of the underground water supply so that wells there frequently produced bitter and undrinkable water. Yet another cause of the high death rate in the early years of most Bessarabian colonies was the poor sanitary conditions. The Neu Elft, Teplitz, and other histories mention that dysentery was a major cause of deaths in the first years of the colony. Here the colonists with their limited understanding of this disease were not able to connect the cause of this problem (poor sanitary conditions) with its result.

21. Trautmann, "Leipzig – 1848 Village History."

22. Kurz, "Neu Elft – 1848 Village History."

became plentiful, the cattle started to thrive, and there was no lack of food."[23] The Wittenberg history comments, evidently on the period from 1816 to 1819, that "there were good crops and the sale price for cattle was high," and then goes on to note good harvests in each of the years from 1819 to 1822, though the price of cattle had fallen from 16–20 silver rubles to 3–4.[24] Another sign of Wittenberg's growing prosperity was that by 1815, they had built a farmhouse to be used for schooling and church services, and in 1819, put up a better building for education and religious needs. Each colony in Bessarabia started its existence having to create everything. There were no fields prepared for agriculture, and no houses, wells, or other infrastructures. Thus, in all settlements, the first years brought great improvements. Nonetheless, progress was neither steady nor uniform, and barring only a few individual examples, neither the colonies nor the settlers could have been described as prosperous by 1820.

Beginning in the 1820s, the German villages began to report problems with pests and drought that produced crop failures. Alt Elft indicated that in 1822, the grain crop generally failed from a "special disease" leading the colonists "to use [eat] potatoes which had not fully ripened because of the bad weather."[25] For 1823, a particularly bad year, Wittenberg/Alt Posttal, Beresina, Borodino, Katzbach, Klöstitz, Krasna, Leipzig, Sarata, and Teplitz all reported problems. For Sarata and Wittenberg, the damage came from an infestation of locusts; in Alt Posttal, Katzbach, and Leipzig, likely suffering from the same infestation, the pests were called grasshoppers. Such infestations continued periodically through the 1860s. For Teplitz, the problem was field mice, and in Krasna, it was gophers, with the village history adopting the Russian word *suslik* to describe the problem.[26]

Using the 1848 Bessarabian village histories as a source, Dwayne Janke has charted the descriptions the different histories make of harvest yields and has drawn a pessimistic conclusion.[27] For the period from 1817 to 1848, Janke argues that on average, "the farmers in Bessarabian German colonies had crop yields less than halfway between poor (barely enough to get their sowed seed back) and fair (producing some grain to sell for income)."[28] Given, however, the imprecise and unquantified descriptions of problems, the existence of wide differences between villages, and the surprising actual harvest results from 1824 (as collected by the Welfare Committee) that coincide with one of the worst years reported in the village histories, I feel Janke has overstated the case of problem harvests.

There were, to be sure, several years of problem harvests and years of total crop losses in the period before 1848 that brought hunger and worry at times to all the German villages. Drawing information from the same village histories, I count that problems with harvests occurred, on average, in roughly a quarter of the

23. Martin, "Tarutino – 1848 Village History."
24. Kurz, "Wittenberg – 1848 Village History."
25. Mayer, "Alt Elft – 1848 Village History."
26. Josef Riehl, ed., "History of the Village of Krasna, Bessarabia," trans. B. Wachter von Budde, Germans from Russia Heritage Collection (Fargo: North Dakota State University Libraries, 1948), https://library.ndsu.edu/grhc/history_culture/history/riehl.html. The Germans typically called these pests *erdhase*. See Rudolf Hofer, "Hoffnungstal, Bessarabia," Germans from Russia Heritage Collection (Fargo: North Dakota State University Libraries, 1983), http://library.ndsu.edu/grhc/history_culture/history/hoffnungstal.html.
27. Dwayne Janke, "Ups and Downs of Grain Production in the Early Years of Bessarabian Mother Colonies," *Bessarabian Newsletter* 11, no. 2 (2007): 4–6.
28. Ibid., 4.

27 years from 1821 to 1848 for which data are reported. For Janke's conclusion to be supported, problems with harvests would need to have occurred in at least half of these years. While that, indeed, was the experience of the four villages with the worst results, it was far from what was reported elsewhere. Counting all years in which any problem with the harvests is reported in the village histories, the average number of problem years for the fourteen villages reporting issues is 7.2 of the 27 years, or 26.7 percent. If one counts instead years where a village reports a major or total crop failure, the average number of problem years falls to 2.2 of the total of 27 years or 8.2 percent. Katzbach, with 15 reported years of reduced harvests, and Alt Posttal and Krasna, with 13 reported years of any kind of problem, indicate the worst experiences. Tarutino, with only 1 reported year of reduced harvest, and Brienne, Leipzig, and Neu Arzis, with 2 years each, reflect the best experience. Four villages—Alt Elft, Arzis, Kulm, and Paris—did not report in their village history any problem years, though it is difficult to presume that they had none. It is not easy to get deeper into the statements of crop damage to the actual harvest experiences of the villages reporting damage. Thus, when the Leipzig history notes that "in 1823–24 grasshoppers did much damage…which resulted in crop failures,"[29] the implications range from some damage to a great deal of damage but not seemingly the total loss of field crops.

Throughout Bessarabia, the years 1823, with ten of the fourteen villages reporting problems, and 1833 and 1847, with nine villages reporting problems, were clearly the most difficult times. Again, the ultimate meaning isn't totally certain. The Alt Posttal and Wittenberg histories separately describe their experience as a single village through the harvest of 1823 and their experiences as different but neighboring villages thereafter, but the treatment given, though similar, is not exactly the same. Wittenberg's history notes "fair" crops from 1819 to 1822, but in 1823–25 "really bad" harvests since "locusts destroyed the fields." Crops improved in 1826–27 and again harvests are called "fair."[30] In the Alt Posttal history, the harvests in the years 1822–24 are called "complete crop failures…no grain and field crops were left" as "field mice and swarms of grasshoppers ate everything," and in 1825–27 "the same thing happened."[31] There is no easy explanation for the sharp difference between the two histories on the experience of 1822 and 1826–27. The differences in the treatment of the bad years of 1823–25 seem also more than just ones of tone: the Alt Posttal history leaves the impression of terrible years with virtually no grain crops harvested, while the Wittenberg history suggests poor harvests but some grain produced. Clearly, the years 1823–25 brought great troubles to many Bessarabian German settlements. The Borodino history reports "total crop failures" in the period from 1823 to 1825 with the 1825 crop attacked by locusts and grasshoppers. Katzbach reports total failures from 1822 to 1824 and problems with grasshoppers from 1825 to

29. Trautmann, "Leipzig – 1848 Village History."
30. Kurz, "Wittenberg – 1848 Village History."
31. Kludt, "Alt Posttal – 1848 Village History."

1829. Krasna reports repeated issues from 1822 to 1827,[32] Leipzig, with grasshopper problems in 1823–24, and Sarata, with major locust problems in 1823 and 1826, also note difficulties in some or all of these years.

We have another quite in-depth look at the harvests of 1825 in German Bessarabia that gives a very different perspective of harvest results and even calls into question the claims of "total" crop failure, though it clearly indicates there were great problems with the harvest of summer wheat. In 1825–26, the Welfare Committee conducted a detailed study of the economic status of the German and Bulgarian colonies in Bessarabia and South Russia. Among the statistics they collected by settlement were the amounts of seed planted and the yields produced in calendar year 1825 for different grain crops (see table 5–1). This study will be considered in broader detail further on in this chapter, but here it is worthwhile to consider these data in light of both the reported crop failures noted for the same year in the 1848 village histories as well as the apparent absence of crop failures in Kulm and Tarutino, whose histories made no mention of problems.[33] The figures from the 1825 Welfare Committee study for seed planted and yields of grain are given in *ćetvert'*, an old Russian measure for grain, which as a dry measure was equal to 209.9 liters and as a measure of weight was equal to 126.4 pounds.[34]

The claim made in the Alt Posttal history that 1825 produced a "complete" crop failure is hardly borne out by Welfare Committee statistics. Indeed, Alt Posttal and Wittenberg appear to have had excellent harvests of winter wheat and rye earlier in the year. In comparison with other Bessarabian German villages, including Kulm and Tarutino, whose histories did not report harvest problems, Alt Posttal and

TABLE 5–1.    Seed planted and yields from three grains in the Bessarabian German colonies, 1825

| | Rye | | | Winter wheat | | | Summer wheat | | |
|---|---|---|---|---|---|---|---|---|---|
| | Planted | Yield | X[a] | Planted | Yield | X | Planted | Yield | X |
| Wittenberg | 9.0 | 182.5 | 20.3 | 53.4 | 772.5 | 14.5 | 193.0 | 1,247.0 | 6.5 |
| Alt Posttal | 8.5 | 148.0 | 17.4 | 42.9 | 528.0 | 12.3 | 154.8 | 1,075.0 | 6.9 |
| Borodino | 116.4 | 1,105.0 | 9.5 | 29.5 | 337.0 | 11.4 | 53.0 | 203.8 | 3.8 |
| Katzbach | 44.5 | 382.8 | 8.6 | 24.5 | 223.9 | 9.1 | 41.0 | 158.3 | 3.9 |
| Krasna | 109.6 | 1,097.9 | 10.0 | 24.9 | 312.3 | 12.6 | 83.8 | 369.3 | 4.4 |
| Leipzig | 137.1 | 550.4 | 4.0 | 36.4 | 170.9 | 4.7 | 49.8 | 90.1 | 1.8 |
| Sarata | 8.0 | 166.4 | 20.8 | 8.5 | 118.3 | 13.9 | 18.4 | 396.8 | 21.6 |
| Kulm | 144.9 | 1,702.5 | 11.6 | 61.8 | 370.9 | 6.0 | 148.1 | 486.5 | 3.2 |
| Tarutino | 119.3 | 973.0 | 8.2 | 268.8 | 1,575.3 | 5.9 | 74.6 | 181.4 | 2.4 |

a. The X columns show the number of times greater the yield is over the seed planted.

---

32. Krasna reports "great damage" from gophers in the harvests of 1822–24 and from grasshoppers in the harvests of 1825–27. Brandes indicates the plague of grasshoppers decimating harvests in the years 1823–25 stretched from Bessarabia to Mariupol' in South Russia (*Von den Zaren Adoptiert*, 216). Dwayne Janke, elsewhere, translating an excerpt from the work of Roger Sears dealing with Russian agricultural problems more broadly than Bessarabia, focuses on locusts. Janke, "Locusts! Winged Invaders of South Russia's Steppes," Black Sea German Research, updated March 2012, http://www.blackseagr.org/pdfs/locusts_janke.pdf).

33. Rempel, *German Farming Achievements*, Table 22, Table 29.

34. Richard Hellie, *The Economy and Material Culture of Russia 1600–1725* (Chicago: University of Chicago Press, 1999), 646–48.

Wittenberg even produced decent harvests of summer wheat in the fall. Despite the positive results from rye and winter wheat, the summer wheat harvests for Alt Posttal and Wittenberg, given the large amounts planted, must have been major disappointments. The mention made in the histories of locust and grasshopper infestations in the region would seem a probable cause. Leipzig, Tarutino, Kulm, Borodino, and Katzbach had significantly worse results, with harvest yields of summer wheat less than four times seed planted. Leipzig barely returned seed planted with a harvest yield of 1.8 and Tarutino did little better with a yield of 2.4. Statistics from the 1825 harvests are also provided for other grain crops including those for oats, barley, and millet. Both Alt Posttal and Wittenberg posted healthy returns, especially for barley and millet with yields of roughly sixteen times seed planted for barley and fifty-two times seed planted for millet, and actual yields of roughly 800 četvert' for barley and nearly that for millet. Although these were grains widely used for feed, the returns speak to a healthy agricultural environment.

The difficulties with the crop of summer wheat evidenced by the Welfare Committee statistics should not be read as indicating these German colonies, with the exception of Leipzig, were experiencing problems in feeding themselves. For most of the colonies rye was the major food grain. Rye had been the major grain crop in northern Germany, and the colonists were keeping to crops they knew well. Only in the villages of Alt Posttal, Wittenberg, and Sarata, with populations predominantly from Württemberg and southern Germany, was the summer wheat planted substantially in excess of rye. If the figures for Alt Posttal, Wittenberg, and Sarata are excluded, the dominant position of rye elsewhere is indicated by the fact that it made up 42.8 percent of the edible grain planted in the other colonies.[35] Indeed, from the perspective of the Welfare Committee, what stood out from these results was that the Leipzig colony was having real problems with returns for all three crops, which put them well below the standards set by other settlements. At this time, Leipzig was the third largest of the Bessarabian German colonies after Tarutino and Klöstitz, with a population of 640, a third larger than Wittenberg or Alt Posttal. This is not to say that the reports of crop failures and infestations of pests in 1825 did not represent painful harvest losses or create hardships in other villages, but that only in Leipzig do such losses appear to approach dangerous levels.

A realistic overview of the progress of the German colonies in Bessarabia through 1848 would be one that stresses steady improvements in economic conditions over time that were regularly stalled or interrupted by setbacks. The problems faced were various. Rinderpest, the cattle plague, is reported in twelve villages[36] and likely occurred in all the German villages. Beresina reports the most in the period from 1821 to 1848, with five outbreaks, and four others indicate four separate outbreaks (Borodino, Krasna, Klöstitz, and Wittenberg). As a rule, outbreaks did not hit numbers of villages simultaneously, though five villages—Beresina, Borodino, Sarata, Tarutino, and Wittenberg—reported outbreaks in 1845, the worst year. Sarata's losses are given in numbers of cattle lost and were large: seven hundred in 1828, five

35. Counting the total rye, winter wheat, and summer wheat planted in all colonies, the figures are: summer wheat 39.5 percent, rye 33.8 percent, and winter wheat 26.7 percent. Excluding Alt Posttal, Wittenberg, and Sarata, the figures for the remaining six colonies are: rye 42.8 percent, summer wheat 28.7 percent, and winter wheat 28.5 percent.
36. The village histories reporting incidences of cattle plague are: Alt Posttal, Berezina, Borodino, Brienne, Krasna, Klöstitz, Neu Arzis, Neu Elft, Sarata, Tarutino, Teplitz, and Wittenberg.

hundred in 1835, and six hundred in 1845. The means by which rinderpest spread was unknown in this period. As a major pathway for the disease is contaminated water, Sarata's problems with finding decent water and the resulting use of the pond created by damming the Sarata River as a general source of water for cattle was likely a cause for the serious problems encountered in that village.

While dry conditions are often mentioned, prolonged drought is mentioned less frequently as a significant cause of crop problems. Draught, however, is noted by several villages as affecting the harvests of 1832–34 and 1846–47. The Tarutino history remembers conditions in 1833 as an "immense drought [that] prevented any harvest" and so brought the cost of wheat to a high of 10 silver rubles for a četvert'.[37] The histories also mentioned difficulties occurring because of heavy frosts (Alt Posttal, 1828–29), harsh winters (Tarutino, 1840–41), fires (Beresina, 1822, 1829, 1842, and 1845), earthquakes (Beresina and Brienne, 1829 and 1838; Alt Elft, 1828, 1830, and 1838; and Kulm, 1839, where it dried up producing wells[38]), hail (Alt Arzis, but the year or years are not specified), a plague that killed horses (Wittenberg, 1847–48), and a south wind that blew salt from the lakes, hurting the fruit crops (Sarata notes this as frequently happening).

## Some of the problems the Bessarabian Germans faced were caused by factors coming from outside the German settlements

Several of the village histories also mention difficulties that arose from the passage of troops through Bessarabia in 1828 and 1829. Russia had restarted its war with the Ottoman Empire in 1828, and Russian troops headed for and returning from the fighting beyond the Danube in Romania were billeted at times in the German colonies in Bessarabia or requisitioned food and horses as they passed though. The Borodino history complains that the passage of troops during harvest time in both 1828 and 1829 hindered field work. The Wittenberg history complains that the villagers were not reimbursed for providing food and shelter. The Alt Posttal history mentions it had to billet soldiers in the village and supply teams of horses to the soldiers. The Beresina history notes that the "numerous military units" that marched through the village in 1828–29 made "many demands."[39] Kern notes in his description of Beresina that the villagers were obliged to use their horses to pull cannons from their village all the way to the Danube.[40]

Supplying the needs of the Russian troops in Bessarabia was not without some recompense though. The Teplitz history mentions that the settlement was repaid for the hardships "suffered during the last Turkish war" by a decree issued by Tsar Nicholas I that exempted the colony from taxes for the years 1828–30.[41] In a curiously similar account, Kern, in his discussion of the Beresina colony, reports a story that Tsar Nicholas I had stopped in the village while traveling to the war front in 1828, had lunch with colonist Jacob Esslinger, and responded to Esslinger's request

---

37. Martin, "Tarutino – 1848 Village History."
38. The Kulm history refers to an earthquake in February 1839, though this may be a misdating of the earthquake that the Beresina history dated precisely to January 11, 1838 (O.S.) at 9:00 in the evening.
39. Foerster, "Beresina – 1848 Village History."
40. Kern, *Homeland Book*, 123.
41. Kludt, "Teplitz – 1848 Village History."

for the colony to be exempt from payments for a few years by granting the request.[42] Tsar Nicholas I did quickly pass through Bessarabia in May of 1828,[43] but I have found no indication in Russian sources that he stopped in or passed through any of the German colonies. There is no mention of a visit by Tsar Nicholas in the 1848 Beresina history, which surely would have noted this extraordinary event for the village. Moreover, the court protocols of access to the tsar in 1828 were quite strict and limited to persons of a noble rank. Even in stopping to rest in the midst of rapid and tiring travel, the tsar was not likely to lunch and converse with people he and his entourage would have considered only marginally above, and not very different from, Russian peasants. The story as a result sounds apocryphal. While Tsar Nicholas I may not have dined with Jacob Esslinger, it does appear that Nicholas I, following the successful Russian military campaign in Romania, did exempt the Bessarabian Germans (and quite likely other Bessarabians) from tax payments for three years. In a complex segment of the Katzbach history, it is mentioned that in addition to extending the ten-year grace period for paying back the funds loaned to establish the colonists in Bessarabia for another ten years, the colonists also received, after the tsar's "completed campaign," three more years free of tax. This is what the Teplitz history also reports, and possibly what the Beresina story sought to explain. The taxes for which the colonies received this three-year grace period were the normal state tax obligations. The German colonies, by the mid-1820s, were obliged to pay such taxes following the end of a ten-year period of freedom from all taxes, granted them to help them become established. Unlike the repayment of the state loan that had provided the colonists with building and farming equipment, which had by 1824 been put off for a second ten-year period, the colonies were, by the time of the 1828 Russian campaign in Romania, obligated to pay the normal annual taxes. The Russian government no doubt also saw the act of granting a grace period from taxes in southern Bessarabia as a means to deal simply with any claims due for requisitions and billeting.

While fighting in Romania, some of the Russian troops became infected with the plague. Returning to Russia, they stopped in the German villages in Bessarabia, where they spread the disease. In Neu Elft, 15 people died, and 180 in Alt Arzis, but the greatest impact was in Klöstitz. There, between July and November 1829, 365 people died of the plague, among whom were 14 people who died on one day, September 14, 1829 (O.S.). Villages were quarantined to prevent the spread of disease. A second disease epidemic occurred in 1831, when cholera spread through Bessarabia and many of the German villages were affected. The likely cause of so many villages suffering episodes of this disease at once was the import of contaminated food into the German villages. Once individual villagers became ill, poor sanitation within the German villages spread the disease further.[44] In total, the village histories reported 415

---

42. Kern, *Homeland Book*, 123. Kern notes that for this story he is quoting a report in the Odessa "Calendar" for 1908.

43. He left St. Petersburg May 7, 1828 (O.S.), and, traveling by coach and horse, reached Braila on the Danube by the 24th of May (O.S.).

44. In general, cholera is caused by the fecal contamination of the food and water supply, but it can be spread by contaminated food, especially sea food brought in from outside an area. A pandemic of cholera spread from India to Russia and thence to Europe in 1817; it is now thought the disease was spread via the dumping of contaminated bilge water kept in ships that had visited India. The Alt Elft history, reflecting some memory of this pandemic, reports the rumor that the epidemic of 1831 came to Russia from Persia. There were also outbreaks of cholera in 1848 in Klöstitz and a more serious one in 1855 during the time of the Crimean War in Alt Elft, Beresina, Klöstitz, and Tarutino.

cholera deaths with nine villages reporting losses. This, however, is only slightly more than the toll from the plague alone in Klöstitz. Alt Arzis and Tarutino suffered the worst from the cholera epidemic, losing 82 and 81 people respectively. The Tarutino and Kulm histories both note that cholera victims were generally adults. The Kulm history emphasizes the intensity of the epidemic: "In one month 30 people died most in the age range of 30–50 years. The disease was deadly, for example, people could be healthy in the morning and working in the fields [and then] suddenly became ill and were dead after a few hours."[45]

## Other problems the Bessarabian Germans faced, they created for themselves

Not all the troubles the German colonists experienced in their first years in Bessarabia were caused by outside factors. Five of the village histories suggest a significant rise in social problems in their communities. The improved economic conditions, the significant increase in personal freedom, the general isolation from outside authority, and—in particular—the ready availability of wine and spirits drew people away from their strict religious practices, from educating their children, from their traditional customs of mutual community support, and also from productive labor. The Tarutino history reports that problems started to arise soon after the difficulties of founding the settlement had been overcome: "After [1818] they started to prosper and with it came corruption of their customs. They hardly cared for church or schooling, indulging in eating and drinking was spreading like cancer; rowdiness and thefts were a daily dilemma."[46]

The Leipzig history scolds the early colonists for being "defiant and [living] sinful and boisterous lives." No one respected authority and "every man thought he was right." Apart from individual failings, Adam Trautmann, a Leipzig church teacher who wrote the 1848 village history, blamed two other causes. Religious life was in "disarray" and the youth of the community, through the poor efforts of the village to provide religious training, were described as being an "ethical ruin" where "licentiousness and demoralization went hand in hand." Trautmann also blamed a disorganized civil government with "cowardly" mayors for not correcting matters. As a result, citizens behaved as though "there was no God and showed no obedience to authority."[47] Evidently, the poor situation in Leipzig gave the Welfare Committee reason to issue a "warning" to the community, which caused the village to improve conditions and behavior. Christian Minderlin, the author of the Brienne history, implies a similar situation there where the intervention of the Welfare Committee together with improved local administration righted a "deeply troubled" community. The Wittenberg history also implies that an intervention of the Welfare Committee prevented the erosion of the healthy customary standards of the community: "Had the authorities not intervened with rules and regulations to upkeep customs and maintain order; and had there not been decent citizens among the settlers, who led with good examples, the customs would have been lost and carelessness would have taken the upper hand."[48]

---

45. Straub, "Kulm – 1848 Village History."
46. Martin, "Tarutino – 1848 Village History."
47. Trautmann, "Leipzig – 1848 Village History."
48. Kurz, "Wittenberg – 1848 Village History."

The Sarata history notes that village authorities there had sought to correct similar social problems. Teens were now forbidden to gather in the evenings "since [this] had brought them to the edge of ruin before," and other regulations were put in place to restrict day-long celebrations of weddings and baptisms that led to "eating and drinking without measure and silly behavior."[49] In Kern's description of the growth and development of the Paris colony, he implies that similar problems may have existed there. Kern notes that "after vineyards were built, the settlers prospered in spite of personal wine use which was fairly high."[50]

## Over time the German colonies made distinct economic progress

The difficulties and setbacks the German colonists faced in establishing themselves in Bessarabia formed a major theme in both the 1848 village histories and in Kern's and other accounts that supplement the village histories with memories of the twentieth-century villagers. The theme of difficulties and setbacks plays counterpoint, though, to another that is at least equally important in describing the early life of the colonies: the gradual improvement in living standards, the production of surplus crops from the fields and fruit from the orchards and vineyards, the growth in the size of animal herds, and the start of local craft businesses. With the development of Odessa as a major entrepôt for agricultural surplus, German farmers had an outlet and economic prosperity grew. When the German colonists came to Bessarabia they planned to recreate the grain farming and vegetable agriculture they were used to in Prussian Poland and Württemberg. Many may have brought seed with them. The steppe earth, as noted earlier, was very different from the wet clays they were familiar with in Poland. Schmidt reports the upper layer of soil had a humus content of 10 percent in comparison to the more normal 2 percent, and this humus rich layer was in many places 1.5 meters deep.[51] Other variables, like the high alkaline content of the soil, its radical drop in fertility when precipitation was low, its resistance to familiar means of improvement such as manuring, and the far broader swings in climate, with extremely cold winters and blazing hot summers, caused familiar grains and crops to do poorly in Bessarabia. The conservative resistance to introducing new crops or introducing different agricultural techniques meant that the adjustment to the new conditions in Bessarabia went slowly among the Germans.

Over time, the Germans became familiar with local plant varieties mastered by the Russians and Ukrainians. Barley, rye, and spelt were replaced by hard winter and hard summer wheats. These did far better in the heat and cold, were more disease resistant, and provided a higher protein content than the grains the Germans were used to. Mutschall's history of Tarutino notes that the impetus for introduction of Arnaut, a hard winter wheat, came from a suggestion made by the Welfare Committee in 1827.[52] Hard wheat varieties also produced higher yields. With the steady growth of grain shipments to Western Europe from Odessa, Germans in Bessarabia gradually came to realize that they had a lucrative market for the surplus

---

49. Natterer, "Sarata – 1848 Village History."
50. Kern, *Homeland Book*, 60. The Lichtental village history also makes reference to the prevention of "dissolute living by gluttonous eating and drinking." Hahn, "Lichtental – 1848 Village History."
51. Schmidt, *Die Deutschen aus Bessarabien*, 43.
52. Wilhelm Mutschall, "History of the Community of Tarutino from 1814 to 1934," *Heritage Review* 43, no. 2 (2013): 5.

from their harvests. However, they would need to use different techniques. The Alt Arzis history notes that the four-crop rotation farmers were accustomed to didn't work in Bessarabia. The Sarata history indicates that fields that had been farmed for five to six years needed to be left fallow for another six to eight years to regain their fertility. Kern reports on a four-year system used in Plotzk at least by 1860 that produced quite positive results. A field was left to hay for three to four years and then summer wheat was planted for two successive years. In the third year, the field was planted mainly with barley, with a third in oats, and in the fourth year, winter rye and winter wheat were planted before restarting the cycle with hay.[53] It took time, however, for the Germans to make these adjustments. The 1825 Welfare Committee study indicates, as noted earlier, that most of the German settlements were still planting rye as their major grain.[54]

Fruit trees, which in Prussia were typically confined to a family's small farmyard, were a specialty in Bessarabia and became, over time, a major money crop for the Germans. Colonists from Württemberg were familiar with growing fruit and may have been the first to understand and master the potential in Bessarabia, though all who had contact with Moldavians and Bulgarians were exposed to the existence of successful orchards. Fruit trees ultimately became plentiful in all the German villages with Alt and Neu Elft, Sarata, and Teplitz particularly noted as centers. The Teplitz history notes with pride that "two farmers reaped a profit [from their orchards] of more than 100 silver rubles in one year."[55] Pear, plum, cherry, apple, and apricot trees initially did well and, as will be discussed further on in this chapter, were grown in large numbers. Several of the 1848 village histories, however, report that their fruit trees weren't long lived. Sarata's history reports that they died after ten to twelve years, Wittenberg's after twelve to fifteen years, and Neu Elft's after fifteen to twenty years. The Borodino, Gnadental, Katzbach, Klöstitz, Lichtental, and Tarutino histories also report that their fruit trees weren't lasting. Solutions were evidently found because the statistical evidence available from later Welfare Committee economic studies show fruit as a significant economic factor for the German settlements in Bessarabia, as it was for Bessarabian farms of all nationalities.[56] Bessarabian melons and tree-grown fruits became well-noted and prized in the Ukraine and Russia, and their perceived value is attested by the fact that the huge open market in Kiev was and is still called the Bessarabian Market (*Bessarabs'kij Rinok*).

Vineyards became an even more important piece of the agricultural economy in every German colony in Bessarabia. Vineyards growing native grapes and the production of wine and brandy from them were long-standing traditional enterprises among the Moldavians and Bulgarians. As noted earlier, German settlements with large numbers of Württembergers such as Sarata and Alt Posttal were early adopters in planting vineyards. The 1825 Welfare Committee economic survey shows these two settlements as leading in the number of grapevines planted at 67,245 and 31,485 respectively, followed by Klöstitz (17,790), Tarutino (16,261) and Beresina (12,749) as the next leading centers. Far and away the major center for the cultivation of

53. Kern, *Homeland Book*, 62.
54. There is a longer discussion of the changing field rotation systems in German Bessarabia in chapter VI.
55. Kludt, "Teplitz – 1848 Village History."
56. The 1848 Sarata Village History suggests, for example, that planting new trees on land that had been unused or left fallow worked best as "new plants replacing old ones, [didn't] thrive well."

grapevines, however, was the colony of Schabo, founded in 1823 along the estuary of the Dniester River below Akkerman. Schabo was settled by French Protestants from Switzerland who had been invited to settle in Russia by the Russian government specifically with the cultivation of grapes in mind. The land on which Schabo was located was already covered with grapevines left from the time of Turkish control. The 1825 economic survey reported fourteen families and thirty-nine people in the Schabo colony,[57] but already 104,000 grapevines, most of which, it is presumed, they found there.[58] Viniculture using both native Moldavian and imported grape varieties did well in the German villages where the sandy soil was closer to the surface. Vineyards became attractive to the Germans when they realized they did better during dry summers when the heat stunted other crops.[59] Apart from home use, wine production was kept in barrels and large jugs in baskets that were sold locally or offered by the mug from farm wagons at local fairs and markets. Except for wine produced in Schabo, wine made in the Bessarabian colonies was not generally exported from the province before 1860.[60]

For millennia, the steppe grasslands had been ideal natural pastures for animals and were used as such by the many nomadic groups who had preceded the Germans. Horses, cattle, and sheep in particular thrived in this habitat. As noted in the 1848 village histories, the most successful Moldavians and Bulgarians the German colonists encountered in Bessarabia were those who owned herds of animals. It would appear that soon after their settlement in Bessarabia, wealthy colonists bought local animals and other colonists did so as quickly as they were able. The Wittenberg history notes that colonists were selling cattle there at least by 1819. Many histories report the importance of animal herds in raising the level of prosperity in their village with Sarata (cattle), Klöstitz (cattle), Brienne (horses), Teplitz (horses and cattle), and Kulm (cattle, horses, and sheep) making especially positive mentions. The Kulm Heimatbuch mentions the importance of Karakul sheep, a hardy breed that did well in the extremes of the Bessarabian climate, though this likely refers to practices in the later parts of the nineteenth century and the early twentieth. The Sarata history notes that the "community used most of their land for grazing cattle," as grain did not do well there. As the size of herds expanded in the settlements, markets were created. Tarutino was permitted to hold a market for cattle and fruit every fortnight on Tuesdays. Alt Arzis and Sarata also were later permitted markets, with the one in Alt Arzis particularly noted for the

57. Kern, relying on local information in his study (*Homeland Book*, 194), reports that only two families had settled in Schabo in 1823, followed by eight more who came in 1826. The Welfare Committee survey based on data collected in 1825 indicates that there were more settlers in place sooner than local tradition remembered.

58. Rempel, *German Farming Achievements*. Details on the number of grapevines in Sarata come from Table 27, details on the number of grapevines in Alt Posttal, Klöstitz, Tarutino, and Beresina from Table 20, details on the number of grapevines in Schabo from Table 34, and details on the population in Schabo from Table 31.

59. Hugo Häfner, in his detailed article on twentieth-century Bessarabian wine production, notes the cultivation of "black Salfiner, Zottler, Sereksia, Blue Portuguese, Black Fat One, Färber and Bordelaise (Bordeaux)" for red wine and "white Salfiner, Grünlauber, Hartschalige, [and] Fruhweiß" for white wine. Häfner, "Wine Growing—An Illustrated Documentation," *Heritage Review* 37, no. 4 (2007): 12. Gotthilf Vogel, in his reminiscences of agricultural life in Kulm, notes growing hirtop grapes. Vogel, "A Year's Review of Agriculture and Grape Growing" in "Heimatbuch der Gemeinde Kulm," *Heritage Review* 14, no. 2 (1984): 30–31.

60. Häfner, "Wine Growing." Much of the wine produced in the German colonies was sold and consumed within Bessarabia. The best wine produced in Bessarabia was produced in Schabo, whose notoriety was helped both by the experience of the Swiss winemakers who immigrated there and by the settlement's easy access to the important Odessa market by boat.

sale of horses. Starting in the period just before the Crimean War, cattle and horses were also driven to Odessa or sold to dealers who drove stock to the markets there.

The Welfare Committee encouraged all the German settlements to plant trees as the steppe lacked woodlands. In the Bessarabian steppelands, wood throughout the nineteenth and early twentieth centuries was an important, scarce, and valuable commodity. A portion of the common land in each village appears to have been devoted to this. In some villages, such as Kulm, where the planted forest area was located in the meadowland along the Kogil'nik River and was established in the early days of the colony,[61] the trees did well and wood served as a saleable asset. However, many of the village histories report that only acacias—that is, American poplars—seemed to do well. Most trees were not able to take deep root and so did not survive beyond twenty years. The Wittenberg history presumes the cause to be the hard-baked clay soil underneath the topsoil, which prevented trees from spreading roots and absorbing sufficient moisture.

A number of the German settlements benefited from the availability of stone on village land and created quarries. These provided stone for building houses in that village as well as a source of village income, as the stone could be sold to other villages that had no sources of building stone on their land. Alt Posttal, Beresina, Borodino, Brienne, Klöstitz, and Teplitz all mention the advantages of finding stone and creating quarries on village land. The Alt Arzis, Friedenstal, Gnadental, and Leipzig histories report having to import stone, and the Paris history notes citizens there had to purchase it.

## The early economic progress achieved by the German colonies is evidenced by the detailed 1825 Welfare Committee survey

The earliest detailed data on the progress of the German colonies in Bessarabia come from the Welfare Committee's thorough survey of the economic health of the German colonies in South Russia and Bessarabia that was compiled in 1826 and based on harvest and other data from 1825. The survey enumerated the population of each settlement and gathered data on the number of cattle, sheep, horses, and pigs, the amount of rye, winter and summer wheat, buckwheat, oats, barley, millet, potatoes, peas, beans, and corn planted and harvested, and the number of apple, pear, plum, and cherry trees as well as grapevines planted in each village.[62]

The Welfare Committee survey confirms that sixteen of the German colonies in Bessarabia were well-established by 1825.[63] Healthy yields were evident for some plantings of grain, despite the reports of crop failures we have seen occur-

---

61. The Kulm history refers to giving attention to the condition of the forest "after the first year of the settlement." In contrast, the Klöstitz and Paris histories, like several others, refer to the recently planted forests, implying they are recent to 1848. The oak forest in Kulm was badly damaged by Russian troops quartering nearby in the late 1870s and was totally destroyed during World War I. The Google satellite view indicates that as of the early twenty-first century, the woods have not been regrown.

62. The Welfare Committee economic survey material quoted and discussed in the following pages is taken from Rempel, *German Farming Achievements*. Data concerning the colonies in Bessarabia come from Tables 16–37 of the survey.

63. In 1825, there were nineteen German colonies in Bessarabia. Details for Schabo, founded two years earlier, suggest that the colony was not yet self-supporting, and those for Sarata, only three years old, were just starting to turn positive. As data on Neu Arzis are for the most part lumped together with those for Alt Arzis in the survey material, except for population counts, I have not separated the two in the tables that follow. Thus, in concluding that sixteen colonies show material progress in establishing themselves, I am excluding Schabo and Sarata and not counting Neu Arzis as a separate colony.

ring in 1825. There were also large numbers of grapevines and fruit trees growing. The livestock count was already decent, with large numbers of cattle holdings in Bessarabia that were well in excess of the livestock counts of eighteenth-century fullholder Prussian peasants. The positive yields in grain produced food supplies well in keeping with Hagen's estimates of Prussian peasant household consumption for eighteenth-century fullholders. The different varieties of grain grown and the large numbers of cattle, sheep, and fruit trees further suggest that the diet of German families in Bessarabia was likely better and more varied than that of peasants in Prussia. The survey does indicate a good deal of variation between the colonies and also implies the beginnings of some specialization. In the survey, most colonies are clustered around the averages for the group, but a few colonies stand out as doing materially better or worse than others.

The data collected by the Welfare Committee show that as of late 1825 or early 1826, the German colonies in Bessarabia plus Schabo had grown to a population of 8,954 people (see table 5–2). The wide differences in population are the most striking figures here. The new and still growing colonies—Katzbach, Sarata, and especially the recently founded Schabo—are the smallest, along with the three villages that split in two. At the other end of the spectrum is Tarutino, the largest colony by a good margin, with 914 citizens. It is about 20 percent larger than the next colony, Klöstitz, with a population of 772, and 40 percent larger than the third and fourth, Leipzig at 640 and Beresina at 638. Tarutino would remain a major center among

TABLE 5–2. **Population counts for the Bessarabian German colonies, 1825–26**

| Colonies | Males | Females | Total | Families | Founding families |
|----------|-------|---------|-------|----------|-------------------|
| Alt Elft | 156 | 166 | 322 | 82 | 63 |
| Alt Posttal | 240 | 211 | 451 | 71 | 69 |
| Alt Arzis | 225 | 232 | 457 | 91 | 123[a] |
| Beresina | 340 | 298 | 638 | 140 | 139 |
| Borodino | 313 | 293 | 606 | 123 | 115 |
| Brienne | 189 | 180 | 369 | 89 | 84 |
| Katzbach | 134 | 124 | 258 | 55 | 55 |
| Klöstitz | 403 | 369 | 772 | 142 | 134 |
| Krasna | 270 | 251 | 521 | 138 | 112 |
| Kulm | 378 | 316 | 604 | 119 | 108 |
| Neu Arzis | 93 | 92 | 185 | 43 | — |
| Neu Elft | 126 | 132 | 258 | 63 | 63 |
| Leipzig | 317 | 323 | 640 | 138 | 128 |
| Paris | 276 | 260 | 536 | 128 | 121 |
| Sarata | 226 | 209 | 435 | 98 | 60 |
| Schabo | 25 | 14 | 39 | 14 | 14 |
| Tarutino | 506 | 408 | 914 | 194 | 136 |
| Teplitz | 191 | 185 | 376 | 113 | 98 |
| Wittenberg | 254 | 229 | 483 | 82 | 69 |
| **Total** | 4,662 | 4,292 | 8,954 | 1,923 | 1,691 |

a. The 123 founding families combine those for Alt and Neu Arzis.

the German colonies throughout the period of settlement in Bessarabia, challenged only starting at the end of the nineteenth century by Sarata and Alt Arzis.

Males outnumbered females in most of the colonies. The difference in number between the sexes is striking for Tarutino, with 24 percent more males than females; Kulm, with a 19 percent spread, and Alt Posttal, with a 13 percent spread, also had male populations that were roughly 10 percent larger than the female populations. One reason for this pattern may be the fact that, as noted in the discussion of the 1815 Kulm census in the previous chapter, the early immigrants included numbers of young unmarried men. In four colonies, however, the opposite pattern existed, with women slightly outnumbering men.

A comparison between the number of families listed in the 1825 survey and the totals offered in the 1848 histories for the number of founding families suggests that a material increase in population occurred since the founding of the colonies. The comparison clearly suggests some population growth. Tarutino shows the greatest growth among the older colonies, with an increase of 42.7 percent in the number of families, followed by Teplitz and Kulm at just over 15 percent. The new colony of Sarata, founded in 1822–23 by sixty families, shows the greatest growth of all, moving from sixty families in 1823 to ninety-eight families at the end of 1825 as it grew toward its allotted total of one hundred farmsteads with new arrivals from Germany.

Earlier in this chapter we looked at yields for grain harvests for some villages to show that reports of crop failures in 1825 were not so extensive. Here, in order to eliminate size bias from the village comparisons, I would like to look at grain yield results on a per-family basis for all the German villages. Table 5–3 shows in četvert' the total harvested grain of each village divided by the number of families.

On average, the 1825 harvest in the Bessarabian colonies produced fair—even decent—results, with only summer wheat coming in at less than four times seed planted. In his culling of the data from the eighteenth-century von Kleist estate records on land in and around the village of Stavenow in Brandenburg, Hagen notes yields for rye, the major grain crop there, typically coming in at three times seed planted, which is far below the 1825 survey yields for rye in the German colonies in Bessarabia.[64] Hagen also calculates from this same data that for a fullholder family of five (including two children over six) in eighteenth-century Brandenburg, the annual household grain consumption would have been around 33 bushels of rye plus 19 of barley.[65] The equivalent Russian measurements would be 5.5 četvert' of rye and 3.2 of barley. Most of the German colonies produced at least 5.5 četvert' of rye, providing both food and seed recovery. Exceptions were Alt Elft, the clearly troubled settlements of Teplitz and Leipzig, and the colonies dominated by South Germans (Alt Posttal, Sarata, Teplitz, and Wittenberg) for whom rye was a less popular grain for human consumption. The average return on barley meets the Brandenburg comparison, but this is only because a few colonies had excellent returns: Only five of the seventeen colonies, or 29.4 percent, averaged harvests of more than 3.2 četvert' of barley per family. On the other hand, the addition of winter and summer wheat crops, not typically grown for peasant consumption in Prussia, would supplement barley in Bessarabia and, for almost all the colonies, would more than cover the

---

64. Hagen, *Ordinary Prussians*, 189–90.
65. Ibid., 211.

TABLE 5–3.    Per-family grain yields for the Bessarabian German colonies, 1825–26

| | Rye | Winter wheat | Summer wheat | Barley | Millet |
|---|---|---|---|---|---|
| Alt Elft | 4.7 | 4.5 | 1.1 | 2.0 | 1.3 |
| Alt Posttal | 2.1 | 7.4 | 15.1 | 11.2 | 10.1 |
| Arzis | 9.1 | 3.6 | 0.8 | 1.1 | 1.4 |
| Beresina | 8.7 | 5.0 | 2.6 | 3.1 | 3.2 |
| Borodino | 9.0 | 2.7 | 1.7 | 2.8 | 2.2 |
| Brienne | 12.2 | 1.6 | 4.1 | 1.6 | 1.2 |
| Katzbach | 7.0 | 4.1 | 2.9 | 2.9 | 2.5 |
| Klöstitz | 9.5 | 3.5 | 4.0 | 3.7 | 3.2 |
| Krasna | 8.0 | 2.3 | 2.7 | 2.2 | 1.8 |
| Kulm | 14.3 | 3.1 | 4.1 | 6.2 | 7.5 |
| Leipzig | 4.0 | 1.2 | 0.7 | 1.3 | 2.4 |
| Neu Elft | 6.5 | 4.5 | 1.4 | 1.0 | 0.9 |
| Paris | 8.6 | 3.1 | 0.5 | 2.0 | 2.2 |
| Sarata | 1.6 | 1.2 | 4.0 | 4.0 | 3.1 |
| Schabo | — | — | — | — | — |
| Tarutino | 5.0 | 8.1 | 0.9 | 3.0 | 2.2 |
| Teplitz | — | 1.8 | 1.6 | 2.0 | 0.4 |
| Wittenberg | 2.2 | 9.4 | 15.2 | 10.2 | 9.3 |
| **Average**[a] | 7.3 | 3.9 | 2.9 | 3.3 | 3.0 |
| **Return over seed** | 9.5x | 8.5x | 3.9x | 7.9x | 27.8x |

a. The figures for yields in četvert' of summer wheat for the villages of Arzis and Brienne were not listed and I have estimated them using the figures given for the shocks of summer wheat that were cut in the harvest for those two villages (which establish that they did have a harvest). The figure for millet yield for Kulm was also left out but was apparently included in the total line for the group of colonies listed along with Kulm. Thus, it was assumed that the difference between the total figure and the sum of the village figures that were provided was the Kulm harvest.

shortfall. Teplitz and Leipzig were exceptions, with poor results in all the grains sown. Perhaps in 1825 Teplitz was still showing the effects of the major loss of adult lives that attended its founding. Leipzig was a large colony but clearly not doing well. It was generally filled with immigrants with a Prussian background and so rye would have formed a basic staple as the colonists sought to recreate their homeland experience. Yet the results for rye, though producing four times the seed planted and four četvert' of grain per family, falls well behind the other non–South German colonies, and in other grains Leipzig barely recovers seed. Finally, given that it reported major crop failures for 1825 in its 1848 history, one is again struck by the very positive results Alt Posttal achieved. On a comparative basis, its results were substantially above the averages achieved in the other colonies for all these grains, other than for rye.

The 1825 survey suggests that the food supply available to the Germans in Bessarabia well exceeded in both amounts and variety what Hagen indicates was typical for peasants on the von Kleist estates in Brandenburg. A major reason for this was the fact that the colonists had far more land in Bessarabia, which allowed for more plantings and room for more animals. A second important reason was that, unlike in Prussia, in Bessarabia they were not obliged to turn at least half of their produce into cash in order to pay land tenure fees and state taxes. When tax payments began, villages were assessed as communities, rather than by individual families. In general, taxes in Russia were well below the demands that Prussia had made. The 1848 Wittenberg Village History lists the various taxes, presumably of the prior year, which add up to 1,864.19 rubles for the community as a whole or 24.21 rubles for each of the seventy-seven families. Brandes, using other sources, notes taxes in 1854 for a Bessarabian German family with 60 desjatina came to 12.28 rubles.[66] Beyond the wider number of grains grown, the colonists also grew buckwheat, beans, corn, lentils, potatoes, and oats. Oats, as well as the extensive amounts of hay harvested, were used for animals. On the smaller plots peasants had before coming to Bessarabia, they were unable to maintain or feed anything more than a few animals over the winter. As a result, meat was not normally part of their diet in Prussia. As will be argued below, this was not the case in Bessarabia. Fruit too, as will be discussed below, formed a greater part of their diet. The data from the 1825 Welfare Committee survey supports the idea that the colonists by then enjoyed a broad and healthy diet. The 1848 Tarutino history reports in this regard that after the first years, "even by poor farming harvests became plentiful…and there was no lack of food."[67]

Although the numbers of animals reported in the German colonies in 1825 were not large, they were already materially larger than the numbers owned by peasants in Prussia and southern Germany. Cattle and sheep widely outnumbered other domesticated animals, though it is likely that as the survey numbers come from the winter of 1825–26, the number of pigs had been reduced, perhaps materially, by the annual fall slaughter.

With fruit trees, too, the numbers reported in 1825 would appear greatly in excess of the number that might have been supported on the small plots peasants owned in southern Germany, or on the somewhat larger plots in the far less fruit-friendly climate of Prussia. Though the chart below combines the totals for all fruit trees, it should be noted that plum trees far outnumbered other fruit trees, forming 69 percent of the total. While the plums they produced would have been consumed in several ways, they also were used for making brandy, as several of the 1848 village histories mention. Table 5–4 shows the number of fruit trees, grapevines, and various domesticated animals calculated on a per-family basis for each of the German colonies in Bessarabia in 1825.

In 1825, cattle formed the largest number of domesticated stock kept by the German villages. Even the recently established colonies of Katzbach and Sarata had relatively large per-family numbers. By 1825, there appears to have been a thriving market for cattle. The Wittenberg history notes that in the period from 1819 to 1825, the colonists depended chiefly on cattle sales to produce income, though prices in 1825 were in the range of 3–4 silver rubles per animal, down from the period from 1817 to 1821, when there were fewer cattle available and the going price was 16–20 silver rubles. Sheep, which by the late 1830s had become a far more prominent part of the economy for the Bessarabian Germans, were in 1825 just beginning to gather attention, with a few

66. Brandes, *Von den Zaren Adoptiert*, 166.
67. Martin, "Tarutino – 1848 Village History."

TABLE 5–4.  **Per-family holdings of fruit trees, grapevines, and animals in Bessarabian German colonies, 1825–26**

| | Cattle | Horses | Sheep | Pigs | Fruit trees | Grapevines |
|---|---|---|---|---|---|---|
| Alt Elft | 8.2 | 1.5 | 2.9 | 0.3 | 16.1 | — |
| Alt Posttal | 16.4 | 3.0 | 3.5 | 1.2 | 15.0 | 443.5 |
| Arzis | 9.1 | 1.6 | 3.1 | 0.4 | 2.2 | 17.4 |
| Beresina | 12.9 | 2.2 | 3.9 | 1.6 | 11.7 | 91.1 |
| Borodino | 11.7 | 2.1 | 1.4 | 1.3 | 10.3 | — |
| Brienne | 8.5 | 1.1 | — | 0.4 | 2.6 | 31.9 |
| Katzbach | 13.1 | 2.2 | 2.5 | 0.6 | — | — |
| Klöstitz | 13.1 | 2.6 | 2.8 | 1.1 | 37.6 | 125.3 |
| Krasna | 10.1 | 1.9 | 1.9 | 0.5 | 32.0 | 67.7 |
| Kulm | 14.4 | 2.7 | 7.5 | 1.2 | 44.3 | 79.2 |
| Leipzig | 8.9 | 1.7 | 4.8 | 1.3 | 13.7 | 9.7 |
| Neu Elft | 8.9 | 1.4 | 2.5 | 0.2 | — | — |
| Paris | 7.3 | 1.8 | 4.4 | 0.6 | 22.2 | 4.6 |
| Sarata | 10.3 | 1.4 | 0.4 | 1.2 | 51.0 | 686.2 |
| Schabo | 0.1 | 0.2 | — | — | 63.1 | 7,428.1 |
| Tarutino | 10.1 | 1.8 | 4.1 | 0.7 | 31.2 | 83.1 |
| Teplitz | 5.9 | 1.7 | 0.4 | 0.3 | 1.4 | 3.6 |
| Wittenberg | 15.1 | 2.8 | 2.1 | 1.5 | 13.5 | 129.3 |
| **Average** | 10.6 | 2.0 | 3.2 | 0.9 | 20.6 | 174.7 |

villages taking the lead. The 1825 survey, however, does indicate that the sheep flocks in German Bessarabia were all "coarsely wooled" and thus were not the Merinos later raised profitably in abundance. The relatively large holdings of sheep in Leipzig, which in other areas had shown such poor results, may be an indication that the Welfare Committee, which regularly encouraged the growth of sheep holdings, had sensed trouble and already begun to intervene in that village's economy.

Hagen's statistics from the eighteenth century from the village of Blüthen in Brandenburg indicate that fullholders there—that is, the most well-to-do peasants— had sufficient fodder to keep five to six animals over the winter.[68] The 1825 statistics from German Bessarabia are from a comparable season, as they date to the late fall or early winter. The average village stock holdings in Bessarabia all exceed Hagen's count from Prussia as they range from a high of 25.8 animals per family in Kulm to a low of 8.3 in Teplitz. Hagen also provides figures for the mature livestock summer-time holdings of Stavenow, Brandenburg, peasant farmers during 1721–71.[69] These indicate that Prussian fullholders had on a per-family average more horses and sheep but significantly fewer cattle than the Germans in Bessarabia in 1825 (see table 5–5).

The larger number of horses kept by the Prussian peasants points to interesting differences from Bessarabia. Hagen speculates that the large number of horses kept in Prussia—as an extreme example in 1754, families from the village of Glövzin kept between six and nine horses—was tied to an increasing market demand driven by

---

68. Hagen, *Ordinary Prussians*, 198.
69. Ibid., 201. This table also indicates a summertime average of 3.8 pigs.

TABLE 5–5.    **Average number of animals, Bessarabian Germans vs. Stavenow peasants**

|  | Horses | Cattle | Sheep | Pigs |
|---|---|---|---|---|
| Bessarabian averages, 1825–26 | 2.0 | 10.6 | 3.2 | 0.9 |
| Stavenow Brandenburg summertime averages, 1721–71 | 5.0 | 4.9 | 8.7 | 2.0 |

the army requirements, and the needs of the peasants for cash to settle tenure and state obligations. In the half century for which he has statistics, Hagen notes that the appraised value of horses "nearly tripled propelled by population growth, rising grain prices and army demand."[70] Extra horses may well have been useful in fulfilling the obligatory labor required to hold tenure on the Stavenow estates. In Bessarabia, in contrast, cattle appear to have drawn greater market interest and have been an important food source as well. This was not true in Prussia, where the limitations on the amount of grain peasants could keep after the needs of food, taxes, and rent made larger herds of cattle more difficult to keep.

In 1825, the German colonies were just beginning to develop extensive vineyards. The average holding of 174.7 grapevines per family, however, is exaggerated by the large number of vines that already existed at the site of the Schabo village. If the Schabo vineyards, which nearly equaled the total held in all the other colonies, are excluded, the average per-family holdings decrease from 174.7 vines per family to 112.2. If the extensive plantings in Sarata are also taken out, the average holdings decrease to 75.4. As noted earlier, the colonies with a Württemberg and Rhineland heritage, Alt Posttal, Sarata, and Wittenberg, led the way in introducing vineyards. The statistics for fruit trees show a much wider variation among the different colonies than for grains or animals. The new colonies of Sarata and Schabo have major leads, though Schabo's results, like those for grapevines, likely reflect not their own plantings but the existence of fruit trees remaining from the prior settlement. Sarata's results clearly show the focus of that community as well as its perhaps above average wealth. Among the older colonies, Kulm, Klöstitz, Krasna, and Tarutino stand out as early adopters. The wine market in Kishinev, dominated by Bessarabian German producers, had sales worth 40,000 paper rubles in 1840. By 1854 these had grown to 53,900 silver rubles.[71] Judging from the 1848 village histories, there were in each village differences in how the settler families adapted to conditions in Bessarabia. The data from the 1825 Welfare Committee economic survey, however, do not take us down to the level of individual family results. When averaged on a per-family basis, however, these data do make clear distinctions between the average successes achieved by the different German colonies in Bessarabia. The tables on the prior pages compare eleven categories from yields of grain to numbers of animals, fruit trees, and grapevines. Defining settlements that rank in the top three of each category as being the most successful adaptors and those who rank in the bottom three as the least successful, Kulm stands out as doing the best, ranking eight times in the top three, and Teplitz as the worst, ranking five times in the bottom three (see table 5–6).

For the Welfare Committee, the most worrisome results of the 1825 survey were those colonies that were having the most trouble adjusting. Teplitz stands at the

---

70. Ibid., 200.
71. Brandes, *Von den Zaren Adoptiert*, 179.

TABLE 5–6.    **Rankings of German colonies in terms of achievement**

|  | Top 3 | Bottom 3 |
|---|---|---|
| Kulm | 8 | — |
| Alt Posttal | 7 | 1 |
| Wittenberg | 7 | 1 |
| Brienne | 2 | 3 |
| Arzis | 1 | 4 |
| Leipzig | 1 | 4 |
| Neu Elft | — | 4 |
| Teplitz[a] | — | 5 |

a. I did not count Schabo, Sarata, or Katzbach in this listing, as these
colonies were each in the first years of settlement.

head of this group. Founded in 1817, it was clearly still suffering from the many early
deaths that caused this group of Württembergers to settle in Bessarabia rather than
to go on to their intended destination in the Caucasus. The Teplitz history notes that
in just a four month period after their arrival, they lost 110 people and that as a result
the "village lost not only many of their best farmers but also was forced to care for
many orphans and work their farms until they became of age."[72] The Leipzig colonists were also having issues adjusting to Bessarabia. The Leipzig history connects
that village's problems with its discouraging start and the moral and religious decay
this produced. In looking for reasons why the same villages were the least productive
in many measurements, it is interesting to note, though, that with the exception of
Leipzig, all the villages experiencing the most difficulties were located on the lower
Kogil'nik where there were greater areas of highly alkaline soil on which the German
colonists were still often finding it difficult to produce crops. Alt Arzis, noting the
"many desjatines of useless land," also suffered from the fact that the former leaseholder did not give up part of the land assigned to them and it was not until 1823
or 1824 that the village gained full control.[73]

## The 1825 Welfare Committee survey also collected data from the German colonies in the Ekaterinoslav, Xerson, and Tauride provinces, which permits comparison with those in Bessarabia

The 1825 Welfare Committee economic survey also collected similar data for
the German colonies in South Russia whose founding predated the colonies in
Bessarabia by ten to twenty-five years. Comparing the per-family averages for the
German colonies in Bessarabia with those in the Ekaterinoslav,[74] Xerson (referred to

---

72. Kludt, "Teplitz – 1848 Village History."
73. Neumann, "Alt Arzis – 1848 Village History."
74. The German colonies in the Ekaterinoslav Province were grouped into three districts: (1) the
    Ekaterinoslav District, made up of the sixteen Xortica Mennonite colonies (731 families) and the
    Jamburg colonists (58 families); (2) the Novomoskovsk District, which included the Josefstal and
    Rybal'sk settlements (116 families) and the Kronsgarten Mennonites (22 families); (3) the
    Aleksandrovsk District, which included seventeen Prussian colonies (451 families), another with
    settlers from Baden (13 families), and the Schönwiese Mennonites (39 families). The three districts
    comprised 1,430 families. As some statistics collected in this 1825–26 survey are tied to differing
    combinations of Ekaterinoslav colonists, the figures shown in table 5–7 are based on results most
    closely identified with these three districts.

as Odessa in the Rempel material),[75] and Tauride[76] provinces offers another perspective on the state of development of the Bessarabian colonies. The four areas have relatively similar population sizes: Bessarabia had 1,923 families, Ekaterinoslav had 1,430 families, Odessa had 2,805 families, and Tauride had 2,486 families. Settlements in the Ekaterinoslav and Tauride provinces were generally founded between 1789 and 1801 and were heavily populated with Mennonites who emigrated from Prussian Poland. The settlements above Odessa had been mainly settled in the period from 1803 to 1809 and were populated with many colonists who had emigrated directly from Western Europe, chiefly Württemberg. Some of the Ekaterinoslav and Tauride settlements, such as Josefstal, Rybal'sk, and the Moločna Mennonites, started life in Russia with smaller allotments of land, but all the rest began with allotments that were as generous as those in Bessarabia. The per-family comparisons among the four regions are seen in table 5–7.

The regional comparisons offer several surprises. Despite their relatively short existence, as of 1825, the Bessarabian colonies had more cattle per family, had the best per-family harvests of summer wheat and millet, and were second best in their harvests of winter wheat and barley and in the number of grapevines. Their second-place position in holdings of grapevines is maintained even if the huge number of grapevines found in Schabo are removed from the Bessarabian average, dropping it to 112.2 per family.

Apart from establishing the early strength of the Bessarabian colonies, the per-family comparisons between the different regions raise two other points of interest for Bessarabia. The significant lead the Odessa Province had built up by developing fruit tree orchards and particularly by planting vineyards is a testament to their early recognition of the great economic potential of the products from these activities. The Bessarabian Germans would ultimately come to see or be led by the

TABLE 5–7.  **Per-family harvest yields and animal, fruit tree, and grapevine holdings in the Ekaterinoslav, Tauride, Odessa, and Bessarabia provinces, 1825–26**

|  | Ekaterinoslav | Tauride | Odessa | Bessarabia |
|---|---|---|---|---|
| Rye Harvest | 10.0 | 14.5 | 11.6 | 7.3 |
| Winter Wheat | 0.03 | 0.5 | 5.4 | 3.9 |
| Summer Wheat | 1.6 | 2.6 | 2.6 | 2.9 |
| Barley | 1.9 | 3.1 | 5.3 | 3.3 |
| Millet | 1.3 | 1.0 | 1.1 | 3.0 |
| Cattle | 5.1 | 6.0 | 4.0 | 10.6 |
| Horses | 3.1 | 3.1 | 2.5 | 2.0 |
| Sheep | 19.8 | 24.1 | 2.6 | 3.2 |
| Fruit Trees | 51.9 | 74.3 | 99.7 | 20.6 |
| Grapevines | 1.5 | 12.7 | 463.3 | 174.7 |

75. The Welfare Committee refers to German colonies placed in the Xerson Province as the Odessa colonies and these are made up of the Liebental District (721 families), the Kučurgan District (492 families), the Glückstal District (430 families), the Berezan District (1,089 families), and the Tiraspol District (73 families).
76. The German colonies in the Tauride Province included the Moločna Mennonites (1,222 families), plus other German colonists located in the Moločna area (852 families), the Berdjansk villages of Württembergers (100 families), and Germans colonies located in the Crimea (312 families).

Welfare Committee to see this potential. Those colonies in Bessarabia that came to this realization earlier found their way to prosperity more rapidly. The Alt Elft and Paris village histories from Bessarabia both noted that they would have prospered earlier if they had planted vineyards and orchards sooner. In both cases this failure is chalked up to the fact that fruit trees and grapevines were "hard to obtain" or "not available." Since the large number of trees and vineyards extant in the 1825 survey in Bessarabia establish the existence of seedlings locally, such excuses appear to reflect difficulties in finding free cash to invest in fruit or perhaps more likely the delay on the part of villagers in realizing the economic potential there. Another reason for the slow development of orchards and vineyards in Bessarabia was that until the late 1830s and early 1840s, the market for products from these activities was strictly local. The growth of the city of Odessa as both a transshipment center and a market in its own right changed many perceptions among farmers in Bessarabia as to where to invest time, energy, and capital.

On the opposite side of the ledger, the economic difficulties of the colonies in the Ekaterinoslav Province stand out clearly in the comparisons with the younger colonies. Of the ten categories examined, the Ekaterinoslav Province is last in four and next-to-last in three. The German communities in this region were dominated by large numbers of Mennonite colonies on generally smaller plots of land, who had, by 1825, already developed a class of landless settlers. This combination drove down the per-family results. In one area, though, the Mennonite communities became leaders among the German colonies. Some Mennonites were already owners of large herds of sheep, an approach that would later prove to be another major source of agricultural strength for many Germans communities in South Russia and Bessarabia.[77]

## The Welfare Committee also collected economic data in 1841, which permits further comparisons between the German colonies in Bessarabia with those in South Russia

It is possible to have a second and later view of economic development in the German colonies in Bessarabia and South Russia. Among the materials Klaus includes in his book is a summary sheet from a Welfare Committee economic survey done in 1841.[78] While the survey from 1841 collects different data elements than the survey from 1825 and organizes them differently, comparisons between the two surveys can be made. These comparisons show the Bessarabian colonies continuing to make strong progress. As the 1841 survey also includes material for the German colonies in the Ekaterinoslav, Tauride, and Odessa provinces included in the 1825 survey, it is also possible to continue to make comparisons between the different regions. The 1841 survey further contains data from the larger Bulgarian colonies in Bessarabia founded at the same time as those settled by Germans, adding another layer of detail and insight for comparison.

The summary of the 1841 survey Klaus presents does not offer detail by village. Instead, for Bessarabia and South Russia, the data are presented in blocks of colonies. The Bessarabian colonies are combined as a Malojaroslav District of eleven

77. The Xortica Mennonite colonies averaged 27.2 sheep per family and the Kronsgarten Mennonites had 68.9. Keeping sheep was an economic strength of the Bulgarian colonies. The Kislava Bulgarians in Tauride Province averaged 64.9 per family and those in Staryj Krym 31.4.
78. Klaus, *Naši kolonii*, Appendix VII.

colonies,[79] a Klöstitz District of nine colonies,[80] a Sarata District of three colonies,[81] and Schabo colony remaining on its own. The 1841 survey includes data from the five additional German colonies established after 1825. The new colonies are: Gnadental (1830), Friedenstal (1833), Lichtental (1834), Dennewitz (1834), and Plotzk (1839–41). Per-family comparisons, however, permit valid comparisons of change. While several data elements are continued from the 1825 survey, such as population and the number of cattle, sheep, horses, grapevines, and fruit trees, other data points are missing or changed. There is no material on grain planted and harvested, for example, but there is information on money earned from the sale of grain and animals, and this is compared to tax obligations, creating a measurement of surplus (see table 5–8).

The total German population in Bessarabia grew from 8,954 to 15,157, an increase of 69.3 percent. While the increase in number (6,203 people) is smaller than those of the other three regions, the increase as a percentage of the 1825 figure is very much in line with that of the two Tauride districts, which together grew 73.0 percent, and slightly larger than that of the four Odessa districts, which together grew 64.8 percent. The increases in population in all four provinces are in some part the result of the arrival of new colonists coming from Russian Poland and Western Europe who founded new settlements. As noted above, there were five such new colonies in German Bessarabia. The large 203.7 percent increase in population of the Bessarabian Sarata District from 1825 to 1841 is greatly due to the addition of the 80 families from Württemberg who created the colony of Gnadental between 1830 and 1833, and the 76 families, also from Württemberg, who founded the colony of Lichtental in the period from 1834 to 1840. But for the Klöstitz and the Malojaroslav districts, much of the growth in population comes from births in the existing colonies. One of the two new colonies added to the Malojaroslav District, Dennewitz, was formed almost entirely from the children of settlers from other German Bessarabian villages.

Looking at the population growth from a larger provincial perspective, variances narrow, with Bessarabia, Odessa, and Tauride showing similar levels of growth that appear mainly driven by natural increases. The Ekaterinoslav Province, which shows the largest growth as a percentage of its 1825 population, was also the region with the greatest number of new colonies and new immigrants coming from outside the region (see table 5–9).[82]

In considering the causes of population increase in the older Bessarabian German settlements in the first half of the nineteenth century, what data we have suggest that natural increase was the primary cause. The unusually detailed sources available for Kulm,

---

79. The Malojaroslav District, named after the official names of Wittenberg and Alt Posttal, consisted of Wittenberg (Malojaroslavec I), Alt Posttal (Malojaroslavec II), Kulm, Tarutino, Krasna, Katzbach, Alt Elft, Neu Elft, Teplitz, Dennewitz, and Plotzk. As the latter had just been founded, with settlers arriving between 1839 and 1841, it is not certain how much detail Plotzk offered or was included.

80. The Klöstitz District, named after the Russian form of Klöstitz, consisted of Klöstitz, Leipzig, Beresina, Borodino, Paris, Alt Arzis, Neu Arzis, Brienne, and Friedenstal.

81. The Sarata District consisted of Sarata, Gnadental, and Lichtental.

82. The significant (153.9 percent) population growth in the Mariupol' District of Ekaterinoslav is clearly related to the ten additional colonies that appear in the 1841 survey. Some of these, like Klein Werder (1831), were colonies founded by families moving from other German settlements in Russia and Russian Poland, while others, like Ludwigstal (1828), were founded by colonists coming directly to Russia from Hesse and Württemberg. Five of the eleven new colonies in the Mariupol' District were founded by families who moved in 1831 from the German colonies originally established in 1767 near Chernigov above Kiev in the Ukraine. Adam Giesinger, "Villages in which Our Forefathers Lived: Early Daughter Colonies near Mariupol," *American Historical Society of Germans from Russia Journal* 2, no. 3 (1979): 1–2.

TABLE 5–8.  **Comparisons of population change in Bessarabia and other South Russian areas**

| Bessarabia | Families | Males | Females | Total | % Change |
|---|---|---|---|---|---|
| Malojaroslav District | | | | | |
| 1825 | 917 | 2,255 | 2,022 | 4,187 | |
| 1841 | 957 | 3,463 | 3,305 | 6,768 | +61.6% |
| Klöstitz District | | | | | |
| 1825 | 894 | 2,156 | 2,047 | 4,203 | |
| 1841 | 1,111 | 3,554 | 3,364 | 6,918 | +64.6% |
| Sarata District | | | | | |
| 1825 | 98 | 226 | 209 | 435 | |
| 1841 | 240 | 658 | 663 | 1,321 | +203.7% |
| Schabo | | | | | |
| 1825 | 14 | 24 | 15 | 39 | |
| 1841 | 40 | 82 | 68 | 150 | +284.6% |
| **Total Bessarabia** | | | | | |
| 1825 | 1,923 | 4,662 | 4,292 | 8,954 | |
| 1830[a] | 2,054 | 5,193 | 4,829 | 10,022 | +11.9% |
| 1841 | 2,348 | 7,757 | 7,400 | 15,157 | +69.3% |
| **Xerson/Odessa** | **Families** | **Males** | **Females** | **Total** | **% Change** |
| Berezan District[b] | | | | | |
| 1825 | 947 | 2,373 | 2,226 | 4,599 | |
| 1841 | 1,632 | 4,568 | 4,290 | 8,858 | +92.6% |
| Liebental District | | | | | |
| 1825 | 721 | 2,939 | 2,837 | 5,776 | |
| 1841 | 1,173 | 4,116 | 4,033 | 8,149 | +41.1% |
| Kučurgan District | | | | | |
| 1825 | 493 | 1,546 | 1,519 | 3,065 | |
| 1841 | 524 | 2,430 | 2,274 | 4,704 | +53.4% |
| Glückstal District | | | | | |
| 1825 | 429 | 1,506 | 1,443 | 2,949 | |
| 1841 | 572 | 2,704 | 2,552 | 5,256 | +78.2% |
| **1841 Xerson/Odessa Total** | 3,901 | 13,818 | 13,149 | 26,967 | +64.5% |
| **Ekaterinoslav** | | | | | |
| Xortica Mennonite District[c] | | | | | |
| 1825 | 789 | 2,098 | 2,102 | 4,200 | |
| 1841 | 808 | 2,993 | 3,036 | 6,029 | +43.5% |
| Josefstal District | | | | | |
| 1825 | 138 | 442 | 420 | 862 | |
| 1841 | 222 | 881 | 883 | 1,764 | +104.6% |
| Mariupol' District | | | | | |
| 1825 | 503 | 1,485 | 1,416 | 2,901 | |
| 1841 | 862 | 3,795 | 3,572 | 7,367 | +153.9% |
| **1841 Ekaterinoslav Total** | 1,892 | 7,669 | 7,491 | 15,160 | +90.4% |

*(continued)*

| Tauride | | | | | |
|---|---|---|---|---|---|
| Moločna Mennonites[d] | | | | | |
| 1825 | 1,221 | 3,321 | 3,107 | 6,428 | |
| 1841 | 2,383 | 6,185 | 5,936 | 12,121 | +88.6% |
| Moločna and Berdjansk | | | | | |
| 1825 | 952 | 3,341 | 3,069 | 6,410 | |
| 1841 | 1,180 | 5,170 | 4,915 | 10,085 | +57.3% |
| **1841 Tauride Total** | **3,563** | **11,355** | **10,851** | **22,206** | **+73.0%** |

a. Population figures from the year 1830 from Welfare Committee statistics are quoted by Brandes, *Von den Zaren Adoptiert*, 154.

b. The Berezan, Kučurgan, Liebental, and Glückstal districts were German villages located in Xerson Province. In 1825, they represented 97.4 percent of the population in the Welfare Committee's Odessa Province. The small Tiraspol group of 1825 is not separately listed in 1841. The 1841 survey does list another group of Xerson "colonists," the 1,691 Swedish colonists ("švedskie") whom I have not considered in this study. By 1841, Berezan had increased from eleven to twelve colonies, Liebental from ten to twelve, and Glückstal from four to five, while Kučurgan remained at six.

c. The 1841 survey figures appear not to include the Catholic colonists in Jamburg who were present in the 1825 survey (in group 1 in footnote 74 on page 114). The Kronsgarten Mennonites (part of the 1825 group 2) seem to be counted in the Josefstal District of 1841, as the total number of colonies remains unchanged. The Schönwiese Mennonites (part of the 1825 group 3) are not specifically identified in 1841 but may be counted in the Mariupol' figures. As such, the districts included in the 1841 survey appear to represent 95.9 percent of the population for Ekaterinoslav Province counted in the 1825 survey. Nomenclature for the districts has changed as well. The 1825 Ekaterinoslav District is in 1841 called and limited to the Xortica Mennonites, the Novomoskovsk District is now called the Josefstal District and the Aleksandrovsk District is now called the Mariupol' District. In 1841, the Xortica Mennonites continued to have seventeen colonies and the Josefstal District four, while the Mariupol' District increased from eighteen to twenty-eight. The Xortica and Josefstal colonies were settled in the late 1780s, and those northwest of Mariupol' between 1789 and 1848.

d. German colonies in Tauride Province appear here in two groups: (a) the Moločna Mennonites, located along the middle Moločna River who settled there in 1803–4; and (b) the non-Mennonites settled along the Moločna River at about the same time, and the Württemberg colonies placed near Berdjansk further southeast just inland from the Sea of Azov that were settled in the early 1820s. These two groups make up 86.7 percent of the 1825 Tauride Province figures for German colonies. I do not include here the third district of Germans in Tauride, those settled in the Crimea, who did appear in the 1825 data, because the 1841 summary merges their data with those of Bulgarian colonies in the Crimea. The Moločna Mennonites grew from thirty-nine colonies in 1825 to forty-four in 1841, the non-Mennonite Moločna colonies remained at twenty-three from 1825 to 1841, and the Berdjansk colonies grew slightly from three to four colonies in that period.

TABLE 5–9.  **German population in the South Russian provinces**

| | 1825 | 1841 | Percent increase | New colonies |
|---|---|---|---|---|
| Odessa | 16,389 | 26,967 | 61.5% | 4 |
| Bessarabia | 8,954 | 15,157 | 69.3% | 5 |
| Tauride | 12,838 | 22,206 | 73.0% | 6 |
| Ekaterinoslav | 7,963 | 15,160 | 90.4 % | 10 |

from Flegel's collection to the actual 1835 and 1859 censuses, indicate that settlement grew mainly from increases in the sizes and numbers of its native families. The number of surnames from the 1859 census not listed in the census for 1835, for example, is less than 10 percent. It is a presumption, of course, but the absence of commentary on significant population inflow from outside of Bessarabia into other early Bessarabian colonies suggests that natural increase was responsible for the large population increases in those settlements as well. Over the forty-four-year period from 1815 to 1859, the number of families in Kulm nearly tripled from 106 to 290, while the total settlement's population increased by a factor of over four from 343 to 1,416 (see table 5–10).[83]

Kulm's population increase of 49.5 percent between 1825 and 1835 is very much in line with the 58.2 percent growth in population between 1825 and 1841 for the overall Malojaroslav District of which Kulm was a part.

The population figures in the 1841 study also count the number of families living in the German colonies that were landless. The figures for the Xortica Mennonites and particularly the Moločna Mennonites show the development of a worrisome phenomenon: large numbers of families in these villages were indicated to be land-less. Among the Xortica Mennonites, 46.7 percent of the families were landless, and among the Moločna Mennonites the figure had climbed to 56.7 percent. Numbers of landless citizens are also indicated in many other colony groups: 35.0 percent in the Liebental colonies, 25.6 percent in the Berezan colonies, and 32.4 percent in the Josefstal colonies in the Ekaterinoslav Province. There were few landless families at this time in the Bessarabian colonies; the 1841 survey counts only fifteen, all of them in the Sarata colonies, and likely working in trades and not landless poor.

Turning to the economic data, the 1841 survey results show that the major direc-tion of development in the Bessarabian colonies was toward investments in fruit trees, grapevines, and sheep (see table 5–11).

The greatest change occurred in the number of sheep held by the Bessarabian Germans. The total numbers held grew 645 percent while the per-family holdings increased 468 percent. The per-family holdings of fruit trees increased 300 percent and per-family holdings of grapevines increased 247 percent. The increases in the number of sheep and fruit trees came mainly from the older colonies, with the Klöstitz and Malojaroslav districts supplying 92 percent of the total for sheep and 79 percent for fruit trees. With grapevines, however, the Sarata District and Schabo, which had 12 percent of the population, provided 35 percent of the Bessarabian total. The growth in all three areas suggests an increased understanding of the different economic possibilities of the farmland they possessed. Although earnings from the sale of fruit and wine were clearly growing by 1841, the most important source of income for Germans in Bessarabia came from sales of animals (see table 5–12).

In 1841 as in 1825, the Bessarabian Germans were the leaders among the Germans in South Russia in both the total numbers of cattle and the per-family holdings of cattle. They maintained this lead despite the fact that the numbers of cattle only increased by 17 percent and the per-family holdings decreased slightly, a sign that

TABLE 5–10. **Number of families and individuals in Kulm, 1815–59**

| | Families | % Increase | Inhabitants | % Increase |
|---|---|---|---|---|
| 1815 | 106 | — | 343 | — |
| 1825 | 119 | 12.2% | 604 | 76.1% |
| 1835 | 200 | 68.1% | 903 | 49.5% |
| 1859 | 290 | 45.0% | 1,416 | 56.8% |

83. The figures for 1815 are listed in Klaus, *Naši kolonii*, 25; those for 1825 from Hans Rempel, "Table 16: Summary of Birth, Marriages and Deaths in the Bessarabian Colonies of Foreign Settlers in Year 1825, Section A: Souls," in Rempel, *German Farming Achievements*; and the Kulm Bessarabia 1835 Census, and the Kulm Bessarabia 1859 Census.

TABLE 5–11. **Per-family holdings of the 1841 Bessarabian districts**

|  | Malojaroslav | | Klöstitz | | Sarata + Schabo | | Total Bessarabia | |
|---|---|---|---|---|---|---|---|---|
|  | 1825 | 1841 | 1825 | 1841 | 1825 | 1841 | 1825 | 1841 |
| Horses | 1,914 | 3,310 | 1,703 | 3,266 | 135 | 1,012 | 3,752 | 7,588 |
| Per family | 2.1 | 3.5 | 1.9 | 2.9 | 1.2 | 3.6 | 2.0 | 3.2 |
| Cattle | 10,101 | 11,205 | 9,899 | 9,244 | 1,014 | 3,419 | 21,014 | 23,868 |
| Per family | 11.0 | 11.7 | 10.3 | 8.3 | 9.1 | 12.2 | 10.9 | 10.2 |
| Sheep | 2,951 | 20,988 | 2,747 | 18,480 | 38 | 3,308 | 5,736 | 42,776 |
| Per family | 3.2 | 21.9 | 3.1 | 16.6 | 0.3 | 11.8 | 3.2 | 18.2 |
| Fruit trees | 19,387 | 79,229 | 13,499 | 36,066 | 3,382 | 29,924 | 36,268 | 145,219 |
| Per family | 21.1 | 82.8 | 15.1 | 32.5 | 30.2 | 106.9 | 20.6 | 61.8 |
| Grapevines | 77,516 | 445,320 | 37,641 | 480,673 | 171,245 | 497,880 | 286,402 | 1,423,873 |
| Per family | 84.5 | 465.3 | 42.1 | 432.6 | 1,529 | 1,778.1 | 174.7 | 606.4 |
| Wine produced | — | 18,694 | — | 4,623 | — | 13,566 | — | 36,883 |
| Per family | — | 19.5 | — | 4.2 | — | 48.5 | — | 15.7 |
| Mills | — | 76 | — | 79 | — | 25 | 43 | 180 |

TABLE 5–12. **Per-family holdings in the South Russian provinces**

|  | Bessarabia | | Odessa | | Ekaterinoslav | | Tauride | |
|---|---|---|---|---|---|---|---|---|
|  | 1825 | 1841 | 1825 | 1841 | 1825 | 1841 | 1825 | 1841 |
| Horses | 3,752 | 7,588 | 6,018 | 14,530 | 4,408 | 8,935 | 7,778 | 15,484 |
| Per family | 2.0 | 3.2 | 2.8 | 4.4 | 3.1 | 4.7 | 3.1 | 4.4 |
| Cattle | 21,014 | 23,868 | 10,101 | 22,660 | 7,320 | 12,136 | 14,918 | 17,916 |
| Per family | 10.9 | 10.2 | 4.7 | 6.8 | 5.1 | 6.4 | 6.0 | 5.0 |
| Sheep | 5,736 | 42,776 | 7,597 | 47,651 | 28,281 | 109,638 | 59,867 | 208,133 |
| Per family | 3.0 | 18.2 | 3.5 | 14.3 | 19.8 | 57.9 | 24.1 | 58.4 |
| Fruit trees | 36,268 | 145,219 | 241,859 | 228,681 | 74,167 | 117,228 | 184,524 | 310,696 |
| Per family | 18.9 | 61.8 | 111.9 | 68.7 | 51.9 | 61.9 | 74.3 | 87.2 |
| Grapevines | 286,402 | 1,423,873 | 1,068,033 | 3,794,931 | 2,166 | 880 | 31,608 | 3,617 |
| Per family | 157.0 | 606.4 | 494.2 | 1,140.0 | 1.5 | 0.5 | 12.7 | 1.0 |
| Wine produced | — | 36,883 | — | 84,626 | — | 0.0 | — | 0.0 |
| Per family | — | 15.7 | — | 25.4 | — | 0.0 | — | 0.0 |
| Mills | 43 | 180 | 90 | 205 | 49 | 111 | 77 | 128 |

investment had shifted to other areas. While the number of sheep dramatically increased in Bessarabia and the per-family holdings passed those in the Odessa Province, sheep herds remained far behind the holdings of the Germans in the Ekaterinoslav and Tauride provinces. The largest herds in Bessarabia were in the Malojaroslav villages, which average 21.9 sheep per family. This compares to holdings of 89.6 sheep per family among the Moločna (non-Mennonite) colonists, 80.6 sheep per family among the Xortica Mennonites, and 44.0 sheep per family among the Moločna Mennonites. For holdings of sheep, the 1841 survey distinguished between improved (*uluc̆ennye*) and ordinary (*prostye*) breeds.[84] Ninety percent of the holdings of the Bessarabian Germans were of the latter variety, whereas all of the Mennonite flocks were the improved and likely more valuable breeds. Sarata, though, assumed a leadership position among the Bessarabian colonies in this category, as all of its sheep were improved breeds.

The number of fruit trees held by the Bessarabian Germans increased substantially, and the growth in the per-family figures moved the Bessarabians into a virtual tie with the Ekaterinoslav Province for third place. The major fruit growers among the regions were the Moloc̆na non-Mennonite Germans in the Tauride Province with 174.6 fruit trees per family, followed by the Liebental colonies in the Odessa Province with 99.9 fruit trees per family. The decrease for 1841 in the absolute number of fruit trees and the significant decrease in the per-family holdings of fruit trees in the Odessa Province seems anomalous. This suggests there were issues with obtaining a complete counting from this region.

The 1841 figures show that the Bessarabian colonies greatly increased their plantings of grapevines, and at 5,000 grapevines per family, the Schabo colony had the largest per-family holdings of any group in any region. The greatest increase in the number of vineyards, however, came from the Liebental colonies in the Odessa Province. Schabo had a total of 200,000 grapevines while the twelve Liebental colonies had 3,379,556 or 281,630 per colony and 2,881 per family a growth of 235% per colony and 147% per family. The Mennonite colonies did not plant grapevines, and the Moloc̆na non-Mennonite Germans and Mariupol' colonists kept only a few so that the efforts of the colonies in the Tauride and Ekaterinoslav provinces were negligible in this area.[85] On a per-family basis, Schabo in Bessarabia was the leading producer of wine, creating 250 barrels or *vedro*[86] per family or 10,000 in all for the village. In terms of total production, though, the Liebental colonies were the largest wine-producing region, totaling 72,394 vedro or 61.7 per family. The Malojaroslav colonies in Bessarabia, the next-largest producer, averaged 19.5 vedro per family.

It is unfortunate that the 1841 survey summary did not include grain yields, as the agricultural economy of the German settlements in South Russia rested on this platform. Grain fed the colonists and their animals, though, as yet, it formed only a small portion of their earnings. As a proxy for some perspective on the growth in grain harvests, the 1841 survey did include a count of the number of mills in use in each of the colony groups, and these may be compared to counts included in the 1825 survey. In all four provinces the number of mills increased.[87] The Bessarabian colonies had the fewest number of mills counted in 1825, but in 1841, the number had almost quadrupled, going from 49 to 180 and giving them the second-highest total among the four regions. The Odessa Province was the leader in both surveys,

---

84. The "improved" breeds likely included Merino, Karakul, and Romanov, whose wool throughout the nineteenth century brought the best prices.

85. This is not true, however, for Tauride Province colonists settled in the Crimea who were not included here, because the figures for 1841 combine totals for the German and Bulgarian colonies. The 620 German and Bulgarian colonist families in Crimea had on average 1,049 grapevines per family, which would have placed them near the leaders.

86. The amount of wine produced is measured in the Russian liquid quantity called a vedro. One vedro is equal to 12.3 liters or 3.25 US gallons.

87. The 1841 survey included wind- and water-driven grain mills and oil mills. The 1825 survey did not count the number of mills for Sarata and Schabo but provided millers and that number is used here.

with 90 in 1825 and 205 in 1841. The growth in the number of mills throughout the German colonies probably testifies to the increasing sizes of grain harvests and with these, the commensurate requirements for processing those harvests. The relationship is however demonstrative rather than arithmetical. Thus, one would not be on good ground to presume that the smaller increases in the numbers of mills that occur in the Odessa, Ekaterinoslav, and Tauride provinces indicate smaller increases in harvest sizes there than in Bessarabia. There may be other reasons for the larger increase in the number of mills in Bessarabia. One explanation for the fact that the Bessarabian German colonies built far more mills in this period than other German colonies may have been that Bessarabia had a far less developed internal infrastructure. Roads connecting the settlements were fewer and more primitive. This meant that the Bessarabian colonies would find it economically more advantageous to satisfy milling needs with several mills within the village rather than encourage the development of larger more efficient milling centers to which farmers would cart their grain.

In comparing all the per-family holdings provided by the data in the 1841 survey, one might conclude that the German colonies in Bessarabia had caught up with and in some areas had surpassed many of the German colonies in other regions of South Russia. To do so, however, would likely exaggerate the actual progress made by the Bessarabian Germans since their arrival in 1814. One would be on firmer ground to suggest that by 1841, most of the Bessarabian colonists were far better acclimated to the steppelands and that their farms, gardens, and orchards were generally showing promise. Though losses from insect, pest, and animal plagues continued, these were setbacks rather than disasters, and in general, farmsteads were producing at least small surpluses. In this view, the Bessarabians were catching up with the older German colonies in South Russia but hadn't yet reached par with them. This conclusion is supported by another data set within the 1841 survey that gathered information on income earned from the sale of grain, animals and their products, and from "various" other sources such as fruit and wine. These are measured in silver rubles and are netted against community tax obligations to give estimations of total village retained surpluses. As with the economic details discussed above, the summary figures for earnings, taxes, and surpluses are not given for individual villages except Schabo but instead are grouped in the blocks of villages noted above.

Table 5–13 shows the reported income from the sales of grain, animals, and other products and nets that income against taxes owed to calculate retained surplus. Consider the surplus per family figure as an assessment of the economic progress of the colonies in Russia. This suggests that the average prosperity varied directly with the settlement age. The Ekaterinoslav and Tauride colonies established first show the highest surplus per family figures, which are rather distantly followed by the Odessa and Bessarabia regions. However, the fact that no grain sales are reported for the Klöstitz District in Bessarabia or the Liebental District in the Odessa Province creates the suspicion that the stated retained net surplus figures for these two groups are lower than what they were in reality. With the 1848 Bessarabian village histories[88] not reporting major crop difficulties for the years 1840–41, it seems probable that the Klöstitz colonies had some profitable grain sales that somehow did not find their

---

88. Teplitz, part of the Malojaroslav District, did report problems with field mice in 1841.

TABLE 5-13. **Retained surplus sources and total and net surplus values**

| | Grain | Animals and wool | Other products | Total income | Taxes owed | Net surplus | Surplus/ family |
|---|---|---|---|---|---|---|---|
| Malojaroslav | 13,836 | 30,582 | 14,817 | 59,235 | 15,154 | 44,081 | 46.1 |
| Klöstitz | — | 16,932 | 4,975 | 21,907 | 17,036 | 4,871 | 4.4 |
| Sarata | 11 | 1,650 | 1,313 | 2,974 | 1,949 | 1,025 | 4.3 |
| Schabo | 1,000 | 50 | 500 | 1,550 | 160 | 1,390 | 34.8 |
| **All Bessarabia** | 14,847 | 49,214 | 21,605 | 85,666 | 34,299 | 51,367 | 21.9 |
| Berezan | 33,128 | 26,559 | 9,019 | 68,706 | 20,097 | 48,609 | 41.4 |
| Liebental | — | 11,116 | 23,735 | 34,851 | 19,438 | 15,413 | 9.4 |
| Kučurgan | 14,387 | 8,711 | 6,193 | 29,291 | 11,185 | 18,106 | 34.6 |
| Glückstal | 5,683 | 8,674 | 3,472 | 17,829 | 11,396 | 6,433 | 11.3 |
| **All Odessa** | 53,198 | 55,060 | 42,419 | 150,677 | 62,116 | 88,561 | 22.7 |
| Xortica Mennonites | 18,533 | 56,205 | 3,234 | 77,972 | 6,437 | 71,535 | 88.5 |
| Josefstal | 1,890 | 3,841 | 379 | 6,110 | 3,241 | 2,869 | 12.9 |
| Mariupol' | 27,851 | 22,129 | 6,797 | 56,777 | 9,439 | 47,338 | 54.9 |
| **All Ekaterinoslav** | 48,274 | 82,175 | 10,410 | 140,859 | 19,117 | 121,742 | 64.3 |
| Moločna Mennonites | 82,992 | 56,555 | 22,889 | 162,436 | 9,313 | 153,123 | 64.3 |
| Moločna non-Mennonites | 81,785 | 54,148 | 8,204 | 144,137 | 16,624 | 127,513 | 122.0 |
| Berdjansk | 4,880 | 3,314 | 152 | 8,346 | 1,200 | 7,146 | 52.9 |
| **All Tauride** | 169,657 | 114,017 | 31,245 | 314,919 | 27,137 | 287,782 | 80.8 |

way into the 1841 survey report. Similarly, the figures for both Sarata and Schabo in earnings gained by the sale of other products seem suspiciously low. The colonies of Sarata and Schabo were both heavily invested in fruit trees and grapevines. Schabo produced on average 250 vedro of wine per family and had 312.5 fruit trees per family, and the Sarata District produced 14.9 vedro of wine per family and had 97.6 fruit trees per family.

The suspicion that the 1841 earnings figures for Bessarabian Germans quoted by Klaus are incomplete is further suggested by earnings figures for 1836 cited by Malinovskij.[89] Using data from the Russian State Historical Archives in St. Petersburg (RGIA), likely Welfare Committee reports to the Ministry of the Interior, Malinovskij reports that in 1836, Germans in Bessarabia earned a total of 203,020 rubles. The total earnings are broken down into four categories (see table 5–14).

It is possible that the 1836 and 1841 data collections were built up from different informational bases and so are not comparable, though on the surface this does not seem the case. The total earnings figure of 203,020 rubles, however, is so much larger than the figure of 85,666 rubles that Klaus reports for 1841 that it casts doubts about the validity of the latter. As other sources indicate, 1836 was an unusually favorable year and so possibly its results exaggerate normal conditions in Bessarabia.[90] It is also

---

89. Malinovskij, *Social'naja i xozjajstvennaja istorija*, 86.
90. Brandes (*Von den Zaren Adoptiert*, 218) notes, for example, that the years 1836–38 had particularly good harvests.

TABLE 5–14.  **Sources of earnings of the Bessarabian Germans, 1836**

| Item | Earnings (in rubles) | % of total |
|---|---|---|
| Animals and meat | 113,333 | 56 |
| Wool | 40,687 | 20 |
| Wine | 40,000 | 20 |
| Grain | 9,000 | 4 |
| **Total** | 203,020 | 100 |

possible, as suggested above, that the Bessarabian totals for 1841 are simply missing data and materially understate earnings from German Bessarabia. The figures from 1836 do mirror the data from 1841 that indicate grain sales to be the smallest source of earnings by the Bessarabian Germans.

Even taken on their own, the 1841 figures for Bessarabia show undeniably positive signs. The Malojaroslav colonies averaged per-family earnings of 32 silver rubles from the sale of animals, likely cattle, which was the third highest earnings figure of any of the individual groups. Their earnings from the sale of other products, likely wine, brandy, and fruit, at 15.5 silver rubles per family were the highest of any group in this category. It would, however, take substantial adjustments to bring the Bessarabian or the Odessa per-family surplus averages up to the levels attained by the Ekaterinoslav and Tauride colonies.[91] It is true that the tax obligations for the Bessarabian and Odessa provinces were higher on a per-family basis than those in the Ekaterinoslav and Tauride provinces, but the difference in no way accounts for the significantly higher net surplus retained in the latter two regions. Taxes for the Bessarabian colonies averaged 14.6 rubles per family and for Odessa 15.2 rubles, while for Ekaterinoslav they were 9.4 rubles and for Tauride 7.6 rubles. The better results in the Ekaterinoslav and Tauride provinces stem from other causes.

Sales of grain and animals and their products were higher and in some cases substantially higher in the Tauride and Ekaterinoslav provinces than in Bessarabia or Odessa. The best per-family results in grain sales came from the Tauride Province, with the Moločna non-Mennonite colonists earning 78.3 silver rubles per family, first among all the individual groups. The Berdjansk colonists were second at 36.1 rubles, and the Moločna Mennonites third at 34.8 rubles. The Mariupol' colonists in Ekaterinoslav also did well, earning on average 32.3 rubles from grain sales. The best in the other regions was the Berezan District from Odessa at 28.2 rubles. Again, as the Klöstitz and Liebental districts reported no earnings from grain, the averages for the Bessarabian and Odessa provinces as a whole appear understated. However, the Berezan figures suggest that even if results were underreported for Odessa and Bessarabia, these provinces were still likely to have been well under the leaders. The best results in the sale of animals and their products came from the Xortica Mennonites from Ekaterinoslav, who earned on average 69.6 rubles per family. Sheep were likely the source of these results, as they were for the Moločna

---

91. If it were assumed that the Klöstitz District earned the same amount in grain sales as the Malojaroslav District and that in the Other Products category the Sarata District and Schabo had a surplus equal to the same per family amount as the very high Malojaroslav District (15.5 silver rubles), the total Bessarabian per family net retained surplus would climb from 21.9 to 29.0 silver rubles, still far below the next higher group, Ekaterinoslav Province with 71.23 silver rubles.

non-Mennonite colonies in Tauride that were second best at 51.8 rubles per family. This is not surprising as the Xortica colonies reported holdings of 80.6 sheep per family, and the Moločna non-Mennonite colonists averaged 89.6, with all the sheep in both groups belonging to improved breeds. The Malojaroslav District in Bessarabia, as noted above, was in third place in per-family earnings from the sale of animals at 32 rubles, followed by the Mariupol' colonists in Ekaterinoslav at 25.7 rubles.

The better overall results from the German colonies in the Tauride and Ekaterinoslav provinces seem driven by two factors. Colonists there had been living in Russia longer and as a result, had had more time to learn the varieties of grain that did well, and the techniques they needed to apply, as well as to learn about and acquire those animals that were best adjusted to the climate and conditions of the steppe. A second factor that is apparently behind the better results of the Tauride and Ekaterinoslav colonies is that they were physically located closer to or had easier river or overland routes to reach large local markets in such towns as Ekaterinoslav, Berdjansk, Xerson, and Nikolayev and, crucially, the rapidly expanding local and international markets in Odessa.

## The 1841 survey also provided data on the Bulgarian colonies in Bessarabia

The advantages of greater familiarity with local conditions can be seen by comparing the results of the Bessarabian German colonies in the 1841 survey to those of Bulgarian colonies also located in Bessarabia. The Bulgarians, natives of the region south of the Danube, were quite accustomed to the general agricultural conditions that existed in Bessarabia. Beginning in 1808, when the Russian army took control of land beyond the Dniester River, numbers of Bulgarians crossed the Danube and were permitted to settle in what became Bessarabia. In doing so, the Bulgarians escaped the control of the Ottoman Turks and settled in a land where their Orthodox faith was to be predominant. When, in 1827–28, Russia again initiated military campaigns in Romania seeking territory at the expense of the Ottoman Empire, more Bulgarians were permitted to move to Bessarabia. Thus, the Bulgarian colonies in Bessarabia had been established over roughly the same period as the German colonies. The Bulgarian colonies were generally located to the northwest, west, and southwest of where the German settlements were created in Bessarabia. Some of the Bulgarian colonies were neighbors of the Germans: Tvardica, Kiriet Lunga, Džoltaj, and Avdarma were just above Wittenberg and to the west of Alt Posttal, Tarutino, and Kulm; and Devlet-Agač was the next village down the Allijaga Valley from Neu Elft.

In the 1841 survey, the Bulgarian colonies were grouped into the Upper and Lower Budjak districts.[92] While the Bulgarians brought more primitive agricultural techniques to Bessarabia than the Germans, they also brought detailed knowledge

---

92. The division between the Upper and Lower Budjak groups is generally a line running east and west from just below the German colony of Wittenberg. The Bulgarian villages of Tvardica and Kiriet Lunga lying north of this line are in the Upper Budjak, while the villages of Čumlekioj and others lying to the south of it are in the Lower Budjak. An exception to this rule, perhaps as the Welfare Committee wished to have roughly equal numbers of Bulgarian colonies in both groups, is the village of Čadyr-Lunga, which, though situated at about the same distance south of this line as Čumlekioj, is in the Upper Budjak district.

of the plants and animals that did well in the steppe conditions. As a result, even as late as 1841, the surplus results for the Bulgarian colonies in Bessarabia were as good as or better than the results of the German colonies.

As with the tables above, the surplus earnings noted below are measured in silver rubles acquired from the sales of produce and animals (see table 5–15).

The Bulgarian colonies, with 5,034 families, were more than double the size of the German colonies at 2,348 families. This accounts in part for the large size of the raw numbers of the Bulgarian totals. The Bulgarians had slightly lower per-person average tax amounts than did the Bessarabian Germans, which was another factor in their better results. However, despite the fact that the Bulgarians lacked the technical skills and better agricultural techniques, and judging from Klaus' descriptions, didn't put in the same general effort as the Germans, they produced better results on a per-family basis. What they did have was local knowledge. This advantage shows up most predominately in the differences in grain sales, where the Bulgarian per-family results were nearly double those of the Germans. Without details on crops and yields, though, it is not possible to understand any of the factors that led to this result. With the sale of animals and wool, the survey provides some detail for the causes of the different results. On a per-family basis, the Bulgarian families earned 15 percent more from such sales than did the Germans. The Bulgarians kept nearly as many cattle as the Germans, 9.6 per family versus the German average of 10.2, so it would not appear that the sale of cattle was part of the better results achieved by the Bulgarians. Rather, the difference seems related to holdings of sheep where both the number and type of sheep kept by the Bulgarians stand out. The Bulgarians had 165 percent more sheep on a per-family basis, an average of 48.4 per family in comparison to 18.2 for the Germans. Moreover, 81.5 percent of the sheep in Bulgarian herds were the improved breeds versus just 10.2 percent for the Germans. As the results for the German colonies in the Ekaterinoslav and Tauride provinces indicated, sheep herds of the improved stock thrived in the steppe climate and sold well in the Russian market. That the Bulgarians grasped this ahead of the Germans

TABLE 5–15. **Surplus earned in the German and Bulgarian colonies in Bessarabia**

| | Grain | Animals and wool | Other products | Total surplus | Taxes owed | Net surplus | Net surplus/ family |
|---|---|---|---|---|---|---|---|
| **German** | | | | | | | |
| Malojaroslav | 13,836 | 30,582 | 14,817 | 59,235 | 15,154 | 44,081 | 46.1 |
| Klöstitz | — | 16,932 | 4,975 | 21,907 | 17,036 | 4,871 | 4.4 |
| Total German Bessarabia[a] | 14,847 | 49,214 | 21,605 | 85,666 | 34,299 | 51,367 | 21.9 |
| Per family | 6.3 | 21.0 | 9.2 | 36.5 | 14.6 | | |
| **Bulgarian** | | | | | | | |
| Upper Budjak | 31,477 | 82,458 | 17,793 | 131,728 | 29,717 | 102,011 | 37.0 |
| Lower Budjak | 27,315 | 38,618 | 5,944 | 71,877 | 30,541 | 41,336 | 18.1 |
| Total Bulgarian Bessarabia | 58,792 | 121,076 | 23,737 | 203,605 | 60,258 | 143,347 | 28.5 |
| Per family | 11.7 | 24.1 | 4.7 | 40.4 | 12.0 | | |

a. This row also includes the small figures for the Sarata and Schabo districts.

in Bessarabia is not likely the result of the fact that they were more wealthy and could buy them more quickly, but because they were more knowledgeable about both the breeds of sheep that did well in local conditions and market interests.

## Some of the 1848 village histories provided economic data or commentary on economic progress

The next look at detailed economic conditions in the German colonies in Bessarabia comes from materials included in three of the 1848 village histories. As part of their accounting for the progress of the colony, the authors of the Wittenberg and Alt and Neu Elft histories provide some details on human and animal populations in 1848. These allow comparisons with data from the Welfare Committee's 1825 survey (see table 5–16).

Both communities that provided 1848 population data show substantial growth from 1825: Wittenberg grew by almost 60 percent and Neu Elft doubled. As data from the 1841 survey indicate, there had been a growing consensus among the Bessarabian Germans that sheep held attractive economic advantages. The significant growth in the number of sheep, which all three villages show and which evidently came at the expense of cattle, suggests a recognition that sales of sheep and wool did well. Given that there is no mention in the village histories of losses of sheep to animal plagues, the growth in the size of village herds may also suggest the recognition that raising sheep entailed fewer risks. For Wittenberg, where per-family measurements are possible with the 1848 data, the average family holdings of horses and cattle are close to the per-family averages of the Malojaroslav District to which it belonged in the 1841 survey.[93] With regard to sheep, there was a 36 percent increase in the per-family holdings from an average herd of 21.9 for the Malojaroslav District in 1841, to a per-family average of 29.8 sheep for Wittenberg in 1848. The nearly eight-fold increase in the number of sheep in Neu Elft from 1825 to 1848 and six-fold increase in Alt Elft in the same period point in the same direction: that these colonies, having grasped the greater advantages of sheep, were moving along the positive economic track we have seen developed by the Germans in the Tauride and Ekaterinoslav provinces and by the Bulgarians in Bessarabia.

TABLE 5–16. **Population data for three Bessarabian German colonies, 1825 and 1848**

| | Wittenberg | | Neu Elft | | Alt Elft | |
|---|---|---|---|---|---|---|
| **Population** | **1825** | **1848** | **1825** | **1848** | **1825** | **1848** |
| Human | | | | | | |
| Families | 82 | 77 | 63 | — | 82 | — |
| Males | 254 | 386 | 126 | — | 156 | — |
| Females | 229 | 382 | 132 | — | 166 | — |
| **Total** | 483 | 768 | 258 | 537 | 322 | — |
| Animals | | | | | | |
| Horses | 227 | 259 | 86 | 206 | 127 | 200 |
| Cattle | 1,237 | 859 | 561 | 818 | 672 | 869 |
| Sheep | 173 | 2,294 | 157 | 1,361 | 241 | 1,653 |

93. The per-family holdings for the Malojaroslav District in 1841 were 3.5 horses per family and 11.7 cattle. These figures compare with 3.3 horses and 11.2 cattle for Wittenberg in 1848.

The Alt Elft history also provides details on fruit trees, grapevines, and grain seed planted in 1848 that show the colony making major investments in fruit and grapevines but not yet in grain (see table 5–17).

Although others of the 1848 Bessarabian village histories do not provide detailed information for 1848, virtually all made some comment on the economic state of their colony at the time the history was written. These documents, as noted earlier, were locally written and followed a pattern of suggested topics.[94] The final topic typically addressed is the current condition of the village. All the villages note losses suffered from a continuing series of crop failures, insect infestations, and animal plagues, some even in the recent past. Nine colonies, for example, reported crop losses or failures in 1847 and eight reported losses from cattle epidemics in 1844–45. Nonetheless, nearly all report village conditions over the past few years as trending positively. It cannot be discounted that the village history authors, in indicating this, sought to please Welfare Committee officials, whose aide is in most histories emphasized, but the repeated refrain likely carried some elements of truth. Neu Arzis reports that even with the hardships, "conditions have begun to improve."[95] Alt Arzis notes "everyone lives contentedly"[96] and the colony now has sixty of eighty-four houses built of stone. Neu Elft calls present conditions "favorable"[97]; Dennewitz calls attention to the "current economic well-being"[98]; and Brienne also contrasts its "present prosperity" to earlier conditions.[99] In describing the current state of economic health of the villages, a repeated refrain is that while one cannot call the village rich or prosperous, in the present conditions, it is doing all right. Borodino notes that with the misfortunes suffered, one could not call the village prosperous "in the full sense of the word"; still, the village "belonged to the more well to do among the Bessarabia communities."[100] Neu Elft mentions that while current conditions are good "one

TABLE 5–17. **Agricultural data for Alt Elft, 1848**

|  | 1825 | 1848 |
|---|---|---|
| Fruit trees | 1,322 | 9,432 |
| Grapevines | 0 | 155,100 |
| Winter rye | 41.1 | 31.4[a] |
| Winter wheat | 45.0 | 19.6 |

a. The 1848 figures for grain planted have been translated in the English-language version of the Alt Elft village history (http://www.odessa3.org/collections/history/link/altelft.txt) into bushels, which I have here put back into četvert'. The Alt Elft history also gives a figure for what is presumably grain for human consumption planted in the spring of 1848, which may include summer wheat, buckwheat and barley, and millet. In 1825, Alt Elft planted 87 četvert' of these grains; in 1848, "2,249 bushels of grains" are noted in the translation, which would be 377.3 četvert'.

---

94. The author of the Friedenstal village history, the church school teacher Jacob Eckert, notes that he had written the history in the "format requested" and indicates that this format was supplied in a letter of January 8, 1848 [O.S.], from Welfare Committee chairman Eduard von Hahn. This suggests a copy of this letter requesting the village histories went to each village. Eckert, "Friedenstal – 1848 Village History," trans. Elvire Necker-Eberhardt (N.p.: Odessa Digital Library, 2000), http://www.odessa3.org/collections/history/link/friedtal.txt.

95. Ziemann, "Neu Arzis – 1848 Village History."

96. Neumann, "Alt Arzis – 1848 Village History."

97. Kurz, "Neu Elft – 1848 Village History."

98. Haas, "Dennewitz – 1848 Village History," trans. Elvire Necker-Eberhardt (N.p.: Odessa Digital Library, 2000), http://www.odessa3.org/collections/history/link/dennew.txt.

99. Minderlin, "Brienne – 1848 Village History."

100. Eckert, "Borodino – 1848 Village History."

cannot speak of actual wealth yet,"[101] and Beresina notes that while the misfortunes experienced "have not let the colonists experience a true sense of well-being…they rightfully expect it in the future,"[102] as their wine industry is doing well.

A second repeated refrain is to indicate the colony's emerging prosperity in spite of past and current difficulties. Alt Posttal notes that the "settlers have come to a degree of prosperity despite the frequent hindrances,"[103] Wittenberg notes that while the colony is not yet in ideal state, "conditions have improved enormously,"[104] and the Paris history indicates that "despite [many difficulties] prosperity…has been raised in the last few years."[105] In some cases, a positive note sounds without a "despite." Friedenstal notes an "obvious upswing" bringing increased wealth to the village and that over the past five years "the earlier sad condition [of the village] has disappeared totally."[106] Tarutino ends its history with perhaps the most positive message, noting that the colony had increased its gardens and orchards and had received great bene-fits from a cattle and fruit market that was held every two weeks. In summing up, the history then generally assigns credit for the village's well-being: "The advancing prosperity of this colony is credited to farming, wine making, raising cattle, and the diligence of the women, who spin wool and weave throughout the winter."[107]

Alt Posttal, Alt and Neu Elft, Dennewitz, and Wittenberg also call attention to the diligence of women "spinning, weaving, knitting and sewing."[108] The implica-tion is that such work saves money by avoiding the need to purchase cloth, though the Neu Elft, Dennewitz, and Wittenberg histories mention that such work was also made for sale. The Wittenberg history made the most detailed reference to the economic value of the work done by women: "The business oriented women raised sheep and in the winter they used the wool to spin, weave and sew clothing for themselves, using flax and hemp to help support the household need. That saved a lot of expenses and even brought extra income."[109]

Beyond the needs of food and clothing that could be supplied from the family farmsteads in Bessarabia, prosperity as described in the village histories also implied the production of surplus. While the focus here is on surplus created in animal stock and products of the land, surplus was also created by the local manufacture of tools and equipment, such as ax handles and wagons, or through the sale of services from shoemaking to carpentry to milling. Surplus animals, fruit, wine, and grain could be capitalized through cash and barter sales made within one's village. Local transactions, though, needed parties interested in both acquiring and selling, matches not always to be found within the village. The regular biweekly regional markets in Tarutino, and later in Alt Arzis and Sarata, increased the odds of finding matches and so became widely attended, popular events. Surplus cattle, horses,

---

101. Kurz, "Neu Elft – 1848 Village History."
102. Foerster, "Beresina – 1848 Village History."
103. Kludt, "Alt Posttal – 1848 Village History."
104. Kurz, "Wittenberg – 1848 Village History."
105. Dieno, "Paris – 1848 Village History."
106. Eckert, "Friedenstal – 1848 Village History."
107. Martin, "Tarutino – 1848 Village History."
108. The Dennewitz history is quoted here (Haas, "Dennewitz – 1848 Village History"). The Alt Posttal history speaks to the work of women creating thread, weaving and processing wool and Alt Elft to the weaving of wool and linen. Neu Elft ties the growing prosperity of the village in part to women's diligence.
109. Kurz, "Wittenberg – 1848 Village History."

sheep, wool, fruit, and grain were offered for sale as well as wine and food products. The following chapter will discuss the broadening of these markets and their success in drawing participants from the neighboring Bulgarian, Gaugaz, Moldavian, Ukrainian, and Russian settlements, as well as other evidences of village prosperity such as the construction of churches, schools, and other public buildings. The point I wish to make here is that through the 1840s, such village and regional markets were the primary places where families acquired cash from surplus for personal uses and tax payments, and that it was the sale of animals and their products, in particular cattle, sheep, and wool, which were the primary sources of surplus income for the Bessarabian Germans. Where the village histories mention values of property or sales, such as in the Sarata and Wittenberg histories, cattle and oxen are the focus. Cattle, as the 1825 and 1841 surveys indicate, were the largest animal holdings of the Bessarabian Germans, and surplus gained from animals, as the 1841 survey shows, was far and away the greatest source of surplus earnings.

Over time, grain sales would supplant earnings from animals. Though the sale of grain had become a source of income for the Bessarabian Germans in the 1840s, this lagged well behind sales of animals and fruit products. In the 1841 survey, surplus grain sales made up 17.3 percent of gross surplus for the Bessarabian Germans. In the best-performing Malojaroslav District, grain sales made up 23.4 percent of surplus, while 51.6 percent of gross surplus came from the sale of animals and wool and 25.0 percent from the sale of fruit and wine. In the 1840s, grain-producing harvests were not certain, and the grain type sown was not always the most productive nor was the grain market yet attractively developed. Although the village histories were no longer frequently reporting infestations of grasshoppers and locusts, years of crop failures from drought or field mice and gophers were not uncommon. A second reason for the modest totals of surplus from grain sales is that such sales appear generally to be local where demand was modest and the prices offered were low. In the 1840s, transportation issues within Bessarabia made the domestic Russian market hard to access. The export market from the port of Odessa was at this time just developing, and only began to heat up at the end of the decade.

Russian, Ukrainian, and especially Jewish grain buyers, called *čumaki* after the heavy oxen that pulled the carts they used, circulated though the southern provinces buying grain to sell in Russian markets or, increasingly, for shipment from Odessa. Ethnic Greek merchants were the major shippers of grain from Odessa, their vessels carrying it to ports in Great Britain, the Netherlands, Belgium, and France. The merchants would sell and then repurchase their cargos several times while ships were en route and so create in crude form a grain futures mechanism to lay off risk. Such sales would later, as communications improved, inform ship's captains as to which port would offer the best price and so determine the destination.[110] Prices for farmers producing grain varied materially. Prices inland, where the grain was grown, could be as much as 3–6 silver rubles per *četvert* of wheat, lower compared to prices offered at the port in Odessa. In the 1840s, Germans in Bessarabia were not yet in the habit of taking their grain to Odessa, because grain surpluses were not constant or were low, the difficulty of making the overland journey to Odessa was deemed too great, or the difference in price between what the *čumaki* offered locally and

---

110. Martin Rothstein, "Centralizing Firms and Spreading Markets: The World of International Grain Traders, 1846–1914," *Business and Economic History*, 2nd ser., 17 (1988): 106–7.

what they received in Odessa wasn't fully recognized. This clearly is the meaning of the passage in the 1848 Sarata Village History that notes "since good grain harvest is rare here, and since the grain would have to be taken to a port, the cost and time, was not worth the effort."[111]

For the Bessarabian Germans, the idea that grain could be an important source of earnings was catching on even as the 1848 histories were being written. Odessa's growth as a grain entrepôt was spurred by Great Britain's repeal of the Corn Laws, the mercantilist restrictions and tariffs on imported grains, in 1846 (fully effective in 1849), which opened that country to the import of far cheaper food grains. The continuing growth of urban centers in Great Britain and the Low Countries brought a steady demand for increasing grain imports. Spurred by a growth in industry and trade, urban centers in northwestern Europe became steadily larger. Local agricultural resources were no longer sufficient there to feed the urban populations and imported grain from Eastern Europe often proved to be cheaper than that grown locally. At the other end of the market chain, success in producing high yields started to become a more regular harvest expectation for the Bessarabian Germans beginning in the 1850s. For the most part, the colonists had mastered growing the hard wheats that did well in the steppe soil and climate. Particularly important was the realization, becoming more widely spread in the late 1840s and early 1850s, that forms of hard red winter wheat brought both greater yields and were greatly sought after in the Odessa market.[112] Insect infestations became less common, as throughout the first half of the nineteenth century. The Russian government had given away or sold crown landholdings of Bessarabian steppeland; more steppeland, as a result, was given over to animal pasture or brought under cultivation. This appears to have reduced in large measure the breeding grounds of the grasshoppers and locusts, making them far less of a hazard. The combination of improved crop knowledge and growing techniques with far fewer insect incursions meant better harvests with higher yields and thus increased surplus.

The Crimean War (1853–56) temporarily stopped the grain shipments to Western Europe, but at its end in the spring of 1856, trade picked up at even higher levels. In the 1850s, most grain sales among the Germans in Bessarabia appear to have been made locally to the čumaki factors, but trips by groups of German farmers to Odessa became, over time, more common. Taking grain to Odessa brought Bessarabian Germans into significantly greater contact with products not produced at home, such as sugar, tea, and tobacco as well as manufactured goods of wide variety, such as cloth and clothing, tools and equipment, jewelry, and luxury items. As a result, trips to Odessa became a two-way economic street, exposing the travelers to the material and technological changes and the new temptations sweeping through nineteenth-century Europe.

## Detailed economic data from the village of Leipzig exists as part of an 1856–57 census

Even with the temporary closure of the port in Odessa during the war, the 1850s appear to have brought economic improvements to the Bessarabian Germans. We

---

111. Natterer, "Sarata – 1848 Village History."
112. Glenn D. Kuehn, "Hard-Kernelled Red Winter Wheat: A Legacy of Our German-Russian Ancestors on the Great Plains of North America," *Heritage Review* 45, no. 1 (2015): 11–12.

can see this in the last set of economic data available on the German colonies in Bessarabia. It is from only one colony, Leipzig, but is unusually rich and detailed. It was collected as part of the 1856–57 census and for some reason was collated with the census material. The economic data are of such detail that it is likely they were gathered on instructions from the Welfare Committee and so likely exist for other colonies as well.

Leipzig, heretofore, had not been one of the more successful German colonies in Bessarabia. It was located on the northern edge of the German settlement area on the eastern bank of the Kogil'nik River about 6 miles upstream from Kulm and 12 from Beresina. In the 1825 survey, Leipzig did poorly in comparison to its neighboring villages, ranking last in the numbers of horses, cattle, and wheat yields, and next-to-last in grapevines.[113] In the 1841 economic survey, Leipzig belonged to the Klöstitz District, which had the poorest results among the Bessarabian German colonies. The 1848 Leipzig Village History focuses on ethical and economic lapses in the colony, but ends with the thought that conditions were improving as Leipzig "[tried] to become as progressive as other south Russian colonies."[114]

While Leipzig's progress through 1848 was evidently not sterling, the data for 1856–57 suggests economic conditions had much improved. The 1856–57 material provided data on the holdings of 213 households, each designated by the name of the primary householder. These are all male with the exception of four households headed by widows. The 213 households occupied 121 of the original 128 farmstead grants.[115] While a material number of the 121 properties (54 or 45 percent) were held by a single property owner, the majority of properties were jointly held by two or more families. In almost all cases the families jointly holding property together were related. A common pattern was a father holding a property jointly with his married sons, such as the Martins in property #76, the Pohls in property #67, the Brauns in property #61, and the Bierwagens in property #24. Variants of this were property #9, where ownership was divided between a widowed mother, Sophia Sommerfeldt Kühn, and her widowed daughter, Friederike Kühn Flegel, or property #112, where ownership was divided between Gottfried Neumann and his father-in-law, Michael Bäsler, on the one hand, and Johann Neumann, Gottfried's cousin, on the other. Another common pattern was that of male siblings inheriting their father's property such as the Lang brothers in property #30, the Kraft brothers in property #38, and the Fruck brothers in property #86. A variant of this pattern was the joint ownership by the Weikum brothers of property #28, although their widowed father, Christoph Weikum, aged sixty in 1856, was still alive and presumably living in retirement with them.

---

113. This point compares the per-family holdings from the 1825 survey for Leipzig with the neighboring settlements of Kulm, Tarutino, Borodino, Beresina, Klöstitz, Alt Posttal, and Wittenberg.

114. Trautmann, "Leipzig – 1848 Village History."

115. The Leipzig village history mentions there were 128 "founding families" (Trautmann, "Leipzig – 1848 Village History"), while Stumpp notes (*Emigration from Germany to Russia*, 532) that there were 126 founding families and the 1856–57 census refers to 128 properties in Leipzig. Only 121 of these properties are occupied in 1856 with no one listed as living on properties 1, 2, 3, 91, 96, 106, and 116. The Leipzig history mentions that in 1841–42, "many…were taken with the wandering fever…and went to Serbia" (Trautmann, "Leipzig – 1848 Village History"). The history further notes that in 1843, 15 families came from Rohrbach and Worms in the Berezan district of Xerson Province to settle in Leipzig. Birth records indicate that some Berezan newcomers, however, were in Leipzig in the summer of 1842. The implication of the 1856–57 census numbers is that even with this addition not all the abandoned farmsteads had been taken up.

There were, in addition, two properties held by families with no evident blood or marital relationships, which suggest a de facto subdivision of the property. Jacob Mädsche and Friedrich Treichel each owned one half of property #64 and Jacob Jabs is listed as renting on the property as well. The Treichel family, one of the founders of Leipzig, settled property #64 but seem not to have done well there. Jacob Mädsche, who came to Leipzig from Worms in the Berezan District in 1843 had no blood or marital connection with the Treichels and would thus appear to have acquired de facto rights to his half the property by an agreement or purchase. The implication of their joint ownership and the continued prohibition against subdividing in German Bessarabia is that legally, the farmstead was a single indivisible entity jointly possessed. The same situation appears in the tangled multi-family ownership of property #10 where Jacob Kühn and Johann Daniel Buchwitz, who were not related and had no earlier family connection to the property, are listed as part-owners. In addition, Christoph Kranich and Joseph Tschikorsky, the latter related by marriage to Buchwitz, are also listed as having homesites within property #10, but show no earlier family relationships with the property. The Jesse family into which both Buchwitz and Tschikorsky married also shows no connection to #10. In 1856, both Buchwitz and Kühn were recently married and perhaps in need of independent property. It may be that property #10 had been abandoned in 1842 and not filled by one of the arriving Berezan families. With the frequency of properties jointly managed by siblings with at times the families at times living in different buildings on the property, it may be that the Welfare Committee became used to the practice of de facto joint ownership or even the establishment of independent homesteads within a property. Given the absence of any relaxation in the rule against subdivision at this time, it is likely that legally the separate sections of the property could not be independently disposed of or further divided.

The ten families noted as possessing a homesite or a homesite with a bit of land to garden on the farmstead of another family are similar to the cottagers described by Hagen as a frequently encountered class in eighteenth-century Brandenburg. The families of the widowed mother and daughter who held property #9 shared that property with the family of Christian Lasson, who is listed as a farmer and shoe-maker with a homesite there and 4 desjatina of land leased elsewhere. A similar example would be Paul Bäsler, who had a homesite on property #13 and, like Lasson, is noted as having several horses, cattle, and sheep, and leasing 4 desjatina of land. Poorer homesite owners also existed in Leipzig. Andreas Höhn had a homesite on property #16 with one horse and three cattle and is described as a day laborer. Johann Treichel, who had a homesite on property #4, owned only four cattle and a thresher from which he earned 20 rubles a year.[116]

In addition to the class of villagers who had a small homesite on the farmstead property of another family, there was a class of renters paying for a place to live and, as they often did craftwork, a place to ply their trade. The thirteen individuals described as renters were of greatly varying economic standing. Some, like Michael Ganske, whose father was a Leipzig founder but "disappeared,"[117] rented on prop-

116.   Johann was the brother of Friedrich Treichel, noted above, who was half-owner of his father's farmstead, property #64.

117.   Flegel, *Extended Relationships*, 201. As the context is the marriage listing of Michael's older brother, Ferdinand, it would seem Michael Ganske's father, also a Michael, was one of those who abandoned Leipzig in 1842–43.

erty #14 and owned no animals, trees, or grapevines. He is described as a laborer and was clearly less well off than the poorest of those listed as having a homesite only. Jacob Jabs, noted above as renting on property #64, was in a similar situation. He is described as a laborer but owned two horses and three cattle. Several of those described as renters were engaged in full-time trade and had reportable annual earnings. Andreas Weber, who came to Leipzig from Borodino, was renting on property #66 and is described as a wheelwright earning 40 silver rubles a year. Even better off was Andreas Hoffmann, a cabinetmaker, who rented on property #65 and earned 50 silver rubles a year from trade. Hoffmann would also have inheritance rights to a share of property #43 then operated by his father, Jacob.

The economic measurements contained in the Leipzig census materials of 1856–57 include counts of the number of animals, wagons, and plows as well as estimates[118] of the number of shade trees, fruit trees, and grapevines. From these it is possible to see what average holdings looked like, as well as families who stood on both margins of the economic scale. Also included are estimates of the value of various business ventures such as mills and, as noted already, the annual or seasonal income of several occupations. The variety of data collected offers some insight into how different households specialized, what economic courses proved successful, how household assets were divided without dividing the household land, and the differences in holdings between the most well-to-do and the poorest households.

Several of the economic categories collected in 1856–57 are the same as those collected in 1825 for Leipzig and in 1841 for the Klöstitz District of which Leipzig was a part, and so permit a comparison of the totals and the per-family averages (see table 5–18).

The 1856–57 data show significant gains in both the total village numbers and the per-family holdings for all categories from the 1825 figures. There were material gains in the numbers of shade and fruit trees, and particularly in the number of grapevines, where it is evident that many villagers had been making investments. The buildup in the size of herds of sheep from 1825 is also significant (+249 percent), but the Leipzig average for 1856–57 still lags behind the low-achieving Klöstitz District for 1841. Sheep would, over time, become an important source of income

TABLE 5–18. **Leipzig data for 1856–57 shows a material improvement from prior surveys**

|  | Horses | Cattle | Sheep | Hogs | Shade trees | Fruit trees | Grapevines |
|---|---|---|---|---|---|---|---|
| Total 1856–57 numbers | 734 | 2,029 | 2,327 | 324 | 15,840 | 8,014 | 121,632 |
| 1856–57 Average per household Household | 3.5 | 9.5 | 10.9 | 1.5 | 74.4 | 37.6 | 571.0 |
| Total 1825 numbers | 229 | 1,225 | 666 | 173 | 184 | 1,887 | 1,342 |
| 1825 Average per family | 1.7 | 8.9 | 4.8 | 1.3 | 1.3 | 13.7 | 9.7 |
| 1841 Average per family for the Klöstitz District | 2.9 | 8.8 | 16.4 | — | 5.0 | 26.9 | 426.5 |

118. That the numbers of grapevines and fruit and shade trees are in most cases estimations is strongly implied by the fact that these numbers are given in even thousands, hundreds, or fifties (thus Wilhelm Pahl is noted as having three hundred shade trees, three hundred fruit trees and eight hundred grapevines). Only in a few cases dealing in small numbers (Jacob Mann, for example, owned eight fruit trees) can there be a presumption of exactness.

for the Bessarabian Germans, including those living in Leipzig, as they had become for Germans in the Ekaterinoslav and Tauride provinces. In 1856–57, though, the economic investment in sheep in Leipzig was still in its early stages.

Data on grain production were not included in 1856–57 census. Had such data been included, they would likely have shown a significant improvement over the poor results on display in the 1825 survey where Leipzig's harvests and per-family yields were among the lowest of all the German colonies in Bessarabia. Grain was an important part of Leipzig's nineteenth-century economy, as Kern notes in his study.[119] The positive influence of grain in the Leipzig economy of 1856–57 is likely reflected in the number and success of the mills owned and operated by Leipzig citizens and possibly by the increase in the average number of horses.

There was also a significant growth in the number of shade trees in Leipzig from 1825 to 1856–57. The Welfare Committee was interested in this category, as the original settlement agreements for the German colonies mandated that each village set aside common land on which to plant and nurture trees. Wood was a valuable commodity on the treeless steppe of Bessarabia, and woodlands became an important means to control soil erosion after the steppe had been plowed. The substantial average number of shade trees by household in Leipzig, 74.4, suggests that in addition to the common area reserved for trees, many farmsteads allocated a part of their own land as well to grow additional trees. The wood from these would have both a household use and an economic value in sale.

The Leipzig data shows a great deal of variation in holdings per household, indicating that clear differences have occurred that separate low-, middle-, and high-income families. While the figures for many villagers cluster around the averages, showing a large middle class in reasonable prosperity, there are some, particularly renters and even some property owners, who were apparently living on the margins with a fair bit of risk. At the other end of the spectrum, some families, notably those who had built and operated mills or who had a useful trade in addition to their farm, were doing quite well and had accumulated sizeable assets in animals, trees, grapevines, the values of mills, or cash (see table 5–19).

TABLE 5–19. **Differences between families in the Leipzig 1856–57 data**

| | Horses | Cattle | Sheep | Hogs | Shade Trees | Fruit Trees | Grapevines |
|---|---|---|---|---|---|---|---|
| J. Bäsler | 3 | 17 | 14 | 2 | 105 | 105 | 800 |
| C. Hinz | 8 | 14 | 23 | 5 | 150 | 20 | 1,000 |
| G. and G. Pahl | 12 | 37 | 42 | 9 | 150 | 200 | 3,000 |
| Rutschke Family | 14 | 47 | 79 | 5 | 300 | 4 | 1,100 |
| S. Fiedler | 5 | 10 | — | — | — | — | — |
| S. Lütke | 4 | 11 | 9 | 2 | — | — | 200 |
| J. Hennig | 4 | 2 | 5 | 5 | 50 | 30 | 105 |
| C. Lasson | 3 | 10 | 9 | — | — | — | — |
| M. Wiersche | 0 | 0 | 0 | 0 | 0 | 0 | 0 |
| Leipzig average per household | 3.5 | 9.5 | 10.9 | 1.5 | 74.4 | 37.6 | 571.0 |

---

119. Kern, *Homeland Book*, 142.

Johann Bäsler and Christian Hinz represent the middle class, at least from the holdings collected in the 1856–57 Leipzig data, with numbers generally above the village averages. The figures for both suggest some specialization: cattle and fruit trees for Bäsler and sheep, grapevines, and probably grain (judging by the number of horses) for Hinz. Gottfried Pahl and his son Gottlieb are among the well-to-do families in Leipzig. They are listed as jointly owning property #85, which included a mill valued at 70 silver rubles. The profits from the mill perhaps provided the cash that allowed them to invest in more grapevines and to keep larger numbers of cattle, sheep, and hogs. Gottfried Rutschke and his sons Gottlieb and Friedrich are listed as each owing a third of property #42 and, at least in terms of the number of livestock owned, they were one of the wealthiest families in Leipzig in this era. They also were wheelwrights, and from their earnings had accumulated the cash needed to build their herds and keep them fed over winter for profitable sale later. The father, Gottfried, is noted as possessing 30 silver rubles, while one son, Gottlieb, had 350 silver rubles, and the second, Friedrich, is reported to have earned 40 rubles for five months of work during the year as a wheelwright.

In contrast at the other end of the economic scale, Samuel Fiedler rented a place to live on property #122 from the Klauss family. With a family of eight to feed, he likely worked as a laborer for the Klauss family and perhaps others. Fiedler, though, was not without assets; he owned five horses and ten cattle, suggesting he earned additional money from using his horses to plow and harvest, and raised some of his cattle for sale. Christian Lasson seems a step up from Fiedler. Lasson, who appears to have come to Leipzig after the founding of the colony, possessed, as noted earlier, a homesite plot on property #9, leased 4 desjatina of land, had three horses, ten cattle and nine sheep, and in addition, had a trade as a shoemaker from which he earned 35 rubles in eight months of work. Lasson and Fiedler are both in better shape than Michael Wiersche, who rented living space from Gottfried Werner on property #74, had no animals, and worked as a farm laborer earning 30 rubles a year.

As with the differences in the situations between Wiersche and Lasson and Fiedler, there appear clear distinctions in the holdings of the less well-to-do in Leipzig that suggest both varying levels of poverty and an ongoing fluidity of family situations that were both rising and falling. Samuel Lütke was, in 1857, roughly at the same economic level as Christian Lasson. Like Lasson, he had a small home-site on another family's farmstead, rented land for crops, and had roughly average village holdings in horses, cattle, and sheep. In 1857, however, Lasson was forty-nine years old, had no other family in Leipzig, and, while evidently starting from very modest beginnings, had reached the upper end of wealth among cottagers with his earnings as a shoemaker. Perhaps he reached the limit of his prospects. Lütke, in contrast, was twenty-nine years old in 1857, was the grandson of an original settler of Leipzig, rented more land than Lasson (6 compared to 4 desjatina), and, as his father owned half of property #119, likely had hopes of further improving his lot by gaining control of more land. In contrast, Johann Hennig is listed as the sole owner of the full property #21, presumably the original allotment of 60 desjatina that he and his younger brothers inherited from their father, Martin Hennig. However, in 1856–57, Hennig's total holdings of 2 cows, 5 sheep, 30 fruit trees and 105 grapevines place his farmstead among the poorest of farmsteads, behind the holdings of Lütke and Lasson, who had only household lots and rented land. It is possible, of course, that Hennig focused on the cultivation of grain and so the differences in net worth from the rest of the village were not as great as they appear. Nonetheless, with one brother, Wilhelm, leaving for Siberia and a second, Samuel, dying later from "heavy drinking,"[120] it may be that the Hennigs were simply not doing well.

Specialization appears to have been a key strategy for families who, in 1856–57, were in the upper layers of holdings of animals, fruit trees, and grapevines (see table 5–20). The brothers Gottlieb and Gottfried Quashnick, who were joint owners of property #97, had two thousand grapevines, well above the Leipzig average, and so clearly were focused on producing grapes and wine from them. The census also noted another family specialty in the listing for their father, Gottfried, now retired though living in the household. Gottfried kept forty-three bee hives, the only apiary noted in the Leipzig data, which was likely a valuable source of income. Samuel Giese with seven thousand grapevines, Joseph Fink with three thousand, and Gottfried Pahl and his son Gottlieb also with three thousand maintained the largest number of grapevines in the colony. The Pahls also had a small mill and had—tied with Wilhelm Müller— the second-largest herd of cattle (thirty-seven) in Leipzig behind the Rutscheke family, who had forty-seven. The 1856–57 Leipzig census suggests that cattle were an important part of the local economy. Of the 213 resident families, 86 had herds of more than ten cattle. Though sheep in general did not yet appear to be a major economic focus in Leipzig, there were some families who were specializing in this direction. Martin Guhlke and his son Jacob, owners of property #54, were leaders with a herd of ninety-eight. Another family strong in this area was Johann Jacob Beierle and his son Johann Peter, joint owners of property #73, with a herd of ninety-six.[121]

The Leipzig data from 1856–57 shows several instances of individuals supplementing farmstead income through various trade work. Jacob Wiege, who worked on property #103 with his father and siblings, also earned 30 silver rubles in nine months of work as a blacksmith. Christian Stelter, sharing property #34 with family members, earned 40 rubles a year as a part-time blacksmith. Shoemakers had roughly similar earnings to blacksmiths. The highest earnings in this trade were attributed to Ludwig Treichel,

TABLE 5-20. **Holdings of wealthier Leipzig families, 1856–57**

| | Horses | Cattle | Sheep | Hogs | Shade trees | Fruit trees | Grapevines |
|---|---|---|---|---|---|---|---|
| G. and G. Quashnick | 3 | 14 | 15 | — | 100 | 30 | 2,000 |
| S. Giese | 8 | 16 | 21 | 1 | 115 | 130 | 7,000 |
| J. Fink | 5 | 8 | 4 | 3 | 110 | 50 | 3,000 |
| G. and G. Pahl | 12 | 37 | 42 | 9 | 150 | 200 | 3,000 |
| M. and J. Guhlke | 7 | 20 | 98 | 3 | 200 | 12 | 1,000 |
| K. Klauss | — | 10 | — | — | — | 15 | 200 |
| Leipzig average per household | 3.5 | 9.5 | 10.9 | 1.5 | 74.4 | 37.6 | 571.0 |

120.  Flegel, *Extended Relationships*, 268.
121.  The Beierle family was among the settlers who came to Leipzig in 1842–43 to replace those who, as noted earlier, had left Bessarabia to try their luck outside Russia. The 1841 Survey indicates that in the Berezan District, herds of sheep had grown to 23.8 per family and were starting to become an important economic factor. The Beierles were economic innovators in bringing this focus to Leipzig.

who received 40 rubles for twelve months of work, and Christian Lasson, who earned 35 rubles for eight months of work. In comparison, the going rate for a farm laborer was payment of 30 rubles a year.[122] Thirty rubles was also the annual income earned by Wilhelm Eberhard, the village scribe, who held the only town position requiring formal education.[123] Johann Beierle, who owned property #37, and homesite-only resident Johann Treichel on property #4 owned early forms of threshing machines, the use of which earned them 15 and 20 rubles, respectively (see table 5-21).

Among the wealthiest citizens in Leipzig, however, were the ten mill owners. Reported annual earnings from milling do not seem large, 15 to 25 rubles,[124] but several mill owners are listed as having large cash hoards, and well above average numbers of animals and grapevines. Mill owners Wilhelm Müller and Daniel Ziehl are reported as each holding 500 rubles in cash, and both had large herds of sheep: Müller had 89 and Ziehl 83, where the average household number was 10.9. Mill owner Gottfried Pahl had 3,000 grapevines and Johann Jesse had 2,000 where the average was 571.0. The mills were clearly costly to build and maintain; the 1856–57 census valued them between 70 and 450 rubles, with the median value being 250 rubles. All of this strongly suggests that the reported earnings were not the actual full earnings of the mill owners, that instead their earnings were much higher and so justified the high costs of building a mill. Higher earnings would also explain the large cash reserves, and the large numbers of animals, grapevines, and other property mill owners had accumulated.

The wealthiest Leipzig resident listed in the 1856–57 census is Karl Klauss, a wine merchant. He is described as earning 80 rubles annually, far and away the largest reported trade income. He also had 650 rubles in cash, the largest cash hoard in the village. While the dimensions of Klauss' business are not clear, it would be fair to

TABLE 5–21. **Wheelwrights and cabinetmakers had the best-paid trade work in Leipzig**

| Profession | Earnings |
| --- | --- |
| **Wheelwrights** | |
| Friedrich Rutschke | 40 rubles (five months of work) |
| Andreas Weber | 40 rubles (twelve months of work) |
| Friedrich Werner | 50 rubles (six months of work) |
| **Cabinetmakers** | |
| Andreas Hoffmann | 50 rubles (twelve months of work) |
| Gottlieb Kautz | 50 rubles (twelve months of work) |

---

122. The renters Johann Bunk, Karl Jeschke, Michael Wiersche, and Christian Wolf are each listed as earning 30 rubles a year as farm laborers.

123. The Eberhard family evidently put much focus on the possibility of outside earnings. In addition to the brothers Daniel (a blacksmith) and Wilhelm (the village scribe), a third brother, Friedrich, was the school master in Grosliebental in South Russia northwest of Odessa and across the Dniester River estuary from southeastern Bessarabia, where he earned 50 silver rubles a year. Their father, Wilhelm, though listed as a resident of Leipzig, was indicated as well to be the "supervisor" for the Jewish colony of Inguletz (now the Ukrainian Inhulets) southeast of Krivij Rig, for which he earned 50 silver rubles a year.

124. Gottfried Lächelt, owner of a horse-driven mill worth 200 rubles, is reported to have had earnings of 15 silver rubles, and Johann Stelter, owner of a grain mill valued at 125 rubles, is also reported to have had earnings of 15 silver rubles. Jacob Freimuth, owner of a windmill valued at 400 rubles, is reported to have had earnings of 25 rubles.

presume that he purchased grapes and made wine from them for sale. Grapevines had become a far more prominent part of Leipzig farming by 1856–57. The total of 121,632 grapevines held by individual properties in Leipzig in 1856–57 was larger than the total number of grapevines in German Bessarabia in the 1825 survey (115,157), and equal to 25 percent of the total 1841 holdings of the Klöstitz District to which Leipzig belonged.

While the data on individual households highlights families who were doing particularly well, the causes that lay behind a family's prosperity aren't always clear. Grain harvests were not part of the Leipzig economic data, but earnings from the sale of grains may have been an important factor for some families. This would seem particularly the case for prosperous families who did not have substantial holdings of animals. Earnings from the sale of grain were apparently one reason that lay behind the wealth of the Karl Pfennig household, owners of property #50. Signs that the household was doing well were their four hundred fruit trees, the highest number of any household in the colony. The family also had a large herd of twenty-four cattle, a number that tied them with two other families for the eighth-largest herd in the village. These factors, however, do not completely seem to explain why Pfennig, as evidenced by his holding 500 silver rubles in cash, was one of the richest house-holders in Leipzig. Aside from wine merchant Karl Klauss noted above, who had 650 rubles, only three others, Adam Hintz, who held 550 silver rubles, and mill owners Daniel Ziehl and Wilhelm Müller, with 500, were reported to have cash amounts of this magnitude. The Pfennig family's possession of five horses, a plow, and two wagons suggests a family further specialized in grain. Karl Pfennig's good economic standing appeared to have been created entirely in Leipzig. He is the son of another Karl Pfennig who immigrated in 1808 in very troubled times from Mecklenburg to Schröttersdorf in South Prussia and was described there by his descendants as being a poor cottager, a *büdner*, and so was not likely to have come to Leipzig in 1814 with means.[125] If grain sales were one important factor lying behind the family's solid economic position, another surely would be that the Pfennigs were particularly gifted in their ability to mix together some combination of thrift, hard work, and talent.

Leipzig, once a laggard among the German settlements in Bessarabia, appears by the late 1850s to have made material economic improvements. Leipzig had now set its feet on a path that would make it, by the end of the nineteenth century, one of the most well-to-do German villages in Bessarabia. Kern notes in his survey that by then "prosperity showed everywhere."[126] The 1856–57 data show that the great majority of villagers had adequate landholdings, and reasonable numbers of animals, fruit trees, and grapevines. The terrible results of the 1825 Welfare Committee survey had generally been left behind. However, with that progress, there also appeared clear signs of class and occupational differentiations. Some families who rented or owned a homesite only and sought to earn a living by selling their labor had fallen

---

125. Flegel, *Extended Relationships*, 523. Flegel here is quoting the Deutsches Auslands Institut Jahrbuch of 1940. The term "büdner" could also mean a stall keeper, another poorly paid occupation. Schröttersdorf was the name given during the period from 1796 to 1807 to four neighboring villages, Maszewo, Chełpowo, Powsino and Biała, clustered on the east bank of the Vistula River just downstream from Płock. When, after 1815, this area became part of Russian-controlled Poland, the Polish village names returned.

126. Kern, *Homeland Book*, 142.

far behind the majority who owned a full farmstead. Others in this group had turned to trades and lived decently by a combination of small farming and trade earnings. Above the broad middle was a small group, roughly 10 percent, who had done particularly well in accumulating substantial holdings of animals, fruit trees, grapevines, or cash savings.

## By the 1850s, the German colonies in Russia were on a solid economic footing

Several explanations have been offered for the early economic success of the German colonists in Russia: the Germans had brought to Russia a more advanced agricultural technology, that they were able to adapt to changing conditions by trying new approaches, that they had a strong community spirit that encouraged mutual aid and the provision of support for those who were falling behind, and that their culture valued and encouraged hard work. The German agrarian economist August Freiherr von Haxthausen, in his published reflections from an extensive trip made through rural Russia in 1843–44, commented on the reasons for the prosperity he encountered in German villages he visited in the Volga region and on the Dnieper River in South Russia. He noted the greater prosperity of the German villages in comparison to neighboring Russian settlements, ascribing the better conditions in the German villages, without digging too deeply into the matter, to their hard work and better tools and techniques.[127] In assessing the Russian state's mercantilist project of settling foreign colonies in South Russia, von Haxthausen in 1843–44 noted of the German colonies: "The majority of the colonies are flourishing; the people after long years of difficulty and poverty, have generally become well off, and some of them rich...I cannot say that I met anyone who wished to return to Germany."[128]

Hans Rempel's study of German agricultural villages in the Black Sea region of Russia, published in 1940, ascribes the German success achieved by 1825 to their adaptability, to their successful introduction of new sustaining crops (particularly potatoes), and to their propensity to establish joint communal protections such as reserves of grain.[129] Rempel does not offer reasons why he thinks the German colonists "were more adaptable and suitable for colonization."[130] Rempel's study makes little or no reference to the fact that in adapting to conditions in South Russia and Bessarabia, the Germans borrowed extensively from the experiences of neighboring peoples. In doing so, the Germans learned to plant strains of hard wheat, learned the advantages of the smaller and hardier breeds of cattle, and in particular learned the advantages raising sheep for the Russian market. The colonies with settlers from Prussia and northern Germany learned the advantages of planting vineyards. Judging

---

127. Haxthausen, *Russian Empire*, 1:349, 420–30.

128. Haxthausen, *Russian Empire*, 2:43.

129. Rempel's views are summarized in the introduction to his work, *Deutsche Bauernleistung am Schwartzen Meer, Bevolkerung und Wirtschaft.* A translation by Roland Wagner ("German Farming Achievements in the Black Sea Region, Population and Economy, 1825") appears in the Odessa3 collection (http://www.odessa3.org/journal/rempel-intro.pdf). While some of the points Rempel makes are colored by his assumption of general German ethnic superiority, his conclusions generally stay within the data presented. In a separate translator's preface, Wagner argues convincingly that scholarship trumps clear expressions of ethnic prejudice in Rempel's work ("Some Reflections on Hans Rempel's *German Farming Achievements in the Black Sea Region, Population and Economy, 1825*" [N.p.: Odessa Digital Library, 2007], http://www.odessa3.org/journal/wagner-forward.pdf).

130. Rempel, *German Farming Achievements*, 11. Rempel is quoting here from G. G. Pisarevskij's 1909 study *Iz istorii inostrannoj kolonizacii v Rossii v XVIII.*

from the 1848 village histories, the Welfare Committee played a significant role in urging struggling colonies to try new approaches. The Klöstitz history, for example, closes with observations of recent village economic improvements and notes in particular the recent plantings of vineyards, for which "we owe thanks to the authorities [the Welfare Committee] that advised of its advantages and encouraged such a goal."[131] We will come back to this point in the following chapter as well. In general, the helpful role of the Welfare Committee has been underplayed in discussions of the growth of the German colonies in Bessarabia.

Adapting to new conditions by making changes to long-established agricultural practices was not easy, particularly for those without great resources for whom false steps and bad decisions meant starvation or death. From this distance, it is not possible to follow the reasoning that helped the Germans in Russia step over the hurdles imposed by the limited understanding of local conditions and the strong pull not to go beyond the familiar crops and techniques they brought with them from Prussia and the Rhineland. To some extent, this may have stemmed from the determination to do better, a sibling to the general and commonly observed cultural pattern of hard work. This may also have resulted from the fact that the great majority of the colonists had undergone the experience of moving within the past two generations and so had some family experience with the issue of adapting to new circumstances. It was likely a process of seeing some take risks and succeed that led others to take similar steps.

Later chapters will consider two other important factors that helped the Germans adapt successfully to Bessarabia and South Russia. One was their familiarity with more sophisticated farming techniques, such as plows that cut deeper, or crops, such as potatoes, that were significant in establishing a healthy food supply. The second and far more important factor was their cultural habit of building social capital within their villages that kept stores of grain for lean years and established funds for orphans and fire insurance that not only protected the weak but created a pool of useful capital for other investments, especially in land.

Yet, important as any factor in explaining the success of the German colonies is the fact that the colonists owned the land they farmed and were living in comparative freedom to develop that land. Any cultural disposition to hard work or to the value of improving one's situation had to be augmented by the feeling that whatever gains were to come from that labor would materially belong to the families who had made those efforts. In Bessarabia, the immigrant colonists were no longer under obligations to any landlord and were no longer subject to high taxes, and so kept the great majority of surplus they were able to produce. Although they started on the empty steppe, this formula led to prosperity.

---

131.   Schaeff, "Klöstitz – 1848 Village History."

# VI

# Settled and Communal Life in Mid-nineteenth-century German Bessarabia

This chapter will discuss what is known about community organization and life in German Bessarabia in the period before 1860. The available data permits some consideration of such topics as the physical structure of the villages, the organization of village administration, village insurance funds, civic building projects, inheritance practices, the beginnings of contacts with settlers of different nationalities, the buildup of social capital within the German villages, patterns of crime and misdemeanors, relations with the Welfare Committee, and the religious revival created by the Separatist movement and the disruptions this caused. The focus will be on the first three generations of German settlers in Bessarabia. The following period after the 1860s brought such significant changes within and to German Bessarabia that it deserves the separate treatment it will receive in later chapters.

This chapter will argue that for the first forty to fifty years, the German colonies in Bessarabia generally sought to continue the patterns of life and cultural norms they had brought with them from Prussia and other German-speaking lands. From one perspective it would appear that the original settlers quite succeeded in creating German villages that in terms of religion, culture, and language were little different from those left behind. In many ways, the German colonies in Bessarabia gave the appearance in this period that they were not in Russia at all.

Yet from other viewpoints, the colonies were becoming very much part of Imperial Russia. Although the steppe seemed empty when the Germans first arrived, it was gradually filling up with villages of other nationalities. Over time, Bulgarians, Russians, Moldavians, Gaugaz, and Ukrainians became neighbors to the Germans. Contact with these communities led the Germans to adopt words from other languages and so create the characteristic German speech of Bessarabia. Germans sold some of their grain by speaking pidgin Russian with the čumaki traders and sold wagons, cattle, and fruit at the Tarutino weekly market to Bulgarians, Gaugaz, and Moldavians, picking up words from those languages in the process. If they read a newspaper, it was a German-language paper from Odessa, but the news was about Russia and borrowed words and terms from Russian. Even before the great national reforms of the 1860s and 1870s, there existed subtle pressures to take steps toward assimilation: to speak some Russian as well as to understand and work within the framework of Russian customs and Russian political, social, and commercial norms. Although the colonies remained very German, they were also starting to be touched by Russia.

The nineteen original German colonies in Bessarabia grew to twenty-five in the period from 1830 to 1842 when six additional German colonies were established on the steppelands to the south, east, and northeast of the first colonies. When the 60-desjatina farmsteads of these six additional colonies were finally fully occupied by 1849, there were 432 more German families settled in Bessarabia.[1] The additional six villages were settled by Germans with backgrounds very similar to those who had settled the original nineteen. Friedenstal (1833) and Plotzk (1839) had large numbers of Germans who came from villages in Russian Poland, having settled there when it was Prussian Poland, and, like the first Germans to come to Bessarabia, had still earlier backgrounds in other parts of Prussia or Württemberg. They had left Russian Poland in the aftermath of the Polish uprising of 1830–31 and the harsh Russian controls that had been established after the Polish rebels were defeated.[2] The majority of the settlers in Gnadental (1830) and Lichtental (1834) came to Bessarabia directly from Württemberg and thus closely resembled the settlers of Teplitz and Sarata. There were settlers from Württemberg among those who founded Plotzk as well. Württemberg was also the origin of most of the settlers who came to Hoffnungstal (1842), but they came to Bessarabia from crowded villages in the Berezan, Liebental, and Glückstal regions of the Xerson Province in South Russia where they had settled in the period from 1800 to 1819.

The sixth additional colony in Bessarabia was Dennewitz (1834), which was established on part of the original Teplitz land and was filled mainly with families, generally second-generation families, from other German colonies in Bessarabia, chiefly Wittenberg, Alt Posttal, Kulm, Beresina, and Tarutino. While the Dennewitz village history describes the settlers as people "who found themselves without land

---

1. There were in fact more than 432 families. The 1848 Friedenstal Village History notes that in addition to the 87 farmsteads, the Welfare Committee settled another 48 residents, "mainly widows and orphans," making 135 families, and that by 1848, another 60 families had been added, giving Friedenstal a total of 195 families. (http://www.odessa3.org/collections/history/link/friedtal.txt).

2. Many Poles had hoped that the large portion of the Napoleonic Duchy of Warsaw, which, after 1815, had remained under Russian control as a quasi-independent state called Congress Poland, would be allowed to form the basis of an independent Poland. Russia, however, had no intention of permitting its old rival to return to life. When Russia's intentions in Poland became quite clear, the Poles revolted.

or farms" seeking a place to "establish themselves...to make a living,"[3] the founders of Dennewitz were not like the renters or homestead-only owners who existed in Leipzig in 1856–57. Rather, the Dennewitz settlers appear to be the reasonably prosperous married sons or relations who came to Dennewitz from some of what the 1825 survey indicates to be the most prosperous German settlements in Bessarabia. Their parents or relations had established successful farmsteads, which, in 1834, they were helping run. Their motivation appears to closely resemble that of founders of daughter colonies after 1865: the desire to have a farmstead of their own independent of their current circumstances. Thus, Dennewitz colonist Johann Hiller, for example, left three brothers behind in Tarutino to run the farmstead established by his father and older brother. Johann Schimke, a Dennewitz colonist from Kulm, was an orphaned boy who grew up on the farmstead of his uncle Christian Schimke, where it was clear that the farmstead was destined to be taken over by Christian's son Friedrich. The Dennewitz colonists brought cash, farm and household equipment, and livestock with them. As a result, Dennewitz rapidly prospered. Dennewitz, thus, quite differed from the other five new colonies. Very much like the original nineteen colonies, these latter went through an initial difficult period of establishing themselves.

After 1840, there was very limited immigration of Germans from outside Imperial Russia into Bessarabia: a few settlers from Württemberg in Plotzk (1840s) and four small villages founded in northern Bessarabia by German speakers coming from across the border in Austrian Galicia and Bukovina (1865–85).[4] After the founding of Hoffnungstal in 1842, there was only a limited immigration of Germans into Bessarabia from the colonies in South Russia.[5] Thus, it is fair to state that after the 1840s the German population in Bessarabia largely grew on its own. The six German colonies founded between 1830 and 1842 were the last colonies to be gifted land in Bessarabia by the Imperial Russian government. When new German settlements were founded in Bessarabia beginning in the 1860s, these were founded by German families collectively purchasing or leasing land from existing landowners.

The six additional large German colonies also changed the linguistic and cultural balance in German Bessarabia. If, among the original nineteen colonies, settlers with Württemberg or upper Rhineland backgrounds formed a slight majority, the very strong presence of such people among the settlers of the six additional colonies quite tipped the balance. After 1850, common Bessarabian German speech and customs increasingly came to have a South German feel. This trend became more pronounced, as the daughter colonies founded after 1865 mixed families of different home villages and different German backgrounds.

Unlike with the original nineteen colonies, the founders of five of the six additional German colonies received no financial support for travel or supplies for building, food, or farming equipment. The founders of Hoffnungstal were an exception as, given their poverty, they received a small, interest-free loan of 100 rubles to help them establish themselves on their own. Colonists elsewhere had to rely on

---

3.  Haas, "Dennewitz – 1848 Village History."
4.  These latter were: Ryschjanowka (1865), Scholtoi (1881), Strymbeni (1881), and Alt Oneschti (1885).
5.  Sofiental (1863), Seimeny (1867), and the Catholic villages of Balmas (1880) and Larga (1890) were founded by settlers from South Russian German settlements who moved across the Dniester River to lease land in Bessarabia.

funds they brought with them. This implies that the standards the Russian government established for immigrants had been further raised. It would appear that in contrast to many of the colonists of the first nineteen settlements, the later colonists, particularly those coming from outside Russia, had sufficient capital to pay for their travel and arrive with funds to help themselves get settled. The Gnadental and Lichtental histories note that colonists had on average 700 and 600 rubles respectively which were "used mainly for the building of homes."[6] One source contemporary with the founding of the new colonies suggests that settlers arriving in Plotzk, at least, purchased their land from settlers already there. The wife of Plotzk colonist Friedrich Schlechter, a late arrival to the new colony, wrote back to family near Murrhardt in Württemberg in January 1841 to say that when they arrived,

> there was just one lot left and it was occupied by a blacksmith from Almersbach... though we didn't have the money to buy it. Instead we purchased a place for 38 fl[orins]. It contains four acres with garden and vineyard. We also have a much larger place with a yard and a small house. Now we will be able to get on quite well until we build a larger house. The farmland contains 120 acres.[7]

While this account appears to lump together more than one event, it would appear that the Schlechters bought several noncontiguous parcels of land in Plotzk. Despite the inability of the Schlechters to purchase the last lot available, they appear to have ended up with something close to the normal allotment of 60 desjatina provided colonists in the first German settlements.

Colonists coming to Plotzk after 1839 received ten "free years" to establish themselves before they would be liable for tax payments. It is not clear whether this or a similar benefit was offered elsewhere. The Gnadental history notes that they received a three-year grace period before taxes were due, but that was because the colonists arrived to face a cholera epidemic and suffered "many poor harvests."[8] The only other benefit mentioned by the new settlements was that in Lichtental, the early colonists were permitted to lease out the unused lands of the village. With the earnings from such leases, the village built up cattle herds, which helped when harvests were poor.

Unlike with the earlier German colonies established in Bessarabia, some of the new colonies were given much latitude by the Welfare Committee in naming the settlements. The Friedenstal 1848 village history notes that an opinion poll was used to determine a permanent name and "the majority chose the name Friedenstal"[9] and proposed it to the Welfare Committee, which approved it. Hoffnungstal also selected its name "at the wish of the first settlers"[10] and this gained approval from the Welfare Committee. Similarly, Plotzk was chosen as a village name because "the community agreed to name it"[11] so. For the colony of Gnadental, however, the village name

---

6.  Koch, "Gnadental – 1848 Village History."
7.  Schlechter, "A Letter," 18.
8.  Koch, "Gnadental – 1848 Village History."
9.  Eckert, "Friedenstal – 1848 Village History."
10. L. A. Kurtz, "Hoffnungstal – 1848 Village History," trans. Irmgard Schlenker (N.p.: Odessa Digital Library, 1996), http://www.odessa3.org/collections/history/link/hoffbess.txt.
11. Wernick, "Plotzk – 1848 Village History," trans. Elli Wise (N.p.: Odessa Digital Library, 1996), http://www.odessa3.org/collections/history/link/plotzk.txt.

was "introduced by the Welfare Committee,"[12] and with Lichtental, the village name came from the district office of the Welfare Committee in Sarata. Only Dennewitz received its name after the fashion of the original colonies: "the name was changed to Dennewitz by the government to commemorate the victory at Dennewitz in Prussia."[13]

## The early German villages in Bessarabia were laid out in a similar fashion

The village plan for most of the German colonial villages initially consisted of two rows of houses separated by a broad passageway or street. Several of these villages— Wittenberg, Alt Posttal, Katzbach, Dennewitz, and Hoffnungstal—also had a stream flowing through that broad passageway.[14] The major exceptions to this rule were the multistreet villages of Sarata, Gnadental, and Lichtental, which were set on the large grant initially given to Lindl for Sarata.[15] Public buildings such as churches, schoolhouses, and town administrative offices were later built near the middle of the passageway or in a middle square in the multistreet villages. Each family had a farmstead of between a quarter to two-thirds desjatina[16] on which they built houses. The Alt Elft history describes these as consisting of two rooms with a kitchen and entry hall. Behind the houses, the Brienne history notes, there were often a vaulted cellar, stables, a threshing yard, and then room for orchards. Schmidt notes that a "typically Besarabian" yard contained "the summer kitchen set apart from the main house."[17] This separation she indicates was mandated from colonial days as a fire protection. The Brienne and Sarata histories also describe the farmsteads as being surrounded by walls 2 *arshin* high (1.4 meters or 4.6 feet).[18] The general appearance suggested villages in German-speaking lands. Haxthausen describes German Mennonite villages in South Russia in 1843 with a similar layout:

> We felt at once transported to the valleys of the Vistula, in West Prussia, so thoroughly German was everything around us: not merely the people, their language, dress and dwellings, but every plate and vessel…the plan of the villages and the detached farmhouses with gardens, plants, vegetables…are all German.[19]

---

12. Koch, "Gnadental – 1848 Village History."
13. Haas, "Dennewitz – 1848 Village History." The battle of Dennewitz, an unsuccessful attempt by Napoleon to retake Berlin, was fought September 6, 1813, in Brandenburg.
14. Several colonies later grew by adding side streets and so lost the single street aspect. This is true of Tarutino, Alt Arzis, Leipzig, Kulm, and Berezina. Though describing Berezina as "laid out in a rectangle with three main streets and six side streets," Kern is referring to Berezina in the twentieth century, not its original layout (*Homeland Book*, 122)
15. The Gnadental history describes the village as "formed like a rectangle consisting of four rows of houses. There are two streets leading through the colony and between them is a large yard in which stands a prayer house" (Koch, "Gnadental – 1848 Village History"). Schmidt includes village plans of Gnadental and Sarata. The latter, though of modern origin, shows basic features of the interesting original design created by Aloys Schertzinger in which houses are set along all four sides of each of the two main squares with yards extending in toward a center point in each square suggesting clock faces (Schmidt, *Bessarabia: German Colonists*, 199).
16. The Friedenstal history describes the size of the farmstead as 90 x 30 faden (using the German term to describe the Russian measurement sažen' of 2.1336 meters or roughly 7 feet), which would be 1.125 desjatina. The Dennewitz history describes farmsteads as 20 x 80 faden or 0.666 desjatina.
17. Schmidt, *Bessarabia: German Colonists*, 197.
18. The Sarata history, using German measurements, describes the walls as "4 fuß high," which would be 2 arshin. An arshin, an old Russian measurement of length, is 71.12 cm or 2.33 feet. Natterer, "Sarata – 1848 Village History."
19. Haxthausen, *Russian Empire*, 1:420–21.

The description Sue Clarkson offers of nineteenth-century German villages in southern Hungary appears close to the pictures presented in the Bessarabian German village histories:

> *The houses were built perpendicularly to the street, and consisted of a series of adjoining rooms, with the parlor on the end which faced the street, and sheds for domestic animals on the opposite end. … Each house plot was surrounded by a fence, and the courtyard within the fence contained grape vines, fruit trees and the household garden.*[20]

The layout of the German colonies in Bessarabia, however, was not something that the colonists created by replicating the villages from which they had emigrated. Instead, the great similarity in appearance among the villages indicates plans established and put into practice by the Welfare Committee. The Friedenstal history notes that the village was "laid out according to government regulations"; the Hoffnungstal history describes the village plan as "required by the upper level government." In describing the Schertzingers' plan of Sarata, Schmidt notes it was made with the help and by implication likely the approval of "Eduard de Pott, architect for the Welfare Committee."[21] The look is not that of villages in Germany, which were often clustered about road junctions or were long "street villages" of houses strung out along a single road. Villages in Germany grew up gradually over time as circumstances permitted. In contrast, the German colonies in Bessarabia had a planned look that bears some resemblance to Russian peasant villages, with a street or passageway separating two rows of houses. However, the neat regularity of the farmsteads, the separating walls, and the wide pathways between the farmsteads, with planned space for public buildings, were quite unlike Russian villages. Surely a keystone of the Russian planning for the layout of the German colonies in Bessarabia was the ownership of equal parcels of land. This was a nearly unique feature of the colonies as "Newtowns." The sites were surveyed and then planned to hold specific numbers of settler families, each with a farmstead of exactly the same size set along the street and rights to equal amounts of land outside the village to farm. Once settled in the villages, the colonists made them look German; the layout of the villages, though, was established according to plans made by the Welfare Committee.

The Bulgarian colonies in Bessarabia were not laid out in the same fashion as the German ones. They were usually rectangular blocks with several crossing streets. This plan was apparently adopted because the Bulgarian colonies were to hold many more families than the German ones and the individual farmstead plots were smaller. Looking at the former colonial villages in Bessarabia via the Google satellite view, it is still possible to see the original layout of the settlements. Comparing Wittenberg or Alt Posttal, for example, to their Bulgarian neighbors Čumlekioj and especially Tvardica, the farmsteads in the German villages are similar in shape to those in the Bulgarian villages but less crowded together and at least a third larger in size.

The Google satellite view clearly shows the pattern of equal farmstead dimensions in the Bessarabian German settlements amidst later additions and diminutions. Even

---

20. Sue Clarkson, "A History of German Settlements in Southern Hungary" (N.p.: The Federation of East European Family History Societies, 2003), http://feefhs.org/links/banat/bhistory.html.
21. Schmidt, *Bessarabia: German Colonists*, 199.

the parallel lines of the farmsteads in Hoffnungstal are visible as marks on the ground despite the fact that the village dwellings were obliterated by the Soviet army when the area was used as a military training ground after World War II. For most of the colonies, the rows of farmsteads that run on both sides of the original street are quite evident, with their equal shapes and regular boundaries running back from the buildings, marking the limits of the first stage of the settlement. In Kulm, Wittenberg, Alt Posttal, Paris, and Katzbach, the street/passageway was so wide that parallel roads have developed along its edges, and some dwellings have now been placed in what was the street. In contrast, in other villages such as Leipzig, Krasna, Alt Elft, Brienne, Gnadental, and Friedenstal, the street was narrower and continues now to serve as a road.

## The farmstead makeup follows a similar pattern throughout the German settlements in Bessarabia

There exists a detailed drawing of a street scene in nineteenth-century Krasna that shows how farmsteads were laid out.[22] Dwellings are pictured as long structures that run back from the street and at their front edge are separated from the wide grassy street by whitewashed stone walls broken with narrow gates for people and wider gates for wagons. Living quarters are on the street side and barns and sheds for animals stretch behind. On one side of the house and barn is a yard, and on the other are gardens and orchards. The general accuracy of the drawing is established by a photo from Krasna taken in 1937 that shows the same long house–barn structures perpendicular to and fenced off from the wide street.[23] Other photos taken in Bessarabia in the 1930s, during the resettlement in September 1940, or more recently, by visitors to the former German villages, offer further images of early German Bessarabia. These include a photo from the church tower in Leipzig taken in the 1930s that looks down a wide street at a series of long, single-story buildings that are set close to the fence bordering the street, much like those in the Krasna photograph.[24] Some of the buildings are houses; others appear to be barns, some of which may have become businesses. There is a picture of more rural Katzbach from the 1920s or 1930s showing the wide dirt street and a neat row of houses set close to the street behind a wall. The houses have two windows facing the street on the ground floor with a single window above in an attic, which looks quite like the houses in the foreground of the Leipzig picture. The main door is in the middle of the long side facing the yard.[25] There is a particularly interesting photo taken in Klöstitz in 1923 of the last remaining house existing from the time of settlement.[26] It shows a thatched roofed two-room, single-story house with a single window and door on its

22. Ted J. Becker, "Long-houses" [image] (N.p.: The Krasna Project, c. 2012), http://14ushop.com/krasna/images/long-houses.jpg.

23. Ted J. Becker, "Krasna overhead1" [image] (N.p.: The Krasna Project, c. 2012), http://14ushop.com/krasna/images/krasnaoverhead1.jpg.

24. This is in the photograph collection of the Bessarabiendeutscher Verein Heimatmuseum. Unknown, "Leipzig - Blick vom Kirchturm" [image] (N.p.: bessarabien.de, c. 2015), http://www.bessarabien.de/heimatmuseum/_k8/leipzig---blick-vom-kirchturm--21.php.

25. A copy of this photograph in on page 227. Details on the original are Unknown, "Gemeinde Katzbach – Teilansicht" [image] (N.p.: bessarabien.de, c. 2015), http://www.bessarabien.de/heimatmuseum/_k8/--20.php. The wall, judging by the height of the men pictured next to it, appears to have maintained the 2 arshin height that the 1848 Brienne and Sarata histories note in their village descriptions.

26. Unknown, "Letzes Häuschen aus der Ansiedlerzeit" [image] (N.p.: KloestitzGenealogy.org, 1923), http://www.kloestitzgenealogy.org/bilder/bildergalerie_kloestitz_gestern/b_k_g.htm.

long side that runs parallel to instead of back from the street like the newer houses beside it. This suggests that not all houses were sited in the same way, as the photo from Katzbach or the drawing of Krasna might imply. Indeed, there is a house in the foreground of the Leipzig picture that, like the old Klöstitz house, is set parallel and not perpendicular to the street, and a house in a picture of Neu Posttal in the same collection that is set similarly.[27]

Allen Konrad provides a good description of such farmsteads when he notes:

> In general…farmsteads in Bessarabia were separated from the street by a…wall, usually of stone. They were cleaned and whitewashed and gave the yard a nice appearance. The entrance to the yard was often provided with two yard gates of wood or iron that were mounted on two pillars. Often you would find a kind of roof connecting the two pillars. The iron gates were made in various designs. The first homes in Kulm stood diagonal in the yard. Later, the houses were situated with the gable toward the street.[28]

## The fields for crops and animal pastures surrounded the village

The farmstead set in the village represented only a small piece of the land given to each colonist family. The bulk of their property lay in the surrounding lands belonging to the colony. Sometimes villages divided up their grant of land into sections of varying qualities and gave families shares in each section. Sometimes families received connected plots of land, but within that plot the quality of land varied. Over time, though, the trend was for families to have connected plots of land rather than pieces scattered throughout the fields belonging to the village.

When the German colonists first came to Bessarabia they followed the three-field crop rotation system long used by peasants in Western Europe. This meant dividing arable land into three sections: one for winter planting, a second for spring planting, and a third left fallow. In the following year, usage would shift a notch: the fallow field from the prior year would be planted with grain in winter, the winter field would be planted in spring (a year after harvest), and the spring field would be left fallow. Thus, there was always at least one field planted, and only a third of the land was in heavy use at any one point in time. The Alt Arzis history refers to the use of an even more conservative four-crop rotation. Hagen notes that in Brandenburg after the mid-eighteenth century, this crop rotation system had been largely abandoned. Instead, there were "fallow free rotations of cereals and fodder."[29] In Bessarabia, though, the German colonists continued to use the more conservative crop rotation system. Undoubtedly in a new land with a different climate, farmers felt this was a safer approach. In one of his articles in the Kulm Heimatbuch,

27. A copy of the Leipzig photograph is on page 227. Details on the original Leipzig and Neu Posttal photographs are Unknown, "Leipzig – Blick vom Kirchturm"; and Unknown, "Leipzig-Blick vom Kirchturm"; and Unknown. "Neu-Posttal - Ansicht vom Kirchturm" [image] (N.p.: bessarabien.de, c. 2015), http://www.bessarabien.de/heimatmuseum/_k8/neu-posttal---ansicht-vom-kirchturm--24.php.

28. Allen E. Konrad, "Bessarabia: Before, During and After the German Settlements" (powerpoint presentation, Germans from Russia Heritage Society Convention, July 22, 2010), 7, http://www.grhs.org/korners/memonly/konrad_doc/Bessarabia-%20Before%20During%20and%20After%20the%20German%20Settlements.ppt (members-only access).

29. Hagen, *Ordinary Prussians*, 196.

Theophil Weiss describes the three-field system that was in use apparently well into the twentieth century on what he refers to as Kulm's *baustückland* or "arable fields":

*1. Winter grains planted: wheat, barley, rape and rye (this latter for fodder)*

*2. Spring grains planted: wheat, barley, oats, millet, rape, mustard, flax, and hemp*

*3. Fallow field crops were: field corn (maize), sunflowers, castor oil plant, soybeans, potatoes, turnips.*[30]

Because the fertility of the highly alkaline soil in Bessarabia varied so intensely with the amount of precipitation, the Germans in Bessarabia were led to make changes in their farming procedures. The Alt Arzis history notes their traditional four-crop rotation and the application of manure provided no help in periods when the fields were long without rain: "The grass and the crops turn yellow and are burned."[31] The Gnadental history notes that since there appeared to be more dry seasons than wet ones, "one can not use the fields too often." This led farmers there to conclude that fields needed to be rested "for 6 to 8 years to regain nutrients."[32] Another change, discussed in chapter V, was to plant strains of hard wheat that handled the dryness better. The Alt Posttal history notes that "of all grains summer [hard] wheat (Arnaut) excels by far because it tolerates heat and even grows with little rain."[33] The Gnadental passage implies that farmers devoted only small plots of land to grain so as to leave large sections fallow for a long time. The grass grown on the fallow fields supported cattle and sheep. In the colonies along the southern tier of the German area where the alkaline content of the soil was higher, farmers adjusted by turning from growing cereals to raising cattle and sheep on the natural grass that thrived on the steppe or to planting vineyards that also handled the drier climate well.

## The Welfare Committee mandated ultimogeniture inheritance, but this seems to have been ignored

Continuing a practice favored by earlier administrators of German colonies in Imperial Russia, the Welfare Committee mandated an ultimogeniture inheritance; that is, a colonist's youngest son was to inherit the undivided farmstead. In Bessarabia, issues of inheritance, however, did not quickly arise as the land grants given colonist settlers were so large that it took time for families to grow into their full utilization. Given the low state of mechanization and high dependence on human, horse, and oxen power, the 60 desjatina allotments given each of the settler families were so large that they needed several working adult families to maximize their economic potential. The German farms in Bessarabia often came to prosperity once a founding family had grown and married children to join in the work or when sibling families replaced their deceased parents. This was the pattern evident in over half of the Leipzig farmsteads recorded in the 1856–57 census discussed in the prior chapter. By having several adult members of a single family engaged in the work of a single

30. Weiss, "Cultivation and Grain Growing" in "Heimatbuch der Gemeinde Kulm," *Heritage Review* 14, no. 2 (1984): 29–30.
31. Neumann, "Alt Arzis – 1848 Village History."
32. Koch, "Gnadental – 1848 Village History."
33. Kludt, "Alt Posttal – 1848 Village History."

farmstead, the Welfare Committee could evidently look past the inheritance rules that had been fixed for the Bessarabian colonies, as they could maintain that the property remained undivided. The Welfare Committee's goal in banning the subdivision of properties was to avoid the problems that were developing in the earliest German settlements in South Russia, particularly in the Mennonite settlements, where partible inheritance was creating some family farms too small to provide adequate support for their owners. Partible inheritance and the resulting development of smaller and smaller farms was also seen as a primary cause of the growth of a class of landless poor who hired out their labor. Klaus, for example, notes holdings of fewer than 10 desjatina in some of the Mennonite communities.[34]

When a male owner of a Bessarabian German farmstead died, the inheritance rules specified by the Welfare Committee stipulated that the land was not to be subdivided and was to pass intact to the former owner's youngest son. According to Klaus, this was covered in Section 173 of the code governing the colonies.[35] This inheritance preference, however, was not created for the Bessarabians but was a continuation of a principle appearing in the earlier *Kolonistengesetz*, the "Colonist Law" compiled in 1764 by the Russian government for the German colonies established on the Volga. While the Kolonistengesetz did specify that a family's land should go to the youngest son, this regulation, as Giesinger notes, was indifferently enforced in the Volga colonies.[36] Ultimogeniture, or inheritance by the last-born male, is not frequently found and clearly was an effort at social engineering made by the Russian administrators. The presumed goal of ultimogeniture would be to keep the property from being subdivided again and again and so keep its owner out of poverty. The older sons were to go into trade or potentially to serve the state.

Despite the existence of the regulation mandating ultimogeniture, it was, as for the Volga Germans, generally ignored by the Bessarabian Germans.[37] Mutschall, in his history of Tarutino, notes that the rule "could not be enforced."[38] Looking at actual practice in Bessarabia as indicated in, for example, Flegel's genealogical lists for families from Kulm, Leipzig, and Tarutino, I can find no example of a single son inheriting to the disadvantage of his brothers and sisters. Indeed, until the prohibition against partible inheritance was abolished in 1870, the almost universal practice among the German communities in Bessarabia was to maintain an undivided household shared by parents with children or by several children and their families. Of the 121 farmsteads listed in the 1856–57 Leipzig Census, just over half (61) are

---

34. Klaus, *Naši kolonii*, 134–35. Small inherited allotments and resulting poverty had become a noticeable problem also among Russian and Ukrainian peasant populations. Land allotted in these peasant communities, though, was not held by individuals or families but collectively "owned" by the community (or mir as it is called in Russian) and all living members of the community had rights to a share. Those families with more sons acquired rights to more land than families with fewer sons, creating inequalities among families. As health standards improved and communities grew in size, individual shares would decrease, creating economic hardship particularly for families with fewer male members. See also Roland Wagner, "A Discussion of Local Government in the German Colonies of the Black Sea Region" (N.p.: Odessa Digital Library, 2001), 6, http://www.odessa3.org/journal/government.pdf.

35. Klaus, *Naši kolonii*, 233.

36. Giesinger, *From Katherine to Krushchev*, 53–54. Some of the German Volga colonies followed the Russian peasant mir system in which community land was regularly redivided among the living male adults.

37. Klaus (*Naši kolonii*, 235) describes ultimogeniture as strongly encouraged by Section 178 of the legal code, which could be broken only when a father deemed the youngest son "incapable."

38. Mutschall, "Community of Tarutino," *Heritage Review* 43, no. 2: 7.

held by multiple owners. Property #86 in Leipzig, for example, was jointly owned by the brothers Wilhelm and Christian Fruck, whose father, Peter, was one of the original settlers of Leipzig and died in 1848. The property appears to have been jointly managed by them until 1873, when Wilhelm died. After that, it was managed jointly by Christian and Wilhelm's son Gottfried until at least 1913. Where a property is listed under one name, it is because that person was the sole survivor in that generation in the family. Property #123 was held in 1857 solely by Michael Jeschke, whose father died before 1834 and whose younger brother Paul died in 1928. The property went to Michael's sons Christian, Ludwig, and Daniel.[39] Property #32 in 1857 was owned entirely by sixty-one-year-old Christian Hinz, one of the original settlers in Leipzig; his married sons Jacob (twenty-eight) and Christian (twenty-one) are listed in the census as joint heirs. In the mid-1860s, the younger brother, Christian, moved his family to the new village of Neu Freudental in the Odessa region of South Russia, and the Leipzig property was managed by Jacob and his sons-in-law at least into the 1920s.[40]

By the 1860s, many farmsteads were supporting more than two families of married siblings, and this produced such overcrowding in the original settlements that married children started to leave. The great emigration out of the original colonies will be the subject of a later chapter. Here, in the consideration of German inheritance practices, it highlights how such emigration became affordable. The prosperity of the German households in Bessarabia rested on a cash-based economy where earnings were achieved from sale of farm produce, chiefly grain, animals, fruit, and wine. Savings put away by a family, as well as the potential value of all the jointly owned property, created the capital base for the family. Under German customs, all children had inheritance rights to a share of that capital, rights which, upon reaching adulthood, they could even exercise while their parents were still alive. As the colonies started to become crowded, younger adults began to think of striking out on their own by activating their inheritance rights. This provided the means to purchase or lease land in Bessarabia or to gain new land by immigrating to other regions in Russia, to Romanian Dobrudscha across the Danube, and to North America across the ocean.

Traditional German inheritance customs gave children rights to equal shares in the value of the family's household effects: its animals, seed, equipment, cash, cloth, and furniture. If taken before the death of the parents, shares would be based on an estimate of the value of the household at that time. One major event that would trigger the early settlement of a child's inheritance share would be a daughter's marriage. William Hagen, in his study *Ordinary Prussians*, describes these transactions in some detail from the records of the von Kleist Stavenow estates in eighteenth-century Brandenburg. Daughters would create marriage dowries by combining an early inheritance settlement (called an *Abfindung*) with the cash savings they had been able to put together plus all the goods they had purchased or made at home. Hagen notes that among women, these were called marriage goods (*Eheguth*), bride's trove (*Brautschatz*), or dowry (*Aussteur* or *Austattung*). Gender-neutral terms were also

---

39. Flegel, *Extended Relationships*, 330, 332. Michael's brother Paul had a son, Karl Jeschke, who in 1857 was listed in the census as a renter on property #64 and was due an inheritance from property #123 when Michael Jeschke died.

40. Flegel, *Extended Relationships*, 194–95, 292–94, 585–86.

used, such as marriage gift or dowry (*Mitgift*) and, commonly, "goods brought in" (*Eingebrachtes*).[41] Part of a daughter's settlement would also typically be the cost of a bridal costume, or "dress of honor" which, though descriptions are missing from the judicial documents that make up Hagen's sources, was a valuable right, as costs, when settled in cash or livestock, were high. As marriage customs for Germans in Bessarabia did not alter from the practices they brought with them from Prussia and Württemberg, such marriage settlements of inheritances continued. For daughters in Bessarabia who did not marry, the Kulm Heimatbuch notes that they "had a life-long right to live in [their] parents' house and received, instead of money, a piece of land" from which they would be able to support themselves.[42] Klaus notes the existence of a regulation dating from 1764 that was to cover inheritances in the German colonies in Russia which sought to guarantee some protection for daughters by mandating that a quarter of an estate was to be held collectively for all daughters.[43] This rule appears to have been ignored in German Bessarabia where the tradition of the rights of all children to equal shares in an estate appears more commonly honored.

On the subject of the division of property to provide a marriage portion for a daughter, Klaus notes that the Russian laws and regulations governing the German colonies sought to establish clear rules that would avoid unnecessary disputes. For example, a dowry settlement was to be considered "forever separated from the fundamental holdings and property of the father" ("navsegda vydelennymi iz korennogo xozjaistva i imuščestva otca").[44] This anticipated and sought to limit, or at least to govern, family disputes about inheritances which, as Hagen notes, were not uncommon in eighteenth-century Prussia. Klaus is here clearly concerned with real property rights, which would not have been an issue in Bessarabia where the land grants could not be subdivided. The principle raised, though, would be equally applicable to any grants of cash, animals, furniture, or other property. When property was promised or even transferred but involved future obligations, a critical death or a change of heart could create disputes. No doubt such inheritance disputes existed in German Bessarabia, but the civil records describing such suits and settlements, if indeed such records continue to survive, are not currently in the public domain. The Kulm Heimatbuch indicates that where "disagreements" arose over the value given property, appraisers would be called in and their "valuation was then binding."[45]

A third situation occurring in both Prussia and Bessarabia that called for an early settlement of a household estate took place when a male parent decided to retire from his labor and pass the ownership and management of the family property on to a child or children. In Prussia, the recipient was typically the oldest surviving son; in Bessarabia, as we have seen, typically this was multiple sons and/or sons-in-law and their families. The retiring parent(s) in Prussia would often take a cottage separate

41. Hagen, *Ordinary Prussians*, 157. There is a detailed account of wedding customs in Kulm in the "Heimatbuch der Gemeinde Kulm," but perhaps as a result of the fact that it is recounted by men, it does not include details of the bridal costume or details of bridal settlements. Th. Weiss, E. Widmer, A. Kugele, J. Roloff, and D. Wölfle, "The Wedding" in "Heimatbuch der Gemeinde Kulm," *Heritage Review* 14, no. 3 (1984): 54–56..

42. Wölfle, "The Establishment of the Village of Kulm," 9. This was evidently not a right that was frequently exercised. As will be discussed in the following chapter, nearly all persons reaching young adulthood married.

43. Klaus, *Naši kolonii*, 236. The law referred to was one dated 19 March 1764 (O.S.).

44. Ibid., 237.

45. Wölfle, "The Establishment of the Village of Kulm," 9.

from the main house on the family's leased land and in some cases a contract was signed obliging both sides to provide each other help and assistance.[46] In Prussia, such formal contracts existed to protect the landlord against the risks of a new tenant being unable to pay rents or against the need to support indigent elderly persons. In Bessarabia, such contracts may also have existed, though I have yet to find references to them. As such transfers of ownership by their very nature awaken worries and create promises that are made and sometimes broken, there is every likelihood that oral or written agreements existed. Should these have become matters of dispute, there would have been references to them in the civil records of the German villages and perhaps in the records of the districts in which the villages were located. Again, however, whether such records continue to exist is not currently known.

Some idea of retiree arrangements in German Bessarabia can be gleaned from details included in the 1856–57 Leipzig Census. The census lists seven retirees, six of whom are noted as the original owners of a property that was at the time of the census owned by their sons or sons-in-law, indicating that a clear transference ownership had occurred. Thus, Johann Patzer is referred to as the original owner of property #49 which was then jointly owned by his two sons Ludwig and Daniel; similarly, Gottlieb Sommerfeld is noted to be the retired owner of property #65, which was jointly owned by his two sons-in-law Ludwig Pahl and Christian Fruck. Several retirees continued to maintain some property in their own right. Johann Patzer had two horses, three cattle, and three hogs, and leased, presumably for the maintenance of himself and his wife, 6 desjatina of land, for which he paid 80 kopecks a year. Gottfried Quashnick, who gave up the ownership of property #97 to his two sons, is listed in the census as having in his own right forty-three beehives and 15 silver rubles. Gottfried Lächelt, who gave up property #57 to his older son Christian,[47] is listed as owning a horse-driven mill worth 200 silver rubles and earned, presumably from this, 15 silver rubles a year. Only in the case of Johannes Fink, a latecomer to Leipzig from Rohrbach in the Berezan District of South Russia, was the property (#104) listed as being jointly owned by the retiree, Johannes, and his son Joseph.

The Kulm Heimatbuch states that property could only be inherited by male heirs. Female heirs, according to the Heimatbuch, were paid off with a settlement of cash or other goods.[48] The 1856–57 Leipzig Census, however, indicates that in practice, some widows retained ownership of their family's property. For example, Christina (Waltz) Pahl, who did not remarry after the early death of her husband in 1848, is listed as the owner of property #80 instead of her twenty-four-year-old son Gottfried. The widow Sophia (Sommerfeld) Kühn and her widowed daughter Friederike (Kühn) Flegel are listed as the joint owners of property #9, which had been settled by Sophia and her husband Michael and would ultimately go to Friederike's children. While Hagen notes that in eighteenth-century Prussia, occasionally widows continued to maintain property originally leased to their husbands, this was not normally the case. Because of the limited availability of land for lease, widows

---

46. Hagen, *Ordinary Prussians*, 157–63.
47. Christian Lächelt had a younger brother, Christoph Lächelt, who is not listed as having ownership rights to property #57, no doubt because he had become the sole owner of property #70.
48. Wölfle, "The Establishment of the Village of Kulm," 9.

in Prussia would have been under significant pressure to remarry, because if they did not, "the deceased farmer's siblings might seek to reclaim it [the leasehold]."[49]

## Village welfare funds in Bessarabia continue practices brought to Russia from the former German-speaking homelands

The inheritance rights of orphans were an area that customarily received a great deal of attention in German peasant communities. German communities traditionally took special care to preserve the rights of orphans to inherit the property of their parents when the orphans reached an appropriate age. Unusually among European peasant communities, German villages would name guardians to oversee the valuation and preservation of the property to be inherited. The function of the guardians was to sell or lease property that could not be cared for by the surviving children. Villages would establish funds for orphans that would hold cash that came from property sales or leases. Such cash might then be loaned out to other villagers and interest earnings would be added to the accounts held for orphans. Hagen, for example, describes the situation of an orphaned girl in one of the von Kleist villages in Brandenburg where a guardian was to convert the mother's estate to cash, which then was to be "securely lent out against landed property to assure the girl her future maternal inheritance."[50]

Such a protective social custom was in evidence in the early history of Teplitz. The 1848 Teplitz Village History reports that many orphans were created as a result of the epidemic that killed 110 people and forced the group from Württemberg to settle in Bessarabia. Thereafter, the village history notes, the economic progress of the village was slowed as surviving adults were "forced to care for many orphans and work their farms until they [the orphans] became of age."[51] As in Prussia, German communities in Bessarabia appointed trustees to evaluate the property of the deceased parents and to lease out property that the surviving children could not farm or manage. The funds earned from such leases went into an account held by the village which would go to the orphans once they reached maturity. Until that time, assets in cash in orphans' funds could be put out on loan to other villagers, with such loans secured by property of those taking the loans. The orphans' funds formed a useful source of capital in the colonies. Initially, the villages themselves were frequent borrowers from the orphans' funds, using these as a source of money to make local capital improvements such as storehouses, schools, and churches. After the mid-1860s, orphans' funds became an important source of capital to be used for early payments of inheritance rights. Families would borrow such capital rather than sell family assets in order to provide inheritance payments to sons and daughters who wished to leave the community and buy land elsewhere.

In 1866, the Welfare Committee ordered the creation of a larger, more centralized orphans' fund. Mutschall suggests this was driven by the concern that not all villages had been treating such funds prudently.[52] From this time, centralized funds were established in Klöstitz, Alt Posttal, Sarata, and Tarutino. Kulm appeared to have been

---

49. Hagen, *Ordinary Prussians*, 163.
50. Ibid., 242.
51. Kludt, "Teplitz – 1848 Village History."
52. Wilhelm Mutschall, "History of the Community of Tarutino from 1814 to 1934," *Heritage Review* 44, no. 1 (2014): 32.

operating for some time a common orphans' fund.[53] The Welfare Committee regulations permitted such funds to offer loans at a rate of 6 percent with the principal paid over a period of ten years. As noted below in the discussion of Klaus' study, the Welfare Committee was at this time concerned with broadening access to banking arrangements within the German colonies.

The Kulm Heimatbuch reports, without indicating dates, that money from the fund for orphans was loaned out at 6 percent interest with 5 percent going back as an interest payment to the fund and 1 percent being kept by the village.[54] Later, interest rates of 10 percent and 12 percent were charged. The money was loaned for a ten-year period with interest and 10 percent of the principal due annually. Those who borrowed from the Kulm fund for orphans had to sign a promissory note endorsed by two solvent citizens, with the loan then approved by the mayor, who was the manager of the fund together with other village officials, collectively called the "community administration."[55]

Peasant communities throughout the German-speaking world also sought to protect themselves from damage caused by fire by establishing communal fire insurance funds. Such funds were created by various village subscriptions with collected funds let out at interest, much like the funds for orphans, but callable in the case of fire to reimburse claims. The Kulm Heimatbuch notes that the Welfare Committee had established a fire insurance office, the *Brandkasse*, in the district office in Klöstitz in 1849.[56] The fact that the Welfare Committee established the Brandkasse well before a centralized fund for orphans would suggest that, unlike the latter, fire insurance funds had only been sporadically created in the German villages.[57] The Brandkasse was funded by a community tax that was assessed, at least in Kulm, by the number and size of buildings to be insured. Villagers were also assigned firefighting equipment that they were to bring to the site of any village fire. Failure to appear promptly at the site of a fire with the assigned equipment would lead to greater future individual tax assessments.

The funds maintained for fire insurance and orphans created a small but useful banking system that provided access to capital for Germans living in the colonial villages in Imperial Russia. As a later chapter will discuss in more detail, such funds were an important source of money for Germans in Bessarabia wishing to buy additional land to create new villages or to emigrate from Bessarabia. Klaus, in the chapter in his study that considers banking arrangements in the foreign colonies in Russia, gives chief credit to the Welfare Committee for establishing and supervising funds for fire insurance and orphans' property that served as sources of loans.[58] While the Welfare Committee did establish district offices with bank-like responsibilities for managing such funds, it is important to remember

53. Wölfle, "The Establishment of the Village of Kulm," 8.
54. Ibid. It isn't clear whether this refers to the pre-1869 village fund or the post-1872 district fund administered in Kulm. After 1872, Kulm had become a district headquarters in its own right.
55. Ibid.
56. Ibid.
57. The 1848 Borodino Village History, in noting the fires that occurred there in 1822, 1829, 1842, and 1845, mentions that new buildings were put up for those who suffered losses. That this was accomplished via the "generous assistance of the community" suggests not a fire insurance program but ad hoc arrangements of mutual aide (Eckert, "Borodino – 1848 Village History").
58. Klaus, *Naši kolonii*, 259. This and the following paragraph are based on the chapter in Klaus entitled "Volostnye Banki" ("Volost Banks"). "Volostnye Banki," in Klaus, *Naši kolonii*, 259–90.

that the concepts of providing such funds and loaning out money in them were customs long practiced in German peasant settlements and brought to Russia by the German settlers.

The Welfare Committee, by 1869, was also responsible for the establishment of a second banking arrangement to serve the foreign colonies in Russia.[59] This was more recognizably a bank in the modern sense in that it took in deposits from individuals and, by loaning out those deposits, earned interest for the depositors and income for itself. All the examples Klaus lists of this second type of bank are from South Russia or from the Volga regions and not from Bessarabia. Klaus describes, for example, a bank of this second type established in the Odessa region taking in deposits as small as 5 rubles and letting out funds securitized by assets worth at least two-thirds of the value of the loan. It would appear that such commercial banks were not established in German Bessarabia until the twentieth century.[60] The Mannsburg Bank, established in that village in 1906, is the first commercial bank that I have found references to that was located in a German village in Bessarabia. By 1925, Mannsburg had a second bank, the Minerva. Commercial banks were also formed at this time in some of the older colonies in Bessarabia: the Bank for Commerce and Industry in Tarutino, founded in 1923, and the Volksbank in Borodino, founded in 1925.[61] Some Germans in Bessarabia did take loans for land purchases from banks in Odessa, but here again references to such are from the twentieth century, suggesting that in the nineteenth century, the reach of commercial lending was more limited. For example, the purchase of the land creating the new village of Marienfeld, Bessarabia, settled in 1911, was based on a loan from the Bank of Odessa taken out in 1910.[62] The Russian Ministry of Finance did set up a Land Bank in 1883 whose purpose was to offer loans primarily to Russian peasants for the purchase of land they were to have rights to as part of the decree that ended serfdom. The German colonists did not as a rule apply for funds here, but the colony of Tarutino did borrow from the Land Bank in 1890 when it acquired 1,200 desjatina north of Leipzig and leased farmland there to landless families from Tarutino.[63]

## The German villages taxed themselves to put up buildings that served communal needs. Such civic efforts also continued customs the colonists brought with them to Bessarabia

In all the colonies, early priority was given to building prayer houses, schools, and common grain storage structures. Later, the German villages built parsonages, civic offices, housing for teachers, and then larger, more elaborate churches. Such

---

59. Ibid. According to Klaus, this type of bank was established at the initiative ("po initiative") of the Welfare Committee.

60. The 1848 Sarata history mentions that in 1846 Gottlieb Beygel set up a trust fund "at the area commerce bank as a free gift" with yearly interest used to pay salaries for teachers. The bank referred to here was a Russian bank in the city of Akkerman some 25 miles east of Sarata. Akkerman, now Bilhorod Dnistrovs'kyi was a provincial district center for southeastern Bessarabia. "Beygel" is likely the family Stumpp identifies as Beyhl (224) and Bechtle (543) (*Emigration from Germany to Russia*).

61. Kern, *Homeland Book*, 192, 125. There was also a credit union in Eigenfeld that in 1922 became the Volksbank, a community bank in Neu Alexandrowka, and the German Agricultural, Commercial and Industrial Bank in the district capital of Akkerman, all of which appear to have been founded after World War I. As noted in footnote 60 above, a Russian commercial bank existed in Akkerman from at least 1840.

62. Ibid., 159.

63. Ibid., 152. This was the village of Neu Tarutino.

buildings were created by common agreement, with labor and costs shared by all the members of the settlement. Wittenberg, in 1815, the same year as its founding, was "equipped a farmhouse to be used for schooling and church services."[64] By 1819, the first school was built, with the building also intended for church services. In 1832–33, a new prayer house was built and the 1819 building renovated for use solely as a school building. Ten years later in 1842, the school was torn down and a larger one built farther away from the stream that ran through the middle of the village.

Kulm's Heimatbuch provides a similarly detailed account of civic building in that village. In 1831, the village completed two new structures, one to be used as a prayer house and the second as a school. Until then, religious services had been held either in the open air or in houses, and schooling had been provided in a rented house. Kulm was thus somewhat behind its neighbors in this regard, as the 1867 Tarutino Parish Report indicates that Tarutino had built a prayer house in 1820, Alt Posttal in 1824, and Leipzig in 1826.[65] The school building in Kulm proved to be too small and in 1842 it was torn down and replaced with a larger building, which included a teacher's living quarters in addition to a classroom. Kulm at this time also had a grain storage building and another used as a civic office. By 1852, the prayer house was crowded at services and the community organized to collect funds to build a larger church.[66] Some 8,000 rubles had been collected by 1860, with 3,500 rubles set out in loans.

The pattern of constructing buildings for religious, educational, and civic use as well as the regular improvement of these buildings, suggested by the materials preserved from Kulm and Wittenberg, appears to have been generally common throughout the German villages in Bessarabia. The village descriptions in the 1848 histories and the historical overviews supplied by Kern refer to many such buildings that were built or improved by common labor and shared expense in the German communities. Counting references in these sources to buildings constructed before 1850, fourteen of the twenty-four colonies had erected prayer houses, and seventeen indicated having built schools. Several also refer to the construction of parsonages, additions to schools that provided living quarters for teachers, or buildings that housed town offices and kept village records. While there are only seven references to grain storage buildings, it would seem likely that most if not all of the colonies by 1850 had constructed or taken over some structure for this purpose. Community grain storage, a shared protection against future poor harvest yields, was an old tradition in German peasant villages. The Welfare Committee, as Klaus notes in several instances, also strongly encouraged this, having found such provision helpful in the German communities in South Russia.[67]

---

64. Kurz, "Wittenberg – 1848 Village History."
65. Unknown, "Tarutino Parish Report—1867" in "Heimatbuch der Gemeinde Kulm," *Heritage Review* 13, no. 4 (1983): 17.
66. Ibid., 10–11.
67. The Welfare Committee may also have had a role in encouraging the construction of buildings for religious services and schooling. The Katzbach village history, for example, ends by thanking the Welfare Committee "for the favored promotion enjoyed by the church and school." Conrad Laib, "Katzbach – 1848 Village History," trans. Karen Retzlaff (N.p.: Germans from Russia Heritage Society, 1996), http://www.grhs.org/vr/vhistory/katzbach.htm. It would not be justified, however, to conclude from this that such civic building existed solely or even chiefly as a result of Welfare Committee encouragement.

## The focus of the German villages on community self-support is also visible in data collected by the Welfare Committee on social capital

There is another glimpse at the buildup of community self-support in the German villages in Bessarabia. This appears in one of the data categories collected for the 1841 Welfare Committee economic survey. This survey gathered information on what the Welfare Committee termed "social capital" (*obščestvennye kapitaly*), which enumerated amounts valued in silver rubles set aside or earned that year (the distinction isn't always clear) for community purposes. As with other data points in the 1841 survey, the information about social capital has been consolidated and grouped by Welfare Committee districts. For Bessarabia, the twenty-four German colonies were placed in one of four district groups: the Malojaroslavec District consisting of eleven villages, the Kljastickij or Klöstitz District consisting of nine villages, the Sarata District consisting of three villages, and the Schabo District.[68] Information on social capital is also provided for German colonies in the Tauride, Ekaterinoslav, and Odessa (Xerson) provinces of South Russia, as well as for Bulgarian colonies in Bessarabia, permitting comparisons across this wider area.

The survey collected data and defined four categories of social capital. The first was the value of stores of food that had been set aside by a community for use in future lean years.[69] This would include the value of donated grain held in village storage sites, the value of produce created on common land in the village, and possibly funds earned from the sale of grain or animals to be held in the village treasury for later purchases of food. The second category was social capital for charitable institutions, which would have included funds set aside for the building of prayer houses, churches, and schools. The third category of social capital was community funds built up from sheep breeding (*ovcevodstvo*). Presumably what is meant here are funds derived from the sales of community-owned sheep or the intrinsic value of such community-owned sheep that were grazed on common land. The Bessarabian Germans are not reported to have derived any common income from this activity but some German communities in South Russia did. The fourth category of social capital referred to funds that came from "quit rent" matters (*ot obročnyx statej*). In German Bessarabia, this would have referred to common funds derived from leasing unused land owned by the colony. The Lichtental village history notes "that for a number of years a large part of the land was rented out," and that the colony earned from this 5,000 rubles, which it used to build a church.[70] Funds appearing in this

---

68. The breakdown showing which villages were located in which districts is indicated in footnotes 78, 79, and 80 in chapter V.

69. The title for this category was "Social capital for the guaranteeing of common food provisions [earned] from publicly [owned] arable land" ("Obščestvennye kapitaly na obezpečenie narodnogo prodovol'stvija ot obščestvennoj zapaški"). It would appear from the title that the Welfare Committee here was thinking more in terms of Russian and Bulgarian community customs than those of the Germans, as it envisions provisions produced on community-held (vs. individually held) land. In the German villages it was often the custom to address this issue by having farmers give up part of their harvest to be set aside for community stores. However, the German colonies in Bessarabia did have community-owned land. The Kulm Heimatbuch, in its description of gathering funds for building the 1868 church, notes that in the 1850s, farmers worked without pay on a portion of the "community pastureland" with the yield going to the building fund, a description that, had it been for food reserves, would directly fit the Russian title here. Theophil Weiss, "District of Kulm and Neighboring Districts" in "Heimatbuch der Gemeinde Kulm," *Heritage Review* 13, no. 4 (1983): 10.

70. Hahn, "Lichtental – 1848 Village History."

category for other regions might also have been derived from performing hired labor on the land of neighboring villages or estates. It is not clear whether funds appearing in this and in the preceding category were meant to represent social capital earned in the past year or the total held by the community, though the latter would appear more likely (see table 6–1).

Leasing community land or earnings derived from community labor formed the major source of social capital in three of the regions, with sheep breeding in Odessa and saved food provisions in the Bulgarian colonies the major source in the other two regions. Though not the leading category, sheep breeding was clearly an important source for building social capital in both the Ekaterinoslav and Tauride provinces. This is not surprising given the data in the same survey indicating the large number of sheep held on average by families in the German colonies in those provinces.[71] It does seem surprising, however, that sheep breeding was such an important a factor in creating social capital in the Odessa Province. There a focus on sheep breeding appears just to have started and there were much smaller herds of sheep than in the Tauride and Ekaterinoslav provinces. The Liebental and Kučurgan districts of the Odessa Province, for example, indicate a combined social capital value of 20,905 rubles built from sheep breeding. As these two districts also indicate total holdings of only 10,835 sheep, this suggests that a material portion of the sheep existing there were either communally owned or devoted to producing community social capital.[72]

Considered on the basis of per-family averages for social capital, the Bessarabia Germans, although among the newest colonies in this survey, had built up the third-highest average social capital, nearly equal to the second-place Odessa Province. Earnings from leases played a significant role in Bessarabia, where they made up

TABLE 6–1.   **Total social capital funds in silver rubles reported for Bessarabia and South Russia**

| | Bessarabia | Tauride | Ekaterinoslav | Odessa | Bessarabia Bulgarians |
|---|---|---|---|---|---|
| 1. Food provisions saved | 3,764 | — | — | 1,837 | 38,854 |
| 2. Charitable institutions | 517 | 2,003 | 897 | 2,437 | 4,040 |
| 3. Sheep breeding | — | 9,987 | 12,713 | 36,244 | — |
| 4. From leases | 24,194 | 11,038 | 37,142 | 2,755 | 18,688 |
| **Total social capital** | 28,475 | 23,028 | 50,752 | 43,273 | 61,582[a] |
| # of families | 2,348 | 3,563 | 1,892 | 2,805 | 10,149 |
| Social capital per family | 12.13 | 6.46 | 26.82 | 15.43 | 6.07 |

a. The data on social capital for the Bulgarian colonies in Bessarabia was not subdivided into the four districts the Welfare Committee used but rather totaled to represent all social capital gathered by the Bulgarian colonies in Bessarabia. As a result, the data for the Bulgarians here is broader than that used in chapter V, which included only data for the Upper and Lower Budjak districts that were located closest to the German colonies in Bessarabia.

---

71. The Tauride Province reported 208,133 sheep or an average of 58.4 per family; the Ekaterinoslav Province reported 109,638 or 57.9 sheep per family.
72. The Berezan District of the Odessa (Xerson) Province also reported an unusually high amount of social capital earned from sheep given its total number of sheep. With a total count of 36,816 sheep, Berezan reported social capital derived from sheep breeding of 15,339 rubles. In the Tauride Province, where sheep herds were much larger, social capital from sheep breeding was far less significant. The Moločna non-Mennonite colonies, with 93,677 sheep, reported 9,750 rubles of social capital from sheep breeding, while the Moločna Mennonites, with 104,875 sheep, reported no social capital from this activity.

85 percent of the total social capital. In Bessarabia, the leasing of unused colony land, an action noted in several of the 1848 histories, would seem to be the source of the funds. The Ekaterinoslav Province also reported that earnings from leases were the major source of its social capital. The figure of 37,142 rubles from leasing is 73.2 percent of Ekaterinoslav's total social capital. Nearly 75 percent of Ekaterinoslav's reported earnings from leasing came from the small Josefstal District villages, whose 222 families produced 27,683 rubles. Given the problems these colonies had in establishing themselves[73] and that in 1841, nearly a third (32.4 percent) of the families were described as landless, the implication is that such earnings in Josefstal were derived from leasing out their own labor.

The absence of any social capital derived from preserving food supplies in the German villages of the Tauride and Ekaterinoslav provinces and the small amount noted for the Odessa colonies is likely additional evidence of the problems of varying food supplies widely reported for these colonies. It is also likely this is the reason the Welfare Committee raised the pressure in the Bessarabian German colonies for establishing grain storage houses. Welfare Committee pressure could also be behind the significant proportion of the social capital attributed to the Bulgarian colonies in Bessarabia that was derived from preserved food supplies: 63.4 percent of all the social capital built up by the Bulgarians came from this source. In contrast, the Bulgarian colonies in the Crimean District of the Tauride Province show very little social capital built up and none coming from this source.

## There are also data collected by the Welfare Committee on actions that disturbed community peace in the German villages

The Welfare Committee's 1841 survey also collected statistics on crimes and misdemeanors. The statistics are organized by district and cover widely varying periods of time. For colonists in the Moločna districts in Tauride—Mennonites and non-Mennonites—the statistics were for the past thirty-seven years; for the Berdjansk District in Tauride, the data were for the past eighteen years. In the Ekaterinoslav Province, the data for the Mariupol' colonists were for the past seventeen years, and for the Xortica Mennonites and the Josefstal colonists, the past ten years. In the Odessa (Xerson) Province, the data were for the past ten years, and for the Bessarabian Germans and Bulgarians, the past five years. The varying periods suggest that this was the first time the Welfare Committee had sought to collect data on crime, so they had asked the different regions to provide what data they had available (see table 6–2).

The data on crime can be generalized into three categories with the largest number falling into the category of crimes against the state or religion (see table 6–3).

Statistics on crime rates from nineteenth-century European rural settings are hard to come by, though general observations suggest they were quite low. Hagen, who had access to judicial records from the Stavenow villages in Brandenburg, concludes that "major crime incidence in the Stavenow lordship was extremely low."[74] This would also be, with one exception, the general conclusion concerning the

---

73. Giesinger, *From Catherine to Khrushchev*, 95. Giesinger notes that these colonies needed "much government help" for some time. As an example of problems, Giesinger reports that there were forty-three landless families in 1857; this, however, would have been an improvement from 1841, when the figure was seventy-two.

74. Hagen, *Ordinary Prussians*, 473.

TABLE 6–2.  **Data on crime for the German villages in South Russia**

| | Bessarabia | Odessa | Ekaterinoslav | Tauride | Bulgarians |
|---|---|---|---|---|---|
| Insubordination to the authorities | 30 | 101 | 125 | 18 | 89 |
| Bribery[a] | 6 | — | — | — | 2 |
| Not catching criminals | 2 | 9 | 4 | 3 | 57 |
| Murder | — | — | — | 1 | 4 |
| Disobedient children | 2 | 20 | 20 | — | 6 |
| Slander | 1 | 46 | 19 | 14 | 3 |
| Rape | 17 | 16 | 75 | 69 | 20 |
| Robbery | — | — | 2 | — | 3 |
| Swindling | 40 | 61 | 49 | 29 | 69 |
| Taking/destroying the property of others | 6 | 1 | 10 | — | 4 |
| Arson | — | — | — | 1 | — |
| Forest crimes | — | 1 | 4 | — | — |
| Crimes against the Faith | — | 23 | 2 | — | — |
| **Total crimes** | 104 | 278 | 310 | 135 | 257 |
| Average crimes/100 families | 4.4 | 8.4 | 16.4 | 3.8 | 4.7 |
| Average/year | 20.8 | 27.8 | 23.1 | 3.8 | 51.4 |

a.  Bribery (lixoimstvo) was the corruption of state officials.

TABLE 6–3.  **Three general categories of crime in the German colonies**

| | Number of Crimes | Percent of Total |
|---|---|---|
| Crimes against the state or religion | 471 | 43.5 |
| Crimes against people | 333 | 30.7 |
| Crimes against property | 280 | 25.8 |

data from Bessarabia and South Russia, where among the German colonies there was a single murder, a single case of arson, and just two robberies over all the years from which data had been collected. The Bulgarian colonies in Bessarabia, which, like the German colonies there, had a low incidence of crime, nonetheless indicated that there had been four murders in the five years of data collected.

The major exception to this pattern of small numbers of violent crimes is the frequency of rape, referred to in the survey as the "illegal satisfaction of passions" (*protivuzakonnoe udovletvorenie strastej*). Rape represented the third highest number of crimes reported, 197 or 18.1 percent of the total. Combining data for all the years reported by the German and Bulgarian colonies, the overall incidence of rape was 1.19 per one hundred families. The incidence of rape, however, varies significantly across the different regions. It is highest in Ekaterinoslav at a rate of 5.6 per year. It was least frequent among the German colonies in the Odessa and Tauride provinces where the rates were 1.6 and 1.9 per year, respectively.

Statistics on rape from the nineteenth century are hard to come by, particularly from rural settings. Where they exist, it is commonly thought that social mores caused incidences of rape to be underreported. It is difficult, as a result, to place these 1841 statistics in any material context. Hagen, in his review of data from the Stavenow estates in Brandenburg, focused not on rape but on the social problems created by children born out of wedlock, or problems created by adultery and incest. Such issues caused by apparently consensual sex occurring outside of the generally accepted moral norms are very different from the problems created by incidences of rape. One possible implication of Hagen's data is that rape was less common. On the other hand, in a world where women's rights were limited, incidences of rape may simply not have been reported.

The 1841 statistics for Bessarabia and South Russia offer no information about the ages of the victims or perpetrators or details on circumstances relating to any of the crimes reported. The few village memoirs written about the German colonies in Bessarabia as well as the 1848 histories pay little attention to crime. The frequency of the incidences of rape reported in the 1841 statistics matched with the absence of commentary on this topic suggest a very serious social problem that was not publicly discussed or possibly even addressed as a social issue to be corrected.

Overall, the lowest incidence of crime was reported from Tauride, which had an average of 3.8 crimes per year. As this represented crimes reported over a period ranging from eighteen to thirty-seven years, the statistics are impressive. Less comforting, however, is the fact that of the 135 crimes reported from Tauride, just over half (51.1percent) were rape. The Bessarabian and Ekaterinoslav Germans had the second- and third-lowest incidences of crime, with the Bessarabian German villages reporting a frequency of 20.8 crimes per year and the Ekaterinoslav villages 23.1 crimes per year. The highest crime rate was reported from the Bulgarian villages in Bessarabia with an average of 51.4 crimes per year. Among the German colonies, the crime statistics for the Odessa Province stand out for special attention. They had the highest number of insubordination crimes at 10.1 per year, the second-highest number of swindling crimes at 6.1 per year, and an average of 2.3 crimes against the faith per year when virtually no other region reported any crimes of this nature at all. In general, it would appear that among the German colonies, the Mennonite villages experienced the fewest incidences of crime. Drawing conclusions from these data, however, should be done cautiously. The apparently unusual statistics for Odessa raise the possibility that the basis for defining what constituted criminal behavior varied among the districts and regions, skewing the results collected here.

Among the Bessarabian Germans, swindling, insubordination to the authorities, and rape form the top three crimes and together make up 83.7 percent of the total crimes reported. Roughly 60 percent of the crimes were committed in the Klöstitz District and the remainder in the Malojaroslav colonies. The Klöstitz colonies had twenty-seven incidences of swindling and thirteen cases of rape, where there were thirteen and four respectively in the Malojaroslav colonies. The Malojaroslav District had twenty-one incidences of insubordination, while there were only nine among the Klöstitz colonies. There were no crimes reported from the Sarata District or Schabo. There is no detail provided on levels of severity of crimes or on punishments. Criminal hearings were evidently held in the separate villages and any punishments, physical or monetary, were assessed there. The Kulm Heimatbuch offers a small detail on this subject when it notes that the village mayor needed to be someone respected by other villagers because he, together with his two assistants, was expected to take control of troublesome situations, hold those accused in custody, and determine and administer punishments. Though not noted in the Heimatbuch, village mayors likely had some general judicial guidance from the Welfare Committee district offices and reported crimes to them as well.

The 1841 Welfare Committee survey also included a listing of misdemeanors reported by the colonial districts. These are much more numerous than crimes (see table 6–4).

With misdemeanors, a somewhat different picture emerges than that evidenced by the statistics on crime. The Bulgarian colonies in Bessarabia materially stand out as having been far more troublesome than the German colonies. The Bulgarians reported 271 misdemeanors per year, a figure that is over eight times the largest number for any of the German colonial regions. The misdemeanor figures for the Bulgarians are driven by large numbers of cases of drunkenness and not fulfilling agreements. The average incidences of drunkenness among the Bessarabian Bulgarians came to 65.6 charges per year, while the number of charges for not fulfilling agreements came to 171.2 per year. The total number of 856 incidences of broken agreements among the Bulgarians contrasts significantly with the 28 reported from the German colonies in all regions. Giving one's word to undertake an action was a serious commitment in German culture. Not fulfilling that commitment brought significant loss of face and status within the community. The problems in the Bulgarian colonies reflect different cultural mores that presumed agreements between individuals could be undertaken as hoped-for results rather than binding actions.

Among the German colonies, the Bessarabian Germans reported the highest number of misdemeanors per year at 33.8. Among the Bessarabian Germans, drunkenness and indifference to farming formed the largest numbers of misdemeanors. As with the statistics on crimes, Tauride experienced the best results among the German colonies, averaging 2.8 misdemeanors per year. Overall, drunkenness was the most

TABLE 6–4.  **Data on misdemeanors in the colonial districts**

| | Bessarabia | Odessa | Ekaterinoslav | Tauride | Bulgarians |
|---|---|---|---|---|---|
| Not fulfilling obligations with regard to fires | 10 | — | 3 | 1 | 77 |
| Indifference to farming | 38 | 36 | 84 | 43 | 52 |
| Civil strife, quarreling | 11 | 3 | 100 | 14 | 14 |
| Drunkenness | 65 | 61 | 73 | 7 | 328 |
| Vagrancy | 19 | 15 | 13 | 2 | 2 |
| Bootlegging | 17 | 15 | 5 | 24 | 1 |
| Not fulfilling the instructions of the authorities | 3 | 71 | 92 | 3 | 19 |
| Not fulfilling agreements | 3 | 6 | 7 | 2 | 856 |
| Not fulfilling financial loan/promissory notes | 3 | 3 | 13 | 4 | 6 |
| **Total misdemeanors** | 169 | 220 | 390 | 100 | 1,355 |
| Number/100 families | 7.2 | 6.6 | 20.6 | 2.8 | 24.9 |
| Number/year | 33.8 | 22.0 | 29.1 | 2.8 | 271.0 |

common misdemeanor across the different regions of German colonies, accounting for 23.4 percent of the total, followed by indifference to farming with 22.9 percent, and not fulfilling the instructions of the authorities with 19.2 percent of the total. Indifference to farming was an issue in all the regions. In Tauride, it was the largest area of problems and was to be found even among the Moločna Mennonites. Though the data points cannot be connected, it would not be surprising to find throughout the regions that correspondences existed between the cases of drunkenness and not fulfilling fire duties, indifference to farming, civil strife, and violent crime.

In the Bessarabian German colonies, the Klöstitz District was, as with cases of crime, the leading source of misdemeanors, with 102 of the total of 169 or 60.4 percent. The Klöstitz colonies had large numbers cited for indifference to farming (33), drunkenness (29), vagrancy (16), and not fulfilling firefighting obligations (10). The Malojaroslav colonies were the leading area for problems of drunkenness (31), bootlegging (17), and civil strife (10).

The total picture provided by the data on crimes and misdemeanors suggests that the German colonies in Bessarabia and South Russia were on the whole peaceful communities free of many social troubles. Given that the data in the 1841 survey provided cumulative figures covering numbers of years, it is striking how far such figures are below twentieth-century statistics. This is particularly true for statistics on violent crime—that is, incidences of murder, robbery, and rape. Normalizing the figures for all the German colonies by creating a one-year average and adjusting that average to the per 100,000 person basis typically used for crime statistics, the German colonies had an average annual figure of 18.9 violent crimes per 100,000 people. The figure for the Bessarabian Germans alone would be 27.2 violent crimes per 100,000 people, all derived from incidences of rape. Such statistics are significantly below the US Census Bureau's state-by-state statistics for 2006, for example, which range from a high of 1,508 violent crimes per 100,000 people in the District of Columbia to lows of 116 in Maine and 128 in North Dakota. Nevertheless, despite the relative peacefulness the statistics from Bessarabia suggest, the relative frequency of both rape and drunkenness indicate that the German villages were not free from violence or social troubles.

## The German villages were given a great deal of local autonomy

Up until 1872, when the Russian government made major changes in its relations with the German colonists, the German colonial settlements in Russia enjoyed a significant degree of local civic and legal autonomy. Each of the German villages was largely responsible for local police and judicial functions. The village government determined whether a crime or misdemeanor had occurred, whether individuals so charged were in fact guilty, and what the resulting punishment should be, and then executed that punishment. Mutschall notes that in Tarutino, punishments were often "blows of the rod." Cases of adultery, though, were deemed religious rather than civic matters "and guilty parties were condemned to punishment in church."[75]

In Bessarabia, as in the Volga and South Russia colonies, the Russian government asked the male owners of land to elect a mayor, to be called a *Vorsteher* or *Schulz*, and

---

75. Mutschall, "Community of Tarutino," *Heritage Review* 44, no. 3: 17. Those guilty of adultery had to stand penitently at the church door after services.

two assistants.[76] These officials had terms of office of generally two to three years.[77] From the perspective of the Welfare Committee, the major duties of these officials were to collect taxes, to enforce the rules the Russian government imposed via the Welfare Committee, and to punish anyone breaking those rules. Taxes were assessed, as in long-standing tradition for Russian peasant villages, to the village as a whole and were based on the total amount of arable land. It was then up to the community to decide how to assign and collect the taxes owed. As Mutschall has noted, "what was to be taxed was left completely up to the community" to decide.[78] We know from the 1848 Sarata history that that village decided every family was to pay a flat rate of fourteen rubles with the remainder of the village tax obligation allotted in proportion to the number of cattle each family owned. In Tarutino before 1872, the number of livestock formed the basis of taxation, so the few families that owned no cattle, horses, or sheep had no tax liabilities.

Many of the duties and responsibilities of the mayor and his assistants involved administering not the orders and regulations of the Russian government, but the rules the communities established themselves. Such rules generally followed German peasant custom and common law. To maintain order and peace in the settlements, the mayors and their assistants relied on remembered customs the colonists had brought with them from Prussia and Württemberg. Such customs were the basis of deciding inheritance and orphan rights as well as rights in business disputes. Mutschall stresses this point, especially with regard to inheritances, for which rights were "not tied to the national laws" but were determined "according to 'local custom'."[79] According to such customary practice, for instance, a widow with adult children was to receive free room and board until her death or remarriage.

The mayor and his assistants were charged with general civic executive authority: the maintenance of peace and customary morality, the organization of fire protection, and the maintenance, when necessary, of a night watch. The mayor was responsible, too, for protecting the rights and assets of orphans and minors. Record keeping was another mayoral responsibility. The actual record keeping, though, was delegated to the village secretary, who maintained the accounting books for taxation, as well as criminal and judicial records. Correspondence with the Welfare Committee, as well as the collection and tabulation of economic data pursuant to Welfare Committee requests, was also the responsibility of the village secretary.

The Kulm Heimatbuch notes that in Kulm, the mayor's office was called the Schulz, the two assistants were *Beisitzer,* and there was in addition a secretary (*Dorfschrieber*).[80] In Kulm, the mayor could arrest citizens and had charge of the

---

76. Giesinger calls this the "long standing Russian means for village organization" which goes back to the *Instrucktion*, the rules formulated for governing the Volga German colonies (*From Catherine to Khrushchev*, 49). The term *Schulz* was commonly used (as was *Schultheiß* from which Schulz is derived) to describe a "mayor" in a German peasant community whose primary function was to pay taxes, with the term coming from the word *Schuld*, meaning "debt." *Vorsteher*, meaning administrator or manager in German, typically referred to an appointed official.

77. In Kulm, the term was two years; in Tarutino, according to Mutschall, it was three. Wilhelm Mutschall, "History of the Community of Tarutino from 1814 to 1934," *Heritage Review* 42, no. 2 (2012): 6.

78. Mutschall, "Community of Tarutino," *Heritage Review* 44, no. 3: 25.

79. Ibid., 24.

80. Wölfle, "The Establishment of the Village of Kulm," 5–7.

community jail (called the "little house") and "could even inflict punishment."[81] In Kulm and likely elsewhere, the mayor and his assistants also had an important role in marriages. They would draw up the marriage contracts in which the assets and holdings of the bride and groom would be listed along with the values attested by village appraisers.[82]

In Mutschall's description of Tarutino, the mayor and his assistants, called the Committee, had to approve any sale of fixed assets. They also made visits of inspection to check the maintenance of houses, kitchens, cellars, food storages, barns, orchards, and gardens. If any kind of disorder was found, the home owner was punished: "10–15 blows while still on his own private property." Mutschall indicates that women were also punished when deficiencies in general household upkeep were noted in the inspections.[83]

According to the rules laid out by the Welfare Committee for the German settlements in Bessarabia, the mayor and his assistants were to be elected by a "majority vote from householders, who, already of legal age, have their own housekeeping and sensible judgment, who lead an irreproachable life, who think and behave honestly, are good husbands, and so distinguish themselves in agriculture, horticulture and cattle raising."[84] In the Kulm Heimatbuch, elections are described as occurring by "balloting with white and black balls or by a show of hands."[85]

Until 1872, the right to vote in village elections and to hold village office remained limited to men who were the heads of families that possessed one of the original household land allotments in the village. These men and their families acquired such possession from having settled the land, inherited it, married into it, or purchased it.[86] Women, such as those listed in the Leipzig statistics of 1856–57 as property holders, did not have the right to vote. Also without voting rights were adult males, married and single, who were living and helping to work a family's common property but were not deemed to be the family's head, as well as men purchasing or renting small plots of land on the allotments of other families. By the early 1860s, people of other nationalities began to seek places in the German colonial villages in Bessarabia. These were Moldavian, Russian, Ukrainian, Jewish, and Gaugaz peoples coming from other villages chiefly in Bessarabia, who took work as herdsmen, farm workers, and shopkeepers. These newcomers were also not permitted to vote in the village assemblies, to hold office, or to share in the community land to graze their animals.

A major reform enacted with Tsar Alexander II's approval in 1864 broadened the right to vote in village communal elections. While focused chiefly on peasant rights of Russians, this reform also took into consideration landless citizens in German colonial villages. The reform recognized the owners of households without land

---

81. Ibid., 6.

82. Such marriage contracts would, after the death of one or both of the parties, play an important role in the allocation of the family assets to be inherited.

83. Mutschall, "Community of Tarutino," *Heritage Review* 43, no. 2: 6–7.

84. Wagner, "Discussion of Local Government." Wagner is here quoting in translation from a document recording the elections of 1862 preserved (or once preserved) in the Odessa Archives, Fond 6, Inventory 1, File 20877. As similar wording is found in the "instructions" to villages from the Welfare Committee (see Schmidt, *Die Deutschen aus Bessarabien*, 62–64). It would seem that both sources refer to rules established by the Welfare Committee.

85. Wölfle, "The Establishment of the Village of Kulm," 7.

86. Mutschall, "Community of Tarutino," *Heritage Review* 44, no. 3: 16. As noted earlier, the land was not legally their personal property. Until 1872, the land was collectively held as communal property by the village.

(called in the German communities *Anwohner* and referred to here as cottagers) and farm laborers who lived in the household of another and did not own a house (called *Einwohner*) and permitted both groups to participate in the village assemblies and vote for village leaders.[87] As the landless did not constitute a material portion of the German population in Bessarabia until well after 1872, it is likely this reform had little immediate impact on the German villages there. Later, when there were more landless families in Bessarabia and this rule might have had an impact, it is clear that they were not given equal voting rights. Rather, it would appear that the landless were allotted a fixed number of votes as a group rather than each landless individual having a vote or a portion of a vote. In this way, the landless, though having some voting rights, did not materially affect elections. Mutschall, for example, notes that in Tarutino toward end of the nineteenth century, the landless as a block had but 4 votes out of a total village vote of 275.[88]

## The Welfare Committee tended to intervene only to improve the economic health of the villages, or when the German villages had conflicts with outside civic authorities or internal unrest

The great degree of local autonomy enjoyed by the German villages in Bessarabia was in part the result of the limited resources of the Welfare Committee and the comfort it felt given the general quiet and busy self-absorption of the colonial settlements. In part, too, such freedom was, in Bessarabia, the result of the Russian government's intentional effort to limit the powers of the Moldavian nobility to regain political, administrative, and economic control over lands lost in the Russian victories of 1808–11.[89] In Bessarabia, the provincial civil government was prohibited from interfering in the civil and economic activities of the colonies or to seek to overrule the parallel authority that had been given to the Welfare Committee.

To establish a local presence among the German colonies in Bessarabia, the Welfare Committee set up a district office in Wittenberg in 1817 and then moved this office to Alt Posttal in 1831. A second Welfare Committee district office in German Bessarabia was established perhaps as early as the mid-1820s in Klöstitz. These two district offices reported to the regional office for Bessarabia in Akkerman, which in turn reported to the headquarters of the Welfare Committee located in Odessa after 1831.

In its management of the German colonies in Bessarabia, the Welfare Committee appears chiefly focused on establishing the economic well-being of the colonies. The Welfare Committee generally left the colonies to themselves except to remind the colonies of economic opportunities or to offer advice or even warnings when it thought a colony troubled by economic or social problems. Most of the 1848 village histories frequently offer up thanks for the leadership and guidance of the Welfare Committee, but references to actual interventions in village life are rare. The Leipzig history, in noting the "licentiousness and demoralization" that threatened the growth and moral health of the community, does indicate that the "authorities…had given

---

87. Wagner, "Discussion of Local Government," 5.
88. Mutschall, "Community of Tarutino," *Heritage Review* 44, no. 3: 20.
89. Jewsbury, *Russian Annexation of Bessarabia*, 135–37.

warning."[90] On the other hand, the problems in Sarata of the "nightly hanging out of teens" or excessive "eating and drinking" appear to have been addressed solely by the community leaders themselves.[91]

One major focus of the Welfare Committee was to gather and analyze demographic and economic data from the colonies. Material from the Welfare Committee archives that Brandes and Malinovskij include in their studies indicate that the Welfare Committee on some regular basis collected detailed statistics from the colonies on population growth, crops planted and harvested, animal herds, production of wine, farm household earnings from agriculture and trade, tax payments, and as we have just seen, data on social and legal issues. Such data very likely became the basis of reports the Welfare Committee prepared for the Ministry of the Interior and then after 1837, the Ministry of State Domains. These reports would form, from a cameral point of view, an account of the state's investments in the colonies. The Welfare Committee also appears to have been responsible for receiving, checking, and passing on the annual tax payments collected after 1830 as well as the amortized repayments of the government's cost in bringing the colonists to Bessarabia that were collected after 1835. For all the freedom the Welfare Committee permitted the colonies in the handling of their internal, local political and social affairs, it should not be presumed that the Welfare Committee confined itself solely to data collection. Staff from the Welfare Committee's district offices would regularly visit villages and so had first-hand knowledge of both the state of affairs in different villages and the general accuracy of the reports the villages prepared.

It would further seem probable that the Welfare Committee staff kept close watch over any relations, especially adverse relations, that developed between the colonies and provincial or other officials or agents of the Russian government. Malinovskij, quoting from Welfare Committee archives in Odessa, describes two incidences where conflicts occurred between Bessarabian German colonists and semi-official representatives of tax farmers who had purchased from the government the monopoly of selling alcohol and then collecting and paying the tax due on such sales. In Russian, a representative of the tax farmers was referred to as a *smotritel'*, a term that described a private citizen who had contractual responsibility for some aspect of governmental business.[92] The colonists had a competing right to the sale of wine and spirits made from wine and this led to conflicts. The smotriteli created issues on their own by carrying on their shoulder the chip of quasi-official authority. This encouraged the attitude that the Germans, like any peasants who raised their voices, ought to be punished just for doing so. Taking the trouble to note even minor disagreements suggests the Welfare Committee's close attention to events in the German villages. Where the disagreements led to charges and punishments, it is

---

90. Trautmann, "Leipzig – 1848 Village History."

91. Natterer, "Sarata – 1848 Village History."

92. In general, a smotritel' or supervisor was someone who contracted with the government to provide services, such as delivering supplies or even managing a railroad station. Agents of the tax farmers were also called smotriteli. Until 1863, in Russia, tax farmers (*otkupščiki*) purchased the right to sell government-produced alcohol and to collect and pay the taxes on such sales. A smotritel', thus, was not a government official, but a private citizen who had responsibility under contract for some aspect of government affairs. The 1815 conflict in Tarutino that resulted in the arrest of Pastor Schnabel also involved two smotriteli who supplied grain to the village and had charge of the grain storage that the hungry villagers had attacked.

interesting to note that the Welfare Committee could not always be presumed to be an ally supporting the colonists.

In 1835, a conflict arose between the smotritel' Kotovič and the sitting Klöstitz *Oberschultz* Engel over the sale of wine. The smotritel' had forbidden such sales while Engel had retorted that he only obeyed the Welfare Committee and "a smotritel' is not an official" (*načalnik*). The Welfare Committee notes indicate that no action or punishment resulted and reported only that the smotritel' replied wryly that Engel had "an insufficient knowledge of the monarchical form of government."[93] A more serious conflict took place in Neu Arzis in 1847 or 1848 when a smotritel' named Kossovskij reported that he felt forced to leave the village under threat of being physically harmed. Kossovskij then brought back provincial police, who arrested Daniel Gunsch, whom Kossovskij identified as a ringleader, and Kossovskij gave him sixty lashes. When this incident was later reviewed by the Welfare Committee, the colonists complained that Kossovskij had interfered with their work preventing them from planting trees and gathering ashes, presumably because he wanted them to do something at his bidding. In its review, the Welfare Committee, as Malinovskij reports, saw the colonists as disobeying the request of an official and so decided in favor of the smotritel'. Interestingly, the report of this incident was sent up to the Ministry of State Domains in St. Petersburg, and Malinovskij quotes a response made by Minister Pavel Kiselev who, though understanding the rights of the colonists, felt that it was more important "to fulfill the instructions of the authorities whose power in no way ought to be weakened by disorder or disturbances."[94]

### The 1848 village histories and Kern's village synopses report the existence of two possibly interrelated social disturbances dating from 1830 to 1848

The social disturbances reported in the 1848 village histories and in Kern's *Homeland Book* were: first, the decision of some villagers to leave Bessarabia and Russia to seek better fortunes in German settlements that had been recently founded in Serbia and Romania; and second, the conflicts created in some settlements by colonists breaking away from Evangelical Lutheran practices to follow competing religious beliefs as Separatists.

The 1848 Leipzig Village History reports that in 1842–43, a number of families gave up their farmsteads and emigrated from Russia with some going to Serbia. The history implies that the Leipzigers who did so were but one group among those from several other German Bessarabian villages. Likely related to this, the Friedenstal history notes that in 1842, some twenty-six families left that village "for Turkish Moldova, Serbia and Wallachia."[95] Kern, in his section on Friedenstal,

---

93. Malinovskij, *Social'naja i xozjajstvennaja istorija*, 100.
94. Ibid., 100–101. Kiselev's letter was dated February 8, 1848 (O.S.). Malinovskij, noting that this reply came at the cusp of the 1848 revolutionary disturbances in Western Europe, implies that this influenced Kiselev's preference for order over rights. However, as Kisilev here fully reflects what is known of the long-term views of Tsar Nicholas I, Kisilev's opinion may well be largely independent of any connection with the 1848 disturbances.
95. Eckert, "Friedenstal – 1848 Village History."

2

mentions that "some of the founders gave up and moved on to Serbia."[96] The Leipzig history suggests the emigrants were motivated by "wandering fever."[97] The Friedenstal history depicts them as coming from the "poorest and laziest"[98] of the settlers there, and implies that they were fooled by attractive promises. The negative characterizations of the emigrants may result from the sad fate that befell them. Such negative characterizations may also reflect the attitudes expressed by the Welfare Committee and behind these, the mercantilist views of the Imperial Russian government, which would consider the emigration of productive farmers as a commercial loss.

Given that many of the Bessarabian colonial families had a history of moving to find better situations as well as the litany of hardships families had experienced in getting settled in Bessarabia, it is not surprising that some would conclude that perhaps they might do better elsewhere. This would be particularly true for families in Leipzig, which had a slow and troubled development. This is, however, the first instance of families leaving the German colonies in Bessarabia. That families were permitted to emigrate from Russia is another indication that the Germans were treated by the Russian government as having special rights. Russian and Ukrainian peasants at this time were not permitted to emigrate. Permission for the Germans to leave would undoubtedly have come from St. Petersburg rather than from the Welfare Committee. Permission to leave Russia came with the stipulation, as the 1848 histories remind us, that that the emigrants would not be allowed to return. To fill the newly vacant farmsteads in Leipzig and Friedenstal, the Welfare Committee brought in families from the now crowded colonies in Xerson (Odessa) Province. The Leipzig Village History notes they came from the villages of (or near) Worms and Rohrbach in the Berezan District. It may well be that families from the Berezan, Liebental, and Kučurgan districts in Xerson who appeared in other Bessarabian villages in the early 1840s were similarly replacements for these emigrants.

The families leaving in 1842 were likely offered some outside financial help to settle elsewhere. The major group apparently was headed for Austrian Serbia. As Serbia began in the 1830s to assert rights of independence from the Ottoman Empire, Austria became increasingly concerned about unrest in territories it held north of the Danube River which had a large Serbian-speaking peasant population. Beginning in the late 1830s, Austria sought to attract German-speaking peasants to that area with offers of land and funding to settle them there. It is unlikely that the emigrants leaving for Serbia were responding to direct contact from Austrian authorities, as the Russian government would have clearly forbidden that. Perhaps those electing to leave Bessarabia had heard of the existence of such offers and thought that by crossing over into Austrian territory they would receive funding. In any case, that they knew of the Austrian offers speaks to the fact that the Bessarabian Germans had and maintained contacts with the German-speaking world outside of Bessarabia, even if much of such news traveled by word of mouth. The references in the Friedenstal history to some emigrants settling in Moldavia and Wallachia likely refer to offers made by Romanian nobles owning land there. The Russian army's victories in 1828–30 had made large parts of Romanian Moldavia and Wallachia

96. Kern, *Homeland Book*, 85.
97. Trautmann, "Leipzig – 1848 Village History."
98. Eckert, "Friedenstal – 1848 Village History."

semi-independent territories under Russian control, making their borders with Bessarabia far more porous.

Both of the Bessarabian village histories indicate that the emigrants of 1842 did not prosper and were not successful in establishing themselves elsewhere. The Leipzig history notes "many found distress and their graves, others wandered homeless."[99] The Friedenstal history adds that the hopes of the emigrants for a paradise "proved to be a vapor."[100] Brandes has built detail around at least one group of those leaving the Bessarabian German colonies in the period between the spring of 1842 and March 1843. This group of some 189 families passed through Russian-controlled Romania, crossed the Danube into Ottoman province of Bulgaria, and reached Adrianople in Thrace. The Turkish governor there settled them in Christian villages in Bulgaria near Silistra along the Danube and gave them three years of tax-free time to establish themselves. Two families, however, were offered settlement in Turkish villages but declined and turned back.[101]

The Friedenstal history and Kern both note that, having left their homesteads in the Bessarabian colonies, the emigrants were not permitted to return. In securing permission through the Welfare Committee to leave, the emigrants had given up their rights of settlement and citizenship. The Leipzig history, however, indicates that some managed to return to Russia but "lived [now] in poverty and misery."[102] The fact that some were able to return to Bessarabia is also confirmed from the genealogies of some of the emigrant families as will be discussed below.

The second social disturbance that is discussed in the 1848 village histories concerns the religious Separatists. It would appear, as argued below, that at least some of the emigrants were Separatists and thus not an independent issue as they are presented in the village histories and Kern. Kern's collection of data on the Bessarabian villages is the major source for information on the Separatists in Bessarabia. The Separatists formed small, loosely organized religious groups who broke away from the Evangelical Lutheran church in several of the German colonies in Bessarabia. In Kern's view, the Separatists held beliefs that were dangerous to the maintenance of religious faith and community peace. In Kern's section on Leipzig, he notes that "the misguided Separatist movement undermined the wholesomeness of the community."[103] In his account of Borodino, another village where Separatism was popular, Kern notes how "the fanaticism of Separatism… destroyed the moral fabric in Alt Elft, Klöstitz and Tarutino."[104] Writing about Klöstitz, Kern mentions that "church life was hindered through the Separatist movement" and "sectists and fundamentalists…took a terrible toll on spiritual affairs."[105]

In using the term "Separatists" to describe this group, Kern links them to groups of Pietists in Württemberg who, in the period from 1815 to 1820, were involved in conflicts with the state-supported Lutheran church there. These conflicts, along with mounting economic difficulties, caused some of these Pietists to immigrate both to

99. Trautmann, "Leipzig – Village History."
100. Eckert, "Friedenstal – 1848 Village History."
101. Brandes, *Von den Zaren Adoptiert*, 369.
102. Trautmann, "Leipzig – 1848 Village History."
103. Kern, *Homeland Book*, 142.
104. Ibid., 125.
105. Ibid., 131, 121.

Russia and to the United States.[106] In Württemberg, many of these people called themselves Separatists (*Separatister*), which reflected their belief that they sought to separate themselves from the Lutheran church or even separate themselves from existing societies to await in greater purity the coming of Christ. The Separatists in Württemberg were largely noted for their millennial views. They passionately anticipated the arrival in their lifetimes of Christ's one thousand-year rule on Earth as suggested in the book of Revelations (20: 1–5), and so focused their thoughts on the end of days, the return of Christ, and eternal salvation. Some of the emigrants leaving Württemberg for Russia between 1817 and 1819 had the intention of settling in the Caucasus region and awaiting there for the end of the world. Some made it to the Caucasus; others who arrived in Odessa ended up founding colonies in the Berdjansk District of Russia's Tauride Province east of Odessa.[107]

Kern's descriptions link these same views to Separatists he describes in German Bessarabia in the 1820s through the 1840s. In addition to their millennial beliefs, the Separatists in German Bessarabia tended to reject formal church ties and refused to celebrate baptisms, confirmations, or church holidays except the Sabbath. They revived the Pietist practices of group Bible reading and textual discussions in which participants shared their personal and emotional religious experiences and revelations. The Separatists in Bessarabia also shared common ground and practices with the popular preaching and teaching of Father Ignaz Lindl in Schwabian Bavaria and neighboring eastern Württemberg in 1815–20. Lindl encouraged some of his followers from Bavaria and Württemberg to immigrate to Russia to found the village of Sarata in Bessarabia in 1822 to create a place where they might have a religious life that was more personal and emotional than that celebrated in the established churches in their former homes. Lindl preached about personal revelation and the coming of Christ bringing eternal salvation to some at the end of days.[108]

The practices that Kern criticizes in several German Bessarabian villages in the 1820s through the 1840s had their origin, according to Kern, in Lindl and Sarata. In his discussion of Alt Elft, Kern notes: "the Separatists Movement, headed by Pastor Lindl in Sarata, created additional worries [in Alt Elft]. Six families joined the Separatists."[109] In terms of actual practices, the Separatists in Bessarabia disassociated themselves with both the village Evangelical Lutheran churches and with religious

---

106.  Zoar, Ohio, was founded in 1817 by a group of Separatists emigrating from Württemberg.

107.  Giesinger, *From Catherine to Khrushchev*, 123–25. Some of the Separatists had the intention of going from Russia to Jerusalem and awaiting Christ's return there. The Russian government blocked these plans and as Giesinger notes, "forced [them] to settle down in the South Caucasus to face the realities of life" (*From Catherine to Khrushchev*, 41). The founders of Teplitz left Württemberg at this time with the intention of settling in the Russian Caucasus. Religious views, possibly even Separatist views in the narrower sense defined above, may have played a role in their coming to Russia. With these and other immigrants to Russia from this time it is important to remember, however, that Walker's study of emigration concluded on much evidence that many Württemberg emigrants bound for the Caucasus were chiefly motivated by economic reasons. Whatever the religious culture of the Teplitz immigrants, Separatist views, in the broader sense that Kern uses, do not appear to have troubled community life there at the time they were creating issues elsewhere in German Bessarabia.

108.  Susan A. Crane, "Holy Alliances: Creating Religious Communities after the Napoleonic Wars," in *Die Gegenwart Gottes in der modernen Gesellschaft: Transzendenz und religiöse Vergemeinschaftung in Deutschland*, ed. Michael Geyer and Lucian Hölscher, 52–53 (Göttingen, Ger.: Wallstein, 2006).

109.  Kern, *Homeland Book*, 54. Kern here is writing not literally but allusively and referring to the spread of Lindl's ideas. Lindl did not preach in Sarata and though his ideas had several connections with those of the Separatists, Lindl never specifically identified his views with the Separatists.

teachings based solely on doctrinal interpretations of the Bible. In his discussion of Leipzig, Kern notes that the Separatists ridiculed the church, and in the section on Klöstitz mentions that the Separatists focused their attention not on a study of the Bible but on the "inner light"—that is, the revelations and religious ideas that arose in their discussions.[110] The Evangelical Lutheran pastor in Sarata named the letters of Lindl and Johan Jacob Wirz as influential, noting wryly people read these kneeling: "Man liest ihre Briefe kniend."[111] Wirz was a Swiss German silk weaver who in 1823 began to write of having divine revelations and developed a group of followers called the Nazarines (*Nazarener*). A Wirz letter from October 1841 urges followers to establish a "new church" and prophesies that Christ would return to earth in 1846. In German Bessarabia, Carl Ehni of Borodino, struck by these prophecies, worked to create such a new church that, following the prescripts of Wirz, would offer its own communion.[112] In his discussion of Borodino, Kern names Karl Ehni as a Separatist leader and criticizes his views noting that for his followers "only his visions mattered, not...the scriptures."[113]

For Kern, this produced superstitious and nonsensical beliefs. Certainly a major reason why Kern, himself a pastor in the Evangelical Lutheran church, viewed the Separatists in such a negative light was that the Separatists rejected the church, its religious services, and the pastors who led them.[114] In his section on the Klöstitz parish, Kern quotes from E. H. Busch's study that the Separatists referred to the church as "the Great Babylonian Whore" whose attendees follow the priests of Baal. Busch notes eighty Klöstitz families who held their own services, avoided eating pork, and elected their own priests. In references that strongly suggest views that go back to Lindl's preaching, Busch further notes that the Separatists outlawed marriage, established "cults" of saints and the Virgin Mary, and believed in the imminent coming of Christ and the end of the world.[115]

Susan Crane, in her discussion of Lindl's preaching, notes that officials in Württemberg and Bavaria criticized the practices of such sectarians for "holding private—and by implication secret—meetings and conducting blessings in houses."[116] Other worries were centered on the emotional effects such meetings would arouse in participants, including the breakdown of the traditional barriers that separated men and women.[117] Crane notes the frequency with which such meetings in Germany involved kissing as a sign of respect for revelations of the Holy Spirit. In Bessarabia, Kern notes in his accounts of several villages that Separatist influences were responsible for creating unstated moral problems in their villages. His implication appears to be that Separatists following the guidance of their

110. Ibid., 142, 130.
111. Brandes, *Von den Zaren Adoptiert*, 283. The quote comes from Hans Petri's book on Lindl.
112. Ibid.
113. Kern, *Homeland Book*, 125. Ehni is also mentioned in the section on Klöstitz where Kern notes that "church life was hindered through the Separatist movement in Borodino led by Karl Ehni" (130). Ehni (1802–1882) was a Borodino colonist who was born in Marbach in Württemberg and came to Borodino as a child, having first moved from the Rhineland to Sulzfeld in South Prussia.
114. Brandes quotes the Leipzig Separatist, M. Kranich, as calling the existing Evangelical Lutheran church "das alte Babel." Brandes, *Von den Zaren Adoptiert*, 283.
115. Kern, *Homeland Book*, 121. The E. H. Busch work referred to is his three volume *Geschichte und Statistik der ev. Luth. Gemeinde in Russland* of 1862–67.
116. Crane, "Holy Alliances," 55.
117. The practice of the Evangelical Lutheran church followed at this time was to separate men and women during services by having them sit in different sections of the church.

own "inner light" were no longer observing conventional relationships or even sexual mores. It would be an exaggeration, however, to infer from Kern's statements that the behavioral problems referred to in several of the 1848 village histories[118] were chiefly the result of the Separatists. The Leipzig history notes troubles in the church and school organizations of the village as well: "The religious areas were in more disarray than the civic difficulties. The chief cause was the ethical ruin of the generation growing up."[119]

These problems, which the history also indicates necessitated Welfare Committee intervention, appear to have far broader causes. The personal freedom granted the colonists in their villages in Russia, a stable food supply, and the production of wines and spirits led to personal and group indulgence. The Leipzig history notes that "under these circumstances licentiousness and demoralization went hand in hand."[120] Such conditions may have encouraged a break with church practices as occurred with the Separatists, but the results described were not solely related to religious issues.

It is difficult to apply precise dates to the period in which Separatist views achieved some popularity in German Bessarabia. Kern gives no specific dates and rarely provides an associated context that might suggest dates. However, in his section on Leipzig, he does mention that the "Separatist Movement interrupted the finishing of the House of God."[121] As the building of the first church in Leipzig began in 1826 and was completed in 1837, this would suggest Separatist activity was strongest in the late 1820s and early 1830s.[122] Such dating would also fit with Kern's descriptions of the troubles between pastors and congregations in Tarutino in the period from 1831 to 1840, as well as with what little is known about the life of Karl Ehni, whose leadership of the Separatists in Borodino Kern stresses.[123]

The Separatist movement in German Bessarabia appears to have significantly quieted if not died out by the time the 1848 village histories were written. Kern, in his discussion of Tarutino, sees the end of troubles created by the Separatists occurring when the Russian government asked the Lutheran church to intervene. It may not have been Tsar Nicholas I intervening as Kern and others state, but it

---

118. The 1848 histories for Brienne, Leipzig, Sarata, and Tarutino each refer to early problems with moral behavior.
119. Trautmann, "Leipzig – 1848 Village History."
120. Ibid.
121. Kern, *Homeland Book*, 142.
122. The "Tarutino Parish Report—1867" places the height of the agitation much later: "The peak of this controversy came during the agitation of a certain Jahn...in 1845" ("Tarutino Parish Report— 1867" in "Heimatbuch der Gemeinde Kulm," *Heritage Review* 13, no. 4: 17). This dating does not fit easily with the dating in several sources that suggest the Separatists left Bessarabia in the early 1840s. I have found no other references to Jahn, whom the parish report calls a school teacher.
123. Kern, *Homeland Book*, 189. Karl Ehni, born in 1802, was in his prime in this period; he married in 1822 and again in 1834, with his second wife bearing a daughter in 1837. Kern notes that the Tarutino congregation declined to give Pastor Helwich horses to visit other congregations and as a result the pastor decided to live on church land apart from the village, where he received his "faithful villagers." His replacement withdrew in 1840 "to Alt Posttal where it was quieter than in Tarutino." Mutschall does not ascribe problems to the Separatists but notes the church and the school in great disorder: "Pastor Helwich found his sextons ignorant and coarse, the school teachers drunk and usurping his authority and income, and his parishioners disrespectful." Mutschall, however, also finds Pastor Helwich part of the problem, as he was "easily offended, irritable, fearing conflict and despondent, hurt by every contradictory statement, he considered himself a martyr, and withdrew into himself" (Mutschall, "Community of Tarutino," *Heritage Review* 43, no. 1: 8–9).

would have been normal procedure for the Welfare Committee to demand that the troubled villages settle themselves or to send officials from the Evangelical Church hierarchy in St. Petersburg to do the same.[124]

It would seem moreover that Separatists formed some of those groups described in the village histories as leaving Bessarabia for Serbia and Romania in 1841–42. Separatist emigrants from Bessarabia are known to have settled in the village of Jakobsonstal just north of Braila in Romania[125] in the early to mid-1840s. Among these were members of the Schorr and Nelitz families of Leipzig, both of whom were described as having been Separatists in Leipzig.[126] Jacob Phillip Schorr and his wife Luise Jastrow Nelitz Schorr were living in Leipzig in July 1840, which we know from a record of the birth of their daughter Christina. Family genealogies give the birthplaces of succeeding children to be Jakobsonstal for the period from 1847 to 1852. A grandson, Jacob Ohlhausen, born in Jakobsonstal has the religion "Ev. L" crossed out on his birth record, suggesting the family continued to be Separatists.[127] The Ohlhausens and other Separatist families from Jakobsonstal later moved back to Bessarabia. They are listed among the tenants and workers on the Bortscheag Estate established by an Alsatian family in 1860 in southwestern Bessarabia. Beginning in 1880, Separatist families bought land near the Bortscheag Estate, helping to found the villages of Albota, Unter-Albota, and Sofiewka. The author of the "Descendants of Ferdinand Ohlhausen Family History" comments that "some research into the history of the Bortscheag Germans finds that many were so-called Separatists and followed Ignaz Lindl's teaching."[128] If some of the 1841–42 emigrants were Separatists, the 1848 Leipzig history's reference only to "wandering fever" as motivation for those leaving the village suggests a continuing sensitivity about the memory of Separatists in the village.

The genealogies of the Ohlhausens and others suggest that Separatist beliefs continued well beyond the 1840s, though the number of adherents declined. A population count by religious affiliation for the years 1851 and 1858 indicates that in 1851 in German Bessarabia there were two hundred male "sectarians." By 1858, though, the number had dropped to sixty-eight.[129] By the twentieth century such beliefs may have disappeared or no longer have been considered outside normal Evangelical Lutheran practice, as Kern makes no notice of troublesome Separatists in his discus-

124. Kern, likely citing stories circulating in Tarutino, indicates that Tsar Nicholas I had been asked but declined to intervene directly into the religious affairs of the village, stating instead that the villagers "have a duty to the crown and the community. Let the church heal them" (*Homeland Book*, 192). Wilhelm Mutschall ("History of the Community of Tarutino from 1814 to 1934," *Heritage Review* 43, no. 3 [2013]: 6) and Brandes (*Von den Zaren Adoptiert*, 284) also quote an alleged order of Tsar Nicholas I that the Separatists were to remain under authority of the Lutheran Church, and that they were "not to be released from their congregational responsibilities." Nicholas I was famous for involving himself in administrative details, but I have been unable to find in Russian sources confirmation of his involvement here.
125. Jakobsonstal was a village on a bluff above the west bank of the Danube River. It is now the suburb called Pisc which is attached to Braila. Jakobsonstal was 11 miles south of Galati and so was quite near the southwestern border of Bessarabia.
126. Elvire Necker-Eberhardt reports that "some of my forefathers (Nelitz/Schorr) had the faith of Bessarabian 'Separatists'." Elvire Necker-Eberhardt's Korner at the Germans from Russia Heritage Society website: http://www.grhs.org/korners/necker/necker.html.
127. Unknown, "Descendants of Ferdinand Ohlhausen Family History" (N.p.: ohlhausen.ca, c. 2011), http://www.ohlhausen.ca/Ferdinand%20Ohlhausen%20Family%20History.pdf.
128. Ibid.
129. Brandes, *Von den Zaren Adoptiert*, 276. The data in this chart appear to come from Welfare Committee sources and lists populations in Bessarabia and South Russia (Neurußland).

sions of the villages of Unter-Albota, Albota, and Sofiewka. In his discussion of the Klöstitz parish, Kern mentions that when the children of the "cultists" declined to participate, the movement "lost momentum."[130]

## Though the German colonies in Bessarabia seem, in the period before 1860, to be isolated islands of German language and culture, they were not immune to influences from the outside

The closed character of the colonies, their special German-speaking civic connection to the Russian state supplied by the Welfare Committee, their general isolation in Bessarabia from both the Russian heartland and Western Europe, and the great differences in religion, culture, and technologies from other peoples living near them in Bessarabia tended to separate the German villages into their own special worlds. Giesinger, writing about all the German colonies in Russia from the Volga to Bessarabia, asserts that the colonists "soon lost contact...with their ancestral homeland" and goes on to characterize the Germans in Russia as

> an introverted people for whom their community was their world. Within this community they preserved to a considerable degree the eighteenth century German peasant culture that they had brought with them, not affected by the social, political and intellectual changes now taking place in Germany, about which they scarcely heard, nor influenced appreciably by the way of life of the alien peoples among whom they lived.[131]

Giesinger appears to be writing here of the German colonies in Russia, at least through the second third of the nineteenth century. I believe Giesinger's characterization to be generally accurate for this period; yet, at least for the Bessarabian Germans, if taken without reservation, it can obscure important changes that were starting to occur. It is not possible to assess with any real accuracy the degree to which contact with greater Germany and its culture had been broken off or the degree to which the German colonists in Russia remained unaware of the great changes occurring in greater Germany and Western Europe in the nineteenth century. The significant loss of family materials occasioned by the Bessarabian Resettlement of 1940 and the even more destructive effects of World War II and the forced removal by the Soviets of Germans from the Volga and South Russia to Siberia and Kazakhstan destroyed or has removed from easy access much of the nineteenth-century records and correspondence kept by the Germans in Russia. We do know that for Bessarabia, and likely elsewhere, ties were not wholly broken. The letter written by the Plotzk colonists Friedrich and Friederika Schlechter to family and friends in Murr, Württemberg, establishes that some connections continued. Similarly, the fact that in the early 1840s, some colonists abandoned Bessarabia for

---

130. Kern, *Homeland Book*, 121. Elvire Necker-Eberhardt has noted in a manuscript on the Separatists she has put online the continuing existence of the Separatists into the twentieth century: "In 1930 Borodino still had 9 [Separatists] Leipzig 24 and Alt Elft and Paris 'ein kleines Häuflein' (a small group)" and that "in Tarutino in 1934 Gottlieb and Louise Tetzlaff...were still known as Separatists." Separatism came to an end in Bessarabia in 1934 when the remaining Separatists rejoined the Lutheran church. Necker-Eberhardt, "Separatists in Bessarabia: A Geneological Nightmare" (N.p.: Germans from Russia Heritage Society, 2011), 6, http://www.grhs.org/korners/memonly/necker_doc/Separatists_in_Bessarabia_sep_10.pdf (members-only access).

131. Giesinger, *From Catherine to Khrushchev*, 55.

Serbia indicates that there was an awareness of the Austrian government's efforts to attract German peasant settlers to its new border region in Serbia.

Before the 1830s, Odessa may have been not much more than a large village, as described by some of the German Separatist families arriving there in 1819, but it grew rapidly and, by the end of the 1840s, was already a major port city with a large German-speaking minority population. By the late 1850s, following the Crimean War, Odessa grew even faster, pushed by the rapid increases in the grain trade with Western Europe. Odessa had several German-language newspapers, some of which must have regularly found their way into nearby Bessarabia. Therefore, perhaps a better characterization of the German colonies in Bessarabia would be that while the isolation Giesinger cites generally describes life in the colonies, the period from the founding of the colonies until the 1860s is one in which that isolation was steadily beginning to erode.

When the Germans first came to the southern Budjak region of Bessarabia, the steppelands were very lightly populated. The Tartar population that once lived there had been forcibly moved to the Crimea, but the area had not been completely depopulated. Many of the 1848 Bessarabian colonial histories mention that on arriving at the site designated for their settlement, they found Moldavians and Bulgarians who were leasing that land or land nearby to graze cattle and sheep. The Budjak did not remain empty for long and as the Germans settled in, they gained more and more neighbors. At the time the German colonies were founded in Bessarabia, other colonies for Bulgarian refugees were established nearby in the Budjak to provide the Bulgarians sanctuary from Turkish control. Soon too, and for similar reasons, the Russian government permitted groups of Gaugaz, Turkish-speaking Christians, coming from what is present-day Romania and Bulgaria, to cross into western Bessarabia and settle on the Budjak. Tsar Alexander I and his successor Tsar Nicholas I made extensive land grants from crown holdings in Bessarabia to Russian noble families, often military officers who had distinguished themselves in the final campaigns against Napoleon or, in the case of Nicholas, families who proved themselves to be loyal supporters of himself and the Tsarist government following his turbulent rise to the throne. Some of these new landowners brought in Russian and Ukrainian peasants to establish small villages and farms or leased their land to Moldavians for use with their cattle herds.

As a result, by the late 1830s and early 1840s, the German colonies in Bessarabia had acquired many non-German neighbors. These were typically mono-ethnic villages that were sometimes larger than the German colonies. At times, neighboring settlements were large farms referred to in Russian as a *xutor* or *xutir* in Ukrainian.[132] In nineteenth-century South Russia, the term xutor described a small farm settlement of several families set off by itself that was often (though not typically in Bessarabia) inhabited by Cossacks. The neighboring villages surrounding Kulm by the mid-nineteenth century provide a good example of the multiethnic mix surrounding the German colonies in Bessarabia. Kulm was set between the

132. The Russian word xutor is derived from the old North German (Scandinavian) word *huntari*, referring to an area ruled by one leader [Max Vasmer, *Etimologičeskij slovar' russkogo jazyka*, vol. 4, *T-jaščur* (Moscow: Progress, 1973), 286–87] and so harks back to the time of the tenth- and eleventh-century Rus, the Swedish trading and raiding group who established a profitable route from the Baltic to Constantinople and in so doing, founded the first East Slavic state and gave the East Slavic people the name Russians.

German colonies of Leipzig 10 versts to the north, Tarutino the same distance to the south, and Berezina also 10 versts downstream on the Kogil'nik River. The same 10 versts southwest of Kulm was the Bulgarian colony of Tvardica, and directly west at about the same distance in the Lunga River valley was the Gaugaz village of Kiriet Lunga. Just to the northwest of Kulm, perhaps 8 versts away, in the ridge land above the Lunga River was the small farming settlement of Xutor Božka, a property belonging to the Russian noble Sokolov family. Russian- and Ukrainian-speaking peasants worked this farm as serf labor. The pathways that connected Kulm to all these villages as well as to Alt Posttal are still visible in the Google satellite view.[133] It was not uncommon for peasants from Tvardica and Kiriet Lunga to bring their grain to be milled in Kulm. Kern mentions that Bulgarians, likely from neighboring Tvardica, came to Wittenberg to purchase the wagons made there. Moreover, in the biweekly markets of Tarutino, Arzis, and Sarata, the trade in animals, grain, fruit, and homemade ware brought together people of many different nationalities from all over the Budjak.

The early cultural contacts the Bessarabian Germans made with other peoples living near them are reflected in linguistic borrowings that the Germans adopted into their speech. Albert Eckert, who has published the most detailed study of German dialects in Bessarabia, notes many loan words, particularly in the areas of food, tools, and animals.[134] Similar examples appear in the studies of Shirley Fischer Arends and Paul Reeb.[135] Food loan words are particularly numerous, such as *arbuse* (watermelon), from the Russian and Ukrainian *arbuz*; borscht, the Russian/Ukrainian beet soup *boršč*; *kasha* from the Russian/Ukrainian word for porridge; and *kvass*, the fermented drink made from grain, called *kvas* in Russian and Ukrainian. Some loan words show more specific origins, such as the name for stuffed cabbage rolls, *halubzy* or *hulooptsi*, which comes from the Ukrainian *golubcy*;[136] or the word for a sweet made of crushed nuts, honey, and grapes, *halva*, which comes from a Turkish word borrowed in Russian as *xalva*. Eckert notes several borrowings from Romanian but generally assigns these to the period after World War I when Bessarabia came under Romanian administration. This conclusion, however, underplays the long contact the Germans had with Moldavians in Bessarabia that is stressed by words borrowed into Bessarabian German from Moldavian and Romanian. One example is *mamaleeka*, the frequently found local polenta, called *mamaliga* in Moldavian and Romanian; another is the word *pet* used at least in the Kulm dialect for a well that came from the Moldavian *peţ*. A tool loan word is the root of Albert Rüb's description of a hand washing device that was commonly found on German farms in Bessarabia which he calls a *rukimoinik*, a term that the Germans took over without alteration from the Russian *rukomojnik*.[137]

---

133. These pathways can also be clearly identified from the path and roadways marked on the 1901 Austro-Hungarian military map ("Bolgrad," Sheet 46-46 in 3rd Military Mapping Survey of Austria-Hungary, http://lazarus.elte.hu/hun/digkonyv/topo/3felmeres.htm)..

134. Albert Eckert, *Die Mundarten der deutschen Mutterkolonien Bessarabiens und ihre Stammheimat* (Marburg, Ger.: N. G. Elwert, 1941), 51–85.

135. Fischer Arends, *Central Dakota Germans*; and Paul Reeb, "Cultural Dynamics in German-Russian Cookery," *Heritage Review* 14, no. 3 (1984): 25–29.

136. The Ukrainian origin of the borrowing into German is established by the pronunciation of the initial Slavic consonant 'g' as 'h'.

137. Albert Rüb, "Things Pertaining to Bessarabian Housekeeping," *Heritage Review* 38, no. 2 (2008): 3–4. The term rukomojnik in Russian means "hand-washer."

Until 1872, the tightly knit linguistic, religious, and cultural linkages of the German colonies in Bessarabia discouraged settlement by other nationalities in the German villages or Germans in the villages of other ethnic groups.[138] The larger Bessarabian German towns—Tarutino, Arzis, Sarata, and Klöstitz—had Bulgarian and Moldavian farm workers and Jewish shopkeepers before 1872, but these were in such small numbers and were living without any pretense or expectation of community rights that their impact was slight. The German villages thus contrasted materially with the larger Bessarabian towns such as Kishinev, Akkerman, Ismail, and Tartarbunar which were quite multiethnic.

The Russian government, at least through the reign of Nicholas I, did not pursue policies of assimilation directed at the non-Slavic peasantry living with its borders. Russian policy was not to push to assimilate these different national groups but to encourage their quiet obedience to the Tsar and the absolutist rule of the state. True assimilation was, in any case, out of the question in nineteenth-century Russia, where ethnic boundaries were perceived as near-permanent markers. As Tolstoy's sarcastic treatment of the character Berg in *War and Peace* indicates, mastering the Russian language and adopting Russian customs did nothing to make someone considered any less German.

As a result, in the first half of the nineteenth century, the different national groups living in Bessarabia were not pressured into learning the Russian language and were permitted to maintain their own customs and village rules and to practice their different forms of Christianity. The German and Bulgarian colonists were especially favored. Their relationship with the Russian government was managed by the Welfare Committee outside the normal provincial civil government. Welfare Committee officials were German speakers who dealt with the German colonies in German. Moreover, these officials considered it an important part of their duties to encourage colonial growth and economic stability via adopting agricultural products better suited to steppe conditions. Thus, the Klöstitz village history points to the strong role the Welfare Committee played in encouraging the successful development of vineyards. When social troubles developed in the colonies either from drinking or the activities of the religious Separatists, Welfare Committee officials intervened not with police actions and punishments, but, as several of the 1848 histories attest, with strong encouragement to local officials to make changes.

By the 1860s, the German colonies in Bessarabia had established themselves on a solid economic footing. In the original colonies, the second and even third generations had become the community leaders. Living together in a single village, families from different places in Prussian Poland and Württemberg were now far more closely interwoven. Intermarriages pulled families together and even brought together couples with Prussian and southern German backgrounds. The merging of families from different backgrounds was reflected in the village dialect. Settlements with a preponderance of colonists with a Württemberg family background (such as Wittenberg, Alt Posttal, and Beresina) had a village dialect in which High German predominated. Villages with a preponderance of colonists with family origins in

---

138.  Daniel Isert is an exception to this rule. He came to Tarutino in 1845 from Prussian Pomerania wanting to set up a mill to pursue his cloth making trade. Tarutino citizens, considering him an outsider, were cool to him and his designs. Isert then moved on to the multiethnic village of Tartarbunar south of Sarata where he bought a water mill and established a successful business.

Prussia, such as Kulm, Leipzig, and Paris, had dialects strongly influenced by Low German. In settlements such as Alt Elft and Brienne, which had large numbers of families from both Prussia and southern Germany, mixed dialects were created that blended words from different forms of German. In describing the German used in Alt Elft, Kern notes the village "had its own distinct dialect, a mixture of Swabian, High German and Platt-German."[139]

The Bessarabian colonies by the 1860s had recreated German villages on Russian soil. The social customs, religious practices, the standards of work and male–female roles, and the mechanisms of mutual aid were not new but just those the colonists had brought to Russia from Prussia and greater Germany. Yet while their villages may have looked like isolated, mainly self-focused outposts of German peasant culture, their settlements in Bessarabia differed greatly from the settlements they had left behind in Prussia and Württemberg. Though the German peasants there lived as a minority population in parts of West Prussia and particularly in the new Posen Province,[140] they were living in Prussia, a country dominated by their culture and language, and often did not feel like minorities. When they traveled into larger market towns they found the German language, culture, and influences all about them. If they traveled west of the Oder looking for work or when they were drafted into the army, they were once again totally in a majority culture. News of Prussia or of other German states easily reached those who were curious. In the Prussian provinces of West Prussia and particularly Posen, even though German peasants were in places outnumbered by Poles, German peasants continued to feel very much a part of developments in both the German language and culture. In Württemberg, peasants never left German culture. In Bessarabia, on the other hand, the German colonists were really minorities. One result was that the colonies tended to look inwardly for support and comfort and hold tightly to habits and customs. Another, ironically, was that such a minority status made them more susceptible to influences from the cultures around them, particularly as they became more comfortable in their new surroundings. As an example, the extensive borrowing of Russian, Ukrainian, and even Moldavian words into the speech of the Bessarabian Germans is not at all matched by the small borrowings from Polish into the speech of the German communities in West Prussia and Posen.

While it would appear that the Bessarabian Germans were able to maintain some contact with greater Germany via letters, German newspapers from Odessa, or news passed via the churches or by word of mouth from village to village, the major influences of change were coming from other cultures, especially from Russia. German colonists dealt with Russian and Jewish tradespeople who passed through the colonies buying wheat and animals or selling small manufactured goods. Bulgarians, Gaugaz, and Moldavians bought animals and goods at the markets in Tarutino, Arzis,

---

139. Kern, *Homeland Book*, 54. He notes a similar situation in Brienne where "a new, compromised dialect emerged" (84). By "Swabian" ("Schwäbisch"), Kern means the Alemannic dialect of German spoken in Württemberg and parts of Baden and Bavaria.

140. In West Prussia, Germans would have been in a minority in the broad central strip running northwest from Kulmerland through Pommerellen. The populous urban centers in the east (Danzig, Elbing, Dirschau, Marienburg, Marienwerder, and Graudenz) were German-speaking, as was the western edge of Schneidemühl and Deutsche Krone. In Posen Province, by 1861, just over 40 percent of the population was German-speaking and this population was concentrated in Bromberg and the Netze Valley to the west. The provincial capital of Posen had a Polish-speaking majority.

and Sarata, wagons in Wittenberg and Teplitz, and pitchforks in Paris. Russian was increasingly the lingua franca in such trades, even if the Russian the Germans knew was just a pidgin Russian of a few words. The passage of Russian troops who fought in Romania in 1827–29 and the outbreak of the Crimean War, fought not far from Bessarabia in 1853–56, made the colonists sensitive to being citizens of Russia. Just being aware of how commerce took place, such as the rules by which alcohol could be bought and sold in Russia brought new influences and created cultural change.

The picture I wish to leave of German Bessarabia entering the 1860s is one of twenty-five colonies doing well economically and growing much larger. They were continuing to live in a German-speaking world and one in which their lives were chiefly guided by the religious and social customs they had brought with them to Russia. They were, however, increasingly exposed to Russian civil, social, and political influences that would only become more predominant and create more impact as time went on. By 1860, the significant population growth in the German settlements in Bessarabia was the greatest force for change in those communities. There were more hands now than were needed to maximize the potential of the farmsteads. As younger members of German families in Bessarabia began to consider what they might do to improve their situations, two other major external factors came into play. The first was that Russian noble landowners found that their increasing needs for cash to meet the lifestyle demands expected of their class created reasons for them to become interested in leasing or selling the underused and less essential property they owned in Bessarabia. The second was that the defeat in the Crimean War led the new Tsar Alexander II to consider ways to reform Russia so as to keep up with the changing sources and means used by France and Great Britain to exert national power. Pursuing such reforms led Alexander II to make fundamental changes to the relationship of the Russian state with the German colonies. These forces and their implications will be the focus of the next few chapters.

# VII

# Demographic Data Reveal Conditions and Customs in German Bessarabia

Demographic data form the most detailed information source that is available about the German colonies in Bessarabia. In the general absence of civic, fiscal, political, and economic records from the German settlements in Bessarabia, as well as first-person accounts via diaries and letters from the citizens themselves, demographic data acquire unusual weight as a historical source. However, demographic data form a very useful source of information. Such data can provide commentary on economic conditions and expectations, as they show both the effect of these conditions and the population's anticipatory reaction to them. Demographic data also have much to say about the maintenance of and changes to customary habits and practices.

Economic conditions, for example, are reflected in data concerning both the ages at which people married and the extent to which members of a generation were able to marry. General data on marriage ages and the frequency of marriage among the peasant population in the eighteenth and nineteenth centuries in Prussia and Württemberg indicate that the ability to marry was directly tied to a couple's financial position and economic prospects, notably the possession of land of sufficient size to support a family. For Prussian and Württemberg peasants, such requirements meant that generally between 10 and 25 percent of adults were not able to marry, and those who did needed time to amass the required land and financial resources. These factors resulted in marriages typically occurring in the late twenties for women and early thirties for men. Such late marriages in turn tended to limit the average family size. As this chapter will show, the data from the Bessarabian German population on the frequency of marriage, the average age at marriage, and the average family size reveal a very different picture. As a consequence, such data strongly imply quite different economic circumstances.

When the German settlers established villages in Bessarabia, they brought with them customs, habits, and patterns from their homelands. As the prior chapter argues, the isolation and self-sufficiency of the German villages in Bessarabia initially strengthened the hold of such customs, but gradually the contact with neighboring peoples and with Russian culture in general began to introduce new elements into the cultural life of these villages. The first names given to children clearly reflect such cultural changes. The first generations continued the patterns of biblical and prior family usages that dominated in the eighteenth century. Gradually, however, Russian names start to appear, as do names made popular by usage among the German nobility and by their currency in popular culture in greater Germany. In contrast, among the Bessarabian Germans who immigrated to North America beginning in the last quarter of the nineteenth century, the influences of the new and different cultures they encountered appear quite rapidly and numerously in children's names. The differing pace of these changes suggests on one hand the power of monoethnic single-language villages to preserve narrow customary practices, and on the other that the power to preserve customary practices is limited when such villages are minority settlements in the midst of a different ethnic culture, and even more limited when families no longer live in villages but on their farmsteads.

Another example where demographic data indicate the process and timing of change is in the selection of marriage partners. Initially, marriage partners of the Bessarabian Germans were primarily found within the same cultural group. Thus, at first, the children of Low German–speaking northern German families and High German–speaking southern Germans married partners who shared their linguistic and cultural background. Over time this pattern broke down and the different German cultures became mixed. By 1860, intercultural marriages occurred frequently in the original settlements, and after 1860, under the influence of the mixing populations in the new villages, it would be hard to speak of any clear patterns at all.

Some hurdles exist in the use of demographic data to shed light on the experience of the Bessarabian Germans. One major problem is that such data are not uniformly rich throughout the period of settlement in Bessarabia. As noted in the introductory chapter, demographic data are detailed and comprehensive only for the period from 1835 to 1885. The data preserved from this period are census data on marriages, births, and deaths collected and maintained by the separate Evangelical Lutheran parishes in German Bessarabia. They are preserved because during the resettlement of 1940, Soviet authorities permitted the German refugees to take such church records with them to Germany. Censuses and any administrative, fiscal, and political records for the period after 1885 were deemed to be state property and had to remain in Bessarabia to face an uncertain fate.[1] While demographic records of some detail exist from the period before 1835 as well as after 1885 for Germans who remained in Bessarabia as well as for those who emigrated from there to North

---

1. The discovery in the 1990s that the state archives of Moldova preserved census records from German Bessarabia collected by the Welfare Committee before 1870 raised hopes that other administrative records concerning the German settlements in Bessarabia may yet survive in archives in Moldova or the Ukraine.

America, the individualized nature of these records creates significant hurdles for those seeking generalized pictures of experience. Unlike the church census records, which have been aggregated to collect births, deaths, and marriages by decade, the existing village records from before 1835 and the family questionnaires filled out by some Bessarabian resettlers upon arrival in Germany in 1940,[2] as well as the US and Canadian census records for Bessarabian emigrants, provide data that can be approached only on the basis of individuals. While concerns regarding completeness exist in dealing with the church data from 1835 to 1885, far greater problems exist with the data available for the period following as well as the period before 1835.

In order to draw reasonable conclusions from demographic data, it is important that the data set fulfill certain basic qualifications: it should cover the full time period studied, it should reflect reasonably complete pictures of families within the population group studied, and finally, it should be reasonably numerous. Even with the richness of the demographic data on Bessarabian Germans, these are not easy conditions to satisfy. Even with the rich data sources available for the period from 1835 to 1885, capturing complete information for families from church data is difficult, as several gaps exist. It is best for data about families living in one of the original settlements, but even for these settlements, many marriages, births, and deaths are missing. For information on families for the periods before 1835 and after 1885, the available data is far more spotty. Not all the pre-1835 records from individual colonies survived the resettlement to Germany and ravages of World War II. The questionnaires covering post-1885 data are not available for the great majority of resettled families, and even for those extant, there are many missing pieces. The families who completed them were working from memory under stressful conditions rather than from records in hand. Moreover, as the focus of the questionnaires was on those arriving in Germany, children who died before the resettlement are frequently not listed and the information typically only goes back a single generation, leaving major gaps for the period just after 1885. Finally, as any data set covering the period from 1815 to 1940 will have to be stitched together from many pieces, doubts always arise as to whether the data are varied and numerous enough to avoid outliers distorting the patterns they show.

In seeking to answer such concerns, I have based the demographic study that follows on five generations of one Bessarabian German family and the families of their marriage partners. This data set aggregates material collected on more than four thousand individuals and covers the period from the first German settlements in Bessarabia through the departure of families during the resettlement of 1940. The data set also includes families who immigrated to North America in the period from 1876 to 1914. The chief advantage of such a data set is its general completeness. It provides information on individuals born and deceased before 1835. For the period between 1835 and 1885, it offers more complete records of marriages and births than the parish records and is more likely to include records of the many children who died in their first years of life, whose names are frequently missing from the parish records. Using one family and its marriage partners as an organizing principle provides a means to bring in individual data from the questionnaires as well as the

---

2. As noted in the introduction, many such questionnaires have been put online on the Odessa3 website (http://www.odessa3.org/collections/bess/koblenz/). While large numbers of the questionnaires are extant, those available online clearly do not represent anything close to the full resettlement population.

US and Canadian census records while still asserting that the data set is not biased by the uniqueness of the examples found.

Family data, of course, are not without their own problems and potential biases. Used to suggest common patterns among the German population as a whole in Bessarabia, family data may distort results by the family's economic or genetic strengths and weaknesses, or by the accidents of their experiences. Nevertheless, the relative completeness of family data gives these data the upper hand. It is also reasonable to argue that the potential for economic and genetic bias is eroded, at least in part, both by the inclusion of the strengths and weaknesses of many other families who became connected to the group via marriage and by the large number of individuals included in the data set.

The data set used in this chapter is based on information from the Raugust family and their marriage partners. This surname form was first established in Bessarabia. As a result, all people with the surname Raugust (or related to those with the surname) are descendants of two brothers, Jacob Raugust and his wife Christina Kujat, and Martin Raugust and his wife Johanna Müller. In 1814, along with their mother, Elisabeth, and their small children, they emigrated from Tscherbin (Szczerbin) in West Prussia and were among the founding settlers of Kulm, Bessarabia.[3] The Raugusts first appear, though with the surname spelled Ragus, in 1772 in the first Prussian census of the former Royal Prussia. They were peasant tenants farming in the village of Maleschechowo (Polish Małociechowo) on the west bank of the Vistula River between the towns of Schwetz (Polish Swiecie) and Bromberg (Polish Bydgoszcz). The lands they worked had been absorbed into Prussia as part of the First Partition of Poland of 1772. The family subsequently moved to Szczerbin. They first appear in Bessarabia in the 1815 Kulm census and are listed as having the surname Raugusch, which, considered with the earlier spelling of Ragus, suggests they came from a Prussian- or even Lithuanian-speaking background. Coming to Bessarabia, however, Jacob and Martin were at the least the third generation of speakers of North German (Plattdeutsch) and should be counted among the large Prussian stream within the Bessarabian German population.[4]

3. Stumpp, in his listing of early German immigrants to Bessarabia, also notes the existence of a Gottfried Raugust (1769–1846), born in or coming to Bessarabia from Gabris, West Prussia, and settling in Katzbach (*Emigration from Germany to Russia*, 399, 525). This listing is in error, and the person Stumpp notes to be Gottfried Raugust is in great probability Gottfried Sawall. The 1835 Welfare Committee census of Katzbach does not list a Gottfried Raugust but does list Gottfried Sawall, and the collected Bessarabian church records of deaths (the St. Petersburg Collection at www.odessa3.org) lists Gottfried Sawall's death as July 1, 1846 (O.S.), with the added note that he was from Gaspies, West Prussia, both facts that closely match Stumpp's listing for Gottfried Raugust. The death notice also gives Sawall's age at death as seventy-six years, six months, and ten days, which would give him a birthdate of December 21, 1769 (O.S.). The absence of any records of a Gottfried Raugust other than Stumpp's listing and the striking similarity in Sawall's dates and birth place to the information Stumpp gives for Gottfried Raugust, suggest that Stumpp has inadvertently transformed Sawall into Gottfried Raugust. In his Katzbach listing (525), Stumpp does list a Gottfried Sawall with the dates (1806–1854), which turn out to be those for Gottfried's son, Martin Sawall.

4. The fact that the Raugusts belonged to the group of Bessarabian German settlers of Prussian origin introduces another potential form of bias into the data set. This is mitigated by the fact that by the second generation in Bessarabia, members of the Raugust family had already begun to marry into families of Bessarabian Germans who came there from Württemberg, either directly or via Poland. The village of Szczerbin from which they emigrated is located in the Netze River valley (Polish Noteć) about 9 km north of Wirsitz (Polish Wyrzysk). After 1772 and up until 1807 and Napoleon's inclusion of this area in the Duchy of Warsaw, Szczerbin had been part of the Prussian province of West Prussia. In 1814, when the Raugust family began their immigration to Bessarabia, Prussia was again in loose control of this area, though the formal legal return to Prussia agreed to by the parties to the Congress of Vienna was not likely known at the time of immigration.

Jacob and Martin Raugust and their descendants managed two homestead allotments in Kulm from 1815 until the resettlement of 1940. Their descendants by the third generation married into families living in Kulm as well as families from the nearby settlements of Leipzig, Tarutino, Alt Posttal, and Wittenberg. The experiences of members of this extended family mirror the major trends of the general history of the Bessarabian German population as a whole. The Raugust brothers appear to have come to Bessarabia as a result of the depredations created by the passage of armies through Prussian Poland during Napoleon's Russian Campaign of 1812 and its aftermath. In Bessarabia they worked to attain at least a middling level of prosperity in Kulm. Many descendants participated in the wide dispersion of Bessarabian Germans, as a growing population with improved financial means permitted the formation of new settlements. Descendants of the two Raugust brothers were among the early settlers of Dennewitz in 1834, and of Mannsburg and Eigenheim in the 1860s. By the resettlement of 1940, members of this family and its marriage partners lived or had lived in over forty-five different villages in German Bessarabia. Descendants were among the emigrants from Bessarabia who established the German villages of Cogealac and Tariverdi across the Danube in Romanian Dobrudscha in 1875 and the German village of Lilienfeld in the north Caucasus region of Russia in 1881. They were also among the first groups from Bessarabia to go to North America, where they established farms in Hutchinson County, South Dakota, as early as 1878. In the period from 1878 to 1914, many members of this family immigrated to the states of South and North Dakota, Montana, and Washington in the United States, as well as to the provinces of Saskatchewan and Alberta in Canada. The great majority of family members, however, remained in Bessarabia.

The data set I have created for the extended Raugust family and their marriage partners includes information on slightly over four thousand individuals. To facilitate comparisons, I have organized the data by generation (see table 7–1). Including the founding group who came to Bessarabia, I will treat in the following study five

TABLE 7–1.   **Basic features of the five generations**

|  | Males | Females | Total |
|---|---|---|---|
| Generation 1<br>Births 1761–1800, with the majority between 1780 and 1800 | 40 | 43 | 83 |
| Generation 2<br>Births 1804–41, with the majority between 1818 and 1835 | 109 | 118 | 227 |
| Generation 3[a]<br>Births 1827–78, with the majority between 1838 and 1862 | 414 | 421 | 835 |
| Generation 4<br>Births 1851–1906, with the majority between 1865 and 1895 | 589 | 565 | 1,154 |
| Generation 5<br>Births 1876–1940, with the majority between 1890 and 1920 | 898 | 880 | 1,778 |
| **Totals** | 2,050 | 2,027 | 4,077 |

a. Membership in a generation is determined by the generation membership of the parents. As a result, overlaps in birth years occur between the generations: individuals born into Generation 3, for example, may have been born earlier than some members of Generation 2.

generations whose members extend from the middle of the eighteenth century to the twentieth century.

## Average life span data

The data for this group of Bessarabian Germans suggest that the average life spans for both males and females gradually increased during the nineteenth century and attained even greater length in the early twentieth. As with data on average life spans among European peasant populations in general, the results are heavily influenced by the high frequency of childhood mortality. Improvements in the average life span tend to reflect both reductions in early childhood deaths as well as improvements in the diets and living and working conditions that prolonged the lives of adults. To reflect both influences, table 7–2, in addition to providing the average life span for all members of each generation, shows both the average life span for the population cohort that lived at least twenty years and the numbers of childhood deaths (defined as deaths occurring before the age of twenty), considered as a percentage of total births.

Several anomalies in the data on life spans for Bessarabian Germans need to be pointed out before considering implications. Generation 1 is totally made up of the reasonably healthy adults who immigrated to Bessarabia. There is every reason to believe, however, that childhood mortality among the siblings of these individuals would be as high as that in the following generations. The near-total absence of data on such siblings (as such data chiefly exist in whatever church records remain from Prussian Poland) thus increases the average life span data for this generation. Were it available, the average life span would presumably be in the forties for both men and women.

The data for Generation 2 also overstate average life spans, though not as radically as for Generation 1. The majority of Generation 2 was born in the period between 1818 and 1835, before the Bessarabian church parish records provide much detail. While family data collected mainly in the twentieth century record many individuals from this generation and are an improvement on both the parish records and the data available for Generation 1, it is very likely that the data available have a bias toward individuals who reached adulthood. As a result, a fair presumption is that

TABLE 7–2. **Average life span data**

|  | Gen 1 | Gen 2 | Gen 3 | Gen 4 | Gen 5 | Combined |
|---|---|---|---|---|---|---|
| Average life span, males | 68.4 | 44.4 | 33.8 | 35.1 | 51.6 | 41.6 |
| Number of data points | 40 | 91 | 345 | 439 | 429 | 1,344 |
| Average life span, females | 57.4 | 41.9 | 32.0 | 37.2 | 55.9 | 42.6 |
| Number of data points | 36 | 92 | 330 | 370 | 378 | 1,206 |
| Average life span, males living 20+ years | 68.4 | 54.7 | 61.7 | 63.9 | 68.3 | 64.5 |
| Number of data points | 40 | 73 | 183 | 226 | 320 | 842 |
| Average life span, females living 20+ years | 57.4 | 49.8 | 56.7 | 64.8 | 70.9 | 63.2 |
| Number of data points | 36 | 45 | 180 | 212 | 268 | 741 |
| Percent who died before reaching 20 | — | 35.5% | 46.2% | 45.9% | 27.1% | 35.5% |
| **Total known life spans** | 76 | 183 | 675 | 809 | 807 | 2,550 |

with health standards and living conditions no better than those of the following Generation 3, childhood mortality for Generation 2 is underreported, and consequently the average life span is likely exaggerated.

The third anomaly is the general underreporting of death dates for Generation 4 and especially Generation 5. This problem is particularly felt with data on members who remained in Bessarabia until 1940. As a result, it is likely that for these generations, the effect of the more complete information on childhood mortality pulls down the figures for the average life spans of both generations. The difficulty of establishing death dates after 1885 is also the primary cause for the declining percentage of data on life spans as a function of the known population (see table 7–3).

Even with these anomalies, some points may be made from relatively firm ground. The enormous impact of childhood mortality on life spans stands out so significantly that it will be taken up below as a separate topic. A second point to notice in these data is that life spans for those who reached at least twenty years of age, and so reached adulthood, show steady and significant increases.[5] As increases in life spans are now frequently understood as being directly related to improvements in health care and economic well-being,[6] the steady increases in life spans among these Bessarabian German adults suggest supportive improvements in both the economic health of their villages and the standards of health and diet within them.

A third point of interest in these data is that by Generation 4, the life spans for women start to exceed those for men. This is true for the data covering the whole data set population, as well as just for the adult subset that lived at least twenty years. That life spans for women exceeded those of men is generally interpreted as a sign that a leading cause of death among young adult females—complications of or resulting from pregnancy and childbirth—had been reduced through improvements in medical care, hygiene, or diet and especially through more sanitary conditions during childbirth itself. The Bessarabian German data set offers some evidence to support such a change. There were fifteen women in this data set who died on the same day they gave birth or within a few days afterward and all but one are from Generation 3 or earlier. An important secondary influence in women achieving

TABLE 7–3.   **Existing data on life span as a function of total known population**

| Gen 1 | Gen 2 | Gen 3 | Gen 4 | Gen 5 |
|---|---|---|---|---|
| 91.6% | 80.6% | 80.8% | 70.1% | 45.4% |

---

5. The average life spans for Generation 1 adults of 68.4 years for men and 57.4 years for women need some comment, as these were not equaled again until Generation 5 for men and Generation 4 for women. The long average life spans of the Generation 1 group may result in part from the fact that it is small in number and so may not be typical of the first generation of Bessarabian colonists as a whole. However, even though this is a small group, the numbers are not driven by a few outliers: thirty of the forty men, for example, lived more than sixty years, and twenty men, half of the group, lived more than seventy. A second explanation may be that, as many in this group came to Bessarabia in their thirties and forties having already survived hardships in Prussia and Württemberg as well as the establishment of the German colonies in Bessarabia, this group was unusually tested and winnowed and thus represents a particularly healthy and hardy segment of their actual generation.

6. See among many examples the study by William Nordhaus, "The Health of Nations: The Contribution of Improved Health to Living Standards" (working paper, Cowles Foundation for Research in Economics, Yale University, New Haven, CT, 2002); and Raouf Boucekkine, Bity Diene, and Théophile Azomahou, "A Closer Look at the Relationship between Life Expectancy and Economic Growth," University of Glasgow, last modified August 14, 2007, http://www.gla.ac.uk/media/media_43616_en.pdf.

longer life spans may be the reduction in female mortality for the age five to fifteen cohort, which historically had been subject to a higher death rate from infectious and parasitic diseases caused by their traditionally indoor lives.

Studies show that from at least the seventeenth century, women from the more well-to-do levels of society tended to outlive men. In considering general populations of varying economic levels, however, it is not common to see women's life spans exceeding those of men until the late nineteenth century and more typically not until the early twentieth.[7] This demographic change occurs in the data set for Bessarabian Germans within the same time frame. Generation 4 members, where this change starts, were for the most part born in the period from 1865 to 1895. That Bessarabian German women on average began to live longer than men implies that positive changes occurred in their health, diet, and living conditions. That such changes were occurring contemporaneously with similar changes in Western Europe and Scandinavia implies that, at least with regard to standards for healthy living conditions and diet, the Bessarabian Germans were keeping up with the most developed areas in the world.

The data showing the longer average life spans for the Generation 4 and 5 populations who lived at least twenty years are greatly influenced by data coming from the Bessarabian German families who immigrated to North America before World War I. The existence of data from the regular censuses conducted by the United States and Canada, together with the public availability of US Social Security death notices, has provided significant help in determining death dates for members of families immigrating to North America. In contrast, data on the great majority of Bessarabian German families who remained in Europe are far more limited. The 1940 resettlement questionnaires, occasional post–World War II village data collections (such as that for former residents of Kulm), and family genealogies form major but often incomplete sources for the larger segment of the population that remained in Bessarabia. The far better data sources from North America result in the fact that immigrants there produce 70 percent of the total life span information for the adult subset of these two generations, as can be seen in table 7–4.

TABLE 7–4.   Average life spans for Generation 4 and 5 adults in North America and Europe

| | North America | | Europe | | Combined | |
|---|---|---|---|---|---|---|
| | Male | Female | Male | Female | Male | Female |
| Generation 4 | | | | | | |
| 20+ population | 70.6 | 72.4 | 54.6 | 52.7 | 63.9 | 64.8 |
| Data points | 132 | 130 | 94 | 82 | 226 | 212 |
| Generation 5 | | | | | | |
| 20+ population | 73.2 | 76.9 | 48.9 | 51.7 | 68.3 | 70.9 |
| Data points | 256 | 209 | 64 | 59 | 320 | 268 |

7.   Arjan Gjonça, Cecilia Tomassini, and James W. Vaupel, "Male–Female Differences in Mortality in the Developed World" (working paper, Max Plank Institute for Demographic Research, Rostock, Germany, 1999). Gjonça, Tomassini, and Vaupel note that "the development of a significant male–female disparity in mortality did not take place until this century" (4). They also note that in England and Wales in the period from 1725 to 1749, available data indicate that women had longer lives, but this pattern had been reversed by 1775. In addition to reductions in mortality from childbirth, Gjonça, Tomassini, and Vaupel also highlight the importance for increased female life spans due to reductions in mortality from disease and parasites among females age five to fifteen.

The significant differences in average life spans between Bessarabian German immigrants to North America and those who remained in Europe are striking. For Generation 5 members who remained in Europe, average life spans are not only more than twenty years lower than for those of Generation 5 members in North America, but are also lower than the results for the European members of Generation 4. Two factors offer some insight into the surprising results for the European figures. The first is that the major sources for death information for European members of Generation 4 and especially Generation 5 are the questionnaires filled out by the emigrants from Bessarabia arriving in Germany in the winter of 1940–41 and casualty reports from World War II. With information thus generally capped at 1945, the available data concentrate those who had comparatively shorter life spans.

The second influencing factor is that, as will be discussed in more detail in a later chapter, the lives of many people in these two generations in Europe were negatively impacted by World War I and the Russian Revolution, which followed it. These events brought significant economic destruction and major physical hardships to the German settlements in Bessarabia. There were nine deaths in this data set reported for soldiers lost in the fighting of World War I,[8] and it is probable that some of the deaths reported in the questionnaires that occurred between 1918 and 1940 were hastened by the hardships associated with trying to reestablish prewar standards of living in a now-impoverished Bessarabia. In contrast, the major wars brought no destruction of property or loss of livestock and food supplies to the Bessarabian Germans in North America. In addition, no members of the North American Generations 4 and 5 lost their lives fighting in either World War I or II.

It is possible to compare the Bessarabian German life span data with data for a Prussian peasant population of a similar culture. Owing to the fortuitous preservation of estate records from the Stavenow estate in Brandenburg,[9] there exist detailed life span data for a population living in circumstances similar to the conditions abandoned by the large Bessarabian immigrant contingent that came from West and South Prussia. The Stavenow records provide life span data from 1694 through 1946 for residents of the villages of Blüthen, Stavenow, Groß Linde, and Mesekow.[10] A Stavenow pastor, Karl Gross, put together the church records matching births and deaths and so created the demographic records. In his book *Ordinary Prussians,* William Hagen collated this data but combined records for men and women. To make comparisons on the same basis, I have similarly adjusted the data presented in table 7–2.[11] These adjustments can be seen in table 7–5.

8. As citizens of the Russian Empire, these nine German Bessarabians died fighting with the Russian army. The thirteen men who died during World War II were soldiers fighting in the German army or older men or boys conscripted into the National Militia "Volkssturm."

9. Many records from Prussian estates were destroyed in the burning and looting of property that accompanied the victorious push of the Red Army into Poland and eastern Germany at the end of World War II. Records from the large Stavenow estate in Brandenburg are among the few large collections of estate records that survive, as they were donated to the Prussian State Archives in Berlin in the 1920s. These records form the basis of William Hagen's excellent study, *Ordinary Prussians.*

10. The Stavenow estate, located in the Prignitz District of northern Brandenburg, consists of the lands and attendant villages surrounding the castle and manor in Stavenow. Stavenow lies just to the southwest of the small town of Karstädt north of the Elbe River, which is partway between Ludwisgslust and Perleberg (see map in Hagen, *Ordinary Prussians,* 14).

11. The Stavenow data is from Table 4.16 in Hagen, *Ordinary Prussians,* 272.

TABLE 7–5.  **Average life spans for Bessarabian generations and Stavenow peasants**

| | Life span: All | Data points | Life span: 20+ group | Data points |
|---|---|---|---|---|
| **Bessarabian Data** | | | | |
| Generation 1 (1780–1800) | 63.2 | 76 | 63.2 | 76 |
| Generation 2 (1818–1835) | 43.1 | 183 | 52.2 | 118 |
| Generation 3 (1838–1862) | 32.9 | 675 | 59.2 | 363 |
| Generation 4 (1865–1895) | 36.1 | 809 | 64.3 | 438 |
| Generation 5 (1890–1920) | 53.6 | 807 | 69.5 | 588 |
| **Stavenow Data** | | | | |
| 1694–1799 | 32.0 | 1,476 | 57.4 | 779 |
| 1800–1899 | 32.4 | 2,049 | 58.6 | 1,081 |
| 1900–1946 | 45.0 | 657 | 61.1 | 475 |

The averages for the Bessarabian German Generation 3, born in the middle of the nineteenth century, are extremely close to the averages for the nineteenth-century Stavenow population: 32.9 years versus 32.4 years for the entire population and 59.2 years versus 58.6 years for those who lived at least until age twenty. This suggests that by Generation 3, the Bessarabian Germans had established living, working, and sanitary conditions as well as a sufficiently healthy diet that placed conditions in Bessarabia on par with those in Brandenburg. Although in Bessarabia the German colonists had to create their villages and farms from scratch, working with heretofore unplowed steppeland in a remote, pestilent, and primitive part of Europe, the colonists had several important advantages when compared to the Brandenburg leaseholders. The German families in Bessarabia had significantly larger plots of land, which they owned rather than leased, and were subject to much lower taxes and fees. Once their farms became established in Bessarabia, the retained food supplies of grains, fruits, and meats appear to have been substantially greater than those for peasants in Brandenburg. As a result, by the mid-nineteenth century, it is likely that the Bessarabian villagers lived in far better economic, dietary, and perhaps even sanitary conditions than the leaseholders on the Stavenow estates. It is not surprising, therefore, to see in the Generation 4 and particularly in the Generation 5 figures material improvements in life span over those of the people living on the Stavenow estates. The North American presence in the Generation 4 and 5 figures is also telling. The Bessarabian Germans came to North America as skilled, independent farmers who brought both sufficient cash and plant knowledge (particularly concerning strains of durum wheat) that proved generally successful.

The German colonies in Bessarabia were surrounded by villages of Bulgarian, Russian, Ukrainian, Gaugaz, and Moldavian peasants. It is not possible, though, to make life span comparisons between the Bessarabian Germans with these neighboring peasant populations. The Imperial Russian government did not conduct a complete census of Bessarabia until 1897. The village and church census records that survived the world wars, revolution, and changes of government in Bessarabia and other regions of Imperial and Soviet Russia have yet to be organized and studied. Such data as are currently available are, like the Stavenow material, local and perhaps accidental, but unlike the Stavenow material, they are often not sufficiently numeric.

What is generally known about life expectancy among the Russian peasantry in the nineteenth century would suggest that average life spans were generally much shorter than those in Western Europe. Statistics, however, are rare, and much is assumed from descriptions of poor living conditions and the heavy labor requirements of serfs. For example, a study of the Russian peasant population on the Gagarin estate of Petrovskoe in the Tambov Province, well to the northeast of Bessarabia, indicates that in the nineteenth century, peasants at birth had an average life expectancy of about twenty-seven years.[12]

On the other hand, data from the United States are both readily available and much studied. US data suggest that positive economic and health conditions fostered longer average lives than was generally the case in Western Europe. For example, studies by the Department of Commerce of US census data show that already by 1850, well ahead of much of Western Europe, women in the United States could expect longer lives than men. The nineteenth-century US averages quoted in the US Department of Commerce figures appear to be chiefly built on data for white persons living in Massachusetts and thus do not reflect wider samples of the US population. If one considers just the average life spans of adults—that is, removing the effects of childhood deaths—the experience of the combined Bessarabian Germans (that is, from both Europe and North America) positively compares with that from the United States. Adult Bessarabian German males of Generation 3, born generally between 1828 and 1861, had a slightly longer average life span (61.7 years) than US males (from Massachusetts) born in 1850 (60.1 years). Similarly, the average life spans for both adult Bessarabian German males and females of Generation 4, born generally between 1865 and 1895, were longer than those for the Massachusetts population born in 1890. For early twentieth-century births, the Bessarabian figures are even better, and now not just the adults but all Bessarabian Germans at birth have better average results than a US population somewhat broader than the Massachusetts group.[13] These latter figures for the Germans are based on the Generation 5 figures, which, as noted earlier, are heavily influenced by the experience of Bessarabian immigrants to North America. The figures for Bessarabian Germans who remained in Europe are much worse, as can be seen in table 7–6.

## Childhood mortality

The high frequency of childhood mortality was a common and painful feature of life among the German colonies in Bessarabia, as indeed it was among families of all nationalities and economic levels throughout Europe at this time. The Bessarabian German figures for average life spans for people born in the nineteenth century are significantly impacted by the large numbers of deaths that occurred in childhood. Nearly half of all of births for Generation 3 (46.6 percent) and Generation 4 (45.9

12. Steven Hoch, *Serfdom and Social Control in Russia: Petrovskoe, a Village in Tambov* (Chicago: University of Chicago Press, 1989), quoted in Edgar Melton, "The Russian Peasantries, 1450–1860," in *The Peasantries of Europe: From the Fourteenth to the Eighteenth Centuries*, ed. Tom Scott (Cambridge, Eng.: Longman Pub Group, 1998), 258–59. Peasant holdings at Petrovskoe in the nineteenth century were about 12 desjatina in comparison to those of 60 desjatina in German Bessarabia.

13. The US data is from US Department of Health and Human Services, National Center for Health Statistics, "Life Expectancy by Age, 1850–2011," organized by Infoplease.org, 2014, www.infoplease. com/ipa/A0005140. The figures for the US population born 1909–11 are from the more than a dozen "Original Death Registration States."

TABLE 7–6.  Average life span data for Generations 3, 4, and 5, and US populations

| | Males | | Females | |
| --- | --- | --- | --- | --- |
| | Total Group | Adults (Age 20+) | Total Group | Adults (Age 20+) |
| US (born 1850) | 38.3 | 60.1 | 40.5 | 60.2 |
| Bessarabian Gen 3 (most born 1838–1862) | 33.8 | 61.7 | 32.0 | 56.7 |
| US (born 1890) | 42.5 | 60.7 | 44.5 | 62.0 |
| Bessarabian Gen 4 (most born 1865–1895) | 35.1 | 63.9 | 37.2 | 64.8 |
| US (born 1909–11) | 50.2 | 62.7 | 53.6 | 64.9 |
| Bessarabian Gen 5 (most born 1890–1920) | 51.6 | 68.3 | 55.9 | 70.9 |
| Generation 5 North Americans Only | — | 73.2 | — | 76.9 |
| Generation 5 Europeans Only | — | 48.9 | — | 51.7 |

percent) were children who died before they reached age twenty. As discussed above, it is very likely that Generation 2 experienced similar results. The Generation 2 childhood mortality rate of 35.5 percent is very likely low as a result of the incomplete birth records available.

Data for childhood mortality within the Bessarabian German data set are not evenly spread between the sexes. For Generations 3 through 5, which have the best data, deaths among males outweigh those among females. The differences in the results for Generations 4 and 5 are striking (table 7–7).

I find no clear explanation for these differences. While the outdoor work of boys made them more susceptible to accidents, the more indoor life of girls made them increasingly prone to illnesses borne by disease and parasites. It is possible the differing results are an anomaly particular to this data set. A second explanation might be a conscious or unconscious prejudice that led families or the recording churches to underreport the deaths of girls, particularly in cases of stillborn children or children who died within a day of their birth. The frequency of childhood deaths among the Prussian leaseholders from the Stavenow estate is remarkably similar to the experience of the Bessarabian Germans (see table 7–8).

For both the Bessarabian Germans and the Prussians, childhood mortality is preponderantly early childhood mortality. Between 72 percent and 87 percent of the total childhood deaths occurred before age five (see table 7–9).

Crowded, small spaces, imperfect sanitary conditions, vague conceptions of how illnesses were transmitted, and of course the great vulnerability of newborn and very young children to disease and parasites all account for the high numbers of childhood deaths. Insufficient nutrition does not appear to have been a factor in

TABLE 7–7.  Counts of male childhood deaths among Generations 3, 4, and 5

| | Childhood deaths | Male deaths | Percent of total |
| --- | --- | --- | --- |
| Generation 3 | 312 | 162 | 51.9% |
| Generation 4 | 371 | 213 | 57.4% |
| Generation 5 | 219 | 126 | 57.5% |

TABLE 7–8.   **Comparison of Stavenow and Bessarabian childhood deaths**

|  | Percent of births died before age 20 |
|---|---|
| Stavenow Group 1694–1799 | 47.2% |
| Bessarabian Generation 3 (1838–1862) | 46.2% |
| Stavenow Group 1800–1899 | 46.3% |
| Bessarabian Generation 4 (1865–1895) | 45.9% |
| Stavenow Group 1900–1946 | 27.8% |
| Bessarabian Generation 5 (1890–1920) | 27.1% |

TABLE 7–9.   **Percent early childhood mortality, Bessarabians and Stavenow peasants**

|  | Percent of childhood deaths occurring before age 5 |
|---|---|
| Stavenow Group 1694–1799 | 75.8% |
| Stavenow Group 1800–1899 | 84.1% |
| Bessarabian Generation 2 (1818–1835) | 73.1% |
| Bessarabian Generation 3 (1838–1862) | 84.9% |
| Bessarabian Generation 4 (1865–1895) | 72.4% |
| Bessarabian Generation 5 (1890–1920) | 87.5% |
| Stavenow Group 1900–1946 | 82.4% |

Bessarabia.[14] Improvements in sanitary conditions likely account for the better results in the twentieth century in lowering the numbers of deaths that occurred in the first years of life. Even so, the numbers of childhood deaths in the twentieth century are remarkably high by current standards. The data for the Bessarabian Generation 5 and the Stavenow village data for 1900–46 indicate that just over a quarter of all births (27.1 percent and 27.8 percent, respectively) resulted in deaths before age twenty. By contrast, the World Bank reports that the probability in 2015 in the United States of a newborn dying within the first five years of life is 0.7 percent per one thousand live births, and 0.4 percent in Germany and United Kingdom.[15]

One common pattern in the early childhood deaths among the Bessarabian Germans was for a couple to lose their first child, suggesting that inexperience was a factor. In examples from Generation 2, the siblings Anna Dorothea, Michael, Johann, Ludwig, and Justine Raugust all lost their first child. Their two remaining siblings, Louise and Karl Raugust, both lost their second child, as did Johann Raugust, who lost both of his first two children. Many such first-child deaths occurred soon after birth. In the Generation 2 examples just cited, four of the five first-child deaths occurred within thirteen months of birth. A second common pattern, though not as frequently met, was for a couple to lose one or both of their last two children, as occurred with the siblings and in-laws Gottlieb,

14. Hagen (*Ordinary Prussians*, 273) implies that it might have been for the Stavenow Prussian families. In speculating about the causes of high childhood mortality in the nineteenth century, Hagen notes the growing number of families without land. Such landless families who worked for others while they farmed small household gardens experienced difficulties feeding themselves in lean years.

15. UN Inter-agency Group for Childhood Mortality Estimation, "Mortality Rate, Under-5 (per 1,000)," c. 2014, http://data.worldbank.org/indicator/SH.DYN.MORT. These statistics are developed by UNICEF, WHO, World Bank, and UN DESA Population Division.

Johann, Michael, Justine Raugust, and Juliana Schimke, and Johann Hoffmann of
Generation 4.

While it was not uncommon for most families across all five generations to
lose at least one child, it is striking that some families seem especially unlucky. In
Generation 3, for example, Wilhelm Mutschall and Elisabeth Widmer of Tarutino
lost seven of twelve children, Christian Lobe and Karolina Tiede of Kulm lost five
of eight children, Michael Kison and Elisabeth Breitkreutz of Kulm lost seven of
nine children, and David Raugust and Justine Vogel of Kulm lost seven of eleven
children. For many families (even those with large numbers of children), however,
the experience was much different. Gottfried Leischner and Karolina Jung of Kulm
and later Logan County, North Dakota, lost only one of twelve children; Samuel
Wutzke and Wilhelmine Kison (the sister of the Michael Kison noted above) of
Tarutino lost one of nine children; and Samuel Graumann and Elisabeth Schlauch,
who spent their married life in Eigenheim and Sangerowka, lost one of eleven children. Given such contrasts, it is hard not to presume that in unlucky families, lower
standards of care, sanitation, and cleanliness played at least some role in the much
higher frequency of childhood deaths.

Overcrowding in the original German settlements, which was a noted feature of
the 1860s and led directly to the founding of new villages, may have been an additional factor in the increased childhood mortality for Generation 2 and 3 families.
For example, when Jacob Raugust, one of the two first Raugusts and an original
settler of Kulm, died in 1842, his homestead and farm were taken over by his adult
sons, Michael and Johann. Michael was already married with a child, and Johann
married the following year. In 1843, the household also included their unmarried
siblings, Ludwig and Justina. As noted earlier, the land grants of 60 desjatina in
the original colonies were large enough to support several adult families working
together. By 1865, however, Ludwig had married, as had Michael's sons, Johann and
Christian, and his daughter, Karolina. All these families continued to live together
in the same homestead. As a result, there were now thirteen adults and twenty-one
children crowded in Jacob Raugust's original homestead. This led Michael Raugust
and his wife, together with their underage children and their married sons and
daughter, to take their Kulm inheritance and lease a homestead in the new village
of Mannsburg, Bessarabia, in 1866. Conditions in this Kulm household before 1866,
though, must have been quite close and crowded. Though presumptive, it is reasonable to ask whether the five deaths of children in this group that occurred in the
period from 1855 to 1863 (four of which occurred between 1860 and 1863) were
influenced by the crowded conditions.[16]

For Bessarabian German families—indeed, for all families of poor to middling
economic status throughout the world—children generally formed the pension
plan of their parents. To have children survive to adulthood was to create economic
support when one became too old and infirm to work. The high childhood mortality
in the nineteenth century, when it was common for only one out of two children to
survive to age twenty, only encouraged families to have more children. One could

---

16. Johann Raugust and Anna Rosina Lobe's sons Johann and Gottlieb both died on January 22, 1860
(O.S.), at ages six years, two months and eleven months, respectively. Other deaths were their son
David, age two, in 1863, and the deaths of Ludwig Raugust and Anna Maria Flaig's daughter
Louisa at age two in 1855 and their unnamed stillborn daughter in 1861.

never be sure which children would survive. However, this became a vicious circle. With the major causes of childhood mortality generally unchecked until the beginning of the twentieth century, more children also often meant more childhood deaths. This pattern that was common across Western Europe was equally descriptive of the Bessarabian Germans.

## Marriage: Rates of marriage, ages at marriage, seasonal timing of marriage, and patterns of remarriage

### Rates of marriage

The data for the Bessarabian Germans strongly suggest that nearly everyone who reached age eighteen married (see table 7–10). Individuals over eighteen who did not marry make up less than 2 percent of Generations 2 through 5.[17]

The figure of 98.4 percent for the number of adults who married may even be deemed low, as a full third of the twenty-four who did not marry died before reaching age twenty-five and may not have considered themselves healthy enough to marry.

Such marriage statistics among the Bessarabian Germans indicate that an extremely high percentage of adults married, at least by comparison to what is known about marriage rates in other European countries at this time. Marriage statistics for European countries for the nineteenth and early twentieth centuries are built generally from church and state registers. Records are often incomplete, and so academic studies tend to build countrywide assumptions from a few more complete data sources. Demographic studies of nineteenth century marital patterns in northern Europe typically suggest that a material portion of the adult population, in the range of 10–25 percent, did not marry. For example, using proxies for the unmarried, such as the number of single women ages forty to forty-nine, the French anthropologists Rallu and Blum estimate that between 10 percent and 12 percent of the late nineteenth-century population of France, Germany, and the Czech lands in Austria did not marry, while the figure was over 20 percent in Scandinavia.[18] John Hajnal, in a 1965 article that Rallu and Blum rely heavily on, postulates that in the nineteenth century, it was common in northwestern Europe (Hajnal specifies the area west of a line running from St. Petersburg in Russia to Trieste in Italy) for

**TABLE 7–10.** Individuals over age 18 who did not marry

|  | Number not marrying | Percent of total |
|---|---|---|
| Generation 2 | 1 | 0.7% |
| Generation 3 | 5 | 1.4% |
| Generation 4 | 3 | 0.7% |
| Generation 5 | 15 | 2.8% |
| **Total** | 24 | 1.6% |

17. All members of Generation 1 were married. I have not included Generation 1 in this table, as our knowledge of immigrant families is confined to those who came to Bessarabia. Thus, we do not have marriage statistics for siblings who remained behind.

18. Jean Louis Rallu and Alain Blum, eds., introduction to *European Population: Demographic Dynamics* (London, Eng.: John Libbey and Company, 1993), 4.

10–20 percent of the population never to marry.[19] Flinn, noting the randomness of the data on which such estimates are built, still came to the same totals of 10–20 percent.[20] Coleman and Salt, in studying British demography, suggest that in the nineteenth century 10 percent of men and 14 percent of women never married.[21] Hagen, in his study of the Stavenow estate population, notes that in the period from 1721 to 1771, about 40 percent of the noninheriting children of landed peasant households were not married, which would suggest that about 25 percent of the total adult population never married.[22] Wolfgang Kaschuba, in his study of Kiebingen, a peasant village in Württemberg, found that perhaps a quarter of that population in the late nineteenth century did not marry.[23] The experience of the German population in Bessarabia, then, would seem to be in sharp contrast to their own past as well as to contemporary German and Western European patterns of the nineteenth and early twentieth centuries.

The high rates of marriage and the relatively young average ages at marriage among the Bessarabian Germans, discussed in the section below, are indications of the availability of land and the growth in material prosperity in Bessarabia. In Prussia, as Hagen notes, peasants, on reaching adulthood, needed to save funds and then wait for the death or retirement of a parent or neighboring leaseholder in order to acquire the rights to land. The acquisition of land rights was the critical factor in being able to support marriage and children. In Bessarabia, the colonists owned tracts of land far larger than the leaseholds held in Prussia and Württemberg. During the first generations in Bessarabia, more hands were needed to exploit the value of the farmsteads, which encouraged marriages. In later generations, the wealth built up in these family farmsteads continued to support the ability to marry as it became possible to purchase or lease land within one of the new villages elsewhere in Bessarabia or to emigrate and achieve similar ends.

### Ages at first marriage
The average ages at first marriage for the Bessarabian German group were generally stable through Generation 4: the low twenties for men and the high teens to low twenties for women. With Generation 5 and the arrival of the twentieth century, they rose slightly (see table 7–11).

The average ages at first marriage for the Bessarabian Germans are substantially younger than those noted for contemporary populations in Western Europe. For example, among the Prussian families on the Stavenow estate in Brandenburg, the average ages through the nineteenth century were over thirty for men and over twenty-five for women. By the twentieth century, the median ages for the Prussian

19. John Hajnal, "European Marriage Patterns in Perspective," in *Population in History: Essays in Historical Demography*, eds. D. V. Glass and D. E. C. Eversley (Chicago: Aldine Publishing Co., 1965), 101–43.
20. Michael Flinn, *The European Demographic System, 1520–1820* (Baltimore: The Johns Hopkins University Press, 1981), 4.
21. David Coleman and John Salt, *The British Population: Patterns, Trends and Processes* (New York: Oxford University Press, 1992), 180.
22. Hagan, *Ordinary Prussians*, 246. As Hagen's data covers a long period in time, I have assumed that he meant to imply that his unmarried group did not later marry.
23. Kaschuba, "Peasants and Others," 251. The Catholic village of Kiebingen, located across the Neckar River from Rottenburg am Neckar, lies in the same area of Württemberg from which many families had emigrated to Poland and Bessarabia.

TABLE 7–11. **Average ages at first marriage, male and female**

| | Male | Female |
|---|---|---|
| Generation 1 | 23.8 | 19.7 |
| Generation 2 | 22.6 | 18.5 |
| Generation 3 | 22.2 | 19.1 |
| Generation 4 | 23.9 | 20.8 |
| Generation 5 | 25.0 | 22.0 |
| **Weighted average** | 23.8 | 20.6 |

TABLE 7–12. **Average and median ages at first marriage, male and female, Stavenow peasants**

| | Males | | Females | |
|---|---|---|---|---|
| | Avg. age | Median age | Avg. age | Median age |
| Stavenow 1800–49 | 31.5 | 28.0 | 27.0 | 25.0 |
| Stavenow 1850–99 | 31.5 | 27.5 | 26.5 | 25.0 |
| Stavenow 1900–46 | 28.5 | 26.5 | 25.0 | 23.5 |

group (which are less dominated by outliers than the averages), though still older, come much closer to the Bessarabian figures (see table 7–12).[24]

The average ages Hagen provided for Stavenow are quite typical of those reported from studies of other groups in Germany and Western Europe for this time. In the village of Kiebingen in Württemberg, Kaschuba found the average age for men at marriage did not fall below thirty until 1875, and the average for women remained above twenty-seven until after World War I.[25] Flinn's data on women from the parishes of Grafenhausen and Öschelbronn in Württemberg covering the years 1750–1849 calculates that the mean ages at the time of first marriage were above age twenty-five.[26] E. A. Wrigley provides data for the United Kingdom from the nineteenth century that indicates that the average ages at marriage fluctuated between twenty-five and twenty-seven for women, with men generally being a year older.[27]

As with the issue of the higher proportion of the population marrying, the lower average ages at first marriage for the Bessarabian Germans are likely the result of the availability of sufficient land and the greater economic well-being of the adult population. These same conditions and opportunities were frequently available to

24. The information for the ages at first marriage from the Stavenow estate comes from Table 4.15 in Hagen's *Ordinary Prussians*, 271. For the Bessarabian group, the average figures are not dominated by outliers; the mean figures fall well within 100 basis points of the averages.

25. Kaschuba, "Peasants and Others," 251.

26. Flinn, *European Demographic System*, Table 7, 127. The mean age for the parish of Grafenhausen was 26.5 and for Öschelbronn was 25.6.

27. E. A. Wrigley, "Family Limitation in Pre-industrial England," *Economic History Review*, 2nd ser., 19, no. 1 (1966): 82–109. The averages ages at marriage for Stavenow and those quoted elsewhere from German lands raise questions about the low average ages reported for Generation 1 of the Bessarabian Germans. The average ages for Generation 1 were 23.8 years for men and 19.7 years for women, vs. 31.5 and 27 in Stavenow (1800–49). One explanation is that the average for the Bessarabian Germans was greatly influenced by the fact that 60 percent of the Generation 1 marriages occurred after arrival in Bessarabia when the availability of land and the need for marital partnerships encouraged early marriages. This doesn't explain early age marriages that occurred in Prussian Poland, such as that between Martin Raugust and Johanna Müller, which took place in 1812 when he was 23 and she was 20.

immigrants in North America. It is not surprising, therefore, to see that the average ages at first marriage in the United States from the last decade of the nineteenth century and the first decades of the twentieth, when census data started to be collected for age at marriage, were quite similar to those for Generation 5 among the Bessarabian Germans (see table 7–13).[28]

There are particularly rich data for the Generation 5 group on ages at marriage for both the European and North American subsets.[29] The average ages at marriage for the two subsets are substantially similar, with Generation 5 members in North America marrying slightly earlier. Both subsets are close to contemporary general population averages for both Western Europe and North America. However, in comparison to earlier generations of Bessarabian Germans, average ages at marriage for Generation 5 have increased by at least a year. This rise is unlike the figures for Europe and North America, where the trend is downward. There are no data coming from Generation 5 participants that would help explain this rise. In the United States, the increase in the average ages at first marriage, noted as starting in the 1970s, has commonly been attributed, at least in part, to the development of strong youth cultures, which in a generally prosperous society emphasize taking time for individual fulfillment and the growth of experiences.[30] Such causes do not seem relevant to the reported experiences of Germans in North America in the early

TABLE 7–13. **US average ages at marriage compared to Bessarabian Germans of Generation 5**

| | Avg. age at marriage, male | Avg. age at marriage, female |
|---|---|---|
| US 1890 census | 26.1 | 22.0 |
| US 1900 census | 25.9 | 21.9 |
| US 1910 census | 25.1 | 21.6 |
| US 1920 census | 24.6 | 21.2 |
| Bessarabian Generation 5 (1890–1920) | 25.0 | 22.0 |
| North American Generation 5 | 24.7 | 21.1 |
| European Generation 5 | 25.2 | 22.4 |

28. The US data is median age and is supplied by the US census. A chart is provided: "Median Age at First Marriage, 1890–2010," United States Bureau of Census, organized by Infoplease.org, accessed 2011, http://www.infoplease.com/ipa/A0005061.html. Anatole Romaniuc and Liubov Chuiko, in their demographic study of Ukrainians in Canada, indicate that not all populations in North America married at young ages. They cite first ages at marriage for Ukrainians in Canada from the early to mid-twentieth century as 29.5 for men and 26.1 for women. They contrast these figures to significantly younger ages at first marriage for Ukrainian peasants in nineteenth-century Ukraine: 20.5 for men and 19.5 for women. They believe the differences were driven by varying economic and demographic circumstances; early marriages in the Ukraine were cultural responses to prospects of short life spans driven by poor working and health conditions, while later average ages in Canada were encouraged by the far better living conditions that promised longer lives with expectations of forming households of their own. Romaniuc and Chuiko, "Matrimonial Behavior in Canada and the Ukraine: The Enduring Hold of Culture," *Journal of Comparative Family Studies* 30, no. 3 (1999): 335–61.

29. Unlike with the average life span data for the Generation 5 families who remained in Europe, the data on average ages at marriage are reasonably rich. Data points for the average ages at first marriage are:

|  | North America | Bessarabians in Europe |
|---|---|---|
| Males | 175 | 260 |
| Females | 178 | 273 |

30. Other major factors attributed to the current increase in the average age at marriage in the United States are the growth in the use of birth control and a decline in the cultural value placed on marriage—factors that are even less relevant to Generation 5's experience.

twentieth century. More likely explanations may be the increased hurdles in meeting eligible partners created by the fact that the Germans were living on separated farmsteads and not in villages, or the time it took for immigrants to build up capital from new farmsteads created in a new environment.

One factor that may have increased the ages at which Bessarabian Germans in Europe married was World War I and the difficulties it brought. World War I brought great hardships that were multiplied with Imperial Russia's collapse, the Russian Revolution, and Bessarabia's absorption into Romania. The war effort took away men, food supplies, and animals. The revolution brought Romanian control and Soviet hostility, which closed Bessarabia off from both its former agricultural markets in Russia and its major supply routes to Western Europe. Moreover, with the collapse of the Imperial Russian ruble, all hard currency savings were devalued or lost. As economic conditions became more difficult, marriages may have been postponed. This is suggested by the contrast in average ages at marriage between Generation 5 Germans in Bessarabia and Germans from this data set who, after leaving Bessarabia in the late nineteenth century, established themselves in Romanian Dobrudscha, which had been less touched by the war (see table 7–14).[31]

Even so, a cultural pattern of early marriage had been set by the generations immediately prior to Generation 5. Given that only a slight increase in average ages at marriage occurred, it is possible that such expectations led couples in Bessarabia to marry before they were more certain of economic security.

In North America, the war brought no economic collapse but indeed the reverse. However, cultural expectations were different and affected marriage customs. In the twentieth century especially, the custom after marriage was for the newly married couple to establish themselves away from their parents in a separate farm homestead or in a place in a town. To achieve this, some savings and independent prospects of income were necessary. In North America, as the selection of children's names noted at the end of this chapter will indicate, Generation 5 couples appear to have had strong inclinations to adapt to local customs. It is noteworthy in this regard that the Generation 5 data on the average ages at marriage for Bessarabian Germans in North America are virtually equal to the average ages at marriage derived from responses in the 1920 census for the US population as a whole.

TABLE 7–14. **Average marriage ages for Bessarabian and Dobrudscha Germans**

|  | Avg. age at first marriage | |
|---|---|---|
|  | Males | Females |
| Bessarabian Germans | 25.2 | 22.4 |
| Dobrudscha Germans | 22.8 | 19.5 |

31. Romania's late entry into World War I (1916) and quick defeat meant that Dobrudscha, unlike Bessarabia, did not undergo significant economic disruption as a result of the war. As the data points from Dobrudscha are not numerous (twelve women and eleven men), the implication they offer—that a better economic fate allowed average ages at marriage to remain low—can only be said to be suggestive rather than evidentiary.

## Seasonal times for marriage

It was typical among eighteenth- and nineteenth-century farming communities for marriages to occur over the fall and winter, during the period after the harvest had been brought in and before spring planting work began. In the farming calendar, which was always filled with work, this was the season of the lightest duties.[32] This pattern is also found among the Bessarabian Germans. As can be seen in table 7–15, November is the most popular month in three of the five generations, and November and February are among the top four months in all five generations.

Although winter months continue to predominate as favored times for marriage in Generation 5, it is clear that customs were changing. June became one of the top four months, and a general broadening in the choice of times for marriage is indicated by the fact that the top four months formed a much smaller portion of the total. Whereas the top four months made up roughly two-thirds of the marriage dates for the first four generations, they dropped to under half of the total for Generation 5. Given the popularity of summer marriages in North America, it might be presumed that the shifting pattern in marriage seasonality seen in Generation 5 was impacted materially by experience from Bessarabian Germans in North America. This does not prove to be the case, however. The marriage patterns for the North American group in Generation 5 were quite similar to that of the European group. The same months made up the top four, though June was second among the North Americans instead of third, and the top four comprised just under 50 percent for both groups. Patterns differ in that for the next most popular months, the Bessarabians in North America had a greater propensity for March and October weddings (10.3 percent and 8.8 percent of their totals, respectively), while the Europeans had greater preferences for May, September, and April weddings (12.9 percent, 8.1 percent, and 7.4 percent, respectively).[33]

TABLE 7–15. **The four most popular marriage months for Generations 1 through 5**

|  | First | Second | Third | Fourth | Percent total |
|---|---|---|---|---|---|
| Generation 1 | October (5) | September (4) | February (3) | November (3) | 65.2% |
| Generation 2 | November (25) | February (23) | January (13) | December (13) | 63.3% |
| Generation 3 | November (56) | December (54) | January (43) | February (37) | 70.4% |
| Generation 4 | February (57) | November (45) | January (34) | December (33) | 67.3% |
| Generation 5 | November (56) | February (56) | June (47) | January (44) | 49.9% |

32. Lucchetti et al. point to this pattern in their study of the timing of rural marriages in France, Spain, and Italy in "Changes in Marriage Seasonality among Some European Rural Populations," *International Journal of Anthropology* 11, no. 2–4 (April 1996): 73–81. This pattern does not appear to hold for marriages in England. W. J. Edwards finds May and June to be the most popular months. Edwards, "Marriage Seasonality 1761–1810: An Assessment of Patterns in Seventeen Shropshire Parishes," *Local Population Studies* no. 19 (1977): 23–27, http://www.localpopulationstudies.org.uk/PDF/LPS19/LPS19_1977_23-27.pdf.

33. It should be noted that while the ages at marriage for many North Americans in Generation 5 are known, this is less true for the marriage months. Only 33.4 percent of the 407 data points on Generation 5 marriage months come from North America, though North Americans make up 41.1 percent of the total population and 39.8 percent of the data points for the average age at first marriage. A major reason for this difference in data between marriage months and ages at first marriage is that US census data provide no information on the month of marriage but do provide ages at first marriage.

The general pattern for Generation 5 suggests that changes in broad cultural patterns common to both Europe and North America were at work. Given the likelihood that in the first four generations, the agricultural calendar played a dominant role in determining preferred months for marriage, one hypothesis might be that fewer members of the group were actively involved in farming and so were less attuned to its seasonal needs. However, while by Generation 5 in both Bessarabia and North America there were more people working in commerce and manufacturing than earlier, the great majority remained engaged in farming. As a result, changes in marriage seasonality suggest instead that by the early twentieth century, agricultural requirements during the period from March through October had become somewhat less demanding. One major cause would have been the continuing growth of mechanical help in performing farm tasks. While we see couples in Generation 5 selecting a far wider range of marriage dates, summer harvest periods continued to be the least popular time for marriage. In all five generations and for both the Europeans and North Americans in Generation 5, the month of August was the least popular marriage date.

### Second marriages

Divorce was not an accepted means to end a marriage for Germans in Bessarabia or for couples in the first generation of Bessarabian Germans to immigrate to North America. In this data set I found only three cases of divorce. All were in Generation 5, all were in North America, and all were among either children or grandchildren of those who immigrated to North America. Instead of divorce, second marriages and subsequent marriages occurred almost entirely as a result of a spouse's death. Patterns of remarriage following a spouse's death among the Bessarabian Germans, however, are in sharp contrast with today's customs. Among the Bessarabian Germans, when a spouse died, especially when there were young children in the household, the pattern was for the surviving spouse to remarry quickly. Thus, after the August 1867 death of Kulm resident Christian Lobe's wife, Justine Tiede, Christian (with five children in his household, including a month-old baby) remarried in November of the same year. Similarly, when twenty-seven-year-old Karolina Raugust's husband, Samuel Kuhn, died in Kulm in November 1872, Karolina, caring for a nineteen-month-old son, married Wilhelm Stelter the following February. It would not be correct to presume from this, I believe, that Bessarabian Germans were less likely to grieve for a spouse who died or were less loving in marital relationships. The pattern of prompt remarriage more likely had an economic root. The family farmsteads in both Bessarabia and North America were agricultural enterprises heavily dependent on the labor of both husbands and wives. The death of a spouse created an immediate and significant economic hardship. A surviving spouse had to set aside grief and look for a suitable new marriage partner in order to keep the farmstead running. If there were young children to be cared for, the need was all the greater.

While the data set indicates that it was common for both widowers and widows to remarry, there are marked gender differences in the frequency of remarriage, the time lag between a spousal death and remarriage, and whether or not the new spouse is marrying for the first time (see table 7–16). Widowers were more likely to remarry

TABLE 7–16. **Patterns in second marriages among the Bessarabian Germans**

| | Gen 1 | Gen 2 | Gen 3 | Gen 4 | Gen 5 | Total |
|---|---|---|---|---|---|---|
| **Second marriages** | | | | | | |
| Males | 8 | 44 | 63 | 49 | 34 | 198 |
| Females | 4 | 32 | 40 | 29 | 21 | 126 |
| Total | 12 | 76 | 103 | 78 | 55 | 324 |
| Percent of total marriages | 26.1% | 42.4% | 30.6% | 17.7% | 7.1% | 17.9% |
| Males as % of second marriages | 66.7% | 57.9% | 61.2% | 62.8% | 61.8% | 61.1% |
| **Average wait to remarry (months)** | | | | | | |
| Males | 5.0 | 7.2 | 12.6 | 9.9 | 10.9 | 9.9 |
| Females | 13.3 | 13.5 | 39.7 | 29.4 | 47.8 | 30.2 |
| Male data points | 6 | 42 | 52 | 42 | 20 | 162 |
| Female data points | 4 | 31 | 33 | 18 | 8 | 94 |
| **New spouse not married before** | | | | | | |
| Spouses of males | 3 of 8 | 20 of 44 | 29 of 63 | 23 of 49 | 17 of 34 | 92 of 188 |
| Spouses of females | 0 of 4 | 9 of 32 | 12 of 40 | 9 of 29 | 5 of 21 | 35 of 126 |
| Percent for males | 37.5% | 45.5% | 46.0% | 46.9% | 50.0% | 46.5% |
| Percent for females | 0.0% | 28.1% | 30.8% | 31.0% | 23.8% | 27.8% |

than widows, they remarried more quickly than widows, and they were helped in both instances by having a larger pool of potential spouses to choose from.

Widowers formed 61.1 percent of the data points on remarriages across all five generations. One reason that males among this Bessarabian German data set made more second and subsequent marriages would seem related to the fact, observed earlier, that adult females stood a far higher chance of dying in the midst of a couple's reproductive years than did adult males. It should be noted in this regard that the number of second marriages as a percent of all marriages peaks in Generation 2, and the total number of second marriages peaks in Generation 3. These high points for the numbers of second marriages occurred in the mid-nineteenth century, when young adult female mortality rates were at their greatest among the Bessarabian Germans. It is tempting to conclude that for Generations 4 and 5, as medical and sanitary conditions improved, fewer deaths were occurring among young adults and as a consequence, there were fewer second marriages occurring.

In making second marriages, males in this data set were more likely to find spouses who had never married before than were females. As the chart above indicates, close to half of the brides of widowers (48.9 percent) were women who were marrying for the first time, while the equivalent figure for the grooms of widows is just 27.8 percent. What underlies these figures is that while there appears to have been no particular difficulties for widows in their twenties or early thirties to find new husbands among those who had never married, it became significantly rarer for widows over the age of thirty-five to do so. On the other hand, widowers in their thirties (and occasionally over the age of forty) found new partners who had never married before. What may lie behind this pattern is the cultural preference for grooms to be older than brides, or perhaps that this preference became more strongly marked the older widows and widowers became. In any case, the remarriage data clearly suggest that young unmarried females were willing to marry older widowers, while young unmarried men were less likely to pick older widows as brides.

Most surviving spouses under the age of thirty remarried. While grooms were typically a few years older than brides at first marriage, it was not extraordinary for widows in this younger age bracket to find new husbands younger than themselves. Anna Dorothea Bobermin Lobe, for example, was thirty with two children, one of whom was barely a month old, when her first husband, Christian Lobe, died in June 1855. By December of that year, she was remarried to the bachelor Martin Raugust, who was ten years her junior. For widows over thirty-five and especially over forty, it appears to have been far more difficult to find a suitable second spouse. This is possibly one reason why forty-year-old Karolina Winter Schimke did not remarry when her husband, Johann Shimke, died in 1878 in Eigenheim. In contrast, her brother-in-law, Wilhelm Schimke, a widower at age forty-four, married the thirty-three-year-old widow Susanne Heiss Vogel after his first wife, Justine Hartmann Schimke, died in 1893.

In general, this data set on remarriages suggests that widows and particularly older widows had a harder time remarrying than did widowers, and as a result more widowers than widows were able to remarry.[34] One indication that widows had a more difficult time finding suitable spouses is seen in the significant difference between widows and widowers in the average length of time taken to remarry. Presuming that for economic reasons both genders had equally strong motivations to remarry after the death of a spouse, it nonetheless took Generation 1 and 2 widows more than twice as long and Generation 3, 4, and 5 widows more than three times as long as widowers in those generations. Several possible causes for these significant differences exist. Whereas widowers, as noted above, often found suitable spouses among women who had yet to marry, widows, especially older widows, were far less likely to find bachelors to marry. The larger pool of potential brides no doubt shortened the time widowers needed to find a suitable spouse.

A second reason for the longer period of time for widows to find new spouses was that the general custom among European peasant communities was for males to take the lead in initiating relationships with the opposite sex. The customary opprobrium directed at women who took more aggressive approaches may have held widows back and made their searches more cautious and deliberate.

A third cause for the gender disparity in the time taken to remarry may have been the cultural preference among potential grooms to seek brides who were younger than themselves. A general custom among both the Germans in Bessarabia and peasant agricultural communities in Europe was for grooms to be older than their brides. It was not unheard of for this pattern to be broken, as the example of the marriage between Martin Raugust and Anna Dorothea Bobermin Lobe, noted above, attests. However, by and large in the second marriages from this data set, grooms were older than brides. The existence of such a pattern suggests that women who became widows after reaching their mid-thirties had no sources for potential husbands other than older widowers. Unfortunately for such widows, two independent factors tended to reduce the number of available widowers in this population

---

34. Flinn, in his study of European demography in the period from 1500 to 1820, notes in passing and without citing data that in Europe during this period, "widows . . . remarried at significantly lower rates than widowers" (*European Demographic System*, 30).

cohort. First, fewer men were widowed in the over-thirty population because fewer older adult married women were dying than among the younger age group. Judging by the data on average life spans noted earlier in this chapter, adult women who survived to their thirties had an extremely good chance of living until at least age sixty. As will be noted later in this chapter, when women reached their mid-thirties, the spacing between children was growing—that is, women of that age and older were bearing fewer children or had ceased to have children altogether. The result was that after their mid-thirties, women were no longer as endangered by the major cause of death among young adult females.

The second reason it was difficult for widows in their mid-thirties to find older widowers was that there were fewer males alive to become widowers. Again judging by the patterns of death among males in the data collected on average life spans for the Bessarabian Germans discussed earlier, while males reaching the age of twenty had a very good chance of living until at least age thirty-five, after that point, the risk of death rose steadily and sharply. The hard farm labor that males needed to perform in Bessarabia began to take its toll. Wear and tear, accidents, and, judging from the 1841 Welfare Committee report on misdemeanors, drunkenness increased the frequency of adult male deaths after age thirty-five. For widows in the cohort age thirty-five to fifty, there were, therefore, two demographic trends at work that made it harder for them to find new spouses: a) the increasing rate in male deaths produced more widows, and thus greater competition among the latter in seeking suitable second spouses, and b) the decreasing rate of female deaths meant there were fewer widowers. This data set suggests that after age thirty-five, when it also became far less likely that a widow might find a younger husband, the older a woman was when her husband died, the more difficult it would be to find another spouse.

## Intermarriage between colonist families from Prussia and Württemberg

Members of Generation 1 were born in settlements in Prussian Poland, Prussia, Württemberg, and southern Germany that were composed of people from a single German cultural group. Those who married before coming to Bessarabia found their marriage partners within their home village or from other settlements like theirs. Some members of Generation 1, though, came to Bessarabia as unmarried young men and women and married within the first five to ten years of their arrival in Russia. Though exposed in Bessarabia to families of different German backgrounds, these people uniformly picked marriage partners who shared the same background as their own families. Individuals with a family history from Prussia or northern Germany married others with similar backgrounds. Württembergers, whether they came to Bessarabia from Württemberg or Prussia, married other Württembergers. Christoph Radke, for example, came to Kulm with his family as an unmarried teenager from Trikowa, West Prussia, where his family, originally from Prussian Pomerania, had been living since before 1765. In 1815, in Bessarabia, he married Marie Hass (or Hasz), who had immigrated to Kulm with her family from Tomischel, near Posen in South Prussia, where her family had been living since at least the 1760s. Similarly, Ferdinand Kuhn, born in Sontheim, Württemberg, who came to Tarutino with his parents as a thirty-year-old bachelor, found a bride who shared his background. In

1816, he married eighteen-year-old Anna Maria Stockberger (or Stadtberger), who was born in Kirnbach, Württemberg.[35]

In the following generation, the first one born and raised in Bessarabia, there appears to be a continued predilection to find marriage partners who were from the same cultural and linguistic backgrounds. As noted earlier, the data set used in this study is heavily weighted toward families with a Prussian background. Unsurprisingly, most of the Generation 2 marriages were between individuals from Prussian families, particularly given that Kulm, Leipzig, and Tarutino, from which most marriage partners were found, were predominantly populated with families with Prussian backgrounds. In Generation 2, marriages did start to occur between Prussian and Württemberg families. They remain, however, a very small part of the total (9.6 percent). Most of these marriages occurred with members of one family, the Lobe family of Kulm.[36]

The conservative nature of the pattern of Generation 2 marriages is further underlined by the fact that there was a predilection for marriages with families with a Prussian background who had come to Bessarabia from the same areas in Prussian Poland. The Raugusts came to Kulm from the village of Szczerbin (Tscherbin) in the Notec River valley east of Bromberg, in what had been West Prussia before Napoleon's victory placed this area in the Duchy of Warsaw. Numbers of families from this area formed a prominent part of early intermarriages, both with the Raugusts and with each other: the Vogels and Graumanns also came from Szczerbin itself, while the Leischners and Grosses came from Szaradowo and the Lemkes came from Schöndorf, villages that were located to the west of Bromberg, not far from Szczerbin. Other marriage partners came from the general region near Bromberg. The Winters, Burghardts, Burgemeisters, Hammels, and Lüttkes came from the area around Thorn, to the south of Bromberg, and the Schimkes and Radkes came from Trikowo, south of Thorn.

In Generation 3, as table 7–17 below indicates, marriages between partners where both were from Prussian families continued to form the majority, making up 68.8 percent of the total. Similarly, marriages where both partners shared Württemberg origins grew from 2.9 percent to 5.4 percent. The pattern of mono-cultural marriages, though, was nowhere near as dominant as in the prior two

TABLE 7–17. **Generation 2 and 3 marriage patterns**

|  | Gen 2 | Gen 3 |
|---|---|---|
| Both partners from Prussian families | 83.8% | 68.8% |
| Mixed Prussian and Württemberger families | 9.6% | 22.9% |
| Both partners from Württemberger families | 2.9% | 5.4% |
| One partner from other German areas (Saxony, Bavaria, Palatinate) | 3.7% | 2.9% |

35. Though not mentioned in either the Kuhn or Stockberger/Stadtberger families genealogies, it is quite likely both families reached Bessarabia after some period of living in settlements of Württembergers in South Prussia.

36. Anton Lobe, with his four sons and one daughter, came to Kulm from the village of Erdmannsweiler, near Łodz in South Prussia. Erdmannsweiler is located in a group of villages thickly settled by Württemberg immigrants to Prussia. Flegel has Anton Lobe's father, another Anton Lobe, coming from Erdmannsweiler, Württemberg (a village close to Königsfeld im Schwartzwald; *Extended Relationships*, 435).

generations. Marriages between Prussian and Württemberger families have more than doubled, growing from 9.6 percent of the total to 22.9 percent.

Part of the material growth in marriages between Prussian and Württemberger families in Generation 3 came from the mixing of population in new villages in Bessarabia. Shortly after their marriage in Kulm in 1833, Generation 2 members Karolina Wilhelmina Raugust and her husband Johann Schimke moved from Kulm to the new village of Dennewitz, established south of Teplitz by the Welfare Committee. Most of the new settlers in Dennewitz came from the villages of Wittenberg and Alt Posttal, which were primarily settled by Württemberg families who had moved to Prussian Poland in the 1790s and early 1800s. Not surprisingly, most of the Schimke children married into Dennewitz Württemberger families. Yet a big part of the intermixing of cultures simply came from the growth in familiarity that resulted from being neighbors and fellow townspeople with families of different backgrounds. Hence the many Generation 3 marriages between people with Prussian family backgrounds were with men and women from Württemberger backgrounds from their home or a neighboring village, such as the Flaig, Kuhn, and Lobe families from Kulm, the Sprecher family from Leipzig, and the Bogner and Seitz families from Tarutino.

Experiences like those of the Schimke family in Dennewitz became significantly more common for Generation 4 people after the 1860s. By then, the crowded original settlements had encouraged many families to participate in one of the land purchases that created the new German villages in Bessarabia. Though families often moved to these villages with relatives and friends, the new villages mixed together families from many different settlements. For example, Karolina, David, and Salome Raugust—Generation 4 children of Kulm native Johann Raugust, who moved his family from Kulm in the 1860s—grew up in the new villages of Mannsburg and Seimental, Bessarabia, where they met and married spouses from families with Württemberg backgrounds.

Sufficient mixing had occurred by Generation 4 that it becomes increasingly difficult to designate individuals from this distance as either Prussian or Württemberger. Therese Graumann and the widower Emmanuel Burgemeister, who married in 1913, form a typical example. Both the Graumanns and Burgemeisters had Prussian backgrounds from families who came to Bessarabia from West Prussia, but allegiances to Prussian speech and culture cannot be assumed. While Therese's father, Samuel, had Graumann and Raugust parents, her mother, Elisabeth Schlauch, descended from a family that came to Bessarabia from Murrhardt in Württemberg via Poland. Similarly, Emmanuel Burgemeister's mother, Karolina Hättig, and grandmother, Katharina Finkbeiner, were from Württemberger families. It is clear that, even in the mid-twentieth century, people were quite aware of the differences in speech and culture that distinguished families with a Prussian origin from others with a Württemberg background. Nevertheless, it seems likely by Generation 3 and more certain by Generation 4 that the awareness of such differences was no longer a limitation in selecting a marriage partner.[37]

---

37. One result of mixed cultures and languages in both families and villages was to produce special speech forms using elements of both dialects. See the commentary on language in Kulm in Wölfle, "The Establishment of the Village of Kulm," 5, where the author notes that in the twentieth century, "through the mixing of the different Platt [Prussian North German] and Swabish [Württemberger South German], a completely new colloquial language arose."

Therese Graumann and Emmanuel Burgemeister were married in Bow River, Alberta, Canada, and their marriage also illustrates a relevant theme in the pattern noted above for Generations 1 and 2: new environments favored marriage partners who had similar backgrounds. This was likely part of the reason behind the frequency in Generation 2 marriages between families who had emigrated from the similar areas in Prussia. It would also explain the frequency in Generation 4 and 5 marriages that occurred in North America for spouses to be selected from other Bessarabian German families or from German families from South Russia. Of the Generation 5 marriages that occurred in North America, over 50 percent were with members of other immigrant German families from Bessarabia and South Russia (see table 7–18).

Having the German language in common was clearly a very important factor in selecting a spouse in marriages that commenced not long after the arrival of Bessarabian Germans in North America. No one from Generation 4 and 5 who came to North America as a young adult or older teen married a non-German-speaking spouse. Indeed, this was probably the cultural expectation the Bessarabian Germans brought with them. For all five generations of Bessarabian Germans in Europe, no one married outside the German-speaking community. Yet in North America, this was not always the case. Those who did not marry German speakers, however, were always the children of the immigrants and typically were born in North America. The experience of Christian Haag and his descendants provides a good example. In the spring of 1878, Christian Haag, age twenty-two, came to South Dakota from Neu Posttal with his aunt and uncle, Andreas Schlenker and Anna Dorothea Schimke, and their children. It is quite likely that he helped them establish their farmstead in Hutchinson County. He is listed right after the Schlenkers in the 1880 census, but by then he may well have been an independent farmer. In late 1880 or early 1881, he married Lydia Isaak, who had come to Hutchinson County from Seimental, Bessarabia, with her family in May 1876.[38] It is doubtful they knew each other personally in Bessarabia, but

TABLE 7–18. **Generation 5, origins of spouses in North American marriages**

| Family origin of spouses | Number | Percent of total |
|---|---|---|
| Bessarabian Germans | 51 | 18.9% |
| Germans from South Russia | 89 | 33.0% |
| Germans from Volga and Russian Poland | 5 | 1.8% |
| Subtotal | 145 | 53.7% |
| Other Germans | 26 | 9.6% |
| Subtotal of German connections | 171 | 63.3% |
| Americans | 89 | 33.0% |
| Unknown | 10 | 3.7% |
| **Grand Total** | 270 | 100.0% |

38. Seimental, also known as Seimeny, was established in early 1860s by Germans on land leased from the Volkonski family. The Isaaks, one of the first families in Seimental, came there from Kulm. Lydia is listed in the Bessarabian parish records as born on August 14, 1863 (O.S.), in Sofienthal, Bessarabia (http://www.odessa3.org/collections/stpete/bess/link/bes186xb.txt). Flegel (*Extended Relationships*, 322) places her birth in 1867 using the ship's manifest from her arrival in New York, but the 1900 and 1910 US census listings establish that the parish record was correct.

they had several second and third cousins in common, as well as the comfort of a common language and the familiar habits and culture they each brought from Bessarabia. In their married life, the Haag family lived in Hutchinson County among many families who had come there from Bessarabia. There were, though, many other families, both recent immigrants and native-born Americans who were not German. Of the Haags' fifteen children, eleven married, and of that group, four married Bessarabian Germans or Germans from Russia, three married people with other German backgrounds, and four married Americans with no connection to German culture. Assimilation had begun.

The marriages of the Haags' children reflect the pattern shown in the data set for North American Generation 5 children in general. Table 7–18 above shows that over a third of the Generation 5 marriages in North America were to people whose surnames indicated something other than a German background. If one considers a subset of the Generation 5 North Americans, those who were born in North America, the figure rises to nearly 50 percent. The assimilation this figure suggests should not be surprising given both the intermixing of many cultural backgrounds in the farming villages in North America where the immigrating Bessarabian Germans settled, and the rapid and near-universal acquisition of the English language by those born in North America.

## Children and patterns of childbearing
### Numbers of children per family: Approximations of average family size
A common demographic feature among farming communities in Western Europe in the eighteenth and nineteenth centuries was for such communities to pass through three general stages with regard to the number of children born:[39]

- Peasant farming communities historically had high birth rates but also high death rates that together produced generally stable population numbers.

- In the late eighteenth and the first half of the nineteenth century, as medical knowledge, health habits, and diet improved, particularly high birth rates continued, but more people lived longer lives and populations grew.

- As parents came to feel that more of their children would survive, the number of children per family began to fall. This appears to have happened first in England in the 1870s but becomes a clear phenomenon in Western Europe from the late 1920s.

As shown in table 7–19, the experience of the Bessarabian German data set falls in line with the second and third stages: Families in the first three generations were large, averaging over six children in each generation, and the total population grew,

---

39. Tomas Frejka, "Parity Distribution and Completed Family Size in Europe: Incipient Decline of the Two-Child Family Model," *Demographic Research* 19, article 4 (2008): 47–72. Frejka's charts show distinct declines after 1930 in the number of women in Denmark, Norway, Sweden, France, England and Wales, the Netherlands, and Austria with three or more children (Panel D, 53). The decline begins ten to fifteen years earlier in Eastern Europe (Czech and Slovak republics, Slovenia, Poland, Lithuania, and Romania; Panel D, 59). Simon Szreter notes that in Great Britain, smaller family sizes began in the 1870s and even earlier among the professional middle class and some textile workers. Szreter, "Debating Mortality Trends in 19th-Century Britain," *International Journal of Epidemiology* 33, no. 4 (2004): 707.

TABLE 7–19. **Average number of children per family compared with childhood mortality rates**

|  | Gen 1 | Gen 2 | Gen 3 | Gen 4 | Gen 5 |
|---|---|---|---|---|---|
| Average children per family | 6.7 | 6.7 | 6.4 | 5.0 | 3.1 |
| Percent childhood mortality | 35.5%[a] | 46.2% | 45.9% | 27.1% | 7.95% |

a. As health-care conditions facing Generation 1 parents had not undergone material improvement from the past, it is likely that the childhood mortality figures for the children of Generation 1 parents were as high as those for Generation 2 and Generation 3. As a result, it is to be presumed that this fact is masked by the incomplete data available for the period before 1835.

but the average number of children per family dropped in Generations 4 and 5 in parallel with declines in childhood mortality.

The average family size (that is, children plus parents) for this data set of Bessarabian Germans ranged from nearly 9 persons in Generations 1 through 3 to 7 persons in Generation 4 and slightly over 5 in Generation 5. This is materially higher than the average family size figures available for nineteenth-century Western European populations, which ranged typically from 4.5 to 6 persons.[40] Studies of the nineteenth-century population in the United States drawn from census materials suggest families there were also larger than those in Western Europe. Michael Haines, in his study of fertility in the United States, indicates the average family size was just under 9 in 1820 and dropped to just over 7 in 1860 and then further to about 5.5 in 1900.[41] This is quite similar to the data set for the Bessarabian Germans, though the progression downward in family size appears to have occurred earlier in the United States. As with the figures on longer average life spans and earlier ages at first marriages, the similarity between nineteenth-century family sizes in the United States and among Bessarabian Germans is another suggestion of comparable conditions. For both groups, the population was dominated by farming families with adequate plots of land and healthy food supplies.

Declining childhood mortality was not the only arguable reason for decreasing family size. It is commonly observed from European and North American experience of the past three centuries that there is a clear relationship between economic level and smaller families. As family income and economic security rise, families tend to have fewer children. It is certainly possible that the rising prosperity among nineteenth-century Bessarabian Germans influenced family sizes. However, without economic data on specific families, such an influence can only be suggested. The opposite economic conditions may also have had similar influences on family size in the twentieth century: periods of economic difficulties seem to have led families to have fewer children. As a result of World War I and its difficult aftermath, German Bessarabia became far poorer as animal stock and savings were lost, and economic conditions were slow to improve as access to former markets had been denied. For Generation 4 and 5 couples living in Bessarabia who married between 1914 and 1930, the average number of children dropped to 2.3 children per family, well below the

---

40. For example, Coleman and Salt (*British Population*, 14), quoting three British sources, see households in Britain containing on average something close to 4.7 persons from the late sixteenth century to the early twentieth century. Silvia Sovič, writing of nineteenth-century peasant families in Slovenia, finds an average family size of 4.9 people. Sovič, "Families and Households of the Poor: The 19th-Century Slovenian Gostači," *History of the Family* 10, no. 2 (2005): 161.

41. Michael Haines, "Fertility and Mortality in the United States," *EH.Net Encyclopedia*, edited by Robert Whaples, Economic History Association. Article published March 19, 2008, http://eh.net/encyclopedia/fertility-and-mortality-in-the-united-states/.

numbers of North American couples of their generations. While not an indication of a clear connection, this lower figure for Germans in Bessarabia does at least suggest that the absence of men fighting in the war as well as the economic and political unrest may have had some impact on creating smaller families.[42]

### Childbearing practices: Average time after marriage to the birth of first child

Once they married, the general practice among Bessarabian Germans was not to delay long in starting a family. Data on the average spacing between the marriage date and the date of the first child's birth do show some differences among the five generations. There was a steady decrease in the number of months between marriage and first birth, as seen in table 7–20.

I have found no comments among the memoir pieces written by Bessarabian Germans that would offer any insight to this pattern. I do note that for the first generations, the average age for women at first marriage was below 20. For Generation 2, it was 18.5, and for Generation 3, it was 19.1. With numbers of women in those generations also marrying at the young ages of 16 and 17, it may be that couples, by themselves or following the advice of parents, decided to wait before starting a family.

Illegitimate births where the parents never subsequently married were quite rare in the Bessarabian German communities. I found only two instances among the 5,854 children born to the five generations in the data set. This contrasts sharply with Flinn's figures of 11.9 illegitimate births per 100 live births in Germany in the period from 1780 to 1920.[43] It also stands in clear contrast with the figures Mack Walker quotes in *German Home Towns* of 1 in 5 births in Bavaria and 1 in 10 births in the Bavarian Palatinate in the period from 1824 to 1833 being illegitimate.[44] Illegitimate births in Germany, as Hagen, Walker, and many other commentators suggest, were

TABLE 7–20. **Average time (in months) between marriage and first birth**

|  | Gen 1 | Gen 2 | Gen 3 | Gen 4 | Gen 5 | Total |
|---|---|---|---|---|---|---|
| Average months | 17.3 | 15.7 | 14.0 | 13.2 | 12.9 | 13.7 |
| Data points | 13 | 97 | 212 | 161 | 249 | 732 |

---

42. As the resettlement questionnaires form the major source of demographic information for this period, and as they do not cover the whole population of the resettling Bessarabian Germans, it is reasonable to presume that the figure of 2.3 as the average number of children for young families of Germans within this group could be an understatement. A primary focus of these questionnaires is clearly living family members who were part of the resettlement. Questions might also be raised about the data on Bessarabian Germans in North America where the US census records form the major data source. The census records are only snapshots taken at ten-year intervals. Children who were born and who died in the intervening years are not captured, as the records of families with genealogies do show. Here, too, a fair presumption is that some children among the North American families who were born and died between census years are missing. As a result, it would not be surprising for the true average family sizes of Generation 4 and 5 families to be slightly larger.

43. Flinn, *European Demographic System*, Table 6.1, 82. Germany, in Flinn's data, has the highest incidence of illegitimate births. Scandinavia is next at 6.8 illegitimate births per 100 live births, followed by Spain with 6.5, England with 5.9, and France with 4.7.

44. Mack Walker, *German Home Towns: Community, State, and General Estate, 1648–1871* (Ithaca, NY: Cornell University Press, 1971), 338. Walker's figures come from Ludwig Zimmermann in *Die Einheits- und Freiheitsbewegung und die Revolution von 1848* in Franken.

more common in situations where marriage was not possible either because the couple did not have the necessary money or property, or did not possess the citizenship rights required to marry.[45] Marriage was not possible in many other cases, such as when one parent (the father, typically) was already married. In Bessarabia and North America, unlike Prussia and Württemberg, property was plentiful, and so marriage was nearly universal. In addition, economically prosperous families had no need to send young women away to work in the households of others (a major factor in illegitimate births where the father was already married). I did find, however, eleven incidences where a baby was born generally two to four months before the couple married.[46] Perhaps as an indication of changing mores, all but one of these occurred in the early twentieth century among members of Generation 5.

Much less rare, though still not frequent, were premarital conceptions. There were forty-two incidences in the data set where a couple's first child was born less than eight months after their marriage. Examples of premarital conceptions occurred among all five generations in the data set, though the great majority were after 1870. Flinn's data for Germany in the period from 1780 to 1820 indicate 23.8 premarital conceptions per 100 first births. As a rough comparison, there were 28 premarital conceptions among the 493 first births in Generation 5. This creates a ratio of 5.7 per 100 first births—far below Flinn's figures for Germany and other countries of a century earlier.[47]

## Childbearing practices: Mother's age at the time of the birth of her first child

The figures for a mother's average age at the birth of her first child remain relatively constant across all five generations. With the exception of Generation 1, it rises slightly from age twenty to a little over age twenty-two (see table 7–21).

The slight rise in the figures for the average age at first birth for women of Generations 4 and 5 is reflective of the similar rise in the average age at which they married: from 19.1 years in Generation 3 to 20.8 for Generation 4 and then to 22.0 for Generation 5. The young average age at the birth of the first child across all

TABLE 7–21. **Mother's average age at first birth**

|  | Gen 1 | Gen 2 | Gen 3 | Gen 4 | Gen 5 | Total |
|---|---|---|---|---|---|---|
| Average age | 21.8 | 20.0 | 20.1 | 21.9 | 22.6 | 21.5 |
| Data points | 32 | 97 | 219 | 251 | 347 | 732 |

---

45. The possession of land (leased land in Germany) was critical for peasant farmers to marry. Citizenship was a critical element for those living in midsized towns that were predominant in Württemberg, as resident noncitizens, such as journeymen, were forbidden rights to marry. As Walker's data indicates, only journeymen whose work passed the standards necessary for them to become masters would be allowed to acquire citizenship and with that, the right to marry. As such towns held themselves responsible for supporting the impoverished only when such poor were town citizens, town boards were very careful to judge the economic viability of candidates for citizenship. This, together with the desires of town boards to limit competition and to maintain income for existing trades, made acquiring rights of citizenship difficult but also increased the frequency of nonmarital relationships (*German Home Towns*, 330, 338).

46. Anna Buchholz, who was born in Paris, Bessarabia, in 1922 seven and a half years before her parents' marriage, represents far and away the most delayed settlement within this data set.

47. Flinn, *European Demographic System*, Table 6.2. Flinn's figures for other countries are 34.5 premarital conceptions per 100 first births in England and 13.7 in France.

generations clearly points to the large family sizes among the German Bessarabians discussed earlier.

### Childbearing practices: Average spacing between children

The average spacing between children fluctuated between 2 to 2.5 years (26 to 31 months), as shown in table 7–22.

It is tempting with the figures for Generation 1 to assume that the spacing was comparatively longer as a reflection of the difficulties in establishing the new colonies. Yet because records for this generation are far from complete for both couples who had children before coming to Bessarabia, and for couples with children born in Bessarabia, the higher average spacing for Generation 1 may just reflect the limitations of the data.[48]

The data on spacing are strongest for Generations 2 and 3, where the most common pattern was for new pregnancies to commence regularly between sixteen and twenty months following the birth of a child, with longer periods typically occurring only for the last several children. When a child died at birth or soon thereafter, however, a new pregnancy was almost immediately begun. As a result, it might be assumed that the high childhood mortality figures for Generations 2 and 3 brought down the average spacing pattern in these generations (i.e., that the early commencements decreased the average). Yet for families with no early deaths or just a single one, such as Gottlieb Schütz and Sophie Lobe of Generation 3 or Johann Kuhn and Henrietta Raugust of Generation 2, the spacing pattern in each closely mirrors the generational averages.[49]

The average spacing between children for Generation 4 (twenty-nine months) is materially longer than the averages of the prior two generations (twenty-six months). The data points behind the Generation 4 figures (117) are large enough to give credibility for the average and so raise interest in potential causes, but in the absence of commentary from families of this generation, causes remain speculative. Given the time frame in which this generation typically started families (1890–1915), it is tempting to see the longer spacing as recognition of the fact that more children were surviving to adulthood, or perhaps that longer spacing tended to result in healthier babies and mothers. The figures from Generation 5 show a similar trend to longer average spacing periods between children. As these data come chiefly from families in Bessarabia and Dobrudscha and are based on spacing information from almost

TABLE 7–22. **Average spacing (in months) between births**

|  | Gen 1 | Gen 2 | Gen 3 | Gen 4 | Gen 5 | Total |
|---|---|---|---|---|---|---|
| Average spacing (in mos.) | 31.0 | 26.0 | 26.0 | 29.0 | 28.5 | 27.9 |
| Data points | 28 | 82 | 172 | 117 | 88 | 487 |

48. As such limitations are typically the result of missing data on children who did not survive, this conclusion would be supported by the comparatively low childhood mortality figures for Generation 1 families: 35.5 percent vs. 46.2 percent for Generation 2 and 45.9 percent for Generation 3 and similar high figures from the contemporary Stavenow population in Brandenburg.

49. The Schütz family, who had no children die, had an average spacing of 25.9 months; the Kuhn family, with one child dying within a month of birth and the next child born 15 months later, averaged 28.1 months. With both families, the longest spacing (37 and 33 months, respectively) was with the last children.

90 percent of the families there with at least four children (the minimum figure used in collecting spacing data), it has credibility. Again, causes are speculative, but as the data especially show long gaps appearing during the war years and through the 1920s, the absence of men serving in the Russian army, the economic difficulties created by the war, and Bessarabia's absorption into Romania would seem likely factors.

Finally, it is important to see that data from several of the categories discussed above appear to move in tandem (see table 7–23). Together, they suggest that changes in the living conditions of the Bessarabian Germans created changes in cultural habits.

The later average ages at marriage and the longer average life spans move in tandem with decreases in childhood mortality, decreases in the average numbers of children, and increases in the average spacing between children. With more children surviving, families seem to have drawn the rational conclusion that they would economically benefit from having fewer children. A second hypothesis frequently made is to presume that the realization that more and more children would survive to lead long lives gave heightened value to individual lives. Parents saw greater benefits in making investments of time and energy in fewer children, and so spacing between children increased. The greater likelihood of becoming an adult and living a long life became one source of encouragement for young men and women not to hurry into marriage. While married couples presumably observed, thought about, and discussed these demographic changes, their observations and conclusions were deemed too personal to put into any public record. The changes must then speak for themselves.

### Childbearing practices: Names given to children

The data set for the five generations of Bessarabian Germans shows constant change in the preferences families had for the first names selected for their children. The names they selected suggest both the increasing impact of outside cultural influences and the wide variety of those cultural influences. Thus, the naming patterns of the Bessarabian Germans undercut arguments that these Germans lived long in isolated islands dominated mainly by the eighteenth-century German culture they brought with them to Russia.

TABLE 7–23. **Common threads in the data on ages and children**

|  | Gen 1 | Gen 2 | Gen 3 | Gen 4 | Gen 5 |
|---|---|---|---|---|---|
| **Average age at marriage** | | | | | |
| Males | 23.8 | 22.6 | 22.2 | 23.9 | 25.0 |
| Females | 19.7 | 18.5 | 19.1 | 20.8 | 22.0 |
| **Average life span for those surviving childhood** | | | | | |
| Males | 68.4 | 54.7 | 61.7 | 63.9 | 68.3 |
| Females | 57.4 | 49.8 | 56.7 | 64.8 | 70.9 |
| Average children per family | 6.7 | 6.7 | 6.4 | 5.0 | 3.1 |
| Average spacing (in months) between pregnancies | 31.0 | 26.0 | 26.0 | 29.0 | 28.5 |
| Average childhood mortality | | 35.5% | 46.2% | 45.9% | 27.1% |

Prominent features of the patterns in these five generations for the first names of both boys and girls are a broadening usage in the number of names, the sources of influence for those names, and a continuing shift in particular favorites. Initially, name usage was limited. Calculated by counting each time a name is used, the ten most popular first names for boys and girls dominated usage through Generation 3. They formed over 70 percent of the total names in use for Generations 1 and 2 and nearly 60 percent for Generation 3. In the following two generations, the usage of different names broadened radically. The popularity of the top ten names fell to less than 40 percent of the names given to children by Generation 4 parents, and then to just a quarter of the names given by Generation 5 parents. Among the favorite names given by Generation 4 parents, three of the boy names and five of the girl names hadn't appeared in the top ten listing before. By Generation 5, not one of the top ten names for both boys and girls had been in that group in Generations 1 through 3 (see tables 7–24a and 7–24b).

In parallel with the decreasing dominance of the top ten names, the total number of different names used in this data set grew substantially. The different names used by Generation 3 parents are more than double those used in Generation 1, and from Generation 3 to Generation 4, the number of names doubled again. Over the whole period from Generation 1 to Generation 5, the total number of different names increased by a factor of nearly seven for both genders.

In Generations 1 and 2, parents gave clear preferences for names that had biblical or religious origins—such as Johann, Maria, Daniel, Gottlieb, Christian, and Christina—or names such as Friedrich, Wilhelm (Wilhelmina), and Louisa that, because of their associations with the Prussian and Württemberg royal families, came into popular use by other classes from those territories. With extremely limited data available for generations prior to Generation 1, it is not possible to speak to the continuance of family traditions. However, it is clear that family traditions existed as there was an early preference shown for names that were handed down from generation to generation within different families. For example, among the grandchildren of Jacob and Christina Raugust, there were three girls named Christina and four boys named Jacob.

Names used by Generation 3 parents, however, start to indicate that broad and sweeping cultural changes were at work, even though these new names did not make the top ten lists.[50] Many names indicate the influence of names used by the German royals and nobility, such as Rudolf, Albert, Alfred, Eduard, Ferdinand, Elizabetha, Katharina, and Theresa. Other names had origins in German heroic tales and folklore, such as Reinhold, Otto, Bertha, and Hulda. Some names, such as Alexander, Olga, and Sophie, would appear to have been borrowed from usage among the Russian tsars and their families. Some part of the popularity of the names Maria and Sophie may be related to the influence of the Dowager Tsarina Maria Fëdorovna, the second wife of Tsar Paul I, who was born the Duchess Sophie Marie, a daughter of Friedrich II Eugen, Duke of Württemberg.

Names underwent significant changes in popularity over the five generations. Johann, Daniel, and Christian, for example, which were extremely popular through

---

50. The generational references in this section are to the habits of the parents belonging to that generation in giving names to children. In speaking about Generation 3 names, for example, the names are those given by Generation 3 parents to their children who were Generation 4 individuals.

**TABLE 7–24A. Top ten boy names for Generations 1 through 5**

|  | Gen 1 | Gen 2 | Gen 3 | Gen 4 | Gen 5 |
|---|---|---|---|---|---|
| First | Johann | Daniel | Johann | Johann | Emil, Erwin |
| Second | Gottlieb | Johann | Daniel | Emil |  |
| Third | Christian | Gottlieb | Christian | Friedrich | Artur |
| Fourth | Karl | Christian | Friedrich | Daniel | Ernest, Oscar |
| Fifth | Michael | August | Gottfried | Artur |  |
| Sixth | August | Martin | Gottlieb, Jacob | Wilhelm | Albert |
| Seventh | Daniel, Martin, Samuel, Wilhelm | Wilhelm |  | Christian | Arnold, Herbert |
| Eighth |  | Friedrich | David | Gottfried, Oscar |  |
| Ninth |  | Gottfried | Wilhelm |  | Otto |
| Tenth |  | Karl | Gotthilf, Gustav | Gotthilf | Gerhardt, Robert |
| **Percent of total** | 85.4% | 71.2% | 55.3% | 36.5% | 24.8% |
| Different names | 25 | 32 | 62 | 121 | 171 |

**TABLE 7–24B. Top ten girl names for Generations 1 through 5**

|  | Gen 1 | Gen 2 | Gen 3 | Gen 4 | Gen 5 |
|---|---|---|---|---|---|
| First | Wilhelmine | Wilhelmine | Maria | Emma | Elsa |
| Second | Karolina | Louise | Louise | Bertha | Ella |
| Third | Justina | Justina | Christina, Lydia | Maria | Alma |
| Fourth | Louise | Karolina |  | Lydia | Erna |
| Fifth | Christina | Christina | Justina, Karolina | Emilie, Ida | Lilli |
| Sixth | Anna | Julianne |  |  | Hilda |
| Seventh | Maria | Maria | Sophie, Wilhelmine | Elsa | Gertrude |
| Eighth | Anna Rosina | Rosine |  | Anna | Ida |
| Ninth | Eva | Susanne | Emilie | Pauline | Frieda |
| Tenth | Julianne | Dorothea, Friederika | Mathilde | Esther, Frieda, Hilda, Magdalene | Irma |
| **Percent of total** | 78.9% | 78.0% | 59.1% | 38.0% | 28.9% |
| Different names | 28 | 38 | 64 | 145 | 191 |

Generation 4, were not even in the top twenty names in Generation 5 usage. Gottlieb, the second most popular name in Generation 1 and third most popular in Generation 2, dropped to twenty-eighth place by Generation 4 and was tied with Christian at sixty-first place in Generation 5. Similar changes in popularity occurred among the names for girls. Wilhelmine, Karoline, and Louise, which were among the most commonly used names in the first three generations, dropped to no higher than twenty-first (Karoline) in Generation 4 and no higher than fifty-first

(Wilhelmine and Louise) in Generation 5. Justine, which was third in the first two generations and fifth in Generation 3, dropped to fifty-first in Generation 4 and wasn't used at all among the 650 girls born to Generation 5 parents. Maria alone continued to maintain popularity throughout the data set. It was in the top ten names through Generation 4 and dropped only to the twelfth position in Generation 5 (see table 7–25).

The striking use of new names that began with Generation 3 is more marked among the names for girls than the names for boys. Several of the names just under the top ten girl names in Generation 3 became highly used in following generations, while similarly situated boy names reflected older fashions and were less used in later generations. The next twenty most popular names for girls in Generation 3 included names such as Emma, Bertha, Pauline, Salome, Sarah, and Ida, which all received more frequent use in later generations. Emma, which was fifteenth in popularity in Generation 3, moved to first place in Generation 4 and third place in Generation 5. Bertha moved from nineteenth place in Generation 2 to second place in the following generation, and Ida moved from twenty-ninth place in Generation 3 to fifth place in Generation 4. With boy names such as Emil, Artur, Oscar, and Otto, there were similar leaps from the lower ranks of Generation 3 to top ten positions in later generations, but these names came from further back in the Generation 3 listings (see table 7–25). The group from eleventh to thirtieth among Generation 3 boy names was filled with names like Nathanael, August, Samuel, Michael, and Emmanuel, which were all frequently used in the first generations but far less frequently used in later ones.

Another way to illustrate the more conservative pace of change in boy names is to note that 45 percent of the top ten names for boys used by Generation 4 parents had never been among the top ten in prior generations, while 60 percent of the top ten names for girls used by Generation 4 parents had never before been among the top ten.

The new names that start to appear in use among the Bessarabian Germans suggest that their isolation and insularity, so notable when they first settled in Russia, was passing. The changing fashions in name use suggest influences from other areas of German culture and other German-speaking populations. The name usage among Bessarabian Germans suggests strong influences from folklore, light romantic and heroic literature, and positive newspaper accounts of people from the lower and middle classes. Thus, in Generations 4 and 5, names such as Egon, Erich, Ewald, Horst, Norbert, Siegfried, Walter, and Werner started to appear with regularity, as did the girl names Alwine, Erica, Gretchen, Helga, Hildegard, Ingrid, Irmgard, and Waltraut.

Borrowings of Russian names started to appear in usage in Generation 3 among the Germans in Bessarabia, and these increased just slightly in Generations 4 and 5.

TABLE 7–25. **Changes in rank of boy names**

|  | Gen 3 rank | Gen 4 rank | Gen 5 rank |
|---|---|---|---|
| Nathanael | 12th | 13th | 35th |
| August | 12th | 34th | 50th |
| Emmanuel | 15th | Not used | 61st |
| Michael | 16th | 54th | 61st |

Names such as Olga, Liudmila, and Irina for girls show clear Russian roots, as do the names Ivan, Viktor, and Woldemar for boys. In contrast to the limited influence of Russian names among the Bessarabian Germans who remained in Europe, there was a strong presence of English first names used by Bessarabian Germans who immigrated to North America (see table 7–26). Though no English name achieved close to top-ten prominence in the listings, many were used at least four times in either of Generations 4 or 5: Clarence, Donald, Harold, Harry, Harvey, James, Melvin, Raymond, and Wilber for boys and Alice, Annette, Bernice, Doris, Evelyn, Gladys, Joyce, Linda, Lorraine, Melitta, Mildred, and Violet for girls. When considered as a portion of the total names used in a generation, Russian names formed no more than 2.5 percent of the names used in any generation, while English names grew in Generation 5 to between one-fifth and one-quarter of the total.

A reasonably typical picture of usage can be seen in the family of Generation 3 members Andreas Schlenker and Anna Dorothea Schimke. Settling in Hutchinson County, South Dakota, in 1878, they were among the early arrivals in the United States from Bessarabia. The Schlenkers brought five children with them to the United States, and four others were born after their settlement in South Dakota. For their children born in the United States, the Schlenkers continued to use popular but traditional German names: Johann, Elisabeth, Dorothea, and Helena. Their children, part of Generation 4, made different adaptations to culture in the United States. For example, Elisabeth Schlenker married Andreas Schaal, whose family had come to Hutchinson County from Teplitz, Bessarabia.[51] All eight of their children were given names that continued German traditions: Rudolph, Pauline, Agnes, Gertrude, Helen, Otto, Rose, and Gerhardt. Elisabeth's sister, Dorothy, married Emil Fuerst, whose family, like the Schaals, had come to South Dakota from Teplitz. Emil and Dorothy Fuerst's three children were given names that, by contrast, had more of an English flavor: Arthur, Lora, and Clinton.[52] In the following generation, naming patterns gave preference to English names. The grandchildren of Andreas and Anna Dorothea Schlenker—part of Generation 5 and all born in South Dakota—favored English names over German: 56.8 percent of the names given to their children were English.

Finally, there is one more influence to consider that likely played a part in the significant broadening in the choice of names that occurred from Generation 3 onward. Generation 3 was the first generation born in Bessarabia where the majority moved away from the village in which they were born. This fact was even more typical for the two succeeding generations, as can be seen in table 7–27.

TABLE 7–26. **Prevalence of Russian and English names among Bessarabian Germans**

|  | Generation 4 | | Generation 5 | |
| --- | --- | --- | --- | --- |
|  | Boys | Girls | Boys | Girls |
| Russian | 1.4% | 2.3% | 2.3% | 1.7% |
| English | 6.7% | 9.1% | 20.7% | 27.1% |

51. All eight surviving children were married to spouses who were born or whose parents were born in German Bessarabia.

52. This example is meant to show only that different immigrant siblings married into families with similar Bessarabian German backgrounds might choose differently in the naming of their children. Of the forty-five Schlenker grandchildren, most (82 percent) were given names with a clear German heritage.

TABLE 7–27. **Percentage of a generation that moved from their birthplace**

| Generation 3 | Generation 4 | Generation 5 |
|---|---|---|
| 68.8% | 70.4% | 90.0% |

As later chapters will discuss in more detail, couples in these generations were more likely to move away from their parents and to establish farmsteads on their own. Whether such movement occurred within Bessarabia, Russia, Dobrudscha, or North America, one important effect of this population movement was to establish a preponderance of nuclear families in Generations 4 and 5 who lived independently, sometimes near their parents but often far away. Such independence tended to decrease parental influence and to increase a couple's personal freedoms and so encouraged the growth of individually determined preferences. This movement from Generation 3 onward to establish farmsteads in new places also increased the mixing of traditions. In Bessarabia, Dobrudscha, and Russia, Generation 4 and 5 individuals were more likely to select a marriage partner from another strain of German culture than their own. In North America, as indicated in table 7–18 above, a similar mixing occurred with the additional twist that 10 percent married Germans, Austrians, and Alsatians who had come to North America directly from Western Europe, and 33 percent married spouses who had backgrounds other than German. The combination, then, of couples sharing different traditions and having increased freedom to determine their own choices would seem fertile ground to explain the reasons couples chose to look elsewhere than past family customs in choosing names for their children.

Plowing on the open Bessarabian steppe

Harvesting grain with a reaper

**A lunch during harvest time**

**Horses at work threshing**

**Threshing**

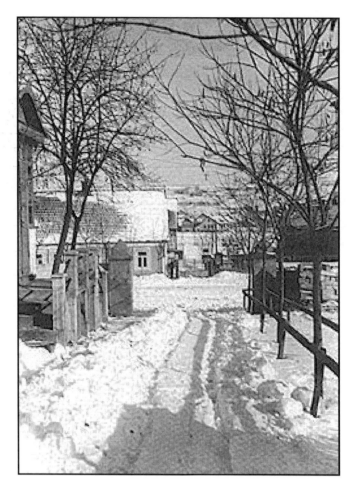

Tarutino in winter

A view of Katzbach

A view of Leipzig from the church tower

View of Leipzig and its church completed in 1908

Lichtental church of 1902

**Wittenberg church of 1869**

The weekly market in Tarutino

Teplitz wagon builders at the weekly market in Arzis

A mother and her daughters at house work

A woman at work in Beresina

The Gnadental teacher, Otto Schaupp, with his class

Sarata cooperative store circa 1923

The resettlement trek

The resettlement trek

# VIII

# The German Colonies Expand in Bessarabia and Russia Starts to View Them Differently: 1860–70

By 1860, the German colonies in Bessarabia had grown into well-settled, prosperous communities. The second and third generations now managed the farmsteads in these villages, typically by splitting the work between the families of at least two siblings. The added adult labor increased productivity and permitted families to achieve more from their 60 desjatina plots. The economic gains had been founded on the profitable sales of animals, grain, and fruit within the province or to exporters for markets outside Bessarabia. The Germans had also established a profitable wine trade and sales of small manufactured goods such as wagons and ax handles mainly within the province. In the period from 1830 to 1870, the port of Odessa built up a flourishing grain trade with urban Western Europe.[1] Significant urban growth, especially in Great Britain, France, the Netherlands, and Belgium, spurred demand. Odessa's easy access to the grain-producing regions of South Russia and Bessarabia, its good harbor, and its status as a free port helped it in responding to this demand. Though by the 1860s it was still rare for Bessarabian Germans to take their wheat to Odessa so as to take advantage of the higher prices which were available there, the growing demand for wheat for export kept prices rising even for sales to the

---

1. The last wish of Père Goriot, the hero of Balzac's 1835 novel of the same name, was to go to Odessa and remake his fortune in the grain trade.

itinerant čumaki traders. The Crimean War (1853–56) had interrupted the trade with Western Europe and slowed economic growth in Bessarabia, but export demand restarted at an even higher level following the war's settlement at the Congress of Paris. The war also brought beneficial infrastructure improvements for citizens of South Russia and Bessarabia. The Russian government improved river transportation north into central Russia and by 1866, had completed railroad links between Odessa and the cities of Kiev and Xar'kov (Ukrainian Kiiv and Xarkiv). Markets for grain (and especially animals and fruit) from the south were now created in central Ukraine, which increased the demand in Bessarabia for the sales of surplus produce and animals. The Bessarabian Germans, with hard work and prudent farm management, were producing surplus well beyond family needs. By the sale of such surplus, the Germans created capital holdings that financed not only improvements to farms and households, but also civic building projects within their villages. When their settlements became more crowded, such capital financed the purchase or leasing of land to create new villages and new opportunities.

The German colonies in Bessarabia were helped in the accumulation of capital by the fact that their citizens owned the land they farmed and that the tax obligations these citizens bore were relatively light. These factors created significant contrasts to the earlier experiences of the colonists in Prussia and Württemberg. By the 1850s, the German colonies had paid off the amortized debt that the Russian government charged them to recover the costs of bringing them to and establishing them in Bessarabia. Thereafter, the colonies were only assessed annual taxes. In comparison, the peasants in the Stavenow villages of Brandenburg appear to have used nearly half of their harvest of rye, their main grain crop, to pay royal taxes and seigneurial duties for the leasing of land the farmed.[2] We have one look at the taxes owed by the Bessarabian Germans thanks to commentary in the 1848 Wittenberg Village History, expressed in table 8–1.

The village history also notes that there were seventy-seven families in Wittenberg, which would make the per-family average annual tax liability 24.21 rubles. The family

TABLE 8–1.   **The annual tax obligation owed by the colony of Wittenberg**[a]

| Tax type | Amount |
| --- | --- |
| Colony authority (Welfare Committee) | 58.17 rubles |
| State police | 18.63 rubles |
| Land and postal fees | 56.58 rubles |
| Local tax | 661.02 rubles |
| Provincial tax | 1,069.79 rubles |
| **Total** | 1,864.19 rubles |

a.  Kurz, "Wittenberg – 1848 Village History."

2.  Hagen, *Ordinary Prussians*, 208–12. In Prussia, peasants paid taxes in cash to the state; the land tax, called the "Kontribution," was paid monthly and the smaller troop quarter and hearth taxes were paid annually. Peasants also made cash payments as part of their rent for the holdings they leased from noble estate owners. Hagen calculated that "the royal and seigneurial exactions cost the typical 18th century full holder about 27 bushels of rye yearly" (211). At the same time, Hagen calculated that family consumption needs for an average household of "four adults (including servants), one retiree and two children" as 33 bushels. The Kontribution alone was supposed to be equal to the value of the seed planted, which with yields of 3.5 times would be a significant debt, though the peasants worked hard to lower that by fudging the calculation.

count here appears to be the number of active farmsteads rather than the number of married couples with children, so the tax liability would be that of a farmstead, which typically supported extended families of several working couples.[3] A tax liability of 24.21 rubles per farmstead is reasonably similar to the average per-family tax liability of 15.83 rubles indicated for the colonies in the Malojaroslavec District, of which Wittenberg was a part, in the 1841 Welfare Committee economic data survey. The Klöstitz District had a similar average per-family tax liability of 15.33 rubles.[4] The 1841 data indicate as well that the Malojaroslavec District's results from the sale of grain, animals, and other products produced average earnings of 61.89 rubles per family. As a result, the per-family average tax liability came to 25 percent of cash earnings. The results from the Klöstitz District were significantly poorer at 19.72 rubles of earnings per family but as they included no figures from the sale of grain, this appears to understate family earnings. Perhaps the best signs that by the 1850s, post-tax retained family earnings in the Bessarabian German villages were healthy are the number of civic buildings, churches, and schools that were built at community cost. In the 1850s, Alt Arzis remodeled its school. Beresina built a school, as did Hoffnungstal, Katzbach, Lichtental, and Borodino. Brienne and Neu Elft built churches in this period. In the 1860s, Alt Posttal, Borodino, and Leipzig built new schools, and Kulm and Teplitz built large new churches.

One important cause of the growing prosperity of the German settlements in Bessarabia was the fact that their farmsteads were being worked by several families of adults. At 60 desjatina, the farmsteads were too large before the advent of mechanized aides for a single couple to maximize their potential. From at least the 1830s forward, most farmsteads were worked by at least two married couples, at first parents and children but then increasingly by married siblings. However, as more of the second generation grew old enough to marry, the benefits of having several married couples living and working together decreased as the farmsteads became more crowded. This situation worsened in the late 1850s and early 1860s as members of the third generation also started to marry. This is evidenced by the example cited in the previous chapter of the Jacob Raugust farmstead in Kulm. In the early 1860s, this farmstead was being operated by the families of three of his sons and two of his married grandsons. By 1865, this farmstead was a crowded home to thirteen adults and twenty-one children. While this was perhaps an extreme example of overcrowding, the general situation it describes was not at all atypical.

## In the 1860s, landless German peasants were perceived to be a significant problem in the German colonies in South Russia but appear to have been much less of an issue in German Bessarabia

The German colonists in South Russia had been allowed, unlike those in Bessarabia, to subdivide their allotments as inheritances. Over time such subdivisions created

---

3. The figure of seventy-seven families in the 1848 history is close to the figure of eighty-two families listed for Wittenberg in the 1825–26 Welfare Committee economic survey.

4. The 1848 Sarata Village History notes that in Sarata every farmstead paid a flat tax of 14 rubles. The remaining tax obligation was then apportioned among the farmsteads according to the number of cattle each had. Cattle were the prime engine of the Sarata economy at this time (Natterer, "Sarata – 1848 Village History"). In contrast, the 1841 survey indicates a tax liability of only 8.12 rubles per family for the three colonies in the Sarata District.

238 GERMANS FROM RUSSIA

smaller farmsteads and ultimately ones insufficient to meet a family's needs. The subdivision of land in inheritance had been a common and expected practice among the Mennonites and the Germans coming from Württemberg.[5] As early as 1814, Russian administrators had noticed and become concerned about the consequences of the subdivision of land in the German colonies in South Russia. As a result, the rules governing the Bessarabian settlements prevented subdivision. Perhaps there had been hopes that the Russian government would continue to find places in Bessarabia to establish new German villages and this would relieve crowding in South Russia. Dennewitz, founded in 1834 and settled by colonists from other Bessarabian villages, may have sponsored such hopes. Crown land in Bessarabia was not to be a solution for the crowded conditions in South Russia, at least in any large measure. Only Hoffnungstal, founded in 1842 in Bessarabia, was settled with Germans from the overcrowded colonies in the neighboring Xerson (Odessa) province. Hoffnungstal, though, marked the end of the Russian government's efforts to create new German settlements in Bessarabia.

Overcrowding in German colonies in South Russia had produced an increasing number of families who were landless and lived by craftwork or working in commerce or, more negatively, were reduced to working as hired help on the farms of other Germans. This latter group tended to be poor and worries about their condition increasingly occupied the attention of the Welfare Committee. The 1841 economic survey counts both landed and landless families and indicates the landless were particularly prominent among the Mennonite colonies but were present in all the German colonies in the Tauride, Ekaterinoslav, and Odessa provinces (see table 8–2).[6]

TABLE 8–2. **1841 landless population in South Russia**

|  | Percent of total families per district |
|---|---|
| **Tauride** | |
| Moločna Mennonites | 56.7% |
| Moločna colonists | 19.6% |
| Berdjansk colonists | 8.9% |
| **Ekaterinoslav** | |
| Xortica Mennonites | 44.9% |
| Josefstal colonists | 32.4% |
| Mariupol' colonists | 11.8% |
| **Odessa** | |
| Liebental | 35.0% |
| Kučurgan | 15.8% |
| Berezan | 25.6% |
| Glückstal | 17.7% |

5. The subdivision of tenures could only have been an aspiration for Germans holding land tenures in Prussia. There, landlords wished to pass on tenures intact to a family who looked able enough to pay the leasing costs and state taxes. As a result, though tenure holders sought keep land rights within their families, the achievable goal was to pass their tenure on to one able child.

6. Klaus, *Naši kolonii*, Appendix II.

In the 1841 survey, there were virtually no landless families reported among the Bessarabian German colonies.[7] The only ones counted were in the three Sarata settlements, which reported 15 landless families among the 225 total families listed in that district. While landless, such families were most likely not impoverished but rather families who were living from the earnings of their craftwork, as were the great majority of the 1858 landless group in Sarata discussed below.[8]

By the 1860s, the difficulties of the poor landless families in the German colonies in Russia had reached major proportions. An article in the German-language *Odessaer Zeitung* in April 1863 complains that the Welfare Committee seemed focused only on the fullholders of the landowning class. The article is sharply critical of the Welfare Committee, whom it charges with neglecting families with smaller holdings or no land, which the article estimates to be two-thirds of the German population.[9] The major theme of Malinovskij's study of the German colonies in the period after 1860 is the growth in number of the landless poor and the increasingly sharp disparity in income and prospects between the landless and landed. Whether or not it was in response to urging from outside sources such as the Odessa newspaper, the Welfare Committee, as Brandes has reported, became increasingly focused later in the 1860s on landless Germans and potential solutions to their plight.[10] Indeed, the first efforts of the central government in St. Petersburg to consider how the major reforms approved in the 1860s by Tsar Alexander II might be applied to the German colonies in Russia began with using the Welfare Committee to conduct a study of the landless poor within the German colonies.

The creation of a growing class of landless poor with its attendant social issues, however important in the study of the South Russian German colonies, does not appear to have been a major story in German Bessarabia. In their separate treatments of landless poverty, Klaus, Malinovskij, Brandes, and Fleischhauer each focus on the large number of the poor in the Moločna Mennonite colonies and the great conflicts that developed between their interests and those of the well-to-do farmers. In German Bessarabia, as will be discussed in detail in following chapters, the pressure of continuing significant population growth was released by the financial ability of families to find additional land elsewhere in Bessarabia, greater Russia, and abroad, and by families, particularly in the larger villages, finding ways to support themselves sufficiently even when they only had small plots or no land at all. For the latter families, this was possible because they found sufficient livelihood in craftwork, or commercial or industrial occupations. Brandes supplies data from the village of Sarata in 1858 supporting the idea that landless were generally employed in craftwork and were not poor. Sarata then had a population of 867, of which 130

---

7.  In 1841, there were also no landless reported among the Bulgarian colonies in Bessarabia.
8.  Kern offers another perspective about who at least some of these landless were. In his discussion of Gnadental, one of the three settlements in the Sarata District, he notes that once the allotted eighty farms of 60 desjatina were taken up, eight "landless families remained, finding work and room and board with established farmers" (*Homeland Book,* 107). This suggests a group of landless farm laborers, much as we have seen in Leipzig. However, as these eight families were new but apparently late arrivals from Württemberg, who had, like earlier arrivals, brought some capital with them, we cannot presume either their poverty or their long-term continuance as farm laborers for others.
9.  Malinovskij, *Social'naja i xozjajstvennaja istorija,* 123. Unless focused on the Moločna Mennonites, the newspaper's estimate of two-thirds of the German population as either landless or smallholders would, if true, represent a revolutionary change from the data reported in the 1841 survey.
10. Brandes, *Von den Zaren Adoptiert,* 340–43.

(15 percent) were landless. Of the group of landless, 114 (88 percent) were willingly (*freiwillig*) employed either in handwork or commerce.[11] The 1858 Leipzig census materials discussed in chapter V support the view that there were then few landless and that by no means were all of the landless poor. Out of a total 219 families, the census counts 14 households of renters and 5 others that owned a homesite but seem to have no rights to land. Of these 19 households, 6 are listed as shoemakers, masons, a wheelwright, and a cabinetmaker and so seem analogous to the Sarata landless: not necessarily poor, just not working the land to earn a living. The remaining 13 Leipzig cottagers, though, did fall at the lowest economic layer of the village, hiring themselves out as farm laborers. One was a drayman, another a field and fruit worker, another a thresher, and several are simply described as day laborers. Four of the renters, though described as laborers, are also noted as earning 30 rubles a year, the amount paid the village secretary. It seems fair to conclude that the Leipzig numbers indicate, at least for that village, that the truly poor, the landless farm laborers and cottagers with small plots, formed a small proportion of the total village population.

It is very surprising, therefore, to see other statistics from 1857 from a different Welfare Committee count that indicate a comparatively large population of landless among the German villages in Bessarabia. The landless in Bessarabia, indeed, appear in far higher numbers than in other areas of German settlement in South Russia. Such a view comes from data Brandes found that compare the landless populations in the different German districts in Bessarabia for 1841 and 1857 (see table 8–3).[12]

The numbers of landless reported here for 1841 do not match the numbers of landless reported in the Welfare Committee 1841 survey noted above. The 1841 survey did report 15 landless in the Sarata District, but it reported none in the Klöstitz and Malojaroslavec districts. The origin of these new 1841 figures is therefore uncertain.[13] At the same time, it is difficult to tie in the landless numbers reported here for 1857 with data from other sources. The figure of 163 landless families in the Sarata District in Bessarabia, for example, is 25 percent higher than the count of 130 made just a year later and cited in another document that Brandes quotes (mentioned above). The 1857 average per village figure of 132.5 landless for the Malojaroslavec District

TABLE 8–3. **Comparison of landless in the Bessarabian districts**

|  | Klöstitz | Malojaroslavec | Sarata | Schabo |
|---|---|---|---|---|
| Colonies in 1841 | 9 | 10 | 3 | 1 |
| Farms | 927 | 78 | 181 | 39 |
| Landless | 151 | 170 | 15 | — |
| Colonies in 1857 | 10 | 10 | 3 | 1 |
| Farms | 999 | 879 | 261 | 65 |
| Landless | 1,180 | 1,325 | 163 | 12 |

11. Ibid., 338. Brandes connects the landless in Bessarabia at this time to the development of trade work and commerce rather than to a growing class of poor.
12. Ibid., 336–37.
13. The 1841 Welfare Committee survey information contained in the appendix of the Klaus study (*Naši kolonii*, discussed in detail in chapter V) counts 957 families in the Malojaroslavec District and 1,111 in Klöstitz, whereas the figures Brandes quotes for 1841 are 954 families in the Malojaroslavec District and 1,078 in the Klöstitz District. This would suggest that the compiler of the data Brandes quotes is working from a different source.

is seven times higher than the 19 counted from the 1857 Leipzig census. The total 1857 figures for landless in the Klöstitz and Malojaroslavec districts are well in excess of any other German district in South Russia. The Moločna Mennonites, the center of the landless problems in 1841, dropped to fourth place in 1857 with 669 landless, behind Malojaroslavec (1,325), Klöstitz (1,180), and Liebental in Xerson (855). Clearly at work here are differing definitions of what it means to be landless. The far more detailed look at the landowning and landless situations within a village's population (available from the 1857 Leipzig census) suggests that the counts of landless in the 1857 numbers that Brandes quotes may well include: a) families who were not listed as farmstead owners but had homesites on another family's farmstead and who also leased several desjatina of land for farming or grazing elsewhere in the community's holdings, and b) families listed as jointly owning a farmsteads. Neither group was truly landless. Perhaps the statistical requirements behind the data Brandes quotes required that only one family be named the landowner while the others were deemed landless. Additionally, given the assumption that Malinovskij makes from observing the landless among the Moločna Mennonites (that a landless state likely means that the family is economically not well off), the numbers quoted by Brandes should not be used to assert that the German colonies in Bessarabia had large numbers of landless poor in either 1841 or 1857.

As will be discussed in later chapters, over the course of the period from 1860 up to the beginning of World War I, it is certainly true that far wider distinctions in wealth and income developed in German Bessarabia. While most of the population remained in a broad middle group that included farmers but also craftworkers and tradesmen, a very wealthy group of farmers, land investors, manufacturers, and commercial traders separated themselves above them. Well below the broad middle group, there appeared a growing class of landless poor. The existence of such a group is evidenced by the efforts of Tarutino to lease and then buy land elsewhere in Bessarabia so as to provide land it might lease to and so sustain its poor. I have not found evidence, though, to suggest that, by the 1860s, this class of landless poor formed a large and influential group in German Bessarabia, as Malinovskij suggests existed elsewhere in parts of South Russia, or as might be presumed from the figures Brandes quotes (listed above). Kern and other village descriptions begin to note material numbers of the poor only after the crushing economic losses caused by World War I and by Bessarabia's separation from its former markets in Russia when it became part of Romania in 1918.

## By the 1860s, farmsteads in the original colonies were becoming overcrowded, and in reaction, some Germans in Bessarabia looked to start new settlements by leasing or purchasing land

As suggested in the chapter considering the demographic data for the Bessarabian Germans, by the early 1860s farmsteads were beginning to become crowded. Married adults of Generation 2 were managing the farmsteads, but some of their children were now grown and married and producing children of their own. The resulting crowded conditions were creating economic and social issues. While two or even three married couples could efficiently manage the 60 desjatina farm, more adults produced too many hands and likely conflicts of interest. It is also likely that some who were part of a jointly managed farmstead wanted the independence to run a farm on their own and so began to look for solutions. No doubt families in the original colonies looked at the possibility of acquiring more land bordering their settlements. This appears not to have been possible in the 1850s and 1860s. The first workable solution found was to lease or even buy land elsewhere in Bessarabia and so create new daughter settlements. That families had the means to take these measures testifies to their financial strength. To fund their land leases and purchases, as well as their move and reestablishment, departing family members used whatever savings they had built up and took out their inheritance share from the value of the family farmstead. The payment of the inheritance shares was sometimes financed by the remaining members of the farmstead by loans taken from the village orphan and fire funds or even from other villagers. The following chapters will detail how this movement, which began on a small scale in the 1860s, later expanded significantly, with far larger numbers of Germans leasing or purchasing additional land in Bessarabia or moving from Bessarabia to do so in the Crimea, the North Caucasus, or Siberia, or to immigrate to Dobrudscha and ultimately, in particularly large numbers, to North America. The first steps of this process were the sixteen new villages established in Bessarabia during the 1860s, a number almost equal to the nineteen original Bessarabian German settlements. Such a mass movement could only have taken place if the families had built up profitable farmsteads, and the German villages had material capital saved by villagers or in insurance funds and the habit of loaning out those funds to maximize their value.

Although the Budjak steppelands in Bessarabia were virtually unoccupied when the German colonists first arrived in 1814, by the 1860s, virtually all the land was spoken for. Upon becoming part of Russia, most of the Budjak became crown land. Tsar Alexander I and his brother and successor Tsar Nicholas I granted large estates carved out of the crown landholdings to Russian aristocrats and nobles, often as recompense for military service. One such was Count Aleksandr Xristoforovič Benkendorf (1781–1844), from a Baltic German family of Estonia, who had been a distinguished general in the Russian army during the Napoleonic Wars and later became the head of the dreaded Third Section secret police for Nicholas I. Benkendorf was granted 41,080 desjatina of land in Bessarabia inland from the Black Sea along the middle stretch of the Alkalija River. Grantees of property such as Benkendorf did not live on their new estates in Bessarabia, which were very distant from St. Petersburg, Moscow, and their home estates. Rather, the Russian owners of estates in Bessarabia sought to turn their grants to profitable use by importing serfs from their other properties to create farming villages, or far more frequently, by leasing out rights to local Moldavians and others to use the land to raise cattle or sheep. As a result, by 1860 much of the land in the Budjak was spoken for but large tracts there were underutilized.

In considering how the German colonists in Bessarabia were able to lease or purchase land or establish nearly permanent leases that frequently led to land purchases, it helps to understand the position of the absentee owners of the land grants. The major basis of the wealth of the Russian nobility was the possession of land. Government service or outright grants of money from the tsar, such as pensions, were the only other socially acceptable means to acquire money. In the second half of the nineteenth century, however, the Russian nobility, like much of the nobility throughout Europe, were experiencing steadily increasing economic pressures. Income from the land they owned was generally flat or at best rising only slightly. In contrast, the costs of maintaining the fashionable lifestyle they expected and wished to lead were undergoing significant increases. Costs for such luxuries as clothing, travel, and housing were rising steeply as technological innovations and access to new luxuries from a worldwide market drove up prices and changed demands. Moreover, competition for such luxuries with families who had recently acquired great wealth from commerce and manufacturing put further pressure on prices. In order to maintain or even achieve what were deemed proper lifestyles for their class and status, many aristocratic families needed to borrow funds or sell property. Many nobles in the second half of the nineteenth century chose another option: living beyond their means, which only worsened their economic position. In Bessarabia and South Russia, the consequence of such lifestyle pressures on estate owners was that from the 1860s to the outbreak of World War I, many noble estate owners became interested in selling or leasing their underutilized property.

Of the sixteen new German settlements established in Bessarabia in the 1860s, thirteen were located in the southern steppelands, the Budjak region, where the original German colonies were established. Settlers for twelve of these came from the established German colonies in Bessarabia.[14] The other German settlement founded in the Budjak was Sofiental, founded in 1862 mainly by settlers crossing over from Xerson Province to lease land, though some Bessarabian German families also joined this group.[15] The three new German settlements founded in the 1860s out of the Budjak region—Neu Strymba, Ryschkanowka, and Scholtoi—were established in northern Bessarabia.[16]

## The new settlements had several features in common

The details that are known about the leases and land purchases made in the 1860s suggest both common attributes shared by the different new villages and features that make them separate and unique. One major common feature was that the groups that banded together to make land purchases or take leases were formed from a mix of families from different German villages in Bessarabia. In other words, these were not "daughter" villages formed as offshoots by residents of a single Bessarabian colony. The land for Eigenheim, founded in 1861 along the northern stretch of the Alkalija River, was purchased by a group of German families who came from Alt Elft, Gnadental, Kulm, Leipzig, Paris, Plotzk, and Tarutino. Mannsburg began in 1863 on

---

14. Dale Wahl indicates there were eighteen new villages established in Bessarabia in the 1860s ("Bessarabian Village Names" [N.p.: Odessa Digital Library, 1996], http://www.odessa3.org/collections/bess/link/bessvl.txt). Two of these, Stanhopka and Tamurka, Kern indicates (*Homeland Book*, 187, 131) were founded by land purchases in the 1890s. The sixteen villages with a clear origin in the 1860s are: Benkendorf (1863), Demir Chadschi (1861), Eigenheim (1861), Hoffnungsfeld (1864), Josefsdorf (1865), Mannsburg (1863), Mintschuna (1868), Neu Posttal (1863), Neu Strymba (1860), Neufall (1867), Ryschkanowka (1865), Sarjari (1860), Scholtoi (1865), Seimeny (1867), Sofiental (1862), and Tchemtchelly (1862).

15. Seimeny's founders also included families coming from across the Dniester Liman in Xerson Province.

16. Descendants of the residents of Scholtoi have put up an extensive website with maps, pictures, and even videos of recent visits to the former German settlement, which is now within the borders of Moldova (http://www.scholtoi.de/index_en.html).

land leased jointly by families who came from Alt Elft, Alt Posttal, Dennewitz, Kulm, and Plotzk. It is not clear whether members of such groups were personally acquainted before their group formed. Indeed, as suggested by the large number of villages represented in the two examples above, the groups were formed by their common interest in establishing a new settlement rather than having shared long acquaintance.[17] The wide backgrounds of the settlers in the new villages also suggests that once a potential was found for purchasing or leasing a plot of land, there were some means for communicating this throughout the different German settlements so as to alert and gather interested families.

Another apparent commonality was that, at least among the those villages where details are available, families purchased or leased large plots of land that were close to the size of the original colonial farm allotments of 60 desjatina. Benkendorf, founded on land leased from the Benkendorf family's grant along the Alkalija River, averaged family plots of 53.5 desjatina. In nearby Neu Posttal, established on leased land, the family plots averaged 67 desjatina, and in Eigenheim, established on land purchased further upstream along the Alkalija River, the family plots averaged 74.1 desjatina.

The large average sizes of farm plots within the new settlements in the Budjak suggest another common feature: that the settler groups were generally made up of families of reasonable economic standing. Kern even describes several of the founders of Neufall, settled in 1867, as "very wealthy."[18] The founding of Demir Chadschi also speaks to wealth in that it was a huge 6,190-desjatina estate that one man, Friedenstal citizen Konrad Renz, purchased in 1861. The land area he bought was 1,174 desjatina larger than the total land area given the colony of Friedenstal in 1833. Renz settled his family on this estate and then sold portions of it to settlers from Alt Arzis and Gnadental, which created the village of Demir Chadschi.[19] Kern also notes about Benkendorf that "it was well known that Benkendorf was a rich community,"[20] though this may relate to a later period in the settlement's history.[21]

## The new settlements also had features that made them different from one another

Not all of the new settlements founded by Germans in Bessarabia in the 1860s were established by settlers who could be described as economically well off. The village of Josefsdorf appears to have been founded by much poorer settlers. They first established

---

17. Kern implies this point when he notes the different backgrounds of the families who leased land to establish the village of Tchemtchelly in 1862. In listing the names of first settlers, he comments that the family names (Knopp, Taschner, Müller, Meilke, Quast) "demonstrate the mingling of north Germans with Swabians" (*Homeland Book*, 78).

18. Ibid., 170.

19. Renz (1818–1894) was born in Worms in the Berezan District of the Odessa Region. Stumpp lists him among the early settlers of Friedenstal (*Emigration from Germany to Russia*, 518). Demir Chadschi appears to be the settlement named Ch (Xutor) Gamaleja on the 1901 Austro-Hungarian military map of Bessarabia (http://lazarus.elte.hu/hun/digkonyv/topo/200e/47-46.jpg), but the village is currently named Zelenaja Balka.

20. Kern, *Homeland Book*, 165.

21. Kern's treatment of the settlement of Benkendorf suggests that it was founded on purchased land that was bought for what would then have been the extravagant sum of 110 gold rubles per desjatina (*Homeland Book*, 165). This would certainly support his statement that this was a rich settlement. Brandes, however, offers a correcting view when he notes the land in Benkendorf was actually purchased in 1896 (*Von den Zaren Adoptiert*, 399). It is more likely that Benkendorf was founded on leased land. An 1896 purchase date also fits better with data on the purchase price for the land, as will be discussed in a later chapter that covers this topic.

their new village in 1865, apparently on leased land.[22] Kern describes the settlers as "members of the poorer segment in the mother colonies."[23] The settlers came from just two neighboring colonial villages, Borodino and Beresina, and so the new settlers may have been well-acquainted before establishing the new village. This fact would also set them apart from the founding groups of the other new settlements of the 1860s, which joined together people from a wide number of different colonies.

Not all the new German settlements created in Bessarabia in the 1860s were founded by Germans from Bessarabia, and not all were located in the Budjak region in southern Bessarabia. The village of Sofiental, as noted above, was founded on leased land in 1863 mainly by families coming from the Liebental District of Xerson Province just across the Dniester from Bessarabia. Sofiental was located southwest of Schabo where, together with Neufall, Neu Posttal, Benkendorf, and Sarjari, it opened up a new area of German settlement in the Budjak well to the southeast of Sarata. In a similar fashion, the new settlements of Mannsburg, Tchemtchelly, Eigenheim, and Seimeny opened up new areas in the Budjak well to the east and northeast of Sarata.

Three new German settlements were founded outside the Budjak. All three of these—Ryschkanowka, Scholtoi, and Neu Strymba—were located in northern Bessarabia near the town of Belz (Imperial and Soviet Russian Bel'cy, now Balti in Moldova). Neu Strymba and Ryschkanowka were located to the north of Belz, Scholtoi to the south east.[24] Ryschkanowka and Scholtoi were both founded by German speakers who had been settled in Austrian Galicia, the part of Poland taken over by Austria in the first partition of 1772, who entered Russian Bessarabia in the 1860s as they searched for land they might farm on lease. In his article "123 Jahre Ryschkanowka," Hugo Häfner describes the Ryschkanowka settlers as having backgrounds much like those of the German Bessarabian villagers in the Budjak: they came originally from both Rhineland and northern Germany, from Württemberg, Hesse, and the Pfaltz, from East Prussia, Pomerania, and Poland.[25] Häfner notes as well that in their passage from Galicia to Bessarabia, most families had spent some time farming in Bukovina.[26]

The third German village founded in northern Bessarabia was Neu Strymba, which was located between Ryschkanowka and Belz. Its founding story is quite different from the other new settlements. Its setters had actually arrived in Bessarabia in 1815. They were from Württemberg, Baden, and the Pfaltz and were on their way to Xerson Province where they were to create a settlement near Tirasopol'. Stopping in their journey to Xerson in Kishinev, Bessarabia, they were lured by the agent of a Russian landowner

22. Though Kern describes the village as "founded in 1865 on purchased land," he goes on to say that "the lease…brought settlers from Borodino and Beresina," and in another sentence that "the villagers did well since there was plenty of lease land available" (*Homeland Book*, 147). This implies that the village purchased the land at some later date.

23. Ibid.

24. The site of Ryschkanowka is now incorporated in the town of Riscani north of Balti. The site of Neu Strymba is now the village of Grinauti located between Balti and Riscani. Scholtoi is today the village of Ciolaci Nou and is located to the southeast of the town of Falesti, southeast of Balti rather than to the north of Falesti as indicated on Stumpp's map "Karte der Deutschen Siedlungen in Bessarabien."

25. Hugo Häfner, "125 Jahre Ryschkanowka" (1990), 188. Digital copy of original article available at http://www.bessarabien.de/upload/ryschkanowka_hk1990.pdf..

26. Bukovina was territory on the northern slopes of the Carpathian Mountains to the northwest of Bessarabia. Once the northwestern section of Ottoman-controlled Moldavia, it was taken over by Austria in 1775, and in the nineteenth century attracted many new German settlers from elsewhere in Austrian-controlled territory, as well as other German-speaking lands.

in Bessarabia into establishing the village of Naslawtscha (now Naslavcea in Moldova) in a bend of the Dniester River upstream from Mogilev in the northern most point of Bessarabia. They had been promised a hundred-year lease of large lots after which they would own the property. In taking up this offer they founded the village of Naslawtscha in 1817. According to Kern, sometime later their landlord went back on the original promises, and leasing rates were increased to the point that the settlers began to complain of hardships. Pastor Faltin of Kishinev intervened on their behalf and families were given 4 desjatina each to live on in Naslawtscha. For some this was too small an allotment and they moved to establish Neu Strymba. Here families leased lots of 9.5 desjatina, but perhaps chastened by their previous experience with not being able to afford leases for large tracts, they declined to lease larger 60 desjatina properties.[27]

## Most of the new settlements were founded on leased land

Of the sixteen new German villages founded in Bessarabia in the 1860s, fourteen were on land leased by the settlers and two were on land that had been purchased.[28] From the perspective of the Germans, leasing land had strong attractions, as it carried far lower current costs. It had to be an attractive option for cautious families who feared their savings and inheritance shares would not be sufficient to support buying land, moving to it, and supporting themselves through the first hard years of establishing themselves there. In leasing and purchasing property, Germans would not at this time have dealt with the actual landowners. For properties they owned but did not live on, it was common for noble landowners to retain an agent to manage that property. The agent would be liable for a fixed payment and would seek tenants whose fees would then both cover that payment and provide a profit. In this way, the noble landlord would not be seen to be in business, an action beneath his station, and the Germans would be dealing with a businessman whose interests lay in short-term gain rather than in the long-term value of the property.

Leasing costs varied, could change, and, as the Naslawtscha settlers learned, carried great risks. The forty-eight families who established the village of Neu Posttal in 1863 paid 1.18 ruble per desjatina with lease terms fixed for ten years. In Seimeny/Seimental, founded in 1867, the new settlers paid 2 rubles per desjatina with prices fixed for twelve years. The Neu Posttal settlers had plots that averaged 67 desjatina, giving them annual leasing costs of 79 rubles, which with taxes due likely put their annual carrying costs over 100 rubles. While the calculation that this was affordable provides another indication of the potential value the Germans put on land, it also suggests that until the new villages were well established, margins with such carrying costs were slim. At the end of the first decade of fixed leasing costs for Neu Posttal in 1873, the landlord raised the price of leasing from 1.18 ruble to 1.65 ruble per desjatina, still below that which the new settlers of Seimeny paid. Nevertheless, Kern reports that with the increase "many families moved away to find cheaper land elsewhere."[29]

27. Kern's treatment of this point is not fully clear: "They refused to lease the 60 desjatines of land against the purchase price…they undermined their possibilities of expansion with this move" (*Homeland Book*, 117).
28. Kern gives the impression that Hoffnungsfeld was founded on purchased land (*Homeland Book*, 87). However, Günther Vossler's study clearly indicates that the village was founded in 1864 on leased land that was purchased by the settlers in 1881. Vossler, "Die Tochterkolonie Hoffnungsfeld," last modified April 15, 2013, http://www.bessarabien.com/upload/hoffnungsfeld_internet.pdf.
29. Kern, *Homeland Book*, 171.

## The attitude of the Russian government to the German colonies in Russia had been slowly changing from the 1830s on and reached climax in two decrees issued by the tsar in the early 1870s

Throughout the 1860s, the Imperial Russian government continued to view the German colonies in Russia through a mercantilist lens as positive economic additions to the welfare of the state. From this viewpoint, the Welfare Committee encouraged the continuing economic growth of the colonies by emphasizing the cultivation of fruit, vineyards, and grains, especially wheat, and the buildup of specialized animal herds, notably sheep. Having passed through periods of economic struggle and some religious controversy, the German colonies in Bessarabia were now developing more vigorously. The intervention and guidance they needed now was more related to managing growth. In both South Russia and Bessarabia, the Welfare Committee, driven by its general concern about landless poverty, gave increasing focus to supporting commercial growth in the larger towns. The Welfare Committee, in its larger study of landless poverty in South Russia, came to see the commercial strength of German villages as a source of employment that would grow even stronger if the German villages served the commercial needs of the surrounding non-German settlements.[30] This idea supported a second goal of the Ministry of State Domains in the 1860s: increasing the numbers of Russian speakers among the Germans. Funds were supplied to build or strengthen central schools. From 1865, the Werner School, established in Sarata in 1844, became the central school for training teachers for German Bessarabia and the German Glückstal District in the neighboring Xerson Province.[31]

The push to increase the use of the Russian language in the German settlements through an increase in the number of teachers who were qualified in that language, though, was not driven solely by an economic focus. It was driven more by major shifts in how the government was coming to see its German citizens. The value of seeing them as different from other state agricultural assets was being questioned, as was the view that letting them establish small, nearly independent islands of Germanness offered no dangers to the state. This brought into question the special rights and privileges, the separate legal and social position of the German colonies. While the Russian government in the 1860s continued to view the German colonies with benign and positive eyes, the thought that the colonies should remain protected and privileged entities no longer seemed compelling. The government's changing position toward the German colonies was not caused by anything happening in or stemming from the German colonies themselves. The major changes to the protected position of the German colonies in Russia resulted largely from the fact that this issue was swept up in the 1860s and absorbed into the government's consideration and implementation of major political, social, and legal reforms affecting the country as a whole. The second major force that helped to shift the Russian government's relationship with the German colonies was the shocking and violent growth of Prussia into Germany, from Russia's client to its potential rival. As Prussia grew and then became Germany, Russians began to see the Germans living in Russia differently.

---

30. Fleischhauer, *Die Deutschen im Zarenreich*, 282.
31. Brandes, *Von den Zaren Adoptiert*, 312.

The fundamental changes to the relationship between the Russian government and its German colonies in Russia were implemented in the early 1870s. These changes were formalized in two decrees issued by Tsar Alexander II in 1871 and 1874. The intention of these decrees was to end the special rules and privileges under which the German colonies were governed and so to integrate the colonies politically and legally as equal and undifferentiated members of the Imperial Russian state. A discussion of the effects of these decrees will form the focus of the following chapter, but they cannot be properly understood without considering the background that led to their implementation. Alexander II's two decrees concerning the German colonies were not welcomed by the German colonists, who viewed them as an abrogation of the promised rights they had believed would never be changed. This coloring of broken promises has continued to be the general theme of accounts of the German settlements in Russia. Such a view, however, reflects the isolated state of the colonists and their surprise and shock when the decrees were issued, making it seem that the decrees were unmotivated and arbitrary acts of the tsar and the Russian government. Such a view also reflects a great misunderstanding by the Germans of the tsar's traditional powers in Russia: no right was ever granted by a tsar that could not be taken away, and the tsar's powers were never to be limited.[32] The surprise and shock that greeted the tsar's decrees resulted from the fact that the gradual changes in the Russian government's attitude toward the German colonies were not clearly perceived in the colonies themselves. Hurdles for the colonists that made it harder for them to understand currents of thought within the Russian government were their physical and cultural isolation, their self-absorption, and their general lack of fluency in Russian. Even the work of the Welfare Committee served to impede the understanding of the changing attitudes of the Russian government toward the colonies. Though the Welfare Committee provided a benevolent German-language connection with the Russian state, it also tended to limit interest in questions of civic affairs to those directly touching on the colonies.

The decrees issued by Tsar Alexander II were not issued to punish the Germans, because he disliked them, or as the result of any sudden, arbitrary, or negative changes in the Russian government's attitude toward the Germans. This chapter will argue instead that the causes for the changes in the relationship between the German settlements in Russia and the Russian government lay in two conclusions the government reached about the colonies during the 1860s. One was that times had changed and large numbers of additional German immigrants were no longer needed or desired in Russia. With the existing German colonies now successfully planted and grown into valuable economic assets of the state, the special treatment the colonies had received to establish themselves no longer seemed required. A second argument made here is that the legal changes made to the position of the German settlements in Imperial Russia follow the logic inherent in other major civic and legal reforms put into place in the 1860s in Russia. Government officials pushing for the reforms convinced Tsar Alexander II that the Russian state would best be served by having a single set of laws and rights that applied to all its citizens. To that

---

32. The wry comment of the smotritel' in chastising the Klöstitz Oberschultz Engel by noting that the latter had "an insufficient knowledge of the monarchical form of government," would seem in the present context to carry a far broader truth (Malinovskij, *Social'naja i xozjajstvennaja istorija*, 100). See note 96 of chapter VI.

end, the government looked at all groups that held special and unique rights and privileges and asked whether the state really benefited by their continuance.

When the German peasants were first invited to come to South Russia and Bessarabia early in the nineteenth century, the Russian government had several primary goals. One was to have the Germans occupy territory taken from the Turks and so help secure a new Russian possession by adding Christian settlers. A second was to promote, for the benefit of the Russian state, the economic development of those lands through the introduction of agricultural skills and techniques not present among other peoples in those lands or among Russian and Ukrainian peasants the government might import.

By the early 1830s, the Russian government's view of the German colonies was changing. The more conservative Tsar Nicholas I had succeeded his brother Alexander I in 1825 and brought to power views that considered Western Europeans less favorably. Nicholas I's instinctive suspicion of Western Europe was heightened by two important events that occurred near the beginning of his reign: the Decembrist revolt and the Polish insurrection. When Alexander I died in December 1825, there was some confusion as to his proper successor, and the political confusion this created emboldened a number of junior officers in the army to revolt in hopes of introducing a more representative government.[33] The hopes of these young officers, the so-called Decembrists, were inspired by their observations of political freedoms that existed in Western Europe. Nicholas I successfully put down this revolt, but the concerns this challenge raised to the autocratic power of the Russian tsars only deepened his worries about unwanted Western influences.

Such opinions were further strengthened in Nicholas I by the major Polish insurrection of 1830–31. Following the French retreat, Russia had, in 1813, taken control of most of the Duchy of Warsaw, by which Napoleon had resurrected the former Kingdom of Poland. The 1815 Congress of Vienna treaty created a semi-independent Russian protectorate state in Poland whose territory was made up of much of the Duchy of Warsaw, including half of what had been South Prussia before Napoleon. Though it permitted the Poles to have a liberal constitution, Imperial Russia treated this protectorate, called Congress Poland, as just another province of the Russian state.[34] Many Poles believed the intention of the Congress of Vienna was to reconstitute a Polish state and so never accepted continuing Russian domination. In

---

33. When Alexander I died in December 1825, he left no children to inherit the throne. The older of his two younger brothers, Grand Duke Constantine (1779–1831), was legally next in line, but at the request of Alexander I, in 1822, Grand Duke Constantine had agreed to renounce his rights to succeed. Alexander I's reasons for requiring this very unusual renunciation have not been clearly established, though Grand Duke Constantine's poor record with the Russian army and unstable behavior likely played a role. His renunciation was not made public while Alexander I was alive, but was well known within the imperial family. When Alexander I died and officials in St. Petersburg, unaware of the renunciation, proclaimed loyalty to Constantine as the succeeding tsar, this caused Nicholas to hesitate in asserting his correct understanding of the succession, and gave opportunity to the Decembrist officers in St. Petersburg to stage their revolt.

34. Congress Poland was officially called the Kingdom of Poland (Korolevstvo Pol'skoe) but to distinguish this entity from the independent Kingdom of Poland that disappeared in the eighteenth-century partitions, it was frequently called Congress Poland, to indicate it was created by the Congress of Vienna. In addition to the areas of Poland that Russia had gained in the eighteenth-century partitions, Congress Poland included the regions of Łodz and Kalisz in Great Poland which had been under Prussian control as part of the province of South Prussia before Napoleon.

November 1830, a major revolt began which took the better part of a year for the Russian government to crush and suppress.

One result of the revolts of the Decembrists and the Poles was that Nicholas I cut back significantly on both immigration to Russia by Western Europeans and travel by Russians to Western Europe. Most of the new German colonies established in Bessarabia during the reign of Nicholas I were founded with Germans who came from other settlements in Russia. Two, Friedenstal (1834) and Plotzk (1839–40), were founded by Germans who came from Russian Poland and were thus escaping the turmoil created by the Polish revolt. A third, Hoffnungstal (1842), was founded by Germans from Xerson Province in South Russia, and a fourth, Dennewitz (1834), with settlers who had come from other German colonies in Bessarabia. Of the six new German colonies formed in Bessarabia after the accession of Nicholas I, only two, Gnadental (1831) and Lichtental (1834), were largely populated by immigrants from the west. In Plotzk, a minority of its new citizens were immigrants from Western Europe. In each of these three new colonies with immigrants from the west, the immigrants all came from Württemberg and Baden. As in the late eighteenth century and early nineteenth century, small landholdings and religious conflicts had continued to stimulate emigration.[35] The government of Nicholas I, like that of his brother before him, saw German peasants from these provinces, perhaps because of their strong religious beliefs, as law abiding, self-absorbed, and conservative, and so not likely to stir the waters of liberal thought in Russia.

By the 1830s, also, Russia's strategic concerns on its southern borders had changed. Continuing their successes against the Ottoman Turks, Russian forces between 1827 and 1829 had pushed Russian areas of control across the Danube to the southwest and across the Prut River to the west of Bessarabia. In doing so, Russia gained control over the mouth of the Danube and the Romanian-speaking provinces of Wallachia, as well as the remainder of Moldavia not part of Bessarabia or Austria.[36] This moved Russia's border with the Ottoman Empire further south from Bessarabia, near the present border of Bulgaria and Romania. Russia, however, held back from absorbing these new territories into the Russian state. Austria, France, and Great Britain were quite concerned about Russia's acquiring territory along the coast of the Black Sea because this brought Russia ever closer to Istanbul and potential control over access to the Black Sea. Instead, Russia acted as though a protectorate had been established. This was likely done with the thought that, as with Congress Poland, over time, such de facto control would pass into de jure absorption. Russia's hopes were not to

---

35. Although Mack Walker's arguments, discussed in prior chapters, for the primacy of economic factors in driving Württembergers to migrate are quite strong, it would appear that (at least from the viewpoint of the Russian government) the founders of Gnadental and Lichtental were chiefly motivated by religious reasons. The Russian government settled them on land that had been set aside for Lindl's followers and joined these settlements together with Sarata to form the Welfare Committee's Sarata District. Such actions carry the implication that the government viewed these new settlers as religious immigrants who were following in the footsteps of the Sarata settlers.

36. Moldavia is a term long used to describe both Bessarabia and a land area of roughly equal size west of the Prut River, as well as the territory north of the latter that was absorbed by Austria in 1775 as Bukovina. The reference here to the expanded area of Russian control refers to the second piece, the territory west of the Prut River. Moldavia was unified from the sixteenth to the end of the eighteenth century under the Ottoman Turks and later by Romania during the period from 1918 to 1940. The current country of Moldova occupies only a portion of ancient Moldavia, the northern two-thirds of what had been Bessarabia. The southern third of Bessarabia (where most of the German colonies were located) is now part of the Ukraine. Moldavia east of the Prut is part of Romania and Bukovina is spilt between Romania and the Ukraine.

be realized, though. When in the early 1850s Russia threatened to push farther, the grounds were created for the Crimean War. Russia lost in that fight, with the result that the Russian border was pushed back to the Danube and the Prut, and even a small part of southwestern Bessarabia slipped temporarily out of Russia's control.

By the mid-1830s, Russia's interest in attracting settlers from Western Europe had almost disappeared. In addition to Nicholas I's concerns about the political risks of the increased exposure to Western ideas, Russia's strategic situation after 1830 provided little rationale for seeking new foreign immigrants. In Bessarabia, the border with the Ottoman Empire was now much further away, and the potential that the Turks might regain control of lost lands seemed increasingly remote. The government no longer had large plots of empty land at its disposal, having granted away much of the Budjak as favors or settled it with colonists. Russia was not interested in attracting foreign settlers to the protectorate lands in Romania beyond the Danube and Prut except for Dobrudscha, which extended the Budjak south of the Danube along the Black Sea coast. Other lands in Romania were already well settled.[37] Inviting foreign settlers to the protectorate lands would likely have had negative diplomatic consequences, as Vienna, Paris, and London were already indicating unhappiness with Russia's extension into southeastern Europe. Moreover, by the 1840s, the focus of Russian expansion was shifting further eastward to the northern slopes of the Caucasus Mountains and beyond them to Central Asia. As Russia gained control of territories here and sought to solidify its position among the largely Muslim populations by establishing Christian villages, it did so with immigrants coming from elsewhere in Russia. German villages in the north Caucasus were founded generally by people from the Volga colonies, supplemented by Germans from South Russia and Bessarabia. As a result, after the accession of Nicholas I, immigration from German lands into Russia slowed to a trickle and then by the mid-1840s ceased altogether.

Although the government of Nicholas I was much less interested in attracting German settlers from Western Europe, it continued to place high value on the German colonies that had already been established in Russia. The Russian government continued to consider the German colonies in Russia, on the whole, as growing economic assets that held positive implications for the Russian state. By the 1840s, the colonies were no longer just potential assets, as they had been in their first years; they were mature assets, with even the youngest colonies in Bessarabia paying dividends to the state in the form of food supplies and taxes. In periods when there were war zones near Bessarabia, for example during the military campaign in Romania in 1827–29 or during the Crimean War of 1853–56, the colonies provided strategic supplies of animals, grain, and other products that the Russian government might buy or even seize as needed.

## One major conclusion gradually reached by the Russian government was that the German colonies were essentially like other peasant communities in Russia

An implicit recognition of the economic value the Russian government attached to the German colonies was the transfer of the reporting relationship of the Welfare

---

37. Beginning in the 1840s, Germans from Bessarabia crossed the Danube and established farms in Dobrudscha. After the mid-1870s, larger numbers came. Separatists from the Bessarabian colonies, as noted earlier, were among the first Germans to come to Dobrudscha.

Committee from the Ministry of Interior to the newly established Ministry of State Domains in 1837. The Ministry of State Domains was set up to oversee the major financial assets owned by the tsar: estates, peasants, mines, and manufacturers. Such assets supported a good portion of the costs of the government as well as the total costs of caring for and feeding the royal family. The most important assets held by the tsar were the huge crown estates worked by peasant serfs. The crown owned a substantial portion of the arable land in European Russia. Figures from 1858 suggest that there were an estimated nineteen million serfs working on crown lands who represented roughly 45 percent of the total serf population in Russia. The transfer of the German colonies, including the Welfare Committee, to the Ministry of State Domains suggests that the financial dividends the colonies were paying were considered important enough to warrant the special financial oversight this ministry was set up to provide. At the same time, however, merging the management of the German colonies into the Ministry of State Domains suggests that the issues associated with these colonies were thought to be essentially similar to those concerning the management of the Crown estates.

Nicholas I had created the Ministry of State Domains in great part because he wanted to have more control over, and so incur less wastage from, the most significant financial assets owned by the crown. The ministry was to report directly to him rather than through the Council of State. Nicholas I's special interest in this ministry was also indicated by his appointment of the very able Pavel D. Kisilev as its first head. Kisilev was perhaps the most talented of Nicholas I's ministers and had a history of handling difficult assignments well. Alexander I had asked him in 1816 to review the many problems the early Russian civil administration was experiencing in Bessarabia. His memorandum had, among other things, been instrumental in the establishment of a strong and independent Welfare Committee headed by an official of sufficient rank to prevent the provincial governors from interfering with the development of the colonies. Kisilev was later in command of the troops occupying Wallachia and Moldavia in 1828 and from 1829 to 1834 served as the governor of the de facto Russian protectorate there. In 1835, he was promoted to the Council of State in St. Petersburg. Kisilev was noted for a number of reforms of the Russian government. Some of his proposals, such as freeing the serfs, were too radical to be considered at this time, but many others, particularly those he introduced during his long tenure as head of the Ministry of State Domains from 1837 to 1856, were much praised by pre-Soviet Russian historians.[38] Among these were the introduction of state assistance for schools and medical facilities in peasant villages. Welfare Committee efforts to improve schools and medical facilities as well as the plight of landless colonists were likely responses to concerns raised by Kisilev. The Kisilev reform that had the greatest impact on the German colonies was the change in the basis of taxation. The tax base assessed to villages was shifted from a per-head tax to an economic assessment more closely linked to the resources held by a peasant community. Taxes were now to be based on land allotments and especially the economic value of the land held for agriculture. While this linked taxation more closely to probable income, and certainly made taxation in the overall perspective more fair, the effect for the German colonists was to increase the amount of

38. Nicholas V. Riasanovsky, *A History of Russia*, 2nd ed. (New York: Oxford University Press, 1969), 364.

taxes paid. Norman Saul has suggested that the taxes assessed the German colonies increased perhaps 25 percent during the period from 1840 to 1860.[39] Saul's estimate doesn't appear to take into account the special taxes and exactions that occurred during the Crimean War.

A central point to be made about the treatment of the German colonies during Kisilev's long leadership of the Ministry of State Domains is that increasingly during this period, the German colonies were seen less as unique assets and more as assets essentially similar to those provided by other peasant communities managed by the ministry. Saul makes this point when he notes: "With their transfer to the new Ministry of State Domains, the central government began to treat the colonists more and more as Russian state peasants."[40] This is not to say that Kisilev thought the Germans should be reduced to serf status and bondage, but that he saw the German peasants and the Crown's Russian peasants as offering similar opportunities for the state that were held back by similar problems for which similar solutions seemed fitting. The logic of this approach, however, implicitly questioned the appropriateness of offering special and unique treatment to the Germans.

Kisilev's major focus was to introduce a more rational management of, and so create better returns from, valuable state assets. As an example, Kisilev pushed initiatives that sought to find ways to provide land for landless Russian peasants or find useful work for them to perform. Noting that among the German Mennonite communities in South Russia there existed a similarly large population of landless poor, Kisilev sought ways to find land for them. Acting through the Welfare Committee, some efforts were made to have wealthy Mennonites transfer unused land for the benefit of the landless.[41] Kisilev was also responsible for increasing the number of primary schools and medical facilities available to Russian peasant communities. His similar support of educational, sanitary, and medical improvements for the German colonies is implied through the comments in the 1848 village histories, noted earlier, that thanked the Welfare Committee for its influence in these areas. More significant improvements in these areas occurred in the 1860s, after Kisilev's retirement. The Central School program was established to create more and better-educated teachers, though little progress was made in the 1860s toward its further goal of providing many teachers among the Germans who were fluent in Russian. Kern notes that the first doctor to practice in German Bessarabia, Dr. Beyer, came to Klöstitz in 1860 and at that time "the district [Welfare Committee officials] began monitoring the health organizations."[42] Tarutino had a doctor resident in the 1860s. The Alexander Asylum in Sarata began in 1864 as a nursing clinic. Kern's description of the Alexander Asylum focuses on its mission as an institution of social welfare

---

39. Norman Saul, "The Migration of Russian-Germans to Kansas," *Kansas Historical Quarterlies* 40, no. 1 (Spring 1974): 38–62, http://www.kancoll.org/khq/1974/74_1_saul.htm. Saul offers this as an estimate for all of South Russia and Bessarabia but does not provide a source or the basis of his calculation/estimation. As noted earlier, even with this tax basis reevaluation, the colonists were liable for materially lower taxes than had been the case for them in Prussia and Württemberg.

40. Ibid.

41. Klaus, *Naši kolonii*, 160–63. Saul also makes this point in "Migration of Russian-Germans" (40–44). Some wealthy Mennonites owned estates with over 1,000 desjatina of land. As noted later in this chapter, Heinrich Goerz, in his study of the Moločna Mennonites, dates much of the effort to help the landless Mennonites in Moločna to the 1860s. Goerz, *The Molotschna Settlement*, trans. Al Reimer and John Toews (Winnipeg, Man.: CMBC Publications, 1993), 133–35.

42. Kern, *Homeland Book*, 129.

established through the efforts of several pastors working in German Bessarabia who had been inspired by the work of Reverend William Löhe in Neuendettelsau in Franconian Bavaria.[43] Through connections with Reverend Löhe, nurses were sent from Bavaria to practice in Sarata. That the Russian government permitted the nurses to come to Sarata, apparently without difficulty, suggests the intervention of the Welfare Committee and the interest of the Ministry of State Domains in promoting improved public health in German as well as Russian villages.

From the point of view of the Ministry of State Domains, the issues raised by the German colonies were increasingly seen as neither unique nor special. The issues of chief importance were those of the agricultural economy: finding and producing successful crops, increasing the number of higher-valued animals, increasing access to and distribution from local markets, maintaining adequate landholdings, and, very humanely, increasing the education, health, and welfare of the farmer-peasants. Such an attitude was certainly encouraged by the fact that the Ministry of State Domains had responsibility for both the crown estates and the foreign colonies. Even though there were great differences between the two, not least in that the German colonies were significantly more productive and had developed supportive social welfare programs of their own, over time, and certainly by the 1860s, senior ministry officials came to think that the economic challenges both groups faced were fundamentally similar. They rationally concluded that it was more efficient for the state to administer Germans and Russians in the same way. Although the German colonists may not have realized this, by the 1860s, their claims to special treatment embedded in the settlement agreements were increasingly considered unnecessary by the ministry that oversaw their affairs in Russia.

## From the 1860s onward, the popular press in Russia portrayed the German population in Russia increasingly in a negative light

The 1860s saw the transformation of Prussia into powerful and dangerous Imperial Germany. Russian popular opinion began to see Germany, no longer as a client state, but as a rival power to Russia. The Crimean War of 1853–56 split the allies who had defeated Napoleon in 1812–14. With Russia no longer closely allied with Great Britain, Austria, and France, Prussia, and in particular its prime minister Otto von Bismarck, saw an opportunity to force many of the independent German-speaking non-Hapsburg states in central Europe into a larger and more powerful Prussian state. Prussia's strength was put forcefully on display with military victories over Denmark (1863–64) and Austria (1866). Following its victory over Austria, Prussia absorbed the remaining free states that had been part of the North German Confederacy. In 1870, Prussia intentionally provoked France to attack, causing Prussia's allies, Bavaria, Württemberg, and Baden, to enter the war on Prussia's side. The stunningly quick and total victory gained under Prussian military leadership then led these south German states to agree to join Prussia to form a new German state.

Before the 1860s, the Russian government tended to regard Prussia as a secondary power in Europe, not one equivalent to itself, France, and Great Britain. Indeed, Russia commonly viewed Prussia as a near-client state, in that Prussian designs in Europe would always need Russian support to be realized. Up until the Crimean

---

43. Ibid., 14.

War, Russia had sought to neutralize both Prussia and Austria by seeming to favor one and then the other, assuming that neither could act without Russia's support and that their rivalry would prevent a combination against Russia. Russian popular opinion of Prussia and the smaller German states before the 1860s tended to admire German cleverness, industriousness, and organization but also saw the German states as too small, weak, and feckless to compete with the major countries: "A nemcev tol'ko lenivyj ne bil. S tex por kak mir stoit, nemcev vse bili. A oni nikogo. Tol'ko drug druga."[44]

Prussia's violent growth into Germany was a shocking development to the Russian government and to Russian public opinion. Germany was now a major power with a first rate military and significant economic resources, a true rival for Russia. Beginning in the 1860s, concerns about Prussia's growth and aggressive actions started to appear in the popular press in Russia. Along with critical articles on Prussia, there were newspaper articles critical of German culture, as well as negative characterizations of notional German habits and behaviors. These were most commonly found in newspapers aimed at a lower-middle-class readership, such as M. N. Katkov's *Moskovskie vedomosti* (Moscow gazette). Following the defeat of France, some concerns were raised within the Russian government about the dangers the German colonies might now pose to Russia. In 1871, following France's capitulation, General A. M. Dondukov-Korsakov, governor general of the provinces of Kiev, Poldolia, and Volynia, wrote a worried memo to the Ministry of Internal Affairs that connected the dots between a now powerful Germany and the existence of German settlers in Russia. He warned the central government that, were there to be a war with Germany, the German settlements in South Russia posed grave political and military dangers.[45]

Articles in the Russian press critical of the Germans living in Russia were most likely to be found in papers that adhered to a conservative and nationalistic line. Such articles tended to center around one of two themes. The first was the relatively higher value of Russian cultural habits as opposed to those of the German colonists. Thus, in 1872, Prince A. I. Vasil'čikov argued that the Russian peasant collective organizational system, the *mir*,[46] was superior to the system practiced by German peasants living in Russia. The mir owned the land, whereas with the Germans, sepa-

---

44. "Only the lazy haven't beaten the Germans. Ever since the beginning of the world everyone has beaten the Germans. They haven't beaten anyone. [They] Only [have beaten] each other." These are opinions of the old and experienced Prince Nikolai Bolkonskij in Tolstoy's *War and Peace* (L. N. Tolstoy, *Sobranie sočinenij v dvadcati tomax*, vol. 4 [Moscow: State Publisher of Artistic Literature, 1961], 141). Less-than-flattering descriptions of Germans appear frequently in this novel written by Tolstoy during the 1860s.

45. Dietmar Neutatz, "Die Kolonien des Schwartzmeergebietes im Spannungsfeld nationalstaatlicher Politik 1861–1914," in *Die Rußlanddeutschen: Gestern und Heute*, ed. Boris Meissner, Helmut Neubauer, and Alfred Eisfeld (Köln, Ger.: Markus Verlag, 1992), 83–86. The note from General Dondukov-Korsakov is part of fond 1282, o. 2, d. 869, bl. 241 of the holdings of the Central Historical Archives in Moscow (CGIA).

46. In the Russian mir system, the village community owned the land rather than families or individuals owning specific fixed allotments. Individual families were given temporary land allotments by the mir. The mir regularly redivided the community's available land among those members alive and capable of working the land. This system sought to benefit the community as a whole by giving advantages to families with larger numbers of working males. The Russian state assessed tax liabilities against the mir as a unit rather than assessing individual families living in the village. As a result, the regular redivisions of land among working males protected the mir's ability to meet its obligations to the state by giving the most land to those who were likely to provide the greatest financial return to the community.

rate families owned property and such property was commonly equally divided at the death of the owner among the descendants. In making this argument, Vasil'čikov highlights the experience of the Mennonite communities in South Russia, where the subdivision of land produced smaller allotments and ultimately many landless peasants.[47]

A second theme that typically appeared in articles critical of the German colonists in Russia was the charge that such Germans lived as aliens in Russia. The German colonists, it was accurately charged, continued to live in an almost totally German world as though they were not actually in Russia. The fact that the Germans had preserved their German speech, religion, and customs was now seen as an affront. Not unlike current debates on immigration in Europe and North America, strong feelings began to be expressed by some nineteenth-century Russian observers that since the Germans were living in Russia as Russian citizens, they ought to speak Russian and adopt Russian ways. Such anti-German portraits were a theme often appearing in the conservative press of M. N. Katkov, N. P. Giljarov-Platonov, and V. P. Meščerskij.

Assimilation, as the term is currently understood, was not the goal of the Russian nationalists. Assimilation, in the sense of losing a prior cultural identity and being accepted and treated as a native in another, was then, and generally is now, nearly impossible in Russia. German citizens in Russia who spoke only Russian and had adopted Russian customs were in the nineteenth century and are today, when recognized by their surnames, called Germans by other Russians and treated differently. What the Russian nationalists wanted was for the German colonists to become less German and more Russian. They would do so by learning to speak Russian, by expressing loyalty to Russia, and giving evidence of Russian patriotism. In doing so they would continue to be Germans living in Russia, but acceptable Germans.[48]

As Russian nationalists began to see Germans as competitors rather than as usefully skilled, well-organized, and better-educated friends, their characterizations of the German colonists living in Russia started to take on negative features. The German colonists, for example, were depicted as "arrogant" and "land-hungry," as well as ungrateful and unwanted competitors. Because the Germans would not learn Russian, they were depicted as "isolated from the surrounding world" and having "a foreign mentality," meaning that they were not just different, they were not Russian.[49]

The conservative nationalists, however, were not the only nineteenth-century Russians with opinions about the German colonists. Another group of commentators in the Russian press of the 1860s onward, often referred to loosely as "Westernizers" (zapadniki), generally sought to improve Russia by adopting economic, cultural, and especially political patterns that existed in Western Europe. In their view, Russia was backward and primitive by comparison with Western Europe. Consequently, they tended to view the German colonists in Russia as positive forces whose presence might change and improve the habits of the Russian peasants, whom they saw as tied to ancient and uneconomic ways. On this side of the debate, the German

47. Neutatz, "Die Kolonien des Schwartzmeergebietes," 83.
48. Ibid.
49. Ibid., 80–81. It might be noted in this regard that Russians colloquially refer to themselves as *naši* ("us, our guys"). To be *ne naši*, "not one of us," is a near tribal expression of distaste for the other. The word for German in Russian, incidentally, is *nemec*, which means, literally, "one unable to speak [our language]."

colonists were seen as prosperous farmers who were diligent, sober, self-confident, and sensible.[50]

The point to be made here in considering the changing public attitudes toward the German colonists is that while the Russian government came to support the nationalist view that the German colonists needed to learn Russian and be treated no differently from other citizens of the Russian state, the government and especially the Ministry of State Domains saw great value in the colonies and so continued to offer support and protection. In the government's view, the economic progress of the German colonies benefited the state and their quiet and withdrawn ways posed no dangers to the state's autocratic power.

As will be noted in more depth in later chapters, when the tide of nationalism rose during the reigns of Alexander III and Nicholas II, the Russian government declined to act on the advice of those who urged that additional restrictions be placed on the German colonists because of their potential disloyalty to the state, or that the Russian government check the alarming growth in the number of German settlements by forbidding the colonists to make additional land purchases. In contrast, the Russian government did not refrain from limiting the expansion of other populations it viewed less favorably. Following the suppression of the Polish Rebellion of 1863–64, the Russian government issued a decree that barred Poles from purchasing land in the provinces of Volynia, Podolia, Kiev, Vilnius, Kovno, Grodno, Minsk, Mogilëv, and Vitebsk. At the urging of officials in the Russian Orthodox Church, the Russian government in 1864 adopted similar restrictions that barred Jews from purchasing land in western Russia.[51]

One part of the background to the Russian government's annulment of the privileges granted to the German colonists lay in the absorption of the Welfare Committee into the Ministry of State Domains and the consequent view that issues concerning management of state peasants and the German colonists were essentially similar. A second part lay in the changing attitudes toward the German colonists that grew out of Nicholas I's concerns with Western influences, and in the changes in Russian popular opinion that resulted from the Russian defeat in the Crimean War and the rise of weak Prussia into powerful and threatening Germany. Far more important in understanding the causes for annulment of those privileges, however, are the Russian government's efforts to reform the Imperial Russian state without harming the autocratic powers of the tsar through making a series of significant civic, legal, social, and economic changes in governance.

## The changes to the legal status of the German colonists in Russia should be understood as just one part of the comprehensive reforms introduced during the reign of Alexander II

The major reforms implemented by Alexander II in the 1860s have their origin in the government's reaction to Russia's defeat in the Crimean War. That war

---

50. Ibid.
51. Richard Benert, "Land Laws Pertaining to Germans in the Southwest Provinces, Kiev, Podolia, Volhynia 1864–1915," *Journal of the Society for German Genealogy in Eastern Europe* 2, no. 1 (March 2000): 16–21. The act barring Jewish land purchases was issued in July 1864 and that barring Poles from purchasing land in December 1865. These prohibitions were extended and strengthened during the reign of Tsar Alexander III by new regulations issued in May 1882 and December 1887.

was fought because the Western European powers of France, Great Britain, and Austria-Hungary wished to check Russian expansion in the Balkans. The military defeat exposed the fact that over the course of the first half of the nineteenth century, in military, technological, and economic terms, Russia had fallen materially behind its Western European rivals. Russia's defeat forced the Imperial government to address Russia's backwardness in military organization, training, and equipment. It also caused the government to understand that Russia's humiliation was clearly related to its comparatively stunted economic growth. Though Russia was large in population by comparison with countries in Western Europe, it lacked the industrial base, the available capital, and the social and political conditions that would create the economic power its rivals enjoyed. Indeed, it seemed that without major changes Russia would only fall further behind. Reforms became possible because the military defeat undercut the arguments of the conservatives who had dominated affairs in the Russian government under Nicholas I and sought to freeze Russian civic, political, and economic life in the state it had reached in 1815.

After study, Alexander II's advisors concluded that the significant growth in both military strength and technological and industrial power now enjoyed by Russia's Western European rivals had been the result of civic, social, legal, and military reforms these countries had implemented. Great Britain and France had sponsored enormous economic growth by giving protection to private property and to capital investment. They lifted restrictions on the movement of people and so permitted the growth of cities and towns, which helped form larger labor pools. They adopted broader and more rational programs of taxation, which increased tax returns and thus grew the state's financial capabilities. France and particularly Prussia had reorganized military service by reducing the term of active army service but applying it to a broader pool of draftees, which created a smaller and less expensive standing army but one that had the capability of pulling back huge numbers of trained reserves when needed. While Western European countries were undergoing significant changes, the government of Nicholas I had sought to freeze the existing social order and so preserve a semi-medieval state that rested economically upon serf labor in the belief that this would be the strongest bulwark to protect the tsar's absolute power and the leading role of the nobility. Tsar Alexander II's advisors sought to make clear that "the catastrophe of the Crimean War underlined the pressing need for fundamental reforms in Russia as well as the fact that the hour was late."[52]

Alexander II, though by nature a conservative man like his father, did understand that Russia had to reform or fall further behind and face increased dangers. Out of many ideas for change that were considered in the period from 1861 to 1874, Alexander II agreed to and implemented by decree five major reforms that are outlined below. A major theme running through these reforms was the attempt to place the relations of all citizens with the Russian state on the same platform. Such a platform was created in two ways: first, by establishing a common legal framework for civil, political, and economic rights; and second, by taking down the special rights or privileges granted to some citizens that stood in the way of commonality.

The decrees of 1871 and 1874 that changed the relationship between the German colonies and the Russian state were among the last reforms made by the government

---

52. Riasanovsky, *History of Russia*, 377.

of Alexander II. From the limited data that have come to light concerning internal discussions within the Russian government about the specific reforms that affected the German colonies, it does not appear that the changes in the rights of the colonies and their citizens were made in any effort to punish or penalize the Germans, or because of any issues or concerns that arose from actions of the Germans. The primary motive for change was that the special rights held by the colonies had come to be thought of as out of keeping with the efforts of the Russian state to create the conditions needed for Russia to remain in step with its Western rivals.

The reforms that Alexander II ultimately approved are best understood as efforts to modify legal and civic practices in Russia, rather than create fundamental (much less revolutionary) change. The reforms did free the serfs and establish several important legal and political rights. They did improve economic conditions sufficiently to allow some parts of Russian industry to compete with its Western European rivals. The military reform did create an approximation of the reserve army system established in contemporary Germany and France. However, the reforms were hamstrung by the desire not to diminish the absolute power of the tsar as well as by efforts to maintain the power and influence of the nobility. As a result, the reforms offered neither sufficient satisfaction nor encouragement to those intended to benefit from them, nor consolation or a justifying rationale to those who opposed them. In spite of the mixed results achieved by the reforms, Russian historians have frequently noted that not since the time of Peter the Great had so many important changes been introduced.[53]

## Among the reforms approved by Alexander II, five stand out
### 1. The emancipation of the serfs (1861)

A decree issued in March 1861 emancipated the native peasant population in Russia. Heretofore, their legal position as serfs was little better than slavery. Peasants were bound to the land on which they were born and were obligated to provide agricultural labor, cash payments, or both to whoever owned the land—generally the crown, a noble family, or the church. While peasants had some legal rights and their labor duties were generally fixed by custom, they were entailed assets of any property. When land was sold, peasants working it were passed by the property rights to the new owner. The emancipation decree freed the peasants by ending their legal entailment to the land and by giving peasant communities a portion of the estates to which they had been tied. Individual peasant families did not receive rights to amounts of land under the decree. The recipients of the land grants were the peasant communities who were expected to continue to divide up the arable land annually among peasant families living in the community. Under the decree of emancipation, landowners received payment from the state to compensate them for the land and the peasant services that had been lost. The newly freed peasants were then to repay

53. S. Frederick Starr, *Decentralization and Self Government in Russia 1830–70* (Princeton: Princeton University Press, 1972), ix. See also Riasanovsky, *History of Russia*, 409.

the government over a period of forty-nine years for the costs the government had incurred in freeing them.[54]

Issues arose, however, as the required repayments to the government were often greater than the former dues owed to the landlords. Additional problems came from the selection of what land on an estate was to be ceded to the peasant communities. As compensation to landowners, they were allowed great discretion in selecting what land on an estate was to be ceded. As a result, the peasant community often received the least desirable allotments, which only increased peasant difficulties in earning enough to make the required repayments. As further concession, landlords were to retain a substantial portion of their former estates. The Soviet economic historian P. I. Ljaščenko has estimated that immediately after the reform, some thirty thousand noblemen kept ownership of around 95 million desjatina of land, averaging 3,166 desjatina per landowner, compared with the 116 million desjatina given over to twenty million freed peasant families, who received on average 5.8 desjatina.[55]

There was also a military aspect considered in the edict emancipating the serfs. Before emancipation, serfs who had been drafted into the army could not return to the peasant communities in which they were born after completing their required twenty-five years of service. Military service had freed them, and landowners, concerned that returning servicemen might create social and political problems, did not want them back. As a result, retired soldiers tended to look for work in cities and, having difficulty adjusting to civilian life, often became vagrants. Now, after emancipation, retired servicemen would be able to return to their native villages, and their readjustment to civilian life would become the problem of the local village mir.

## 2. The creation of representative organizations of local self-government (1864)

A decree of January 1864 established local councils of elected officials who would be responsible for the administration of government at the district level. These local councils, called zemstvos, were established throughout most, but not all, of European Russia.[56] Before 1864, local government had been the responsibility of provincial officials who were appointed by the central government in St. Petersburg. Now the local zemstvos were to be indirectly elected by all classes, with representation proportional to landownership. Each zemstvo was made up of separate districts, each termed a volost, that under the guidance of its zemstvo were responsible for local schools, public health, roads, and prisons. To take on these responsibilities, the zemstvos were

---

54. While Russia's defeat in the Crimean War is popularly understood to have played a major role in leading Alexander II's advisors to advocate emancipating the serfs, there is much disagreement among Russian historians as to the extent to which the defeat served as the impetus for emancipation. Certainly the defeat opened the way to a vigorous analysis of Russian problems and deficiencies and also undercut the arguments of Russian conservatives that nothing ought to change. It is also generally accepted that after 1840, or at least 1850, there was a broadening agreement that serfdom had outlived its economic usefulness. This was the basis of Kisilev's proposal for a limited emancipation that Nicholas I had considered seriously.

55. Riasanovsky, *History of Russia*, 414.

56. The word is derived from the Russian word for land, *zemlja*. Zemstvos were not created throughout all of Russia. In the Baltic states where the local nobility already had developed local councils, these were preserved. In the nine provinces created from Russia's share of the partitions of Poland and from Russia's absorption of Congress Poland, all with large Polish-speaking populations, no zemstvos were created. Russia had just put down another Polish revolt and had no desire to offer a new platform for Polish national rights to be asserted.

given a limited ability to assess and collect taxes. Though this reform was a major step toward creating local self-government, it was insufficient to produce material changes in local conditions. The provincial and central governments retained great and controlling local power. With representation tied to landholding, the nobility who wished few changes were typically the leading powers in local zemstvos. While the zemstvos could raise funds via taxes, the limits placed on this right meant many local needs could not be addressed.

### 3. The creation of a semi-independent judicial system (1864)

A decree of December 1864 made the judiciary a separate function and semi-independent of government. All citizens of Russia now were to have equal standing before the law. The former complex system, under which there were some twenty-one different ways to initiate a legal case, was now abolished. In its place, the decree established two procedures that were to cover all legal matters: justices of the peace were charged with handling minor civil and criminal cases, while trial by jury was introduced for major crimes. The reform of the legal system was the most successful of the major reforms of Alexander II. Riasanovsky notes with only slight exaggeration that, at least in form, it "almost overnight transformed the Russian judiciary [system] from one of the worst to one of the best in the civilized world."[57]

### 4. Financial, infrastructure, and land ownership reforms (1860–85)

A decree of June 1860 that was revised and strengthened in 1866 established the Russian State Bank and created the ability of that bank to sell bonds in Russia and abroad to finance needed state improvements. Unlike Western Europe, which had many private banks to supply capital to businesses engaged in trade and industry, Russia had almost no institutions to provide short-term credit. To meet this need more broadly, the Russian State Bank was established. The reformers also hoped to use this bank, like the Bank of England, to put the Russian currency on a firm basis, though this goal was not really achieved until 1897 when Russia adopted the gold standard. Under the rubric of this decree, beginning in the early 1860s, the Ministry of Finance began to invest in the construction of railroads to support both internal and external commerce. With costs of construction beyond the current means of the Russian government, the Ministry of Finance began to sell Russian railway bonds in Western Europe and North America, which proved a successful way to raise capital. To support peasant ownership of land, the Ministry of Finance founded the Peasant Land Bank in 1882 with the goal of providing mortgages to enterprising peasants who wanted to purchase land available on the market. However, the Ministry of Internal Affairs was concerned that such a bank would give peasants advantages over noble landowners who were heavily indebted. To mitigate this possibility, the Ministry established in 1885 the Nobles Land Bank to provide access to additional capital for nobles threatened by foreclosure.

---

57. Riasanovsky, *History of Russia*, 418. Even with later attempts at clawbacks, such as the effort to control political protests by asserting that criminal charges made as a result of any actions taken to undermine or change the government were subject to military courts-martial rather than the normal judicial system, the new system was not generally undermined.

## 5. Reform of the Russian military (1874)

This was the last of the great reforms, and it went into effect with a decree released in January 1874. All male citizens without regard to class were now subject to military service. In the past, only peasant males were subject to be drafted. Previously, the Russian army had been kept at an enormous size. Russia's goal had been to maintain a standing army equal to the combined size of the Prussian and Austrian armies. Now, the size of the standing army was to be significantly reduced. Copying the successful Prussian model, this reform sought to create a much smaller active duty force with a huge trained reserve that could be called up as needed. The Prussian model was dependent on a railway-based logistics system that Russia, still lagging far behind the rest of Europe in railway construction and hampered by the huge size of even European Russia, could adopt more in theory than in reality. The term of military service, which after emancipation had been reduced from twenty-five to ten years, now became six years of active service followed by nine years of reserve duty. Exemptions from possible service obligations were provided to men who were the only sons of their parents. Reduced terms of service were also provided to the educated—those educated at university had only six months of active duty, those with a secondary education had a two-year requirement, and those with a primary education had a four-year requirement. Such service requirement reductions, as the following chapter will note in more detail, referred only to education in Russian-language schools.[58] The military reform introduced elementary education for all draftees, which often provided the only real education received by many peasant soldiers.

## The reforms that affected the German colonies in Russia came out of studies made by the Russian government in the late 1860s that were closely tied to the concerns and principles underlying the earlier Alexandrine reforms

As noted above, a major theme running through Alexander II's reforms was to place all Russian citizens on more or less equal legal footing with the government. All citizens were now equal before the law, and all citizens were eligible to vote for representatives serving in the zemstvo government. The reformers were following here the progressive social practices of Western Europe, in which central governments sought to simplify civil regulation and make it uniform and universal by ending the multiplicity of differing local practices and rights. Acting under this principle, the Russian government took away the special rights of the noble and middle classes when it made their members subject to military service, and when it took away the rights of the noble class to purchase a local monopoly of distilling alcohol.

The groundwork for Alexander II's decree of 1871, which revoked the special privileges of the German colonies in Russia, came from a series of studies made by the Ministry of State Domains in the period from 1865 to 1866 that looked first at the administration of the German colonies and then at the problem of landless Germans in South Russia. In 1867, questions raised by these studies led to a

---

58. Mutschall's history of Tarutino notes that in 1880, graduates of German schools with Russian-language instruction, such as the one in Tarutino, would benefit from this reduced service requirement, though at a later date this privilege was taken back. Wilhelm Mutschall, "History of the Community of Tarutino from 1814 to 1934," *Heritage Review* 45, no. 1 (2015): 19–20.

further study now undertaken jointly by senior members of the Ministry of State Domains, the Ministry of the Interior, and the Ministry of Justice that considered how, in light of the Alexandrine reforms, the German colonies in Russia should be treated.

This process began in 1865, when the Minister of State Domains, A. A. Zelenoj, asked that a study be made of the Welfare Committee's administration with two questions in mind: (1) How well had the local legal and police functions operated in the German colonies; and (2) How well had the colonial self-administered government functioned. Vladimir Islavin, a former head of the Welfare Committee, was put in charge of this study.[59] The study, finished in 1865, concluded that many of the recent complaints filed about Welfare Committee actions were reasonable and well founded, and that visits to offices showed work in disarray and that many of the section leaders did not speak or understand German.[60] One outcome of this study was that the sitting head of the Welfare Committee, Alexander von Hamm, was relieved of duty and replaced. Perhaps also as a result of this study, the special administration for smaller colonies was abolished in December 1866 and its responsibilities were merged into the Welfare Committee.

Also in 1865, Zelenoj established a second study committee that dealt with issues in the German colonies. He asked this second group to consider what might be done to help poor, landless Mennonites who had been vigorously complaining about their situations. German Mennonite colonists, particularly in the Moločna district of the Tauride Province, had experienced substantial population growth, which, combined with widely varying agricultural success among different families, had created material disparities in wealth. A survey completed in 1865 in the Moločna District indicated that 64.6 percent of families were landless or owned only tiny cottage plots, while the great majority of allotted land was held by just 26.2 percent of families.[61] Such a state of affairs existed in spite of the fact that there were "still 15,820 dessiatins of unsettled land" which wealthy Mennonite landowners had been using for grazing.[62] In August 1865, this study committee, with Islavin as its head, visited the Moločna District to see and hear the grievances of the Mennonites first hand. As a result of the study, the Ministry of State Domains ordered in February 1866 that some 16,000 desjatina of communal lands in the Moločna District were to be given to over 1,300 landless families in equal distribution.[63]

59. Islavin had been head of the Welfare Committee from 1856 to 1858; in 1867, he held the rank of Privy Counselor (Tajnyj sovetnik) in the Ministry of State Domains, the third highest rank among Russian officials, which was equivalent to that of a Lt. General in the army.

60. Brandes, *Von den Zaren Adoptiert*, 348–49. In the discussion of the several government committees and commissions that led to the development of the Decree of 1871 that follow, I have relied largely on Brandes (349–55), as well as the following: Brandes, "Wirtschaftliche Entwicklung und soziale Differenzierung in der Deutschen Kolonien Neurußlands und Bessarabiens bis zur Aufhebung der Kolonialstatus" in Meissner, Neubauer, and Eisfeld, *Die Rußlanddeutschen*, 69–78; Neutatz, "Die Kolonien des Schwartzmeergebietes," 79–99; and Fleischhauer, *Die Deutschen im Zarenreich*, 281–82.

61. Goerz, *Molotschna Settlement*, 130. Goerz quotes results of the survey showing that "in 1865 there were in Molotschna 1,384 landowners [families], 2,356 landless, 1,063 cultivated cottage lots (Anwohner); in addition some 490 families lived in cities or in Russian villages."

62. Ibid., 131.

63. Ibid., 133. The number of landless families is implied by Goerz when he indicates that "this amounted to 12 dessiatins of land for every family." Families who formerly sold their farmsteads and those who lost them "due to shiftless[ness] and neglect" were excluded from this land distribution.

In the course of making these studies, questions of a broader nature appear to have been raised: The focus of the Alexandrine reforms was to end parallel sets of rights and regulations, so shouldn't these reforms affect the colonies administered by the Welfare Committee? In January 1867, Zelenoj established a special commission to consider these larger issues. To give their deliberations weight and their conclusions the likelihood of action, he included representatives from the ministries of interior and justice as well as from his own Ministry of State Domains. That the work of this commission represented a continuation of the earlier studies is implied by the fact that the commission was headed by Lieutenant General Arkadij Rosset and included Vladimir Islavin. Both had played prominent roles in the earlier studies. The new commission's secretary was Alexander A. Klaus, who had been secretary to the earlier study of the Moločna landless poor.[64] Klaus was the author of the 1869 study on foreign colonies in Russia, *Naši kolonii*, which has been frequently cited.

The conclusions reached by the 1867 commission argued that Russia would benefit from a close alignment between the legal rights given to the colonists and those new rights established for the freed serfs, taking the position, long held in the Ministry of State Domains, that the groups were made up of similar populations facing similar problems and opportunities. With this in mind, the commission specifically recommended that, insofar as possible, the treatment of the German colonists under Russian law should be equivalent to similarly situated Russian citizens. Such a conclusion reflected the philosophy that the welter of differing rights held by separate groups of citizens was an unnecessary encumbrance and inefficiency for a modern state. With regard to the landless poor, the committee concluded that the disinclination of the colonists to leave their overcrowded villages, even in the face of great need, was a primary cause of their poverty. It was observed that the poorest villages swarmed with small tradesmen and craftworkers unable to earn a decent living with their many competitors. The committee recommended that efforts be made to settle poor landless colonists in nearby Ukrainian and Russian villages, which would give the Germans a broader area to apply their occupations and so to earn adequate livings. It further noted that mixing the populations would encourage the use of the Russian language, a goal of the Central Schools established in 1865.

Zelenoj, agreeing with these conclusions, gave them to a second team of officials from his own ministry as well as from the ministries of justice, the interior, and finance to create the necessary regulatory language. Zelenoj then presented these recommendations to Alexander II in 1870. On June 2, 1871 (O.S.), Alexander II approved the recommendations and, in signing the document, transformed them into law. The document thus became a formal decree, called in Russian an ukaz, which was publically issued by the government on June 4, 1871 (O.S.).

Much of the literature that has focused on the experience of the German colonies in Russia has depicted the Decree of 1871, and the later one of 1874 on military requirements that also had a great effect on the Germans, as major breaches of trust

---

64. A. A. Klaus was an official in the Ministry of State Domains and held at this time the rank of Court Counselor (Nadvornyj sovetnik), a rank equivalent to that of a lieutenant colonel in the army. Brandes identifies Klaus as the son of an organist from one of the Volga colonies who had attended a gymnasium (that is, a Russian high school) in Saratov and had worked afterward in a Saratov trusteeship office (*Von den Zaren Adoptiert*, 354). The detail Brandes offers puts to rest Fleischhauer's assertion that Klaus came from South Russia (*Von den Zaren Adoptiert*, 281).

with the colonists. The decrees eliminated many of the special rights and ended the special treatment the Germans thought had been given them in perpetuity when they immigrated to Russia. The Russian government's motivations for issuing these decrees has often been viewed as resulting from concerns generated by the founding of a powerful and rival German state, from the unease awakened by the success of some colonists, and from the unhappiness expressed by many Russians that the Germans had long lived in Russia without showing any signs of assimilation. Seen in this light, the decrees became the initial acts of formal anti-German policies instituted by the Russian government.

Brandes, Fleischhauer, Giesinger, and Neutatz form a minority among commentators when they emphasize that the Russian government acted from benign motives and that the "changes Alexander made in the status of the colonists came in connection with the great reforms of his reign."[65] Many other commentaries, often written by the descendants of Germans who emigrated from Russia to North America, seek to connect the decrees to Russia's anti-German policies or fears about Germany's growing power. Harry Scholz, in his Chapman College thesis, sees the origin of the decrees in anti-German Russian nationalism that became heated after Prussia's victory over France.[66] Karl Stumpp concludes that there was a direct connection between the Prussian victory over France in 1870, the founding of Imperial Germany in the following year, and the cancellation of the special privileges that had been granted "for all time."[67] The Roll family account of the German colonies in Russia notes that "soon the Russians became jealous and pressure was brought to bear on the government to withdraw the special privileges."[68] The Weisenberger family history saw the origin of the decrees in the increased resentment felt by Russian peasants toward the privileges granted the German colonists and the growing political tension between Russia and Germany.[69]

Such views do not appear supported by the charge given the interministry commission, whose recommendations led to the Decree of 1871, nor are such views supported by the timing of events that led to the issuance of the decree in June 1871. The commission finished its meetings sometime in 1869, well before the start of Prussia's war with France, which began in August of 1870. The passage from design recommendations to final regulations typically took one to two years for the other Alexandrine reforms, so the process of realization for the Decree of 1871 seems to have followed a normal course rather than been spurred by external events. Moreover, the drafting group, who took up work in 1869 when the commission had developed its conclusions, had no charge to change or alter the recommendations of the commission. Its function was to turn those recommendations into regulatory language. Concerns about the power of Prussia/Germany and negative Russian attitudes toward unassimilated Germans were surely present in Russia in 1871. Both

65. Giesinger, *From Catherine to Khrushchev*, 224.
66. Harry G. Scholz, "The German Colonists of Russia: The Repeal of Russia's Law of the Colonists in 1871 and Its Effects on the German Colonist Population" (Orange, CA: Chapman College, 1969), 10–12.
67. Karl Stumpp, *Die Rußlanddeutschen: Zweihundert Jahre Unterwegs* (Freilassing, Ger.: Pannonia-Verlag, 1965), 28–29.
68. Brent Mai, "Ukraine German-Russians," Roll Family website, c. 2014, www.rollintl.com/roll/grsettle.htm.
69. Karen Abel, "The Weisenberger Website," http://home.att.net-needler. This website has since been taken down.

attitudes, though, became prominent themes of commentary only later in the 1870s, particularly after the 1878 Treaty of Berlin, which thwarted Russian plans in the Balkans. They were given an even stronger push when Alexander III succeeded his father following the latter's assassination.

The motivation for the Decree of 1871 seems clearly related to the goal of making uniform the legal status, rights, and duties of both landowning and landless peasants of all ethnic backgrounds in Russia. This is also the conclusion of Dietmar Neutatz, based on a study of the notes from the meetings of the interministry commission. Neutatz also emphasizes that the commission minutes reflect neither fear nor hatred of the Germans living in Russia, but instead the desire to help the Germans do better and achieve more within the developing Russian state. He thus concludes that the motives of the participants on the commission were not driven by a spirit of repression or Russification but by goodwill and concern for the welfare of the German colonists: "Die Beratungen der mit der Ausarbeitung des Gesetzes betrauten Kommissioner atmeten nicht den Geist von Repression und Russifizierung, sondern von Wohlwollen und Fürsorge."[70]

---

70. Neutatz, "Die Kolonien des Schwartzmeergebietes," 81. Ingeborg Fleischhauer has argued similarly that the Russian government's policy on nationalities at this time "was based upon utilitarian and pragmatic considerations and implemented in a somewhat liberal manner." Fleischhauer, "The Case of the Russian Germans," *Journal of Modern History* 53, no. 1 (March 1981): 1066.

# IX

# The Decrees of 1871 and 1874 Significantly Changed the Legal Rights and Responsibilities of German Settlements in Russia

The ukaz, or decree, issued June 4, 1871 (O.S.), was concerned with what the Russian government called the "foreign colonies." In addition to the German colonies along the Volga in South Russia and Bessarabia, the Decree of 1871 addressed itself to the rights of the Bulgarian colonies in South Russia and Bessarabia, as well as those of the Tartar colonies in the Crimea. The decree rescinded the varying special rights that had been provided to these colonies, which had been maintained in force by governments under Catherine the Great, Paul I, Alexander I, Nicholas I, and Alexander II.

The focus of the Decree of 1871 was to change the legal standing of the colonist citizens of Russia. They were no longer colonists but became either "settler owners" (*poseljane-sobstvenniki*)—that is, farmers who were owners of land—or "rural residents"—that is, non-landowning peasants. These were the same legal categories that had been assigned to the emancipated Russian peasants. The Decree of 1871 then:

1. Rescinded the privileges granted the different colonies as part of the settlement offers made when the colonists agreed to immigrate to Russia;

2. Eliminated the Welfare Committee through which the colonies had received special governance separate and independent from the provincial governments;

3. Eliminated the Welfare Committee districts and merged local village government into the volost and zemstvo systems, which reported to the district and provincial governments (former colonies with over three hundred citizens were not to be included in a volost with a majority different from themselves);

4. Introduced the reformed judicial system by establishing justices of the peace who were to try civil and criminal cases on the basis of Russian law;

5. Stipulated that Russian was to become the language of local government and that each community was to have a secretary able to record meeting results in Russian;

6. Stipulated that apart from religious education, which might continue to be conducted in the native language of the village, all secular education would have to be based on instruction in Russian.

As it would take time to implement fully all the terms of the Decree of 1871 (over a decade for some features), the immediate effect of the decree can be understood as generally aspirational. Nevertheless, the intention of the decree was to institute major legal and cultural changes in the "foreign colonies." The process of the largely successful implementation of these changes became a significant feature of the history of the German villages in Bessarabia from 1871 onward.

With regard to the German colonies in Russia, the Ministry of State Domains had long viewed the colonists as facing fundamentally similar challenges and having similar opportunities as Russian peasant communities. After the emancipation of Russian peasants, the ministry considered both groups as sharing the same legal status. To the Germans, however, the thought of being placed on the same legal footing as Russian peasants no doubt seemed a diminishment of both rights and status. This is Giesinger's implication when he notes that the decree "pulled them [the Germans] down to a basis of equality with the Russian peasants."[1] Virtually all accounts of the Decree of 1871 by Germans testify to the fact that surprise and shock greeted its announcement. It would not seem that the German colonists were aware of the deliberations that led to the decree or of the opinions held in the Ministry of State Domains. If they had been, reactions to the decree might have been more organized and vigorous.

## Early consequences of the Decree of 1871

The most significant early consequence of the Decree of 1871 for the German villages was the start of the process by which local governments and local judicial practices became incorporated into the volost (district-level) organizations of Russian provincial governments. While the Welfare Committee disbanded quickly, the adoption

---

1.  Giesinger, *From Catherine to Khrushchev*, 225.

of the use of the Russian language and Russian civil and legal procedures in local government occurred more slowly. Mennonite villages of South Russia often had some citizens who had been educated in Russian, which helped smooth for them the introduction of the new organization of governance. In Bessarabia, this does not seem to have been the case. There, it appears that for some time the local village government and courts continued to use their customary rules and practices with sessions held in the German language. However, leaders in the Bessarabian German villages who filled posts in civil government and acted as justices of the peace came under increasing pressure to learn Russian and apply Russian civil administrative procedures and Russian civil law. There is little data on the implementation of the changes mandated by the Decree of 1871 in German Bessarabia. It would not be surprising to learn that the process varied materially by village and that difficulties sometimes arose where German customs varied from Russian legal practices. By the early twentieth century, however, the meetings of civil government and the records of decisions of the justices of the peace in the German villages in Bessarabia were at least partially in Russian and followed patterns generally identical to all other villages throughout the province.

The Decree of 1871 paid special attention to the situation of landless colonists. It sought to address the issues of their poverty by giving them shares of land that would come from community reserves of unused land. Where the subdivision of farmsteads had been forbidden, the decree now permitted farmsteads to be subdivided, though it continued to forbid subdivision of farmsteads with less than 20 desjatina. The decree also sought to ensure that the landless poor would have full rights to vote and participate in the local volost governments. However, apart from permitting the subdivision of farmsteads, the provisions of the Decree of 1871 affecting the landless do not appear to have had much impact in German Bessarabia. Brandes has noted that the landless played little role in the Bessarabian community affairs, though he doesn't specify why this occurred.[2] Perhaps this is a reference to the common practice after 1871 of giving the landless cottagers limited voting rights. While the final decades of the nineteenth century saw steady increases in the numbers of landless poor in German Bessarabia, they never became a significant subsection of village populations. Many Germans deemed "landless" in Bessarabia were not poor. They were family members who shared management of a family farmstead and whose interests were represented in local government by an older sibling or parent.

For all the changes the Decree of 1871 brought, it did not touch the religious rights of the German colonists, nor did it end several unique customary and legal practices that existed in the German colonies. The rights of Germans in Russia to practice their Protestant and Catholic beliefs and to do so in the German language remained unchallenged. Similarly, German citizens could continue to educate their children in those beliefs and, in so doing, educate them in the German language. The Decree of 1871 did not sweep away all the legal particularities of the German colonies. In the context of discussing common pasturing land, Brandes asserts that land used for the houses and gardens of the landless poor in German Bessarabia remained owned by the community, which implies that the existing community efforts to help

---

2. Brandes, *Von den Zaren Adoptiert*, 355.

the landless poor were not overturned by the effects of the Decree of 1871.[3] The village fire protection offices, called the Brandkasse, also continued in effect. These organizations assessed contributions from town building owners that were used in times of need to repair buildings damaged by fire or to purchase and maintain fire-fighting equipment. Similarly, the decree did not end or change the rights of villages to maintain funds to benefit orphans. The decree did not disturb the rights of the German communities to loan out money held in the fire and orphans' funds or to set varying terms for the repayment of such loans. The village mandates to establish and maintain forest enclosures also continued in force. Such mandates had been part of the settlement agreements in Bessarabia and evidence the concern of the Russian government with fostering the growth of trees on the steppe and reducing problems caused by the absence of wood.[4]

While legally the Decree of June 1871 went instantly into effect, the implementation of all of its provisions actually took several decades. Fleischhauer has asserted that such a delay resulted from the fact that the Russian government decided to postpone much of the implementation of the Decree of 1871 until 1881 so as to smooth the transition.[5] Fleischhauer, however, provides neither sources for this assertion nor evidence of the decree's postponed implementation. More credible explanations for the delays in the implementation of the provisions include the great difficulty of making the complex transition the decree mandated quickly, the general absence of local officials able to speak and write fluently in Russian, and the struggle to apply Russian civil procedures and laws in the new volost governments and courts. Another reason for delays in implementing procedures required by the Decree of 1871 was the Russian government's absorption in devising and then implementing the great military reform of 1874.

Contrary to Fleischhauer's assertion of a ten-year delay in the implementation of the decree, it is clear that some provisions of the decree became effective soon after issuance. For example, the Welfare Committee appears to have quickly disbanded and closed its doors. The Welfare Committee's Bessarabian district offices in Alt Posttal,[6] Klöstitz, and Sarata, and its regional office in Akkerman are not referred to after 1872, and the term of office of the last head of the Welfare Committee, Vladimir Öttinger, officially ended in 1871. In its listing of town officials, the Kulm Heimatbuch indicates that a clear break occurred in 1872. Gottlieb Radke, elected to the normal two-year term in 1872 as the Schulz, had his term abruptly end when he was replaced later in the same year by Christian Lobe, who governed under a different title, the Oberschulz. The village secretary, Friedrich Scheller of Tarutino,

3. Ibid., 359.
4. Brandes gives another incidence of the retention of formerly held rights when he notes that the Decree of 1871 kept in effect certain lease arrangements under which German settlements, chiefly in South Russia, had been allowed to increase village holdings ("Wirtschaftliche Entwicklung und soziale Differenzierung," 76).
5. Fleischhauer, Die Deutschen im Zarenreich, 284–85.
6. In writing about the Welfare Committee's district office in Alt Posttal, Kern notes that "only Klöstitz and Sarata had [other] such offices." In the following paragraph, he confusingly adds: "Over the years, more district offices were established and when they were closed in 1918 only Alt Posttal, Wittenberg and Katzbach still belonged to Alt Posttal" (Homeland Book, 64). As the Welfare Committee and its administrative structure clearly ended in 1872, Kern appears here to be referring here to both the Welfare Committee district office in Alt Posttal and the volost office established there after 1872 that combined that village with Wittenberg and Katzbach and remained in existence until Bessarabia's absorption into Romania in 1918.

who held this post from 1865, continued in office after 1872, but now under the title of District Secretary.[7] The Kulm Heimatbuch also indicates that up to 1872, Kulm belonged to the Malojaroslavec District, meaning a district of the Welfare Committee, and that in 1872, Kulm became a volost in its own right.[8] These references certainly suggest that in 1872, important pieces of the Decree of 1871 were implemented in Kulm.

Data in the Kulm Heimatbuch, however, suggest that a meaningful integration of Kulm into the provincial volost system of civic administration, as well as the justice of the peace system of courts, was delayed until 1880, when Friedrich Frey was brought in as the Volost Secretary. Frey, a native of Neudorf in Xerson Province, replaced the above-mentioned Friedrich Scheller. The implication in the Heimatbuch is that Frey's command of the Russian language and perhaps Russian civil procedures were the reasons for his appointment. As Volost Secretary, Frey would maintain records and provide correspondence for and translate correspondence from the provincial and district civil administration, as well as conduct and report hearings of the justice of the peace.[9] While the connections between the provincial and zemstvo officials in Bessarabia and the German settlement volosts may have been limited in the early 1870s, it is clear that some existed. The conscription obligations mandated by the Decree of 1874, which reformed the military, were communicated and implemented throughout German Bessarabia by the end of 1875. Frey's appointment in Kulm establishes that some approximation of the volost system and the justice of the peace judicial system were implemented by at least 1880. In spite of Frey's appointment, the meetings of village volost government and court proceedings continued to be held in German. It was not until the first decade of the twentieth century that volost meetings in Kulm appear to be conducted at least in part in Russian.

It is clear, however, that in some of the German colonies there was, at a much earlier date, a growing awareness that a knowledge of the Russian language was both necessary and of practical value. Mutschall's history of Tarutino suggests that as early as 1857, the village secretary, Johann Kutz, was teaching Russian to a few students, and that in the 1860s, Pastor Pingoud "started teaching a bit of it in school" and "as time passed, the Russian language acquired a modest place in the school."[10] The existence of more than a handful of Germans fluent in Russian does not appear to occur before the 1890s. Mutschall notes that in the period before the 1871 decree, German villages, led by their pastors, strongly resisted the Welfare Committee's encouragement to make Russian the general language of instruction in the German village schools.[11]

---

7. Wölfle, "The Establishment of the Village of Kulm," 7.
8. Ibid., 6. As a result, the change in title for the village secretary was to Volost Secretary.
9. It is not clear where Frey acquired his education in Russian. He did not come directly to Kulm from Neudorf in Xerson Province. Though he appears in Neudorf as the orphan son of Michael Frey in the 1858 Neudorf census data listed in Stumpp (*Emigration from Germany to Russia*, 711). Friedrich Frey married Christina Koch of Gnadental, Bessarabia, sometime before 1876 and is shown as living in Alt Elft, Bessarabia, in 1876 when their first child was born March 1, 1876 (O.S.). Reuben R. Drefs, trans., "Bessarabian Village Birth Records, 187×," ed. Marty McMahon (N.p.: Odessa Digital Library, 1998), http://www.odessa3.org/collections/stpete/bess/link/bes187xb.txt.
10. Wilhelm Mutschall, "History of the Community of Tarutino from 1814 to 1934," *Heritage Review* 44, no. 2 (2014): 22.
11. Ibid., 21.

I have not found data that suggest that authorities in any of the Bessarabian German villages in the 1870s and 1880s possessed sufficient knowledge of Russian or a background in Russian legal or civic procedures to implement the requirements of the Decree of 1871 fully. It would also appear that civic meetings and court sessions in the German villages were held in German during these two decades. The volosts, however, clearly were established. The villages of Kulm, Tarutino, and Krasna, perhaps because they were large and situated so close to each other, each became a volost in their own right around 1872.[12] Other volosts were made up of several villages joined together, with Alt Posttal, Klöstitz, Sarata, and Arzis each serving as centers of volost administration. When a volost included more than one village, non-German settlements were sometimes made part of volosts centered on a German village. This was especially true for many of the new German villages founded further east of Sarata in Bessarabia. There, volost boundaries very likely included neighboring non-German settlements. Kern notes, for example, that Neu Posttal became a volost center in 1880 with the volost territory incorporating settlements in a radius of 15–20 kilometers. As such, this volost would have included the German village of Benkendorf and the Russian village of Demidovka.[13]

Fleischhauer's assertion that the Russian government delayed the implementation of the Decree of 1871 for ten years may have been based on her reading of a provision in the decree that granted Germans unhappy with the decree a special right to emigrate. The Decree of 1871 permitted the former colonists, for a period of ten years after 1871, to leave Russia without paying to the state "any part of their acquired capital."[14] Prior to this special exemption and after its ten-year period expired, German colonists who elected to emigrate from Russia were required to pay a tax based on all the capital they had acquired in Russia, and a tax on any belongings they took with them.[15] It is going beyond the evidence to suggest that by offering special rights to emigrate, the Russian government delayed implementing all aspects of the Decree of 1871 for ten years. What this provision suggests instead is that the government intended to implement the decree as rapidly as feasible, but wished to offer this simplified means to a passport as a safety valve.

While it is likely that German settlers throughout Russia reacted negatively to the Decree of 1871 and the loss of their special rights, apart from the Mennonites there do not appear to have been any formal protests. I have not found indications that the Bessarabian German communities followed in any great detail or interest the announcement and implementation of the major Alexandrine reforms in the 1860s. It does not appear that the district offices of the Welfare Committee in Bessarabia provided any hints in the late 1860s of coming changes when it became apparent to senior members of the Welfare Committee in Odessa that such were forthcoming. Thus, when the Decree of 1871 was translated, it surely came as a great surprise to

12. Wölfle, "Heimatbuch der Gemeinde Kulm," *Heritage Review*, 13, no. 4: 6. Wölfle asserts that Kulm and Tarutino were the only German settlements in Bessarabia to be volosts in their own right. The chronicle of Krasna, however, notes that Krasna formed its own volost (Riehl, "History of the Village of Krasna"). Leipzig also later became a separate volost, but this did not occur until 1909 when it was separated from the volost centered in Klöstitz.

13. Kern, *Homeland Book*, 171.

14. Ralph Koprince, "The International Passport System of Late Imperial Russia," *Heritage Review* 14, no. 4 (November 1984): 19. Koprince here is quoting from a translation of the 1871 decree.

15. Ibid., 17–18.

the German communities in Bessarabia and awakened many concerns. However great the surprise the decree created, the general reaction was passive. As Giesinger has surmised, it was likely dominated by thoughts of waiting to see how the decree would be implemented and what the new administrative systems would be like.[16]

## Reactions were far stronger to the announcement of the major military reform

The military reform was announced in a decree dated January 1, 1874 (O.S.). As noted in the previous chapter, this was one of the major reforms enacted under Alexander II and one that affected men of all social classes and nationalities throughout Imperial Russia. Heretofore the German colonists, though citizens of Russia, had not been subject to conscription into the Russian army. The Decree of 1874 took away what the German colonists considered one of the major rights they had been granted in the different settlement agreements that had brought them to Russia. Moreover, under the terms of this decree, most German conscripts from the former colonies would have to serve the maximum term in the army: six years of active duty plus another nine years in the reserves. Shortened service was linked to the levels of education a conscript had attained. Education, however, was defined as education in Russian. For Germans conscripted from the Bessarabian villages, and likely for most Germans from South Russia and the Volga, such education as they had received had been provided in German and so was not counted. From the perspective of the Imperial Russian government, such treatment of conscripts from the German colonies was not at all prejudicial. Education in Russian was now the civic standard for the country as a whole, and conscripted Germans were likely to have outcomes similar to the conscripted Russian peasants whom the government regarded as their legal and social equals.

Given the huge size of Imperial Russia, the absence of infrastructure connecting its many parts, and the historically slow movement of its still relatively undermanned civil service, major changes in policy could not be rapidly implemented. It took the Russian government the better part of two years to implement the Decree of 1874 reforming military service. Under this decree, conscription obligations were established on a provincial basis tied to the estimated male population of the province. The obligation of each province, or *gubernija* in Russian, was subdivided into the county-like regions,[17] each called an *uezd*, of that province and these obligations were then subdivided among the volosts. The province of Bessarabia was divided into eight regions. In 1874, almost all the German settlements in Bessarabia were located in the Akkerman uezd.[18] The Russian government was able to establish provincial conscription requirements in 1874. These were then divided among the regions and volosts by the end of 1875. By the end of the following year, Germans from the Bessarabian settlements had been called up as part of the first conscription allotment and began their service in the Russian army.

---

16. Giesinger, *From Catherine to Khrushchev*, 226.
17. In the ancient European provinces of Russia such as Moscow, Tula, and Kaluga, the gubernija were subdivided into regions, each call a *provincija*, and then into uezdy.
18. The Akkerman region was located in the south central and southeastern part of Bessarabia where the original German colonies had been placed. The three German settlements founded in northern Bessarabia noted earlier were located in the Bel'cy region.

The military reform enacted by the Decree of 1874 has frequently been cited as the critical factor that caused Mennonites as well as many non-Mennonite Germans in Bessarabia and South Russia to emigrate. Commentaries offered by immigrants to North America from the German communities in Russia almost always mention the loss of the exemption from military service as an important if not primary cause of why they left Russia. A North Dakota Studies article on the Germans from Russia gives the revocation of the exemption from military service as the first reason why "Germans began to leave Russia."[19] The Baumstark family history, for example, notes that main reason the family left South Russia was to avoid conscription.[20] Hugo Raugust, in giving reasons why his grandfather Christian Raugust left Russian Bessarabia, put "required military service" at the head of the list.[21] Norman Saul, in his essay "The Migration of Russian Germans to Kansas," argues that "the removal of the special exemption [from military service] must be considered a catalyst for the idea of emigration."[22]

Such references offer little doubt that non-Mennonite Germans in Russia were very unhappy with the military reform of 1874 and the loss of the exemption from conscription it mandated. However, their religious beliefs, their behavior in Prussia prior to coming to Russia, and their behavior after 1874 in Russia and North America do not make it clear why required military service became the focal point of their discontent. In contrast to the Mennonites, members of the Evangelical Lutheran and Catholic churches in Bessarabia and South Russia were not professed pacifists. The doctrines of these churches did not preclude members from serving in the military and fighting in wars. In Prussia, from the early eighteenth century through Prussia's temporary demise in 1806, each district was responsible for producing a quota of young men for the army. It is likely that members of the German families who came to Russia had served in the Prussian army. This was not the case for those who came directly to Russia from Württemberg, where a permanent army of volunteers and mercenaries was the rule and conscription was not practiced. However, the economic pressures that were created by the small family plots in Württemberg led many young men there to elect soldiering as a career. Following the imposition of the military reform of 1874 in Imperial Russia, there is no history of non-Mennonite Germans from Bessarabia or South Russia protesting conscription or asserting rights that would prevent them from being conscripted.[23] Similarly, in the United States and Canada, sons and grandsons of immigrants from Bessarabia and South Russia elected to serve or accepted being drafted into service to fight in World War I and World War II.

While the objections to service in the military were prominent on the lists of reasons why families chose to emigrate, there is little explanation offered as to why this was so. Some of the reasons might be guessed at. The Russian army had a

---

19. D. Jerome Tweton, "Germans from Russia Now Second Largest Immigrant Group," *GRHS News*, December 2005, http://www.grhs.org/data/grhsnews/Dec2005.pdf.

20. Heinz Baumstark and Ann Justiss, "Little History of Baumstark," ver. 26, last modified on November 1999, http://heinz-baumstark.homepage.t-online.de/meineHTML/history-e.htm.

21. Hugo Raugust, "The History of Christian Raugust and Wife Carolina Raugust (nee) Gross," unpublished document in the author's possession.

22. Saul, "Migration of Russian-Germans to Kansas."

23. There are several stories of young men emigrating from Bessarabia to North America in the spring before the annual conscription calls were made. Such stories do attest to the desire not to have to serve in the Russian army, but not necessarily to objections to the concept of military service per se.

terrible reputation for the abuse of recruits, particularly those with a non-Russian national background.[24] Corruption in the purchase of supplies and incompetence in their delivery made life in the army notoriously difficult and hard.[25] Russian military doctrine from the time of Catherine the Great through the end of the Soviet period put great reliance on the technique of using overwhelming numbers to beat better-trained and better-equipped opponents. A major consequence of this doctrine was that the Russian military leadership was willing to put up with large numbers of casualties.[26] Germans could well also object to the fact that religious services in the Russian army were solely under the control of the Russian Orthodox Church. With the conflicts of the Russo-Turkish wars of 1827–29 and 1877–79 taking place in Romania, and with Bessarabia serving as a staging, supply, and hospital area for the fighting, the Bessarabian Germans gained first-hand (and not positive) experiences with the Russian army at war.[27] Moreover, many German families who immigrated to Bessarabia came there as the result of the impoverishment caused by the requisitioning of food, supplies, and animals and the destruction of personal property that accompanied the passage of French troops to and from Russia in 1812–13. Memories of these experiences together with the knowledge that the prosperity they had achieved in Bessarabia was in part the result of not having to send sons into the army because of their military exemption were likely other factors that lay behind the clear antipathy expressed by the Germans about the loss of their exemption from military service.

Norman Saul is one of the few commentators who addresses why the reaction to military conscription was so strong among the Germans in Russia. In his view, Germans in Russia strongly opposed the military reform of 1874 because service in the Imperial Russian army was considered in a highly negative light: "Hostility to the Russian army was quite high…because of conditions that prevailed for recruits, perhaps exaggerated by rumor, bias against advancement by non Russians and the predominance of Russian Orthodox religious services."[28]

Another reason the German colonist families were not keen on military service was that they had not yet bought into the idea that, as citizens of Russia, they should

---

24. This has been a long-term problem in the Russian army where the custom of *dedovščina* or the rights of older soldiers to haze recruits cruelly and often violently, was deeply ingrained. This continues to be a problem to the present day. See: "The Consequences of Dedovshchina," 2004, Human Rights Watch, https://www.hrw.org/reports/2004/russia1004/6.htm; and Jake Rudnitsky, "Full Metal Torture," *Vice*, April 1, 2006, http://www.vice.com/read/full-v13n4.

25. Bruce W. Menning, *Bayonets before Bullets: The Imperial Russian Army 1861-1914* (Bloomington: Indiana University Press, 1992). In his study of the Russian army, Menning refers to the Russian supply services as "incompetent" in 1877 at the beginning of the Russo-Turkish War (64), and in reviewing that war, Menning calls the supply system "corrupt" with "supplies usually late, inadequate, spoiled or non existent" (83).

26. The Crimean War, the campaigns of the Russo-Turkish wars of the late 1820s and late 1870s, and the Russian campaigns in Central Asia in the 1860s were notorious for the high casualties suffered by Russian troops. In the latter conflicts, the lesson from the American Civil War of the near impossibility of successfully attacking positions that were moderately defended by soldiers with rifles had not been absorbed. The third battle of Plevna (1877) produced over twelve thousand Russian casualties alone (see Menning, *Bayonets before Bullets*, 70–74). The horrors of the Russo-Turkish War of 1877–79 were the central theme of Vsevolod Garšin's much noted short story "Četyre dnja" [Four days] of 1877 and Vasily Vereščagin's paintings such as *Pobeždennye* [The vanquished] in 1877–79. Both Garšin and Vereščagin were on active duty with the Russian army in this campaign.

27. Mutschall notes a hospital for war wounded established in Tarutino in 1878 ("Community of Tarutino," *Heritage Review* 44, no. 2: 17).

28. Saul, "Migration of Russian-Germans."

support its interests, feel loyal to, and even fight for its causes. Until the Decree of 1871, the German communities were only marginally assimilated. Instead, they were islands of German culture, where the religion, language, and customs they brought with them still reigned supreme. Connections with Russia appear to have been weak and just forming.

However, of all the explanations that have been put forth as to why the non-Mennonite Germans who left Russia tended to put military service at the top of their lists of causes for emigrating, the best explanation, I believe, is that conscription came to symbolize the erosion of all the special rights taken away by the decrees of 1871 and 1874. While the full consequences of adopting the volost system of civil government and the standard Russian judicial system were slow in making themselves felt, conscription and its consequences were apparent immediately. The erosion of the rights and privileges given to them as immigrants coming to Russia perhaps symbolized that the special, protective, and isolated world they had created in Russia was now passing, and that a different, unknown, and possibly less attractive period was beginning. This appears to be the conclusion plant biologist William Sumner Harwood drew from speaking with German immigrants from Russia in the Dakotas during the early 1890s. In an article he wrote for *Harper's Weekly* on the farmers he encountered in the Dakotas, he concludes that they immigrated because they "found their rights slipping away from them; found that in their courts, their language, their religion, they were becoming assuredly more and more Russian than German."[29]

In spite of the widespread unhappiness with young men facing conscription as well as the diminution of village independence, the great majority of Germans in Bessarabia and South Russia did not emigrate but remained in Russia. From 1876 through the end of World War I, Germans were conscripted into the Russian army and participated in its campaigns and wars fighting as part of the Russian army in World War I.[30] Albert Kern lists the names of 963 Germans from the Bessarabian villages who were killed or missing in action. In his accounting, the greatest losses were suffered by Leipzig with 47 men killed and Klöstitz with 44.[31]

The non-Mennonite German communities in the Volga, South Russian, and Bessarabian regions did not, apparently, make any formal protests against the Decree of 1874. These communities had no tradition of protesting the actions of the government and, moreover, lacked the organization to act en masse as the Mennonites had. It is nonetheless clear that the non-Mennonite Germans were quite unhappy with the Russian government for taking back rights they thought had been given to them in perpetuity, and, in so doing, "disregarding the promises" made by the tsars from Catherine the Great forward.[32] In taking this position, Germans in Russia were indicating their continued isolation and the limits to their knowledge about Russia

---

29. W. S. Harwood, "A Bit of Europe in Dakota," *Harper's Weekly*, July 11, 1896, http://library.ndsu.edu/grhc/history_culture/history/eureka.html.
30. Kern notes that Karl Bierer of Alt Arzis had been drafted into the army early enough to participate in the Russo-Turkish campaign of 1877–79, where he served as a medic in a hospital in Bender, Bessarabia (*Homeland Book*, 82). Kern's assertion that Bierer had been drafted in 1873, however, is surely in error, as the decree affecting the Germans was not issued until January 1874, and conscription among the Germans in Bessarabia did not appear to have begun until 1876.
31. Ibid., 203–322.
32. Raugust, "History of Christian Raugust."

and its government. The Germans had a fundamental misunderstanding of a basic principle of the Imperial Russian state: tsars never accepted any limitation to their power. They might have, at will, changed or taken back any grant, privilege, or right; they never gave promises in perpetuity.

For its part, the Imperial Russian government assumed that the non-Mennonite Germans would simply accept the change. No concern is evidenced that the Germans would not. Moreover, as the military reform enjoyed the strong support of senior Russian political and military officials and was considered crucial for achieving the political and diplomatic aims of the government, it is unlikely that even organized and massive opposition would have swayed the government. The intention of the reform was to create a modern citizen army along the lines successfully used by the Western European powers. The organizational reform would create a smaller active duty force that used modern weaponry and would be supported by a huge, trained citizen army reserve that could rapidly be brought up to speed when dangers presented themselves.[33]

## The most negative reaction to the military reform was among the Mennonites

The Mennonites were pacifists who believed that it was wrong to take up arms even in self-defense. Indeed, one reason many Mennonites immigrated to Russia was that when Royal Prussia, where they had been living, was absorbed into Prussia in the First Partition of Poland, they feared that in becoming citizens of Prussia, they would become subject to conscription. When rumors about the military reform in Russia began to circulate, the Mennonites had even sent delegations to St. Petersburg in 1871, 1872, and 1873 in an effort to have their communities exempted from military service.[34] In parallel with sending delegations to St. Petersburg, the Mennonites also wrote to German coreligionists in North America inquiring about conditions there and even opened tentative discussions with government bodies in Canada and the United States about the conditions under which they might immigrate.[35]

In response to their inquiries, in 1872, Canada offered the Mennonites terms for immigration that included exemption from military service, as well as self-rule for their communities and rights to maintain their German language were they to immigrate to the province of Manitoba. In early 1874, the state of Kansas passed a law directed at attracting Mennonites there, which exempted from military service all persons whose religion prohibited them from bearing arms. In the United States

33. The Napoleonic wars showed the superiority of the mass citizen army over the smaller, professional, and/or mercenary forces that dominated eighteenth-century warfare in Europe. The best military strategists after this period, such as Swiss Antoine-Henri Jomini and particularly Prussian Karl von Clausewitz, emphasized the concept of war as a struggle between societies. The efforts of the Prussian general staff and its mid-nineteenth-century head, Helmuth von Moltke, to increase the effectiveness of Prussia's army through a better selection of recruits and by improved training and weaponry proved a decisive difference against the French in 1870. The Russian military concluded that only by adopting similar approaches could Russia continue to defend itself and pursue its objectives as a major European power.

34. Giesinger, *From Catherine to Khrushchev*, 227.

35. Scholz, "German Colonists of Russia," 14; Goerz, *The Molotschna Settlement*, 143–48; and Alberta Pantle, "Settlement of the Krimmer Mennonite Brethren at Gnadenau, Marion County," *Kansas Historical Quarterly* 13, no. 5 (1945): 259–85. Pantle gives the example (260) of Cornelius Jansen, a merchant in Berdjansk in South Russia, who wrote at this time to John Funk, the editor of the *Herald der Wahrheit*, a Mennonite newspaper in Elkhart, Indiana, asking about conditions for settlement in the American Middle West.

at that time, state militias formed the only potential nonvoluntary military service. After the American Civil War, the few state militias in existence were formed on a voluntary basis; however, as the right to form a militia belonged to the state government, it was legally each state's right to determine who should serve.[36]

The Russian government was concerned about both the potential for unrest in and emigration from the Mennonite communities. Shortly after the Decree of 1874 was issued, the government published an addendum that extended the Mennonites' exemption from military service for another six years. This extension was presumably an attempt to keep the Mennonites calm while the government sought a solution. As noted earlier, in order to assuage those especially upset, the Decree of 1871 had opened a ten-year door to emigration by eliminating the tax that had functionally made emigration unaffordable for most. It would appear that the Russian government especially feared a mass exodus of the Mennonites.

By April of 1874, however, some five thousand Mennonites had applied for passports allowing them to emigrate from Russia. News of this greatly alarmed the Russian government, and it acted relatively quickly in an effort to prevent or at least minimize any emigration. In April 1874, the Minister of War, Dmitry Miliutin, sent General Eduard I (von) Totleben, a Baltic-German military engineer who was the much-praised Russian defender of the fortress of Sebastopol in the Crimean War, to visit the Mennonite communities in South Russia. Totleben's report to the Minister of Interior, A. E. Timašev, dated April 30, 1874 (O.S.), indicates that he met with three groups of Mennonites: (1) a small group of more radical Mennonites who expressed a readiness to leave for the United States immediately, (2) much larger groups who wished to remain in Russia if a compromise could be found, but who would not accept the decree's demand for military service as written, and (3) a small group Totleben took to be speculators interested in purchasing properties given up by those who emigrated.[37]

Goerz, in his history of the Moločna Mennonites, indicates that Totleben visited and spoke to large audiences, first at Xortica in the Ekaterinoslav Province and then on April 21, 1874 (O.S.), in Halbstadt, a Moločna community in Tauride.[38] Totleben told both audiences that the Russian government wished them to stay in Russia and that it was to their great advantage to do so, but that the government "could not avoid imposing personal state service on them."[39] Totleben, however, offered a compromise. Mennonite youth who were conscripted could be exempted from bearing arms. They might, instead, serve in noncombat roles, such as working in naval workshops, in firefighting brigades, or in the special mobile detachments of the forestry service, whose main task would be planting trees on the steppelands of South Russia. Goerz implies that the Mennonites took these as different potential choices, since when the Halbstadt assembly responded to Totleben three days

36. Mennonite scouting parties from Russia were in the United States in 1872 and 1873 looking at land then available for settlement. Pantle ("Krimmer Mennonite Brethren," 262) notes a scouting party in Kansas in 1873 that met with state officials and inquired whether it was possible for them to enact a law that would exempt the Mennonites from military service. Both Minnesota and Nebraska also enacted such laws in 1877.

37. Fleischhauer, *Die Deutschen im Zarenreich*, 312. Fleischhauer evidently saw a copy of this document during her service with Stumpp's group in the Ukraine during World War II.

38. Halbstadt, now the town of Moločans'k in the Ukraine, is downstream on the Moločna River from the city of Tokmak.

39. Goerz, *The Molotschna Settlement*, 145.

later, they "unanimously chose forestry." The forestry service was preferred because it permitted the Mennonites to keep their youth together in service.[40] The Mennonites asked to be able to maintain control over the education of these conscripts, promising, as part of this, to teach them Russian.

Apparently this compromise was not a preapproved alteration to the Decree of 1874 but was part of the negotiating latitude given to, or taken by, Totleben. This may be inferred by the opposition to this compromise expressed by Minister of War Miliutin. The short biography of Totleben in the *Russkij biografičeskij slovar'* [Russian biographical dictionary] indicates that Totleben met personally with Alexander II on April 10, 1874 (O.S.), just before his visits to the Mennonites and that upon completing his mission, he reported back to the tsar from Warsaw.[41] It isn't clear whether Miliutin's objections were procedural—not wanting the compromises Totleben offered to become formal acts of law that might set precedents for other groups—or philosophical—not wanting to offer compromises at all. Alexander II, however, approved the compromise Totleben had offered, and it became law when issued as a separate decree on May 14, 1875 (O.S.).

One motivation Alexander II might have had was the Ministry of Interior's discovery, around the time of Totleben's visit, that agents working for state governments in the United States and provinces in Canada were circulating in these Mennonite communities talking up the benefits of immigration. To this point, Russia had not experienced any substantial emigration. Until the emancipation of the serfs, Russian peasants, as the property of the estates they worked on, were barred from emigration. Following emancipation, free peasants could emigrate but were faced with the substantial tax on capital gained during the time they had lived in Russia. The Decree of 1871 granted the German colonists a ten-year exemption from this tax, but the Imperial Russian government was not eager to have them leave. In 1874, the Russian government's view was still tied to the mercantilist concept that the assets of the state were the sum of the productive capacities of its citizens. Citizens who emigrated were thus removing productive assets from Russia. Official negative attitudes toward the idea of German emigration were intensified by the discovery of (in the government's view) illegal foreign agents in South Russia who sought to lure away citizens.

Something of this view was reflected in the biographical sketch of Totleben made in the early twentieth century.[42] In this sketch, Totleben is pictured as visiting the Mennonites in 1874 with the goal of limiting emigration. Acting on reports of the existence of foreign agents, Totleben moved vigorously to arrest any that could be found.[43] Totleben warned the Mennonites in his speeches that life in North America would be worse for them, that the land there was poor and the settlements were

---

40. Ibid., 146.
41. Aleksandr Aleksandrovič Polovcov, ed., "E. I. Totleben," in *Russkij biografičeskij slovar'*, Vol. 20a, *Tobizen–Totleben* (St. Petersburg: Tipografija Glavnago Upravlenija Udělov, 1901), 202.
42. Ibid.
43. Brandes indicates that in response to inquiries from the Mennonites, Canada had sent a recruiter in the summer of 1872 to Russia to encourage Mennonite immigration to Canada (*Von den Zaren Adoptiert*, 367). In April 1873, the Russian Foreign Ministry, in response to seeing written inducements to immigration (*Auswanderungspropaganda*), had warned the British Embassy in Russia against involving its agents or consuls in the emigration movement (366, note 2). The reason for warning the British was that under Confederation Act that created Canada in 1867, Great Britain remained in control of Canadian foreign affairs.

endangered by wild natives. Goerz provides a small extract from Totleben's speech in Halbstadt, in which Totleben warns the Mennonites that they might be drawn into a war he imagined brewing between Canada and Great Britain: "You have northern Canada in view—fine, but apparently over there a war with England is not far away and you will then be right in the firing line."[44]

The biographical sketch praises Totleben for limiting the emigration of Mennonites from Russia. It notes that the great majority of Mennonites elected to remain in Russia with less than a tenth choosing to emigrate. Scholz states that while Totleben had permitted those holding passports to leave the country if they wished, he also had those Mennonites who seemed most active in stirring up interest in emigration arrested and exiled.

## The decrees of 1871 and 1874 did mark the start of major changes for Germans in Bessarabia

In the chapter that follows, one focus will be on cultural currents that had a generally negative impact on the Germans in Bessarabia: the growing pressure to assimilate, to speak Russian, and to support Russian national interests, as well as the increasing expressions of irritation among Russian conservatives, especially in South Russia, that the Germans there were an alien presence, unwanted competitors for land, whose efforts at land purchase should be blocked. In spite of such negative influences, the reaction of the majority of the German population in Bessarabia was to passively adapt. They had built up successful and thriving, if now more crowded, settlements. Except for the military reform and the start of conscription, it was far from clear in the 1870s how the consequences of the Decree of 1871 would really affect the German settlements. Throughout the remainder of the nineteenth century and up to the start of World War I, it would appear that the major goals of the Germans living in Bessarabia continued to be satisfied. They continued to live in German-speaking villages preserving their German customs and practicing their Evangelical Lutheran and Catholic religious beliefs. Their economy, with its strong basis in profitable agriculture, continued to thrive. There were great opportunities to purchase or lease additional land in Bessarabia to form new villages and so relieve the critical problem of crowding. The Germans had the financial means to act when landowners were willing to sell or lease. It is clear that the effects of the decrees of 1871 and 1874 were not destabilizing agents. After their issuance, the German communities in Bessarabia continued to grow and prosper.

One clear change that occurred after the issuance of the decrees was the start of a steady emigration of Bessarabian Germans out of Bessarabia, and especially out of Russia, first to Dobrudscha across the estuary of the Danube into Romania and soon thereafter, and in far greater numbers, to North America. Were the decrees the critical force that started the emigration? There is simply too little information to answer this with confidence: few accounts exist from those emigrating that speak to their motivations. However, as emigration from Bessarabia out of Russia started to occur in more than marginal numbers only after the decrees were issued, it is tempting to think the two events were related. It would appear certain that one reaction to the issuance of the two decrees was to foster much discussion

---

44. Goerz, *The Molotschna Settlement*, 145.

in the German communities about their potential consequences. The Decree of 1871 included a provision that allowed the Germans to emigrate without being subject to a special tax imposed on some estimate of the economic gains they had achieved. It is reasonable to presume that as a result, the topic of emigration came up. As well, the fact that several immigrant families in North America remembered the military reform and conscription as a major reason their ancestors left Russia strongly suggests, at least for some emigrants, negative reactions to the decrees were important influences in their decisions to leave Russia. Yet, as we will see in the following chapter, there are several other factors that have weight as proximate causes.

Dobrudscha had attracted small groups of emigrants from German Bessarabia as early as the Separatists in the 1840s. Later, small groups of adventurers had moved there in the 1860s, followed by much larger groups beginning after 1875. Dobrudscha, though attractively close, had drawbacks, not the least of which were the limited opportunities to buy land and the fact that the provinces of Romania on the other side of the Danube from Dobrudscha became war zones in 1877. North America, though far away, offered more land and fewer perceived risks of war.

The first Bessarabian Germans to come to North America settled in the southeastern part of the Dakota Territory in the period from 1876 to the mid-1880s. In this area, which after 1889 became the southeastern part of the state of South Dakota, Bessarabian Germans formed, together with other Germans from South Russia, a significant portion of the population in Yankton, Bon Homme, Hutchinson, and Charles Mix counties.[45]

## The trail forged for Bessarabian Germans from their villages in Russia to the Dakotas was established by a group of Germans from the Berezan District in the Xerson Province in 1872–73

The southeastern Dakota Territory became the first destination of the Bessarabian Germans in North America, because in the spring of 1873, a group of Germans from the Berezan District in Xerson Province of South Russia settled there and the positive news they sent back attracted other Germans living in Russia. The story told by members of this group is one of the few detailed accounts of the emigration of Germans from Russia to North America. It is worthwhile looking at details of this story, not just because many Germans from Bessarabia and South Russia followed them to the very same section of the Dakota Territory, but because their story provides some information on both their motivations for emigration and on how they left Russia. It is also not without importance that their decision to leave

---

45. Few families from the German colonies in Russia had come to the United States as early as the 1840s. The Germans coming from Russia to settle in the Dakota Territory in 1873 represented the first group emigrating in material numbers. They were Evangelical Lutherans like the majority of the Bessarabian Germans and so, apparently, not associated with and perhaps not even aware of the efforts of the Mennonites of South Russia who had sent scouting parties to the United States and Canada in 1872. In "Migration of the Russian-Germans," Norman Saul states that the first Mennonite Germans to emigrate from Russia were Mennonites from the Tauride Province of South Russia who settled in Marion, Harvey, and McPherson counties in central Kansas in 1874 (38). The first Volga Germans to come to the United States were fourteen scouts representing eleven German villages who arrived in New York in July 1875. Their efforts brought Volga Germans to Kansas in the in the spring of 1876.

Russia was made just after the promulgation of the Decree of 1871 and before the promulgation of the Decree of 1874.

The Germans who came to the Dakota Territory in 1873 were from the neighboring villages of Johannestal, Rohrbach, and Worms in the Berezan District.[46] The chain of events that brought them to the United States began in 1849 when twenty-eight-year-old Johann Ludwig Bette left Johannestal and moved to the United States with his wife and several other families from the area. The Bette family had been early settlers in the Johannestal colony, having come there in 1819 from Smoljarina in Prussian Poland.[47] During the 1840s in South Russia, the first effects of growing prosperity and large families created both the financial means and pressures to move from one's birthplace in order to establish a farm of one's own. Johann Ludwig Bette, however, took an unusually distant and unique path by leaving Russia to settle in Sandusky, Ohio, where he had found a German Evangelical Lutheran community. In the United States, he anglicized his name to Louis Beatty and farmed, ultimately buying land on Kelley's Island offshore from Sandusky in Lake Erie. There, using knowledge gained in Russia, he established a vineyard and produced wine and so helped to establish a successful wine producing area that continues to the present day. He seems to have prospered in Ohio.

In the summer of 1872, Ludwig Bette, now about fifty-seven years old, returned to Johannestal.[48] This was a year after the issuance of the Decree of June 4, 1871 (O.S.). An account of Bette's return to Johannestal implies that Bette had been invited to return to Russia by local German "large landowners"[49] who were quite possibly concerned about the consequences of the 1871 decree and were considering alternatives. Although the military reform had not been released, it would appear there was talk of it and concerns raised about it, because Bette's brother-in-law, Johannes Sailer, is quoted as saying, "No, I won't become a soldier."[50]

Bette seems to have talked up life in America and so increased interest in emigration among several Johannestal families. His middle class "fine clothes and a hat," out

---

46. Johannestal, now the village of Ivanivka in the Ukraine, is located in the steppe land north of Odessa about 6 miles northeast of Riasnopil' and 15 miles southeast of Berezivka. Rohrbach, now Novosvitlivka, is about 4 miles north of Riasnopil', and Worms, now Vynohradne, is 2 miles northwest of Rohrbach.

47. Stumpp, *Emigration from Germany to Russia*, 715. Smoljarina, which Stumpp thought was in the Prussian province of Posen, is possibly the village of Smolarnia north of the Notec River about 4 miles west of Trzcianka in (post-1815) Posen Province. Johann Ludwig's father Andres was apparently one of the few Prussian Germans in Johannestal, which was filled largely with settlers with backgrounds in Württemberg.

48. Friedrich Mutschelknaus, "Migration of the First German Russians to Dakota: Memories of the Years 1872-73," *Dakota Freie Presse*, November 11, 1924, http://library.ndsu.edu/grhc/history_culture/history/migration.html. I rely here and in the following paragraphs on a description of Bette's return to South Russia and the subsequent emigration of families from Russia to South Dakota written by Mutschelknaus, one of the immigrants of 1872–73 and a son of one of its leaders.

49. Mutschelknaus describes Bette as invited back to Johannestal, implying that he had remained in written contact with his native village (his in-laws, at least, continued to live there). Bette's passage back to Russia may have been paid by those inviting him. The brief description of Bette's dress, "an American wearing fine clothes and a hat," however, implies Bette had some means of his own and Mutschelknaus describes him as "well-to-do."

50. The fact that rumors about the still-unannounced military reform fed concerns about its potential provisions is confirmed by Goerz, who notes (*The Molotschna Settlement*, 141–43) that the German Mennonites were aware of rumors from 1870 onward that the military reform would subject them to conscription and had sent delegations to St. Petersburg to protest. The context of Sailer's remark (quoted above) appears to refer to his intention for his sons and grandsons, as he was in 1872 too old to be called to serve.

of keeping with country dress in South Russia, and perhaps "some careless remarks comparing the United States with Czarist Russia" aroused the suspicion of local Russian authorities, and as a result Bette needed to change into more traditional peasant clothes to avoid further questionings and trouble.[51] As a result of Bette's positive descriptions of America, a group of some 175 people from Johannestal, Rohrbach, and Worms decided during the summer of 1872 to immigrate to the United States that fall.[52]

A second account of this immigrant party from the Jahraus family gives the impression that Bette led the group of immigrants: "In 1872 a certain Johann Ludwig Bette, a former colonist, persuaded the Jahraus family to join his group of emigrant colonists who were making passage to the USA."[53] The Decree of 1871 and rumors of conscription were certainly also major factors. The Jahraus family claims the decree had reduced the colonists in Russia "to the level of Russian peasants and… [made them] subject to be drafted" and the Mutschelknaus account raises objections to the conscription the family correctly assumed was coming. Though neither account mentions overcrowding or the desires of families to have farms of their own, these were also factors of life in the Berezan colonies and were frequently expressed desires of young families throughout the German settlements who were living with siblings on parental homesteads.

The local Russian authorities created difficulties in providing passports, causing the emigrants to travel to Nikolaev, Xerson, and Odessa to have this issue resolved.[54] The group traveled in four separate parties, each starting from Odessa where they went by train to Hamburg. From there, the Mutschelknaus party went by ship to Hull on the east coast of England, then by train to Liverpool, and by ship to New York. They left Odessa in October and arrived in New York in early December having been delayed by a terrible Atlantic storm that wrecked their ship and forced them back to Ireland to wait for another.

The four groups arrived at different times in New York and made their way to Sandusky, Ohio, where they spent the winter of 1872–73. The fact that they regrouped in Sandusky establishes that Bette either led or was greatly involved in their immigration. In the spring of 1873, the group sent out twelve scouts to locate a place for the group to settle. The scouts were armed with directions and letters from the Reformed minister in Sandusky, Pastor Schaf, asking the pastors of other Reformed Lutheran churches to give them aid and help them find land for sale. The scouts visited sites in Michigan, Illinois, and Wisconsin but couldn't find plots large enough to accommodate the whole group at prices they could afford. The scouts then looked in northeastern Nebraska but settled on land just across the Missouri River

---

51. Police reports about Bette may have been one of the sources of information reaching General Totleben that led him to conclude that there were "agents" from North America seeking to attract immigrants to the United States or Canada.

52. The number of people and the division of the travelers into four groups comes from a short account provided by the Jahraus family at http://www.familykaul.com/Jarhaus.htm.

53. Ibid.

54. Mutschelknaus, "Migration of the First German Russians." This parallels the experience of the Mennonites, as Goerz also notes problems in receiving passports (*The Molotschna Settlement*, 143). Nikolaev and Xerson were cities of increasing importance in Xerson Province, and Odessa was its capital. The trail the emigrants followed to acquire passports suggests the decision was continually pushed up the chain of command with the final decision likely made by the provincial governor of Xerson Province after consultation with the Ministry of Interior.

in the southeastern part of the Dakota Territory. Some of the scouts stayed there to plant a grain crop for the group while the remainder went back to Sandusky to lead everyone to the Dakota Territory. The immigrants had sufficient funds to hire their own railroad cars for the three-day trip from Ohio. They stopped in Chicago, where, having written or telegraphed ahead, they were met by businessmen who had arranged lodging and possibly supplies for them. Arriving in Yankton in a discouraging April snowstorm, they settled on individual plots offered under the terms of the Homestead Act of 1862 northwest of Yankton on the west bank of the James River between what later became the towns of Lesterville in Yankton County and Scotland in Bon Homme.[55]

In three years, the first German emigrants from Bessarabia to North America began to arrive in Yankton by train from New York and settled lands just north and west of the Johannestal group in Bon Homme and Hutchinson County. They did not come to this part of Dakota Territory by accident. They came because they had somehow heard that the Johannestal group had established themselves there and that prospects for farming were attractive. The Bessarabian Germans came there because they wanted to settle near other Germans who shared their language, customs, background, and religion. News was clearly passed by letters. The Mutschelknaus account reports writing a letter to relations in Johannestal when the group reached Sandusky in the winter of 1872–73 which, when it arrived in Russia, was of such interest that "Pastor Birdbath read [the] letter from the pulpit."[56] The Evangelical Lutheran Church was also an important conduit of information and help. The letters carried by the scouting party, who spoke little or no English, appear to have been critical in connecting that group with coreligionists who could help them understand local conditions and suggest where to look. Letters via church connections were the likely connection to the businessmen in Chicago. Clearly other letters were written once the group reached the Dakota Territory. It is very likely that reports from the Johannestal group settling in the Dakota Territory reached Bessarabian Germans in Russia via church connections, possibly via rumors, or by copies or extracts of the letters that were passed among the churches in South Russia and Bessarabia.

Though the Johannestal group was settled in North America well before the Decree of 1874 was released, both accounts indicate that one reason for emigrating from Russia was concerns held about conscription. The Jahraus account also references the loss of "freedoms" and the fact that the Germans had been "reduced" to a legal equivalency with Russian peasants, an issue at the heart of Decree of 1871. At the same time, however, both accounts attest to the attractiveness of Bette's descriptions of life in the United States as strong reasons for their emigration. They both imply that finding good land on which they could establish new farms was quite important. These two accounts are interesting as they carry family memories impressed at the start of German immigration to North America from Russia. They are but two accounts and so cannot be generalized to stand for the many whose rationale we do not know. They do reflect several themes that bridge the gap from a consideration of the decrees of 1871 and 1874 to the following chapter's consideration of the material

---

55. Settlement of just this area was greatly facilitated by the completion of a railroad connection to Yankton from Chicago in early 1873.
56. Mutschelknaus, "Migration of the First German Russians."

numbers of Bessarabian Germans who immigrated to North America from 1876 to the start of World War I in 1914.

Germans in Russia saw the decrees as marking a turning point in their history in Russia. Whether they had lost freedoms remained to be seen, but the settlements as isolated German islands living under special rules were passing into history. Though the Ministry of State Domains saw the Germans colonists in Russia as being socially and now legally equivalent to the native Russian and Ukrainian peasant population, the Germans took umbrage at this. They generally thought the Russian peasants were a more primitive cultural group who, even freed from serfdom, were economically far worse off than themselves. A common opinion among the German colonists was that things Russian were inferior and things German better. By the 1870s, the German colonists did not seem to have developed deep attachments to the Russian state. They were grateful for the land, the help and counsel of the Welfare Committee, and particularly grateful to have been left alone, but they were not eager to fight for Russia. Moreover, rumors about the terrible conditions under which Russian soldiers served, the corruption that cheated soldiers of supplies and food, and the notorious hazing that new conscripts were subjected to made the prospect of conscription very unattractive.

By the 1870s, the older German settlements in Bessarabia were facing real problems with overcrowding as there were now too many married siblings living on the original plots of land. As families continued to have large numbers of children, and better health conditions and knowledge of disease prevention meant more children survived childhood, the German population kept steadily increasing. One answer had been discovered in the 1860s: families could rent or purchase additional land in Bessarabia. This course of action was possible because Germans interested in acquiring land to start new farmsteads had access to capital from family savings and loans from orphan and fire funds, which gave younger family members the means move out of crowded homesteads and establish farms of their own elsewhere. One clear impact of the decrees of the early 1870s was that it was a force that caused people to start thinking about the possible advantages of life outside of Russia. The prosperous, quiet, isolated way of life the Germans had enjoyed in Russia would now undergo changes, perhaps not in positive directions. Emigration out of Russia, not seriously thought about earlier, now became a possibility worth considering.

# X

# The German Emigration from Bessarabia 1875–1914: Pushes and Pulls

There are no accurate counts of the number of Germans who emigrated from Bessarabia in the major period of emigration that dates from 1875 to 1914 and it is not likely that it will be possible to make an accurate accounting, at least in the near future. The absence of individualized census data from Russia, as well as adequate census data from the places to which Bessarabian Germans immigrated, creates insurmountable hurdles. It is not known whether any true census data—that is, collections of the names and ages of presumed complete village populations— exist for German Bessarabia from the post–Welfare Committee period after 1872. While there exist significant data on Germans from Russia in US census collections after 1880, these do not differentiate Germans from Bessarabia from Germans from other parts of Imperial Russia. For example, August Isaak—who in 1878, immigrated with his wife, Louise Wittchen Isaak, and three sons to Hutchinson County, South Dakota, from Danielsfeld, Bessarabia—is only identified as coming from Russia. To identify him specifically as a Bessarabian German from Danielsfeld, his data from the United States must be matched with data from Bessarabia, if such exist. This means that counts of Bessarabian German immigrants must begin with (or at least correlate to) knowledge of the persons and families in Bessarabia. Some records were kept by the German churches in Bessarabia, but after 1880, they are quite incomplete and, for a number of villages, not extant. It is possible that records of passports issued or exit taxes charged survive in Moldova, the Ukraine, or Russia, but these have yet to come to light. The result at present is that counts of German emigrants from Bessarabia cannot be placed on any firm ground.

What do exist are guesses made from partial data. Not surprisingly, these vary materially and so raise issues and doubts. Most of the emigration from German Bessarabia occurred in the period from 1875 to 1914, and estimations of the number of emigrants range from 15,000 to 25,000 people.[1] The 1897 census of Imperial Russia counted 59,998 Germans living in Bessarabia. If the estimates of the number of German emigrants from Bessarabia are even roughly accurate, they suggest that had no emigration occurred, the Bessarabian German population would have been between 80,000 and 120,000 people by 1914. It is thus reasonable to make the limited statement that with estimations of between 15,000 and 25,000 Bessarabian German emigrants before the start of World War I, the great majority of the German population remained in Bessarabia.

## Germans who emigrated from Bessarabia had several destinations to choose from

For Germans thinking they would find better circumstances outside of Bessarabia, one option was to move to another region in Imperial Russia. Land became available in the Crimea, particularly after the 1880s, when Russian nobles sought to sell lands there that had not been developed. Other properties came up for sale in the Crimea when Tartars elected to leave for friendlier treatment in Ottoman-controlled Bulgaria and Turkey. Another area within Russia that attracted emigration from Bessarabia was Siberia. Between 1890 and 1914, some Bessarabian Germans elected to resettle on lands near Tomsk and Slavgorod in the Barnaul Region, near the border with Kazakhstan. Wishing to increase the European population in Siberia and to take advantage of unused arable land there, the Russian government provided both free land and funding to help families move and establish themselves there. The limited data available on the immigration of Bessarabian Germans to places elsewhere within Imperial Russia, however, suggest that perhaps the most popular destination was to the North Caucasus region, along the upper Kuma and Terek rivers in Astrakhan Province and along the central Kuban River in Stavropol' Province. These were lands brought under firm Russian control in the early 1860s as a result of the Russian army's campaigns against the fierce, warlike, and generally Muslim "Circassian" tribes.[2] When Russian control was established, the defeated tribes retreated deeper into the mountains, or were dispersed, exiled, or even massacred

---

1.  An additional and far smaller emigration from German Bessarabia took place after World War I in the period from 1920 to 1930. Brazil and Argentina were the primary destinations at this time. Given that this wave of emigration was limited, perhaps a tenth of the size of the earlier emigration, and closely connected to the impoverished conditions of postwar Romanian Bessarabia, I will leave the discussion of it to a consideration of those conditions in chapter XII.

2.  The Circassia (Čerkesija) was a unifying term Russia gave to the North Caucasus region populated with many independent tribes, such as the Shapshug, Natuhay, Ingusheti, Chechens, and Dagestani. Sometimes joining together, sometimes fighting alone, these tribes fought a generally losing battle against the Russian army from 1825 to 1861. This long and brutal conflict was famously chronicled in the stories of some of Russia's best writers: Alexander Pushkin, Mixail Lermontov, and Leo Tolstoy. Russia's twenty-first-century struggles with the Chechens, Dagestani, and Ingusheti indicate that efforts begun by Imperial Russia in the nineteenth century have yet to be completed or accepted.

by the Russian army. In an effort to attract peaceful farmers from European Russia to settle the newly acquired and less populated territory, the Russian government offered land at no cost. Bessarabian Germans came to the North Caucasus region as early as the late 1860s. They were moving there in material numbers in the period from 1875 to 1885, and the limited data available show they were still moving there up to the eve of World War I. Friedrich Renz provides one example that suggests that multiple moves within Imperial Russia took place. Born in Friedenstal in 1870, he married Katharina Joergens (or Jergenz) of Seimeny, Bessarabia, in Akkerman in 1893. Renz moved his family to Asneumann in the Crimea sometime before 1904 and then moved to Eigenheim in the North Caucasus region, where he was living in 1910.[3]

Dobrudscha was another destination outside Bessarabia that attracted Germans. Lying east and south of the great bend in the lower Danube at Galati, the province of Dobrudscha was neighbor to Bessarabia and continued the rolling, generally treeless Budjak steppelands of southern Bessarabia. Throughout much of the nineteenth century, Dobrudscha was controlled by the Ottoman Turks. In 1878, Imperial Russia took Dobrudscha as part of the spoils of the Russo-Turkish War of 1877–78 but immediately ceded it to the new country of Romania in exchange for parts of southeastern Bessarabia that Russia had lost in the treaty ending the Crimean War. While Dobrudscha was controlled by the Ottomans, settlers could take what empty land they wished, paying the Turks a tenth of their harvest. In the period from 1841 to 1856, Germans from Bessarabia and South Russia moved to the northern, forested section of Dobrudscha and created new villages or attached themselves to existing Moldavian villages. A second and much larger emigration of Germans from Russia occurred in the period from 1873 to 1883.[4] These Germans founded villages on the central steppelands of Dobrudscha, north and west of Constanța. The villages of Cogealac (1874) and Tariverdi (1878) were the largest. As the following examples attest, the Germans who immigrated to Dobrudscha were drawn from many different villages in Bessarabia: Mathais Widmer from Wittenberg (1874 in Cogealac); Martin Raugust from Kulm (1875 in Tariverdi); Friedrich Wilhelm Kuck from Klöstitz (before 1877 in Cogealac); and Johann Heim from Tarutino (before 1879 in Tariverdi). It would appear that Dobrudscha also drew many Germans from South Russia and Russian Bukovina.

Bessarabian German immigration to Dobrudscha fell off after Romanian control was established. New immigrants arriving under Romanian rule were obliged to purchase land from the state, though they were given a twenty-five-year period to pay off their debt. Under Romanian rule, immigrants were also limited in the amount of land they might take. Each person in a family was allowed to claim 10 hectares, up to a total family limit of 50 hectares (45.7 desjatina). The Romanian government also subjected the German settlers to conscription and, like the Russian government in Bessarabia, put increasing pressure on the Germans to

---

3. The movements of the Renz family locations are indicated by the children's birthplaces. The Renz family data come from the questionnaires filled out by his descendants on arrival in Germany in 1940. E. Wise, "Alexanderfeld Bessarabia – A Koblenz Extraction" (N.p.: Odessa Digital Library, 2001), http://odessa3.org/collections/bess/koblenz/link/alexfldk.txt.

4. I rely here on Lester Siebold's synopsis of Paul Trager's study *Die Deutschen in der Dobrudscha*, which is unavailable to me. The two-part synopsis, "Black Sea Germans from the Rumanian Dobrudja," is available to GRHS members at http://grhs.org/korners/blumhagen/blumhagen.html.

learn to speak Romanian. By the mid-1880s, there was less land available for new German settlements or for the expansion of older ones. This factor, together with the distaste for conscription, led some Germans in Dobrudscha to leave Romania for North America. The fact that they moved to villages in North America where relations or fellow villagers from Bessarabia had also moved suggests that correspondence was maintained between the Dobrudscha immigrants and their families and friends in Bessarabia.

North America was the most popular destination for Germans who elected to emigrate from Bessarabia. There was a steady stream of Bessarabian Germans leaving Russia for North America from 1876 until World War I closed off all emigration from Russia. The first group of Bessarabian Germans that I can establish arriving in North America was a party of fourteen families and two single men who sailed together on the North German Lloyd ship, the SS *Mosel*, from Bremen. They reached the Castle Garden immigration receiving center in New York City on May 1, 1876.[5] The group was made up of five families from Teplitz, three from both Dennewitz and Kulm, and two from Friedenstal, with the single men coming from Neu Elft and Teplitz.[6] With wives and children, the party came to eighty-four people. I will take up patterns of settlement by the Bessarabian Germans in the United States and Canada in more detail later in this chapter, but here it should be noted that some elements of those patterns can, not surprisingly, be seen with this first group.

- Families typically did not come to North America singly, but in groups that often included relatives and friends. In this first group, among the families from Kulm, Daniel Gross was the first cousin of Louise Gross, the wife of fellow passenger August Schulz, and among the Teplitz families, three of the wives were Zachers from related families. It was also typical for such travel groups to include families from several villages who were not likely acquainted. Seeking to limit risk by traveling from Bessarabia with other Germans, they formed a group. Their ability to do so reminds us that some means of regular communication existed to pass news among the various German villages in Bessarabia.

- To leave Russia, the Bessarabian German immigrants traveled by train from Odessa to Bremen or Hamburg in Germany. They began their journeys even though some of the children were very young and some of the women were pregnant. Sophia Schulz from Kulm successfully made the trip at age two months, and Karl Christian Heihn was born during the ocean crossing on the SS *Mosel* and arrived in New York at eight days old.

- The traveling parties settled in or near the same area on the farming frontier in North America where others from Bessarabia and South Russia were known to have gone in the immediate past. This suggests correspondence kept the immigrants up to date.

---

5. The passenger list from the manifest of the SS *Mosel* is preserved in Microcopy 237, Roll 403, p. 7 in "Passenger Lists of Vessels Arriving in New York 1820-1897" (Washington, DC: National Archives Microfilm Publications, 1957). Immigrants arriving in New York in the 1870s were received at Castle Garden (also referred to as Castle Clinton), the fort at the tip of Manhattan that was used until the Ellis Island center was created in 1892.

6. The families were: (a) from Teplitz, Balthazar Furst and his married son, also Balthazar Furst, Jacob Klein, Christian Kremer, and August Meisenhalter; (b) from Kulm, Daniel Gross, Johann Isaak, and August Schulz; (c) from Dennewitz, Christian Friedrich, Georg Schiewe, and Christian Weber; (d) from Friedenstal, Friedrich Heihn, and his married son, Karl Heihn; and (e) from Tarutino, Christoph Warnke. The single men were Christoph Kraft from Neu Elft and Georg Schaal from Teplitz.

The first Bessarabian German immigrants went to the southeastern corner of the Dakota Territory.[7] As that area filled up with immigrants over time, the farming frontier moved north, staying to the east of the Missouri River. When what became central South Dakota filled up, the frontier moved in the mid-1880s to the border with North Dakota and crossed into that state in the late 1880s and into the 1890s. In the mid-1890s, immigrants started to look for land in the drier areas west of the Missouri in North Dakota and then crossed into eastern Montana. With the turn of the century, Bessarabian Germans and Germans from South Russia found better farm lands in central Washington, and that became the locus of immigration. From the mid-1890s on, German immigrants in North Dakota had also started to look across the border to Saskatchewan and Alberta in Canada. These were not just new immigrants but also some who had started farms in North Dakota gave those up to move. Similarly, in the middle of the first decade of the twentieth century, new German immigrants to Washington and the young adult sons of farmers just establishing themselves there sought land across the border in central Alberta in Canada.

Given the difficulties of matching data from Bessarabia with census and immigration data in North America, it is not possible to establish the heaviest periods of immigration. It is possible using Flegel's more limited but very focused data from the villages of Kulm, Tarutino, and Leipzig to suggest that there was a steady flow of emigration from German Bessarabia from 1876 to 1914. As discussed in detail later in this chapter, Flegel's data indicate that at least for these three villages, the heaviest period of immigration to North America occurred between 1885 and 1905. It would appear that most immigrants began their travels in the late winter and spring and so arrived in North America from May through September.

The process by which Germans in Bessarabia decided that they would be better off if they emigrated from that province instead of looking for land in Bessarabia or within Imperial Russia was likely driven by varying combinations of pushes and pulls. Pushes were the negative aspects of life in Bessarabia and Russia that urged people to leave. Pulls were the attractive aspects of the places they immigrated to that drew them there. For the vast majority of emigrants, we do not know how they individually weighed the different pushes and pulls or how these may have changed over time. We can only identify them and consider the potential power that lay behind each.

## There were several pushes that caused Germans in Bessarabia to consider emigration

The preceding chapter considered pushes created by the decrees of 1871 and 1874: the introduction of unwanted conscription into the Russian army, and the merging of the German villages into the new civic and legal systems introduced through the Alexandrine reforms of the 1860s that would force those villages to become more

---

7.  When the Dakota Territory was formed in 1861, it incorporated the lands from the Louisiana Purchase that would become the states of North and South Dakota, as well as large parts of what would become the states of Montana and Wyoming. The Dakota Territory included the land east of the Missouri River that Minnesota gave up in 1858 when it became a state. North and South Dakota were carved out of the Dakota Territory, becoming states on November 2, 1889. By 1872, however, counties had been formed and named, and sectional boundaries had been drawn in the Dakotas east of the Missouri, so it is proper before statehood to give the name of counties where the Bessarabian Germans settled.

Russian and less German. We know that these pushes, particularly army conscription that came with the Decree of 1874, carried great weight. In the few cases where immigrants to North America or their descendants offer a commentary on rationale, the desire to avoid conscription is prominent. Such weight is increased, as the immigrants were on good ground when they believed that in coming to the United States or Canada, they would not be subject to conscription. While conscription was used by both the North and South during the American Civil War, it had ended when the war was over. In the period before World War I, the national armed forces in the United States and Canada were recruited on a volunteer basis. It is true that the different states in the United States could organize militia forces via conscription and did so during the Civil War. After the war, the few state militia forces that remained in existence were formed on a volunteer basis. However, to make immigration to their states more attractive to potential Mennonite settlers from Russia, the states of Kansas, Nebraska, and Minnesota enacted laws in the 1870s that exempted persons from military service those whose religion prohibited them from bearing arms.

Concerns about conscription would not have been a major factor for those Germans who chose to immigrate to other regions of Imperial Russia. Germans who took this route knew it could not be avoided. It is far less clear how the issue of conscription might have affected those Germans who elected to immigrate to Dobrudscha. In the period before 1878, the Ottoman government did not conscript in this region for military service, though it held a right to do so. Once Dobrudscha became part of Romania, conscription was introduced by the Romanian government. The new Romanian army did not carry the black marks earned by military service in Imperial Russia and so might have been seen less negatively. If, however, the real issue about conscription was that the German population had not become sufficiently attached to the country they were living in to be willing to support its interests by serving in the military, then the threat of conscription in Romania could well have been one of the pushes that urged Germans to consider moving to North America.

It is more difficult to assess the power of whatever push was created by the Decree of 1871, which brought the German villages into Russia's civil and legal systems. As discussed later in this chapter, it is true that over time, pressure to assimilate and particularly pressure to learn the Russian language was increasingly felt in German Bessarabia. Such pressure eroded the perception that the Germans could live in a separate German world in Russia. Some immigrants to the Dakotas did tell W. S. Harwood that they left Russia because they felt "they were becoming more Russian than German."[8] Nevertheless, it is difficult to imagine that Germans leaving for North America were under the impression that they would be able to create in their new destinations similarly isolated German islands. Perhaps this was so in Dobrudscha for a short while, but after 1878, when Romanian control was established, Germans were brought under increasing pressure to learn Romanian and to consider themselves Romanian citizens and not just Germans who happened to be living in Romania.

In the United States, there was little overt pressure to assimilate, at least before World War I. However, the very nature of the settlement policies in the United

---

8. Harwood, "A Bit of Europe."

States purposefully encouraged assimilation and the mixing of different immigrant populations. In order to claim land in the Dakotas under the Homestead Act of 1862, immigrants had to live on the land they claimed. This purposefully prevented a duplication of the setting the Bessarabian Germans had left behind in Russia: monoethnic settlements surrounded by their farm land. Instead, with immigrants forced to live on their land, new settlers of different linguistic and ethnic backgrounds were generally and accidentally mixed together. Later, when towns and villages were formed to serve the settled farmers, they were even less likely to be monoethnic. English became a necessary lingua franca for communication in the Dakotas and Washington between the German settlers from Russia and the Norwegians, Irish, and many newcomers from other parts of the United States.

## Overcrowding in the German villages in Bessarabia was perhaps the most significant push

The most significant force pushing Germans to consider emigration from Russia, however, was likely overcrowding in Bessarabia. Population increased steadily in German Bessarabia throughout the nineteenth century. In addition to the population data collected by the Welfare Committee in the surveys of 1825 and 1841, discussed earlier, Brandes has collected population statistics for Bessarabia from a number of sources through 1897. Laid out together, these show a steady growth in the number of Germans in Bessarabia (see table 10–1).

As noted in the preceding chapter, after 1850 the immigration of new German families from outside of Russia into Bessarabia generally came to an end. There were German immigrants to Bessarabia coming from overcrowded conditions in South Russia, and, as noted earlier, a few German speakers crossed the border from Austrian Galicia to establish villages in northern Bessarabia. As a result, the chief

TABLE 10–1. Percent changes in German population from 1825 through 1897

| Year | Population[a] | Percent change |
|------|-----------|----------------|
| 1825 | 8,525 | — |
| 1834 | 10,038 | +17.7% |
| 1841 | 12,578 | +23.3% |
| 1851 | 19,139 | +52.2% |
| 1858 | 24,296 | +26.9% |
| 1862 | 27,535 | +13.3% |
| 1890 | 43,582 | +58.3% |
| 1897 | 59,998 | +37.7% |

a. Brandes, *Von den Zaren Adoptiert*, 336, Table 51, and 462, Table 100. Brandes does not cite sources for specific numbers. For 1825, I have used the number from Hans Rempel's study of the 1825 Welfare Committee survey (*German Farming Achievements*, Table 16); Brandes offers a slightly higher number for this year (8,960). Brandes does not provide a figure for 1841; the figure I have used is from Klaus (*Naši kolonii*, Appendix II, 25). For 1890, I have used the Brandes figure from Table 100 instead of the figure for 1890 in Table 51 (43,842), as the latter includes the French from Schabo. This, of course, raises the question of whether other figures used from Table 51 (1834, 1851, 1858) are slightly high because of this issue. This may also explain the different figures for 1897. For 1897, I have used the figure of 59,998 from the data compiled by the DAI before the Soviet takeover of Bessarabia (Allen Konrad, trans., "Bessarabian German Population Statistics 1827-1938" [N.p.: blackseagr.org, 2011], http://www.blackseagr.org/pdfs/konrad/Bessarabian%20German%20Population%20Statistics%201827-1938.pdf). Brandes and other sources have a slightly higher figure for 1897 of 60,206. See also http://demoscope.ru/weekly/ssp/rus_lan_97.php?reg=31.

cause of the substantial growth of the German population in Bessarabia was the continued pattern of families having large numbers of children. The first three generations in the demographic study discussed in chapter VII averaged over six children per family, and the average for Generation 4 was five children.[9] Household size also increased because throughout the nineteenth century, health standards improved, which both increased the number of children able to survive childhood and lengthened adult life spans.

Until the issuance of the Decree of 1871, Bessarabian German families were forbidden from subdividing the 60-desjatina plots of land they had received when they came to Russia. After 1871, while subdivision slowly became more common, the availability of land for sale or for lease in and out of Bessarabia offered other solutions that, given the growing prosperity, could be afforded. Nonetheless, as having large numbers of children remained the rule, younger generations felt a steady pressure to find solutions.

The farmsteads of 60 desjatina, which had seemed so large by comparison with the holdings families had in Prussia and Württemberg, became more crowded over time. The creation of the Dennewitz colony in 1834 suggests that some perception of crowding was extant twenty years after the first colonies were founded.[10] From the late 1840s onward, Bessarabian German farms were typically managed by two families: parents and a married son or daughter, or by two married siblings. The survey of Leipzig indicates that by 1857, crowding was such that some siblings were choosing to move out of their parental family's homestead by purchasing or leasing small cottage plots of land elsewhere in the village. These formed a base for plying a trade, such as shoemaking, or served as a homestead for older surviving parents, who had given away most farm assets but continued to live on the farmstead in retirement, as Hagen describes was custom in Prussia.[11] By the 1860s, however, as more siblings married and started their own families, all within a single farmstead, many farmsteads were starting to edge toward overcrowding.

The example of the crowded conditions experienced by the Raugust family in Kulm in the 1860s, noted in the chapter on demography, may be extreme, but it was likely not far from the norm. The farmstead originally established by Jacob Raugust was in the early 1860s being managed by the families of four of his married children. The household was supporting thirteen adults together with twenty-one children. Crowded conditions and the desire to have a farm of one's own were the likely causes of the first significant expansion of the German colonies in Bessarabia in the 1860s, when thirteen new German villages were founded in the Budjak. As large families continued to be the norm, pressure built in the original settlements for adult children to pick up stakes and start independent farmsteads elsewhere. Kern notes this pressure in describing the foundation of the village of Fundu-Saratzika in Bessarabia (1891–92) when he indicates that the desire for freedom from overcrowding was the motivation for founding

---

9. See table 7–19 for the average number of children in the study group, table 7–8 for decreased childhood mortality, and table 7–2 for increased life spans.

10. Dennewitz was established by the Welfare Committee on land originally set aside for Teplitz, whose population, diminished by epidemic on arrival in Bessarabia, was not able to use it fully. The Dennewitz settlers were second generation families—that is, the sons and daughters of primary householders from Alt Posttal, Beresina, Kulm, Tarutino, and Wittenberg. They clearly saw the formation of this new settlement as an opportunity to have a farmstead of 60 desjatina in their own right.

11. Hagen, *Ordinary Prussians*, 248–59.

many new settlements both inside and outside of Bessarabia: "The founders came from Brienne, Kulm, Borodino, Tarutino and Paris. They were people looking for more land, while longing for freedom from the confines of the mother colony."[12]

The growth in population that took place in the older German settlements in the period from 1850 to 1879 can be attested by netting the number of births listed in the Evangelical Lutheran Church parish records against the number of deaths. The church records stop in the mid-1880s when the civil volost recordkeeping took over. The Odessa compilation has usefully grouped data by decade, and on this basis, the net gain of births over deaths (seen in table 10–2) shows substantial and regular increases in population.[13]

The church data on births and deaths should be taken with a grain of salt, as they are far from complete. If anything, such data undercounts, as it includes no information from the Catholic settlement of Krasna and is strongest only for the older German Protestant settlements that were grouped in the original parishes of Alt Elft, Arzis, Klöstitz, Sarata, and Tarutino. Information from the new settlements that were founded in the 1860s and 1870s is quite spotty. Nonetheless, a net gain of some 23,553 people occurring primarily in the older German settlements does underline the point at hand: those older settlements were becoming more and more crowded in the period from 1850 to 1879. The net gain in population is substantial, coming to 39.2 percent of the total number of Germans counted in Bessarabia in the 1897 census.

The net gain in population figures from the church records of births and deaths suggests that so long as the German population in Bessarabia continued to make farming and the raising of animals its primary economic activity, the Germans could not survive in their original settlements and maintain the broad spread of economic achievement, much less continue to improve on this. The reaction to crowding caused by population growth in the German settlements was for young adults, both married couples and singles, to leave with the goal of establishing separate farms elsewhere. The following chapter will discuss the explosive growth in the new German villages in Bessarabia that occurred particularly in the 1880s and 1890s. The smaller but still material number of Germans who left Bessarabia to establish new farmsteads and villages elsewhere is a branch of the same tree. In both cases, movement from

TABLE 10–2. **Bessarabian German population gains, 1850–1879**

| Decade | Births | Deaths | Net gain |
|---|---|---|---|
| 1850–59[a] | 13,861 | 7,363 | 6,498 |
| 1860–69[b] | 14,722 | 7,043 | 7,679 |
| 1870–79[c] | 17,154 | 7,778 | 9,376 |
| **Total** (1850–79) | 45,737 | 22,184 | 23,553 |

a. Reuben Drefs, trans., "Bessarabian Village Birth Records, 185x," ed. Marty McMahon (N.p.: Odessa Digital Library, 1998); and Drefs, trans., "Bessarabian Village Death Records, 185x," ed. Marty McMahon (N.p.: Odessa Digital Library, 1999).

b. Reuben Drefs, trans., "Bessarabian Village Birth Records, 186x," ed. Marty McMahon (N.p.: Odessa Digital Library, 1997); and Drefs, trans., "Bessarabian Village Death Records, 186x," ed. Marty McMahon (N.p.: Odessa Digital Library, 1999).

c. Drefs, "Birth Records, 187x"; and Drefs, trans., "Bessarabian Village Death Records, 187x," ed. Marty McMahon (N.p.: Odessa Digital Library, 1999).

12. Kern, *Homeland Book*, 157.

13. The collected listings of births and deaths from church records are found at http://www.odessa3.org/collections/stpete/bess/.

crowded villages was possible because the Germans in Bessarabia had, by 1875, built up assets in cash and animals that would allow those wanting to leave to take their inheritance share and use that to move and to establish a new farm, even one quite far away in North America.

## The policy of Russification instituted by the governments of Alexander III and Nicholas II was another push causing Germans to think of leaving Russia

In addition to the pressures that built up from overcrowding and the concerns about conscription, there were other reasons that were pushing German citizens to develop worries about their future in Russia and so lead them to think of emigration. One of these was the policy of Russification implemented by Tsar Alexander III (1880–94) and continued by his son Tsar Nicholas II (1894–1917), which stressed the need for all citizens of Imperial Russia to learn the Russian language and to adopt Russian customs.

Tsar Alexander II was assassinated in St. Petersburg on March 1, 1881 (O.S.), when a student radical threw a bomb under his carriage. It was a traumatic event for Russia and for the Russian government. The new government of Alexander III was fearful that the reforms enacted during the reign of his father had awakened desires for reform well beyond the interests or even the capacities of the Russian government to deliver. Many in government concluded that the assassination proved the reforms had gone too far. Moreover, Alexander III was a man of very different temperament, capabilities, and outlook than his father. Riasanovsky describes Alexander III and his son and successor Nicholas II as "narrow-minded and convinced reactionaries [who] not only rejected further reform, but also did their best to limit the effectiveness of many changes that had taken place."[14]

A major focus of the government of Alexander III was to secure the tsar's unchecked autocratic power. Alexander III thought the reforms made by his father had been inspired by dangerous Western ideas that were at root inimical to preserving this power. He saw the Russian nobility and the Russian Orthodox Church as the natural allies of autocracy and sought to buttress and strengthen the status of these groups. Greatly influenced by his tutor K. P. Pobedonoscev, who argued that Western institutions and practices could not be easily adopted in Russia, Alexander III believed that only institutions that were slowly grown and absorbed into national life would flourish and last. Alexander III placed a high value on supporting Russia's ancient customs and traditions, which he thought gave Russia a unique and special place in the world. In this regard, he looked favorably on Great Russian nationalism, seeing it as a counterweight to Western influences and to the pull of nationalistic ideas among the many non-Russian peoples living in Imperial Russia.[15] Support for

---

14. Riasanovsky, *History of Russia*, 433.
15. The term "Great Russian" (*velikorusskij*) used here and in the succeeding paragraphs refers to the cultural habits and customs of people who spoke the dominant East Slavic language used in Imperial Russia. Such people are often loosely referred to as "Russians" in English. Imperial Russia contained other East Slavic–speaking peoples and cultures to the south and west of the Great Russian heartland. These other East Slavs were identified by terms that included the word "Russian" so that it was necessary to attach adjectives to distinguish them. While the Great Russians thought of the other East Slavic populations as brother and sister Slavs, they also considered them as lesser and subject peoples. The other East Slavic people in Imperial Russia were the Ukrainians, often called "Little Russians" (*malorusskij*) in nineteenth-century Russia, and the Byelorussians, called the "White Russians" (*belorusskij*).

Great Russian nationalists also gave influence to those who habitually defended the centralized, autocratic power of the Imperial Russian government. A similar conclusion was reached in the twentieth century by Communist and post-Communist governments in Russia, who saw in the promotion of Great Russian nationalism an antidote to forces, created by nationalistic interests rising among many of the different ethnic groups living within Russia, that threatened—in their view—to pull the state apart.

One consequence of policies that sought to support Great Russian nationalism was that support for the languages and cultural traditions of other peoples living within the boundaries of Imperial Russia was viewed negatively. Great Russian nationalists thought these minorities should assimilate and adopt Great Russian ways and manners. Policies of Alexander III and Nicholas II, which encouraged the use of the Great Russian language in education and in all dealings with the state, and which encouraged the adoption of the Orthodox faith by the non-Orthodox, have been collectively referred to as policies of Russification by historians. Such policies also included attempts to discourage or at times even prohibit the purchase of land or the free movement within Russia by people not deemed Great Russian.

The policies of Russification were hardly felt to be positive by the non–Great Russian peoples living in multiethnic Imperial Russia. The largest ethnic groups impacted in European Russia were the Ukrainians, Jews, Finns, and Poles. The most restrictive rules were applied to Jews, who were confined to certain settlement areas in Western Russia, forbidden to acquire property, and made subject to brutal harassment. Jews were killed and their homes and businesses were burned during periods of pogrom—that is, anti-Semitic riots where the government typically looked the other way.[16] Other groups receiving particularly harsh treatment were the Muslim tribes in the newly conquered lands in the Caucasus and in Central Asia to the east of the Caspian Sea, some of whom were forcibly converted to Russian Orthodoxy and others exiled to Siberia.

The Germans in Russia were thus far from the largest minority group, and the treatment they received from the Russian government was far from the most onerous or restrictive. Nonetheless, coming after a long period of nearly independent isolation in which the Russian government played a generally benevolent role, the policies of Russification pursued by the governments of Alexander III and Nicholas II were ill-received by the German communities. The greatest impact that Russification policies had on German citizens in Imperial Russia was to increase significantly the teaching of Russian in the German settlements and ultimately to increase the number of Germans who could speak Russian. In 1880, there appear to have been relatively few Germans in Bessarabia able to speak Russian with any fluency. As noted in the preceding chapter, in 1880, Kulm was unable to find a local citizen well enough versed in Russian to be the Volost Secretary and so brought in Friedrich Frey, a native of Xerson Province who had been living in Neu Elft. Once the volost elementary school system was introduced in the German settlements in

---

16. Two pogroms took place in the provincial capital of Bessarabia, Kishinev: one in April 1903 when the anti-Semitic newspaper *Bessarabec* fanned fears that Jews had killed two children, and a second in October 1905 in conjunction with the riots that followed Russia's defeat by Japan. Some fifty people were killed in the first and nineteen in the second, with as many as seven hundred houses damaged or destroyed.

Bessarabia, generally by the mid- to late 1880s, all village children were exposed to some education in Russian. By the first decade of the twentieth century, volost meetings in German Bessarabia were held at least in part in Russian, indicating that some German adults had acquired fluency. In 1911, when Johann Roloff entered government service in Kulm as an apprentice, Russian had become the official language of government in Kulm.[17]

By 1914, though German remained the language of everyday farm work, business, and family life, most adults in German Bessarabia were able to speak and understand some Russian and typically had some reason to use that language at least occasionally in their lives. By that time, the German villages in Bessarabia were no longer isolated islands of German language and culture only tangentially related to the Russian sea about them. Clearly, too, the direction of change was toward the increased use of Russian and an increased assimilation into Russian culture. It is not surprising then that Germans in Bessarabia felt their world was becoming more Russian and less German. Such feelings might easily become another of those pushes which led Germans in Bessarabia to consider emigration. While no doubt those who left Bessarabia for North America realized that they would have to adapt to a different culture in North America, they perhaps hoped that in the underpopulated plains of the western United States and Canada they might be able to replicate the experience of their ancestors, who in first coming to Bessarabia had been able to establish little islands of Germanness that preserved their language and culture. Perhaps, in addition, there were some Germans with more exposure to Russians and Russian culture who were motivated to leave Russia as they realized that even were they to adopt Russian ways, they would never be fully accepted as Russian; whatever the adaptation required in North America, it would not be as negative as the prospects some Germans felt they faced in Russia.

## Another push to emigrate came from the increasingly negative coloring Germans were beginning to attract in Russia

The policy of Russification was broadly supported by Russians within Imperial Russia. In the areas of Imperial Russia where Germans were settled, the slow progress of Germans to adapt to Russian ways started to attract negative comment. The observations that the Germans were not learning to speak Russian, were not adopting Russian customs and allegiances, and were not adopting the Russian Orthodox faith created reactions of distrust and resentment. At times these were interwoven with the growing irritation that German competition in land purchases created among some Russians, which resulted in several attempts limit by law such purchases. At other times such negative coloring given Germans in Russia was linked to the emergence of a powerful Imperial Germany which was seen as a rival and threat to Russia and the achievement of its ambitions.

The following sections will consider details connected to the resentments expressed by Russians about German land purchases as well as the growing fears, expressed particularly in the Russian conservative press, that the German presence in Imperial Russia formed at best a negative influence and at worst a dangerous strategic threat. While few Germans in Bessarabia possessed sufficient Russian to read

17. Daniel Wölfle, "Johann Roloff" in "Heimatbuch der Gemeinde Kulm," *Heritage Review* 13, no. 4 (1983): 22.

the Russian press, it appears that many were at least vaguely aware of the negative commentary that was being expressed about Germans. Before exploring some of the specific complaints raised about Germans, it is worth while noting the potential effect of just the general negative noise that was developing. Among the pushes that led Germans to leave Bessarabia and Russia for North America may have been the growing negative atmosphere itself rather than concern about how any specific threat might apply.

### The Russian gentry and upper middle class became increasingly unhappy about German land purchases

Toward the end of the nineteenth century, access to capital allowed Germans to purchase land in South Russia to create new villages. In doing so, Germans began to be competitors to gentry and upper-middle-class Russians also interested in acquiring land. Such competition helped drive up prices, and, especially for the gentry, also unpleasantly crossed and upset class boundaries. Complaints were raised about the German competition, and calls were made to limit or even forbid German land purchases. Such criticism likely raised concerns in the German communities that their peaceful isolation in Russia under a protective government was now over. Now no longer cared for by the Welfare Committee, they might in a hostile atmosphere become subject to restrictions and penalties that would harm their potential for growth and prosperity. The criticism of German land purchases began to appear in the 1880s, particularly in the Ekaterinoslav Province of South Russia. The frequent German presence in the land market was creating an unwelcome competition for the Russian gentry and the upper middle class. Complaints were raised in zemstvo meetings. The root of the these complaints appears to have been an issue of class: the Germans were foreigners of a lower class, but because of their access to capital and because of the chronic indebtedness of the gentry, the Germans had major advantages when they entered the land market. Germans were able to buy land the Russian gentry either wanted and couldn't afford, or didn't want to sell but had to. The Russian gentry and upper middle class leaned toward conservative nationalism, and so their complaints were often couched in nationalistic terms: the Germans, foreigners, were buying up "native" Russian land that only Russians ought to possess. In October 1880, the zemstvo in Ekaterinoslav made a recommendation to the central government to bar individual Germans from owning more than 10 desjatina of land.

The Ekaterinoslav zemstvo argued that Russians couldn't compete against the Germans in land acquisition. Touching on a vein of worry felt by Russian conservatives up to the present day, the Ekaterinoslav zemstvo went further to assert that the Germans were following a plan with dangerous "political goals."[18] After 1883 the Russian nationalist press started to take up this theme in earnest and began to campaign to prevent the Germans from making a "peaceful conquest" of southwest Russia. For example, Aleksej Suvorin's influential conservative paper *Novoe Vremja* [New times] from the mid-1880s on regularly railed against what it viewed as the "Germanizing" of the western regions of Russia.[19] The antidote prescribed against

18. Neutatz, "Die Kolonien des Schwartzmeergebietes," 84.
19. Fleischhauer, *Die Deutschen im Zarenreich*, 354.

this was for the Russian government to enforce regulations restricting the right of Germans to purchase land as well as their right to use the German language in public.[20]

As a background to the protests issued from the zemstvo of the Ekaterinoslav Province, there were striking gains at this time in both the number of German settlements and in the land area they occupied. Fleischhauer cites the following statistics (table 10–3) for new German settlements in the late nineteenth-century Ekaterinoslav Province.

The increase in the land area occupied by the German settlements in the Ekaterinoslav Province is by a factor of nearly 1,000 percent in just twenty-seven years. During the same period, the land area held by the nobility in Ekaterinoslav Province decreased 32 percent from 339,269 hectares to 231,169.[21]

There were edicts passed in the 1860s restricting Poles and Jews from purchasing land in the western provinces of Imperial Russia. These were extended in March 1887 to apply more generally to "foreign subjects" living in twelve border districts that included parts of Bessarabia. In June 1888, the effect of this decree was extended to all foreign settlers in southwest Russia. In March 1892, the prohibition against owning or leasing property out of one's town of domicile in these regions was extended to include any Russian nationals not of the Russian Orthodox faith.[22] Although the Germans in Bessarabia and South Russia were throughout this period technically included among the foreign subjects, settlers, and non–Russian Orthodox who were barred from purchasing land, these restrictions were never enforced against them by the central government. However, the fact that Germans were not made subject to restrictions on the purchase of land doesn't mean that such restrictions were not repeatedly asked for by provincial governmental officials. In 1891, the Provincial Zemstvo of Ekaterinoslav petitioned the Ministry of Interior to make the restrictions against land purchases by foreigners clearly apply to purchases desired by German-speaking citizens of that province. In 1893, the Nobles Assembly of the Ekaterinoslav Province repeated the same recommendations. In 1897 and 1902, the governor of the neighboring Xerson Province, which also had experienced a large growth in the number of German settlements, reported on the competition between Germans and Russians in land purchases and recommended that restrictions be applied against Germans to limit but not totally prohibit their further acquisition of land.

The Ministry of the Interior, while certainly sensitive to requests from local officials, appears to have viewed the growth in the number of farmsteads owned

TABLE 10–3. **New German settlements in Ekaterinoslav, late nineteenth century**

| Year | German settlements | Land area (hectares) |
|------|--------------------|----------------------|
| 1861 | 2 | 5,123 |
| 1871 | 39 | 27,016 |
| 1888 | 73 | 51,182 |

20. Neutatz, "Die Kolonien des Schwartzmeergebietes," 82.
21. Fleischhauer, *Die Deutschen im Zerenreich*, 322.
22. Neutatz, "Die Kolonien des Schwartzmeergebietes," 82–83. Scholz also makes this point (*German Colonists of Russia*, 16).

by German citizens as positive developments for Russia's economic strength. The German farms were generally created on lands that were at best only partially developed. Once created, the German farms were highly productive and so supplied a healthy income to the Russian state via taxes on the farmsteads and on the sales of surplus grain and animals. The Ministry of the Interior, I believe, held a mercantilist view of the German settlements in Russia throughout the period up to World War I. In this view, a government would strengthen state power, increase its tax receipts, and improve the country's general prosperity by encouraging the growth of its food supply, agricultural exports, and manufacturing. Such a view is certainly reflected in the comments made in 1863 by a Russian army staff colonel in Xerson Province describing the German colonists in South Russia as

> *our Americans who change our wild desert into marvelous villages with gardens and lea, our capitalist farmers who become richer and richer from year to year, occupy more and more land, attribute value to the land, and raise the price for labor by their extraordinary demand.*[23]

Not only did the Ministry of the Interior decline to take the requested action against the Germans, it intervened to reverse restrictive actions that local governments had implemented. Among these were actions taken against Germans by the governors of the provinces of Kiev, Poldolia, and Volhynia. In the late 1890s and first years of the first decade of the twentieth century, governors in these provinces, using latitude granted in a decree of 1886, barred some Germans from purchasing additional land. When the Germans protested, the Ministry of the Interior reversed the actions of the provincial governors in May 1905.[24]

Pressure to restrict the rights of Germans in Bessarabia and South Russia to purchase land reached its highest level on the eve of World War I. Spurred by the continuing heavy activity of German farmers in the land market and especially by the growing tensions between Russia and Germany, the new Russian parliament, the Duma, passed a law in 1912 barring Germans in Russia from making further land purchases.[25] Andreas Widmer from Tarutino, vice president of the Akkerman Zemstvo from 1903 and one of two Germans from Bessarabia elected to the first Russian parliament in 1906, led a campaign in 1913 urging the tsar not to approve this new law. Widmer argued that the economic progress Germans had made in Russia strengthened the country and so benefited its advancement.[26] It would appear that, again, officials of the Ministry of the Interior in St. Petersburg agreed with Widmer's position and declined to provide support for the Duma legislation. I have found no evidence that Germans in Bessarabia were prevented from purchasing

---

23. The quote is from A. Šmid, ed., *Materialy dlja geografii i statistiki Rossii*, vol. 2, *Xersonskaja gubernija* (St. Petersburg: Tipogr. Tovariščestva "Obščestvennaja Pol´za", 1863), quoted in and translated by Detlef Brandes in "A Success Story: The German Colonists in New Russia and Bessarabia: 1787–1914," *Acta Slavica Iaponica Tomus* 9 (1991), http://library.ndsu.edu/grhc/history_culture/history/brandes.html. Colonel Šmid's own German background may have colored his remarks, but the admiration he expresses about the enterprise of the German colonists was central to the mercantilist view of the benefits Germans brought to Russia.

24. Benert, "Land Laws," 17–18.

25. In Bessarabia alone, Germans had bought land to found more than twenty-four new settlements in the period between 1908 and 1914.

26. Kern, *Homeland Book*, 126.

land in the period between 1912 and the start of World War I. Indeed, Germans in Bessarabia founded two villages in 1913 and two more in 1914 before the commencement of fighting in August 1914.[27]

Even though the Ministry of the Interior declined to support restrictions on German land purchases and local restrictions were only a rare event, the talk of them and the continuing agitation for them must have created a source of worry for Germans in Bessarabia and South Russia. The possibility that the Russian government might change its mind and curtail the rights of Germans to acquire additional land and form new settlements would threaten to increase overcrowding in the existing villages and so cause future poverty. As a result, it would be surprising if fears of such an eventuality were not one of the pushes that led Germans wanting to acquire land to think about the possibility of doing so outside of Russia.

**Increasing expressions of anti-German sentiment**

Another reason that may have led Germans in Russia to begin to think of emigrating after 1880 was the increasing expressions of anti-German views. At times these were wrapped in the arguments made for barring German land purchases, but frequently such views stood on their own. As noted earlier, already by the 1860s the non-assimilating habits of the German colonists had sparked expressions of displeasure from conservative Russians. The Germans were seen as rejecting assimilation and so rejecting Russia: the accusations were that Germans didn't learn the Russian language, maintained different customs, and practiced different religions. Even though the German-language press in Russia, such as the *Odessaer Zeitung*, adopted a patriotic pro-Russian stance, Russian nationalistic critics accused the German press in Russia and the German population of only pretending to be Russian.[28]

Some of the anti-German feeling among nationalist and conservative thinkers in nineteenth-century Russia stemmed from the belief that the Germans were limiting the rightful economic development of the Russian peasantry or were providing no useful improvements. The Germans were driving up land prices to what were viewed as unaffordable heights, thus preventing Russian peasants from making land purchases that might lift them to a better stage of economic development. This, however, was a more theoretical and hopeful argument than a realistic one. Russian peasants were not generally in a position to compete for land purchases as the terms of their freedom from the state of serfdom entailed large buyback payments to the government. The Russian government had fronted the payment made to the nobility in compensation for granting the serfs freedom in 1862, but the required debt payments and interest had only driven most of the Russian peasant communities deeper into poverty. In the period before World War I, most Russian peasants were able to maintain only meager levels of savings. Moreover, until 1906, the peasant communities, not individual peasant families, held title to the land and the mir regularly redistributed holdings to match the community's male population. The frequent redistributions undercut motivation to make improvements to the land cultivated. The peasant communities—both in their prior history under serfdom and in their

---

27. Wahl, "Bessarabian Village Names." Neu Dennewitz and Parapara were founded in 1913 and Ebenfeld and Neu Kureni in 1914.
28. Neutatz, "Die Kolonien des Schwartzmeergebietes," 83, 88.

current poverty—had no traditions of holding communal savings as insurance, and thus, Russian peasants frequently had no realistic local access to capital via debt.

The argument that the Germans in Russia provided no useful improvements to the state appears even in the moderate journal *Vestnik Evropy* [The Messenger of Europe], which in an 1868 article argued that, "the colonists [had] taught [the Russians] nothing," and hadn't fulfilled their obligations.[29] This, however, was not an argument frequently made, as the general productivity of the German colonies, the large yields of their harvests, and large herds of animals, as well as their introduction of improved techniques were widely acknowledged.

Because most of the Germans in Bessarabia and South Russia lived by farming and raising animals, educated Russians considered them peasants, that is, part of the peasant class. This was also the class distinction made by the Russian government. One focus of the Decree of 1871, as noted in the prior chapter, was to place the German colonists on the same legal and civic footing as Russian peasants. Unlike Russian peasants, however, the Germans frequently prospered. By the end of the nineteenth century, many Germans had achieved a status roughly equivalent to levels of the middle class: they owned their land outright, they produced grain and animals well beyond their own needs, and by selling such surplus, they acquired saved capital and the spending power to acquire manufactured goods that improved their homes and farmsteads. To Russians, particularly Russians of the slowly impoverishing upper classes, the prosperity of the Germans created an unpleasant class confusion. This was surely part of the unhappiness expressed about the success the Germans were achieving in the land market. For nobles, competition with the German colonists was unseemly, especially as the lower class Germans had advantages the gentry didn't in entering the land market.[30]

The German farmers in Russia maintained beliefs and behaviors that set them apart, not only from Russian peasants but from the behavioral patterns of many Russians of all classes. The Germans maintained beliefs in the perfectibility of man that encouraged individuals in efforts of self-improvement, thrift, and sobriety— behavior patterns that Max Weber refers to as the "Protestant Ethic." As the statistics on drunkenness from the 1841 Welfare Committee study and various reports of similar problems in the 1848 village histories indicate, the German farmers in Bessarabia were not always successful as individuals or communities in pursuing these goals; however, such goals were commonly held as ideals and often put into practice by Germans in Russia. These were not the ideals encouraged by Russian

---

29. Klaus, *Naši kolonii*, 447. Klaus is quoting from *Vestnik Evropy* 3 (1868): 758.

30. Because the Germans had easy access to capital when they entered the land market in numbers, they drove up land prices. The loss of the inefficient but free labor with the end of serfdom meant that profitable agriculture became more capital-intensive for Russian noble landowners. In order for them to make any new land purchases profitable, they would need to make equipment and technique upgrades, much as the Germans had. Many Russian noble landowners, however, were not interested in or adept at changing the techniques of their peasant laborers. As successful agriculture came to demand more efficient use of labor via the use of new machinery, the farms of the Russian gentry—still dependent on the now paid-for labor of Russian peasants—did not do well. Riasanovsky's history covers this well:

> Forced to adjust to more intense competition and other harsh realities of the changing world, members of the gentry had little in their education, outlook, or character to make them successful capitalist farmers. A considerable number of landlords, in fact, preferred to live in Paris or Nice, spending whatever they had, rather than to face the new conditions in Russia. Others remained on their estates and waged a struggle for survival, but as statistics indicate, frequently without success. (Riasanovsky, *History of Russia*, 470)

Orthodoxy, nor were they viewed positively by many in Russia. Instead, the Russian Orthodox Church urged communicants to accept the situations into which they were born as God's will. To strive to change that situation encouraged the sins of pride and greed. Among the Russian peasantry, those who pushed ahead to better themselves incurred the resentment and jealousy of other peasants.[31] Russian peasants who held land of at least 6 desjatina were considered sufficiently well-off to hire additional labor for their farms and as such were commonly called *kulaks*, from the Russian word for "fist" (as in tightfisted).[32] This term was a derogatory term meant to criticize, though it had none of the criminal, even life-threatening aura the Communists later gave it. The Germans with comparatively larger farms who frequently hired labor from nearby non-German villages were certainly viewed by Russians of all classes as kulaks, not just for their success, but also for their striving after success. This different life focus was seen as something that was common to Germans and marked their differences from many Russians. The nineteenth century saw the rise of strong nationalistic passions throughout Europe. Such passions often came to have a xenophobic cast: cultural differences were considered to be cultural challenges. Thus, for some Russian commentators, the German cultural values of self-improvement, thrift, sobriety, and focus on the future drew suspicion, criticism, and even enmity.

Following Prussia's stunning total victory over France in 1870 and its merging with the remaining non-Austrian southern German states to create Imperial Germany, Russian nationalists also started to worry that the German colonies in South Russia and Bessarabia might raise potential dangers for the Russian state as supporters and outposts of the powerful new Germany. Such concerns were magnified when, in 1878, Germany blocked Russia from solidifying the gains its military had won in Romania, and especially after 1890, when Germany declined to extend the Reinsurance Treaty with Russia.[33] In response to the lapse of the Reinsurance Treaty, Russia turned to a former enemy, France, and established an alliance under which each promised to support the other in the case of an attack by Germany. Anticipating the increasing likelihood of a military conflict with Germany, Russian conservatives worried that the growing number of German-speaking settlements in Bessarabia and South Russia now posed major security risks for Imperial Russia. Conservative nationalists worried that large areas of Russia might become Germanized—that is, become German-speaking—with the result that Russia might lose control of them or that Germany might desire to absorb them or use their existence as a rationale for conflict. At the same time, Russian nationalists began to worry that the existence of a large population of Germans of uncertain or doubtful loyalty to Russia living

31. Neutatz, "Die Kolonien des Schwartzmeergebietes," 84.
32. The agricultural reforms of Russian Prime Minister Pyotr Stolypin defined possession of 6 desjatina of land (about 16 acres) as a minimum holding of a well-to-do peasant. These reforms were implemented in the Decree of November 6, 1906 (O.S.), which had the goal of breaking up the ancient Russian peasant landholding system called *obščina* based on collective village landownership and frequent redivision. The German colonists of Bessarabia, in contrast, held grants of 60 desjatina of land per family (160 acres) in their original settlements and tended to replicate farmsteads of this size in later purchases.
33. In the multicountry negotiations in Berlin in 1878, Germany blocked the creation of Russia's hoped-for Russian-dominated Greater Bulgaria. Instead, the independent country of Romania was formed out of the northern section of the putative Greater Bulgaria. Russia was awarded northern Dobrudscha, though it gave this to Romania in trade for parts of Bessarabia that Russia had lost as a result of the settlement of the Crimean War.

near the borders of Imperial Russia could pose a dangerous military risk for Russia in any conflict with Germany.

The point to be made here is not how realistic such fears were, but that they existed and were expressed. Such fears likely gave rise to at least some concerns that Germans remaining in Russia might face increased legal difficulties or social unpleasantness. Such concerns became another reason, another push, for Germans to think about emigration. I would, as a result, criticize an argument made by Fleischhauer, who sought to minimize the consequences of articles in the press that expressed worries about the presence of German settlements in South Russia.[34] Fleischhauer asserts that Russians clearly distinguished between the *germanskij* (Germans of Germany, Reichsdeutsch) and the *nemeckij* (Germans in general, not state-specific, Stammdeutsch) and asserts that the negative points of view were directed toward the germanskij. While the Russian language does contain both adjectives, they were not used to distinguish between Reichsdeutsch and Stammdeutsch, but were synonyms used to describe things German wherever met. In the late nineteenth and early twentieth centuries, the adjective "germanskij" carried an academic and even fusty overtone roughly analogous to the use of the term "Teutonic" in English, though carrying also the tone of marking things that were quintessentially or even passionately German.[35] Moreover, late nineteenth-century Russian nationalists didn't think that Germans living in Russia were any less dangerous than Germans living in Germany; on the contrary, those living within Russia's borders posed potentially greater dangers.

As fears of Germany grew, the conservative press in Russia repeatedly returned to the theme that the Germans living in South Russia represented political and security threats.[36] It was intimated that the Germans might be spies; that Germany might be supplying financial support to Germans in South Russia which, the papers implied, was the reason they had the money to be able to compete for land against Russian purchasers; that Bismarck was directing the actions of the colonists; or that following Bismarck's orders, the Germans in Russia had a mission to create an occupied German ring around the Black Sea coast.[37]

When tensions in Europe mounted in 1908–9 following Austria's annexation of Bosnia-Herzegovina, fears grew in Russia concerning the large German population in Volhynia, the region north of Bessarabia that bordered the Austro-Hungarian Empire. Russian nationalists worried that the presence of this population would be a temptation to Austria or Germany and that in case of conflict, this population would not side with Russia. In 1909, as agitation about the German population in Russia was increasingly discussed in Russian newspapers, Count Bobrinskoj, speaking in the Duma, charged that the Germans had conducted a "strategic colonization of the western borderlands." General Trepov, then governor of the provinces of Kiev, Podolia, and Volhynia, wrote to the prime minister, Piotr Stolypin,

---

34. Fleischhauer, *Die Deutschen im Zerenreich*, 391.

35. Dal', *Tolkovyj slovar'*, 358. The classic prerevolutionary Dal' dictionary defines *germanizm*, his only word based on this root, as "a passionate adherence of Germans [*nemcev*] and things German." Russians of the nineteenth century through the present day rarely distinguish in ordinary speech between Germans of Germany and Germans in general.

36. The newspapers *Novoe vremja*, *Svet*, and *Moskovskie vedomosti* were leaders in this regard.

37. Neutatz, "Die Kolonien des Schwartzmeergebietes," 83–84.

arguing for the need to develop stronger controls over Germans in the area.[38] As noted above, in 1912, such worries led the Duma to pass an edict reworking and strengthening the restrictions on purchases of land that would clearly bar Germans in South Russia and Bessarabia from making land purchases. However, by August 1914 and the onset of World War I, the law had yet to win the tsar's blessing and go into force.

The worries expressed by Russian nationalists were not well-founded and so indicate how little they actually knew of attitudes within the German communities in Bessarabia and South Russia. Once reaching Russia, the German colonists had not maintained close ties with Prussia or Württemberg. There are few references to even personal contacts maintained with family members who remained in Germany. This is not surprising given the semiliterate abilities of many of the first generation of colonists. Religious needs were satisfied by the German Evangelical Church headquarters in St. Petersburg. The Prussian government paid no attention to the colonists once they had left Prussia, any more than to Prussian citizens who had abandoned Prussia for the United States. The Heimatbuch of Kulm gives the impression that, until the last decades of the nineteenth century, narrow village life in Russia dominated the worldview and interests of the colonists. To the extent that the colonists followed or were even aware of news outside of Russia, it would have been through German-language newspapers printed in Odessa that sought to give a pro-Russian cast to politics and international events. Later in the nineteenth century, newspapers and books printed in Germany started to become available in Bessarabia and South Russia, and a few German students from Russia went to Germany for higher educational opportunities. However, there is no evidence that the Germans in Russia in any material way sought closer connections with the state of Germany or displayed disloyalty toward Russia.

While after 1880 it is clear that the German government was aware of the existence of the many German colonies in Russia, it did not seek to represent their interests and appears not to have sent or hired agents to establish contacts among them. On the contrary, the German government appears to have had worries that should they appear to establish closer connections with Germans in Russia, Russia would create problems for Germany by interfering with Germany's relations with its unhappy Polish-speaking population. This is the meaning of German Chancellor Bethmann-Hollweg's comment in his letter of December 6, 1910, to Count Friedrich von Pourtalès, the German ambassador to Russia during a period of mounting tensions before World War I: "Zu einer strikten Neutralität müßten uns… die Schwierigkeiten veranlassen, die wir bezüglich unserer eigenen fremdsprachigen Bevölkerung zu überwinden haben."[39]

It is not clear how deeply knowledge of the worries and concerns expressed by Russian nationalists penetrated into German communities in South Russia and Bessarabia. The German-language newspapers in Odessa did carry stories about efforts to restrict the rights of Germans to purchase additional land and did cover the debates in the Duma on such restrictions. They did not generally reproduce

---

38. Ibid., 86. Both the Bobrinskoj and Trepov references are from Neutatz.
39. Ibid., 87. "We must maintain a strict neutrality [toward such German-speaking citizens of Russia]…[not to do so] will create the need to overcome difficulties with regard to our own foreign-speaking population."

articles from or provide coverage concerning charges in the conservative Russian press that asserted the potential security risks and disloyalty of German citizens of Russia. The German communities would naturally have been very interested in the potential for restrictions on land purchases and were likely to have passed stories and commentary along via news reports and rumors. It is hard not to assume that, at least via rumors, some sense of the growing anti-German feelings expressed by Russian conservatives in the period up to World War I reached German communities. It seems likely that those Germans who elected to leave Russia were influenced by some combination of concerns relating to overcrowding, to conscription, to the Russian language replacing German, to possible restrictions on land purchase rights, to Russian anti-German attitudes, and to the potential for war. All of these touched on questions of the future for Germans in Russia.

## There were also pulls that attracted Bessarabian Germans to the idea of immigrating to North America

At the same time, it is important to bear in mind that there were positive attractions drawing people to consider immigrating to North America. As there were pushes encouraging people to think of leaving Russia, there were also pulls drawing them to new places and opportunities. The United States and Canada wished to attract people from Europe to settle the relatively unpopulated plains east of the Rocky Mountains. In 1862, in the midst of the Civil War, the United States passed the Homestead Act to encourage settlement on the plains west of Minnesota, Iowa, and Missouri. Mercantilist economic thinking stood as one rationale for passing this act. It reflected a desire to make the country stronger by attracting hardworking farmers to populate and make prosperous land where heretofore only American Indians lived, hunting game and farming small, generally temporary sites along the rivers. In part, though, the Homestead Act was also a response to political and economic conditions in the northern United States in 1862.

Congress and supporters of this act wanted the broad, still underpopulated areas of the West settled by people not economically dependent on slavery, so that the new states that would arise there would be non-slave states. Other supporters of the act were Americans who held a Jeffersonian ideal of the United States and wanted the country populated by a class of generally self-sufficient small farmers. Such Americans were disturbed to see the significant growth of manufacturing in the Northeast, and with it the appearance of a powerful, rich class of factory owners and financiers and a large, poorly paid, and turbulent working class. Such Americans saw the Homestead Act as a means to shift the balance of power in the United States back in favor of small, independent agriculturalists.

To attract settlers from Europe, the Homestead Act offered land on very generous terms, far more cheaply than it could be purchased in Bessarabia. Kern reports the costs of purchasing land in Bessarabia as rising from around 40 to 45 rubles a desjatina in 1880 to 500 to 1,000 rubles in the period from 1912 to 1914. Under the Homestead Act, there were two methods by which new settlers might acquire land, both far more dependent on labor than on money:

1. Preemption

   Anyone over twenty-one could purchase 160 acres, roughly the size of the Russian grants of 60 desjatina made to German settlers in Bessarabia in 1814, at $1.25/acre if after six months of occupation they could show proof of residence and cultivation by putting up a habitable dwelling and having made some land improvements.[40]

2. Homesteading

Anyone over age twenty-one could obtain 160 acres of land by (i) paying a $14 fee and filing a claim, and then (ii) within six months plowing at least 10 acres, putting in a crop, and establishing residence on the land. After residing on the land for five years and within seven years of paying the initial fee, the individual needed to pay an additional "proving up" fee of $4 in order to receive a patent and ownership title to the 160 acres.

A family could earn the right to own 160 acres by homesteading and then earn a second 160-acre plot via preemption. Additional plots of 160 acres might be earned at low cost under the provisions of the Timber Culture Act of 1873. These additional claims were called Tree Claims. Large areas of the Dakotas, Nebraska, and Kansas were prairie lands for the most part devoid of trees. To make a tree claim on a 160-acre section, an individual needed to plow and sow at least 5 acres in each of the first two years. Following that, to establish the claim they also needed to sow 10 acres of timber seeds or plant cuttings within two years and then keep those 10 acres in good condition for eight years. American thinking here followed a similar course to that of the Russian mercantilists, who in 1814 required that a portion of the allotment given to a German colonial village in Bessarabia be improved by planting and maintaining a forest area.

Land at such prices would be attractive to those in Bessarabia who owned property, as well as those who were renting but had access to some capital. An article in the February 17, 1910, issue of the *Dakota Freie Presse*, a German-language paper of Neu Ulm, Minnesota, wondered rhetorically whether poor farmers in Bessarabia would remain there when conditions were so attractive in the United States: "Things [in Russia] are getting rougher from year to year, land is getting ever scarcer and higher. The poor people on rented farms can no longer get ahead." Referring more to conditions in South Russia than in Bessarabia, the author of the *Dakota Freie Presse* article then drew the following conclusion: "Many in the old homeland have no land and cannot possibly acquire any of their own. Why should a man stay in Russia and work for somebody else if he can establish a lovely home of his own here?"[41]

The costs for each of the three methods of acquiring land in the western United States were materially lower than the costs of buying land in Bessarabia. The American government had intentionally set low prices for available land and included work-to-earn provisions as a means to attract immigrants, who were willing to do the work and live on the land, rather than land speculators. Despite the attractive

40. It was $2.50/acre if the land was considered a railroad tract. In order to encourage development of the American West, the Homestead Act granted huge tracts of land to railroad companies to encourage railroads to be built with private funds. The railroads were given every other section of land on both sides of the proposed rail lines. These were the railroad tracts, which the railroads then sold to recover their construction costs.

41. Quoted in Richard Sallet, *Russian-German Settlements in the United States*, trans. Lavern J. Rippley and Armand Bauer (Fargo: North Dakota Institute for Regional Studies, 1974), 65. Sallet's work was originally published in German in 1931 under the title *Russlanddeutsche Seidlungen in den Vereinigten Staaten von America*. The unidentified author of the article published in the *Dakota Freie Presse* February 17, 1910, whom Sallet quotes, is referring to the high cost of both buying and leasing land in Russia, which the author imagines will make those in need of land turn to hiring themselves out to richer farmers.

prices and conditions, the terms for land in the United States were not without negative features for Germans in Russia. North America was extremely distant, and realistically, immigrating there meant cutting off easy connections with one's family and friends who remained in Russia. Some stories of the Indian Wars appear to have reached Russia and are likely to have raised worries. General Totleben, for example, used the specter of wild natives to try to discourage the Mennonites from leaving in 1874. Another major negative factor was that Germans emigrating from Russia would not be able to duplicate the tight-knit German-speaking communities that had been founded there. The Homestead Act required settlers to live on their land claims rather than in centralized villages as a means to create a mixture of settlers on the new lands. The United States government didn't want the development of unassimilated, non-English-speaking, isolated village communities (the problem the Russians had created for themselves with Germans in Russia). By parceling out land in 160-acre sections, a German family from Russia might be living next to a family from Ohio or one from Norway. It was hoped that by this means, English would be learned and used, furthering the goal of immigrants becoming Americans.

Canada established a program similar to the Homestead Act of 1862 to attract immigrants to Canada. Under the Dominion Lands Act of 1872, plots of 160 acres in Canada's western provinces were offered for free after a claimant paid a C$10 administrative fee. In order to gain title a settler needed to provide proof that the land claimed had increased in value via cultivation or the construction of buildings. Less concerned than the United States about the creation of unassimilated citizens, the Canadian government allowed immigrants to develop monoethnic, non-English- or non-French-speaking communities. Another difference from the system employed by the Homestead Act in the United States was that settlers in Canada were allowed to claim a neighboring 160 acre plot by paying another fee of C$10.

Canada drew far fewer settlers among the Germans from Russia than did the United States. Canada was somewhat more difficult to get to and perhaps less familiar to Germans in Russia. Most of the Germans from Russia who settled in Canada did so by immigrating first to the United States and then moving from there to Canada. The heaviest period of German Russian immigration into Canada occurred between 1904 and 1914, with most coming from North Dakota, Montana, and Washington. Those who moved to Canada appear to have been motivated both by the rising cost of land in the United States and the fact that much of the best land for farming in the United States had been taken up by the turn of the century. Immigration to Canada from the United States slowed significantly after 1910, as it became apparent that infrastructure in Canada had not caught up with settlement, and new communities had trouble getting grain to a market.[42]

As the following chapter will discuss, World War I destroyed the agricultural economy in Bessarabia and impoverished many German households there. With the value of any saved rubles wiped out by the war's inflation and by the Russian Revolution, few Germans in Bessarabia could find the means to pay passage to North America. Moreover, after World War I, the United States changed its immigration policies and established country-based quotas for immigrants, making it

---

42. Sallet, *Russian-German Settlements*, 32–34. Sallet notes that in December 1912, "farmers in Saskatchewan and Alberta were forced to utilize some of their threshed wheat as fuel because they could neither get heating material nor could they market their wheat" (34).

far more difficult to gain visas for entry. Brazil and (to a lesser extent) Argentina, however, were interested in attracting settlers, and Brazil hired agents to find interested families in Bessarabia. Kern, in his survey of Bessarabian villages, notes that during the years of poor harvests from 1924 to 1928, small numbers of Germans in Bessarabia left for Brazil. In speaking from his personal experience in the village of Neu Borodino in June 1925, Kern notes that he "had taken over the rectory a few weeks back [in June of 1925], when the exodus to Brazil increased. As so often happens in lean years, immigration brokers appear and make a profit by recruiting the disillusioned."[43] In his discussion of Leipzig, Bessarabia, Kern notes that "in 1925–26 the poorer population began immigrating to Brazil, in 1927 they went to Canada."[44]

## The fact that transportation to North America was well organized and affordable increased its attraction for immigrants

The path to North America from Bessarabia before World War I began by traveling to the railroad station just north of Leipzig. From there, travelers went by rail via Bender to Odessa. The Odessa main line carried passengers via Warsaw into Germany on a two-day journey that typically ended in Bremerhaven or Hamburg. There, German steamship companies would offer housing and board in dormitories as part of the ticket price for transit while the immigrants were waiting for the next ship to the United States. If there were thoughts of staying in Germany, these were soon dropped as unrealistic. German agricultural lands were also crowded, forcing the young to leave for the cities. Farm land was not generally for sale, and where it was available for rent, it might only be had on the quite onerous terms of tenure that many of the ancestors of the Bessarabian Germans had abandoned.

The ability of families to emigrate from Russia was dependent on their ability to pay the costs of both traveling and reestablishing themselves on farms in North America. Bessarabian German emigrants from Russia financed these costs from savings and from their inheritance shares due from parental households. Loans were not possible as the emigrants were leaving Russia, though families may have taken out loans to pay out inheritance shares to emigrating relatives. While, as we will see, the costs of emigration were not huge, they were large enough to allow us to presume that the great majority of emigrants had at least modest assets. Such a financial hurdle, however, did not preclude landless Germans with some assets from emigrating from Russia. Both Sallet and Saul note the presence of such landless emigrants, generally from South Russia, among the Germans coming from Russia to North America.

The few accounts of immigrants to North America attributed to the actual immigrants themselves do not provide cost estimates, much less financial records of the funds needed to travel and reestablish themselves on a different continent. Some do provide costs for portions of their travel. With information available from other sources on travel costs, it is possible to estimate the amounts Germans from Bessarabia needed to finance immigration. These data suggest that a married couple without children needed assets ranging from perhaps a bare minimum of 500 rubles to a more likely norm of over 1,000 rubles to make this journey. In the 1880s, passage

---

43. Kern, *Homeland Book*, 130.
44. Ibid., 143.

in steerage to the United States from Bremen cost between US$25 and $35 per adult.[45] The costs of travel to Bremen from Russia and travel from New York to the Dakotas came to perhaps another US$40 to $50, bringing the total travel cost of immigration to about $100 per adult.[46] The cost to purchase a non-railroad tract under the preemption option of the Homestead Act would come to $200, while a railroad tract would cost $400. If a settler chose to acquire land by homesteading, a tract would cost $14. A couple, then, would need to have had a minimum of $325, assuming they could feed themselves on their journey and pay the costs of setting themselves up on $125. It is far more likely they needed between $600 and $900, and of course more than that if they brought children with them. As the ruble was not on the gold standard until 1897, exchange values with the American dollar and German mark varied widely and would also depend on whether the rubles were paper or metal, the quality of precious metal (if the latter), and of course on the bank's or money changer's interest in holding Russian currency. A San Francisco, California, Russian Orthodox church ledger from 1882 that accounted for the salaries of Russian priests used an exchange value of one Russian ruble being the equivalent of US$0.77. Using this exchange value as an example, an immigrating couple would have needed minimum assets for the journey of between 800 and 1,200 rubles.[47]

There exist some immigration manifests from the 1890s onward that in addition to documenting the names of the arriving immigrant passengers also include estimates made by United States immigration officials as to the amount of cash the immigrants were bringing into the country. In a few cases, such manifests are extant for Bessarabian Germans. One such is for the passengers of the SS *Fürst Bismarck*, which arrived in New York on May 27, 1898, and carried fourteen families from Kulm and Leipzig, Bessarabia, as well as two boys traveling with this group. The two boys had little money; a fifteen-year-old from Kulm had $35, and his nineteen-year-old companion from Leipzig had $7.50. They likely had agreed to work for one of the families, who would pay for their travel and feed them for some agreed on period. The fourteen families carried widely varying assets. The two most well-to-do families each brought $1,500, while the poorest family had but $50. The average amount of assets held by each of the fourteen families was $673, with seven families

45. Deborah Dwork, "Health Conditions of Immigrant Jews on the Lower East Side of New York: 1880–1914," *Medical History* 25, no. 1 (1981): 1–40; "Roll Family Genealogy—Emigration and Travel Experiences," The Roll "Fame" Family, accessed July 6, 2015, http://www.rollintl.com/roll/emigration.htm; and Michelle Stone, "John Jacob Kreischer and Katherine Gilcher: Their Story and Family in Syracuse and Onondaga County, New York," Ancestry.com, accessed July 6, 2015, http://freepages.genealogy.rootsweb.ancestry.com/~mstone/kgbook1.html. Dwork reports that "steerage costs from Hamburg, Bremen or Antwerp [to New York] cost $34, from Liverpool $25." The Roll family genealogy reports travel costs of $38.90 in 1912 for one adult from Libau (Liepaja), Latvia, to Boston. Stone reports steerage costs from Bremerhaven to New York in 1883 as between $25 and $30.
46. The Roll Family Genealogy cited in footnote 46 above also notes train expenses from Boston to Lincoln, Nebraska, of $25.10 and travel expenses to Latvia from Saratov as $6.65, making the total costs from Dönhof, South Russia, to Lincoln, Nebraska, come to $84.65 (in 1912 dollars). My rough figure of $100 is thus based on the assumptions that it took: (a) up to $25 to travel to Bremen, Hamburg, or Bremerhaven, (b) under $50 to travel in steerage to the US East Coast, and (c) up to $30 to travel from port of arrival to the Dakotas or Washington State.
47. "From the Financial Statement for 1882," Holy Trinity Cathedral, accessed July 6, 2015, http://www.holy-trinity.org/history/1882/01.01.budget.html. The exchange rate used by the Holy Trinity Cathedral in San Francisco in 1882 of 1 Russian ruble equaling US$0.77 should be seen as a utilitarian calculation tied to a specific time and place. The Russian Orthodox church in Russia paid for the salaries and housing allowances of the Russian priests and deacons serving this church. The parish administration of the Holy Trinity Cathedral then exchanged the rubles into dollars that the clergy could use in their daily lives..

holding $600 or more and seven holding $550 or less. The immigration notes for four of the five Kulm families who arrived a month earlier on the SS *Patria* give an average holding of $443, with a high of $900 and a low of $50.[48]

Other immigration manifests with data on arriving Bessarabian Germans offer similar pictures of asset holdings. The number of data points, though, is far too low to draw definitive conclusions. They do suggest that many Bessarabian German families arrived with sufficient funds to travel west, to make claims on large tracts of land, and to purchase food and equipment. Some families clearly arrived financially well prepared to establish themselves, but others were going to struggle in their first years. To give perspective, statistics collected by the United States Bureau of Labor indicate that for 1901, the average annual family income for a family of five varied between $715 in the South Central states and $891 in the Western states.[49]

### The attractions of immigrating to buy land in North America appear to be strongest for those in Bessarabia who wanted to buy rather than lease land but were finding the rising costs of buying land in Russia too steep

Using data discussed below and in more detail in the following chapter, the costs of immigration to North America would seem to fall in between those of leasing and purchasing additional land in Bessarabia. This again suggests that immigrants to North America came from at least the middling economic levels in late nineteenth-century Bessarabian German society. The costs of immigration were steep enough to make this a high hurdle for the poorest Germans. If they had some means, the poor were more likely to opt for the less expensive opportunity of leasing land in Bessarabia. In the late 1870s, the costs of land purchase and the cost of immigration were roughly similar. Toward the end of the nineteenth century and into the early twentieth, however, the costs of land purchase in Bessarabia rose materially, while the costs of immigration remained generally flat. As a result, it would seem logical to conclude that over time, this growing cost differential became another pull or attraction drawing interest in immigration to North America. In the 1880s, for example, the costs of land purchase in Bessarabia varied between 40 and 90 rubles per desjatina. To buy 60 desjatina, the standard household land area of the original colonies and roughly the same as the 160-acre allotments offered to new settlers under the Homestead Act in the United States, it would cost between

48. A photocopy of the unsigned immigration manifest, the "List or Manifest of Alien Immigrants for the Commissioner of Immigration," for the *Fürst Bismarck* passengers can be found in T 715, Roll 0022, p. 620 in "Passenger Lists of Vessels Arriving in New York 1897-1957" (Washington, DC: National Archives Microfilm Publications, 2010). In several cases, an immigration official has crossed off an earlier notation to substitute a new number. For example, the Johann Krause family of Leipzig was originally noted to have $150, but this was later changed to $125. The David Kuhn family of Kulm was originally listed as having $500, but this was later changed to $800. Such multiple listings suggest that the immigrants were given a second opportunity to assess what they actually had, perhaps after exchanging foreign currency for dollars. For a listing of the names of these arriving passengers from the *Fürst Bismarck* and *Patria*, see footnotes 68 and 66 later in this chapter.
49. US Bureau of Labor, "Wages and Hours of Labor 1890–1905. Retail Prices of Food 1890–1905," *Bulletin of the Bureau of Labor* no. 65 (July 1906): 187. The average annual expenditures for food ran between $292 in the South Central states and $338 in the North Atlantic states.

2,400 and 5,400 rubles at these prices.[50] As several land purchases in Bessarabia were made with loans, one might assume a family didn't need to have the full purchase price available. Nonetheless, presuming a down payment of 45 percent, as was the case in Mannsburg land purchase of 1881,[51] capital requirements per family for land purchase were at least in the order of 1,100 rubles plus the cost of moving and setting themselves up on unplowed land. As land purchase prices in Bessarabia rose rapidly over the next thirty years, reaching 250–500 rubles around 1910, the capital requirements for those purchasing land rose accordingly. Reported rates for leasing land in Bessarabia were significantly lower, in the area of 2–3 rubles a desjatina per year in the 1880s, rising to 4 to 5 or 11 rubles a desjatina in 1899–1905.[52] Thus, equivalent annual costs for leasing 60 desjatina would have been 300–660 rubles. As the following chapter discusses in detail, those leasing land in Bessarabia were often, though not always, coming from poorer families, whose savings and inheritance shares were insufficient to meet the costs of land purchase.

## Estimates of the numbers of Germans who emigrated from Bessarabia

There are no reliable counts of the numbers of Germans who left Bessarabia for other parts of Russia, for Dobrudscha, or for North and South America. There are only estimates, most of which are quite rough. The most serious attempt at estimating the number of emigrants was made by Karl Stumpp (see table 10–4). His estimates are based, apparently, on counts of actual emigrants from some villages, which he then expanded to theoretical totals based on general population data he had collected from German Bessarabia. As a result, because his figures are not given in round numbers, they appear to represent actual counts, whereas they are in fact general estimates, or educated guesses. Stumpp's extensive work in the 1920s and 1930s collecting data on Bessarabian German population figures, however, does give his estimates some credibility. If anything, Stumpp's numbers may be conservative estimates. Data collected by Brandes suggests, for example, that Stumpp probably undercounted the number of Germans who emigrated from Bessarabia to other regions in Imperial Russia.[53] Stumpp's general conclusion, however, that the great majority of the total number of emigrants from German Bessarabia between 1875

---

50. Kern reports costs for the land purchased for Mannsburg in 1881 as 38 silver rubles per desjatina (*Homeland Book*, 169). The land purchased for the village of Neu Posttal bought in the same year was 89 rubles per desjatina (171). A more detailed discussion of land prices in Bessarabia will be found in the next chapter.
51. In Mannsburg, the total costs for the 3,000 desjatina purchased came to 114,000 silver rubles. Kern notes that a mortgage for 63,000 rubles was arranged (*Homeland Book*, 169), thus implying that 51,000 silver rubles or 44.7 percent of the cost was paid collectively by the purchasers in 1881 when the land was bought.
52. In reporting a leasing rate of 11 rubles a desjatina in Maraslienfeld in 1914, Kern is pointing out the heights to which leasing rates might go (*Homeland Book*, 184).
53. Brandes cites archival material on internal immigration within Russia that counts the number of families and individuals leaving the Bessarabian German mother colonies for other places within Imperial Russia during the period from 1859 from 1890: 2,583 families, in total 12,839 people. Most of these—1,271 families containing 8,276 people—moved to daughter colonies in Bessarabia; the remainder—1,292 families containing 4,563 people—went to other sites in Imperial Russia. We know from genealogical data that some of the latter group ultimately immigrated to North America, but as this group of 4,563 emigrants to other sites in Russia is already higher than Stumpp's total of 3,848 to Siberia and the Caucasus, this strongly suggests Stumpp's estimate of internal immigration is low (Brandes, *Von den Zaren Adoptiert*, 397–98).

TABLE 10–4.  **Stumpp's estimates of the total German emigration from Bessarabia**[a]

| Destination | Quantity |
| --- | --- |
| North America | 11,326 |
| Siberia | 2,402 |
| South America | 1,898 |
| Caucasus | 1,446 |
| Romania | 1,342 |
| Other countries | 402 |
| Germany | 354 |
| **Total** | 19,170 |

a. Kern, *Homeland Book*, 5. Kern miscalculates the total number of emigrants, reaching a figure of 19,152 instead of 19,170. With the exception of the figures for South America, Germany, and other countries, all the other emigration totals would refer to emigration that occurred before World War I.

and 1930s went to North America seems to be accepted by all who have commented on this issue.

Elvire Eberhardt, in assessing the size of the Bessarabian German emigration, thought Stumpp's estimates to be reasonable, at least for North America, based on her consideration of the sizes of villages in North America with large Bessarabian German populations.[54] Some estimations of the numbers of emigrant Germans from Bessarabia are far larger. Jakob Becker, for example, believed that 20,000 Bessarabian Germans came to North America and another 15,000 went to Dobrudscha.[55] Becker's numbers seem quite high. The Bessarabian German population that settled in Dobrudscha, for example, was limited to a small number of villages. The majority of these people remained in Romania until 1940. The German army count of German refugees from Dobrudscha transported from Galati in the fall of 1940, which appear to be the total German population then in Dobrudscha, came to just 2,504 people. This gives more credence to the general tenor of Stumpp's estimate of 1,342 Bessarabian German immigrants settling in Dobrudscha.[56]

Census materials from the United States and Canada offer some help in estimating the number of Germans born in Russia who immigrated to North America. The 1900, 1910, 1920, and 1930 censuses indicate languages spoken and countries of origin. However, while these census records show an origin in Russia and German as the family language, they give no help in identifying the region in Russia the immigrants came from. The 1920 US census counted 116,535 persons who had been born in Russia and spoke German as their first language.[57] This would include Germans from Bessarabia, along with German Lutherans, Catholics, and Mennonites from

---

54. Elvire Necker-Eberhardt, "The Bessarabian Dialect in Medicine Hat Alberta" (PhD diss., University of Alberta, 1973), 23.

55. Jakob Becker, *Wie's daheim war: Der Schicksalweg der Bessarabiendeutschen* (Asperg, Ger.: Verlagsdruckerei Wilhelm Altvater, 1950), excerpt in *Bessarabian Newsletter* 7, no. 2 (2005): 9.

56. "Tabulation of Evacuated Ethnic Germans as well as Wagons and Horses Brought into Romania," #T-81, VOMI 920, Record Group 1035, Film Roll 317, Series 535, Frame 2447168 in Konrad, "Evacuation from Bessarabia and Bukovina." The figure of 2,504 is from the German army count during the resettlement.

57. Sallet, *Russian-German Settlements*, 17. This may be the source of Alvar Carlson's estimate of 120,000 German-Russian immigrants in the United States. Carlson, "German-Russian Houses in Western North Dakota," *Pioneer America* 13, no. 2 (1981): 49–60.

South Russia, and Germans from the Volga region. It would not include German immigrants who died before 1920 or those who moved on to Canada. As a result, this total cannot be considered a count of German immigrants from Russia, though it does offer a rough estimate of what that number might be.

Estimations from Canadian census materials of German immigrants from Russia are even more broadly based and so less pertinent to the questions raised here. For example, Valerie Knowles notes in her study only that the majority of Germans in the Canadian western provinces came from Russia, Austria-Hungary, and the Balkans. This study assumes that for the period from 1890 to 1914, 35,000 German speakers from these regions in Europe settled in Manitoba, and perhaps around 100,000 settled in Saskatchewan and Alberta.[58]

There is very little credible information on Bessarabian German immigration to South America. Details discussed later in this chapter will indicate that some immigration to South America occurred before 1914, typically when families turned away at immigration in New York went on to Argentina. It would seem, however, that the major immigration to South America by Germans from Bessarabia occurred in the 1920s when Brazil offered inducements to settlement there. While Kern notes that following failed harvests in 1925 he saw "droves" of the emigration-minded from Neu-Borodino and Leipzig come for papers, the infrequency of noting this elsewhere implies the total emigration was relatively small.[59] In contrast, the editors of *Volk auf dem Weg: Deutsche in Rußland und in der GUS: 1763–1997* [*A People on the Move: Germans in Russia and in the Former Soviet Union: 1763–1997*], a study of Germans from Russia based on materials collected by Karl Stumpp, estimate that "in 1940 approximately 350,000 to 400,000 Germans from Russia lived in the USA, in Canada 200,000, Mexico 30,000, Brazil 200,000, Argentina 200,000, Paraguay 4,500…included in these numbers are those…who immigrated overseas in the 1920s. These could be estimated at 150,000 to 200,000."[60]

Such estimates of the German immigrants to the United States and Canada from Russia appear exaggerated and make sense only if they count the number of immigrants and their descendants, not the immigrants themselves. For Latin America, the numbers estimated for Brazil, Argentina, and Mexico do not seem credible even if descendants are included. There do appear to have been small numbers of immigrants from South Russia to South America before World War I. After the end of that war, the Russian Revolution trapped the German population in South Russia and the Volga in the Soviet Union, almost totally closing off emigration from there.

With regard to Bessarabian German immigration to South America, even if Stumpp's number of 1,898 leaving for South America is low, without more evidence it would be unrealistic to assume it topped 4,000 people. It would seem more likely that the high estimated numbers of Germans living in Latin America really refer

58. Valerie Knowles, "The Arrival of the Europeans," chap. 2 in *Forging Our Legacy: Canadian Citizenship and Immigration, 1900–1977* (Ottawa: Citizenship and Immigration Canada, 2000), http://www.cic.gc.ca/english/resources/publications/legacy/chap-2a.asp.

59. Kern, *Homeland Book*, 131. Under Leipzig he notes that "in 1925–26 the poorer population began immigrating to Brazil. In 1927 they went to Canada" (143).

60. Eduard Markstädter et al., eds., *Volk auf dem Weg: Deutsche in Rußland und in der GUS: 1763–1997*, 5th ed. (Stuttgart: Landsmannschaft der Desutschen aus Rußland, 1997). A translation by Ingeborg Smith (*A People on the Move: Germans in Russia and in the Former Soviet Union: 1763–1997*) can be found at http://library.ndsu.edu/grhc/history_culture/history/people.html.

to Germans coming from Germany. With that presumption, however, the figure for Brazil, where immigration studies have been made, appears far too high for immigrants from Russia and far too low for German immigrants from all sources. For example, Luebke, in his study of Germans in Brazil, estimates that between 1820 and 1914 perhaps 400,000 Germans had settled in Brazil, the vast majority coming from Germany.[61] By 1940 the number of ethnic Germans in Brazil would have been in the millions.

## Data from Kulm, Leipzig, and Tarutino allow a closer look at immigration timing and patterns

It is possible to gain at least a limited picture of the patterns and size of the German emigration from Bessarabia by organizing material on emigrants found in Flegel's extensive genealogical study of citizens of the villages of Kulm, Leipzig, and Tarutino. Flegel provides an excellent starting point by identifying many of the families from these villages who immigrated particularly to North America. By following the traces of such families in the 1900, 1910, and 1920 US censuses, the 1911 and 1916 Alberta censuses, and in the shipping manifests that list the names of passengers arriving in the United States, coherent pictures emerge of the following:

- The relative time flow of immigration based on arrival dates in North America
- Where in North America immigrants first settled and the frequency and destinations of secondary movement when the first settlement was given up
- Group patterns of immigrants traveling from Bessarabia to North America

Rather than organizing the material Flegel has collected into counts of individual immigrants, I found it more useful to consider it from the perspective of separate immigrant families and single immigrants. This places the central focus on the adults who made the decisions to leave Russia. Counts of the total numbers of immigrants arriving in North America overweight the effect of families immigrating with their children. Total immigrant counts, thus, skew attempts to understand the timing of when immigration decisions were made. A second major problem in placing the focus on counts of the total numbers of immigrants is that it is difficult to put together accurate lists. The number of living children at the time of immigration is the problem. Ship manifests are extant for less than a third of the immigrants. Moreover, as the data in Flegel as well as church data from Bessarabia become spotty after 1885, counts of the full sizes of immigrating families are more elusive. The best census data comes from the 1900 and 1910 US censuses. These, however, cannot be relied on to give the sizes of immigrating families as they do not include immigrant children who moved away from family homesteads in the United States or who died after reaching the United States. Indeed, the issue of the actual numbers of immigrants will remain less significant until there are accurate population counts from the Bessarabian German villages for the period from 1876 to 1914. Without such counts, even the basic question

---

61. Frederick Luebke, *Germans in Brazil: A Comparative History of Cultural Conflict during World War I* (Baton Rouge: Louisiana State University Press, 1987).

of the number of those leaving as a function of total village population cannot be considered.

Using Flegel as a starting point, I have identified 480 immigrant couples and single immigrants with backgrounds in the Bessarabian German villages of Kulm, Leipzig, and Tarutino.[62] The dates from which these parties set out from Europe break down into the following patterns, with 94 percent occurring in the period from 1876 to 1914 (see table 10–5).

The United States was the primary destination: 432 couples and single immigrants, 90 percent of the total of 480, came to the United States. It should not be concluded, however, that the United States overwhelmingly formed the dominant destination for all emigration from these three villages, or that these figures accurately reflect the pattern of emigration from these villages, much less from German Bessarabia as a whole. It only appears so because the best data tracking Germans who left Bessarabia exist in records in the United States. The United States and North America, as Stumpp's estimates indicate, may well have been the destination of most Bessarabian German emigrants, but without better data from these three villages on the families who went to the Crimea, the Caucasus, Siberia, and Dobrudscha, we cannot know with any accuracy the relative weight of any destination. It is important to note that not all of the immigrant groups counted in the numbers above came directly from Bessarabia. Among the 432 individuals who came to the United States, there were 18 Tarutino families who traveled from the Russian Caucasus and 18 Kulm families who emigrated from Dobrudscha. They are not counted separately as immigrants to the Caucasus or to Dobrudscha because there are limited or no data on when, how, or with whom these first moves from Tarutino and Kulm occurred. We know of them as immigrants from data that exist on their travel to the United States.

Other destinations included in the total of 480 are: Canada (31), Dobrudscha (12), and South America (5). Canada was the primary destination of immigrants coming after 1918. Of the 27 couples and single individuals leaving Bessarabia after 1918, 20 went to Canada. Prior to 1918, Canada was counted as the initial destination for only 11 of the 443 immigrations to North America. Canada, however, was the beneficiary

TABLE 10–5. **Emigration by period from Kulm, Leipzig, and Tarutino**

| | Kulm | | Leipzig | | Tarutino | | Totals | |
|---|---|---|---|---|---|---|---|---|
| Years | Number | % | Number | % | Number | % | Number | % |
| 1876–1880 | 82 | 35.1 | 8 | 6.3 | 9 | 7.5 | 99 | 20.6 |
| 1881–1890 | 46 | 19.7 | 22 | 17.4 | 9 | 7.5 | 77 | 16.0 |
| 1891–1900 | 48 | 20.5 | 50 | 39.7 | 41 | 34.2 | 139 | 29.0 |
| 1901–1914 | 49 | 20.9 | 38 | 30.2 | 51 | 42.5 | 138 | 28.8 |
| 1918–1940 | 1 | 0.4 | 6 | 4.8 | 4 | 3.3 | 11 | 2.3 |
| 1945+ | 8 | 3.4 | 2 | 1.6 | 6 | 5.0 | 16 | 3.3 |
| **Totals** | 234 | | 126 | | 120 | | 480 | |

62. The great majority of these immigrant parties are individuals listed in Flegel who were born in one of these three villages or whose parents were. I have supplemented this listing with data on immigrants from the Raugust family and families they married into who have Kulm and Tarutino origins but were not collected by Flegel (these data are summarized in table 7–1).

of a number of secondary migrations: 23 families who settled first in the United States ultimately moved on to Canada.

The heaviest volume of emigration occurred in the period from 1890 to 1914. Nearly 60 percent of the total counted from these three villages left Europe during this time frame. For those with backgrounds in Leipzig and Tarutino, this pattern was even more prominent, as nearly 75 percent of the emigrants from these villages left between 1890 and 1914. Emigration by people with Kulm backgrounds not only began earlier but was significantly larger. Slightly over a third of those with Kulm backgrounds started their journeys in the early period from 1876 to 1880, while only 6 percent of those with backgrounds in Leipzig and 7 percent of those with back- grounds in Tarutino date from this period. A second striking feature is the compar- atively large number of emigrants coming from Kulm. Kulm's total is nearly equal to the combined total of emigrants from Leipzig and Tarutino. Kulm was likely the smallest of the three villages and, judging from the Kulm Heimatbuch account, the least diversified in employment opportunities. It is not possible to know with the data available where to put weight in estimating causation. For all we know, the large number of early departures, which may have been an accidental occurrence, was the major factor that encouraged later emigrants. For all three villages, the bulk of emigration, 95 percent, occurred before World War I.

Though Tarutino was one of the largest German villages in Bessarabia, with roughly three times the 1940 population of either Kulm or Leipzig,[63] Tarutino sent out the smallest number of emigrants from the three villages—just 120 emigrant groups. Tarutino's proportionately small number may be linked to the fact that Tarutino had developed into a thriving manufacturing and commercial center. This provided economic options within the village outside of agriculture, and so permitted villagers not wishing to leave the opportunity to remain in Tarutino and earn a reasonable living. Another factor that may have kept emigration from Tarutino down is that Tarutino—nearly uniquely among Bessarabian German villages—used its civic wealth to provide opportunities for its poorer citizens. Tarutino leased land located north of Leipzig that its citizens could sublease and so acquire new farmland. This leased land ultimately became the village of Neu Tarutino and provided another Bessarabian option for those who might otherwise have considered emigration.

Where ship manifests are extant, attesting the arrival of Bessarabian German immigrants in the United States, it is the common pattern to see the immigrants arriving in groups with other families from the same village. In many cases, they shared family relationships. For example, the first group to arrive from Bessarabia that reached New York on May 1, 1876, on the SS *Mosel*, discussed earlier, consisted of fourteen families: five from Teplitz, three from Kulm, three from Dennewitz, two from Friedenstal, and one from Tarutino.[64] Seven of the families were linked

---

63. In the resettlement population count made in 1940 by the German army, Tarutino had a population of 6,186 people in comparison to Kulm and Leipzig, which had populations of 1,814 and 2,257, respectively.

64. While this example and a few others to follow do discuss families with no strong connections to Kulm, Leipzig, and Tarutino (in this case, the families from Dennewitz, Friedenstal, and Teplitz, as they were part of the source material and do illustrate the point being made), such families were not included in the data set of 480 emigrations that is being discussed so as to maintain focus on data from the three villages.

by blood relationships. The evidence from ship manifests, though limited in data points, suggests that groups of three to seven families were normal. Traveling in groups provided comfort and mutual support and limited some of the risks of the long-distance journey. On arrival in North America, it was also quite common for those listed together on a ship's manifest to be found in the next census to have settled in the same county or in neighboring counties. The settlement frontier in the United States in this period was quite broad, giving new arrivals many choices. The fact that groups arriving together tended to settle together suggests this too was thought of as a means to reduce risk. That Bessarabian Germans most frequently went to places where other Bessarabian Germans had settled also suggests that there were regular communications from the United States back to Bessarabia that told new immigrants where they might find acceptable land and even people from home. These immigrants clearly placed value on being near others who spoke their language and shared their customs and who might, in case of need, provide support.

Such predilections are evident in following five families with Kulm backgrounds who arrived in New York on April 17, 1898, on the SS *Patria* from Hamburg. Three of these families settled in Adams County, Washington, and another went to neighboring Lincoln County.[65] The four couples who went to Washington State included two pairs of siblings. The fifth family, Johann Winter and his wife, Wilhelmina Knopp Winter, settled in McLean County, North Dakota, where the 1900 census lists him as living beside or with his father, Daniel Winter, who had immigrated to the United States in 1893. Three weeks later, on May 8, 1898, the SS *Pennsylvania* arrived in New York from Hamburg carrying four Leipzig families, two of whom were related.[66] The 1900 census indicates that three of the families settled in the Spring Valley district of Dickey County, North Dakota, while the fourth, the family of Christoph Bäsler, went on to Morton County, North Dakota, where Christoph's brother, Adam, had established a farm in 1892.

A more complex but fundamentally similar picture comes from considering the relationships and destinations of the fifteen families from Kulm, Leipzig, and Tarutino who arrived in New York on the SS *Fürst Bismarck* on May 27, 1898.[67] Eleven of these families, all with Kulm backgrounds or connections, settled in Adams County, Washington, or in the neighboring Lincoln County. The remaining four families settled separately in North and South Dakota. The manifest filled out by immigration officials for this group is unusual in that it indicates the destinations

---

65. The three Adams County settlers were Christian Hille and Maria Leischner Hille, Gottlieb Lobe and Wilhelmine Gross Lobe, and Gottfried Gross (the brother of Wilhelmine Gross Lobe) and Justine Stern Gross. Gottlieb Leischner (the brother of Maria Leischner Hille, who settled with her husband in Adams County) and Elisabeth Fächner Leischner settled in Lincoln County.

66. The four families are those of August Guhlke and Friederika Kuck Guhlke, Jacob Hilscher and Julianne Wolf Hilscher, Christoph Bäsler and Maria Hinz Bäsler, and Michael Ragout and Katharina Beglau Ragout. August Guhlke was the uncle of Michael Ragout.

67. The fifteen families are: Johann Bich and Rosine Isaak Bich (Kulm), Christoph Haas (Kulm), Nathanael Haas and Louise Schmied Haas (Kulm), Christoph Kraft and Pauline Pries Kraft (Leipzig), Johann Krause and Sophie Bich Krause (Tarutino and Kulm), August Kuhn and Louise Lobe Kuhn (Kulm), David Kuhn and Karolina Löffelbein Kuhn (Kulm), Johannes Löffelbein and Christine Röder Löffelbein (Beresina), Samuel Pahl and Rosina Sprenger Pahl (Leipzig), Gottlieb Radke and Louise Stelter Radke (Kulm), Daniel Roloff and Sophie Stelter Roloff (Kulm), Friedrich Schneider and Salome Haas Schneider (Kulm), Gottlieb Schütz and Sophie Lobe Schütz (Kulm), Johann Stelter and Caroline Tiede Stelter (Kulm), and Ludwig Tiede and Wilhelmine Radke Tiede (Kulm).

each of the families had in mind when they arrived in the United States. This again supports the presumption that letters from earlier Bessarabian German immigrants had come to Russia, advising prospective immigrants on the locations of attractive, available land.[68] Land opportunities in central Washington State were evidently the current recommendation, as four of the five families with Kulm backgrounds who had come on the *Patria* a month earlier also settled there. The group arriving on the *Fürst Bismarck* contained several family interrelationships: there were five sibling pairs and four parents traveling with married adult children.[69]

The four families who did not settle in central Washington clearly had foreknowledge of other areas thought attractive, and the 1900 census lists them as living near other Bessarabian Germans they may well have known in Russia. Nathanael Haas, who elected not to settle in Washington with his father and younger siblings, settled in Dickey County, North Dakota, near his cousin, Martin Haas, who had gone there in 1894. Johann Krause, who had grown up in Tarutino, settled in Oliver County, North Dakota, where the 1900 census indicates he was a neighbor of Joseph Liebelt, also of Tarutino.

Another common pattern was for family members to immigrate to the United States serially over time and settle quite near each other. This again implies the existence of correspondence between family members in North America and those in Bessarabia. In some cases, the short spacing between the arrivals of different family members may imply that the first to arrive had agreed to a role of finding and establishing an attractive place to settle, or that the positive impressions of the first arrivals spurred on relatives who had already been thinking seriously of emigrating. One example of such serial immigration is the Buchwitz family from Leipzig. Twenty-one-year-old Daniel Buchwitz came to North Dakota in 1904 and established himself on land in Township 135 of Morton County. In the following year, his unmarried twenty-year-old brother, Johann, came over and established himself in Township 134 of Morton County. In 1906, their parents, Daniel and Louise Buchwitz, together with the four younger siblings of Daniel and Johann, arrived to establish themselves also in Township 135 of Morton County.[70]

A variant of the pattern of serial emigration was for family members to leave Russia over a broad period of time and yet still end up in North America reasonably close to each other. This again implies continuing communication between Russia

---

68. Only two families indicated to US immigration officials materially different places from where they were found in the 1900 census. Johann Bich and Gottlieb Radke both indicated they would be going to Kulm, North Dakota, when instead they joined the main group to settle in Adams County, Washington.

69. The five sibling pairs were: (1) Johann Bich and Sophie Bich Krause; (2) Nathanael Haas and Salome Haas Schneider; (3) Louise Lobe Kuhn, Sophie Lobe, Schütz and Justine Lobe Haas (the wife of Christoph Haas, who died before her husband and children left Russia); (4) Gottlieb Radke and Wilhelmine Radke Tiede; and (5) Louise Stelter Radke and Sophie Stelter Roloff. The four groups of parents with adult children were: (1) Christoph Haas and his son, Nathanael Haas, and daughter, Salome Haas Schneider; (2) August Kuhn and his son, David Kuhn; (3) Johannes Löffelbein and his daughter, Karolina Löffelbein Kuhn; and (4) Johann Stelter and his daughters, Louise Stelter Radke and Sophie Stelter Roloff. August Kuhn was for some reason not included in the immigration manifest, but was listed on the departure manifest in Hamburg.

70. The arrival dates and settlement sites come from the 1910 US census. Daniel Buchwitz Jr. had by 1910 married Fredricka Hintz and was living independently of his parents. In the census, Daniel Buchwitz Sr. is listed as a neighbor of the families of Christian Röhl, his contemporary from Leipzig who came to the United States in 1886, and Friedrich Röhl, another Leipzig man and contemporary of the younger Daniel Buchwitz.

and the United States. One example would be the passage to the United States of the Radke family of Kulm. Louise (Radke) Roloff and her husband, Daniel, came to the United States in 1885, first to Parkston, South Dakota, and then in 1886 they moved to near Kulm in La Moure County, North Dakota. Louise's four half siblings[71] moved to the United States between 1888 and 1903, and all settled in the area near Kulm, North Dakota, where the boundaries of La Moure, Logan, Dickey, and McIntosh counties come together.[72]

This immigration pattern of sending a family member or members ahead to establish a family footing, which made the transition there of others in the family easier, may also have been tied to a strategy of disposing of family property in Russia on the best terms possible. Brandes, quoting Mennonite sources, offers a description of this strategy that might well have been used by the Bessarabian Germans:

*Besides, this will enable our people to save a great deal of their property, because the father may send his son who is in distress to be drafted in Military Service, to this country and sell his property in Russia gradually, knowing that a place is sure to him near his son and brethren, and so the difficult departure will be made easier.[73]*

In the great majority of cases, the immigrant travel groups of Bessarabian Germans were dominated by adults of roughly similar ages (see table 10–6). The largest demographic block was composed of families led by married couples between the ages of thirty-one and forty-five. This block made up 40 percent of the total number of immigrations. The second largest block was composed of younger married couples under the age of thirty-one, in some cases immigrating in the year they were married. This block formed 31 percent of the total.

The limited evidence provided by the ship manifests suggests that many young, single men and most young, single women traveled to the United States in parties made up of other Bessarabian German immigrants. Where the young, single immigrants were in their teens or very early twenties, the possibility increases that such immigrants had indentured themselves by promising to work in the United States

TABLE 10–6. Demographic categories for the Kulm, Leipzig, and Tarutino emigrants

| Marital status | Kulm | Leipzig | Tarutino | Total | % |
|---|---|---|---|---|---|
| Single, under age 31 | 20 | 15 | 10 | 45 | 9.4 |
| Married, under age 31 | 76 | 40 | 33 | 149 | 31.0 |
| Married, 31–45 | 88 | 50 | 55 | 193 | 40.2 |
| Married, over age 45 | 50 | 21 | 22 | 93 | 19.4 |
| **Total** | 234 | 126 | 120 | 480 | |

71. Louise was the child of August Radke and Louise Vogel. Her half siblings were the children of August and his second wife, Christine Vogel.
72. Louise's half sister Karolina and her husband, Samuel Fregien, came to McIntosh County in 1888. Her half brother Johann and his wife, Karolina Mund, came to McIntosh County in 1890. Her half brother Karl came to Logan County in 1892, and her half brother Daniel and his wife, Sarah Römpfer, came to Logan County in 1903. Flegel also reports that the father of these siblings, August Radke, came to the United States in 1878 (*Extended Relationships*, 550), but does so in error, confusing him with his cousin, also named August Radke, who did come to Hutchinson County, South Dakota, in 1878 (as correctly reported in *Extended Relationships*, 549).
73. Brandes, *Von den Zaren Adoptiert*, 366.

in exchange for financial help with paying the costs of immigration. It is possible that nineteen-year-old Jacob Krause of Leipzig and fifteen-year-old Johann Heinke of Kulm, who were part of the May 1898 *Fürst Bismarck* group discussed above, had made such an arrangement. The immigration manifest states that they only had assets of $42.50 between them. Twenty-one-year-old Emilie Rauter, who arrived on the SS *Fürst Bismarck* in May 1901 as part of a group of four families from Kulm, may have come under similar circumstances. She is listed in the immigration manifest as being with the family of Michael Knopp, and so possibly had agreed to help the Knopps establish themselves as a means to pay for the costs of passage.[74]

Older emigrants were also present in material numbers among those coming from Kulm, Leipzig, and Tarutino. Groups in which they formed the dominant demographic segment make up 19.4 percent of the emigrant parties. One such is the party of four families from Kulm, who were noted above as arriving with Emilie Rauter on the SS *Fürst Bismarck* in May 1901. Here each of the married couples was over age forty-one. Daniel Mann of Leipzig is another example. He was fifty-one years old when he brought his wife and five children to Adams County, Washington, in 1909. In the 1920 census, Daniel is listed as the head of the household in which unmarried sons Wilhelm, age twenty-eight, and Daniel, age twenty-five, as well as several younger children were living. The presence of older children still living in the household, whose work increased its economic viability, was very much the pattern in establishing farms in Bessarabia, though postponing marriage was not. A third son, Jacob Mann, had by 1920 married and established himself independently in Adams County.

In some cases, the life history of an older immigrant to the United States spans the full history of the Bessarabian Germans: birth in Prussian Poland, active adulthood in German Bessarabia, and old age in the United States. The widow Louise Pelz Hass was born in 1808 in Lipnice near Konin in South Prussia and came to Leipzig as a girl. She married Gottlieb Hass of Kulm, which is where they raised their family. After her husband died in 1865, she came to the United States in 1880 as a dependent member, probably of her daughter Louise Hass Isaak's household.[75] Friedrich Koth from Kulm was another Bessarabian German immigrant whose life history stretched from Poland to the United States. Friedrich, though age seventy when he arrived in the United States in 1878, appears to have been the leader of a party that included his wife and four unmarried children under age twenty-one.[76]

74. The Knopps settled in Kulm, North Dakota. A year and a half after her arrival in New York, Emilie Rauter married Gustav Leischner in Odessa, Washington, so if she worked with the Knopps in North Dakota, it was not for long. Emilie clearly had known Gustav in Bessarabia as he was the same age and was also from Kulm (Bessarabia); he had come to the United States three years earlier in 1898. The immigration manifest for the *Fürst Bismarck* that arrived in New York on May 3, 1901, is available in T 715, Roll 190, p. 481, in "Passenger Lists of Vessels Arriving in New York 1897-1957" (Washington, DC: National Archives Microfilm Publications, 1957).

75. In a naturalization record made in Yankton County, South Dakota, in May 1885, Louise Pelz Hass declared she had arrived in the United States in November 1880. Her attachment to the household of her daughter Louise Hass Isaak is suggested by the fact that while six of Louise Pelz Hass's children immigrated with their families to southeastern South Dakota in the period from 1878 to 1881, only Louise and her husband, Johann Isaak, came in 1880.

76. Friedrich Koth's son, also a Friedrich Koth, came to the United States in December 1878, the same year as his father, but independently of the latter, as only the younger Friedrich Koth is listed on the manifest of the *Bolivia* arriving in New York from Glasgow, Scotland.

Friedrich was also born near Konin in South Prussia in 1808 and died the year he came to the United States in Parkston, South Dakota.

In following the emigration of Bessarabian Germans from Kulm, Leipzig, and Tarutino to the United States, there is a distinct pattern to the timing of arrival and the places of settlement. The first groups to come to the United States, those arriving in the period from 1876 to 1881, all settled in the southeastern corner of South Dakota, chiefly in Hutchinson (then called Armstrong) and Bon Homme counties. While throughout the emigration period there are many examples of relations traveling together and settling in North America near each other, this is particularly true of the first groups, many of whom came from Kulm. The brothers and Kulm natives Gottfried and Gottlieb Hoffmann and their families arrived in New York on November 8, 1878, on the SS *Mosel* coming from Bremen. They settled around Parkston in Hutchinson County, near their sister, Wilhelmine, who had arrived a month earlier from Kulm with her husband, Johann Gottlieb Hildebrand. The families of two other Hoffmann sisters also settled nearby: Rosine Hoffmann and her husband, Friedrich Hildebrand (Johann Gottlieb's brother), and Magdalene Hoffmann and her husband, Karl Lobe. In 1880, two other sisters and their families—Justine Hoffmann Henke with her husband, Jacob, and Julianne Hoffmann Stelzer with her husband, August—came to Parkston from Kulm. Jacob Henke's brother Martin and his family were on the *Mosel* with Gottfried and Gottlieb Hoffmann in 1878 and came to the Parkston area as well.[77] The 1880 census lists on the same page, and thus presumably as neighbors in Township 99, Range 60 of what was then Armstrong County, the families of Daniel Schimke, Friedrich Schulz, Gottlieb Winter, Johann Gottlieb Hildebrand, Gottlieb Hoffmann, and Friedrich Hinz, all from Kulm, Bessarabia.[78]

By the early 1880s, southeastern South Dakota was filling up, and new arrivals had to move with the frontier. New settlers coming from Kulm, Leipzig, and Tarutino next favored northern South Dakota, particularly Campbell and McPherson counties, and then spilled across the border into North Dakota. A common first step at this time was for new arrivals to go initially to southeastern South Dakota and then, when they saw the lay of the land, to move on. This tells us that the information reaching German Bessarabia concerning the location of advantageous settlements where new arrivals ought to go in the United States wasn't always current. Johann and Karoline Mutschall Fischer sold their share of Property #83 in Tarutino in the fall of 1885 and took their young children to the United States, reaching New York in November of that year and going first to now heavily settled Scotland in Bon Homme County, South Dakota. In 1887, they moved to North Dakota and established a farm near Kulm in La Moure County.

By the mid-1880s, the area that became North Dakota in 1889 had become the focus of settlement for Germans newly arrived from Russia. North Dakota attracted settlers up until 1914, with the heaviest areas of settlement occurring in Dickey, La Moure, Grant, Morton, Wells, Sheridan, and Adams counties. The popularity of

---

77. The manifest for the SS *Mosel* lists 395 passengers, 126 of whom were Germans coming from Russia, all in steerage and many from Bessarabia. Listed on the same page with Gottfried Hoffmann are the families of Daniel Hille, Gottlieb Graumann, Gottlieb Döring, and August Isaak, all from Kulm, and Christian Sprecher from Leipzig. All settled in southeastern South Dakota.
78. United States 1880 census for Township 99, Range 60, Armstrong County, Dakota Territory, Schedule 1, 24–25.

Bessarabian German immigration to North Dakota is underlined by the naming of Kulm, North Dakota, in La Moure County, Leipzig and New Leipzig, North Dakota, in Grant County, as well as the Roloff Township in McIntosh County and the Haag and Janke townships in Logan County.

By the late 1890s, as lands east of the Missouri River in North Dakota filled, the immigration frontier moved farther west. Some Bessarabian Germans in the late 1890s and into the first decade of the twentieth century settled in the drier lands west of the Missouri River in southern and central North Dakota. More popular were lands in central Washington, particularly Grant, Adams, and Lincoln counties. The provinces of Alberta and, to a lesser extent, Saskatchewan in Canada now began to attract Bessarabian German settlers, both as an original destination and as a secondary one.

As noted earlier, 432 (90 percent) of the couples and single immigrants from the Bessarabian German villages of Kulm, Leipzig, and Tarutino settled in the United States.[79] Of these, 410 (94.9 percent) made their first settlement in United States in one of three states: North Dakota, South Dakota, or Washington (see table 10–7).[80] The data concerning these immigrants indicate that the heaviest period of German emigration from these Bessarabian villages occurred after 1890. As this corresponds to the period when North Dakota was the settlement frontier, it is not surprising to see that in the chart below, North Dakota attracted the greatest number of first settlements in the United States: 233, or 51.6 percent. South Dakota is second with 146 first settlements, 33.8 percent of the total in the United States, and Washington third with 41 or 9.5 percent.

Only 5 of the 480 emigrant parties from Kulm, Leipzig, and Tarutino went to South America. This suggests caution in considering the large estimations of Bessarabian Germans immigrants there. Of the 5 South American parties, 2 emigrated before World War I and went to Argentina. One of these occurred because the family was refused admission to the United States. Karl Schelske was a Kulm native who took his family to Markosovka in the North Caucasus region of Russia in the late 1870s. Together with several members of the Borth family,

TABLE 10–7. **First settlement locations by emigrants from Kulm, Leipzig, and Tarutino**

| Years | North Dakota | South Dakota | Washington | Other states | Total |
|---|---|---|---|---|---|
| 1876–1880 | — | 90 | — | — | 90 |
| 1881–1890 | 39 | 33 | 2 | — | 74 |
| 1891–1900 | 101 | 17 | 16 | 7 | 141 |
| 1901–1950 | 83 | 6 | 23 | 15 | 127 |
| **Total** | 223 | 146 | 41 | 22 | 432 |
| Percent | 51.6% | 33.8% | 9.5% | 5.1% | |

79. Of the 480 emigrant couples and singles from Kulm, Leipzig, and Tarutino, 12 went to Dobrudscha in Romania and 5 went to South America. The remaining 463 went to North America, of which 31 went directly to Canada and the remaining 432, or 90 percent went to the United States.

80. Other states where emigrants from Kulm, Leipzig, and Tarutino first settled were: Oklahoma (7), Nebraska (3), Idaho (3), Colorado (2), California (2), Oregon (1), Texas (1), New York (1), New Jersey (1), and Michigan (1).

originally from Tarutino, and the Flegel family, originally from Kulm and Leipzig, the Schelskes in November 1908 joined a large group of Germans from the North Caucasus who sought to immigrate to the United States. In the immigration inspection in New York, now at Ellis Island, Karl or someone in his family was rejected for health reasons for admission to the United States. Karl Schelske then led his family on to Buenos Aires.[81] The remaining three parties who went to South America were all from Leipzig and went to Brazil in the mid-1920s.

## Several return visits were made to Russia by North American immigrants

The data on emigration from Russia by Germans connected to the villages of Kulm, Leipzig, and Tarutino also provide a few pictures of Bessarabian Germans making return visits from North America to their former homes in Bessarabia and Russia. The small number of return visits suggests these were quite special events. Kulm native Gottfried Knopp, for example, came to the United States in 1886, first settling in Bon Homme and then Hutchinson County, South Dakota. In 1888, he had established himself permanently near Kulm, North Dakota. In 1908, twenty years later, he returned to Russia, presumably to visit Mannsburg, where his father's family had moved between 1865 and 1869.[82] As Knopp's father died in Mannsburg in 1907, his visit to Bessarabia was possibly to deal with the consequences of settling his father's estate.[83] Henrietta Mutschall also made a return visit to Russia. Her family came from Tarutino but had moved to the Russian Crimea, where she was born in 1869. In 1890, she married Wendelin Oster, and in 1893, the Osters came to the United States and ultimately settled in Payette County, Idaho. In 1911, the Osters returned to the Russian Crimea where they adopted their eight-year-old nephew, Wilhelm Aberle, orphaned by the death of his parents, and brought him back to the United States.[84]

Samuel Krüger made two return visits from North America to Bessarabia, including an unusual extended visit that lasted as long as three years in the period from 1910 to 1913. He had emigrated from Tarutino in 1898 to North Dakota with his new bride, his parents, his older brother, and his younger siblings.[85] It would appear that Samuel, together with his father, Michael, and older brother, Friedrich, took land, possibly at least initially to be jointly worked, in two townships in Logan County, North Dakota.[86] In February 1907, Samuel Krüger, traveling alone, returned

81. Flegel, *Extended Relationships*, 617. Karl Schelske's son, Johann Schelske—who with his wife and three children was traveling with his father, stepmother, and his younger siblings—also went on to Argentina but returned to enter the United States in 1909 (the 1910 US census gives 1909 as his date of immigration).

82. Ibid., 369. In his notes on Gottfried Knopp, Flegel mentions he "visited Russia" and that he was wealthy enough in 1915 to winter in Cuba.

83. Gottfried Knopp had two brothers and two sisters who were living with their families in Mannsburg.

84. Flegel, *Extended Relationships*, 513.

85. Flegel reports that Samuel Krüger came to the United States in 1897, which is also what Krüger states on his 1906 passport application. However, the manifest of the *Kaiser Wilhelm* shows that Samuel Krüger, his wife, Maria, his parents, and younger and older siblings all arrived in New York on May 4, 1898. Samuel Krüger's 1909 passport application gets closer to this date as he states that he arrived in New York in April 1898.

86. The 1900 US census lists Samuel, Michael, and Friedrich consecutively as though they were living together in both townships 8 and 12 of Logan County.

from Hamburg to New York, presumably coming from Bessarabia.[87] In 1910, Samuel, together with his twelve-year-old daughter, Bertha, returned to Bessarabia for a period Flegel reports to be three and a half years,[88] with Samuel's father and brothers presumably taking care of his family in North Dakota.[89]

Such return visits to Bessarabia carry several implications. They strongly suggest the likelihood that emigration from Russia to North America did not break off all contact and communication between families and friends. Letters were exchanged, and the natural longing to see relations and friends again spurred interest where means permitted. The visits were all by settlers in the United States; there were no visits to North America by Germans intending to return to homes in Russia. Such visits imply that the visitors had accumulated in North America sufficient saved capital to make them no longer dependent on the annual farm return. To make a trip to Russia, it would have been necessary to have accumulated sufficient capital not just to pay for travel, but, as it would have taken several months to travel back to Russia and then return home, for the traveler not to be dependent on current year farm income. As noted above with regard to Samuel Krüger, other family members or friends would be called on to maintain the travelers' farms and property in North America, and such caretakers would expect major shares of the farm income earned.

One interesting implication of such visits back to Russia is that they imply significant changes had taken place in the worldview of the travelers. Having come to North America, the immigrants had learned not just how to travel, but how to be comfortable doing it; they had acquired a broader view of the world and their own possibilities within it—a broader view, that is, than was generally present in German Bessarabia. They were helped in this, of course, by legal conditions in the United States and Canada that, unlike Russia, freely accepted the possibility of travel and relocation. The great majority of Germans in Bessarabia never traveled far from home villages. There were few accounts of trips outside of Bessarabia apart from carting produce to Odessa, military service, emigration to establish new settlements on lands in the Crimea and Caucasus, and the handful of students sent away for university training. Such travel occurred as a result of necessities, not for pleasure. I have found no accounts prior to World War I of Bessarabian Germans making pleasure visits to other regions in Russia or to other countries in Europe, much less to North America. The North Americans who went back to Russia were different people and lived in quite a different world.

---

87. The manifest for the SS *Kaiserin Augusta Viktoria* of the Hamburg America Line, which departed Hamburg on February 16, 1907, lists a Samuel Krüger as passenger. That this is the Samuel Krüger discussed here is verified by the match in ages, the hometown listing of Lehr (Lehr, North Dakota, on the Logan–McIntosh county line, was the closest settlement to the Krüger landholdings in townships 8 and 12 of Logan County), and Samuel's 1906 passport application.

88. Flegel's shorthand footnote reads "1910 to Bessarabia w/ dau Bertha 3 ½ yrs visit" (*Extended Relationships*, 400). It is not certain what caused Samuel Krüger to make two visits to Bessarabia, one of which was an extended visit that began in 1910. His oldest brother, Wilhelm, had retained the family property in Tarutino; it is possible Samuel went to help maintain that on a positive footing.

89. Other examples of return visits to Bessarabia are those of Jacob Schlaps of Beresina, who came to the United States in the early to mid-1880s and then returned by 1885. He married in Beresina and continued to live there until 1891, when he emigrated a second time, now with his wife and parents. In 1885, back in Russia, he told several people about opportunities in the United States. This led Daniel Roloff and his wife to immigrate there in 1886 [Otto Spurling, "Pioneer Biography of Daniel Roloff, Kulm, North Dakota," *Heritage Review* 40, no. 1 (2010): 11]. Another example is that of Gottfried and his son, Reinhold Siewert, who returned, likely to Neu Elft, Bessarabia, in 1910.

Some accounts of travel back to Bessarabia from North America are more diffi-
cult to work out. Kern, for example, notes in his description of the village of Kulm
that he had a chance meeting there in 1929 with a US senator "involved…with
U.S. immigration policy."[90] He gives the senator's surname as Raugust and implies
he had come back to visit his birth place. The person Kern recalls is undoubtedly
William Raugust, born in 1895 in Eigenheim to a family originally from Kulm.
Though not a US senator, William Raugust was a member of the Washington State
Senate. The details Kern provides, however, suggest that he did not meet William
Raugust in Bessarabia but most likely in Germany after World War II. Raugust
was appointed to the state senate in Washington in 1950, and his only known trip
to Europe occurred in 1951.[91] It is possible that Kern is mixing here the stories
of two different people from Kulm families he had met on their return visits to
Europe. North Dakota immigrant Emanuel Graumann, born in Eigenheim to a
family coming from Kulm, did pass through Kulm during his visit to his brother in
Eigenheim in 1927, and perhaps he was the American Kern remembered meeting
in Bessarabia at that time.[92]

I have found only one instance of a Bessarabian German immigrant to North
America giving up on the new world and returning permanently to Bessarabia. Jacob
Wiest, a forty-three-year-old Leipzig resident, brought his family to the United
States in 1898 and established a homestead in Morton County, North Dakota. In
1908, his wife, Karolina, died, and Jacob subsequently married her widowed sister,
Sophie. Their combined families appear in the 1910 US census in Morton County.
In 1910, however, Sophie apparently died, and Jacob in that year returned to Leipzig,
Bessarabia, with most of his children. Selling his property in North Dakota made
Jacob sufficiently prosperous to purchase property in Kurudschika north of Leipzig,[93]
as well as to donate a clock for the Leipzig church tower at a cost of 360 rubles.[94]
Following the end of World War I and the huge economic losses it created for
Bessarabian Germans, Jacob's sons, Michael and Heinrich Wiest, left Bessarabia for
Brazil around 1925. By 1927, Michael had returned to the United States, and the
1930 census indicates he was a laborer working for the railroad in Adams County,
Washington. His brother Heinrich and family left Brazil in 1929 and returned to
farm in Mercer County, North Dakota. Jacob Wiest remained in Bessarabia and
died in Kurudschika in 1934.

90. Kern, *Homeland Book*, 136.
91. William Raugust was elected to the Washington State House of Representatives in 1943. In 1950,
he was appointed to the Washington State Senate representing the 8th District in 1950 following
the death of the district's sitting senator. He subsequently was elected to consecutive terms in the
Washington State Senate until 1967. The fact that Kern identifies Raugust as a senator must place
the date of their encounter to sometime after 1950. Raugust did have interest in immigration policies and testified on this topic in 1949 before the Foreign Affairs Committee of the US House of
Representatives.
92. Graumann immigrated to the United States in 1906, but had an unusually difficult experience in
gaining admission. He first arrived with his wife and two sons in New York in November 1905,
but one of the family was rejected for reasons of health, and so all returned to Hamburg, where in
December 1905 they took a ship to Buenos Aires, Argentina. In 1906, the family returned to New
York via Liverpool and gained entry.
93. Kern reports that the contract to purchase 1,681 desjatina of land from the Countess Hatzfeld-
Trachtenberg for the village of Kurudschika was settled in 1909 (*Homeland Book*, 141). It would
appear that Wiest, arriving in Leipzig in 1910, was able to join the eighty-four families participating
in this land purchase.
94. Flegel, *Extended Relationships*, 769.

# XI

# German Bessarabia, 1870–1914: Economic Growth, Increasing Prosperity, Territorial Expansion

Though from time to time harvests failed and communities were occasionally plagued with cattle pests, the period from 1870 to the beginning of World War I was generally one of prosperity and steady economic growth in German Bessarabia. Agriculture remained the dominant economic focus, and grain, especially wheat, continued to be the leading cash crop. The middlemen who traveled from village to village buying grain were replaced by agents of the large Odessa merchants. These agents had established themselves at the Leipzig railroad station on the new rail line, finished in 1877, that ran from Reni on the Danube to Bender on the Dniester. Farmers earned more as grain prices became more competitive and more closely matched those offered in Odessa. Grain sales to Western Europe continued to be a major draw for Bessarabian wheat. Breeding stocks of cattle, horses, and sheep were another important focus of German farms. Sales of these animals and their products, which earlier had been confined to local and regional purchasers, now found broader national interest with the railroad linkage. During this period, milk and products produced from it started to replace meat as the most profitable use of cattle. New breeds of horses and sheep spurred sales of these animals. The cultivation of vineyards and the production of wine continued to flourish. Sales of wine, which also had been generally a local business, now found regional markets. Tarutino, Arzis, and Sarata, helped by their weekly markets, were growing into large villages with commercial businesses. Commercial strength created reserves of capital, which in turn helped develop light manufacturing concerns. The manufacture of farm machinery developed into a steady, if local, business. The craftwork produced on individual farmsteads, such as making wagons in Wittenberg, roof tiles and pottery in Klöstitz, or pitchforks in Paris, also found a wider market, as not just other Germans but families from neighboring Bulgarian, Gaugaz, and Moldavian villages became interested customers.

The continuing growth of prosperity and opportunity meant that, with differences in merit and differences in fortune, increasing disparities in wealth also began to appear. Most of the German villages were dominated by a broad band of middle income families; however, they now also contained poor, sometimes landless citizens, and at the other end of the economic spectrum were some quite well-to-do families. A few families were so successful financially that they were able to establish themselves on large farming estates independent of the old villages. Poorer families supported themselves by the traditional craftwork such as shoemaking, tailoring, coopering, or doing paid agricultural work for the more well to do. In the 1870s, Tarutino, perhaps uniquely among the Bessarabian German villages, began to lease land outside its borders that it would in turn sublet to its poorer citizens to help them. Tarutino did this at different sites until 1890 when it bought land north of Leipzig for this purpose to found the settlement of Neu Tarutino.

A major factor underlying both economic and social trends in the period from 1870 to 1914 was the continuing population growth in the German settlements. The 1860s saw the original German colonies in Bessarabia grow to such large population sizes that overcrowding started to develop. Answers to the overcrowding were available. In this period, Russian noble owners of underused land in Bessarabia were increasingly interested in selling or leasing their land. The saved wealth built up in successful farmsteads together with the access to capital from village insurance funds and land bank mortgage funds allowed Bessarabian Germans to take advantage of land opportunities and establish new villages. However, the continuing pattern among Bessarabian German families of having many children kept a steady pressure on the older villages to find additional opportunities to acquire or lease land.

Beginning in the 1870s, new pressures were added to those of a rising population. By issuing the Decrees of 1870 and 1874, the Imperial Russian government fundamentally ended the special status of the German colonies in Russia. The decrees set in motion forces that would increase the process of assimilation and make the Germans subject to conscription in the military for the first time. As Germans in Russia became more active in the land market, their efforts to acquire land began to incite hostility from competitors numbers of whom wished to limit the rights of Germans to buy additional land. Following the creation of the powerful new state of Imperial Germany, other Russians became worried by German land purchases, seeing in these the potential creation of a disloyal, German state within Russia's borders. As the prior chapter has argued, the continuing increase in population in the German settlements, abetted by these additional factors, were together the proximate causes for large numbers of Germans electing to emigrate. Perhaps as many as fifteen thousand Bessarabian Germans left Russia for North America. An additional estimated four thousand Bessarabian Germans, driven chiefly by issues of overcrowding, also left Bessarabia to establish themselves on available land elsewhere in Russia.

The main focus of this story, however, is that of the Germans who remained in Bessarabia until the exodus of 1940. While the changing climate for Germans in Russia at the end of the nineteenth century may have caused many Germans in Bessarabia to wonder what the future might hold for them, the great majority decided that the risks of looking for land elsewhere were too high in light of the opportunities available to them in Bessarabia.

The one census conducted by the Imperial Russian government counted 59,998 Germans living in Bessarabia in 1897. Estimates of the Bessarabian German population presume it increased to between 65,000 and 70,000 by 1914. As their populations continued to increase, many of the German villages in Bessarabia sought to buy or lease land nearby to increase their size. Lichtental bought an additional 1,642 desjatina; Friedenstal added 1,800 desjatina in two separate purchases; and Hoffnungstal was able to add another 915 desjatina. Borodino residents took advantage of inexpensive nearby leased land opportunities. Finding available land for sale or rent near the older, settled villages wasn't typically possible, however. Kern reports that the village of Krasna had only been able to purchase another 600 desjatina near Klöstitz and two pieces of 300 desjatina, one near Friedenstal and the second near Paris.[1]

One factor limiting additional land purchases that extended the size of existing villages was the fact that land near existing villages had such an obvious intrinsic value that sellers raised their prices. In 1910, the citizens of Mannsburg, for example, were able to buy an additional 700 desjatina of land nearby but had to pay the astounding price of 1,000 rubles per desjatina, when land elsewhere in Bessarabia was for sale at between 300 to 500 rubles a desjatina. Though I cannot offer examples, another limiting factor may have been the difficulty of gaining total village agreement to put up the money to buy additional land nearby. The general pattern across German Bessarabia was not for villages to pool funds and so expand, but for individuals, acting on their own, to form groups of Germans from different villages to purchase blocks of land elsewhere in Bessarabia and so create new villages.

## For many Bessarabian Germans, the answer to overcrowding in the old villages was to lease or buy land in one of the new settlements established elsewhere in Bessarabia

These new villages were established as opportunities for land purchase or lease came up. The founding families typically came from different home settlements and then acted together as a group. When after 1860, Bessarabian Germans began to purchase or lease land to form new villages, this set in motion major social changes. The number of German villages in Bessarabia increased dramatically. Nearly 70 percent of the German villages established in Bessarabia by 1914 were created in the period from 1870 to 1914. As the founding families came from many different original settlements, the German population in Bessarabia now became more thoroughly mixed together. Such mixing tended to establish the dominance of the South

---

1. Kern, *Homeland Book*, 200.

German speech throughout German Bessarabia, which was brought to Bessarabia by immigrants with origins in Swabia and the upper Rhineland.

When opportunities to purchase or lease new land came up, the typical response was for small numbers of families to form a group and act together. There are few data describing how such groups generally formed. The implication from the data available is that families interested in taking up offers to lease or join in the purchase of additional land found each other via information shared through common connections such as the churches or the markets. That they were generally made up of families from different villages is a frequent theme of Kern's. Gnadenfeld, for example, was founded on land bought in 1879 by families from Kulm, Neu Elft, Tarutino, Katzbach, Dennewitz, Leipzig, and Wittenberg; Basyrjamka was founded in 1891 on leased land by families from Dennewitz and Neu Posttal; Sofiewka was founded in 1892 on land purchased by families from seven of the mother colonies and three daughter colonies; Sangerowka was founded in 1898 on land leased by families from four of the mother colonies and three daughter colonies.[2] The tendency to form new villages with settlers coming from several different places in German Bessarabia continues the pattern of new village formation that was established in the 1860s.

In the 1870s, the number of new German settlements in Bessarabia modestly increased, but in the following thirty-four years to 1914, there was an explosive growth in the number of new villages founded, as shown in table 11–1.

In 1860, there were 27 German settlements in Bessarabia; in 1870, the total had grown to 39. Using Kern's figures for new villages founded after 1870, there were 118 German villages in the province in 1914; 77 percent of these were founded after 1860, 67 percent after 1870.

In his comments on founding the new villages, Kern leaves no doubt that overcrowding and the resulting limitations on the amount of land families had at their disposal were the major causes for this population movement. In his description of the settlement of Alexandrowka, founded in 1908, Kern notes that the "farms in the mother colonies were constantly shrinking," implying that families in the older

TABLE 11–1. **Number of new settlements from 1870 to 1914**

| Years | Kern Total[a] |
|---|---|
| 1870–1879 | 5 |
| 1880–1889 | 20 |
| 1890–1899 | 25 |
| 1900–1914 | 29 |
| **Total** | 79 |

a. Kern, *Homeland Book*, 200. Kern provides foundation dates for most of the German settlements in Bessarabia in his settlement descriptions or in his listings of the villages in the different Bessarabian parishes.

2. Ibid., 101, 164, 51, 174. The origins of the Sofiewka settlers were Alt Posttal, Beresina, Katzbach, Kulm, Neu Elft, Tarutino, and Wittenberg, plus Unter and Ober Albota and Neu Odessa. The origins of the Sangerowka setters were Alt Elft, Dennewitz, Paris, and Teplitz, plus Neufall, Neu Posttal, and Tschemtschelly.

settlements by this time were frequently subdividing their land.[3] In discussing the history of Brienne, Kern notes that the "lack of land" led families to leave the village, and in his account of Plotzk, he adds that "the land shortage led to migration and the founding of daughter colonies."[4]

Roughly 70 percent of the new German villages founded after 1870 were located in the Budjak steppe region of southern Bessarabia and thus relatively near the original German settlements. The five areas most thickly settled with the new villages were:

1. North of Leipzig, Borodino, and Hoffnungstal, along or near the upper reaches of the Skinoza, Saka, and Čaga rivers.
2. North of Lichtental and Sarata, along or near the upper reaches of the elegider and Sarata rivers.
3. Along the middle and upper reaches of the Alkalija River and east of this along the coast line of the Dniester Liman above Akkerman.
4. Along the Black Sea coast as it runs southwesterly from the mouth of Dniester, and inland from the coast in the steppelands above and around the limans formed by the estuaries of the Alkalija, Xodžider, Sarata, and Šagan rivers all to the east of the Kunduk Liman. Later settlements were made in the steppelands west of this liman.
5. North of Bolgrad in the valleys of the western tributaries of the Jalpux[5] River, especially the Lesser (Malaja) Sal'a and the Albota.

Almost a third of the new settlements founded between 1870 and 1914 (twenty-four of the seventy-nine) were established in hilly, wooded central Bessarabia, north of the Budjak steppe region. As with the new villages founded here in the 1860s, some of these new villages in central Bessarabia were established by Austrian farmers who had crossed over the Prut River from Austrian-controlled Galicia, and two were founded by Germans moving to Bessarabia from Xerson Province. The majority (seventeen of the twenty-four), however, were founded by families coming north from the original German settlements in the Budjak. There were three major areas of German settlement in central Bessarabia:

1. To the east of Leova in the lower valley of the Sarata River[6] and further east and north of there along the remains of the Trajan Wall.[7]

---

3. Ibid., 45. Kern, in this passage about Alexandrowka, comments that letters from immigrants who had settled in North America were decrying the fact that their children were "slowly losing their native tongue since they had to learn English." This certainly suggests that one reason Germans in Bessarabia had for remaining in Bessarabia was their desire not to lose contact with their native roots.
4. Ibid., 84, 62. Kern could see both sides of this point. In his discussion of migration from Brienne, Kern ties roots of migration to the pre-1870 Welfare Committee regulation that stipulated land could not be divided and should be passed as such to the youngest son. In writing of other German settlements, Kern ascribes the cause of population movement to tight conditions and increasingly smaller holdings after 1870, when some families could and did subdivide their original holdings.
5. This river, named the Jalpug on several Western European maps, is the Jalpux on Berg's map. The 1902 Austro-Hungarian military map "Bolgrad" (sheet 46-46, in 3rd Military Mapping Survey of Austria-Hungary, http://lazarus.elte.hu/hun/digkonyv/topo/3felmeres.htm) also uses this form, spelled Jalpuch.
6. This Sarata River flows southwest into the Prut below Leova and so is not the Sarata River that flows south past the German colony of Sarata to the Kunduk Liman and Black Sea.
7. The current archeological interpretation of the Trajan Wall is that this earthen mound and its protective ditch were constructed in the fourth century CE as a defense against invading Goths moving into this area from the northwest. The wall may even have been built under Roman leadership by other Goths who had already settled in Roman Dacia, but the association with the Roman Emperor Trajan, whose reign began at the end of the first century CE, is now considered legendary.

2. Along the Lopušna River and an eastern tributary of the Nyrnowa River all
   east of the Prut River and the town of Husi. Several of these settlements
   were populated by Austrians who had come there from Galicia.[8]

3. Along the Botna River near the town of Zajm southwest of Bender, along
   the Botna's tributary (the Bakalia), as well as along the Kalindir and Byk
   rivers west of Bender. German Catholics from Krasna and from the Xerson
   Province across the Dniester created the largest settlements in this area.

These new German villages were distinctly smaller in size than the original
mother colonies. The seventeen colonies surveyed by the Welfare Committee in 1825
averaged 5,691 desjatina of assigned land.[9] By 1940, the seventeen mother colonies
had increased slightly to an average of 5,859 desjatina.[10] Klöstitz was the largest at
9,872 desjatina, followed by Beresina at 8,445. In 1940, Neu Arzis was the smallest
of these mother colonies at 3,065 desjatina, preceded by Neu Elft at 3,612 desjatina.
In comparison, the three largest of the new settlements founded between 1870 and
1914 on purchased land were roughly the size of the smallest of the mother colonies.
Tschiligider was the largest of the new settlements with a land area of 5,157 desjatina;
it is followed by Mariental with 3,294 and Neu Posttal with 3,217. Moreover, the two
largest of the new villages, Tschiligider and Mariental, were never able to fill out their
land area. Tschiligider, founded in 1884, either wasn't able to subdivide and sell all of
its land, or its largest landowners wished to keep major tracts underused for future
potential. This is apparent from the fact that the Romanian government took back
underused land in the 1920s and reduced the village land size to 1,888 desjatina.[11]
The land that became Mariental was purchased in 1910 by citizens in Mariewka as
additional land for the town to grow into, but this land was not settled before World
War I and remained vacant until 1925.[12]

## Before 1900, the majority of the new German villages in Bessarabia were first established on leased land

This is evident in table 11–3, which outlines data from Kern on the numbers of new
settlements formed from leased land and purchased land. It is also emphasized in
data Brandes cites from Velicyn's 1893 study of Germans in Russia. In comparing
leased holdings to the total landholdings of German villages in different South

8. While Strymbeni and Alt Oneschti were mainly populated by Austrians, Neu Oneschti and Mariental were founded by Germans who had moved there from the Budjak region.
9. The average figure of 5,691 desjatina per settlement is derived from the figure of the total land area assigned the seventeen mother colonies as reported in the 1825 Welfare Committee study, which gave that area as 96,750 desjatina. This data is from Hans Rempel's 1940 compilation of that study: "German Farming Achievements," Table 18, Part 1, Section E2. These figures include the breakup of Wittenberg, Alt Elf, and Alt Arzis, but do not include Sarata and Schabo.
10. Several of the mother colonies had grown in size, as noted earlier, through purchases of neighboring land. The 1940 figures are from Kern's parish listings of village sizes in hectares adjusted to desjatina.
11. As will be discussed in more detail below and in the following chapter, in the 1920s, the Romanian government, in an effort to put landless farmers in improved situations where they would be able to support their families, confiscated underused land throughout the province to use for this purpose. The citizens of Mariewka were thus fortunate to have been able to hold on to the land that became Mariental.
12. Kern, *Homeland Book*, 159. Kern, perhaps using different sources, gives the land area of Mariental here as 3,600 hectares (3,293.7 desjatina), but in his discussion of Mariewka, lists it as 3,400 desjatina (149). One reason for the delay in settlement was that Mariental was far away from Mariewka (some 50 miles as the crow flies). In 1910, Mariewka citizens also had bought 3,500 desjatina across the Dniester River in Xerson Province where they had established what Kern calls "the progressive colony of Olgental" (149).

Russian provinces in 1890, Velicyn indicates that leased landholdings in German Bessarabia formed a larger percentage of total holdings than those for Germans in any of the other South Russian provinces (see table 11–2).[13]

While new villages founded on leased land in German Bessarabia form a clear majority before 1900, in the following fourteen years the pattern dramatically changed (table 11–3). After 1900, there was only one new village formed on leased land, while there were twenty-seven new villages begun on purchased land, almost as many as the total number of leased land villages (thirty-two) formed in the period from 1870 to 1889.[14]

The trend toward purchased land is further emphasized by the fact that seven of the thirty-two new leased land villages established before 1900 were transformed into purchased land settlements. In two cases, Kurudschika and Rosenfeld, this involved a significant change in population as new arrivals willing and able to purchase land largely replaced the former lessees. In the other five villages, the majority of those who had been leasing participated in the land purchases.[15] Thus, the actual count of leased and purchased land settlements existing in German Bessarabia in 1900 and in 1914 is shown in table 11–4.

The trend toward purchased land as the primary basis for the establishing the daughter settlements is further indicated by the fact that, as will be discussed in more

TABLE 11–2. **Leased land as a percentage of total German landholdings in 1890**

| Province | Leased land | Total land | Percent leased |
|----------|-------------|------------|----------------|
| Bessarabia | 85,112 | 296,442 | 28.7 |
| Xerson | 220,123 | 871,646 | 15.5 |
| Ekaterinoslav | 98,834 | 636,885 | 15.5 |
| Tauride | 102,447 | 1,024,095 | 10 |

TABLE 11–3. **Villages founded on leased vs. purchased land in German Bessarabia**

| Years | Leased land | Purchased land | Mixed | Total |
|-------|-------------|----------------|-------|-------|
| 1870–1879 | 4 | 1 | 0 | 5 |
| 1880–1889 | 9 | 11 | 0 | 20 |
| 1890–1899 | 18 | 6 | 1 | 25 |
| Subtotal | 31 | 18 | 1 | 50 |
| 1900–1914 | 1 | 27 | 1 | 29 |
| **Total** | 32 | 45 | 2 | 79 |

TABLE 11–4. **Actual leased vs. purchased land villages in German Bessarabia 1900 and 1914**

| Year | Leased Land | Purchased Land | Mixed | Total |
|------|-------------|----------------|-------|-------|
| 1900 | 24 | 25 | 1 | 50 |
| 1914 | 25 | 52 | 2 | 79 |

---

13. Brandes, *Von den Zaren Adoptiert*, 425.

14. The data in table 11–3 comes from Kern. I have not included in this chart land purchased by a single family forming a personal estate. Thus, Tamurka, an estate of 1,000 desjatina bought by Johann Gerstenberger in 1895, is not included, though Gerstenberger's children and their families formed a small hamlet on this land. For the same reason Korntal II is not counted.

15. These are the villages of Basyrjamka, Emmental, Larga, Mariewka, and Manukbejmka.

detail below, six settlements founded in the 1860s on leased land also transformed themselves into purchased land settlements in the period from 1881 to 1898.[16]

However, at the beginning of this period in 1870 and well into the 1890s, forming new daughter villages on leased land was a dominant pattern. The reasons for this are not hard to see. Leasing costs were low (see table 11–5), and families taking up leased land thought they could afford these from the profits of grain and animal sales. Another factor appears to have been that landlords, who for the most part lived outside Bessarabia, were not at first interested in selling. Many had been leasing land for grazing; renting land to farmers brought higher prices and longer contracts and was therefore more attractive than leasing for grazing. When land did become available for sale, financing hurdles slowed the ability of Bessarabian Germans to take advantage of such opportunities.

Kern notes that the Balmas settlers came over the Dniester River from Xerson because "where one paid ten rubles per desjatina in other regions…a desjatina of land could be rented in Bessarabia for three rubles."[17] Of the Sangerowka settlers, Kern says, "the leases were cheap, so nobody wanted to buy the land."[18] Some leased land villages were well to do and villagers saw no reason to consider buying the land: Tchemtchelly, noted for horse breeding; Alt Oneschti, located on two major land routes in Bessarabia; and Kamtschatka with its commercial fishing stand out in this regard. After 1918, the fact they had not purchased the land created major problems for these leased land villages. Now, as part of Romania, all former leasing arrangements were terminated. The Romanian government confiscated from landowners property that had been leased. To help landless families, such confiscated land was used to create the new "hectare communities." These gave families typically 5.5 desjatina of land; enough, it was intended, for families to feed themselves. Before the war, German families in leased land villages had been farming far larger plots of land. Being grouped with the landless and given these small plots, albeit now as owned land, represented a considerable diminishment for them and caused some impoverishment.

Leasing land, for all its attractive pricing, carried significant drawbacks for the lessee. While lease arrangements were typically for long periods of time, such as a decade, when the term ended the landowner could, and frequently did, raise the

TABLE 11–5. **Leasing costs for land in Bessarabia**

| Village | Years for data | Lease costs per desjatina |
|---|---|---|
| Neu Posttal | 1864–1874 | 1.18 rubles |
| Seimeny (twelve-year) | 1867–1879 | 2.00 rubles |
| New Posttal (renewal) | 1874–1880 | 1.65 rubles |
| Balmas | 1880–1890 | 3.00 rubles |
| Maraslienfield | 1880 | 3.00 rubles |
| Maraslienfield | 1886 | 3.50 rubles |
| Katlebug | 1895–1898 | 1.75 rubles |
| Katlebug | 1899–1905 | 3.25–3.65 rubles |

16. These are the villages of Benkendorf, Eigenheim, Mannsburg, Neu Posttal, Seimeny, and Sofiental.
17. Kern, *Homeland Book*, 197.
18. Ibid., 174.

leasing charges. Moreover, any improvements made to leased land farmsteads really benefited the landowner more than the lessee. Improvements could not be taken with the lessee if that family moved, and as such improvements increased the value of the land, they also increased the landowner's rationale for raising the leasing charges.

The problems of the tenants who founded the leased land village of Maraslienfeld in 1880 provide a good illustration of what could happen. Though the 6,000 desjatina of this estate were leased at what Kern calls a low rate of three rubles per desjatina in 1880, the landowner, Grigorij Marasli, soon "began to raise his prices."[19] Marasli then farmed out the administration of his estate to guarantee a return. However, when crop failures occurred and the lessees pleaded for reduction in their fee, the fixed cost the administrator had guaranteed Marasli blocked any relief. Problems couldn't be resolved, and the lessees ultimately left and were replaced by other Germans for whom the administrator "increased the leases every decade."[20] Leasing costs rose to 4.5 rubles per desjatina and then to 11 in 1914. Families who took out leases could be very sensitive to cost increases; even small increases might make the arrangement unaffordable. When the Neu Posttal lease was renewed in 1874, the leasing cost was raised from 1.18 rubles per desjatina to 1.65. The result, as Kern reports, was that "many families moved away to find cheaper land elsewhere."[21]

Most of the new villages that remained on leased land were noted for their general poverty. Kern frequently mentions that the leased villages were not as well off as those on purchased land. In his discussion of Jacobstal, Kern notes that "there were quite a large number of lease communities which never rose from near poverty levels."[22] Kern describes Hirtenheim as established in 1887 on land in "such state of neglect" that settlers initially were barely able to pay their leasing costs. Later, as conditions improved, the villagers are described as "better off" than the citizens of the crowded older settlements but still not well enough off to purchase the land they leased.[23] Kern describes the German speakers who came from Austrian Galicia to lease the land that became Strymbeni in west central Bessarabia in 1881 as poor. Then, indicating that their situation had improved only slightly, Kern describes them achieving only "a certain prosperity."[24]

It is not clear why the new German settlements that remained on leased land were less prosperous than those on purchased land. There is no indication that there were differences in the quality of the land between leased and purchased villages. The numerous settlements that passed from leased to purchased land attest to that. The fact that some leased communities like Alt Oneschti, Kamtschatka, and Tchemtchelly grew to be notably prosperous also supports the idea that there were not intrinsic differences between the lands offered for lease and those that might be bought. The fact that such wealthy leased villages could not see beyond the cheapness of their leases was a source of puzzlement to Kern. Perhaps because he was thinking of the unhappy post-1918 future of the leased communities, Kern wondered why the settlers of Strymbeni did not buy: "[They] had improved their lot so much compared

19. Ibid., 184. Grigorij Grigorevič Marasli (1837–1907), the son of a wealthy Greek grain merchant in Odessa, was the appointed mayor of Odessa from 1878 to 1895.
20. Ibid.
21. Ibid., 171.
22. Ibid., 103.
23. Ibid., 113–14.
24. Ibid., 119.

with their former existence in Galicia. It is a mystery why no villagers arranged for contracts for deed. There were more than enough banks available to grant them favorable terms."[25]

One cause for the apparent economic differences between leased and purchased land communities might be the fact that families who did well financially in leased land villages often left, using their saved earnings to buy land in one of the new purchased land settlements. When a landowner remained uninterested in selling, such as Count Navrotsky, who leased the land in the Alkalija Valley where the villages of Strassburg I and II were created, Kern reports that "most German renters worked their way up and later purchased land [elsewhere] in daughter colonies like Mannsburg and Romanowka."[26]

When leased land villages lost their more successful citizens, those remaining were often not just those less willing to take risks but also the less industrious. Over time and with a regular outflow of successful farmers, this tended to make the average village income less and less competitive with purchased land villages. Leased land villages seem to have been hurt, too, by the fact that those leaving took with them examples of best practices, as well as sources of credit. Another factor that appears to have been if not a negative, then perhaps a less positive influence on earnings in leased land villages was that because the land was not owned, it was not cared for with the same attentiveness as land that was owned. Again, improvements ultimately benefited the landowner rather than the lessee.

## Only village-sized plots were available for sale in Bessarabia, and this limited land purchases to groups who had been able to solve the financing issues

It is not surprising that some of the citizens of leased land communities developed interests in purchasing the land they were leasing. However, landowners weren't interested in selling individual parcels, only larger parcels of land. By the early 1880s, the ways and means for ordinary German farmers to put together the sums of money needed to purchase large parcels of land were becoming clear. In 1880, forty families bought a 2,500 desjatina estate that had been the site of a failed leased community and so founded Eigenfeld; and in 1881, the leased land villages of Mannsburg and Neu Posttal were transformed into purchased land communities of 3,000 and 3,217 desjatina respectively. The transformations of these three villages were accomplished by different means, and the paths by which these purchases were achieved provide insight into the way purchasing land became ever more frequently seen in German Bessarabia as the predominant way to found new villages.

Forty families from ten different mother colonies grouped together to purchase the land that created Eigenfeld. They appear to have paid the purchase price by combining funds from their own savings, from the inheritance shares owed to them by their families, or from loans taken out from village fire and orphan funds—that is, without the help of sources outside of the German villages.[27] Such funding methods

25. Ibid.
26. Ibid., 178. Kern notes similarly that residents of the leasing community of Katlebug moved on to purchase land in Basyrjamka or Andrejewka (168).
27. At least that is the presumption given by Kern's description of the founding of the village (ibid., 99–100). Kern often notes when mortgages or other outside means of financial help were in use.

imply that the purchasers were reasonably well-to-do families. In 1880, few families in German Bessarabia had accumulated large assets or had access to such within their villages, which may explain why up to this time so few of the new villages were founded on purchased land.

Mannsburg had been founded in 1863 by families leasing 5,000 desjatina of an estate owned by Baron von Günsburg.[28] On October 31, 1881 (O.S.), a group that appears to represent the great majority of the families then leasing signed an agreement purchasing 3,000 desjatina of this property at the cost of 114,000 silver rubles. Part of the cost was financed by a forty-three-year mortgage note of 63,000 rubles with the remaining 51,000 silver rubles paid at signing by the sixty-seven families, who thus put up on average 761 silver rubles. Having this sum at hand shows that, like the Eigenfeld purchasers, these families had achieved some prosperity as lessees in Mannsburg. With an interest rate of 7.5 percent, the annual mortgage costs work out to an average of 73.82 rubles for each of the sixty-seven purchasers. The 3,000 desjatina they bought gave an average family allotment of 44.8 desjatina with the mortgage cost becoming the equivalent of paying 1.53 rubles per desjatina, making this an attractive price to buy with leasing costs rising. What made this deal work for the Mannsburg purchasers was their ability to get a mortgage. Kern does not name the offering bank, but it may be Xerson Zemstvo Bank in Odessa. Mortgages were also involved in the purchases of the land that created the villages of Hoffnungsfeld in 1881 (1,961 desjatina) and Gnadenfeld in 1879 (1,930 desjatina).[29] Brandes asserts that in the period up to 1890, two-thirds of the purchased land in Xerson, Bessarabia, and Tauride was financed by mortgages from the Xerson Zemstvo Bank.[30]

In his notes on the different German settlements in Bessarabia, Kern mentions the existence of mortgages frequently enough to create the presumption that they were commonly used. Mortgages could vary in length. Those who bought out the leased land at Hoffnungsfeld in 1881 paid almost 40 percent of the cost at purchase with the remainder to be paid out by 1915.[31] The purchasers of land at Eichendorf in 1908 took out a sixty-six-year mortgage.[32] In contrast, those buying the land that created Marienfeld in 1910 took on a mortgage of only twelve years, and those buying the land for Neu Dennewitz in 1912 had just a ten-year mortgage.[33] The data on mortgages are so occasional that it is not possible to go far in discussing usage. Data provided by Kern suggest that mortgages were not always necessary, that some families by the 1890s had become sufficiently well-to-do so as to be able to make land purchases for new villages without taking out a mortgage. This is the impression Kern leaves in describing the purchase of the land to create Jekaterinowka in 1907. The twenty-five families buying the land were each responsible for 19,226 rubles and 60 kopecks when they signed the contract,[34] giving the impression they paid the total cost at purchase. The well-to-do farmers who bought land to form the communities

---

28. Baron Goracij (Horace) Evzelevič Günsburg (1833–1909) was a wealthy St. Petersburg merchant. The village of Mathildendorf founded in 1898 on 800 desjatina was also purchased from him.
29. Ibid., 87, 101. Hoffnugsfeld was settled on leased land in 1864, and the land was purchased in 1881.
30. Brandes, *Von den Zaren Adoptiert*, 380.
31. Vossler, "Die Tochterkolonie Hoffnungsfeld."
32. Gutsche, "Bessarabian Village Reports."
33. Kern, *Homeland Book*, 160, 159, 49.
34. Ibid., 138. Kern doesn't give the number of purchasers, but the total price of 3,100 desjatina bought at 155 rubles per desjatina divided by the figure of 19,226 rubles that Kern states each paid indicates there were twenty-five.

of Halle in 1894 and Pomasan in 1910 do not appear to have used or needed mortgages to support their individual purchase costs. Those who bought at Friedrichsdorf
in 1911 also appear to have acquired the land without a mortgage. However, when
the seller died in 1913, the settlers were faced with a major problem: under Russian
law, the heirs could legally buy the land back at the original cost plus the value of
improvements. Given the increases in land prices and their desire to keep the land,
the settlers agreed to pay the heirs a higher price and took out a mortgage to pay
the difference.[35] As will be discussed in the following chapter, World War I brought
difficulties for mortgage holders in Bessarabia. With men away in the army and
the government finding it necessary to take crops and animals for the war effort at
near confiscatory prices, some villages had difficulties keeping up with their mortgage payments and banks holding the mortgages occasionally sought to institute
foreclosures.

## Gottfried Schulz created a financing option that opened the way for many Bessarabian Germans to establish themselves in new villages on purchased land

Different means were used to transform Neu Posttal from a leased land to a purchased
land village in 1881. This village had been founded in 1864 when forty-eight families
leased 3,217 desjatina of land. Perhaps ten years later, the leasing price was raised
from 1.18 rubles per desjatina to 1.65 and many families moved away. Though new
families subsequently moved in to take up some of the now empty farmsteads, the
turnover was apparently unsettling and did not bode well for the ongoing welfare
of the community.

One of the lessees who did not leave when the leasing fee was raised was
Gottfried Schulz. Schulz was born in Dennewitz in 1846 and sometime between
August 1866 and September 1868 moved to Neu Posttal.[36] In 1881, through some
combination of his own assets, very likely a short-term mortgage, and loans, he
came up with 286,313 rubles and bought the entire 3,217 desjatina estate that made
up Neu Posttal.[37] Schulz then divided the property into forty-five farmsteads of 71
desjatina each, set aside the remaining land as community property and then sold
each of the farmsteads at a profit. Some of the buyers were families who had been
leasing in Neu Posttal, but it would appear that many were families who came from
elsewhere in Bessarabia and wanted to own land. The result was that Neu Posttal,
now on purchased property, became a thriving and stable community.

---

35. Ibid., 87.
36. The dates for his move to Neu Posttal are suggested by the birthdates and birthplaces of his chil-
    dren. The oldest child of Gottfried Schulz and Elisabeth Brost Schulz, August Schulz, was born in
    Dennewitz on August 30, 1866 (O.S.). Their subsequent six children were all born in Neu Posttal,
    the first born there being Gottfried Schulz on September 12, 1868 (O.S.).
37. Kern, *Homeland Book*, 171. I have presumed Schulz's use of a mortgage to buy the land area of Neu
    Posttal as there is no indication that he was anything more than a successful farmer before this
    time. Kern, in his description of the leading men in the village of Halle, established in 1894, notes
    that Schulz, one of the founders here, was the "son of the chief administrator of the communities
    of lower Bessarabia" (73). Schulz's father, Gottlieb Friedrich Schulz, was born in 1816 in Sofiental
    in what was then Russian Poland. He appears in the 1835 Kulm census as a 19-year-old living with
    his parents and brothers, and is listed by Stumpp as one of the founding members of Dennewitz
    (*Emigration from Germany to Russia*, 517). The job description Kern refers to would indicate work
    for the Welfare Committee, and while it would not likely be the source of great wealth, it would
    be a source of wide political and economic contacts and so might have been helpful to Gottfried
    Schulz.

In buying up the land that put Neu Posttal among the purchased land settlements, Gottfried Schulz created a new and easier means for many Bessarabian German families to buy farmsteads. Schulz later used this method at least three other times to turn leased land villages into ones based on purchased land. In pursuing his own financial goals, he created opportunities for many Bessarabian German families to buy farmsteads in one of the purchased land communities he helped to establish. Schulz's method was to buy a large plot of land and then resell plots as individual farmsteads. He took on the financial responsibility for the major land purchase and with it the risk that he might not recoup his investment and so be able to repay the mortgage used to make the purchase. Families who bought one of the farmsteads only took on the liability for that limited plot. They did not need to take a share in the collective liability for the full cost of the entire village land, as did the families who together took out a mortgage that bought the land for the creation of Friedrichsdorf, Gnadenfeld, and Mannsburg. Schulz's business method, thus, made buying land simpler and the financial obligations more specific, affordable and less worrisome. As land prices and the cost of large mortgages rose, Schultz's business model helped many Bessarabian Germans continue to move out of crowded conditions onto purchased land. Schulz became quite wealthy through these transactions. Although Brandes refers to Schulz as a "notorious land speculator" ("berüchtigter Aufkäufer"),[38] Kern's praise is justified as Schulz materially helped the transition from leased to purchased land for many Germans.

In 1894, Schulz found a similar opportunity in the leased land community of Seimeny along the coastline of the Dniester Liman, north of Akkerman. He bought, for 360,000 rubles, the 3,000 desjatina the community had been leasing and divided them into fifty-four farmsteads, and resold these, it would appear, mainly to newcomers coming from both German Bessarabia and German settlements across the Dniester in Xerson Province.[39] Starting a pattern he would repeat in later land purchases, Schulz held on to at least one of the farmsteads in Seimeny and, with the help of his sons, developed the land for the family's further profit. In 1898, Schulz bought 2,875 desjatina that had been the leased land settlement of Sofiental, southwest of Schabo. The settlers who had leased land here came from Xerson Province. Again, Schulz divided the land into similarly sized farmsteads and resold the properties, keeping at least one of the properties for himself, which Kern notes "provided a feeling of security" for others buying property there.[40] In Sofiental, many of the families who had been leasing land wished to stay as landowners and had the means to do this, though other Bessarabian Germans also joined them as Schulz advertised the land for sale in Alt Posttal, Wittenberg, Neu Elft, Dennewitz, and Plotzk. In 1899, Schulz repeated this pattern for a fourth time when he put up 237,600 rubles to buy the 2,300 desjatina that had been the leased community of Basyrjamka along the estuary of the Alkalija River, south of Neu Posttal. The failed harvest of 1899 appeared to be the impetus for putting together an offer for the land at Basyrjamka,

38. Brandes, *Von den Zaren Adoptiert*, 398.
39. Kern, *Homeland Book*, 77. As none of the family names of the pre-1894 lessees are repeated among the family names of purchasing families still living in Seimeny in 1940, the implication is that most of the purchasers were newcomers.
40. Ibid., 177.

though as Schulz's sons had been among those leasing land, Schulz likely also had their interests in mind.

In purchasing such large properties on the basis of redividing and selling them, Schulz was taking a reasonable market risk that would bankrupt him if he failed to sell sufficient properties at his desired prices. Schulz's pattern of looking for properties that were currently settled on a leased basis was very likely a useful hedge against this risk. Leased land provided a pool of potential purchasers who knew the land and, whether they bought or left, had, as lessees, already made some basic investments in farmstead buildings and in preparing the steppeland for farming and animals. In addition, Schulz's experience with Neu Posttal must have offered comfort that he could bear the risk. In Neu Posttal, even though most of those who had been leasing elected not to buy, the available farmsteads were soon bought up by other Germans from the older communities. This established that there were many Germans who were eager to buy land and could afford to do so. Finally, while Schulz's habit of keeping some property in each of these villages may have been done for reasons of personal economic gain, it was also a smart action as it seems to have given comfort to purchasers that Schulz thought the land was worth owning or that his presence would help guarantee the sustainability of the settlement. The profits gained from these land sales made Schulz wealthy. As evidence of this wealth, in 1907, Schulz bought a nearly 800-desjatina plot of land just north of Basyrjamka on which he established his single family estate, which he called Schulzenheim.[41]

## Land prices in Bessarabia steadily rose in the period from 1870 to 1914.

Prices in the 1880s ranged from 30 to 89 rubles a desjatina. After 1900, prices often were over 200 rubles a desjatina, and at the height of market frenzy after 1910, prices soared over 400 rubles a desjatina and for desirable land could even reach 1,000 rubles. There are data available on the costs for twenty-four different German land purchases in Bessarabia that occurred before World War I and led to the establishment of new villages (see table 11–6).

The rising prices would seem to reflect not just inflation but also a growing market demand for land coupled with decreasing amounts of land available in the general vicinity of the German settlements in the Budjak. The unusual variances in land prices can sometimes be explained by location. For example, the relatively low price of 30 rubles per desjatina that Johann Seefried paid in 1889 to buy the land that became Neu Sarata was in part the result of the fact that this land was located in central western Bessarabia, not close to the major German colonies and in an area where market interest was just beginning.[42] Similarly, the enormous price of 1,000 rubles per desjatina that Mannsburg residents paid for an additional 700 desjatina was likely the result of their willingness to pay well above market rates for land adjoining the existing village land.

---

41. Ibid., 176.
42. Johann Seefried of Neu Elft, like Schulz, bought the land for resale. Johann Seefried was the son of Lukas Seefried and seems to be following a business plan similar to that used by his father in establishing the settlement of Jargara. Lukas Seefried bought the land for this settlement, located some 5 miles south of Neu Sarata, in 1882 and, keeping some of the land for his own estate, sold the remainder to settlers coming from Neu Elft and Beresina.

TABLE 11–6. **Rising land costs in Bessarabia 1860–1912**

| Town | Year | Cost per desjatina | Land size | Number of families | Average land per family |
|---|---|---|---|---|---|
| Freudenfeld[a] | 1860s | 12 | 2,000 | 32 | 62.5 |
| Gnadenfeld | 1879 | 45 | 1,930 | Unknown | Unknown |
| Mannsburg | 1881 | 38 | 3,000 | 67 | 44.8 |
| Hoffnungsfeld[b] | 1881 | 39.5 | 1,961 | 40 | 47.6 |
| New Posttal | 1881 | 89 | 3,217 | 45 | 71.5 |
| Lichtental | 1886 | 75 | 642 | Unknown | Unknown |
| Neu Sarata | 1889 | 30 | 2,433 | 48 | 50 |
| Neu Tarutino | 1890 | 75 | 1,200 | Unknown | Unknown |
| Seimeny | 1894 | 120 | 3,000 | 54 | 55.6 |
| Romanowka | 1895 | 109 | 1,492 | Unknown | Unknown |
| Friedensfeld | 1897 | 60 | 740 | 2 | 320 |
| Balaktschelly | 1898 | 140 | 1,500 | Unknown | Unknown |
| Stanhopka | 1899 | 140 | 102 | Unknown | Unknown |
| Basyrjamka | 1899 | 99 | 2,400 | Unknown | Unknown |
| Lichtental[c] | 1890s | 140 | 1,000 | Unknown | Unknown |
| Benkendorf[d] | 1890s | 110 | 2,246 | 42 | 53.5 |
| Alexanderfeld | 1907 | 160 | 2,683 | 48 | 55.9 |
| Eichendorf | 1908 | 140 | 2,271 | Unknown | Unknown |
| Jekaterinowka | 1908 | 155 | 3,100 | 25 | 124 |
| Kisil | 1908 | 250 | 1,125 | 15 | 75 |
| Mannsburg | 1910 | 1,000 | 700 | Unknown | Unknown |
| Orak Estate | 1910 | 235 | 791 | 1 | 791 |
| Gretscheni | 1911 | 300 | 1,449 | 1 | 1,449 |
| Kaschplat | 1912 | 408 | 200 | 4 | 50 |
| Baimaklia | 1912 | 500 | 1,150 | 6 | 1917 |

a. Freudenfeld was in fact a leased land village. The land price given here is the price the landowner, a Mr. Kipperwasser, paid sometime in the 1860s. Thirty-two Bessarabian German families leased land here, forming the village, according to Kern, in 1879 (*Homeland Book*, 100).

b. Vossler, "Die Tochterkononie Hoffnungsfeld." Here 1,904.5 desjatina were divided into farmsteads.

c. Kern (*Homeland Book*, 183) does not provide a date for this sale but has noted that Lichtental farmers made the purchase from Countess Tolstaya (Lady Stanhope). As Lady Stanhope agreed in 1898 to sell the land for Balaktschelly and Stanhopka nearby at the same price of 140 rubles, this sale may date from 1898.

d. Kern indicates the village was founded in 1863 and implies that it was at that time that "forty-two families purchased 2,246 desjatines of land at 110 gold rubles per desjatine" (*Homeland Book*, 165). Brandes has indicated the village was founded on leased land in 1863 (*Von den Zaren Adoptiert*, 399) and that the land was purchased some time later. As the price of 110 gold rubles per desjatina seems egregious for the 1860s, this makes sense. Given what is known of land costs in Bessarabia, such a price would more likely place the sale sometime after 1890.

## As land prices went up, the average number of purchasers per new settlement declined, though the average amount of land each family bought grew

For those villages where it is possible to match the number of new inhabitants with the amount of land acquired, it is possible to see patterns over time. The data available are for thirty-nine villages[43] relatively evenly spread across the period from 1870 to 1914, but they come almost entirely from purchased land settlements (see table 11–7).[44]

These data suggest that over this period, new villages in German Bessarabia were increasingly formed by smaller numbers of families. While the land areas of these new villages were decreasing over time, the sizes of the average family allotments in them were growing larger. This data set is not large enough to draw firm conclusions, but as 86 percent of this data set concerns purchased land villages, including all twenty-one of the villages in the period from 1900 to 1914, it does point toward several tendencies in the creation of purchased land settlements. With land prices steadily rising and reaching quite expensive heights after 1900, these data suggest that fewer and fewer families could afford to enter the market. Toward the end of this period, it would seem that purchasers increasingly belonged to the most well-to-do segments of Germans in Bessarabia. Families able to purchase land, however, took advantage of these conditions and purchased larger and larger plots for themselves. Another implication of these data is support for the immigration trends seen in the data from Tarutino, Kulm, and Leipzig, considered in the previous chapter. After 1890, there was a major upsurge in emigration from these villages to North America.[45] One possible reason behind this upsurge in the numbers moving to North America is that the costs of purchasing new land in Bessarabia had begun materially to surpass those of immigration.

The rising costs of purchasing land in the new villages also carry other interesting implications that will be considered later in this chapter. As the costs of forming new villages continued to increase and so limit participation, many families, especially those in the still-crowded mother colonies, needed to look for other opportunities if they had no desire to emigrate. These data may help explain why more families after 1890 were turning to commerce and manufacturing for employment. These data also provide one means for understanding the growing income differences that had begun in German Bessarabia, especially after the beginning of the twentieth century.

TABLE 11–7. **Average plot sizes increase as the number of purchasers decrease**

| Period | Villages with data | Average total land | Average number of families | Average family plot size |
|---|---|---|---|---|
| 1880–1889 | 9 | 1,973 | 36.2 | 57.1 |
| 1890–1899 | 9 | 1,695 | 32.0 | 53.0 |
| 1900–1909 | 10 | 1,668 | 27.5 | 60.7 |
| 1910–1914 | 11 | 1,285 | 15.0 | 85.7 |

43. Included in this data set are figures for Mannsburg, Neu Posttal, and Seimeny, each founded in the 1860s on leased land, but the data used here is from the 1880s and 1890s when these villages were transformed into purchased land villages.
44. The average total land in table 11–7 represents the average of the total amount of land purchased or leased by the village and, like the figures for the average family plot size, is in desjatina.
45. See table 10–5.

## Demographic data on those who purchased land suggest similarities with data on those who headed family parties immigrating to North America

In several cases, Kern lists the names of the village founders. Combining this data with other demographic sources, it is possible to determine the average ages of the founders of five new villages, all founded after 1908 (table 11–8). The demographic picture that results shows a consistent pattern: the founders were middle-aged men and women typically in their late 30s to very early 40s.

The average ages of these village founders at the time of settlement show a distinct similarity to the data pulled from the Kulm, Leipzig, and Tarutino demographics on the average ages of male adults at the time they emigrated from Bessarabia to North America.[46] Also like the emigrant parties, the groups establishing new villages in Bessarabia included many with family relationships. The Parapara settlers of 1912–14 particularly stand out in this regard. This group included the three Schlaps brothers, the three Vossler cousins, and at least seven connections by marriage.

There are three other distinctive demographic features that can be deduced from the lists of founders of purchased land villages that Kern provides. The first, which also typified the founders of leased villages, is that each group was formed by families coming from several different existing Bessarabian settlements. This suggests groups were formed as opportunities came up, and that some form of communication existed among the different German settlements to draw out families who were interested and prepared to act.

A second distinctive demographic feature of founding families is that some of them were headed by women. The Ketrossy founders, for example, included Luise Necker Stelter, who bought 40 desjatina, and Lydia Necker, who bought 35. The Kolatschowka purchasers included Marie Widmer. Kern describes the Lunga purchasers as consisting of "17 men and one woman."[47] Like the women who led family groups immigrating to North America, these women were widows who had become heads of household. While the amounts of land purchased by the two women in the Ketrossy group were the smallest plots held by the founders, they were still full-size farmstead lots, not just cottager land. It was not common for women to be the heads of household or to purchase land in their own right, but the important point to be made is that they could and did.

A third demographic point to be made about the purchasers of land for new villages, particularly those in the early twentieth century, is that they tended to be

TABLE 11–8. **Average ages of the founders of five new villages**

|  | Glückstal | Ketrossy | Kisil | Neu Alexandrowka | Parapara |
|---|---|---|---|---|---|
| Number of founders | 20 | 16 | 14 | 13 | 25 |
| Data points on founders | 18 | 16 | 12 | 13 | 22 |
| **Average age** | 37 | 40 | 38 | 40 | 41 |

---

46. See table 10–6.
47. Kern, *Homeland Book*, 148.

wealthy. In his discussion of Fürstenfeld II, Kern describes the purchasers who bought 3,000 desjatina of land for that village in 1911 as "mostly wealthy farmers."[48] In his discussion of Baimaklia, where the 1,200 desjatina of land was purchased for 500 rubles per desjatina in 1912, Kern notes that "only very rich people could afford that much money."[49] How much money was involved is apparent from Kern's listing of the amounts of land bought in Baimaklia. Ludwig Mayle of Alexandrowka and three others each bought 100 desjatina at a cost of 50,000 rubles; Johann Herberg of Neu Posttal purchased 300 desjatina, spending 150,000 rubles.

However, not everyone bought large lots when such new villages were founded, and this cautions one not to presume that everyone in the purchasing group was especially well-to do. In his discussion of Neu Nikolajewka, for example, Kern lists the amounts of land bought by each of the founding members. Some are quite large, with two purchasing 150 desjatina of land and two others purchasing 100 desjatina each; most (eleven of the eighteen listed purchasers) bought decent-sized lots of 40 or 50 desjatina. One purchaser, though, bought a parcel of only 25 desjatina and two others bought parcels of just 15 desjatina.[50] Similarly, among the purchasers of land to create Glückstal, there are some who bought plots of 10, 14, or 15 desjatina when many were buying plots of 50, 75, or 100 desjatina.[51] Nevertheless, it seems fair to draw as a general conclusion that as prices climbed, the numbers of those who could afford to be among the purchasers decreased. And prices did climb. While the price paid by the Baimaklia purchasers may have been at the upper end, it was not unique. In the same year, Germans paid 408 rubles per desjatina for the land that established the village of Kaschpalat south of Klöstitz. In 1910, Christian Kroll paid 235 rubles per desjatina for the Orak estate and in 1911, paid 300 rubles per desjatina for Gretscheni, both located in far southwestern Bessarabia. Riehl's "History of the Village of Krasna" notes that in the period from 1906 to 1914, the "price of land started to increase dramatically" so that it was common that "200–300 rubles were paid" for one desjatina.[52]

The creation of seventy-nine new farming villages in the period from 1870 to 1914 was one of the most striking features of the evolution of German Bessarabia. It addressed, at least in part, the major problem of overcrowding that the original colonies were facing by the time the third generation appeared. It permitted many German families to establish themselves on large farms of at least 40–50 desjatina, and so repeat the same economic growth cycle their grandparents and parents had achieved by turning large family plots of land into economic engines creating surplus. It also permitted a continuing and growing prosperity in the older colonies, which they had left, by allowing these original colonies to maintain many large farmsteads for a while longer. The ability of the Germans in Bessarabia to create so many new settlements demonstrates that many German families in Bessarabia had been able to build a strong economic base that supported a reasonably broad, stable middle income group. Only at the end of this period does it begin to seem that just the wealthy could participate in this process.

48. Ibid., 156.
49. Ibid., 47.
50. Ibid., 115.
51. Ibid., 112.
52. Riehl, "History of the Village of Krasna."

In establishing the new settlements, it was necessary to develop the land for agriculture, to build houses and barns, and to construct churches and schools. It was possible to accomplish these goals and to put the new communities on solid economic ground, as the period before World War I was one of rising economic prospects for Germans in Bessarabia. With the continuing strong demand for Bessarbian grain in both Western Europe and Russia itself, as well as the strong markets for animals and their products, for fruit, and for wine, the new communities were able to add materially to the accumulated wealth of German Bessarabia. In doing so, the new communities became important factors in growing consumer demand in Bessarabia, which in turn awakened a commercial and manufacturing potential that really came to life in this period, particularly in the older, original German settlements. These topics will largely be the subject of the remainder of this chapter; however, before leaving the topic of the founding of new German settlements in Bessarabia, I would like to address two other related issues that offer important perspectives.

## The land purchases after 1870 in Bessarabia occurred at a fortunate juncture of interests: Overcrowding now pushed German buyers to consider new solutions at a time when they began to have sufficient assets to enter the land market and landowners at this time started to be interested in selling rather than leasing

It was fortunate that when Bessarabian Germans began to consider the possibilities of establishing new settlements, many of them had also developed sufficient savings and had access to capital via village funds that permitted them to think of leasing or purchasing additional land. Moreover, Bessarabia in 1870 still had large tracts of relatively unused land owned by absentee landlords. The huge amount of empty or underused pasture land in the Budjak region that had come into the crown's hand with the absorption of Bessarabia and the expulsion of the Tartars had largely been given away by the tsars as awards for service. The recipients of these land grants in the Budjak lived elsewhere and using estate administrators, leased their holdings, often as pasture land, for income. After the end of the Crimean War, Odessa merchants who had grown wealthy in the grain trade with Europe began to be interested in purchasing land. As the land market had been active in their native Xerson Province for some time, they looked for land in Bessarabia, where, evidently, there was more land available.[53]

When in the 1860s and 1870s, Bessarabian Germans began to look to ease their overcrowding by creating new villages, they found landowners now interested in leasing land to them. One reason for this fact is that leasing land for farming brought better and possibly steadier returns than leasing it for pasturing. A second, much repeated in Kern's village descriptions, was that for a landowner, lessees improved the land, and as land values rose, the fees charged for leasing might increase dramatically. The example of the village of Maraslienfeld, noted earlier, is striking. There, leasing

---

53. Although Kern in his discussion of the village of Balmas notes that leasing land in Bessarabia was materially less expensive in 1880 at 3 rubles a desjatina vs. 10 in Xerson (*Homeland Book*, 197), this does not appear to be the case with land purchase costs. Material provided by Brandes indicates that land costs were always much higher in Bessarabia than in the other South Russian provinces. See table 11–11 below.

costs rose from 3.5 rubles per desjatina in 1880 to 4.5 in the late 1880s and reached 11 rubles per desjatina by 1914.[54]

As the nineteenth century progressed, however, leasing land in Bessarabia no longer tended to satisfy the economic needs of the landowners, particularly the noble landowners. The costs of maintaining the lifestyle standards expected of the nobility were sharply increasing in the second half of the nineteenth century. Standards, particularly in such areas as clothing, personal jewelry, dining, travel, and even servant attendants, could no longer be easily met by goods that might be produced on one's estate. They had become dependent on manufactured goods and upon services that were purchased with money. Moreover, the costs of such goods and services kept rising. This was in part the result of the invention of new luxury goods and technology, and great improvements in the means of travel that created increased expectations of visiting desired places in Western Europe. The increased costs of the noble lifestyle were also driven by the fact that the wealthy end of the growing middle class competed with the nobility for luxury goods, which only served to limit access and raise prices. In their efforts to maintain expected lifestyle standards, the nobility were disadvantaged by the fact that their wealth was often based on land and its agricultural potential. The income to be derived from agriculture could not keep up with now steeply rising costs of desired goods and services. It is more likely that with only small increases in the prices for grain, estate incomes based on selling produce only had slight upside potentials. In contrast, the great fortunes that were now produced from commerce and manufacturing gave to those families enormous potential for access to desired goods and services. Therefore, to maintain their expected life styles, many of the nobility were tempted to sell assets not deemed critical, or live beyond their means. The transition in the late nineteenth century to a money-based economy was not going well for the Russian nobility. The payments received by the nobility when the Russian serfs were freed were, on the whole, not put to good financial use. Riasanovsky, as noted earlier, observed that the Russian nobility was ill-suited to compete as successful farmers: "Many preferred to live in Paris or Nice, spending whatever they had."[55]

One major result of such pressures was that by the late 1890s and into the twentieth century, landlords in Bessarabia clearly had become more interested in selling property than in leasing it. Kern saw their motivations for selling land to Germans as driven by the needs of their expensive lifestyles. In discussing the sale of 1,493 desjatina that created the village of Lunga in 1907, Kern portrays landowners in both Bessarabia and Russia in general as selling "land to finance their 'living high off the hog'."[56]

What we know about those who sold land in Bessarabia to Germans, however, suggests more complex motives than just satisfying extravagant lifestyles amid declining assets. Princess Anna Grigorievna Gagarina-Sturdza inherited from her

---

54. Ibid., 184.
55. Riasanovsky, *History of Russia*, 470.
56. Kern, *Homeland Book*, 148.

Sturdza grandparents extensive lands.[57] Kern notes that she had 40,000 desjatina north of Hoffnungstal and more near Odessa. From these properties, Germans leased 2,000 desjatina in 1895 to form the village of Helenowka. In 1909, another 2,000 desjatina were sold to Germans who created the village of Annowka. Princess Anna Gagarina-Sturdza lived much of her adult life in France, residing there with her parents, clearly living off the income from their estates in Russia.[58] As the family continued to own a great deal of land until the Russian Revolution, when it was confiscated, the family does not easily fit into the portrait of impoverished nobles forced to sell their land. It does, however, suggest a family with needs for income in excess of the returns produced by the lands they owned and so an interest in selling some family assets.

Alexandra von Cancrin (1856–1934), who sold nearly 9,500 desjatina to Germans in Bessarabia in the period from 1893 to 1912, forms a similar example. She inherited extensive lands in Bessarabia from her grandfather, Georg von Cancrin (1774–1845), Minister of Finance under both Alexander I and Nicolas I. She married Philip Stanhope in 1877, later the 1st Baron Weardale, a Liberal member of the British Parliament. She lived in Britain after 1877. She had been married earlier to Count M. I. Tolstoy, a distant relation of the great writer Count Leo Tolstoy. German references to her in Bessarabia often refer to her as Countess Tolstoy (or properly, Tolstaja), although her marriage to Philip Stanhope was clearly known, as the name of the village of Stanhopka indicates. She made some seven known sales to the Germans (table 11–9).

TABLE 11–9. **Alexandra von Cancrin Stanhope's sales to the Germans**

| Date | Town created | Land sold | Value of sale |
|------|-------------|-----------|---------------|
| 1893 | Romanowka | 1,492 desjatina | 162,628 rubles |
| 1890s[a] | Part of Lichtental | 1,000 desjatina | 140,000 rubles |
| 1898 | Balaktschelly | 1,500 desjatina | 210,000 rubles |
| 1898 | August Würth estate | 125 desjatina | Unknown |
| 1898 | G. Gerstenberger estate | 453 desjatina | Unknown |
| 1899 | Stanhopka/Sarazika | 2,000 desjatina | 280,000 rubles |
| 1910 | Pomasan | 1,482 desjatina | Unknown |
| 1912 | Parapara | 1,444 desjatina | Unknown |

a. Kern, *Homeland Book*, 183. The date of this sale appears to be in the 1890s although Kern attributes it to 1886.

---

57. Ibid., 97–98. Her land ownership came via her grandmother Maria Sturdza, the only daughter of Alexander Sturdza, who held lands in Bessarabia in inheritance from his ancient Moldavian noble family. Maria Sturdza married Prince Evgenij Gagarin and their son, Grigorij, reflecting the wealth in lands inherited from his mother, altered his name to Gagarin-Sturdza. Anna Grigorievna was his daughter. The connection with the Gagarin family made her a princess, not a countess as indicated by Kern.

58. Ibid., 98. In treating the sale of land for Annowka, Kern describes Princess Anna Gagarina-Sturdza as the separated wife of an Odessa eye doctor. This may be apocryphal. I have not found trace or mention of him, and it was uncommon for members of the nobility in Russia to marry men in professions. In any case she was not married to him in 1909 when she sold the land for Annowka. Gagarina-Sturdza was interested in art and had exhibited as a painter. In 1908 in France, she married the sculptor Denys Puech, then Director of the Villa Medici.

These land sales place her large holdings in six separate areas in Bessarabia,[59] only parts of which were sold off by 1914. Alexandra von Cancrin Stanhope was a very wealthy woman who, though having received likely more than a million rubles from land sales just to the Bessarabian Germans, had other large tracts of land that provided her with income at least until the beginning of World War I.

Several other landowners in Bessarabia with whom the Germans dealt were neither Russian nobles nor noted for extravagant lives. Their willingness to sell land to the Germans, however, does suggest their need for cash. The land for the village of Lunga was purchased in 1907 from the estate of Stephanos Ralli, a wealthy grain merchant of Greek origin, who had invested in land in both Bessarabia and Xerson.[60] The family of Grigorij Marasli, noted earlier as the owner of lands that were leased to form the village of Maraslienfeld, was similarly a family of wealthy Greek Russian grain merchants who had invested earnings from the grain trade in Bessarabian land. The land for Neu Sarata was purchased in 1889 from an estate owned by Alexander Stoilov (1810–1891), a Bulgarian journalist who wrote under the name Alexander Exarch. Stoilov, with the financial support of the Russian government, published a Russian-language journal in Constantinople. He was by no means a wealthy man and had evidently bought the land in Russia as an investment but had not kept up payments. Kern notes, for example, that this land was under threat of foreclosure at the time of the sale to the Germans.[61]

For a history of the Germans in Bessarabia, the most important point to be made here is of the fortunate timing of different needs. The overcrowding in the original Bessarabian German settlements occurred at the same time that the Germans had built up significant assets from the sale of surplus from their farms, allowing them to enter the land market. The nobles and merchants owning semi-vacant land near the Germans in the Budjak and elsewhere in Bessarabia had at this time developed needs for cash that led them to become interested in leasing and selling land to the Germans. Data that Brandes collected suggest that the willingness of landowners to sell land may have been strong throughout the last half of the nineteenth century. Significant land sales to Germans existed before 1880, and in the Xerson, Ekaterinoslav, and Tauride provinces, more land was sold before 1880 than in the period from 1880 to 1890. German land purchases in Bessarabia contradict this pattern. It would rather seem that Germans in Bessarabia reached the point where they could afford to become materially active in the land market only by 1880, and thus were slower to do so than Germans in the South Russian provinces (see table 11–10). The data from Brandes confirm material in Kern that land purchases by Germans in Bessarabia were modest before 1880 and grew steadily thereafter. The

59. The Romanowka land was west of Mannsburg on the plateau between the valleys of the Alkalija and the Xodžider Rivers. The land bought by the Lichtental citizens is described as near Neu Arzis, placing it west of the Čelegider River (hence the German Tschiligider) and likely not continuous to the land sold to the Würth and Gerstenberger families. The village of Balaktschelly was located well to the west of Romanowka in the valley of a western tributary of the Xodžider River, upstream from the German village of Rosenfeld. The estate lands bought by the Würth and Gerstenberger families were on opposite sides of the Čelegider River somewhat upstream from Lichtental. The land bought by the Stanhopka settlers and Gottlob Eckert to found the Sarazika estate was along the Sarata River north of Sarata, and the land bought to create Pomasan and Parapara was in the far south of Bessarabia on the plateau lands north of Kilia on the lower Danube.

60. Kern (*Homeland Book*, 148) refers to Ralli as "Count Rally"; however, I have not found evidence that the family had been granted noble status by any of the Russian tsars.

61. Ibid., 160. Kern, perhaps misled by Stoilov's penname, Alexander Exarch, thought him Greek.

TABLE 11–10. Land purchases made by Germans in the South Russian provinces

|            | Bessarabia | Xerson  | Ekaterinoslav | Tauride |
|------------|-----------|---------|---------------|---------|
| Up to 1879 | 27,994    | 272,440 | 300,198       | 470,074 |
| 1880–1890  | 52,180    | 190,805 | 237,853       | 199,440 |
| **Total**  | 80,174    | 463,245 | 538,051       | 669,514 |

figures in Brandes, however, indicate that before 1890, land purchases by Germans in Bessarabia were only a fraction of those made by Germans in South Russia: 17 percent of the size of German land purchases in Xerson and 12 percent of those in Tauride.[62]

Data from a 1913 study quoted in Brandes suggest that one reason land purchases by Germans in Bessarabia lagged behind those of Germans in other South Russian provinces was because average land prices in Bessarabia were much higher (see table 11–11).[63]

## One significant group of land purchases in German Bessarabia was made by a class of wealthy Germans who purchased land to create independent family estates

The second issue I wanted to address that emerges from the study of the great expansion in the number of German villages in Bessarabia in the period from 1870 to 1914 is that the land purchases reveal the emergence of a class of particularly wealthy Germans. These were individuals buying land not to establish new villages but to create large single-family estates. Some of these were individuals who had made their mark in Bessarabia, like Gottfried Schulz. Others were Germans from South Russia who recognized the opportunities existing in Bessarabia and bought land there to take advantage of them.

Large single-family estates established by Germans in Bessarabia date from the 1840s where three were established in the vicinity of Klöstitz. Johann Friedrich Hoffmann, who was not a Bessarabian colonist but the manager of an estate in Xerson Province near Odessa, bought a plot of 1,098 desjatina south of Klöstitz in the valley of the Čaga River in 1845 and established the estate of Lambrowka. Hoffmann's father, an estate manager in the Crimea, bought a separate 500 desjatina plot of land near Klöstitz. The two Hoffmann plots came together under single ownership when Johann Friedrich's son Alfred inherited them.[64] Another large family estate, called Friedrichsfeld, was established near Klöstitz at about the same

TABLE 11–11. Average prices for a desjatina in the South Russian provinces

|      | Bessarabia | Xerson | Ekaterinoslav | Tauride |
|------|-----------|--------|---------------|---------|
| 1860 | 35        | 29     | 21            | 14      |
| 1870 | 50        | 39     | 33            | 21      |
| 1883 | 95        | 55     | 50            | 39      |
| 1889 | 105       | 94     | 86            | 76      |

---

62. Brandes, *Von den Zaren Adoptiert*, 420. The figures in this chart are in desjatina.
63. Ibid. The figures in this chart are rubles per 1 desjatina. Brandes is quoting from a work published in 1913 on agriculture in Xerson Province.
64. Kern, *Homeland Book*, 133.

time by Friedrich Bodamer. Bodamer, born in 1811, was the son of a Klöstitz colonist who evidently came to Bessarabia with sufficient assets to set his family on firm economic ground more quickly than others.[65] By 1850, the family was able to buy a village-size plot of land of 7,000 desjatina that was turned into the huge family estate of Friedrichsfeld.[66] The third large estate near Klöstitz was established by Johann Gottlieb Gerstenberger sometime in the 1860s when he bought a plot of 3,000 desjatina.[67] Unlike the Bodamer money, the Gerstenberger wealth appears to have been built up solely in Bessarabia. Johann Gottlieb's father, Friedrich, had come late to Beresina after the farmsteads had all been allotted and so began life in Bessarabia as a landless resident.

There were no other German single-family estates of such size in Bessarabia. As noted in a previous chapter, Konrad Renz of Friedenstal did buy 6,187 desjatina in 1861 but did not use this purchase to create a single-family estate like Friedrichsfeld. Instead, he sold off some of the land in large sections to Germans from Alt Elft and Gnadental, sold other pieces to non-Germans, and leased out further portions. Out of these plots of land was formed the village of Demir Chadschi, south of Gnadental. In 1882, Lukas Seefried of Neu Elft bought 640 desjatina, a much smaller plot of land, in western Bessarabia and, like Renz, while using part as his family's land, sold off much of what he had purchased to other German families, forming the settlement of Jargara. As noted earlier, Gottfried Schulz established a very successful business after 1881 of buying large plots of land for resale to groups of Bessarabian Germans who wanted to establish themselves in new villages. Schulz would typically keep a lot in these villages for himself and so over time became, according to Kern, the largest German landowner in Bessarabia. It wasn't until 1907, however, that he established a single-family estate when he bought 798 desjatina just north of Basyrjamka to form Gut Schulzenheim.

Gut Schulzenheim typifies the scale of most of the German single-family estates established in Bessarabia: impressively larger than the normal family holdings, even the large plots of over 100 desjatina that had been purchased in some of the new villages, but materially smaller than the three huge estates established around Klöstitz. These later single-family estates were created after 1889 and were typically

---

65. Horst Gutsche, "The Bodamer Family of Kloestitz," *Bessarabian Newsletter* 5, no. 3 (December 2001): 39. While Friedrich Bodamer may have become wealthy because he had been an especially successful farmer in Klöstitz, it is also likely that the Bodamers arrived in Bessarabia in 1815 with substantial assets. Friedrich's father, Johann-Ulrich Bodamer, was the grandson of one of the wealthiest commoners in Baden, Hans-Jacob Bodamer, a lawyer and timber company administrator who had been able to purchase land for each of his sons in Grünswettersbach near Karlsruhe. For those who had the means, investing in cattle was the quickest way to build wealth in colonial Bessarabia. Table 19 of the 1825 Welfare Committee report indicates that Klöstitz had the second highest per-family holdings of cattle at 13.1 head per family. Kulm was highest at 14.4. Rempel, *German Farming Achievements*, Table 19.

66. Kern is the source of this dating, but Kern's comparison of the Bodamer holdings in 1850 to those of Gottfried Schulz raises questions. Kern comments on Friedrichsfeld that "by 1850, only Gottfried Schulz...owned more land in Bessarabia" (*Homeland Book*, 133). However, as in 1850 Gottfried Schulz (1846–1925) was only four years old and not the wealthy landowner he later became, it is possible that Kern meant to compare either Bodamer's holdings as of 1850 with those of Schulz at a later date or that 1850 is a misprint.

67. The purchase appears to have taken place sometime before June 17, 1870 (O.S.), when Johann Gottlieb's son Gottfried was born. The church records list Gottfried as having been born in or near Klöstitz whereas all of the earlier Gerstenberger children are listed as having been born in Beresina. Drefs, "Birth Records, 187x."

over 500 desjatina, with the Tamurka estate of Gottfried Gerstenberger at 1,000 desjatina forming the upper end of this category (see table 11–12).[68]

In many cases, it is not clear how these German families acquired the wealth needed to purchase such large estates. Kern implies, vaguely, that Johann Gottlieb Gerstenberger was frugal and that Konrad Renz prospered because "his honesty, daring and diligence gave him the opportunity."[69] Where the sources of family wealth are more clear, the dominant causal factors are not farming but commercial activities: Gottlob Eckert of Lichtental made his money by supplying the Russian army with wagons during the Russo-Turkish War of 1877–78; Johannes Ensslen, though well-to-do by inheritance, was the manager of an estate in the Crimea; Fuchs owned a brick factory; the Schulz wealth came from land speculation; and the Kroll wealth came in part from leasing land. Where farm work is mentioned as a source of wealth, it is raising and selling cattle. Regarding the 600-desjatina Negrowo estate of the Ensslen brothers, Kern mentions that "cattle could be purchased cheaply and fattened up before fetching good market prices in the cities," and that the younger Christian Kroll was able to make the land purchases he did because "his livestock produced a considerable income."[70]

TABLE 11–12. **Large single-family German estates in Bessarabia**

| Year purchased | Founder(s) | Size |
| --- | --- | --- |
| 1889 | Ensslen Brothers[a] | 600 desjatina |
| 1891 | Gottlieb Schimke | 500 desjatina |
| 1895 | Johann Gersternberger | 1,000 desjatina |
| 1898 | Gottfried Gerstenberger | 453 desjatina |
| 1898 | Gottlob Eckert | 830 desjatina |
| 1900s | Gottlieb Gassert | 500 desjatina |
| 1902 | Singer Brothers | 360 desjatina |
| 1907 | Gottfried Schulz | 798 desjatina |
| 1912 | Nathanael Reiman[b] | 366 desjatina |
| 1912 | Eduard Fuchs | 178 desjatina |
| 1912 | Johannes Ensslen | 183 desjatina |

a. The Negrowo estate bought by the Ensslen brothers of Alt Posttal did include some German lessees who continued to lease plots of land after the Ensslens purchased the land, so while this estate was mainly a single-family enterprise, it was not completely so.

b. Reiman and Fuchs were brothers-in-law of Johannes Ensslen, married to daughters of Gottlieb Ensslen of Negrowo (see note 75). Together with Johannes Ensslen's other two brothers, Immanuel and Gottlob Ensslen, they jointly bought in 1912 land along the Black Sea coast and divided it into individual family estates. Kern does not give the original size of Johannes Ensslen's estate or the sizes of the estates of Immanuel and Gottlob Ensslen. He does note that after the Romanian land reforms that took underused land for landless farmers, Ensslen was left with 100 hectares. As these reforms generally confiscated more than half of an estate's land (for example, the neighboring Reimann estate, originally 400 hectares, was reduced to 100 after the land reform) Ensslen's estate as a result can be presumed to have been at least 200 hectares or 183 desjatina (Kern, *Homeland Book*, 166).

---

68. Christian Kroll of Alt Posttal was also very active in the land market, but he continued to live in Alt Posttal and leased out the 214 desjatina he bought in 1898 near Neu Arzis and the 500 desjatina he bought later farther north near Bender. Kroll's son, also named Christian, bought the 791-desjatina Orak estate in the Kahul district of southwestern Bessarabia in 1910, and in 1911 bought the 1,449-desjatina Gretscheni estate, also located in the Kahul district. The latter he seems to have leased or used as grazing land rather than developing it himself (Kern, *Homeland Book*, 96).

69. Ibid., 95.

70. Ibid., 105, 96.

In the period before World War I, a few Germans in Bessarabia had acquired sufficient wealth to set themselves apart from the village communities on separate family estates. Such actions were not just a display of wealth but also served to mark a social distinction. It is tempting to see these family estates as recreations of the social patterns the Germans remembered from Prussia and Württemberg, where the nobility lived on estates separate from the peasant villages. The estate owners may have seen themselves becoming a new nobility among the Germans in Bessarabia. This thought is underlined by the fact that on several of the estates, the owners leased land to other Germans, such as in Demir Chadschi and the Kroll estate. In any case, the emergence of single-family estates in Bessarabia signals the existence of new economic and social distinctions. It is a sign that the general egalitarianism of the early days of the German colonies had passed and a wide range of social levels was now emerging.

## The period from 1870 to the start of World War I was one of positive economic growth for most Germans in Bessarabia

The Germans in Bessarabia were able to make significant increases in their land-holdings in the period before the start of World War I, because as a group, they benefited from several positive economic factors. Despite growing competition from North America, the amount of grain sales to Western Europe continued to increase in this period even though such competition brought down prices. The demand for grain in Western Europe was pushed by the continued growth in urban popula-tion as the Industrial Revolution, which had already transformed Britain, wrought similar changes in France, the Low Countries, and Germany. Economic growth in the German villages in Bessarabia was also helped by improvements in local infra-structure and the adoption of new and better technology. In 1877, a rail line was completed that connected Reni, at the junction of the Prut and Danube Rivers, with Bender on the Dniester. A rail bridge at Bender connected this rail line with another that ran north from Odessa to Kiev and thus to major centers in Imperial Russia. A major station along the Reni–Bender line was a station just north of Leipzig around which the multiethnic village of Romanowka developed.[71] Instead of selling grain to merchants who visited the different German villages, or attempting the multiday, sometimes dangerous, cart trek to Odessa, Bessarabian German growers now carted their grain to Romanowka and sold it there to agents of the Odessa merchants. Doing so brought better prices than had been offered by the middlemen who had earlier traveled among the different German villages or set up temporary stalls in the market towns of Tarutino, Arzis, and Sarata.

Farmers continued to suffer from the cruel whims of nature. Crop losses and even total crop failures occasionally occurred. Tarutino reported failed harvests from 1891, 1892, 1899, and 1905. The year 1905 was so bad that Kern reports that care packages were sent from Germany and North America to help the town.[72] The year

---

71. There was a second rail station on the Reni–Bender line within reach of the Bessarabian Germans, the Kulm ("Kulmskaja") station located across the ridge line perhaps 6–7 km west of Kulm. This station served several Bulgarian villages in the valley of the Lunga River and its tributaries and was popular with the Germans after 1918. Until 1914, the Leipzig ("Leipcigskaja") station was far and away the major railway transport point for German Bessarabia.

72. Kern, *Homeland Book*, 192. I have found no reports of grain troubles from Alt Posttal or Kulm, both neighboring Tarutino, from the 1890s or 1905.

1899 appears to have been particularly troublesome as Balaktschelly, Basyrjamka, and Beresina each noted failed harvests then.[73] Eigenheim reported failed harvests in 1884 and 1892. Many of the older villages, such as Klöstitz, Kulm, and Tarutino, had built grain storage facilities against such eventualities. In years following bad harvests, such storage facilities eased the pain of reduced food supplies or even prevented catastrophe when shortages were great. During the period from 1870 to 1914, reports of poor or failed harvests, however, were few. Instead, plentiful harvests were responsible for grain sales becoming a significant economic underpinning of Bessarabian German economic strength.

The increased yields of Bessarabian German harvests were the result of over a half-century's familiarity with the Budjak climate including seed stock that performed well and a better understanding of soil types, planting times, and pest control. Glenn Kuehn has argued that familiarity with the winter hard wheat variety Krimka, called in North America Turkey Red after it was brought and used by Germans from Russia, was a critical factor in producing a high-yielding, much-desired wheat for export in Bessarabia.[74] With only limited data on wheat grown by Germans in Bessarabia, it is not possible to draw firm conclusions or stress connections to particular seed stock or grain selections. It is interesting to note that the data on grain planted in the Sarata Volost from 1880 and 1890 that Malinovskij provides, described in the following pages, indicates that spring wheat, likely Arnaut, continued to be the dominant grain sewn with winter wheat growing in popularity.

Another major factor for the period after 1870, though, was increased mechanization, which both reduced the amount of required physical labor and increased yields. Kuehn notes the appearance in Russia of horse-drawn reapers in the 1850s and reaper-binders in the late 1860s.[75] By 1876, Gnadental had an automated mowing machine. The prevalence of such mowing machines among the Germans in Russia has been treated as sign of their relative prosperity in comparison to neighboring Bulgarian and Russian farmers. Detlev Brandes notes an 1889 study from the Berdjansk District in the Tauride Province of South Russia that found there was one mowing machine for every two German farmers in comparison to just one for every seven Bulgarian farmers and one for every twenty Russian farmers.[76] During the later nineteenth century, Karl Gutsche of Dennewitz created and sold threshing machines that replaced the flail in separating the harvested wheat from its shells. Farmers could now process up to 130 kilograms of wheat a day with reduced loss of grain. Kern reports that large farms had two or even three of these machines.[77] Steam threshing machines started to replace these machines in the years immediately preceding World War I. Kaschpalat, founded in 1912 and clearly a wealthy

73. Rudolf Weiss, "Wichtige Ereignisse aus der Geschichte der Bessarabiendeutschen" (N.p.: Bessarabiendeutscher Verein, 1949), http://www.bessarabien.de/geschichte.php. Originally published in *Kalender 1949: Jahrbuch der Deutschen aus Bessarabien und der Dobrudscha* (Hannover, Ger.: Hilfskomitee der ev.-luth. Kirche aus Bessarabien, 1949). The calendar listing of major events in German Bessarabia collected by the Bessarabiendeutscher Verein notes 1899 as the "Großes Hungerjahr," the great year of hunger. Malinovskij, however, concludes that the intermittent years of famine when crops failed and the transport system failed to bring grain to the affected areas, creating great hardship in central Russia and to some degree South Russia, was not an issue in Bessarabia (Malinovskij, *Social'naja i xozjajstvennaja istorija*, 145).

74. Kuehn, "Hard-Kernelled Red Winter Wheat," 11–13.

75. Ibid., 12.

76. Brandes, "A Success Story."

77. Kern, *Homeland Book*, 55.

settlement, is reported to have had in operation "four steam threshers soon after its founding."[78] Improved plows, better tools and techniques, and mechanization all helped to increase yields. Lichtental reported a record harvest of 150 pud (about 2,457 kilograms) per desjatina.[79] Krasna achieved record harvests in 1906 and then again in 1910.

Malinovskij has provided data that offers an idea of the earning potential of different grains grown by Germans in South Russia and Bessarabia in the period from 1880 to 1895. One data set he quotes is for the Sarata Volost, showing the number of desjatina sewn with different grains in 1880 and 1890. Matching these general figures with a second data set showing average yields in the region per desjatina in pud and prices paid per pud, both from 1895, gives an idea of the earnings potential for the volost (see table 11–13).[80] It is a rough idea, of course, given that the prices and earnings are for the general area of South Russia and Bessarabia rather than Sarata, and are for 1895 rather than for 1880 or 1890.

Given the limited focus of these data, one cannot push them too far. The information does suggest, at least, that average grain yields in these years were such that farmsteads planting 20 to 40 desjatina could expect reasonable surplus earnings. It would appear that farmers assigned different importance over time to different grains, planting varying amounts from year to year, quite possibly showing sensitivities to price changes. The data Malinovskij provides, however, is too narrow in terms of the years covered and too broad in terms of the areas considered to draw conclusions about general trends in the region or specific ones about Bessarabia. Malinovskij does highlight, for the Moločna, Xortica, Orlov, and Kronau areas, the

TABLE 11–13. Data on grain sewn in Sarata Volost in 1880 and 1890, average yields and prices in 1895 across Bessarabia and South Russia, and the potential value for Sarata Volost crops of 1890

| | Sarata Volost | | South Russia and Bessarabia, 1985 | | | Sarata Volost, 1890 |
| --- | --- | --- | --- | --- | --- | --- |
| | Des. sewn, 1880 | Des. sewn, 1890 | Yield/des. | Price/pud | Earnings/ des. | Potential value[a] |
| Spring wheat | 2,491 | 2,246 | 34.3 | 0.65 | 22.30 | 50,074.57 |
| Winter wheat | 228 | 1,108 | 54.4 | 0.65 | 35.36 | 39,178.88 |
| Rye | — | 245 | 49.9 | 0.50 | 24.95 | 6,112.75 |
| Oats | 686 | 370 | 32.5 | 0.50 | 16.25 | 6,012.50 |
| Barley | 1,144 | 1,761 | 55.2 | 0.50 | 27060 | 48,603.60 |
| Corn (maize) | 53 | 1,134 | 60.7 | 0.50 | 30.35 | 34,416.90 |
| Flax | 213 | 82 | 15.3 | 1.00 | 15.30 | 1,254.60 |

a. This column speculatively shows the potential total value in rubles for the whole Sarata Volost from the sales of different grains by applying the number of desjatina sewn in 1890 in the Sarata Volost against the generalized South Russian and Bessarabian 1895 figures for yields and prices per desjatina for those grains. The values are speculative both because of the mismatch in years between the amounts sewn and the yields and prices and because they assume the cash potential for selling the total yield.

78. Ibid., 89. The wealth of Kaschpalat's founders is certainly implied by the fact that in the year of its founding, four settler families were able to afford the purchase of 200 additional desjatina of land at the high price of 408 rubles a desjatina.

79. Ibid., 182. A pud is equal to 16.381 kg or 36.11 lbs.

80. Data on the grains planted in the Sarata Volost are from Table 59 in Malinovskij (*Social'naja i xozjajstvennaja istorija*, 132), and the information on yields per desjatina in pud and prices per pud are from Table 61 and Table 60 (134). Malinovskij's sources are articles published in the *Odessaer Zeitung* from 1880, 1890, and 1895.

increased interest in winter wheat starting in the 1880s, which the data from the Sarata Volost and Kuehn's arguments would seem to support.

In pursuing profit in agriculture, Germans in Bessarabia also started to look to crops other than wheat. By the first decade of the twentieth century, oil-bearing plants—linseed, canola, soy, and castor—were profitably grown and sold by the Germans. In many of the large villages, oil presses had been built to process these crops. Kern notes that in Gnadenfeld, and thus perhaps elsewhere, a three-field method was widely used: Year 1: corn, castor, and soy beans; Year 2: winter and summer wheat; and Year 3: oats, barley, and flax.[81]

Vineyards, a success in German Bessarabia from the early days of the colonies, continued after 1870 to be a focus of many German farmers. Wine, as a Paris history notes, was frequently sold and consumed locally,[82] but some villages shipped wine to Odessa where it was blended with other varieties produced in South Russia and sold in great bulk as Bessarabian or Moldavian country wine. Hugo Häfner reports that at the weekly Arzis market, there were plenty of small wine "bars" selling home-produced wine for 70 kopecks to a ruble for a 12-liter bucket.[83] No doubt similar sales took place at the markets in Tarutino, Sarata, and at the Leipzig railway station. Vineyards and wine production were important parts of the village economies in Brienne, Eigenheim, Gnadenfeld, Gnadental, Klöstitz, Teplitz, and Tarutino and were the predominant focus of all agricultural work in Schabo and Schabo-Possad. Kern notes that in Gnadental in 1900, 625,000 liters of wine were produced; Häfner notes that the daily shipments of wine out of Schabo in autumn were in the neighborhood of 100,000 liters.[84] Wine producer interests in German Bessarabia varied at this time. Many producers apparently focused on large volumes without much attention to quality. Some producers, particularly in Schabo, were focused instead on raising the quality and reputation, and thus the price of the wine they sold. In efforts to further the abilities of German wine producers in Bessarabia, a wine growing association was created in Gnadental in 1891. About this time, the Akkerman Zemstvo, with an eye on the economic advantages of wine production, established courses on wine production in Akkerman, Seimeny, and Tarutino. However, wine production in Bessarabia suffered a significant setback when the vine louse, phylloxera, appeared and spread in the period after 1890, killing many vines.[85] Grape vines were saved or restarted by grafting grape rootstock from plants resistant to the phylloxera that came ultimately from North America. Häfner reports that to foster this restart, Teplitz natives Johannes Kämmler and Immanuel Wagner in

---

81. Kern, *Homeland Book*, 101–2.

82. "Paris," Bessarabiendeutscher Verein, modified October 10, 2014, http://www.bessarabien.de/upload/paris_1816.pdf, 3.

83. Häfner, "Wine Growing," 11–12.

84. Kern, *Homeland Book*, 108; and Häfner, "Wine Growing," 19. Häfner here also notes that Schabo and likely other German villages in Bessarabia had a profitable trade in edible grapes much in demand in the Odessa market.

85. Kern, *Homeland Book*, 94. Kern mentions that the phylloxera louse appeared in Teplitz in 1890 and destroyed 112 desjatina of the vineyard. Brandes quotes the complaint of a Sarata grower after his vineyards were destroyed that where once there were thousands of buckets of wine produced, for several years no wine from one's own vineyards could be consumed: "Nach einigen Jahren konnte man in Sarata, das jährlich Zehntausende von Eimern produzierte, kein Gläschen Wein vom eigenen Gewächs mehr trinken" (*Von den Zaren Adoptiert*, 179).

1905–6 "ordered 30,000 grape plants from Avignon in France" and sold these at 1 kopeck a piece.[86]

Another very important part of the agricultural economy in German Bessarabia was stock breeding. As noted earlier, cattle, horses, sheep, and their products had been important sources of income from the first days of the German colonies. Stock breeding efforts were often successful as the steppe grasslands were ideal places for stock raising. The German farm economy in Bessarabia was greatly influenced by the introduction of new breeds of livestock during the period from 1870 to 1914.

Kern reports in his account of Lichtental that after 1870, cattle raised primarily for their meat were replaced by a different kind of cattle bred with increased milk production in mind. He notes that the "white-blue steppe cow" became less popular and was generally replaced in herds by the "red cow of Molotschna."[87] This latter was a crossbreed developed by the Mennonite farmers in the Moločna District of the Tauride Province of South Russia from Hereford cattle. The growing interest in developing cattle for milk led to other changes such as the effort to grow clover as feed, as Kern notes when he described a similar switch in Gnadental from the meat-producing "blue steppe cow" to what he calls the "Angus" bred for milk production.[88] In his discussion of Brienne, Kern dates this change away from "steppe cattle" to the turn of the century and also mentions it in his discussions of Basyrjamka and Friedenstal.[89] As milk and its products started to become a commodity, family farm dairy production began to be replaced by larger enterprises. The Kulm Heimatbuch reports that in 1907, a Russian established a dairy organization "throughout southern Russia" based on local independent processors who would buy milk and then turn the milk into butter and cheese and ship these to Odessa.[90] In 1909, Borodino established a farmer's cooperative that included a dairy; another cooperative dairy appears to have been established in Gnadenfeld before 1914. Such cooperatives, more frequently organized after World War I, were favored as they raised the earnings farmers received for milk by absorbing the business and profits of middlemen who heretofore bought directly from farmers and processed milk in small batches themselves.

Raising horses for sale was another area of economic specialization adopted by Germans in Bessarabia from the time of their first settlements there. As with cattle,

---

86. Häfner, "Wine Growing," 14. Häfner quotes from his Teplitz grandfather Stephan's book on wine production that urges planting "vineyards anew on a proven American hybrid varieties basis." Kämmeler's and Wagner's plants from France would have been grafts that also had a North American origin. The French were reselling grafts from America which had been successful in combating the phylloxera outbreak there. Häfner also offers a listing of the grape varieties preferred by Bessarabian German vintners before the phylloxera outbreak (11–12) and those after (13–14). Included in this article is a listing of white and "blue" grape varieties grown for wine in Bessarabia as well as table grape varieties grown in Bessarabia.

87. Kern, *Homeland Book*, 182–83.

88. Ibid., 107.

89. Ibid., 84. In his discussion of Basyrjamka, Kern notes the importation of "red Angus bulls from Holstein" to create a valuable milk producing cow (165), and in the section on Friedenstal, he notes that "the meat producing steppe cattle" were replaced by dairy cattle (85). Discussing Gnadenfeld, Kern notes that the community "experimented with several cattle breeds until the black and white cow (Holstein) was chosen" (102).

90. E. Selcho, "Craftsmen and Craft Occupations" in "Heimatbuch der Gemeinde Kulm," *Heritage Review* 14, no. 2 (1984): 21. The "dairy" that processed the milk it bought required only "a fireplace to warm the milk, a hand-operated cream separator, a hand-operated butter churn, cans and other containers."

after 1870 new breeds of horses became popular for their increased local utility and thus economic potential. Kern mentions in his discussions of Eichendorf and Friedenstal a growing focus on a horse that combined a mixture of Arabian and Orlov genes. He describes this horse attractively as "a light fast colonist horse," one "capable of traveling 80 kilometers in 6–7 hours."[91] The black Nonius was another new breed brought to German Bessarabia toward the end of the nineteenth century.[92] Developed originally as a draft horse for military use, the Nonius was stronger and hardier than the small, locally bred Moldavian horses that had been predominant among the Bessarabian Germans. Horses were a major item sought by buyers at the weekly markets at Arzis, Sarata, and Tarutino. In his account of Arzis, Kern notes that interest in the horses for sale at its market was quite widespread. Buyers came from the Russian province of Volhynia to the north, as well as from Romania and Bulgaria.[93]

The karakul sheep was yet another specialized breed of animal whose economic potential attracted a good deal of interest among Germans in Bessarabia after 1870.[94] The villages of Basyrjamka, Borodino, Eichendorf, Friedensfeld, Gnadenfeld, Kulm, and Neu Nikolajewka were noted for raising karakuls. Kulm employed shepherds who specialized in working just with the karakuls. The thick wool from these sheep was used extensively in the production of carpeting and other heavy fabric materials such as blankets, felting, and hats. For the most part, it would seem that the Bessarabian Germans sold their karakul wool to middlemen who supplied factories elsewhere in Russia. While there were several wool and dye factories established before 1914 in Bessarabia, particularly in Tarutino, these did not specialize in working with the karakul wool, which is difficult to process.

Even though farming and stock breeding dominated the economic activities of Germans in Bessarabia before 1914, most of the original settlements and even some of the larger, new villages, such as Mannsburg, Neu Posttal, and Eigenheim, had citizens whose livelihood depended on commerce and trade. Such individuals were different from those who, both before and after 1870, supplemented their farming income with craftwork such as blacksmithing, carpentry, cabinetmaking, shoemaking, coopering, harness making, and tailoring, in that they fully lived off the income of their trades. The milling of grain is a good example. All of the larger villages, both old and new, had mills to grind grain into flour. Where the movement to oil crops had started, commercial presses were built to process them. In Alt Posttal, and so likely in other villages, mills that had been powered by horses and wind before 1860 were at the end of the century powered by steam and some by motor. The Schock Brothers built a huge mill outside of Leipzig, taking advantage of the rail station; Klöstitz had a motorized mill and two oil mills. The Kulm Heimatbuch reports that before 1909, a Leipzig man created the first steam-powered mill.[95]

---

91. Kern, *Homeland Book*, 48, 85. The Orlov was a horse developed by A. G. Orlov from Voronezh Province of Russia by crossing Dutch, Danish, English, and Mecklenburg breeds with Arabians.

92. The Nonius (or Noniusz) was developed at the Austro-Hungarian Imperial stud farm at Mezohegyes, Hungary.

93. Kern, *Homeland Book*, 81.

94. Karakul (sometimes spelt "caracul" in English) sheep have an ancient lineage: their existence is attested from before 1000 BCE. The name is evidently based on that of a town, Qaraqul, in the valley of the Amu Darja River, which is part of current Uzbekistan.

95. Selcho, "Craftsmen and Craft Occupations," 22.

In the older and larger villages, some light manufacturing started to appear after 1870. In a few villages, the interlocking craft skills that had once supplemented farming became so well-developed that the village became a craft center, where trade supported full-time, independent producers of a similar product. Such were the wagon-building craftsmen of Teplitz, Wittenberg, and Alt Posttal. Kern asserts that the unpainted Teplitz wagons were well-known both inside Bessarabia and beyond.[96] Alt Posttal had fifty-six blacksmiths specializing in wagon work, as well as eighty-three wheelwrights. Wittenberg had thirty-three blacksmiths producing wagons that Kern suggests enjoyed a more limited renown than the wagons of Teplitz, being well sold "especially in Bulgarian villages."[97] The picture Kern paints of the wagon trade is not one of a contemporary industrial enterprise: a single organization emphasizing cost efficiencies that produced predesigned wagons from the same machinery. It is rather an older picture of many skilled, independent, but loosely connected craftsmen—blacksmiths, wheelwrights, and joiners—who created similar high-quality but not identical products.

Population increase, with its attendant issues of land usage and land sufficiency, was an impetus to the growth of such craft industries. One example is provided by the special trades involved with wagon construction. German wagons had won a solid reputation in Bessarabia. There was a demand for them not just in the German villages, but also in the surrounding Moldavian, Russian, Ukrainian, Bulgarian, and Gaugaz villages, and in some cases, beyond the local Budjak region as well. This created steady employment in Teplitz, Alt Posttal, and Wittenberg, maintained village prosperity, and allowed sons to remain in their native villages. The wagon building crafts in these three villages, however, did have some negative health consequences. Because these crafts kept men working closely together in poorly ventilated shops filled with soot and dust, respiratory ailments were common, and all three villages had major problems with tuberculosis.[98]

Other villages specialized in different crafts. Here too the pattern of individual producers working separately and competing against each other had the effect of raising standards of quality to make the village products desirable and so create profitable, steady employment. In Paris, the specialty was making wooden pitchforks from ash, black locust, or acacia, which were "boiled, bent, and hardened with fire."[99] This may well have been only a winter occupation supplementing income from farming; Kern notes, for example, that "money lenders advanced the craftsmen enough money to purchase the materials so they could work during the winter

96. Kern notes that "the villagers of Teplitz were famous from the Prut River to west Siberia, where their 'made in Teplitz' wagons were used" (*Homeland Book*, 93). After purchase, it was evidently common for Germans in Bessarabia to paint their wagons a "traditional" green.
97. Ibid., 66. There were two Bulgarian colonies quite near Wittenberg: Tvardica about 5 km north and Kiriet Lunga (identified by Kern as "Ceader-Lunga") about 7 km north, where Kern notes that "Wittenbergers controlled the entire market."
98. Ibid., 64, 95.
99. Ibid., 60. He is quoting here Paris native R. Weiss. The history of Paris proudly notes the importance of the pitchforks to the Paris village economy and that they were known and valued even outside Bessarabia: "Weit über die Grenzen Bessarabiens waren die 'Pariser Gabeln' bekannt und beliebt" [The Paris pitchforks were known and popular far beyond the borders of Bessarabia] ("Paris," Bessarabiendeutscher Verein).

months."[100] In Borodino and especially Klöstitz, villagers specialized in making pottery that would be sold in the weekly markets of Tarutino, Sarata and Arzis. This was presumably a full-time occupation for some. In listing village trade occupations, Kern mentions that Borodino had three potters and Klöstitz eight.[101] In Klöstitz, the skills developed in making pottery led from individual craftsmanship to the development of manufacturing concerns that made stove, oven, and roof tiles. Roof tile manufacturing had also begun in Mannsburg and Lichtental before World War I, and small factories producing tiles for stoves, as well as roofs, were established in Sarata, Tarutino, and Arzis. Brick factories were established in Hoffnungstal in 1909 and Basyrjamka before 1914.

Small concentrations of manufacturing concerns began to develop in the German market towns of Arzis, Sarata and Tarutino. The weekly markets brought in cash and created many opportunities for small commercial businesses such as arranging loans and credit for warehousing, stabling, and transportation. The Tarutino market and likely those in Arzis and Sarata operated from 7:00 AM to noon for sales by individuals to other individuals and after noon for larger transactions made between factors, dealers, and those making wholesale purchases.

The public markets also created the infrastructure needed to establish viable manufacturing concerns: credit, customers, and transportation. In 1860, Karl Isert established a fulling and dying factory in Tarutino.[102] Five years later, Leopold Steinke had established a woolen cloth factory in Tarutino that in the 1880s was noted for its spinning facilities.[103] Steinke, born in the German villages around Warsaw, came to Tarutino after 1863 from Plotzk, where he had been the village secretary.[104] Steinke's move to Tarutino attests to the fact that the Tarutino community was now willing and likely interested in accepting new people who would start new ventures;[105] Steinke's choice of Tarutino attests to his positive view of the commercial opportunities there. Other wool and dye facilities were created later in Tarutino by August Erdmann and the Scherible brothers. Adolf Steinke, possibly a relative of Leopold, established a cloth spinning factory in Sarata, which in 1886 had five spinning machines, a loom, and two to six other workers and made cotton yarn.[106] Teplitz also had a cloth factory. It was founded in 1895 by Rudolf Jesse, who

100. Kern, *Homeland Book*, 60. Kern's emphasis on the need for short-term loans to buy the wood and other materials suggests that the craftsmen may be poor or even landless and so without the funds themselves.

101. Ibid., 124, 130. Kern may be referring here to craftwork in the 1930s, but it is clear that there were potters working in Klöstitz before World War I.

102. Brandes, *Von den Zaren Adoptiert*, 272, note 4. Brandes reports that the Isert brothers also established a cloth fulling factory in the Akkerman region, though as Tarutino was in the Akkerman region this may refer to the Tarutino factory. The Iserts were evidently relations of Daniel Isert, who sought to establish a small cloth factory in Tarutino in 1845. Daniel Isert moved to Tatarbunar, as he apparently found Tarutino unwelcoming (Kern, *Homeland Book*, 188).

103. Brandes (*Von den Zaren Adoptiert*, 272, note 4) and Kern (*Homeland Book*, 192) date this factory to 1865, though Brandes in his text (*Von den Zaren Adoptiert*, 272) dates the Leopold Steinke factory to 1886.

104. Steinke's residence in Plotzk and his position as the village "Schreiber" are attested from the church data registering the birth of his son Karl Adolph of November 18, 1863 (O.S.). Steinke was married to Pauline Isert and so was connected to the Isert clothworking family.

105. This was not always so. Mutschall has noted that at first Taurutino did not welcome outsiders. Mutschall, "Community of Tarutino," *Heritage Review* 44, no. 3: 24.

106. Brandes, *Von den Zaren Adoptiert*, 272.

came there from Dunaevcy in Russian Podol'e, north of Bessarabia. Brandes reports that the factory was still operating in 1934.[107]

Another major focus of light industry in Bessarabia was the manufacture of agricultural tools and machinery. In 1846, Samuel Meske established a locksmith-metalworking business in Alt Arzis, which he grew into a foundry that produced plows and other agricultural tools.[108] Kern reports that there were several factories specializing in agricultural machinery in Sarata, one established by Karl Layher in 1884 and others established by Friedrich Lütze, Jacob Steib, and Emanuel, Rudolf, and Eduard Heer.[109] Layher's career, like that of Leopold Steinke noted above, indicates that enterprising individuals could move not just to newly formed daughter settlements that focused on agriculture, but also to the largest of the mother colonies and focus their energies on commerce and manufacturing. Brandes notes that Layher, a native of Lichtental, made his initial capital as an innkeeper in Akkerman, and then used that capital to build a steam-driven mill with partners in 1880. Layher bought out his partners in 1883 and by 1886 had earned enough to buy an estate.[110] The most important agricultural implements manufacturer in prewar Bessarabia appears to have been the Hobbacher factory in Sarata, established in 1901, which Brandes indicates was producing two-thirds of the agricultural implements sold in Bessarabia with annual sales of 212,000 rubles.[111]

Malinovskij, speaking of South Russia and Bessarabia in general, notes that in the 1870s, many of the agricultural machines in use were foreign made. Over the course of the remainder of the nineteenth century, there was a major switch to implements made in Russia, often by companies run by Russian Germans.[112] Brandes calls particular attention to the Höhn factory in Odessa, founded by Karl Höhn, who moved the family foundry there from Hoffnungstal in German Bessarabia in 1866. In 1912, the Höhn factory produced eighty thousand plows, thirty thousand harrows, six thousand mowing machines, and three thousand seed-planting drill machines. The Höhn factory was noted for its plows, like the "Kolonistenpflug" and "Neurußischenpflug," whose names (the colonist plow, the new Russian plow) suggest that they were designed for and so beneficial for use by the German settlers in New Russia, that is, South Russia. Josef Meske, who continued his father's foundry business in Alt Arzis, produced a plough that sought to improve on the Höhn ploughs.[113] Malinovskij saw the German settlements in South Russia and Bessarabia as the leaders in introducing new and more efficient technology to the region. They were the first to use electrical power in mills and manufacturing facilities in 1895, diesel tractors in 1897, and steam-powered threshing machines in 1898.[114]

---

107. Ibid.
108. Kern, *Homeland Book*, 82.
109. Ibid., 186.
110. Brandes, *Von den Zaren Adoptiert*, 272. Brandes's information comes from Viktor Žukov's *Formirovanie i razvitie buržoazii i proletariat Bessarabii: 1812-1900* [The creation and development of the Bessarabian bourgeoisie and proletariat: 1812-1900] (Kišinev: Štiinca, 1982). This is also Brandes's source for the information on the Isert brothers fulling mill noted above in footnote 111.
111. Ibid.
112. Malinovskij, *Social'naja i xozjajstvennaja istorija*, 151. Malinovskij identifies the popular foreign agricultural equipment producers as American, but the manufacturer he names, Hornby & Son, is actually a British company.
113. Brandes, *Von den Zaren Adoptiert*, 273, 272.
114. Malinovskij, *Social'naja i xozjajstvennaja istorija*, 151.

The creation of manufacturing and other businesses in Tarutino, Sarata, and Arzis brought more people with other backgrounds into these settlements, now large villages. Not only were non-Germans working in German-owned factories, but non-Germans owned and operated businesses in their own right. Malinovskij offers data from the Alt Arzis Volost of 1884 indicating such (see table 11–14).[115]

What is especially noteworthy here is that 39.1 percent of the forty-six businesses were owned by non-Germans. The mean ruble output of the German-owned businesses was lower than one might expect because the German businesses at this time were dominated by one large and spectacularly successful one. Georg Keck owned a steam-propelled mill employing six workers with an annual output of 100,000 rubles. He also owned a grocery with an annual output of 3,000 rubles and a wine business with annual sales of 250 rubles. Together, these three businesses accounted for 57 percent of the total commercial and industrial output of the town.[116]

Malinovskij presumes that non-Germans also lived and worked in Sarata. He notes that in 1878, Sarata had a wool-weaving business that used new, imported spinning machines driven by horse power. The two-story building also had five living accommodations for the workers. Malinovskij concluded from the "very modest" scale of the establishment that the "workers were people who had come to the town from elsewhere and were not colonists" ("rabočie prišlye, a ne kolonisty").[117] In this regard, Malinovskij may be beyond the support of his evidence. It is not clear from this comment that the workers were not German. Indeed, the modest accommodations at this Sarata business sound very much like those noted earlier that were placed on the second floor of village school buildings to accommodate Germans from elsewhere employed as teachers. It is clear, however, that craft, commercial, and trade work in some of the larger German settlements employed non-Germans. Brandes notes that Tarutino asked permission from the Welfare Committee to permit four Jewish families to build houses in the community in 1869.[118] Brandes has also noted that before World War I, there were 1,906 Jewish residents in Tarutino.[119] Given the growing number of Jews living in Tarutino, Mutschall indicates that "the community allowed the Jewish synagogue to have a lot…for the construction of an

TABLE 11–14. **Manufacturing businesses in the Arzis Volost in 1884**

| Nationality of owner | Number of businesses | Annual sales | Mean sales of one business |
|---|---|---|---|
| German | 28 | 127,700 rubles | 4,570 rubles |
| Jews | 10 | 43,900 rubles | 4,400 rubles |
| Bulgarian, Russian, and others | 8 | 8,900 rubles | 3,900 rubles |

115. Ibid., 155, Table 68. Malinovskij found this material in the state archives of the Moldavian SSR, before the breakup of the Soviet Union.
116. Ibid.
117. Ibid. By "ne kolonisty," Malinovskij means not German.
118. Brandes, *Von den Zaren Adoptiert*, 457. The Welfare Committee gave its blessing to this but asked that no more Jews be allowed to settle there in the future. With Tarutino's continued commercial growth, this restriction was overlooked, as is emphasized by the count of Jewish inhabitants in 1890s reported in the next sentence.
119. Ibid., 272.

elementary school."[120] Brandes comments that by 1890, Tarutino was "a lively small commercial town" with 230 businesses.[121]

Arzis built rental housing for its non-German residents and the lease earnings from these became another source of community income.[122] Kulm had non-Germans living and working in the community. The Kulm Heimatbuch reports Bulgarians working as farm hands and shepherds and on a skilled level, a Jewish butcher named Dudel, who lived in Beresina and would visit Kulm weekly in the period from 1885 to 1900 to sell lamb.[123] Though permitted to live in the German villages, non-Germans were not permitted to become citizens or to vote in community elections until after the reform of 1871 had been implemented.

Initially in Tarutino, nonnatives were not welcomed as residents. Mutschall reports the common attitude was that Tarutino should be for those from Tarutino.[124] There were Germans from other villages or elsewhere in Russia who were welcomed, such as the factory owners Karl Isert and Ludwig Steinke or the town secretary and lawyer Andreas Widmer, because, as Mutschall asserts, they brought special advantages. This implies that other nonnative Germans may not have been so welcomed. Over time, in the last decades of the nineteenth century, attitudes had much changed in Tarutino, and the town became more accepting: "One after another, Russians and Bulgarians, who had lived with farmers by renting…[now] purchased property lots with houses and gardens. …Once the way had been cleared by this precedent, Jews also followed."[125]

It was possible for non-Germans for to make purchases of property in Tarutino, but these were done, Mutschall notes, "without legal documents," and so these residents were not legal "members of the community." Yet, even this barrier was broken when, after Ludwig Briske's property became vacant through insolvency, a Russian merchant named Grebnikov was allowed to purchase it legally and become a member of the Tarutino community and even sell it later to the Sokolovs, "another Russian family."[126] Even those accepted in a semi-legal state of residency were harbored, protected, and helped. When the Russian government sought to limit the number of Jewish residents in towns by not permitting new Jewish residents after 1882, Tarutino sought successfully to get around the limitations and prevent the expulsion of some one hundred families.[127] Responding to a request from the provincial governor of Bessarabia, Tarutino also granted a lot for the building of a small Russian Orthodox Church. On its own, the town later granted additional land for the construction of an Orthodox school and for a parsonage for the attendant priest.[128]

Virtually all the German villages supported craftworkers—shoemakers, weavers, joiners, masons, smithies, and coopers—who mainly supported the needs of that village. As noted in the discussion of the 1858 census materials from Leipzig, it would appear that in some cases such craftwork had become a full-time occupation;

---

120. Mutschall, "Community of Tarutino," *Heritage Review* 45, no. 1: 25.
121. Brandes, *Von den Zaren Adoptiert*, 272.
122. Ibid., 82.
123. Selcho, "Craftsmen and Craft Occupations," 21.
124. Mutschall, "Community of Tarutino," *Heritage Review* 44, no. 3: 24.
125. Ibid.
126. Ibid.
127. Ibid., 21.
128. Ibid., 25–26.

in other cases it supplemented income from a family's farmstead. There is another look at this issue from data Malinovskij quotes from archival sources covering the Klöstitz Volost in 1884 (see table 11–15).[129]

This is unlikely to be the complete number of craft- and tradeworkers in the Klöstitz Volost in 1884. For those that Malinovskij does list, the profit margins are very healthy and the profit reported would sustain a family.

Non-German tradesmen were also frequently seen. When such tradesmen appear in Kern's descriptions of the different German villages, they are generally treated negatively. These tradesmen were middlemen, typically Russians or Jews, who had from the earliest days of the German colonies visited the settlements to buy animals and produce and sell manufactured goods. Kern's negative portraits overlook the fact that the middlemen offered convenience and assumed the risks that the goods they carried for sale would be wanted and could be sold at a profit. Instead, he is focused on the fact that the lower prices such middlemen offered when buying or the higher prices offered when selling were far less attractive than the prices Germans might have received in the larger market towns such as Reni, Bender, or Odessa. Kern's attitude no doubt reflects that of the farmers, his parishioners, who traditionally, and not just in German Russia, felt disadvantaged by the lack of choice that gave the middlemen an economic opportunity and advantage. Perhaps in his tone, there is also the suspicion of being taken advantage of by people not of one's tribe, people presumed thus to be inherently less trustworthy and sympathetic. In any case, the feeling that the prices middlemen offered to both buy and sell were disadvantageous led to the creation and expansion of cooperative stores in German Bessarabia during the first decade of the twentieth century. Owned by the community, these stores shared profits and sought to offer attractive prices. Hoffnungstal established a cooperative store in 1907, Eigenfeld created one in 1908, and as noted earlier, another was founded in Borodino in 1909 that included a dairy. While the concept of cooperative stores reached its peak in the period after 1918, the initiatives began before 1914 with the stores noted above, as well as with the additional cooperatives established in Kulm, Lichtental, and Sarata.

As with purchasing land for the new villages, ready access to capital formed a major help for Germans in Bessarabia seeking to establish and run manufacturing and commercial facilities. The wealthy settlements of Eigenfeld, Mannsburg, and Schabo were the first to establish banking businesses. The bank in Mannsburg was

TABLE 11–15. Earnings from craftwork in Klöstitz Volost, 1884

| Craft/Trade | Number built | Sales | Annual profit | Profit margin |
|---|---|---|---|---|
| Wagon builder | 40 | 720 rubles | 200 rubles | 27.8% |
| Wagon builder | 20 | 360 rubles | 80 rubles | 22.2% |
| Wagon builders (2) | 92 | 1,652 rubles | 368 rubles | 22.3% |
| Smithy | — | 1,300 rubles | 142 rubles | 10.9% |
| Tavern keeper | — | 2,000 rubles | 200 rubles | 10.0% |

129. Malinovskij, *Social'naja i xozjajstvennaja istorija*, 156. His data comes from the same fond and opis in the Moldavian SSR archives that contained the material from Alt Arzis in 1884 noted above in table 11–14.

founded in 1906, and the Credit Shareholder's Financial Institute was established in Schabo in 1911. Private credit, though, was also quite common in the period before 1914. Germans in Russia, as Detlev Brandes has observed, greatly benefited from the fact that they could rely on an "extreme solidarity in their social and economic life."[130] Brandes argues that the Germans, unlike many other ethnic groups in Imperial Russia, would vouch for each other's creditworthiness, which gave them expanded access to public and especially private credit, or access to such credit at better costs. Such credit was often costly, but it could be afforded. Germans in Bessarabia and South Russia, Brandes notes, might get credit "with an interest rate of 10% to 12%," when others might have to pay 24 percent.[131] In his discussion of the village of Kulm, Kern makes a similar point, though he quotes even higher interest rates: "The old-fashioned villagers kept their coins in a sack under their straw mattresses, but they charged 20–36% on their loans. The accessibility to money was important in Bessarabia, and the loan was well worth the interest."[132] Discussing the improved financial conditions in the settlement of Krasna, Kern adds that "many of the grain farmers prospered, and there was always money available for loans."[133]

Manufacturing and commercial opportunities grew in the German Bessarabian settlements in response to the abilities of these communities to develop their agricultural and livestock-based economies into successful, cash-rich positions. The continued population growth also provided a labor pool of people not able to start farmsteads in the new villages, who might staff manufacturing and commercial businesses. Wealth tended to be concentrated in the older mother colonies. These towns had produced sufficient wealth to support both the explosion of new settlements in Bessarabia, as well as the large emigration out of Bessarabia and for all that, continued to do well. However, the original colonies weren't the only German settlements doing well. Some of the new villages like Eigenfeld, Mannsburg, and Neu Posttal had also developed beyond their agricultural base to become manufacturing and commercial centers rivaling the older towns. Others among the new villages, like Benkendorf, Halle, and Pomasan, were wealthy but remained totally focused on agriculture and raising stock. The wealthiest individuals, such as the Schultz, Gerstenberger, and Kroll families, bought large estates and remained focused on agriculture and livestock, having invested their capital in land. Nonetheless, because the older, larger settlements, such as Tarutino, Sarata, Arzis, Leipzig, Beresina, and Teplitz, continued to excel in agriculture and livestock, it was here that the strongest manufacturing and commercial businesses were located, and as a result, here that the greatest concentration of wealth occurred.

## Making an economic success from farming required people to master many different skills

The agricultural year was filled with a long series of tasks. Many were specialized and demanded that the farmer master different and special skills. Farmers were less likely to focus on growing a single crop, as is more common today. Rather, they tended to keep several economic irons in the fire and so grew and worked with many different

---

130. Brandes, "A Success Story," 272.
131. Ibid.
132. Kern, *Homeland Book*, 136.
133. Ibid., 200.

crops for sale and home use. If one was to be successful, such a strategy increased both the labor requirements and the number of skills that needed to be mastered.

In thinking about how Bessarabian German farmers established a region of general economic prosperity, it is important to remember just how many balls they were keeping in the air. Rudolf Hofer places us well in this world with the calendar of work he describes in his account of life in Hoffnungstal, Bessarabia. The picture he paints is from the 1920s and 1930s, but it could well be from the 1880s.

> *In the spring before the field work began, all the plows and machinery had to be checked over and fixed if broke. The wheels on the wagons had to be checked over and oiled. The farmer was always ready but he had to depend on the weather for seeding to start.*

> *Seeding usually started in March if the earth was free of frost and the ground was dry. Oats were sowed first, then barley, corn, soybeans and sunflower seeds. The crops were rotated each year. By the end of April all the crops were seeded. In addition watermelons and pumpkins were planted. The grape plants for the Vineyard were in need of spring care as the branches had to be trimmed. Men from the neighboring non-German villages came to shear the sheep. After lambing time the sheep went out to the pasture and stayed there during the summer. The shepherd was usually a non-German. The cows were gathered after milking time in the morning during the summer months and taken to the pasture. They returned each evening.*

> *Each spring it was time to trap and drown the 'Erdhase' a type of gopher or jumping mouse. The creature would eat the grain both above and below ground. It was a mandatory order set by the Village Elders to catch a certain amount of these varmints.*

> *Next came the processing of the manure. It was removed from the barn stalls and moved to the threshing area where it was packed down every other day with a rolling stone until it was 6–8 cm high. Then it was cut with a spade into…30 x 30 cm squares. The squares were placed in rows for drying by air and sun. After 10 days the squares were packed in pyramids for the final drying. [They were] then placed in a shed and used as fuel to heat the houses during the winter….*

> *Next was the haying time. This was the middle of June until the middle of July.*

> *This was also the time for the first grain to be harvested. First came the winter wheat, then barley, oats and summer wheat. The grain was cut by a horse drawn machine. It was then raked by the farmer into piles for drying, then in an extended wagon hauled home for threshing. The grain was unloaded at the threshing floor and spread out with pitch forks. A pair of horses would then pull a heavy cement stone that would tear and loosen the kernels from the straw. The stones were followed by a sled which had studded sharp metal knives. This would cut the straw into smaller pieces which was used for fodder for the animals. The other straw had to be turned*

*several times by hand. It was then removed and stacked for bedding for the animals. The grain was pushed into a pile and cleaned by hand turned machine called a 'putzmukle'.…*

*Fall left still much to be done. Potatoes, vegetables and fruit were planted for the farmers own use, not to be sold. Then it was time for the sunflowers. They were harvested, the heads were beaten with a stick in order to release the kernels or seeds. This was a family task and usually done in the evening.*

*The grapes were harvested in September and October. We ate all we could and then the rest would be pressed and made into wine. This was stored in the cellar, along with the barrel of sauerkraut and pickles which was also packed in barrels.*

*In the middle of September, winter wheat was planted if the ground was ready. Corn was harvested in mid October. It had to be picked by hand and taken home by wagon. Stripping off the leaves of the corn was always done in the evening in a get together with neighbors and friends. The leaves were used as filler for our mattresses called 'strocksuck'. This is what we slept on. An alternative for the corn leaves was straw for mattresses. The fall plowing continued until the frost came.*[134]

## The wealth built up in the older German settlements in Bessarabia is reflected in the major and costly civic projects they undertook during the period from 1870 to 1914

Civic building projects were major accomplishments of the villages (see table 11–16). Their completion reflected the ability of the settlement to agree on the need and benefits, to save the funds that sometimes came from citizens volunteering their labor for money-earning activities, and then often to use their own collective labor to do the work required to construct the building or facility. On completion, the civic projects reflected not just the common will, patience, and determination of the community, but its collective wealth.

In 1914, Tarutino, then perhaps the largest and the wealthiest of the German settlements, reported having civic assets of 475,800 rubles and an annual civic income of 43,139 rubles.[135] By the same year, Brienne had collected 32,000 rubles that it intended to use to build a larger church. In 1914, a major new improvement in infrastructure was completed in Bessarabia which offered the promise of increased economic growth via better access to the major Russian markets. A new railroad line was completed that linked Akkerman on the estuary of the Dniester with the existing Reni-to-Bender line. This new railroad line ran through or close to many German settlements, both old and new. The linkage between the two rail lines came at, and so expanded, the Leipzig station at Romanowka. Major stations on this new rail line were at Mannsburg, Sarata, Alt Arzis, and Beresina. However, the financial gains promised by this improved access to Russian markets were not realized. The fall of 1914 brought the start of World War I and extremely difficult times for Bessarabia.

---

134. Hofer, "Hoffnungstal Bessarabia."
135. Mutschall, "Community of Tarutino," *Heritage Review* 44, no. 3: 20.

**TABLE 11–16.** **Major civic projects in the mother colonies from 1870 to 1914**

| Year | Civic Project |
| --- | --- |
| 1870–72 | Beresina builds a new city hall |
| 1880 | Gnadental builds a new church at a cost of 25,000 rubles |
| 1882 | Tarutino builds a water supply system to serve the town at a cost of 34,630 rubles |
| 1886 | Plotzk builds a new prayer house |
| 1889–91 | Beresina builds a new church with seating for 750 |
| 1891 | Alt Arzis builds a new school |
| 1894 | Katzbach builds a new church seating 600 at a cost of 19,000 rubles |
| 1894–96 | Alt Elft builds a new church seating 800 |
| 1895 | Beresina builds a new school |
| 1895 | Kulm builds a new school |
| 1902 | Borodino remodels its church, increasing seating to 750 |
| 1902–4 | Lichtental builds a new church seating 960 at a cost of 31,920 |
| 1904 | Hoffnungstal builds a new church seating 700 at a cost of 15,500 rubles |
| 1904 | Lichtental builds a second school at a cost of 9,000 rubles |
| 1904 | Tarutino remodels the aqueduct at a cost of 34,630 rubles |
| 1904–6 | Paris builds a new church at a cost of 37,000 rubles |
| 1908 | Leipzig builds a new church seating 1,000 at a cost of 39,000 rubles |
| 1911 | Alt Posttal builds a new home for its teachers |
| 1911 | Tarutino builds a high school at a cost of 80,000 rubles |
| 1911 | New Elft remodels its church and adds an organ |

In 1918, the rail lines were in disarray, Bessarabia was absorbed by Romania, and the Soviet Union, in punishment, cut off rail connections with Russia.

## There were several positive consequences to the increased economic strength of pre–World War I German Bessarabia but there were also consequences that were negative or mixed

Though general prosperity in German Bessarabia was increasing during the period from 1870 to 1914, it is important to remember that this was accompanied by increased economic differentiation. For families that remained in the crowded older settlements, it became common at least by the 1890s for farmsteads to be divided up among children, making farmsteads smaller. More individuals and families also rented cottager lots offering just a house and small garden land. More families in the older villages, as noted earlier, needed to support themselves with craftwork or factory or business employment. There were thus richer and poorer families spread throughout the same village. Among the new farming villages too, and especially among the new villages on leased land, there were poorer families who struggled to get by. In Kern's description of the leased village of Jakobstal, he states that "there were quite a large number of lease communities which never rose from near poverty levels."[136] In addition to poor farmers, there were also poor farm workers. Interwoven in the different activity descriptions in the Kulm Heimatbuch, for example, are references to "hired men." Sometimes these were Germans, though mainly they were

---

136. Kern, *Homeland Book*, 103.

Bulgarians or Gaugaz. These were laborers who lived on the farmstead and helped in its many jobs.

Contemporary or near contemporary descriptions, such as those of Kern and Mutschall, however, do not give the impression that the gap between the richest and poorest in the towns was so huge as to create social or political tensions. A contributor to the Kulm Heimatbuch notes without commentary the existence of poorer houses within the village, just as another commentator notes that Kulm couldn't be compared economically or socially with such places as "Tarutino, Arzis, Sarata, Neu Posttal, Teplitz, etc."[137] The point made here are that differences worth noting existed, but that these were not so great as to divide the village or German Bessarabia into radically different or even hostile worlds. Such a view undercuts, at least for Bessarabia, a major thesis in Malinovskij's study. To Malinovskij, the period from 1860 to the start of World War I in German South Russia is marked by a sharp differentiation between a minority of wealthy farmers and a far greater majority of landless, exploited German farm workers. In Bessarabia, apart from the handful of estates, the major economic differentiation appears to have been that between farmers of different landholdings and, in the larger towns, between workers of different professions. There does not appear to have been a class of landless German farm hands of any material size. Similarly, in the limited data available, there are no reports of social or political conflicts generated by economic differences among the Germans.

In considering the general and growing prosperity of the German villages in Bessarabia, it is important also to remember that such improvements existed within a provincial world far from Europe's mainstream. The significant financial, organizational, and technological changes that were making deep impacts in Western Europe were slow in reaching distant places in provincial Russia such as Bessarabia. By the beginning of the twentieth century though, some pieces of the new life-altering technologies were appearing in German Bessarabia. The prosperous villages of Krasna and Romanowka are reported to have had steam-powered threshing machines by 1914, and Kulm had steam-driven grain and oil mills by 1914. Gasoline-powered, motorized mills were beginning to appear alongside steam-driven mills at this time. The Kulm Heimatbuch reports that in 1909 a telephone line was run to the village and a phone had been installed in the volost chancellery.[138] This would suggest the likelihood of a telephone connection at least to the Leipzig rail station and Tarutino. Factory owner Karl Layher of Sarata and the large estate owner Alfred Hoffmann, whose lands were just outside of Klöstitz, brought the first automobiles to German Bessarabia before the start of World War I. By at least 1912, Sarata had a motorized bus providing public transportation within the town.

The growing prosperity in many German villages in Bessarabia also provided a platform from which some Germans might make an impact in the social, economic, and political life of Russia outside of the German communities. Dr. August Läger of Alt Posttal finished high school in Akkerman and studied medicine in Moscow and St. Petersburg. He practiced medicine in Klöstitz, and after being called up in 1904 to serve in the army during the Russo-Japanese war, established a practice in the city

---

137.  Oskar Koch, "Contributions to the Homeland Book" in "Heimatbuch der Gemeinde Kulm," *Heritage Review* 14, no. 2 (1984): 25.
138.  Wölfle, "The Establishment of the Village of Kulm," 6.

of Ošmjany (now the Bielorussian Ašmjany).[139] Gottlieb Graumann of Kulm was
educated in Russia outside Bessarabia and became an officer in the Russian Army,
where he served in its engineering corps and by the time of World War I, rose to
the rank of colonel. Andreas Widmer of Wittenberg and Tarutino (1856–1931) was a
talented Bessarabian German who created a career in Russian politics. Widmer, born
and educated in Wittenberg, moved to Tarutino in 1873 to work as an assistant to
Karl Raugust, formerly the chief clerk of the Welfare Committee district office and
then chief town clerk of Tarutino. Widmer married Raugust's daughter and after
Raugust's death, succeeded him in his post. Tarutino by then had become a volost,
and Widmer became the volost clerk. Widmer, representing Tarutino, then became
a member of the Akkerman Zemstvo, the regional government to which most of
German Bessarabia belonged and served as a member of the regional land office.[140]
While initially the volost organizations in German Bessarabia might have made do
by holding meetings in German before Russian was mastered, zemstvo meetings
were always held in Russian. This implied that Widmer could speak, read, and write
a credible Russian. In 1903, Widmer was elected vice president of the Akkerman
Zemstvo, and in 1907, among other duties, he was put in charge of the prison in
Akkerman.

In 1906 and 1907, Widmer was elected as one of the delegates representing
Bessarabia in the first meetings of the all-Russian representative assembly, the
Duma. In response to massive public gatherings of protest, strikes by workers, and
even occasional mutinies in the Russian armed forces, Tsar Nicholas II agreed to
form a "consultative" national assembly. The government's hopes for a passive and
supportive assembly were not realized, and the short and stormy sessions of both
Duma meetings did not satisfy the government, the Duma representatives, or the
electorate. Widmer was one of four representatives to come from the German colonies in Russia.[141] In the Duma meetings, Widmer sided with the centrist Octobrist
Party,[142] which supported the reforming governments of Sergej Witte (1905–6) and
Pjotr Stolypin (1906–11). Breaking with those governments, Widmer did vote with
other Octobrists to protest both the banishment of striking railroad workers to
Siberia and other government measures they deemed extralegal.[143]

---

139. I rely here on the account in Mutschall, "Community of Tarutino," *Heritage Review* 45, no. 1: 22.
140. Mutschall, "Community of Tarutino," *Heritage Review* 44, no. 3: 21. Mutschall refers to the
land office as the *uprava*. Uprava, however, was in pre-1914 Russian terminology a general term
describing any government office having authority over some specific area. The specific office in
question, the land office, was the *zemskaja* uprava.
141. The other delegates from the German colonies were Jacob Dietz, "a lawyer and newspaper editor,"
Heinrich Schellhorn, "an owner of a printing firm" (both from the Volga region), and Johann
Münch, a teacher from the Liebenthal colonies in Xerson Province of South Russia (Giesinger,
*From Catherine to Khrushchev*, 241; and Malinovskij, *Social'naja i xozjajstvennaja istorija*, 187).
142. The Octobrist Party, or more formally the Union of 17 October (Sojuz 17 Oktjabrja), named after
the date of Tsar Nicholas's 1905 decree extending weak constitutional rights to the Russian popu-
lace, held moderate views. Dietz and Schellhorn from the Volga region (see note 149 above) sided
with the more liberal Cadet party (Constitutional Democratic Party), which saw the October
Decree as a first step to the creation of a constitutional republic.
143. Fleischhauer, *Die Deutschen im Zarenreich*, 403. When Fleischhauer singles out Widmer as the
only German Duma delegate "without [a background of] high professional training" ("der einzige
deutsche Abgeordinete ohne höhere Berufsausbildung"), she is calling attention to Widmer's
comparative lack of formal education but failing to credit his extensive practical and political
education gained working in several offices for the Akkerman Zemstvo.

The April 28, 1906 (O.S.), edition of the moderately liberal newspaper *Bireževye Vedomosti* [Exchange gazette] published an interview with Widmer and Johann Münch, a German Duma representative elected from Xerson Province, in which they offered their main views. On a question of major interest to the newspaper's readers, both Germans supported the family ownership of land rather than the communal collectives typical of the Russian peasantry. As for their own focus, both were chiefly concerned with legislative issues they felt important to the German population in Russia: the creation of regulations regarding what costs could be charged for leasing land, the discontinuance of Russification in the schools, and the creation of a ban on speculative land purchases.

Widmer's senior position in the Akkerman Zemstvo and his election to the Duma, like the career successes of Graumann and Läger, testify to the fact that by the beginning of the twentieth century, Bessarabian Germans might participate in the national life of Imperial Russia. German Bessarabia was no longer an archipelago of isolated islands of rural, agricultural German culture. It was now, in its prosperity, producing some educated middle class citizens who shared political and economic aspirations with other such middle class citizens from a wide variety of different cultural backgrounds in Imperial Russia. In the period just before the start of World War I in Russia, such goals centered around creating a constitutional monarchy, the government of which would be constrained by laws created by a representative assembly. Such a system, it was widely felt in the middle class, would bring to Russia both the freedoms and the wide ranging prosperity then enjoyed in Western Europe.

If in some senses German Bessarabia by 1914 seemed to be moving toward increasing similarities with conditions in Western Europe and North America, it is also important to see that from other perspectives, despite the steady economic progress made in the period from 1870 to 1914, German Bessarabia was losing ground.

The German villages in Bessarabia continued throughout this period to look much better fed, much healthier, and much more well-to-do than the contemporary tenant peasant villages in West Prussia and Posen Provinces of Imperial Germany from which many of the Bessarabian Germans had come. At the same time though, from the perspective of Germany's many thriving urban centers, German Bessarabia (in the years just before the start of World War I) would have looked increasingly like a backwater. The large urban centers in Germany, Western Europe, and North America lived almost entirely in a money economy, producing little or nothing of what they ate, wore, or used in their daily lives. Agricultural lands in Western Europe and North America were increasingly also joining this economy by producing more and more for the market and less of what they themselves wore, ate, and used. Such changes were only in the beginning stages in German Bessarabia. Similarly, the significant changes that had occurred in manufacturing, transportation, communication, the use of electrical power, and even the development and spread of leisure activities were only just starting to make themselves felt in Bessarabia. To be sure, German Bessarabia was also generally free of industrial pollution, urban crowding, difficult and dangerous labor conditions, increasing crime, and social strife. German Bessarabia also did not have the massive differences in wealth that industrialization and loosely fettered capital growth had brought to Germany, Western Europe, and North America. Though appearing a backwater, German Bessarabia before World War I might thus have also had a rosy cast to observers from Germany: a world that brought to mind Germany's own past, a world that was rapidly receding from view.

# XII

# German Bessarabia 1914–40: The Disaster of World War I and a Partial Recovery as a Province of Romania

The beginning and end of the period covered in this chapter are marked by cataclysmic events for Germans in Bessarabia: the start of World War I in 1914 and the mass decision to leave Bessarabia in 1940 following the Soviet takeover of the province. The topics covered here are dominated by economic, political, and social issues that were generally driven by causes and forces external to Bessarabia. There is again little information coming from within German Bessarabia on the perceptions individuals held of such issues or the strategies they developed as they sought to deal with them. General descriptions of the German villages illustrate that in the aftermath of the destruction caused by World War I a gradual postwar recovery took place, but this brought the economy and social conditions to different and less prosperous places than they had reached in 1914.

This period brought significant changes to German Bessarabia. The war brought great economic losses to most German households. At the beginning of his book *Bloodlands: Europe between Hitler and Stalin*, Timothy Snyder well captures a sense of the magnitude of the disaster World War I brought to Europe when he states that "no adult European alive in 1914 would ever see the restoration of comparable free trade; most European adults alive in 1914 would not enjoy comparable levels of prosperity during the rest of their lives."[1]

The war took many Bessarabian German men into the Russian army and away from their farms. It closed off the western markets that were the chief end of grain sales for the Germans. The war also brought inflation and scarcities. It forced the Imperial Russian government to devalue the Russian currency and to confiscate grain and animals to meet wartime needs. When the state could no longer sustain the war effort and collapsed in revolution, the Imperial Russian currency lost all value. The massive economic troubles were compounded by social disorder. As Imperial Germany had become Russia's military enemy, fears arose that Germans living in Russia were not loyally supporting the war effort. Germans were threatened with land confiscations. German farmsteads were attacked by those who were suspicious of the German-speaking population, or who were angry at the apparent German victory, or who felt that in this atmosphere they could get away with banditry. When the southern front came near the border of Bessarabia, the province suffered from the depredations of hungry soldiers retreating from the front and bandits operating in the freedom of civil disorder.

When Russia collapsed in revolution, Romania sent in troops and annexed Bessarabia. This brought civil peace and spared Bessarabians the trauma of the civil war that broke out in much of the remainder of the former Imperial Russia. It also spared Bessarabians the land confiscations, the famines, and the resulting deaths that accompanied the introduction of Soviet agricultural policies in South Russia. Romanian control, however, could not restore the trading links that had created prosperity in prewar Bessarabia. The prewar infrastructure in Bessarabia had connected it with Russia, not Romania, so Romanian Bessarabia was at first an isolated area. Moreover, the export paths for shipping grain to Western Europe from Romania were far less developed, and efforts to open new avenues for farmers from Bessarabia were opposed as unwanted competition by land owners in Romanian Wallachia and Transylvania. The former markets for Bessarabian grain, animals, and wine in Russia were generally closed off by the Soviet Union, which wanted thereby to create support in Bessarabia for attachment to the Soviet Union. In the years immediately following the end of the war, trade in Bessarabia was almost exclusively local. As a result, economic recovery was very slow to develop. Gradually, with the reestablishment of civic order, a recovery did occur. However, the economic vitality and high standard of living of the first decade of the twentieth century could not be recaptured.

The major economic losses that occurred during the war, the slow postwar recovery, and the poor harvests in the 1920s created a far larger class of poor and landless people among the Germans and widened the differences between the poor and those who were better off. To help the landless poor, the Romanian government confiscated underused plots of land and established new villages of small farms on them. The major sources of land for this program were the large private estates. This program, however, had major negative consequences for German villages that had been leasing the land they farmed. Though not underused, such leased land had been

---

1.  Timothy Snyder, *Bloodlands: Europe between Hitler and Stalin* (New York: Basic Books, 2010), 1.

parts of the large private estates. The former leased-land villages were grouped with the new villages the government was creating for the landless poor. Families in both groups were now typically allotted 6-hectare (5.5-desjatina) plots of land they would own, which were much smaller plots than families worked in prewar leased-land villages.

Crowding continued to be an issue in postwar German villages as populations grew. Purchasing land to form new villages, however, was no longer an option. Underused private estate land, the major source of land Germans might purchase to create new villages, no longer existed after the Romanian government's confiscations. Even if land had been available, in the immediate postwar period, few if any Germans had spare capital to invest in such. The Imperial Russian ruble had been devalued and then with the collapse of the state it no longer had monetary value. Village savings for orphans, fires, and civic projects had become mandatory contributions to the war effort. Personal needs had wiped out many family savings. The former sources of village credit were temporarily gone.

Emigration was possible but it was no longer as easy to undertake or as attractive an option to gain access to land. There were now new and difficult hurdles. With the loss of savings, there was little money to pay for the costs of travel and reestablishment in another land. There was no thought of going to find land in Russia. First convulsed in revolution and then brought under Soviet rule, private or government land available for settlement no longer existed in Russia. The routes to North America, where Bessarabian Germans had gone in the past and still had strong links to, were now more difficult to travel. The steamship companies in Germany that had made a business of transporting immigrants at attractive costs only partially restarted after the war. The United States enacted new rules that restricted immigration. Immigration to South America, particularly Brazil, was possible after the war, but it was not well known as a destination. In the 1920s, Brazil, did seek to attract German settlers from Bessarabia by offering to pay the transportation and resettlement costs for interested families. Despite hiring local agents to attract settlers among the Bessarabian Germans, their efforts drew only small numbers, chiefly among the very poor. Without other options, as population recovered to prewar totals, family farmsteads were divided to accommodate children.

With trading links to Russia and Western Europe via Odessa closed off by the Soviet Union, new trading links were gradually formed within Romania and then later were established with Germany and other countries in central Europe via the Danube River. Agriculture remained the major economic focus for Germans in postwar Bessarabia. With local markets in Bessarabia and Romania the prime focus, profits for farmers were necessarily modest and never regained their prewar levels. Manufacturing and commercial opportunities were greatly reduced by the war and only grew slowly afterward. It was only in the early 1930s that disposable income among the Germans in Bessarabia reached the point that commercial and manufacturing businesses could gain solid footing. From the late 1920s, co-op dairies began to flourish in several German villages. At this time, numbers of new, though small, factories appeared in the larger German settlements. Construction materials, agricultural tools, and textiles were the chief products and local markets the chief focus. That a clear recovery was in progress in the 1930s is evidenced by the start of many civic construction projects, such as new churches, schools, and administrative buildings. Such civic projects, a major feature of community strength in the period before the war, had totally stopped in 1914. These are all signs that the German villages were getting back on their feet, but with economic life based on an agricultural foundation that was mainly reliant on local and national markets, the pace of economic development was slow.

Throughout the period following the end of World War I massive political and economic pressures continued to build. Sometimes, as with the Great Depression, these directly affected and changed life in Bessarabia. At other times, as with the growing prospects for war, these pressures served only to raise fears and worries. The economic depression that started in 1929 chilled domestic economic growth and brought steep new tariffs to protect domestic agriculture and industry, thus cutting international trade. For German Bessarabia, where international trade had been a major cause of economic growth, the economic depression kept agricultural, manufacturing, and commerce focused on local, regional, and Romanian markets and thus lengthened the long period of recovery.

The growth in political pressures stemmed from the fact that the Treaty of Versailles had not settled nationalistic aspirations in Europe. Political leaders in Germany and Russia fanned resentment about the treaty terms these countries had been forced to accept that created truncated national territories and left unfulfilled national dreams. The initial refusal of the victorious allies to soften the terms of the treaty and then their irresolute responses to German aggression kept increasing the worries that continued peace could not be maintained.

In 1932 unhappiness with the German government's response to the economic depression, on top of a lack of general acceptance of the concept of democracy and much dissatisfaction with how democratic processes were working, led German voters to bring to power the aggressive National Socialist party. The Nazis revived the German economy and raised hopes not just for the recapture of lost territories, but for the reestablishment of Germany as a dominant power in Europe. The existence in Russia and Germany of self-righteous, militaristic governments with aspirations beyond their borders encouraged the resumption of armed conflict in Europe. In 1939, Nazi Germany and the Soviet Union agreed on a mutual division of interests in Eastern Europe and formalized this in the Molotov-Ribbentrop Pact. This treaty allowed Germany to launch an attack on Poland in 1939 without concerns that the Soviet Union would intervene on Poland's side. The Soviet Union gained from this the right to try to take back without German interference parts of Imperial Russia that had been lost in the struggles of the Russian Revolution. In 1939, the Soviet Union joined the German attack on Poland and occupied and annexed Poland's eastern region. In 1940, the Soviet Union launched attacks on independent Finland and the three Baltic countries and then later, in June of 1940, on Romanian Bessarabia. Romania capitulated and Bessarabia became part of the Soviet Union. Germans in Bessarabia were now faced with a terrible choice. The agreement between Nazi Germany and the Soviet Union would allow the Germans to leave Bessarabia and move to Germany. They would have to choose between abandoning their homes, farms, animals, and the work of over 125 years of settlement and emigrating, or staying but still losing much of their property and personal rights to the consequences of becoming part of the Soviet collective farms.

This chaotic period of great change for German Bessarabia began with the start of World War I. What had seemed settled, secure, and certain was undermined and replaced with insecurity, uncertainty, and the unknown. The Imperial Russian state that nurtured and protected the colonies was gone and replaced at first by civic disorder and lawlessness. Disorder was then replaced by a Romanian government with different attitudes toward the Germans, different rules, and a different language. Instead of being a semi-important border province of a major European state, Bessarabia became an isolated backwater of a minor state with an uncertain future. The war devastated the Imperial Russian economy and wiped away savings through forced contributions to the war effort and through inflation. The deaths and injuries of men serving in the Russian army, the loss of animals to wartime requisitions and banditry, the loss of the European grain market, and the postwar loss of the Russian market for produce significantly injured the agricultural economy of German Bessarabia. The consequences of this damage dramatically altered the common expectation within the German settlements in Bessarabia that reasonably hard work would bring prosperity and that with such prosperity, one's children would have similar opportunities.

## Entering World War I proved to be a fatal error for Imperial Russia and brought terrible economic consequences and wrenching social, political, and linguistic changes for Germans in Bessarabia

These significant and difficult adjustments for Germans in Bessarabia were part of the enormous upheavals caused throughout Russia by the Imperial Russian government's huge miscalculation. Imperial Russia made what proved to be a fatal error when it acted on its alliance with France and Great Britain and mobilized its troops to attack Germany and Austria in the fall of 1914. The conflict that erupted was not the short, decisive war of territorial advantage that it assumed would occur when the war started. Instead, there followed a long, expensive, and exhausting struggle ultimately fought for political, even national, survival. Imperial Russia could not sustain the effort. While Russia had made great economic progress and significant improvements to its military organization, training, and weaponry since the Crimean War, its progress had not matched the advancements that had occurred in Western Europe. At first, the enormous size of the Russian army was able to hold in check the better-equipped Germans and Austrians despite suffering early defeats in battles in East Prussia and Galicia. But over time, the continuing large losses in manpower as well as the demands of equipping and feeding this army proved overwhelmingly difficult for Russia's limited industrial base and even more limited transportation system. The Russian war effort was also hindered by the endemic corruption and disorganization of the Imperial Russian state.

For the Germans, as well as communities of all nationalities in Bessarabia, the start of the war brought heavy blows. Large numbers of German men were conscripted into the Russian army or recalled to service. This left the management of many farmsteads to women, the elderly, and the very young. Significant reductions in crop yields were a direct result. The start of the war took away the profitable market for grain in Western Europe since the Russian government needed all available grain to supply its army and to feed its domestic population. To support the war economy, grain purchases were made at fixed prices that were below the former market prices. Similarly, the Imperial Russian government sought to purchase horses, cattle, and sheep, and their products at fixed and reduced prices for the war effort. When its efforts to purchase animals and grain proved insufficient to the needs of the war effort, confiscations started.

Following the start of the war, economic conditions for Germans in Bessarabia steadily worsened. The German inhabitants of the village of Nasarewka, built on purchased land along the Dniester River, were unable to keep up payments of the mortgage taken out to buy the land for their village. In response, the Russian bank holding the mortgage auctioned off the property, and the land was purchased by the Russian Farmer's Bank. Kern notes that the war brought several such defaults.[2] Smaller harvests and the fixed prices established for grain and animals by the government significantly reduced family incomes. This in turn caused families to cut back on their purchases and so hurt local tradesmen and manufacturing. Reduced harvest yields in combination with the increasing demands for grain and animals ultimately shrank the food supply. With its purchase and confiscation of horses and wagons, the war effort in turn created major local transportation problems.

The worsening war conditions created special economic problems. Price fixing and the growing scarcity of goods created the conditions for monetary inflation. Cash that families had saved in banks or under mattresses steadily lost purchase value. Villages that had saved funds for civic projects were put under pressure to use these for the war effort. Brienne, for example, had, by the start of the war, put together a fund of 32,000 rubles to be used for building a new church, but instead, "the money had to be used for the purchase of supply wagons during World War I."[3] As had happened during prior wars with the Ottoman Empire, some of the costs of supporting Russian troops stationed in Bessarabia had to be borne locally. Tarutino and Kulm were responsible for housing and feeding soldiers stationed there during the war. The Kulm Heimatbuch reports that during the war, soldiers who were in need of firewood decimated Kulm's once 48-desjatina oak forest that had been established in 1815 as part of the original settlement terms.[4]

Once Russians came to see Imperial Germany as a major European power and a rival to Russia, worries had arisen concerning the loyalty of Germans living within Russia. The start of World War I only intensified such concerns. Not willing to trust fully in the loyalty of Germans in the Russian army, the Russian government in 1915 transferred many soldiers with a German background to the Caucasian front.[5] After the war began, worries about loyalty were focused especially on Germans living near Russia's borders. Terrible consequences resulted for some German villages in northern Bessarabia near the border with Austria-Hungary when the Russian government acted on such concerns. In 1915, Germans in the villages of

---

2. Kern, *Homeland Book*, 112.
3. Ibid., 84.
4. Theophil Weiss, "Oak Forest of Kulm" in "Heimatbuch der Gemeinde Kulm," *Heritage Review* 14, no. 2 (1984): 35.
5. Malinovskij, *Social'naja i xozjajstvennaja istorija*, 195.

Neu Strymba, Ryschkanowka, and Scholtoi were evicted from their homes and sent into exile in Siberia. Younger men from Ryschkanowka and probably from the other villages were conscripted into the Russian army. Kern argues that the position of the villages close to the Austrian frontier was a major reason for this harsh treatment. Kern implies that the Russian government's concerns about loyalty drove their actions, noting as a rationale that at least in Neu Strymba, many of the Germans there "still had Austrian citizenship."[6] Giesinger's history of Germans in Russia ties these actions to an imperial decree dated February 2, 1915 (O.S.), which as a security measure permitted the expropriation of lands purchased by Germans in the western border provinces, including Bessarabia. Evidently, the order wasn't immediately enforced because the government "feared the economic repercussions."[7] In July 1915, expropriations carried out under this order took place in Volhynia, the Imperial Russian province north of Bessarabia. There more than 150,000 Germans lost their land and farms and were exiled to Siberia. As the expropriations in German villages in northern Bessarabia, which Kern mentions took place in an area close to the regional border with Volhynia, it is possible they were part of the same program of expropriations as those in Volhynia and so would likely have taken place in the late summer of 1915. With continuing Russian defeats and the beginnings of issues with desertion, government officials thought to increase the army's performance by offering the confiscated lands to Russian soldiers as a motivation to fight. As word of this reached other German communities, fears that they also might lose their land grew.

Not all the Germans living in northern Bessarabia had their land taken. In applying the Decree of February 1915 that permitted the expropriations, the Imperial Russian government distinguished between Germans who had been given land as the result of the colonial settlement agreements and those who had more recently come to Russia and bought or leased land on their own. Germans belonging to the former group were spared. This is evident from the differing fates of two groups of Germans living in the village of Neu Strymba, near Belz. The residents of Neu Strymba included a number Germans who had come to Bessarabia as colonists in the period between 1803 and 1808, before its annexation by Russia. Instead of pushing on to Xerson Province, where they had been promised land by the Russian government, they foolishly agreed to lease land in Bessarabia and founded the village of Naslawtscha along the Dniester River just upstream from Mogilev-Podol'skij (Mohyliv-Podil'skyi). Their leasing arrangements did not turn out well, and many of these Germans had been reduced to poverty. Following the intervention on their behalf by the German pastor in Kishinev, in the 1850s, the provincial government in Bessarabia granted them small plots of land of 9.5 desjatina per family some 80

---

6.  Kern, *Homeland Book*, 117. After the end of World War I, survivors of the banishment made their way back to the three villages and rebuilt their homes and farms.
7.  Giesinger, *From Catherine to Khrushchev*, 250. Any expropriation was to be paid for by bonds that would mature in twenty-five years. Giesinger also states that this decree led to the "panic selling of land" and the "neglect of farming operations" in some German areas in Russia by those fearful of expropriation. Kern's descriptions of Bessarabia German villages, though, do not offer evidence that such panic selling or neglect of ongoing farming operations occurred in Bessarabia.

kilometers farther south, creating the village of Neu Strymba.[8] The German population of Neu Strymba was later increased by arrivals from Austria who leased land. In
1915, when the Russian government used the decree permitting expropriation to exile
Germans, the Neu Strymba descendants of the families who had been granted the
9.5 desjatina of land were spared.[9] It would appear from the treatment of Germans
in Neu Strymba that the basis under which the land was held was an important
element in determining who would be exiled. It is not clear, however, whether other
factors such as the length of time a German family had lived in Russia or whether
they continued to hold Austrian citizenship were considered material.[10]

There was another government decree issued December 15, 1915 (O.S.), which
laid the groundwork for a massive program of expropriation and exile of German
citizens in Russia. This decree would have affected all Germans from the western
provinces of Russia, including "lands acquired by grants from the crown, not just
the bought lands covered by the first decree."[11] However, plans to exile all Germans
living in the western border provinces of Imperial Russia never reached fruition.[12]
By the end of the summer of 1916, the Russian military effort was collapsing with
mass desertions of troops. In early 1917, the Imperial Russian government and the
autocratic rule of the tsars had ceased to exist and had been replaced by a provisional government created by the Duma. By the fall of 1917, the Bolsheviks had
assumed power, plunging Russia into revolution and chaos, under the cover of which
Bessarabia would become part of Romania.

Although the great majority of the Germans living in Bessarabia were unaf-
fected by the two expropriation decrees of 1915, it is certain that many knew of
the existence of these acts and worried about their potential effects.[13] Once the war
began, Germans in Bessarabia reported feeling uncomfortable speaking in German
when they were outside of the German villages and sometimes even within them.[14]
Mutschall, noting such fears in Tarutino, comments that "no word of German was to

---

8. Kern, *Homeland Book*, 116. On their way to Russia, these Germans from Württemberg, Baden, and
the Pfalz met a Bessarabian landowner who had evidently promised them an attractive lease-to-own
arrangement with a one-hundred-year period. Later, their leasing contract was radically changed to
the benefit of the land owner and his agent, impoverishing the lessees.

9. Ibid., 117.

10. In this regard, it is interesting to note that the Germans who had remained in Naslawtscha in the
northern corner of Bessarabia (spelled Nasławczy on the Austro-Hungarian military map of 1895,
now the Moldovan village of Naslavcea)—that is, those families who had not moved on to Neu
Strymba in the 1850s but continued to lease land in the village their families had founded in the
first decade of the nineteenth century—were also not exiled.

11. Giesinger, *From Catherine to Khrushchev*, 250–51.

12. The Imperial Russian Decree of December 15, 1915 (O.S.), offers a clear precedent for Stalin's
efforts in the summer of 1941 to exile to Kazakhstan all Germans living in the Ukraine. As with
the Decree of December 1915, Stalin's effort was undertaken when German armies in World War II
had broken through Russian defenses and were pressing toward areas with large German-speaking
populations.

13. Kern, in his discussion of the German People's Council of Bessarabia, notes that "the Liquidation
Laws [the two degrees of 1915 permitting expropriation]...left the Germans uncertain" (*Homeland
Book*, 28). Artur Kraenbring cites preparations for exiling Germans in "The Russian Laws of
Liquidation of 1915 and the Impact of Their Application in the Bessarabian German Enclave,"
*Heritage Review* 41, no. 1 (2011): 19–21.

14. This was also true in multiethnic North American villages and towns. Many anecdotes, especially
from people who were children in German-speaking families in the United States and Canada
during World War I, report that it was at this time that they, individually, or their families moved
from speaking German to speaking English.

be spoken on the street, and no more than three people were to walk together."[15] In part to ensure that young men called into the army could speak Russian, the Russian government increased demands that schools in such multilingual areas give greater emphasis to the teaching of the Russian language. The war brought anti-German feelings in Russia to new heights. Wild rumors circulated that the German colonists were helping the German army. Some Russians, acting under the influence of strong nationalist fervor, now felt it acceptable to be rude and even threatening when they encountered Germans. Beyond just unpleasant social behavior, Germans in Bessarabia began to feel that they were not always secure even in their own villages. Kern reports that many of the women and children remaining in the village of Nasarewka, isolated and distant from other German settlements in Bessarabia, "did not feel safe there…[and] fled to other German communities which were not so isolated."[16] While other Bessarabian German villages also reported some problems with looting, robbery, and the destruction of property before the end of 1916, for the most part, such occurrences took place during 1917 when both the war front and the government had collapsed.

By the winter of 1916, the war had reached a critical phase for Russia. The 800-mile frontline that stretched from Latvia to the northwestern edge of Bessarabia represented an overwhelming commitment for Russia's military. The center of this line was already several hundred miles within Russia's prewar borders. Military losses, though never fully tabulated, were evidently stunning. Current estimates are that more than seven million Russian soldiers were killed, wounded, or captured. Losses of this size would have come to roughly 5 percent of the male population of the prewar cohort of males age fifteen through forty-nine.[17] By the winter of 1916–17, the Imperial Russian government was no longer able to keep soldiers at the front supplied with weapons or food. Riasanovsky estimates that up to 25 percent of Russian soldiers were sent to the front unarmed, with arriving soldiers needing to acquire their weapons from casualties.[18] Food supplies both at the front and among the population at large were in short supply because of Russia's still-primitive transportation system, its poor administrative leadership and organization, and its endemic corruption.

The painful histories of the Crimean War and the 1905 Russo-Japanese War were being repeated. Now Russian failures had more serious consequences. As the winter of 1916–17 progressed, desertions by Russian troops mounted. Tsar Nicholas II, thinking that his presence at the front would rally the troops, left Petrograd.[19] In late February 1917, riots and demonstrations broke out in Petrograd centered on the low supplies of food and coal. Troops sent in to quell the disorder quickly joined

15. Mutschall, "Community of Tarutino," *Heritage Review* 44, no. 2: 18.

16. Kern, *Homeland Book*, 112. The location of this village is in some dispute. Kern describes Nasarewka, also referred to as Glückstal, as located "on the banks of the Dniester River." Stumpp's map locates it well inland from the river along the railroad line running northeast from Belz. Dale Wahl, in his collection of material on Bessarabian village names, identifies Glückstal as the current Valea Norocului, which is located east of Belz on a tributary of the Solonec River ("Bessarabian Village Names"). Each of these locations has no other German villages close by.

17. Nik Cornish, *The Russian Army and the First World War* (Stroud, Eng.: Spellmount, 2006), 235–37. Among the casualties were 985 men from German villages in Bessarabia whom Kern lists as dead or missing while fighting with the Russian army in World War I (Kern, *Homeland Book*, 203–322).

18. Riasanovsky, *History of Russia*, 464.

19. After the start of the war, the capital was patriotically renamed Petrograd, as St. Petersburg (Sankt Peterburg) seemed too Germanic.

the rioters. Finding no one to support it, the Imperial Russian government lost its will and collapsed. A new semirepresentative provisional government was formed from the Duma legislature. Although this new government sought to establish a far more democratic and liberal state, it also sought to continue the war and so failed to address the country's pressing needs of food and safety. But the war effort in 1917 simply could not be continued. Supply and leadership problems remained unsolvable, and desertions continued on a large scale. In late October (under the Julian calendar), the tiny, radical, and dictatorial Bolshevik party, promising food and an end to the war, overthrew the provisional government and plunged Russia into a bitter revolutionary struggle that would not end until 1921.

In Bessarabia, although the provincial governor remained in office following the collapse of the imperial government in February 1917, the governor had little support and so had little power. Civic disorder and looting broke out, largely fanned by retreating and/or deserting troops returning to or passing through the province. The general home front population came to realize that the country was at a major turning point. In Bessarabia citizen groups formed at many levels and connections within society and began discussions on such topics as how to reestablish local order and what might be the political future of the province. Such meetings should be assumed to have taken place throughout German Bessarabia in churches and in civic groups as well as in the Akkerman Zemstvo. Fleischhauer notes that in June 1917, Andreas Widmer of the Akkerman Zemstvo met with German representatives of the Bender and Ismail zemstvos to discuss the implications of the changing political situation in Bessarabia.[20] Kern has noted that there was also a meeting in Odessa on May 14–16, 1917 (O.S.), of over two thousand delegates from German communities in Bessarabia and South Russia called to discuss ways to maintain the linguistic and educational rights and aspirations of the many German communities in this region.[21]

## In 1918, Bessarabia became a province of Romania

In June 1917, a committee made up of representatives of Moldavian soldiers stationed in their native province met and proposed the formation of a national assembly that would declare Bessarabia's autonomy. In the fall of 1917, in a fluid situation that reflected the potential of many different possible futures, a delegation of Bessarabian politicians met with the Kerensky government in Petrograd and discussed possible outcomes for Bessarabia. They even met there with Nikolai Lenin, who allegedly advised them not to waste their time in Petrograd. Also in the fall of 1917, a Ukrainian assembly meeting in Kiev declared Bessarabia part of the Ukraine.

Following the Bolshevik seizure of power, called the October Revolution, the provincial governor of Bessarabia resigned, and power essentially devolved to the regional zemstvo organizations. Elections were held for a popular assembly called the Sfatul Tarii ("the Council of the Country" in Romanian/Moldavian), and this assembly met in November and December 1917 in Kishinev, now again called by its Moldavian name Chisinau. The Sfatul Tarii was dominated by Moldavians, who were the largest ethnic group in the province, but had representatives from the Russian, Ukrainian, Bulgarian, Gaugaz, Jewish, and German communities. The

20. Fleischhauer, *Die Deutschen im Zarenreich*, 548.
21. Kern, *Homeland Book*, 28.

assembly voted to declare Bessarabia an independent democratic state and called for the election of a formal national assembly to enact land reform, demobilize the Russian army still active in Bessarabia, and protect the rights of all national groups living in this new state. However, during the time the Sfatul Tarii was meeting, Bolshevik troops entered the province. The Red Army entered Chisinau on January 5, 1918 (O.S.), and soon established its control over the city. Most members of the Sfatul Tarii fled; those captured by the Bolsheviks were sentenced to death. Alarmed at the arrival of the Red Army, appeals went out to Romania from leading members of the Sfatul Tarii asking Romania to intervene. Romania rapidly responded, and by January 13, 1918 (O.S.), Romanian troops had entered Bessarabia and taken control of Chisinau.

The Romanian government was not interested in supporting the creation of an independent Bessarabia. It wished, instead, to make Bessarabia part of Romania by joining Bessarabia to the western half of ancient Moldavia, already part of Romania. In this way it would re-form the ancient province of Moldavia under one government. Following the Romanian army's establishment of control over Bessarabia, the Sfatul Tarii continued to meet in Chisinau. The assembly, however, clearly understood the purpose of the Romanian army's presence and the goals of the Romanian state. With these in view, the Sfatul Tarii voted on March 28/April 9, 1918 to have Bessarabia unite with Romania.[22] The assembly was not unanimous in this view, and union with Romania was opposed by nearly all the non-Moldavian delegates. Though there were only three votes against union with Romania, over a third of the delegates, including those representing the German communities, either abstained or made themselves absent. On December 9, 1918, the act of union voted for by the Sfatul Tarii was approved by the king of Romania, and so Bessarabia became legally joined to Romania.

To become permanent, the Romanian hold on Bessarabia needed the approval of the major powers. Romania's resourcefulness and nonthreatening appearance won support in turn from both the Central Powers and the Allies. In the Treaty of Brest-Litovsk, which was signed by the Bolshevik government with the Central Powers in March 1918, Romania was left in control of Bessarabia. This treaty allowed Russia to exit the war at the loss of large sections of what had been Imperial Russia's western provinces. Romania was at this time formally allied with the Central Powers, a position it had entered in 1916 after its army had been soundly defeated by German troops. In March 1918 the Central Powers were chiefly concerned with pursuing the war in the west and with establishing control over the large new territories they had acquired at Brest-Litovsk. As a result, they were content to let Romania hold on to Bessarabia. When the Central Powers were defeated in the west in November 1918, the Romanians claimed they had been forced into participation with the Central Powers after the defeat of their army by Germany. The Western Allies at Versailles, focused more on the dismemberment of Austria-Hungary and the worrisome aims of the Bolshevik government, were lenient with Romania. Under the terms of the

22. Soviet authorities changed the dating system in Russia from the Julian to the Gregorian calendar effective January 31/February 14, 1918. By March 1918, this change in dating was percolating through the former provinces of Imperial Russia, including Bessarabia. Although Romania did not formally change to the Gregorian calendar for another year (March 31/April 14, 1919), from the spring of 1918 onward, Gregorian dating started to appear commonly in Bessarabia. Reflecting this, dates given in my text from this point forward will use the Gregorian calendar.

Treaty of Versailles, Romania was allowed to claim both Bessarabia from Russia and Transylvania from Austria-Hungary.

The German communities in Bessarabia were represented in the Sfatul Tarii by Alexander Lösch. He indicates that he abstained from the March 1918 vote on the question of merging with Romania because he had not been empowered to vote on this issue by the German communities.[23] A year later, on March 7, 1919, an assembly of Germans from the different settlements in Bessarabia met in Tarutino to discuss the issue of Bessarabia becoming part of the Romanian state.[24] Calling themselves the Congress of German Colonists, this group voted unanimously to support the union of Bessarabia with Romania. Noting that a majority of the population of Bessarabia were Romanian-speaking Moldavians, the German Congress concluded that such a union was supported by natural ties. The Congress was also careful to point out that the Sfatul Tarii resolution, under which Bessarabia offered to merge with Romania and which the Romanian government accepted in December 1918, included support for the right of each of the different "nations" in Bessarabia to be "ruled, educated, administered and judged in its own language and by its own sons."[25]

It would appear that for the Germans the issue of sovereignty was closely connected to concerns about security and civic order. As the military forces of the Romanian government formed the one source able to provide security under the rule of law in Bessarabia, it was a very attractive answer. Concerns about security and civic order had been magnified in Bessarabia because in 1917, dangerous conditions had developed after the fall of the Imperial Russian government. In this period of civic disorder, Germans in Bessarabia were especially hurt. With the collapse of both the Russian war effort and its civil government, Bessarabia saw a steady stream of soldiers fleeing from the front, often passing through the province to return to their home villages farther east beyond the Dniester. Frustrated by army's inability to supply food, hardened by conditions at the front, and in the absence of civil or military officials to check their actions, the deserting soldiers looted as they went. German villages, like those of other national groups in Bessarabia, were not spared. Indeed, German villages may have been especially targeted. Kern notes pillaging by soldiers in 1917 in the villages of Alexanderfeld, Kaschpalat, and Demir Chadschi. In his account of Alexanderfeld he adds that "the Russians vented their spleen in 1917 when envious soldiers devastated the village."[26] Alexanderfeld was a relatively new (1907) and isolated village located to the northwest of Bolgrad (now Bolhrad) in the southwestern corner of Bessarabia, distant from other German villages. However, troubles also occurred in areas where there were many German settlements: Germans living in Tschiligider next to Gnadental had to flee "to neighboring

23. Quoting from the work by M. Adauge and A. Furtuna, *Basarabia si Basarabenii* (Chisinau: Uniunea Scriitorilor din Moldova, 1991), the Wikipedia article on "Sfatul Tarii" notes: "The representatives of the German minority abstained from the vote on April 9, with Alexander Loesch declaring that they do not have the empowerment of the German community to vote and that 'this question can be answered by the Congress of the German Colonists'" (https://en.wikipedia.org/wiki/Sfatul_%C8%9A%C4%83rii). Adauge and Furtuna's study cites newspaper sources to provide the date of the meeting of the Bessarabian Germans and the major resolutions that came out of that meeting.
24. Ibid.
25. Ibid.
26. Kern, *Homeland Book*, 45.

villages to save their lives," and the Bodamer estate of Friedrichsfeld just south of Klöstitz was "pillaged and torched."[27]

Many of the Russians, Ukrainians, and Bulgarians in Bessarabia were not happy with Bessarabia's union with Romania. As a result, these populations formed sympathetic ground for the efforts of the Bolshevik government to try to regain control of Bessarabia. By late 1919, the Bolsheviks were in firm control of the Ukraine and started to look seriously at ways to end Romanian control beyond the Dniester River. Retaking Bessarabia, however, presented special challenges for the Soviet leadership. Unlike in Poland, where the boundaries of the new Polish state with Russia were uncertain and the Soviets had the opportunity to reclaim as much territory as their military could win, the Soviets could not directly attack Romanian Bessarabia without raising issues of international intervention. On the other hand, if a civil war were to erupt in Bessarabia, that would be a different story and might give them cover to intervene and invade. To that end, the Soviet government sought to sponsor civil disturbances. As agents, the Soviet government found allies in the Russian and Ukrainian communities who were unhappy with Romanian sovereignty. The Soviet efforts produced several small-scale brigand attacks directed against Romanian government offices. Such attempts at civil disturbances, though, made no real popular headway and failed to threaten Romanian civil control. The last and most serious of these was the rebellion in Tartarbunar that occurred September 15–18, 1924. Seeking to create a reason for Soviet intervention, a group of Russian Bessarabians took over the town of Tartarbunar and a neighboring village where they sought to create local counsels (*soviets*) and Red Guard units. The Soviet army at this time made threatening maneuvers on their side of the Dniester River but waited on events. After a day, the rebellion was quickly put down by Romanian army forces, in part with the help of a small armed unit of German militia from Sarata.[28]

The Soviet Union saw itself as the inheritor state replacing Imperial Russia in its rights to territories and had no intention of giving up its quest for regaining control of Bessarabia. Realizing that civil disruption would not dislodge Romanian control of Bessarabia, the Soviet Union, following the unsuccessful rebellion in Tartarbunar, changed strategies. Later in 1924, it carved out from the Soviet Ukraine an area along the eastern bank of the Dniester River and formed from this the Moldavian Autonomous Soviet Socialist Republic, which became a distinct and independent territorial unit within the Soviet Union.[29] The official language of this political unit was to be called Moldavian. By this action, the Soviet Union sought to portray the language of the majority population in Bessarabia as a separate language distinct from Romanian with the implication that the Moldavian people formed a separate ethnic group different from Romanians.[30] The Soviet Union intended by these actions to show its refusal to accept the loss of Bessarabia and to seek whatever

---

27. Ibid., 132, 134.
28. Alexander Bross, the son of a prewar school teacher in Kulm, notes that his brother, Emil, died in September 1924 from "a wound that he received from a battle near Tartarbunar" and that "his name is mentioned annually on the [Romanian] national holiday." Alexander Bross, "Johann Georg Bross" in "Heimatbuch der Gemeinde Kulm," *Heritage Review* 13, no. 4 (1983): 19.
29. While the Moldavian ASSR had a large Moldavian-/Romanian-speaking population, the majority of its citizens were Ukrainians and Russians.
30. To buttress this claim, Soviet linguists based written forms of Moldavian on dialects furthest removed from written Romanian.

advantages might come its way by trying to create conflicts between Moldavians and Romanians.[31] Soviet maps for this period show the Bessarabian portion of Romanian Moldavia marked as "Bessarabia" and, though lying outside the borders of the Soviet Union, was depicted in the same color as the Soviet Union and not that of Romania.[32]

The attitudes of the German population to the question of who should be ruling Bessarabia appear to have been dominated by concerns of security and stability. As noted above, they took almost a year to affirm the union with Romania, waiting to see whether it would last. The hopes expressed in that affirmation that German might return to be the language of civic affairs and education were not to be realized. The Romanian government quickly instituted policies that encouraged the use of Romanian in education and made its use mandatory in local government. As is suggested by the rapid response of the German militia in Sarata to the rebellion in Tartarbunar, the Germans seem to have decided that the order and peace that came with the Romanian control of Bessarabia was preferable to supporting the civic disorder that would be part of any attempt to overthrow that control.

### By the close of World War I and Romania's assumption of control over Bessarabia, German Bessarabia had, in economic terms, taken an enormous step backward

With many German men conscripted into the Russian army, harvests had been reduced and prewar levels of animal stock could not be maintained. As the Imperial Russian government sought to meet the demands of feeding the huge army, it began war requisitions by buying grain and animals at below-market prices. As shortages inevitably developed, farm families in Bessarabia began to worry about their own needs and became reluctant to sell. In response, the government, feeling its needs to be paramount, began to confiscate grain and animals. This created an economic cycle that fed on itself: as goods disappeared from the market due to being confiscated or hidden, prices rose on those goods still available for sale. Inflation was worsened as the government debased the currency to make available funds go further. The monetary situation became still more difficult after the provisional government took power in 1917 and issued paper rubles of its own. By the time of the Bolshevik takeover at the end of 1917, paper rubles issued by the imperial and provisional governments, as well as those issued locally by banks in Odessa, had only speculative value that varied with whatever parties in a transaction might agree to. Kern, in his discussion of Neu Posttal, reports that in 1917, "the newly introduced Kerensky ruble was worth less

---

31. Russia made a nearly identical strategic move following the collapse of the Soviet Union when the former Soviet Republic of Moldavia declared itself to be the independent state of Moldova. Guided by units of the Soviet army loyal to the emerging state of Russia, the Russian and Ukrainian majority living in the former Moldavian ASSR on the east bank of the Dniester declined to join Moldova and formed instead the small, independent, and very corrupt state of Transdnistria. Russia's strong influence in Transdnistria is maintained by the continuing presence of its army there. Bessarabia's history as part of Imperial Russia, the desire expressed by the majority of Moldavian delegates to the Sfatul Tarii to be independent of Romania, and the Soviet strategy of stressing that Bessarabia's Moldavians spoke a different language from Romanians all appear to stand behind the decision of Moldova in 1991 to reject a union with Romania and to declare its language, Moldavian, different from Romanian.

32. See, for example, "Lenninskij plan elektrifikacii rossii," Map 29 in *Atlas istorii SSSR, čast' III*, eds. A. M. Pankratovyj, I. A. Golubcov, and A. V. Foxt (Moscow: Glavnoe upravlenie geodezii i kartografii MVD SSSR, 1958), 33.

than the Odessa ruble." He also notes that German troops appeared in 1918 to buy grain there with "their deflated money."[33] Ruble coins retained value, but only with respect to their content of precious metal. With personal needs now taking up much that their farms produced and savings wiped out by the currency devaluations, most Germans had limited cash. Making mandatory payments, such as those for taxes and mortgages, now became significantly harder even though inflation had reduced the value of any fixed ruble charge. Much of whatever trade continued to exist in German Bessarabia was local in nature. The significant reduction in consumer spending crippled commerce and manufacturing. Even where trade existed, barter based on the exchange of goods tended to replace cash as the basis of exchange.

As noted above, in 1917–1918 the passage of soldiers abandoning the front to return home resulted in looting. Remaining grain stores and animals were now at risk. With the disappearance of regional civic government in this period, local robbers and bandits added to the problems caused by looting soldiers. Danger faced those who ventured to take goods outside their villages, and occasionally bandits felt powerful enough even to launch attacks on the villages themselves. With nearly one thousand Bessarabian German soldiers in the Russian army killed or missing in the fighting and perhaps as many crippled from wounds, there was no possibility for many farms of returning smoothly to prewar states when the war was over.[34] There were other severe problems as well. The Soviet Union, angry at Romania's continued control of Bessarabia, shut off most trade with Bessarabia, cutting off the province from what had been a major market before the war. Even without this action, there were no longer any easy means to transport goods to Russia. The war had destroyed the railroad infrastructure. Virtually no railroad stock remained in Bessarabia after 1919, and the railroad beds were torn up in many places.

In 1919, with food and animal stocks low, no railroad transportation into or out of Bessarabia, no markets but local ones available, and prewar savings gone, the once prosperous German Bessarabian agricultural economy was nearly destroyed. In the spring of 1919, when all the surviving men were able to return from the fighting, Bessarabian Germans were making their first major spring plantings since 1914. In economic terms, 1919 has something of the feel of the first years of German settlement in Bessarabia: farmers were seeking to build up surpluses from scratch. After 1919, economic conditions in Bessarabia did slowly improve, but the German villages were never able to regain the prosperity attained before the start of the World War I.

There are several reasons why the economic recovery that did occur in German Bessarabia after 1919 was slow to develop. It took time after the end of the war for farmsteads to recover and even to satisfy basic needs of subsistence, much less to build up a surplus that might be sold. With the disappearance of agricultural surplus and the loss of savings, commerce and manufacturing shrank to almost nothing. The strength of the prewar economy was built on the trade of agricultural products and animals to international markets in Western Europe and to domestic markets in Imperial Russia. Both of these markets ceased to exist after 1917, and with their

---

33. Kern, *Homeland Book*, 172. Evidently French and Greek troops also temporarily appeared in Bessarabia at this time, as Kern notes the higher value accorded to the currencies they possessed.
34. Ibid., 203–322. Kern has provided a village by village listing of World War I deaths and MIAs that total 985.

disappearance, prices for grain fell drastically.[35] Kern mentions in discussing Neu Posttal that grain prices postwar "had sunk to one fifth of their former level."[36]

When Bessarabia became part of Romania, its access to larger markets now had to pass through Romania. A single rail line formed the major connection for transportation. The old Russian rail line went from Leipzig to Reni along the Danube just east of its junction with the Prut River. To reach Romania, the rail line had been extended in 1876–67 by a bridge over the mouth of the Prut built by the French engineer Gustav Eiffel. Here transport was further slowed as the rail gauge changed from the wide-gauge Russian train lines to the narrow-gauge Romanian lines. By 1918, not only was much of the rail line from Leipzig torn up or in need of repair, but the Eiffel Bridge leading to the Romanian port city of Galati (Galatz) was also down. Romania's efforts to reconnect the rail links to Bessarabia went slowly. Romania was not a wealthy country, and with uncertain prospects for returns, few foreign investors were drawn to funding infrastructure projects in Romania.

Rebuilding the infrastructure to reestablish connections between Bessarabia and Romania was also slowed by the fact that the Romanian government did not consider this its highest priority. The new province of Moldavia, combining Bessarabia with its long-separated neighbor west of the Prut River, was the poorest, the most agricultural, and the most isolated part of postwar Romania. Neither great economic nor political returns were to be had from major governmental investments here. As a backwater far from the political center, Bessarabia became an unattractive assignment for government officials. As a result, the province of Moldavia received little in the way of enlightened governmental help in emerging from the disastrous effects of World War I.[37] Pressure from wealthy landowners in Romanian Wallachia was another factor in slowing Romanian efforts to revitalize Bessarabian infrastructure. These landowners had dominated the Romanian domestic grain market as well as the minor international grain trade that used the Danube River to reach central Europe. The Wallachia landowners had great political weight in postwar Romania and were not eager to encourage the development of competition from Bessarabia.

German Bessarabia's recovery was also slowed by the fact that the grain exporting business from Romania to Europe was significantly less developed than the exporting business from prewar Odessa. Grain from Romania was shipped by river boat on the Danube upstream to Serbia, Hungary, Czechoslovakia, Austria, and Germany. The trade was modest in volume and limited by the small capacities of the ports and ships. Because trade up the Danube was tiny compared to that through the Black Sea, Romania had not developed a commercial financing capability to support and smooth the flow of trade. Limited trade also kept shipping costs expensive, which made grain exports even less competitive. At the same time, demand at the other end of this supply chain was far smaller than the demand once served by the trade from Odessa. Central Europe was less developed industrially and needed fewer external sources to supply its urban needs for grain. In contrast,

---

35. Some minor (and from the official Soviet point of view, illegal) trade of grain, fruits, and wine existed with the Soviet Ukraine, with goods produced in Romanian Bessarabia shipped across the Dniester River

36. Ibid., 172.

37. This is the conclusion of Cristina Petrescu in "Contrasting/Conflicting Identities: Bessarabians, Romanians, Moldovans," in Nation-Building and Contested Identities: Romanian and Hungarian Case Studies, ed. Balázs Trencsényi et al. (Budapest: Regio Books, 2001), 160–61.

prewar Odessa had developed a business model based on a sophisticated banking and factoring commerce that determined destinations en route, with large shipments supplying major urban centers in Western Europe. Even though Soviet Russia and Romania restarted grain shipments to Western Europe following the war, Eastern European grain never regained its prewar position. The costs per unit exceeded (and so had difficulty competing with) grain shipped from North America, Argentina, and Australia.

Another factor in German Bessarabia's slow recovery from the deep problems created by World War I and its aftermath was that German farms were smaller and on the whole less productive than before. As will be discussed in more detail later in this chapter, the German population in Bessarabia continued to grow at a steady rate after World War I. It numbered just under sixty thousand in 1897 when Imperial Russia made its single empire-wide census and had likely reached the neighborhood of seventy thousand by 1914. By 1930, it was over eighty thousand, and by the time of resettlement in 1940, over eighty-eight thousand. Such population growth occurred in spite of conditions present during and immediately after World War I that would tend to slow population growth. The demographic data from the Raugust family and its marriage partners considered earlier in chapter VII suggest that, with many young men away during the fighting, as well as with the troubled and uncertain economic conditions, the frequency of marriages dropped off significantly. After 1918, when married couples were reunited and new marriages started to take place again, there appears to be some tendency to increase the spacing between children.[38] This would be a common reaction to poor economic conditions and uncertain financial prospects. Such patterns would generally suggest a slowdown in the growth or even a decrease in the size of the German population in Bessarabia. Yet, in spite of the poor economic conditions and the tendencies of Bessarabian German couples to marry later and have fewer children, the German population continued to grow, perhaps not at the rate experienced before the war, but at a rate well exceeding replacement.

As children born in the first decades of the twentieth century reached adulthood, they now had to be absorbed in the existing German villages. The strategies used before the war to deal with population growth were no longer feasible or attractive. Before the war, land purchases made to found new German villages in Bessarabia had been the primary response to overcrowding. Now there was little land for sale. As noted earlier, the Romanian government had nationalized much of the underused land that, before the war, had belonged to the owners of large estates in Bessarabia. Such land confiscations were used to provide small holdings for the landless, including landless Germans. Moreover, even if land had been available for sale after the war, most German families no longer had the means to undertake such expense. Family cash savings had generally been wiped out, and village insurance

---

38. Examples of these patterns would be the Leipzig family of Daniel Wiege and Salomea Sprecher, who were married in 1910. They had a daughter, Paulina, in 1911, and a son, Nathanael, in 1913, but their next child was a daughter, Ida, born in 1919, who was followed by another daughter, also named Ida, who was born in 1923. Tarutino residents Albert Winkler and Olga Widmer offer another example. They were married in 1913 and had a daughter, Sinaide, born in 1914, and a second daughter, Laura, born in 1915, but their next child was a daughter, Edith, born in 1920. Such patterns are by no means universal, and several examples of patterns more typical of those frequently found before the war are also present, such as the family of Adam Bohnet and Lydia Raugust, natives of Kulm but adult residents of Nikolajewka, Bessarabia, who had children in regular two-year intervals from 1915 to 1932.

funds that had been available for loans had been swept away by contributions to the war effort and the devaluation of the Imperial Russian currency.

The loss of family savings also generally closed off emigration, the second most popular prewar means of dealing with overcrowding. Small numbers of Bessarabian Germans did leave in the 1920s for Brazil. Their costs for passage and establishing themselves in the New World were paid for by the Brazilian government. Without a history of settlement in South America and thus without knowledge of conditions there or the helpful presence of other Bessarabian Germans already established there, the attractions of moving to Brazil appear to have been strongest for those in the most desperate of straits. As noted in the preceding chapter, the number of people who took advantage of the Brazilian offer appears to have been small. Even smaller, perhaps less than one hundred, were those who went to North America, almost always to join relatives there. With the easy railroad passage through Russia into Germany no longer available and the German steam ship companies in Bremen and Hamburg no longer focused on carrying emigrants, passage to North America was more difficult, more expensive, and thus, in far poorer Bessarabia, no longer a credible option for Germans. Emigration to new settlement frontiers in Russia, an option that drew some from German Bessarabia before the start of World War I, was an unthinkable option after the war. The Bolshevik takeover of the government brought on a punishing civil war that lasted until the end of 1920 in the Ukraine and Crimea and 1921 in western Siberia. Once Soviet control was established, the bleak tales that reached Bessarabia of mass starvation in the Ukraine caused by forced grain requisitions chilled any thoughts of finding a better life in Soviet Russia.

As German families continued to grow, the most popular recourse was to subdivide the existing family holdings to create smaller, separate farms rather than jointly farming the original family holding as had been done in the first three generations. This suggests that families holding a plot of land now had too many adults to make a joint operation feasible. Kern provides a glimpse of how far subdivision had progressed when he reports that in postwar Lichtental "there were many divided properties: 31 half farms, 18 one-third farms, 15 quarter farms, 4 one-sixth farms, and 2 one-eighth farms."[39]

## Data on population counts and village land areas collected by Karl Stumpp in the 1930s indicate a general reduction in average family landholdings

Far more substantial evidence of the diminution in the average family landholdings appears in data Karl Stumpp collected. In a document that was prepared in 1939 for the Deutsches Ausland-Institut (DAI), possibly in anticipation of the consequences of a Soviet takeover of Bessarabia, Stumpp breaks down the German settlements in Bessarabia into seven categories. The data in this document are sufficiently detailed to suggest that they come from Romanian census materials and even local informants. Included here is material on the average sizes of family landholdings that allow us to make comparisons with other earlier data sources. Stumpp divided the

---

39. Kern, *Homeland Book*, 183.

settlements in Bessarabia with a German population into the following seven groups (see table 12–1).[40]

Stumpp's categories and data offer a useful overview of the German settlements in Bessarabia in the 1930s and highlight some of the major changes that occurred since 1914. The mother colonies were the twenty-five original villages founded by 1842. The two categories of containing seventy-seven daughter villages comprised the new villages founded on purchased land after 1860. The wealthy daughter portion of this group was largely made up of villages founded by smaller groups of purchasers after 1890 and also included seven single-family estates.

The thirteen new hectare villages were those established in the period from 1920 to 1923 under the terms of the Romanian Agriculture Decree of March 13, 1920. This act formed new villages in which landless farmers were granted plots of 6 hectares (5.5 desjatina). The land used to create these new settlements had been confiscated under this act from estate lands held by both settled and absentee landlords and included land taken from some large Bessarabian German estates, such as Schulzenheim.[41]

TABLE 12–1.   **Stumpp's 1939 categorization of population and landholding in German settlements in Bessarabia**

| | No. of villages | Total population | Area in hectares | Per-family holdings in hectares |
|---|---|---|---|---|
| Mother colonies | 25 | 45,440 | 158,666 | 21 |
| Wealthy daughter communities | 22 | 3,286 | 31,510 | 57.5 |
| Mid-size daughter communities[a] | 55 | 23,110 | 92,570 | 24 |
| New hectare communities[b] | 13 | 2,764 | 3,950 | 6 |
| Lease hectare communities | 25 | 8,090 | 9,594 | 7.2 |
| Ethnic minorities[c] | 7 | 1,392 | 725 | — |
| Urban dwellers | 5 | 561 | — | — |
| **Totals** | 152 | 84,643 | 297,015 | — |

a.  Stumpp calls this group "Daughter colonies with average agricultural property" ("Landed Property Situation"). I do not use the term colonies, as Stumpp does, for this group, for the new hectare settlements (see footnote 42 below), or for the wealthy or mid-sized daughter settlements. The term colony best describes the first German settlements made under the direction and sponsorship of the Russian government.

b.  Stumpp calls this group "Daughter colonies—Hectarres for communities founded 1920-1923" ("Landed Property Situation"). These were the new settlements founded for the landless poor under the terms of the Romanian Agricultural Decree of March 13, 1920, and commonly referred to by Germans in Bessarabia as the hectare villages.

c.  Stumpp calls this group "Hectare Communities" ("Landed Property Situation"). I have not followed this usage as it confuses this group of cottagers employed in trade living as minorities in other villages in Bessarabia and having only small holdings of land about their houses with the farming settlements established for landless Germans by the Romanian government in 1920-23 that are commonly called the hectare villages.

40.  Karl Stumpp, "Lists Concerning [the] Landed Property Situation in Bessarabia," in Allen Konrad, trans., "Bessarabian Resettlement – Propaganda and Reports, from DAI T81-321" (N.p.: Odessa Digital Library, 2004), http://www.odessa3.org/collections/war/dai/link/dai321b.txt. Though dated to 1939, the population figures suggest that Stumpp's report is based on data from the mid-1930s.

41.  Kern notes that two of the heirs of August Schulz, the son of Gottfried Schulz, were able to purchase back some 650 hectares of the Schulzenheim property lost to the confiscations taken during the land reform. This was not common as Kern further notes that "Schulzenheim…was one of the few estates which survived the liquidations of the land reform" (*Homeland Book*, 176).

The twenty-five lease hectare villages were those German villages, such as Katlebug, Sangerowka, and Scholtoi, that had been founded before the war on leased land, but came under the terms of the Agricultural Decree of 1920 because the land had never been purchased. Under the decree, the leased land on these estates was considered part of large estates and so was taken from the owners and was no longer available for leasing. As a result these villagers were treated as landless farmers and were given small portions of the land they had formerly leased which they now held as owners. In the new settlements founded under this decree for families that had been truly landless, the allotments were 6 hectares of land per family (5.5 desjatina). Unfortunately for the German villages that had been leasing land before the war, this was far less land than they had been leasing. Stumpp's average figure of 7.2 hectares (6.6 desjatina) per family for the leased-hectare villages, however, suggests that families from the formerly leased-land villages were able to hold on to slightly more than the permitted 6-hectare allotments. Three of the villages listed in Kern's study as leased land villages evidently found ways to acquire land as they are included in Stumpp's listing among the midsized daughter communities with modestly greater per-family holdings than the hectare villages: Jakobstal with an average of 12.6 hectares, Kurudschika with 16.2 hectares, and Neu Tarutino with 20.

The ethnic minority group comprised seven villages including Mansyr, Missowka, and Sarjari where the German population, averaging almost two hundred per village, formed a sizable block but were not in the majority. For the most part, the Germans here held only small plots of land. Stumpp provides landholding figures for this group only on a per-head basis, which is why nothing is listed in the per-family column in the chart above. The per-head land allotment figure of 0.51 hectares stresses that Germans in these villages, as Stumpp notes, were largely cottagers employed by others as "handicraft workers, laborers and day-laborers."[42]

The urban-dwelling group of Germans were those located in five large towns—Cetatea-Alba (the former Akkerman), Bendery, Chisinau (the former Kishinev), Leowa, and Tartarbunar—where they formed only tiny parts of the total population. The 80 Germans in Leowa formed the highest percentage in any of the five towns: 1.23 percent of the population of 6,495. In the other four towns, Germans were never more than 0.4 percent of the population.

Stumpp's data generally suggest that family landholdings had been greatly reduced from the holdings noted when the villages were first settled. For twelve villages from the wealthy and midsized daughter categories, it is possible to compare the data Stumpp offers for per-family landholdings from the 1930s with similar data in Kern on family landholdings from the time these villages were founded. The comparisons indicate a variety of outcomes. Generally, family holdings in the 1930s were about half as big as when the village was founded. However, there are wide differences, as in some villages per-family holdings dropped only a little from the original family farmstead sizes, while in others the per-family holdings were just small portions of the original allotments (see table 12–2).[43]

---

42. Stumpp, "Landed Property Situation." Stumpp also notes here that these villagers were "extremely poor and perilously on the way to losing their ethnic heritage."

43. For purposes of comparison, I have changed Kern's figures for the original per-family holdings, which were given in desjatina, to hectares to match those provided in Stumpp.

TABLE 12–2. **Declines in the per-family landholdings for some daughter settlements**

| Village | Founded | Original per-family holdings (hectares) | 1930s per-family holdings (hectares) | 1930s holdings as percent of original |
|---|---|---|---|---|
| Alexanderfeld | 1907 | 61.1 | 26.7 | 43.7% |
| Baimaklia | 1912 | 143.4 | 23.4 | 16.3 % |
| Basyrjamka | 1899 | 65.6 | 42.0 | 64.0% |
| Benkendorf | 1863 | 58.5 | 35.4 | 60.5% |
| Gnadenfeld | 1879 | 33.0 | 30.0 | 90.9% |
| Jekaterinowka | 1908 | 135.5 | 19.8 | 14.6% |
| Kaschpalat | 1912 | 43.7 | 32.4 | 74.1% |
| Kisil | 1908 | 82.0 | 34.0 | 41.5% |
| Mannsburg | 1881 | 48.9 | 33.6 | 68.7% |
| Neu Posttal | 1881 | 77.6 | 66.0 | 85.1 % |
| Neu Sarata | 1889 | 54.8 | 28.0 | 51.1 % |
| Seimeny | 1894 | 60.7 | 29.0 | 47.8% |
| **Average** | | 72.1 | 33.4 | 46.3% |

When considered more closely, it is clear that the outliers result from factors other than population change. For example, in the two villages that show the greatest diminution in the size of family holdings—Baimaklia and Jekaterinowka, where holdings in the 1930s were just 16.3 percent and 14.6 percent of the original per-family holdings, respectively—the diminution in average family holdings was chiefly affected by the land reform act rather than by family land division. Kern notes of Baimaklia that four of the original six wealthy purchasers lost everything but the land around their houses to the land reform. All of the Baimaklia purchasers, such as Gottfried Schulz, were property owners elsewhere in Bessarabia. In Jekaterinowka, 1,100 hectares, a full third of the land that had been bought by the village in 1908, had been taken by the land reform act.[44] In both cases, these villages started with large per-family allotments that likely were not fully in use in 1920 when the act went into effect, and so came to be treated as underused estate land. In the cases of Gnadenfeld and Neu Posttal, where the per-family allotments do not appear to have changed much from the time of the original settlement of these villages, the figures reported by Stumpp for the 1930s per-family holdings distort the comparison because the total village landholdings had grown. Both of these villages made additional land purchases after their original settlement. Gnadenfeld more than doubled its size by adding another 2,084 hectares after 1879. With its growth in population, it maintained a similar figure for the average family holding only because it increased the land area owned by the village. Similarly, Neu Posttal also appears to show average family farmsteads only slightly down from the figures of 1881 when the village was founded on purchased land. Neu Posttal's figures, however, don't take into account the fact that the village, following its founding, managed to purchase another 1,372 hectares. Although Neu Posttal lost 700 hectares to the 1920 Romanian land reform, the net growth of 672 hectares helped the village maintain its average land allotments as its

---

44. Kern, *Homeland Book*, 47, 139.

population grew. If the data from these four outliers are taken out of the picture, the average family holdings of the remaining eight villages were in the 1930s just over half (54.9 percent) of what they were when the village was originally settled.

In the group Stumpp calls the mother colonies, the twenty-five villages that were the original German settlements in Bessarabia, the drop in the size of the average family farmsteads is even greater. This group continued to hold the majority, 53.4 percent, of the total landholdings and a similar percentage, 53.7 percent, of the total population of the combined German settlements. Until 1870, these villages were still living under the mandates of the original settlement agreements and so were prevented from subdividing the original farmstead plots of 60 desjatina (65.6 hectares) of land. The data Stumpp cites from the 1930s indicate that the average family holding of 21 hectares in the mother colonies had dropped to roughly a third of the original plots. As these villages faced a much greater buildup in population pressure than the daughter settlements, it is not surprising that they showed a greater diminution in the average size of family holdings.

Stumpp notes three of the mother colonies that trend differently. Again, special circumstances they exhibit suggest their actual experience may not be so radically different from the general trend of much smaller average holdings. Stumpp's material cites Dennewitz, with an average of 41 hectares per family, and Plotzk and Schabo, with averages of 60 hectares, as having materially higher family farmstead sizes than the other mother colonies. Schabo's first settlers had been given unusually large family allotments of 100 desjatina (109 hectares) to compensate for the poor, sandy soil. Thus, average family holdings of 60 hectares are not a sign that no diminution occurred, but rather reflect an experience that was more in line with that of other mother colonies. Plotzk stands out among the mother colonies because after its original settlement, Plotzk was able to purchase a significant amount of additional land. This increased its size by some 1,311 hectares, slightly over 50 percent of its original size. Like Gnadenfeld and Neu Posttal, Plotzk was able to maintain similar average family allotments because the additional land area matched its population growth. Dennewitz, the home of Gottfried Schulz, was one of the most prosperous of the German settlements in Bessarabia. With large areas of good pastureland, Dennewitz was able to maintain large numbers of animals. The wealth it had built up from livestock allowed families to offer members of younger generations the financial ability to purchase lands elsewhere or to emigrate. Kern calls particular attention to the widespread movement of Dennewitz's emigrants.[45] World War I, of course, brought this to an end. Yet by maintaining an average of 41 hectares per family in the 1930s, the slippage that occurred in Dennewitz was not at all as serious as what occurred in the other mother colonies. Even considering the outliers, then, it is fair to conclude that continuing population growth combined with the loss of past outlets for that growth via emigration or the purchase of additional land resulted in a pattern of subdivision that created smaller and smaller average family farmsteads.

The villages with the greatest decreases in the average size of the family farmsteads were ones that had leased large plots of land before World War I. In Katlebug, for example, Kern notes that before the war, families were leasing large plots of land, typically in sizes ranging between 50 and 150 desjatina (between 54.7 and 164.0

---

45. Ibid., 55–56.

hectares). When the Romanian land reform act confiscated lands that had been leased, Katlebug farmers were considered landless and were given 6-hectare family plots they would now own. For the citizens of this hectare community, as Kern observes, this was "not enough to make a living," and, as a result, "the standards of living were severely diminished."[46] Kamtschatka, Tchemtchelly, and Sangerowka, all relatively well-to-do leased-land villages before the war, were similarly affected. In Helenowka, a purchase agreement had been drawn up but was never signed and finalized, which Kern correctly observes proved "disastrous for both sides."[47]

In some cases, Romanian officials, acting under the powers of the 1920 land reform act, took land from German villages in error, as the land in question had been purchased. Long and costly court battles ensued in efforts to recapture the lost land. This was the case for the village of Jekaterinowka, founded on purchased land in 1907 north of Leipzig. The land had been communally purchased by the new settlers, which evidently led the Romanian authorities to conclude that the individual citizens of Jekaterinowka did not fully own distinguishable plots of land. As a result, 1,100 hectares were taken away from the village and used to establish 6-hectare plots for landless families by extending the southern edge of the neighboring non-German village of Gradišče. A Romanian court ultimately ruled that the Jekaterinowka villagers had been unjustly treated and awarded a payment of sixteen million lei. Half of the award, though, went to lawyers. As the settlers from Gradišče could not be displaced, the Jekaterinowka villagers were granted plots of land from the Casa Noastra land bank farther east. In another case, the purchased land of the village of Fürstenfeld II was evidently confused with the leased land of nearby Fürstenfeld I and was confiscated. Though it was returned, Kern notes "it took a long and costly court battle in Bucharest" to make this happen.[48] Tarutino was less successful in regaining ownership of land bought by that village to create Neu Tarutino. Land in Neu Tarutino was owned by the village of Tarutino and then leased from 1890 onward to landless families who would move there from Tarutino. The Neu Tarutino land was confiscated in 1920, and legal efforts to obtain its return were still in progress in 1940 when the Soviet Union took control of Bessarabia and the concept of private ownership of land became meaningless.[49]

## There are several reliable population counts of German Bessarabia from the 1930s

Though Stumpp's document does not provide a figure for the total German population in Bessarabia, it does provide population numbers for each of the seven

---

46. Ibid., 168.
47. Ibid., 147. It is worth remembering that land sales not made were disastrous for landowners as well. Following World War I, the Gagarin-Sturdca family, from whom the land in Helenowka had been leased, continued to live in France, but now without income from Russia. Their landholdings in Bessarabia had been confiscated to create hectare communities or to be held for future use by the Romanian Land Bank (the Casa Noastra). They also owned land near Odessa that was confiscated by the Soviet government.
48. Ibid., 156.
49. Kern's notation that the legal case on ownership of the Neu Tarutino land was still in progress at the time of the resettlement is found on p. 152 of the *Homeland Book*. This presumes that Tarutino had lost the land to the land bank and was seeking to get it back in court, and that Neu Tarutino lessees had been given 6-hectare plots to own. It is thus surprising and puzzling to see that Stumpp lists Neu Tarutino as a midsized daughter settlement with average family holdings of 20 hectares, as this implies that its citizens had owned that land ("Landed Property Situation").

categories of German settlements. His data add up to a total German population of 84,643. Ute Schmidt, in her study of German Bessarabia, cites a Romanian census of 1930 that counted 81,089 Germans then living in Bessarabia.[50] A decade later, in 1940, the German army's count of the German population in Bessarabia who were evacuated during the resettlement indicated that the population had grown to between 88,545 and 91,049.[51] Stumpp's figures would thus appear to come from the mid-1930s. Though Stumpp does not specify the origin of his data, the detail offered on total village property and average family holdings strongly suggests that it was based on local census materials collected by the villages for the Romanian government, possibly for tax purposes. There is a fourth population count that is provided by Kern and that he dates to the end of 1939 and is tied to church records. Kern breaks his study into groups of parishes, and at the beginning of each parish section, he lists villages and their populations. By adding together the population counts of all the villages in each of the parishes, a total population figure of 87,399 is reached.[52] As this total is relatively close to the figures counted by the German army during the resettlement ten months later in the fall of 1940, it seems on solid ground.

It is possible to compare the three most populous of Stumpp's categories with data from Kern. The comparisons indicate that Stumpp's population figures, if assumed to date from the mid-1930s, correlate well with Kern's, as they come in only slightly lower than Kern's figures for 1939 (see table 12–3).

TABLE 12-3.  **Stumpp and Kern data on the German population in Bessarabia in the 1930s**

|  | Stumpp | Kern | Number |
|---|---|---|---|
| Mother colonies | 45,440 | 46,227 | 25 |
| Mid-sized daughter colonies | 23,110 | 23,226 | 55 |
| Lease hectare | 8,090 | 8,158 | 25 |

50. Schmidt, *Die Deutschen aus Bessarabien*, 78. This census shows that most Germans continued to live in the Cetatea-Alba District, the former Akkerman District, when Bessarabia belonged to Imperial Russia. Schmidt notes that 55,598 people, or 68.6 percent of the total German population, lived in the Cetatea-Alba District. The second largest grouping of Germans in Bessarabia in 1930 was in the Bender District, where there were 10,524 Germans, or 13.0 percent of the population.

51. As will be discussed in more detail in the following chapter, several tabulations of the number of Bessarabian resettlers made by the German army at the Danube River ports in the fall of 1940 give a count of 88,545. One of them, however, adds with an asterisk to that number "to this should be added 2,504 refugees who came from the Galatz Camp." This would increase the number to 91,409. What is not certain is whether the additional 2,504 persons came from Bessarabia, Dobrudscha, or Bukovina. It is clear the author of this report thought they ought to be included in the Bessarabian totals. SS Obersturmführer With, "Report on Bessarabia 2 December 1940," #T-81, VOMI 902, Group 1035, Roll 317, Serial 535, Frames 2447147–2447150, in Konrad, "Evacuation from Bessarabia and Bukovina."

52. As a heading to the first parish he considers, Albota, Kern indicates the figures are of December 31, 1939 (*Homeland Book*, 42). Unlike most data sources based on material from Evangelical Lutheran sources, Kern also provides data on the Catholic parishes in German Bessarabia (196). My count assumes that Kern's figure for Gnadental of 1,210 is for 1939, not for 1839 as is stated at the beginning of his village description (106). That 1839 is a misprint is strongly suggested by the fact that later in his discussion of Gnadental, Kern notes that in 1833 the village "had 80 families and a population of 455" (107).

## Beginning in the late 1920s, German Bessarabia started to make an economic recovery

The recovery did not start until late in the 1920s as Christina Petrescu notes. In her article, focused largely on the 1920s, she stresses the fact that farmers of all nationalities in Romanian Bessarabia were largely cut off from their former markets and so now were mainly producing grain and fruit not for trade but for each farm's own consumption "as food and fodder."[53]

Gradually a market for agricultural and animal surplus began within the province and then, as transportation improved, interest developed for sales within Romania and finally via Romania for sales to Western Europe. While from the late 1920s the agricultural economy in Romanian Bessarabia grew, it never regained the activity and profits of the prewar period. However, it was not without innovations, as in a few cases some progressive German farmers established totally new areas of great opportunity. As in the prewar period, grain sales formed a significant part of the agricultural economy, and these grew steadily throughout the 1930s. For German farmers in Bessarabia, the entry points for the grain market were the villages with railroad depots. It should be noted, though, that individual family grain sales generally never recaptured prewar sales: with the increased division of land, farms were smaller, and so individual farmers brought smaller amounts to market. These all are themes worth discussion, but the place of first importance belongs to the repair and rebuilding of the railroad. The railroad was the key to the establishment of trade links with markets outside of Bessarabia.

The restoration of railroad service to Romania brought back the thriving commercial market in Romanowka at the edge of Leipzig, though now the small Kulm station, next on this line to the south and dormant before World War I, also attracted German business. When the railroad line joining Leipzig and Akkerman was repaired, it created new commercial opportunities to villages farther east. Farmers, who before the war had to cart grain to Leipzig or sell to middlemen, now brought their grain to nearer rail depots. Beresina had donated land for the track and so acquired a station and thus captured a major opportunity. Tarutino, in contrast, had been slow to see the importance of the railroad, and with the line running through Beresina, Tarutino was bybassed and missed out on an opportunity. The stations at Arzis and Sarata greatly enhanced commercial businesses there. Mannsburg was another village where the presence of a railroad depot created a profitable transshipment point for grain. In his discussion of Mannsburg, Kern notes that with Odessa now cut off as a market for grain, "the millions of tons of grain grown by [the surrounding] communities were converted to money here."[54] The limitations of demand, however, could create wide fluctuations in the prices given for grain. Theophil Weiss, in the Kulm Heimatbuch, reports that farmers bringing grain to the Kulm rail station for sale could find that "within a day's time different prices were paid for the same type of grain."[55] There existed no futures market at work to provide farmers with prices that could be fixed during the growing season. The only choice was for farmers to cart their grain to railheads and take the fluctuating prices offered

---

53. Petrescu, "Contrasting/Conflicting Identities," 160.
54. Kern, *Homeland Book*, 169.
55. Weiss, "Grain Selling and Prices" in "Heimatbuch der Gemeinde Kulm," *Heritage Review* 14, no. 2 (1984): 33.

there. Weiss also notes that the German Farmer's Economic Association did try to find ways to establish less erratic market opportunities but that these came to no avail.[56] In Weiss's opinion, this attempt failed because the Economic Association had no money, by which he means that it didn't have the funds to buy grain in bulk and so could not seek more stable pricing as the cooperative dairies had done. In contrast and on a much smaller scale, Weiss notes that he, acting with three other Kulm farmers, did achieve that goal with another crop. Acting collectively, they set aside 324 hectares for oil crops, mainly soybeans, and the group sold the oil to Germany, receiving a good price without the use of middlemen.[57]

The revitalized railroad stations became additional market places that developed and encouraged many other businesses. The stations were not just places where grain or animals might be brought for sale and shipment. At the stations, farmers received cash. This attracted not only craftsmen and peddlers who set up at the stations, but greatly supported the growth of merchants in these villages who, with prospects of increased business, could take on the risk of having increased stock for sale. The railroad stations similarly drew and supported the credit business. The transaction sales of grain and animals created business for banks, helping both sides by smoothing cash flows for buyers and allowing farmers to take and settle loans that built their stock or improved their equipment. Thus, it is not surprising to see that when German Bessarabia began to recover in the postwar period, there was a steady growth in commercial businesses and banks. Mannsburg had two banks. Kern notes that Arzis had "developed from humble beginnings…into the commercial center of the German settlements," that the Beresina depot "attracted various merchant enterprises," and that in Sarata "the train depot furthered trade and industry."[58] Railroad stations augmented the weekly markets that continued to take place in Tarutino, Arzis, and Sarata and, like the weekly markets, drew buyers and sellers from both the surrounding German villages and neighboring non-German ones as well.

Despite the general prohibition by the Soviet Union of trade with what it viewed as Romania's illegally controlled Bessarabia, it is apparent that at least some grain sales to the Soviet Union did occur. Theophil Weiss implies in an article in the Kulm Heimatbuch that among the purchasers of local grain, some sales were made to the Soviet Union.[59] Among the purchasers of Bessarabian grain were the large flour mills in Germany. This suggests efforts to cut through middlemen and to buy directly and more cheaply from the farmers themselves. Such trade with mills in Germany, however, does not appear to have been major. By the mid-1930s much grain was being sold to local grain mills, notably ones in Arzis, Beresina, or Borodino.

In contrast to grain sales, the Bessarabian Germans were much more successful in establishing dairy businesses to control prices and maximize return. As noted earlier, from the 1870s onward, dairy cattle were largely replacing the meat-producing steppe

56. Ibid.
57. Ibid. Weiss dates this to 1940: "cultivated 300 hectares of soybeans, 20 ha of rape seed, and 4 ha of sunflowers in 1940." Given that harvests after July 1940 in Bessarabia were treated as owned by the Soviet Union, Weiss seems to be describing crops "cultivated" in 1939 and then processed and sold in early 1940, before the Soviet takeover of Bessarabia.
58. Kern, *Homeland Book*, 82, 123, and 187.
59. Weiss, "Grain Selling and Prices," 33. In contrasting the uses of the Leipzig and Kulm railroad stations, he notes: "the surplus grain was usually shipped to Russia from Leipzig and to Romania from Kulm."

cattle in the herds kept by German farmers. Prior to 1914, individuals in Borodino and Klöstitz and perhaps other villages created dairy businesses by producing and selling milk products. In the period after the war, though, dairy businesses became a much more significant part of the economy in German Bessarabia. Many German villages now established dairies, which were often cooperatively owned to control product purchase prices. These not only packaged milk but also produced butter, cheeses, yoghurts, and other milk products like kefir. Following the end of World War I, dairies were built or expanded in Eigenheim, Brienne, Friedenstal, Neu Arzis, Teplitz, Eigenfeld, Gnadenfeld, Gnadental, Hoffnungstal, Mannsburg, and Lichtental. Kern reports that Gnadental had established a market for its dairy business in the port city of Galatz on the Danube and by 1927 was taking in 3 million lei a year in earnings.[60] Eigenfeld had developed a market for the products of its dairy to the north in the provincial capital of Chisinau, where, as Kern notes, prices were better and more stable than they were locally.[61] In Lichtental, the dairy business was so attractive that the village supported three separate firms; Mannsburg supported two.[62] A Dane, who had settled in Brienne after the war, established a large, profitable dairy business called Danemarca. Teplitz developed into one of the major dairy centers in Bessarabia, producing in the period from 1937 to 1939 between 500,000 and 700,000 liters of milk and between 27,000 to 30,000 kilograms of butter.[63]

A second agricultural product that became very important for German farmers in postwar Bessarabia were beans that produced edible oils such as linseed, castor, canola, and soy. In contrast to the wildly fluctuating prices for grains in the postwar period, the market for the oil from these beans was far steadier, and with a growing demand, such crops even enjoyed a regular rise in prices. In his account of the village of Seimeny, Kern notes that while the subdivision of farms together with slow economic growth hurt farm income, the majority of farmers in this village did reasonably well by "turning to grains rich in oil content."[64] Discussing Plotzk, Kern notes that "after grain prices plummeted following WWI, the cultivation of oil producing plants increased dramatically"[65] and that in Balaktschelly, "oil produce was added in the 1930s [and] oil producers brought stable prices."[66] To substantiate the improvements in Leipzig after the war, he notes that "more and more farmers switched to more productive, modern machinery and planted linseed, castor beans and soy beans."[67] The beans were pressed in local mills, and the oil was sold to

60. Kern, *Homeland Book*, 107. Though in context it isn't perfectly clear whether Kern means 3 million lei or 3 million liters of milk, the former seems more logical. The value of Romanian lei, unlike that for the nineteenth-century Russian ruble, can be estimated, as in the 1920s it did have an international exchange value. In this decade, the value of the currency was pegged to a notional gold standard that was based on the value of gold reserves taken to Russia in 1916 when the Central Powers were beating back the attack of the Romanian army. The Soviet Union declined to return this gold to Romania following the war, but Romania continued to consider it as Romanian-owned and based currency values on its assumed possession. As of February 1929, 167.2 lei was deemed the equivalent of US $1. (See E. Blejan, B. Costache, and A. Iarovici, "International Reserves of the National Bank of Romania 1920-1944" [Bucharest: Banca Nationala A Romaniei, December 2006]). In 1929, then, 3 million lei would equal US $17,942.58.
61. Kern, *Homeland Book*, 99.
62. Ibid., 183, 169.
63. Ibid., 93.
64. Ibid., 78.
65. Ibid, 62.
66. Ibid, 181.
67. Ibid., 142.

enterprises in Romania. As noted earlier, Theophil Weiss, working with three other farmers in Kulm, had developed special contracts with buyers in Germany. Possibly farmers in other German villages in Bessarabia did so as well. But farmers could not always rely on oil-producing plants. Weiss also notes that some farmers in Kulm who had been discouraged with the fluctuation in grain prices had in 1930 planted castor oil plants but later discontinued this "as there was no market for it."[68]

German farms in Bessarabia continued to raise cattle, horses, sheep, and poultry and to sell these for profit in local markets at rail stations and at the weekly markets at Arzis, Sarata, and Tarutino. Raising livestock and their products for sale was the major economic focus for some German villages. Basyrjamka, Dennewitz, Friedenstal, and Teplitz, as well as the large, single-family estates, stand out in this regard. In most of the German villages, though, it was, as Kern says of postwar Borodino, a "secondary enterprise" to growing grains and oil-producing plants. In the period after World War I, the chief purposes in raising livestock appears to have been to satisfy family needs and to supplement family income via sales of milk to local dairies or sales of the animals themselves. This is suggested by data from three villages where it is possible to make comparisons between livestock holdings from the 1920s and 1930s with those from the early life of these villages. The per-capita holdings suggest that over the 100- to 120-year period, there was very little change in the numbers of horses, moderate decreases in the per-capita cattle numbers, and moderate increases in the holdings of sheep (see table 12–4).[69]

As Borodino, Leipzig, and Plotzk did not develop dairy businesses, the drop in the per-capita figures for the number of cattle seems to suggest that in these

TABLE 12–4. **Herd sizes and per-capita animal numbers for three German villages in Bessarabia; nineteenth century vs. twentieth century**

|  | Population[a] | Horses | Cattle | Sheep |
|---|---|---|---|---|
| Borodino 1825 | 606 | 264 | 1,438 | 169 |
| Per capita |  | 0.44 | 2.37 | 0.28 |
| Borodino 1939 | 2,719 | 1,200 | 515 | 2,879 |
| Per capita |  | 0.44 | 0.19 | 1.06 |
| Leipzig 1825 | 640 | 229 | 1,225 | 666 |
| Per capita |  | 0.36 | 1.91 | 1.04 |
| Leipzig 1927 | 2,200 | 995 | 1,239 | 3,801 |
| Per capita |  | 0.45 | 0.56 | 1.73 |
| Plotzk 1839 | 175 | 112 | 231 | 227 |
| Per capita |  | 0.64 | 1.32 | 1.30 |
| Plotzk 1939 | 298 | 360 | 257 | 782 |
| Per capita |  | 1.21 | 0.86 | 2.62 |

a. The population figures for Leipzig in 1927 and Plotzk in 1839 are estimates.

---

68. Weiss, "Grain Selling and Prices," 33.
69. Data for twentieth-century holdings come from listings in Kern for Borodino (*Homeland Book*, 124) and Leipzig (142), and data for both the nineteenth- and twentieth-century figures come from Kern's listings for Plotzk (62). Data for 1825 for Borodino and Leipzig are from the 1825 Welfare Committee census. Kern separately provides figures for the numbers of horses (254), cattle (1,118), and sheep (644) from Leipzig in 1827 that are not materially different from those of the Welfare Committee study of 1825.

farming villages, the costs of keeping numbers of cattle beyond family needs were calculated as unproductive. The moderate rise in the total village counts for sheep underlines Kern's comment that raising livestock tended to be a secondary occupation. The per-capita numbers of sheep do not suggest that any of these villages specialized in keeping large herds of sheep. In contrast, Theophil Weiss suggests that in Kulm the extensive pasture land had made the breeding of karakuls quite profitable. Karakul values were such that breeders here generally employed their own shepherds. However, even in Kulm, raising sheep remained an occupation of secondary importance to raising crops.[70] In Plotzk, while the per-capita figures for both horses and sheep doubled, the 1939 totals are not large and don't suggest livestock as a major focus.

The 1825 Welfare Committee study did not collect data on holdings of poultry, but two data points provided by Kern suggest that raising poultry had become an important village occupation in the postwar period. In quoting statistics developed for the 100-year anniversary of Plotzk in 1939, Kern notes that village poultry holdings had grown by 1,000 percent from 436 to 4,600.[71] In describing the damage caused by a cloudburst in September 1927 that destroyed the dam Leipzig had built on the Kogil'nik River, Kern notes that the village lost 14,713 head of poultry.[72]

The continued population growth in German Bessarabia, which was a major factor in the decreasing average sizes of family landholdings, encouraged some households, particularly after the economy started to improve in the late 1920s, to support themselves at least in part via craft and trade occupations. Carpenters, smiths, shoemakers, tailors, and saddlemakers formed the largest number of trade workers, but different villages also supported butchers, potters, masons, basket makers, cart- and wheelwrights, bottle makers, and even tombstone carvers. Kern collected for his village descriptions the numbers and occupations of trade workers in twenty villages, and the Heimatbuch provides similar figures for Kulm (see table 12–5). The data for these villages suggest that trade workers generally made up between 1 percent and 5 percent of the village population, with villages on average supporting over eight separate trades.[73]

Alt Posttal's numbers reflect the profitable investment that village's population made in wagon work, where 84 percent of its large number of trade workers employed themselves as wheelwrights (83) and blacksmiths (56). If the figures for Alt Posttal, with its unusually large number of trade workers, are excluded, the remaining villages average 26.2 trade workers or 2.0 percent of the village population. Kern and the Kulm Heimatbuch do not date their listings, though it is probable that they come from the 1930s. The number of different trades tends to vary directly with the size of the village. The larger villages were clearly able to support more specialized trades, although, as the figures for Eigenheim and Seimeny suggest, the

70. Weiss, "Sheep Breeding" in "Heimatbuch der Gemeinde Kulm," *Heritage Review* 14, no. 2 (1984): 34.

71. Kern, *Homeland Book*, 62.

72. Ibid., 143.

73. The figures for Kulm are from Selcho, "Craftsmen and Craft Occupations," 19–22. In his description of Gnadental, Kern notes only that "there were 12 professional tradesmen in the village" (*Homeland Book*, 108). Thus, the number of different trades in the chart is left blank. Finally, I have counted locksmiths separately from blacksmiths as both the *Heimatbuch* and Kern, in his description of Lichtental, note the specialization of the former.

TABLE 12–5.    **Village comparisons of the numbers of trades and trade workers**

| Village | Number of trades | Trade workers | Village population | Percent in trade |
|---|---|---|---|---|
| Alt Posttal | 7 | 165 | 1,564 | 10.5% |
| Benkendorf | 5 | 6 | 461 | 1.3% |
| Borodino | 9 | 43 | 2,719 | 1.6% |
| Brienne | 8 | 46 | 1,820 | 2.5% |
| Dennewitz | 4 | 15 | 554 | 2.7% |
| Eigenfeld | 6 | 12 | 688 | 1.7% |
| Eigenheim | 9 | 24 | 572 | 4.2% |
| Gnadental | | 12 | 1,210 | 1.0% |
| Gnadenfeld | 9 | 9 | 735 | 1.2% |
| Hoffnungstal | 7 | 30 | 1,930 | 1.6% |
| Jekaterinowka | 4 | 9 | 706 | 1.3% |
| Klöstitz | 11 | 55 | 3,312 | 1.7% |
| Krasna | 5 | 36 | 3,511 | 1.0% |
| Kolatschowka | 6 | 8 | 665 | 1.2% |
| Kulm | 11 | 84 | 1,711 | 4.9% |
| Lichtental | 12 | 31 | 1,900 | 1.63% |
| Neu Arzis | 5 | 13 | 849 | 1.5% |
| Neu Sarata | 5 | 19 | 570 | 6.7% |
| Sangerowka | 5 | 8 | 372 | 2.2% |
| Seimeny | 13 | 20 | 597 | 3.4% |
| Wittenburg | 4 | 43 | 1,451 | 3.0% |
| **Average** | 7.25 | 32.8 | 1,328.4 | 2.5% |

relative isolation of a village was another factor that encouraged the development of many different kinds of trade work. These figures also suggest that while each of these villages could support some trade work, such occupations could not absorb large numbers of families looking for ways to find income beyond the diminished potentials of their farmsteads.

The most prosperous villages in postwar German Bessarabia were those that were able to create and sustain businesses in commerce and manufacturing beyond the level of individual trade and craftwork. Villages that had been prosperous before the war but whose economy continued to be chiefly dependent on growing crops and raising animals, such as Kulm, fell behind. The continuation of the weekly markets after the war in Tarutino, Arzis, and Sarata helped sustain some businesses through the difficult first years and then, as the economy improved, helped to grow new businesses. All three of these villages had, in the 1920s, merchants who bought grain and animals from farmers, merchants who sold dry goods to farmers, and banks to help all parties. Stumpp, in his 1939 overview of German villages in Bessarabia, notes that Alt Posttal now had a weekly market.[74] For Mannsburg, Arzis, Beresina, and Leipzig, the rebuilding of the railway line from Akkerman to Leipzig, finished at the start of the war but destroyed by 1918, allowed them to develop and grow commercial

---

74. Stumpp, "Landed Property Situation."

businesses around their rail stations. Over time, Arzis and Sarata seemed to benefit more from being major rail connections than from their weekly markets. As will be discussed in more detail in the next pages, each of these larger and more economically successful villages was greatly helped by the development of manufacturing.

Some villages developed strong commercial bases without the advantages of weekly markets or the railroad. Eigenfeld, founded in 1880 on the Sarata River well north of Sarata, had established itself before the war as a center of commerce serving the new German villages established farther north of it. Critical to Eigenfeld's economic strength was the village's ability to keep its cooperative store in good health after the war. Kulm, which had also established a consumers cooperative before the war, saw it fail afterward, likely because it could not draw sufficient business with the easy availability of the weekly market in Tarutino and the two rail stations in Leipzig. In Eigenfeld's case, the cooperative store linked to a cooperative dairy dominated the local market. This combination gave this midsized village (688 people in 1940) the commercial strength to establish a bank, which helped farmers finance building and equipment needs.

Eigenheim, established in 1861 on the Alkalija River north of Mannsburg, also drew on the commercial strength of its cooperative store to create economic vitality. Eigenheim was also helped by other factors. It was a center of local government, a volost office under the Imperial Russian government and a communa office in Romanian times. With Mannsburg 25 kilometers to the south, too far for easy access, Eigenheim had space to become a local commercial center, too. It successfully maintained a bank, and its commercial businesses drew much business from the much larger Ukrainian Cossack village of Starokozača just to the north. Commerce in Neu Sarata was similarly helped. It was founded in 1890 on the Sarata River, a tributary of the Prut.[75] Its commercial businesses were helped by the village's strong farmer's cooperative and by its designation as a communa center under the Romanians, which drew in trade from surrounding non-German villages. Like Eigenheim, Neu Sarata was also able to support a commercial bank.

Cooperatively owned stores were a positive economic force in several other German villages, with Hoffnungstal (1907), Gnadenfeld (1908), Kulm (1908), and Eigenfeld (1908) having established cooperative stores even before the war. After the war, cooperative stores were set up in Eigenheim and Neu Sarata, as noted above, as well as in Gnadenfeld, Kolatschowka, Mannsburg, Wischniowka, and Lichtental. Lichtental actually set up three cooperative stores. The cooperative store movement sprang up as a response to the general negative reactions among the German farmers to the low prices offered by middlemen to buy produce and animals and the high price markups they perceived on products sold by middlemen. Kern's village descriptions are peppered with negative commentary about both the pricing markups made by traveling merchants and peddlers, and the differences between what farmers received for grain sales and what, in turn, the grain merchants earned when they resold that grain. Culturally, the Germans tended to undervalue the risks such middlemen bore and so considered their prices unfair. Cooperatives could potentially increase the prices received for grains and animals by pooling surplus for sale and so

---

75. As noted earlier, this Sarata River, flowing westward to the Prut, is located in central Bessarabia west and north of the main area of German settlement, and, thus, is different from the river with the same name that flows south from Eigenfeld through Sarata to the Black Sea.

via negotiation, timing, and the sale of larger quantities achieve the best prices. On the other side of sales transactions, cooperatives sought to reduce consumer purchase costs by pooling funds and buying commonly needed items directly and in bulk from wholesale merchants. To succeed, cooperative stores needed a customer base that was without other attractive options, as the failure of the Kulm store suggests. In order to succeed as sellers of grain and animals, cooperatives needed a solid financial basis to be able to buy when farmers needed to sell and then hold for ultimate sale until attractive prices could be found. As noted earlier, Theophil Weiss ties the failure of the Economic Association cooperative in Kulm to the fact that "it simply had no money."[76] E. Selcho indicates that postwar problems with the Kulm cooperative store were also the result of its having an insufficient financial basis. To build up its stock for sale, the store needed to borrow at disadvantageous terms. With interest costs running at 20 percent, this additional cost increased the prices of the goods the Kulm store had for sale, to the detriment of its business.[77] When in 1936 the cooperative had to go out of business, Johann Roloff, with sufficient funding, "opened his own business in the same room and prospered."[78]

Cooperative dairies appear to have had the most success in managing for Bessarabian German farmers the sale of agricultural products. They bought up raw milk from local farmers to sell in bulk or to process and sell as milk-based products. The key elements in their success were that they processed the milk they bought, had a ready local market for the products they created, and then grew as over time they found and serviced larger regional markets. The successes of the Gnadental dairy in creating sales of 3,000,000 lei (1927) and the Teplitz dairy in producing 500,000–700,000 liters of milk (1937–39) were noted earlier. Having established regional contracts for dairy products, as Eigenfeld did with Chisinau and Gnadental did with Galatz, was an important factor in growing a cooperative dairy business into a major economic force for the village.

The villages that built the strongest economic positions after World War I were those with strong commercial bases where manufacturing and milling had taken root before the war. After the war, manufacturing and milling grew to be major focuses of these villages. Critical factors appear to have been the existence of weekly markets, a healthy commercial life that included access to financial help from local banks, and the location of a rail station in the village or close by. Even though it missed out on having a railroad station, Tarutino led this group. Stumpp in 1939 referred to Tarutino as the "political, economical and cultural center of ethnic Germans in Bessarabia"[79] Several other German settlements with railroad stations grew in the 1930s into large commercial and manufacturing villages. The most notable were Arzis, Beresina, Leipzig, Mannsburg, and Sarata. Borodino, without its own rail station, also grew into a commercial and manufacturing center. Stumpp's 1939 survey calls attention to three villages with significant milling facilities for grain: Arzis, Beresina, and Borodino. Stumpp calls Beresina's mill "the largest…in Bessarabia which supplies its flour also to Romania."[80] Kern notes that Beresina's Progress Mill

76. Weiss, "Grain Selling and Prices," 33.
77. Selcho, "Craftsmen and Craft Occupations," 22.
78. Ibid.
79. Stumpp, "Landed Property Situation."
80. Ibid.

was the largest in German Bessarabia, as it had an adjunct in Arzis and "a running capital of 9 million lei."[81] Kern describes Borodino's mill, operated by the Schock brothers, as the second largest.[82] Leipzig and Mannsburg also had major milling facilities.

In Tarutino, manufacturing rather than milling concerns dominated, and the factory owners there pursued many different interests: there were four cloth and dye factories, a paper factory, a brewery, a soap factory, a concrete tile factory and a foundry making agricultural machinery.[83] Sarata also was a manufacturing center. Firms making farm machinery there had been established before the war and these businesses grew and expanded after the war. Sarata, however, was surpassed by Arzis in this field. Kern notes that "Sarata, Tarutino and Arzis were farm machinery producers, although Arzis took the lead later."[84] In economic development, Arzis led in more areas than just the production of farm machinery: Arzis was able to create a web of commercial and industrial enterprises and so became, after Tarutino, the most active business center among the German villages in the postwar period.[85] Stumpp notes that Arzis had a major grain mill, likely the Kogil'nik Mill, which Kern indicates had been founded in 1930. Arzis also had a branch of the Akkerman-based Aswadurow Mill. In addition, Arzis had the Meske agricultural machinery factory, the Kraft tool and dye plant, the Bergman cloth factory, the Widmer and Häckner chemical plant, and the Maas clock manufacturing company. Arzis also developed a substantial warehousing business near its railroad station.[86] The warehouse was in part communally owned with rents used to fund the needs of the village church.

In the postwar period, several other villages, though focused chiefly on agriculture and livestock, also built small manufacturing facilities. Jekaterinowka had a small dye factory and a wool processing plant. Klöstitz citizens were active in making pottery for the Tarutino and Arzis markets and had small factories that made roof and oven tiles. Lichtental and Kolatschowka also made roof tiles. Basyrjamka, Benkendorf, Eigenheim, Friedenstal, Gnadenfeld, Hoffnungstal, Lichtental, and Neu Posttal had manufacturers making bricks. The neglect of buildings during the war, as well as the continuing division of family properties postwar with children wanting a separate house of their own, created a growing demand for concrete and tiles. The widespread appearance of such businesses, together with the weight of the products they made, suggests that such businesses had generally a local focus and produced relatively small outputs.

While the villages with the strongest manufacturing and commercial bases grew during the postwar period and tended to be among the largest German villages in Bessarabia, they were not the only large villages. Several of the mother colonies that continued to be mainly focused on agriculture and livestock also maintained large populations (see table 12–6).[87]

---

81. Kern, *Homeland Book*, 125, 123.
82. Ibid., 125.
83. Ibid., 192.
84. Ibid., 186.
85. Arzis by this time had so grown in size and importance that it no longer was commonly distinguished as Alt Arzis from its much smaller sister village Neu Arzis.
86. Ibid., 82.
87. The population data is from Kern's parish listings dating to 1939–40 (*Homeland Book*, 42, 52, 63, 68, 79, 97, 106, 108, 120, 135, 137, 145–46, 153, 163, 179, 189, 193, 196).

TABLE 12–6. 1930s populations of villages focused on commerce and manufacturing and of those focused on agriculture and livestock

| Manufacturing and commercial focus | | Agriculture and livestock focus | |
|---|---|---|---|
| Tarutino | 3,746 citizens | Krasna | 3,511 citizens |
| Borodino | 2,719 citizens | Klöstitz | 3,312 citizens |
| Beresina | 2,653 citizens | Teplitz | 2,498 citizens |
| Leipzig | 2,302 citizens | Friedenstal | 2,149 citizens |
| Sarata | 2,193 citizens | Brienne | 1,820 citizens |
| Arzis | 1,789 citizens | Kulm | 1,711 citizens |

## Differences in wealth increased in postwar German Bessarabian villages

The villages with strong manufacturing facilities and extensive commercial businesses were on the whole in the healthiest economic shape by the end of the 1930s. The overall financial strength of these villages, though, masks a widening difference in them between families doing very well and families doing less well. Stumpp notes this disparity particularly for Leipzig, where he saw very poor families living "next to well-to-do."[88] Income disparities certainly existed in the villages more focused on agriculture and livestock, but such disparities do not appear to be as broad. The wider disparities in the towns with strong manufacturing and commercial businesses are not surprising given that cultural expectations permit factory owners and the heads of commercial businesses to pay themselves a good deal more than they paid their employees.

I have argued in this study that at the time of the first settlements, there was only a modest differentiation in wealth among the German colonists in Bessarabia; however, throughout the course of the nineteenth century and up to 1914, there was a steady growth in income disparity. Differences in how hard individuals and families worked, knowledge of what succeeded, skill at implementing this knowledge, and luck all played roles in creating widening differences in family fortunes. At the end of the period before World War I, the very richest German Bessarabians were living on large family estates separate from the villages or owned land and houses in more than one village.

In the period after World War I, several of the causes for such differences in wealth and the ways in which these differences became visible changed. Numbers of those who had fallen further behind in the postwar period were hurt by factors and influences separate from their own diligence, skills, and knowledge. Farmsteads were hurt by absent or wounded men, by war deaths, by damages from looting and banditry, and by not having purchased the land that they were farming. Some families were hurt by failing to understand and adapt to the changed market for agricultural products. Others suffered from the division of family properties, with their shares of land becoming too small to produce significant surplus. Not everyone recovered from the economic losses created by the war and its aftermath. Among those who had, the frequent division of family holdings into small properties meant that even where farmers were successful, the economic profits were more modest.

---

88. Stumpp, "Landed Property Situation."

The frequent references to struggles and tough times in Kern and other postwar sources suggest that the number of poor in German Bessarabian villages had grown.

In the postwar period, the richest Germans in Bessarabia were the owners of factories and successful commercial businesses who now lived in the large villages where their business were located. Before the war, the wealthiest families had separated themselves from the villages, but now the most well-to-do lived mixed in among the cottager houses of families who worked in their businesses and the farmsteads of families who continued to earn their living from agriculture. This increased the visibility and emotional reality of differences in wealth. The perception of such differences was also enhanced by the presence and display of luxuries purchased and imported into Bessarabia from Romania, Western Europe, and North America.

In the postwar period it was still quite possible to make a comfortable living from agriculture and raising livestock, but that required having on average larger holdings of land, possessing the funds to purchase the mechanical help of tractors and steam threshers, and finding an interested and steady market for grains, plant-based oils, or dairy products. While after 1918 growing disparities in income continued to develop within villages, it should also be noted that such disparities now existed very apparently between villages. The small-plot hectare villages were the poorest and had fallen the furthest behind. The large villages with both agriculture and strong manufacturing and commercial businesses had the wealthiest Germans in Bessarabia but also had the greatest internal differences in income. The existence of such disparities had the potential for creating social and political tensions in these villages. By 1940 and the resettlement, though, such tensions appear not to have surfaced into public actions.

The only German villages that had prosperous citizens without also having many very poor families were a few of the new daughter villages established on purchased land where families had been able to maintain large plots of farmland after the war. Included in this number were some of the single-family estates founded in the nineteenth century that had survived the Romanian land reform. Here the children of the founders formed small hamlets of large family farms. The numbers of such prosperous villages of generally similar levels of income made up only a small part of German Bessarabia. In Stumpp's 1939 accounting of the German villages in Bessarabia, there are 22 villages in this category, 15 percent of the total number of 149 villages. These 22 villages accounted for only 3.9 percent of Stumpp's total population.

While in the postwar period, some villages became noticeably very poor and growing income disparities appeared more visibly among the Germans in Bessarabia, this should not obscure the fact that many Germans did recover their economic footing after the war. By the 1930s, many of the German villages had recaptured at least the appearance of healthy and semiprosperous places. Improved circumstances led several of the German villages to resume or initiate major civic projects. The undertaking of these construction projects implies that a modest economic recovery was in fact taking place. Brienne, which by 1914 had collected 32,000 rubles toward the construction of a new and larger church but had lost these funds to the war effort, was able to pick up this project again in the late 1920s. In 1934, Brienne laid the cornerstone for the new church. Hoffnungsfeld completed its new church in 1936. Eigenheim built a new church between 1938 and 1939, and Lunga completed its new church and school in 1938, finishing construction that had begun in 1907.

Also in 1938, Neu Posttal dedicated its new Deutsches Haus, which was constructed to house its German cultural association, a building Kern indicates cost 1 million lei.[89] Alt Posttal set a cornerstone for a large new church in November 1938 and by 1940 had spent 3 million lei when the project had to be abandoned because the villagers had decided to join the resettlement. By the fall of 1940, Brienne had not completed its new church. Although by this time Brienne had spent some 1.5 million lei, this project, too, was abandoned as the villagers joined the resettlement.

## Social life in postwar German Bessarabia increasingly reflected the impact of broad cultural connections that reached outside of Bessarabia

As with other rural societies in Europe and North America, German Bessarabia, noticeably by the 1930s, was becoming culturally less isolated. This is suggested by the development of entertainments and social organizations that show interests extending beyond one's family, one's village, one's culture, and one's isolated province or country. Such broadening is, unfortunately, not yet substantiated by memoirs and letters, but only indirectly suggested by descriptions of town life and its cultural institutions and by photographs.

Beginning in 1919, Tarutino had a regularly published newspaper, the *Deutsche Zeitung Bessarabiens*. Dr. Hans Wahl describes it as founded by "teachers at the Tarutino High School" and linked in outlook with "the educational institutions [in Tarutino] and the Lutheran church."[90] A second newspaper, also published in Tarutino, was started in the 1930s, the *Deutsches Volksblatt*. Wahl describes this paper as pursuing the popular German "renewal movement," which tied it with "National Socialist ideological goals."[91] At least by the 1930s, Tarutino had a cinema, a swimming pool, a sports field, and even a tennis court.[92] Sarata had bookshops, and Lichtental had a professional photographer.[93] As evidence of patterns of social life reaching beyond one's family circle, Klöstitz now had two restaurants, Arzis, Mannsburg, and Tarutino had sports clubs, Katzbach had a football (soccer) club, Alt Elft, Teplitz, Beresina, and Eigenfeld had village brass bands,[94] and Neu Elft had an orchestra. Kulm had installed kerosene street lamps in its center where the church and community buildings were located, drawing people out of their homes in the evening.[95] Reading circles were founded in several smaller villages, such as Balaktschelly, as a means to share access to books and periodicals. This reflects a broadening interest in and curiosity about the world beyond one's village, attitudes Giesinger found so absent in the nineteenth-century German villages in South

---

89. Kern, *Homeland Book*, 172. Kern's text also includes a picture of the Neu Posttal Deutsches Haus.
90. Hans Rudolf Wahl, "A Lecture Delivered in Neu Wulmsdorf, Germany, on Saturday, May 31, 2014, on the Occasion of the 200th Anniversary of the Founding of Tarutino," *Heritage Review* 44, no. 4 (2014): 7.
91. Ibid.
92. Ibid.
93. As few photographs exist from pre–World War I German Bessarabia, Kern's notation of Lichtental's photographer in the context of postwar businesses and trades suggests that this was distinctive (*Homeland Book*, 183).
94. Teplitz had a history of brass ensembles. A brass band was created in the 1860s and then given up by 1876, but revived in the 1890s. Another was founded in 1908 and a third in 1927.
95. Daniel Wölfle, "Michael Guse" in "Heimatbuch der Gemeinde Kulm," *Heritage Review* 13, no. 4 (1983): 20.

Russia and Bessarabia. Marienfeld, located north and distant from the main German settlement area, established a community library with "subscriptions to magazines and newspapers."[96] Borodino had a library with a modest collection of three hundred volumes, Teplitz and Mannsburg had libraries with over eight hundred volumes, and Neu Posttal had an even larger collection of over one thousand books. Teplitz sources, proud of the breadth of outside interests among its citizens, gave Kern data from the 1930s on the different subscriptions individuals there had with various German publications from Bessarabia, Romania, and even from Germany.[97]

A special feature of the postwar cultural broadening that occurred in German Bessarabia was the reaching out to Germany for cultural infusions through the import of literary works, music, songs, and drama. In part, this turning to Germany for imports of German culture was a response to growing pressure applied by the Romanian government to teach and use the Romanian language. Under such pressure to assimilate, Germans in Bessarabia felt more keenly the need to educate their children in the German language. The pressure to assimilate also clearly played a role in encouraging Germans of all ages to develop an interest and pride in German culture by learning German songs and drama and reading German literature. Perhaps another factor leading Germans in Bessarabia to focus more on preserving their language, religion, and customs was the increase, materially in Tarutino and Arzis but present in most of the mother colonies, in the number of non-Germans living in their villages. The push to offer school instruction only in Romanian became a touch point. Teplitz reports that while in general in the German Bessarabian villages there was a 1:1 ratio of teachers with a German linguistic background to those with a Romanian background, the number of classes given in the German language was steadily reduced. In 1931, there were six hours of classes in German per week, but in 1939, only two.[98] In response, in the 1930s, German villages began to hire their own teachers to handle course work in religion and language in village schools or to provide such instruction outside the state schools in the village churches.

To promote a better understanding of and pride in German culture, several villages formed German cultural societies. In Borodino, a German cultural organization called the Heilbronn was established, which ultimately created a library of some three hundred volumes. In the mid-1930s, Kulm built the German Community Hall to provide additional schooling in German as well as for religious meetings.[99] Neu Posttal, as noted above, built a German cultural club building, the Deutsches Haus, to provide an attractive place for youth organizations to meet, as well as a place to hold confirmation classes and to put on performances of drama and music.[100]

---

96. Kern, *Homeland Book*, 159.
97. Ibid., 94–95. Fifty-nine subscriptions were to the Tarutino *Deutsche Zeitung Bessarabians*, four to the *Banater Tageblatt*, four for the *Schwäbischer Merkur* from Stuttgart, and others for the *Siebenbürgisches Tageblatt*. The latter was the paper of the German political party in Romania.
98. Ibid., 94.
99. The information on the Heilbronn Society is from Kern (*Homeland Book*, 125), and on the Kulm German Community Hall from Wölfle ("Michael Guse," 20).
100. Organizations that sought to celebrate Pan-German traditions and in particular to educate the youth of German-speaking families in those traditions and even inculcate a sense of pride in them became a common feature within the German-speaking world during the nineteenth century. Greatly influenced by the work of the Grimm brothers, such groups sought to awaken greater appreciation for German folk culture through preserving German songs and folklore. To isolated groups, such as the Bessarabian Germans, forming these organizations were clear responses to the growing pressure of other languages and cultures.

## Although postwar German Bessarabia exhibited striking changes, the dominating features of village life remained focused on an agricultural economy, on German customs and culture, and on religious life

By 1940, the world of pre–World War I German Bessarabia must have seemed strange and distant, since so many changes had taken place after 1914. While the economy had partially recovered, it had not returned to pre-1914 levels, and moreover, economic conditions were now far more varied, complex, and uncertain with new markets, new agricultural products, and new customers. Between 1887 and 1940, the German population in Bessarabia had increased by half from nearly sixty thousand to just short of ninety thousand people. With purchases of new land and emigration no longer answers for the growing population, farmsteads were subdivided. Smaller plots of land led to smaller family incomes. More adults now sought trade work to earn a living or had given up full-time farming altogether to work in one of the manufacturing or commercial businesses that were established in one of the larger villages.

Contacts with Germany had significantly increased after World War I. German-language newspapers published in Bessarabia and Romania and sent from Germany and Austria were now more widespread. Business contacts were developed in Germany and Austria, as well as in the German-speaking regions of Romania. By 1940, Bessarabian Germans were far less isolated and far more aware of political events taking place in the world beyond the province. One result of this was that Bessarabian Germans were likely feeling far less secure. Political rivalries in Europe created worries that war could break out again and rising currents of nationalism at home in Romania brought concerns as to whether they could sustain the dominance of the German language and culture in their villages. The Romanian government was increasing the pressure to assimilate, and the larger villages were gaining material numbers of non-German citizens. Bessarabian Germans were going to unprecedented lengths to pass on the German language and culture. Greater numbers of students were now traveling to Germany, Estonia, and Latvia for further education, and larger numbers of pastors, doctors, dentists, and businessmen born or at least educated in Germany were appearing in Bessarabia.[101] All of this broadened the awareness in German Bessarabia of events and political currents in Germany and Western Europe where annual threats of war finally led to the break out of actual fighting in the fall of 1939. The Soviet Union had not lost its interest in recapturing Bessarabia. Bessarabian Germans appear to have been quite aware of the horrible fate of Germans, very much like themselves, who were living in villages beyond the Dniester River in the Soviet Ukraine. There, people suffered through several periods of famine after the war, at least two of which were created by the Soviet government's policies. In Bessarabia, worries no doubt grew as to whether such things might happen to them.

---

101. Some of the grandchildren of Gottfried Schulz living on the Schulzenheim estate were educated in Riga (Kern, *Homeland Book*, 176). Alfred Hoffmann of the Hoffmann estate near Klöstitz provided money for scholarships to send young Germans from Bessarabia to study in the university town of Dorpat in Estonia (134). Pastor Gotthold Winter of Sarata, who studied at the Treffner classical high school in Dorpat and later at the Lutheran seminary there, may have been one of Hoffmann's beneficiaries (181).

Despite the increased contact Germans in Bessarabia had established with the world beyond the province, the distance separating the generally agriculture-based villages of German Bessarabia from village life in Germany, Western Europe, and North America was becoming wider rather than decreasing. The isolation of Bessarabia within Romania, the limited schooling opportunities, the transportation system that (but for the railroad) was entirely based on muddy or dusty roads and horsepower, the general absence of electricity, and chiefly the overreliance on agriculture as a basis for its economy tied German Bessarabia more to the world that was fast disappearing in Western Europe's rearview mirror. To most Germans living in Bessarabia before June 1940, however, this was neither a problem nor a liability. To be left alone, to be able to maintain their customs and language, to worship in their own churches, and to prosper by the work of their own hands were aspirations as positive for them as they had been for the ancestors who had traveled far to settle Bessarabia. The domineering presence of agricultural life and the demands it made had not fundamentally changed since the Germans first came to Bessarabia.

The world the Germans had created in Bessarabia, however, was about to end. While in early 1940, Germans living in Bessarabia were far more aware of the world outside the province than at any time in their history, it is doubtful that any were anticipating the cataclysmic events that would occur later in the year and quite undercut their resolve to maintain their settlements in Bessarabia, and so end the 126-year-old German presence in the province.

# XIII

# The Resettlement

In the fall of 1940 on relatively short notice, virtually all the Germans living in Bessarabia willingly gave up their homes, farms, equipment, savings, and businesses, and abandoned Bessarabia. Their decision to do so reflects their collective vote of no confidence in their future in Soviet-controlled Bessarabia. In June 1940 the Soviet Union, having earlier invaded and taken over the former Imperial Russian provinces of Estonia, Latvia, and Lithuania, sent troops into Romanian Moldavia. In just five days and with hardly any fighting, Romania surrendered, and the Soviet Union annexed the two territories Romania had gained in the Versailles Treaty: the Imperial Russian province of Bessarabia, as well as what had been the northern half of the prewar Austrian duchy of Bukovina, located just to the north of Bessarabia.[1] Following agreements established during the negotiations for the Molotov-Ribbentrop Pact of August 1939, German and Soviet authorities met in Moscow in September 1940 and set specific terms under which German-speaking citizens living in Bessarabia and Bukovina could elect to leave and move to Germany. Civil and military officials from Germany were then allowed to enter the region and, together with Soviet military officials, informed the Germans in Bessarabia and Bukovina of the terms and their right to emigrate. Those electing to participate in the resettlement—Umsiedlung, as this process was called in the documents—traveled by trucks, railway trains, and horse-drawn carts to ports on the lower Danube in Bessarabia or in neighboring Romania. There, the German government had arranged for river transport to take them and the few belongings they were allowed to bring with them to processing centers in greater Germany. In a sad irony, the resettlers were ultimately given land in what had been, in the eighteenth and early nineteenth centuries, Prussian Poland—the same region many of their ancestors had left 126 years earlier to move to Bessarabia. They were settled in homes and on land confiscated mainly from Polish peasants whom the German government had forced out

---

1. The province of Bukovina is situated on the northwest border of Bessarabia and contains the northeastern slopes of the Carpathian Mountains and the plains bordering these. Part of the Ottoman Empire until 1775, it then became a duchy within the Austro-Hungarian Empire. The southern half of Bukovina had a majority Romanian-/Moldavian-speaking population, but the northern half was largely Ukrainian-speaking.

in its efforts of ethnic cleansing that sought to make the German population of this territory a lasting majority.

In order to participate in the resettlement, a Bessarabian German adult had to make an active election by signing a document. Only a few participants in this resettlement left insights into the rationale that led Germans in Bessarabia to elect to leave, and these all suggest that the prospects of the loss of land and liberties were major fears. That in general Germans in Bessarabia were deeply concerned about and likely frightened by what they anticipated Soviet control would mean for them is strongly suggested by the fact that virtually the entire Bessarabian German population, when offered the chance, elected to leave. In so doing they were willing to abandon homes, crops in the field, animals, equipment, as well as most possessions of any monetary value. While Soviet authorities were quick to establish state ownership of the financial and manufacturing businesses in Bessarabia, by September 1940 they had not yet collectivized agriculture. At this time, the Bessarabian Germans were harvesting grain they had planted in the spring and no doubt considered their own property. Germans in Bessarabia, however, were likely quite aware of the fate of the German population in neighboring Ukraine. These Germans, earlier immigrants to Imperial Russia than the Bessarabians, had been part of the Soviet Union since 1919. As discussed in more detail below, the German population in the Ukraine suffered greatly under Soviet rule, and stories of their experiences had been carried to Bessarabia by Germans fleeing from the Ukraine. G. Wernik, in his account of the resettlement of the Hoffnungsfeld village, notes that they "had heard various horrible reports from those fleeing the Russian 'Paradise' which was separated from [them] by the small Dniester River."[2] However positively the Soviet authorities in Bessarabia had sought after July 1940 to describe their prospects, Bessarabian Germans weren't attracted. By September 1940, when the offer to leave was first formally declared, the great majority of Germans in Bessarabia had concluded that Soviet intentions for them were so unappealing, and even frightening, that it would be preferable to give up their houses, farms, and occupations, and go. For those Germans harboring any thoughts of remaining in Bessarabia, once it became clear that the great majority were electing to leave, they may have come to feel that they had no other choice.

## The experiences of Germans in the neighboring Soviet Ukraine greatly influenced Bessarabian German attitudes

Given the fate of the German communities in the Soviet Ukraine across the Dniester River, Germans in Bessarabia had good cause for concern. Soviet rule brought famine, political terror, and ultimately the loss of land and the reduction of German farmers to the status of serfs bound to state-controlled collective farms. Soviet rule also suppressed religious services and cultural activities. The Soviet government generally did not permit the public practice of religious belief. In German villages in the Ukraine, many churches had been turned into civic buildings and could no longer be used for religious services. Religious services could continue in homes, but local governments put pressure to limit these to single family observances, viewing

---

2. G. Wernik, "Resettlement Chronicle of Hoffnungsfeld, Bessarabia," #T-81, Roll 599, Serial 816, Group 1035, Item 1266, Frames 5386381-5386389, trans. Allen Konrad, December 2012, http://www.grhs.org/korners/memonly/konrad_doc/Resettlement%20Chronicle%20of%20Hoffnungsfeld,%20Bessarabia.pdf (members-only access).

larger groupings as potentially anti-Soviet political gatherings. Religious belief and practice, as a result, had to go underground. Similarly, efforts to introduce or continue language and cultural connections with German organizations outside the Soviet Union were viewed as anti-Soviet activities subject to harsh penalties including exile.

As in Bessarabia, the economic strains of World War I had impoverished many citizens in the German communities in the Ukraine. However, unlike in Bessarabia, the postwar period had not brought real improvements. Soviet economic policies were responsible for creating widespread famine. In the fall of 1921, Soviet authorities in the Ukraine began to requisition large amounts of grain, often via confiscations, despite the fact that the harvest that year had been greatly reduced by drought. The Soviet government wanted the grain for export to the West. Grain sales were to be a major source of foreign exchange the Soviet Union needed to introduce its plans for increased industrialization. The grain requisitions brought famine in the winter of 1921–22, which worsened throughout 1922 with a second year of drought and continued grain confiscations for export. The famine in the Ukraine and elsewhere in the Soviet Russia was widely reported and resulted in the deaths of perhaps 1.2 to 2 million people.[3] The American Relief Administration, headed by Secretary of Commerce Herbert Hoover, was a prominent factor in providing food for over 2 million people in the Ukraine during this period.[4]

An even more devastating famine occurred in the Ukraine in 1932–33 during the forced collectivization of agriculture in the Soviet Union. In 1932, the Soviet government implemented a plan under which the state took over all agricultural production. Using a legal theory that all land, and thus everything existing on it, was state property, what had been heretofore privately owned farmland, farm equipment, and animals were confiscated. Using the same justification, the government bought up or simply confiscated grain stockpiles that had been maintained by villages and families. The Soviet government's intention was to turn farmers into wage-earning workers on collective farms. These collective farms, called in Russian kolxozy,[5] were large-area, state-controlled, industrialized manor farms. Allegedly, the collective farms were communes owned by their members, but they were in fact enterprises tightly controlled by the Soviet state based on a new industrialized form of serfdom.[6] The state assigned production quotas, was the sole legal purchaser of the produce created by the collective farms, and set the prices at which it bought that produce. Fearful that farm workers would rebel against this system with their feet and seek to leave the collective farms for better prospects in the towns and cities, the Soviet

3.  Roman Serbyn, "The First Man-Made Famine in Soviet Ukraine 1921-23," Ukrainian Weekly 56, no. 45, (November 1988), http://www.ukrweekly.com/old/archive/1988/458814.shtml.

4.  Fridtjof Nansen, the Norwegian explorer, scientist, and statesman, won the Noble Peace Prize in 1922, in great part for his work as High Commissioner of Relief for Russia. The Commission had sought to lessen the famine by importing grain from the west for Russia. Soviet delegates to The Hague Economic Conference in the summer of 1922 shocked Western representatives when they announced that, despite the ongoing famine, the Soviet Union intended to resume grain exports.

5.  The singular noun kolxoz is a contraction from the words kollektivnoe xozjajstvo, a "collective farm," with the adjective offering the implication of collective management.

6.  From the 1920s onward, there also existed farming operations operated by and legally owned by the Soviet Government—that is, without the fiction of collective ownership by the working farmers. These were called sovxozy from the contraction of sovetskoe xozjajstvo or "Soviet farms." Farmers here were considered farm workers and were deemed analogous to industrial workers in factories. Sovxozy and kolxozy existed side by side in the Soviet Union. Soviet agricultural theorists considered kolxoz farms an intermediary stage to the ideal sovxoz.

government instituted a system of internal passports that prevented collective farmers from leaving their villages. The net effect was to create a vast class of modern-day serfs locked into their villages. Collective farmers under this system would not be guaranteed an adequate food supply, as the government took preset amounts from each harvest, nor could collective farmers benefit financially from their labor, skills, or agricultural knowledge as the government "purchased" all produce at prices it set.

The Soviet government's intention was to maintain a steady, low-cost food supply in the industrializing cities and to continue to profit by selling grain in the West. A major pillar of the new Five Year Plans was that grain sales in the West would provide the income needed for the state to buy sophisticated industrial equipment for the development of Soviet factories. The overarching theoretical goal for these policies was to allow the Soviet Union to "leap" through the Industrial Revolution in a single generation. Creating the collective farms was thought to be essential because through them the Soviet government could maintain total control over the access to and the pricing of agricultural products. As with Imperial Russia, the major economic activity of the Soviet Union in the 1930s was still agriculture. To meet the state's needs for grain and animals, collective farm production targets were set as part of the Five Year Plans that were to govern all economic activity. The nationwide farm production goals were then divided up regionally and ultimately each collective farm was assigned specific quotas. The Five Year Plans could not be adjusted for local disruptions caused by weather, insects, or work force issues. Thus, if the quota exceeded the collective farm's internal needs for food, the collective farm community had to deal with reduced food supplies or even starve. If a collective farm missed its quota, its leadership would be held responsible and fired, exiled, or even shot.

As some compensation for their lost property, collective farmers were allowed to farm and keep small animals on tiny personal plots of land about their houses which often proved to be important sources of their own and their community's food supply. For Germans in the Soviet Ukraine, collectivization brought ruin: it took away their farms, equipment, and animals, as well as their stores of grain for food and seed, and gave them in return high labor quotas from which they gained little personal benefit.

The forced introduction of collective farms in the Ukraine did not go well. Farmers of all ethnic backgrounds resisted and the government's determination to implement the program quickly resulted in a terrible famine. Farmers sought to sell their animals or kill them before they were confiscated. Soviet officials sought to collect family grain holdings into larger grain storage facilities, but as Ukrainian peasant farmers historically had considered their family grain stores as critical protections against famine, not all grain stores were turned over to the state. Soviet authorities considered this behavior to be anti-Soviet and started to make forced searches and seizures of grain.[7] When the collective farms began operations, productivity was low and results were poor. Farmers, deprived of their land and its benefit to them, refused to work or made only halfhearted efforts. Soviet agriculture officials, fearful of harsh

---

7. Soviet propagandists sought to create a modern, Socialist farm hero from these events in the celebration of the almost entirely fictional Pavlik Morozov. Inspired by the goals of the state and its need for grain elsewhere, Morozov, in this legend, turned in his father for hiding grain from the authorities. Murdered by his grandfather after his father was sent to Siberia, Morozov was portrayed as a martyr.

punishments if they failed to meet the quotas assigned to them under the division of the Five Year Plan targets, took the grain and animals they needed to meet the quotas. If the farmers refused to produce enough to feed themselves over and above the state requirements, then they should suffer and so learn. Such actions produced a famine of enormous proportions, a major humanitarian disaster of nearly unprecedented size created and driven by the uncorrected actions of the Soviet government. The existence and consequences of this disaster were not reported in the Soviet Union, nor were they reported by Western news media, which by this time had been allowed to establish branches in Moscow. As a result, and unlike in the 1920s, there were no efforts outside of the Soviet Union to provide relief. The Davies and Wheatcroft study, the most comprehensive look at the famine of 1932–33 in the Soviet Ukraine, estimated that 5.5 to 6.5 million people lost their lives in those years in the Ukraine as a result of the collectivization of agriculture and the resulting famine.[8]

Conditions in the Ukraine during the early 1930s were worsened by the Soviet government's attempts to use class resentments to smooth the transition to collective farms. The government created a campaign that encouraged farmers to feel that the problems they were experiencing were the result of the greedy, speculative behavior of well-to-do farmers. In this way the Soviet government hoped that poorer farmers would support the government's intention to create egalitarian collective farms. Given the almost universal negative reaction to the process of collectivization, the campaign against so-called well-to-do farmers did not achieve the government's aims. It did, however, create increased suspicions that sadly had the effect of forging barriers that discouraged many from defending those singled out by the campaign, or helping others later once the terrible famine had begun. German farmers in the Ukraine were particularly targeted in this campaign. Wealthier farmers, branded as *kulaks*, were demonized. On December 27, 1929, Stalin announced a policy that aimed at the "liquidization of kulaks as a class."[9] The term *kulak* comes from the Russian word for fist and was used in pre-revolutionary Russia to describe tight-fisted people who were thought not to be open-hearted and generous to those less fortunate. It reflected the negative attitudes commonly felt among the Russian peasants toward those who had gained some economic status. While derogatory, before Soviet times it did not carry the sense of being inhuman or criminal. Soviet propaganda shifted the meaning of the term kulak to describe such people as heartless exploiters and enemies of the peasant class. Rather than the policies of the Soviet government, such people were deemed responsible for the sufferings of the poorer peasants and so deserving of punishment. It is in this sense that the term entered Western European languages.[10] The threshold for meeting the definition of a "well-to-do" kulak was quite low. For example, just before the start of World War I, holdings of as little as 6

8. R. W. Davies and S. G. Wheatcroft, *The Years of Hunger: Soviet Agriculture 1931-3* (Houndmills, Eng.: Palgrave-Macmillan, 2004).

9. J. V. Stalin, *Works*, vol. 12, *April 1929–June 1930* (Moscow: Foreign Languages Publishing House, 1953), 184–89.

10. The definition of "kulak" in the 1956 *Webster's New World Dictionary* follows the Soviet usage: "a well-to-do farmer in Russia who profited from the labor of poorer peasants." The Soviet cast for this word is quite clear in D. N. Ušakov's highly respected Soviet dictionary of the Russian language, where the third meaning of the word kulak is: "zažitočnyj krest'janin, eksploatirujuščij odnosel'čan" (a well-to-do peasant who is exploiting [his] fellow villagers). Ušakov, ed., *Tolkovyj slovar' russkogo jazyka*, vol. 1, *A–Kjuriny* (Moscow: Sovetskaja Ènciklopedija, 1935), 1543.

desjatina characterized well-to-do Russian peasants.[11] It is not surprising that there were many Germans in the Ukraine who had landholdings larger than 6 desjatina inherited from the colonial land grants and who therefore were punished as kulaks.

There has been no comprehensive study made to date of the human cost of the anti-kulak campaign in the Soviet Union. As with the human cost of creating the collective farms, the political overtones of such costs made them too dangerous to calibrate in Soviet times. Western estimates of the human cost of the anti-kulak campaign suggest that perhaps two million peasant farmers were deemed kulaks, dispossessed of land, and sent to labor camps in Siberia or shot.[12]

Fleischhauer, Giesinger, and Schmidt offer much commentary on the sufferings that German citizens of the Soviet Union experienced during the 1920s and 1930s. Giesinger summarizes German experience in this period darkly and succinctly: "The Communist era had dealt Russia's German population blow after blow: the terrors of the civil war period were followed by the famine of 1921–22; the ordeals of collectivization, with confiscations, arrests and deportations, were followed by another famine of 1932–33."[13]

Giesinger estimates that "at least 100,000" Germans were punished as kulaks and sent to the labor camps to be "reeducated."[14] This estimate presumes that those punished amounted to perhaps a tenth of the total German population in the Soviet Union (the 1926 Soviet census counted 1,238,539 ethnic German citizens). Data offered in the footnotes of Flegel's genealogical listing of the citizens of Kulm, Leipzig, and Tarutino give a sharp and individual meaning to the general assertions of German suffering in the Soviet Union. Flegel provides information on the tragic fates of some descendants of the families from these Bessarabian villages who moved to the north Caucasus prior to the start of World War I and so became Soviet citizens after the war.

- Alexander Flegel from the German settlement of Markosovka in the north Caucasus was sentenced to six years of labor in 1933 as a kulak. He was released a sick man in 1937 then rearrested and forced with others to "walk the plank" to his death in the Caspian Sea.[15]

- Johanna Flato, also of Markosovka, was driven from her home in 1933 with four young children. She attempted to find food and shelter in the city of Mineral'nye Vody and "never returned."[16]

- Jacob Beierle of Kronental, also in the north Caucasus, who in 1933 at age sixty ran a general store there, was "dispossessed and executed outside of [the] village."[17]

---

11. As noted earlier (chapter X, footnote 31), the agricultural reforms of the Russian Prime Minister Pyotr Stolypin introduced in the Decree of November 6, 1906 (O.S.), defined the minimum holding of a well-to-do peasant as possession of 6 desjatina of land (about 16 acres).

12. Orlando Figes, citing Soviet archives that were made available after 1990, indicates that more than 1.8 million Soviet citizens were sent to labor camps in 1930–31 as part of the anti-kulak campaign. Figes, *The Whisperers: Private Life in Stalin's Russia* (New York: Metropolitan Books, 2007), 240.

13. Giesinger, *From Catherine to Khrushchev*, 298. The arrests and deportations refer to actions that for the most part took place in the period from 1930 to 1931.

14. Ibid.

15. Flegel, *Extended Relationships*, 172.

16. Ibid.

17. Ibid., 53.

Another problem faced by Soviet citizens of German heritage was that the Soviet government suspected that their ethnicity might lead them to be interested in maintaining contacts with people or cultural life in Germany. Pursuing such interests in the government's eyes, however, made one automatically a disloyal Soviet citizen. As a result, Soviet Germans had increased chances of running afoul of the police and facing harassment, arrest, and exile. Such special attention and its consequences became yet another black mark against Soviet rule as stories about Soviet life circulated in Bessarabia.

The rationale for the concerns of the Soviet government and the extreme nature of its actions were closely connected to its founding and lifelong assumption that it could only achieve its ends through force. The Soviet government had come to power as a minority government and from the start sought to maintain its power by assuming dictatorial control. In doing so, however, the Soviet government went to extremes: it declared itself to be the sole legitimate source of information and forcefully sought to prevent the dissemination of any opinions that might cast doubt on its actions, their rationale, or legitimacy. It willingly used terror, including arbitrary arrests, exile, and executions, to back up its power and enforce conformity of opinion. The Soviet government was always suspicious that its citizens would not give it support, and in the 1930s such concerns were greatly magnified following the obvious difficulties and failures accompanying the implementation of the first Five Year Economic Plan and the collectivization of agriculture. Tensions reached a fever pitch in the mid-1930s when Stalin began a series of fearful purges that decimated the leadership of the Communist party and the Red Army and in addition imprisoned many of the intelligentsia. Stalin's goal, to use a hideous phrase of the time, was to "liquidate" all possible challengers to his power. Describing this period, Riasanovsky summarizes, "no free discussion could take place in the Soviet Union, and almost every personal opinion became dangerous."[18]

The anti-kulak campaign, the collectivization of agriculture, and the purges swept hundreds of thousands of Soviet citizens into the Siberian labor camps and penal colonies. Camp population grew from perhaps 200,000 in 1931 to 1.1 million in 1934 and then to over 1.8 million in 1939.[19] As noted above, Germans from the Ukraine who were being punished as kulaks were among these prisoners. Germans living in the Ukraine were also arrested during the period of the purges on the supposition that they harbored anti-Soviet views, or that contacts they maintained with people living outside the Soviet Union would encourage them to develop such views. The *Odessa Book of Mourning* (*Trauerbuch Odessa*), written after the breakup of the Soviet Union and based on archival material from the Soviet Ukraine, notes the wide range of worries felt by Soviet authorities that might lead to arrests for ethnic German Soviet citizens in the Odessa region. These included:

---

18. Riasanovsky, *History of Russia*, 560.
19. There are several counts of the Soviet prison population included in the major seven volume post-Soviet history of the Gulag, *Istorija stalinskogo Gulaga: Konec 1920-x – pervaja polovina 1950-x godov*, ed. Ju. N. Afanas'ev, and V. P. Kozlov. The most detailed for the 1930s are in volume 4. The numbers quoted here are population counts as of January 1 for each year held in NKVD "correctional-labor camps and colonies" from the *Istorija stalinskogo Gulaga*, Vol. 4, *Naselenie Gulaga: čislennost' i usloviia soderžanija* [The population of the gulag: the numbers and the conditions maintained], ed. A .B. Bezborodov, V. M. Xrustalev, and I. V. Bezborodova (Moscow: ROSSPĖN, 2004), 129–30.

- The private exchange of correspondence with relatives and friends outside the USSR, especially those living in Germany and the United States;

- Public mention of memories of good relations with Austrian and German troops during their occupation of the Ukraine in 1918;

- Visits to the German consulate office in Odessa;

- Participation in meetings for religious worship;

- The return of those exiled as kulaks to their former native villages.[20]

Each of these terrible events in the Soviet Ukraine—the famines, the anti-kulak campaign, the forced creation of collective farms, and the purges—motivated some people to flee. Free emigration, however, was not a right given to Soviet citizens, and Soviet border guards were ordered to capture—and if necessary wound or kill—those trying to escape. Nonetheless, numbers of Soviet Ukrainian citizens of all ethnic backgrounds did manage to escape. Crossing the Dniester River, which formed the border between Romanian Bessarabia and the Soviet Ukraine, was the most practical means to flee southwestern Ukraine. Above the Liman Gulf, which formed the estuary of the Dniester River, there were several places up to the city of Tiraspol' where the river was only 150–200 meters wide. North of Tiraspol' there were many places where the river narrowed to fewer than 100 meters. Numbers of German villages had been established close to the lower Dniester River, so it is not surprising that Germans were among those who were able to escape. I have not found, however, any credible counts of the people, much less the Germans, who fled the Soviet Ukraine before 1940. There were more than just a handful, as the stories of the trials and sufferings of individual Soviet Germans were widely circulated throughout German Bessarabia in the 1930s. News concerning conditions in the Soviet Union clearly also reached Germans in Bessarabia from Romanian and German newspapers and via radio. As many older Germans in Bessarabia were fluent in Russian, news from the Soviet Union also came through Russian-language newspapers and over radio broadcasts from Odessa or through contacts individual Bessarabian Germans had with the large Russian and Ukrainian populations in Bessarabia. Thus, well before the Soviet Union took over Bessarabia in 1940, it is probable that many Bessarabian Germans were aware of the great difficulties people in the Ukraine had been experiencing. It would not be surprising to conclude, as a result, that many Bessarabian Germans had already developed negative attitudes toward the Soviet Union and its policies toward its citizens.

---

20. M. Weiss, "Excerpt from *Odessa Book of Mourning: Stalin's State Terror against the Germans in the Odessa and Nikolajew Districts of Ukraine* 1928-1953," *Heritage Review* 37, no. 3 (2007): 11–13. The examples Weiss chooses are from the Selz and the Razdelnijan districts of the Ukraine, located on the eastern side of the Dniester estuary across from Bessarabia, in which there were several German Catholic villages settled in 1805 by colonists from Alsace and Baden. He is translating from Anton Bosch, Anton Bertsch, and Michael Wanner, *Trauerbuch Odessa: Stalins Staatsterror an den Deutschen in den Gebieten von Odessa und Nikolajew Ukraine*, 1928-1953, Rußland-Deutsche Zeitgeschichte 5 (Nürnberg: Histor. Forschungsverein der Deutschen aus Russland, 2006), 53–76. A German-language newspaper published in Moscow in the 1990s lists Germans executed during the height of Stalin's purges, August 1937 to September 1938. Among these are 1,727 from the Odessa region or "Oblast." H. Ehrman and R. Heinle, "Odessa Province Executions 1937 – 1938" (N.p.: Odessa Digital Library, 2000), http://www.odessa3.org/collections/war/link/executel.txt.

## The Molotov-Ribbentrop Pact opened the way for a swift Soviet takeover of Bessarabia and the resettlement of the German population

The Soviet ultimatum of June 26, 1940, the Romanian decision not to fight, the instant appearance of Soviet troops,[21] and the sudden annexation of Bessarabia by the Soviet Union on June 28, 1940, likely came as a surprise to inhabitants of Bessarabia. For the Soviet leadership, however, it was not a sudden, accidental, incautious, or unplanned event. In August 1939, when the Soviet Union agreed to support Nazi Germany's intended attack on Poland and so to share in the new partition of that country, additional agreements were reached that anticipated a further division of interests in Eastern Europe following a German-Soviet victory in Poland. The August 1939 treaty, often called the Molotov-Ribbentrop Pact after the names of the two foreign ministers who were the chief negotiators, contained a secret addendum. One part of this addendum stipulated that Finland, the three Baltic countries, and Bessarabia—that is, Imperial Russia's former European possessions not then part of the Soviet Union—were not areas of concern for Germany. In other words, the Soviet Union gained from this agreement the right to retake these areas by force without fear of German retaliation. As a quid pro quo, the agreement also freed Germany to attack France, Denmark, Norway, the Low Countries, and the UK without fear of the two-front war that had divided and hurt German efforts in World War I.

In September 1939, threats made by the Soviet Union caused the Baltic countries to agree to cede land for Soviet bases and to permit Soviet troops and naval personnel to be stationed on them. The Finns, similarly threatened, refused to agree, and in November 1939 the Soviet Union attacked Finland. Though Finland lost its second largest city, Viipuri (now Vyborg), and the Karelian Isthmus, it succeeded in retaining control over the bulk of its territory and confirmed that in a treaty signed in Moscow in March 1940. On June 15, 1940, the Soviet Union invaded Lithuania and, on the next day, Latvia and Estonia. On June 26, 1940, the Soviet Union also issued an ultimatum to Romania to cede Bessarabia and the northern half of Bukovina or face attack. Romania did so in one day, and Russian troops entered Bessarabia on June 28th.

It is commonly thought that the 1939 Molotov-Ribbentrop Pact anticipated the resettlement of Germans living in Bessarabia once the Soviet Union had established its control there. The text of the pact, however, contains no such agreement. It would appear that instead Germany and the Soviet Union had discussed this issue and had agreed verbally that a resettlement of Germans wishing to leave could take place, but under terms to be negotiated after the Soviet Union invaded Bessarabia. Even so, allowing ethnic Germans to leave Soviet territory was an unusual position for the Soviet Union to take. It had never permitted a general emigration. Elsewhere within the newly acquired territories, Finns, Poles, Slovaks, and Romanians were not offered such rights. Very likely when Germany asked for this right, the Soviet Union saw this as a price to be paid for making a powerful and dangerous Germany comfortable with its intention to retake former territories of Imperial Russia. The Soviet Union

---

21. Soviet paratroopers were dropped on June 28 along the Danube frontier in order to seal off the border with Romania.

also appears to have thought that only a minority of the Germans would actually choose to leave.

Materials contained in German archives that date to shortly after the Soviet takeover of Bessarabia imply that the Nazi German government was confident the Soviet Union would permit the resettlement of Germans from Bessarabia. The archives are those of the Deutsches Ausland-Institut (the Institute for Germans in Foreign Lands, referred to hereafter as the DAI), an organization concerned with maintaining connections with Germans living outside of Germany. The archives contain a circular letter dated July 5, 1940, eleven days after the Soviet takeover of Bessarabia, that was written to reassure recipients living in Germany who might "be concerned about" the plight of "close relatives and good friends in Bessarabia."[22] The letter states that "Soviet authorities have guaranteed the safety of the Bessarabian Germans" and that, anticipating the potential of a resettlement, "in many places the swastika flag has been hoisted," showing the loyalty of the Bessarabian Germans to the "National Socialist motherland."[23] That the potential of resettlement was in fact a real possibility is indicated by the further assertion that "negotiations concerning the resettlement of the Bessarabian Germans will take place soon."[24] The circular letter further indicates that the DAI Director of the Research Department, Karl Stumpp, would participate in the negotiations, that the resettlement would hopefully take place in the fall, and that a place for resettling the Bessarabian Germans coming to Germany had provisionally been selected in the former Prussian Poland: "It is hoped that the resettlement will be completed before the start of the coldest part of the year. It will provisionally take place in Warthegau."[25]

A second circular letter, dated July 15, 1940, steps back from the claim that a resettlement of the Bessarabian Germans was certain to happen. Likely in response to criticism that the first notice had gone beyond the terms of the formal agreements, the second letter acknowledges that the prior communication had been "too positive."[26] The second circular goes on to state that "a command to resettle has not been given" and that the logistics and, by implication, whether a resettlement would actually take place "is not yet determined."[27] Karl Stumpp, on the following day, July 16, 1940, wrote a letter from Berlin to DAI colleagues in Stuttgart that indicates,

22. "Circular to Bessarabian Germans Present in the Reich," #T-81, Roll 321, Group 1035, VOMI 947, Frame 2452667–2452668 in Konrad, "Propaganda and Reports." The circular letter is signed "Research Department of German Nationality in Russia." As Karl Stumpp was the Director of the Research Department, he is likely the author of the letter or responsible for the accuracy of the details it contains.

23. Ibid. No basis is given for making these assertions. The Soviets did not appoint "ethnic Germans as commissars in various towns" as the letter notes. The general political attitude of Bessarabian Germans at this time toward the Nazi party or the "National Socialist motherland" is far from clear. I have found no other sources stating that Germans in Bessarabia greeted arriving Soviet troops with the Nazi swastika flag.

24. Ibid.

25. Ibid. Warthegau, or more properly the Reichsgau Wartheland, was the name given by the Nazi German government to territory it had reincorporated into Germany after the German defeat of Poland in 1939. The Warthegau was similar to but not exactly the same as the Prussian and later Imperial German province of Posen (1814–1918), which the Treaty of Versailles had awarded to Poland following the end of World War I. Warthegau extended from Poznan in the west to Łodz in the east and so comprised much of what had been called Great Poland (Wielkopolska) before the eighteenth-century partitions.

26. Karl Stumpp, "2nd Circular to all Bessarabian Germans in Germany," # T-81, Roll 321, Group 1035, VOMI 947, Frame 2452663-2452665, in Konrad, "Propaganda and Reports."

27. Ibid.

however, significant preparations were underway in Berlin regarding a resettlement possibility. In this letter, Stumpp notes that a negotiating team from Germany would be "traveling to Moscow on Monday," July 22, 1940, to discuss a resettlement.[28]

The two circulars and the Stumpp letter establish that by the time of the Soviet annexation of Bessarabia, the German government had initiated plans for a resettlement of the Bessarabian Germans in Germany and had developed specific ideas of where the resettlers might be placed, a fact that the first circular had too hastily announced. Stumpp's information that a German negotiating team would go to Moscow proved to be correct. On July 22, 1940, a team led by Wilhelm Nöldeke did in fact arrive in Moscow to begin negotiations.[29] The DAI documents thus strongly suggest that plans for a resettlement of the Bessarabian Germans had been initiated well before the Soviet takeover. The speed with which the Soviet Union accepted a German delegation to discuss resettlement terms for Germans in territories over which it had just taken control also suggests the idea was neither a surprise to them nor unfavorably received. A fair conclusion to draw from the statements in the DAI documents as well as from the Soviet willingness to enter into discussions about a potential resettlement of Germans living in Bessarabia and Bukovina so soon after the Soviets had established control over these territories is that as part of discussions leading to the up to the signing of the 1939 pact, a verbal understanding had been reached that the Soviets would allow Germans in Bessarabia and Bukovina to be resettled under terms to be negotiated later.

During the summer of 1940, after the Soviet takeover of Bessarabia, rumors about an offer to resettle Germans in Germany were clearly circulating in Bessarabia. An account of the resettlement in the Kulm Heimatbuch indicates, for example, that Kulm villagers had heard from reports on the radio that they "were to be resettled."[30] As Soviet authorities soon after the annexation sought to confiscate radios capable of receiving distant broadcasts, this account implies that the radio broadcasts referred to took place in July 1940, and thus that suggestions of resettlement were circulating not long after Soviet control of Bessarabia had been established.[31] It is, of course, not at all certain how credible the statements and rumors about resettlement seemed to the Bessarabian Germans. In actuality, in July and August, there could have been no certainty that a resettlement would take place. The negotiations in Moscow were not easily resolved and it took until September for final terms to be reached. The Soviet Union, holding strong cards, was not willing to give up much, so it became a question of how much the German side would agree to.

The Treichel account of the resettlement in the Kulm Heimatbuch goes on to note that in mid-August two Soviet officials arrived in the village and asked him whether

28. Karl Stumpp, "Letter dated July 16, 1940 to Deutsche Ausland-Institute—Stuttgart," #T-81, Roll 321, Group 1035, VOMI 947, Frame 2452655, in Konrad, "Propaganda and Reports."

29. Wilhelm Nöldeke (1889–1971) was a German diplomat who from 1934 to 1939 was head of the German consulate in Katowice, Poland, the former Kattowitz of Imperial German Silesia. After World War II, he was the West German ambassador to Denmark (1951–54).

30. David Treichel, "Resettlement and Colonization" in "Heimatbuch der Gemeinde Kulm," *Heritage Review* 14, no. 4 (1984): 35. This account was written sometime after World War II. Talk of resettlement would have had to come from German radio broadcasts, as the Soviets had yet to agree on terms and would not in any case have wished to encourage such thoughts.

31. This is also the implication of Treichel's account, which places hearing the radio reports of a potential resettlement soon after the Soviet June 28 takeover. Treichel describes the mood at the time as one of uncertainty: "one was completely unprepared to be placed in a new situation, and did not know what attitude to assume" (Ibid).

his "people wanted to emigrate," to which he cautiously replied that "some would not mind going." When Treichel was then specifically asked whether he would go, he answered evasively: "If the rest go, I will go too."[32] Although Treichel indicates that this conversation was with "two persons of the Russian Resettlement Commission,"[33] this was not likely the case. A resettlement agreement had not yet been reached in mid-August, and once the agreement was reached in early September, it was very quickly implemented by a joint commission with officials from both the Soviet and German governments. Rather, the Russian officials appear to have arrived ahead of the agreement but with the knowledge that the negotiations on resettlement were underway and probably with the intention of taking an inventory of German property and possessions. The reported conversation implies some foreknowledge on both sides of the impending resettlement. The fact that they asked Treichel for his thoughts as to how Germans, or at least the Germans in Kulm, would react and then how he personally would act, indicates that they were aware that the negotiations with Germany had a reasonable probability of reaching agreement. Their questions also imply that part of their task was to assess how many Germans might agree to resettle. Treichel's caution in answering the questions suggests, among other things, that he was not certain resettlement was yet freely on offer. The fact that he was being asked the questions by the Russians, Antonov and Šoltonosov, also indicates that the Soviet representatives were aware that talk about resettlement was broadly current in German Bessarabia.

On August 2, 1940, the Moldavian ASSR, the regional government that the Soviet Union had established on territory on the eastern bank of the Dniester River as symbol of its interest in regaining Bessarabia, was dissolved and in its place the much larger Moldavian SSR was established out of most of Romanian Bessarabia. The Moldavian SSR was created as a full republic, constituting one of the fifteen allegedly semi-independent republics that formed the USSR, the Union of Soviet Socialist Republics. However, the Budjak region, the southern third of Bessarabia where most of the German settlements were located, was not made part of the Moldavian SSR but was attached instead to the Ukraine, as it continues to be today.

Well before the Soviets divided Bessarabia between the Ukraine and the new Moldavian republic, they had moved forcefully to establish their control over the territory. Immediately following the Soviet invasion, the borders were sealed, any equipment thought to be of potential military value was confiscated, leaders of political parties were arrested, independent newspapers and radio stations were closed down, and any public protests in opposition to Soviet control were put down with arrests and some executions. Bessarabian Moldavians who had taken steps to flee to Romania, but had not left Bessarabia, were arrested; many others who had hoped to flee were now stymied, with any sign of their interest a potential cause for arrest. The second stage of the absorption began in late July and early August. Soviet authorities then started the process of nationalizing manufacturing and commercial businesses, confiscating their monetary assets and commercial stock. The former owners were sometimes thrown out and sometimes asked to stay on as managers, while workers at such facilities were told they were now employees of the state.

---

32. Ibid.
33. Ibid.

By September, when Germans in Bessarabia were officially told of the opportunity they had to resettle, they were aware of at least some of the consequences of the other choice, remaining in Bessarabia under Soviet rule. Those consequences were well in line with the stories that they had heard earlier from people who had escaped from the Soviet Ukraine. By early September, the process of nationalizing factories had reached the German settlements, and owners there now lost control of their cash assets, their stocks of raw materials and finished goods. We know this because in early October, Soviet members of the Joint Commission on Resettlement declined an appeal made by factory owner Alfred Jesse of Teplitz, who wanted his factory and its materials counted in the valuations of German property. In rejecting this appeal, the head of the Soviet delegation indicated that such property had belonged to the state prior to the resettlement agreement: "a resettler whose stocks and factory have been nationalized cannot be given an account for these."[34] By September German farmers in Bessarabia had been told by Soviet officials that the Soviet government now owned their land and had become the sole legal purchaser of the grain their farms produced. Moreover, the Soviet government would buy such grain at prices that it alone would set.[35] During the summer of 1940, Germans were not targeted for arrest and exile as security risks; however, other ethnic groups were, especially Moldavians. By September 1940 Soviet authorities in Bessarabia had begun to arrest and deport Moldavians to Kazakhstan beyond the Ural Mountains.[36] By June 1941 the number deported reached an estimated ninety thousand people.[37] While such deportations did not reach a mass level until after the German resettlement, the deportations had begun and were likely to have been observed or at least reported in the German villages. As a result, Germans had reason to consider the dangers they too might face if they remained in Bessarabia.

---

34. Mrs. Finkenauer, "Minutes #20: Concerning the discussion on 7 October, 1940, at 5:00 PM," # T-81, VOMI 920, Group 1035, Roll 317, Series 535, Frames 2447370–2447375, in Konrad and Straeuli, "Bessarabian Resettlement Minutes."

35. Wernik in the "Resettlement Chronicle" reports: "For grain delivered…we received receipts for a joke of a price of 36 kopek for a pud of barley and 80 kopek for a pud of wheat" (4).

36. Between June 28 and July 4, 1940, there were 1,122 persons arrested, many of whom were shot. These were people the Soviets deemed hostile, as they had been officials in the Romanian government, members of the police, priests of the Romanian Orthodox Church, or former members of the Sfatul Tarii who had voted to have Bessarabia become part of Romania (Igor Cașu, "Stalinist Terror in Soviet Moldavia" in *Stalinist Terror in Eastern Europe*, edited by Kevin McDermott and Matthew Stibbe, [New York: Manchester University Press, 2010], 40). The next major category of arrests were Moldavians who sought now leave Soviet Moldavia for Romania.
Following the Soviet annexation, there had been much protest in Bukovina, which had never been part of Imperial Russia (it had been part of Austria-Hungary before World War I). Ethnic Romanians there, unhappy with the Soviet takeover, sought to cross into southern Bukovina, which was to remain part of Romania, or went out in street protests. Soviet troops guarding the new border fired on those crossing, killing some. The Soviet response was to initiate mass deportations. Moldavians in Bessarabia were also a target of these deportations. Survivors of the mass deportations were only allowed to trickle back to Moldavia and Bukovina after the mid-1950s.

37. The best material in English on Soviet deportations of Moldavians in 1940–41 is in Cașu ("Stalinist Terror," 41–43). Cașu's figures combine arrests and deportations from Bessarabia with those from Bukovina. Cașu quotes a report sent to Stalin, Beria, and Molotov that indicates that by June 1941, 31,419 Moldavians had been arrested, most of whom Cașu assumes were deported. An additional 53,356 Moldavians were placed in forced labor gangs and sent to work in other parts of the Soviet Union.

## Once the terms for resettlement were agreed to, the process was immediately implemented

On September 5, 1940, the Soviet Union and Germany reached an agreement on the resettlement of Germans from the newly acquired areas of Bessarabia and northern Bukovina. Implementation was to be carried out by the Joint Commission on Resettlement staffed by administrative and military personnel from both nations. German villages in Bessarabia and Bukovina were to be visited by members of the Joint Commission and German citizens were to be informed of the terms that had been agreed to in Moscow. If Germans then chose to resettle, they were to sign or give vocal approval in an affidavit attesting their agreement to the terms. On its surface, the resettlement agreement appeared to offer seemingly reasonable terms to those agreeing to leave, especially considering the agreement contemplated a process that would be completed by no later than November 5, 1940, just two months after the agreement was signed.[38]

With several important limitations, departing Germans would be allowed to take with them personal items of daily use such as clothing, dishware, hand tools, and household furniture, as well as very limited numbers of livestock.[39] The substantial amounts of property that would have to be left behind would be assigned a monetary value. The Soviet and German members of the Joint Commission were tasked with agreeing on the current monetary worth of the personal assets left behind: buildings, furniture, cash and bank deposits, equipment, animals, grain, furniture, and vehicles, as well as the nonnationalized land and businesses. The Soviet Union would then make a payment to the German government equal to the total amount of the property valuations, which the resettlers were told would be distributed to them in Germany.

Despite the seeming fairness of the agreement's terms, there were certainly reasons for Bessarabian Germans intending to leave to feel that they would lose most of the value of what they and their families had built up in Bessarabia. Their farmland, what the Germans themselves would have considered their most valuable asset, was not even to be considered, as the Soviet Union had "nationalized" farmland via confiscation in order to establish the future collective farms. Houses, farm buildings, and livestock were the next most valuable property left behind by the resettlers. Establishing fair monetary values for houses, farm buildings, and even livestock would be difficult. There existed no open market in the Soviet Union that might set values. With the potential of large numbers of people leaving in a short period of time, the numbers of valuations would overwhelm the commission members and make it difficult to use any but the broadest and most general standards. The Soviet commission members would have significant incentive to minimize the amounts of any valuations. At the same time, the German government's representatives, though they sought to counter the expected low valuations that the Soviet side put forward, were not familiar with historic housing or livestock values in Bessarabia and were

---

38. The "Resettlement Terms" (Umsiedlungsvertrag) for the Bessarabian Germans are listed in Kern (*Homeland Book*, 9–13), Schmidt (*German Colonists*, 318–21), and, more completely, in German at http://jethon.de/html/umsiedlungsvertrag.html.
39. These latter were per farm: Two horses or oxen, one cow, one pig, five head of sheep, and ten head of poultry.

themselves operating under strong incentives to finish the process of resettlement and valuation quickly.

When it came to actually making the property valuations, there were so many to do that the accounting appears not to have gone down to the level of specific properties, that is, to the holdings of specific individuals or families. Instead, valuations were made at the level of a village as a whole: the total number of houses, animals, and pieces of equipment. Most of the valuations, moreover, were not done until the resettlers had left their villages. As a result, a pessimistic but realistic assessment during the sign up period would have concluded that those electing to resettle would never receive adequate compensation for the property left behind. But then, choosing to leave was never really a financial decision. Choosing to leave was to abandon Bessarabia with only a dubious promise that some compensation would be made for what was left behind and an equally uncertain promise about the conditions they would find for themselves in Germany. The decision to leave was based on the assessment that under Soviet rule, there would be no acceptable future for the Germans in Bessarabia. It wasn't just that their landholdings and businesses had been or would be taken away, but that their religious freedom, their rights to practice and preserve their culture, their freedom and legal rights to pursue individual or collective family economic goals would radically change or disappear altogether under Soviet rule.

Complex logistics were required to move the Germans out of Bessarabia. The resettlers were to travel from their home villages to the Danube River ports of Kilija and Reni in Soviet Bessarabia or to Galati (Galatz in German) in Romania, just upstream from Reni and across from the mouth of the Prut River. The German government had arranged for ships to transport the resettlers from these ports upriver to Germany. The resettlement agreement contemplated three modes of travel to the river ports: horse-drawn carts provided by individual families for themselves, motorized trucks provided by the German government, and railroad transport.

## The Soviets placed significant limitations on all items of value that the resettlers might take with them

Germans leaving Bessarabia were able to take with them provisions for the journey and such personal possessions, clothing, and household furnishings limited to the extent that there was room to load such into a wagon or onto a truck or that might fit in the baggage compartment of a train. Those traveling by truck and especially by railroad had greater limitations placed on what they might bring, given the smaller baggage capacities of those vehicles. For those making the journey to the Danube by horse-drawn wagon or by truck, the agreement allowed them to bring, as noted above, limited numbers of livestock. With issues of providing fodder on the journey, limitations in the numbers of animals that could be transported to Germany, and the general need for speed, most Bessarabian German farmers sought to sell livestock before leaving or left their livestock behind for valuation. Transshipment reports indicate that the majority of livestock shipped were horses (22,505), and that these reached the Danube ports by hauling the farm wagons filled with people and their belongings.[40] Some farmers, though, did manage to bring a few of the valuable karakul or merino sheep.

The Soviets placed the heaviest limitations on the amount of cash, financial instruments, precious metals and stones, jewelry, and artwork the resettlers might bring with them. Each person might bring in cash no more than 2,000 Romanian lei but in paper currency only.[41] This was a modest amount roughly the equivalent of the 1929 values of US $12 or UK £2.5 . Each person could bring no more than 500 grams of objects made of silver and no more than a carat's worth of precious stones or pearls. Augmenting the limit of 500 grams of precious metals, each person might also bring one item made of gold or silver from out of a list of such things as watches and their chains, wedding rings, and silver cigar boxes. Not surprisingly, there appear to have been some efforts to smuggle out gold and silver coins and even bullion that had been assets of the German-owned banks.[42] It would appear that most people were forced by these financial limitations to leave behind in Bessarabia all assets of any substantial financial value: money amounts in hand in excess of the 2,000 lei limitation, all money held in gold and silver coins, items made of gold and silver in excess of 500 grams, money held in bank deposits, stock investments, blank checks, all dividend and interest bearing documents, and insurance policies. In addition, families had to leave behind virtually all of their animals as well as their machinery and tools of all types, including tractors, threshing machines, motorcycles, and any machinery operated by gasoline, steam, or electricity. While these would be included in the valuations made by the Joint Commission, the departing Germans had no way of knowing what these values might be or how they would be be translated into compensation.

It is to be presumed that many sought to evade the agreement's limitations by hiding in their luggage and on their persons all sorts of prohibited items. As noted later in this chapter, there were many sales of household items and livestock to people from neighboring non-German villages as well as to Soviet officials. The resettlement agreement permitted people to take funds earned from such sales with them, but Soviet customs officials at the border sometimes raised issues on this score. I have not found commentary on the general success of the resettlers in bringing with them personal assets above the permitted amounts.

Not counted in the valuations (and so not included in compensation) were family landholdings; factories and their stock; commercial businesses and their assets including bank assets, village savings funds maintained for the construction

40. "Tabulation of Evacuated Ethnic Germans as well as Wagons and Horses brought into Romania," #T-81, VOMI 920, Group 1035, Roll 317, Series 535, Frame 2447168, in Konrad, "Evacuation from Bessarabia and Bukovina."

41. Amounts received in authorized sales of property could be added to this total, thus raising the limit above 2,000 lei.

42. In notes made by the German staff working in Sarata to organize the sign up for resettlement, there is a curious reference to a transport of gold. This suggests that the German staff, with the help of Bessarabian Germans, sought to take gold bars out of Bessarabia, likely assets German banks had held in Bessarabia that had somehow escaped nationalization. This is suggested by a reference made to a Johann Jesse, whom the German staff thought troublesome and disloyal. Jesse, the report noted, threatened Eduard Isert, the village leader of Tartarbunar, that he would stab Isert and reveal "all to the NKVD [the Soviet secret police]." The village report goes on to say that Jesse "wanted to reveal the secret movement of gold to Mannsburg." Jesse, evidently, only threatened this action rather than accomplished it. "Sarata Dorfbericht [Village report on Sarata]," #T-81 VOMI 920, Group 1035, Roll 316, Frame 2446879, in Wise, "Bessarabian Village Reports."

or improvement of churches or other civic buildings, such as schools and medical facilities; and the village insurance funds for fire protection and orphans. As noted above, the Soviet Union took the position that as of June 26, 1940 (the date of Soviet control), private ownership of land had been abolished, and factories and businesses employing anyone other than family members had been nationalized. All civic assets were to be taken over by the Soviet government. While the funds the German communities had maintained for fire protection and orphans would be deemed under Soviet law as an illegal and unnecessary privately organized activity, the funds themselves would be absorbed as government property. Civic property and the civic buildings including churches built by the Germans would not be valued for compensation. The Soviet side, at least in the Moscow negotiations, expected that the majority of the German population would not leave their homes and so no doubt argued that the civic assets in buildings and land would continue to be used by the German settlements in Soviet Bessarabia.

## Implementation of the resettlement agreement occurred rapidly and under stressful conditions

The Russian-German commission arrived in Tarutino, Bessarabia, on September 15, 1940, and immediately began discussions on clarifying and carrying out the terms of the resettlement agreement. At the same time, staff members of the Joint Commission began the process of visiting each of the different German villages to give notice and explain the terms of the agreement. Villagers typically had just a few days after the visits by the staff members of the Joint Commission to make up their minds. If they elected to leave, they would then have to sign the affidavit, quickly pack up what they chose to take with them or sell what they could not, and then set off. Officials from the German army had earlier planned the evacuation routes and overnight stopping points. The schedule the German army had worked out was organized by villages, giving only one departure date for small villages and up to three time slots for larger villages so that those electing to resettle would travel together with fellow villagers but only had a few fixed opportunities to leave for the ports on the Danube.[43]

The original plan was to move all the resettlers from their home villages to the Danube ports by means of trucks that the German government would provide, but the road system in Bessarabia was so poor that this proved impossible. While trucks did bring a little over a third of the resettlers to the ports, horse-drawn wagons were the major conveyance. The wagons, either family-owned or rented, traveling together in convoy groups, made up 40.2 percent of the total (table 13–1).[44]

Reni was the primary destination of the truck and wagon convoys and the only destination for those who went by rail. Problems arose when luggage became separated from its owners because a train had too few luggage cars, or the luggage had to wait for a separate truck. Another major problem resulted from the fact that Eiffel's railroad bridge, which connected Reni with Galati, had been destroyed during the Soviet takeover of Bessarabia. There are several references in the minutes of the Joint Commission meetings to delays and difficulties in getting the resettlers to ships in

43. Special slots were given to the seriously ill who traveled separately from the main groups.
44. "Totals According to Mode of Transport," #T-81, VOMI 920, Group 1035, Roll 317, Frames 2447168, in Konrad, "Evacuation from Bessarabia and Bukovina."

TABLE 13–1. **Mode of transport used to reach the Danube Ports**

| Type | Number of People | Percent of Total |
|---|---|---|
| LKW[a] | 30,614 | 34.6% |
| Railroad | 21.011 | 23.7% |
| Treks (rented wagons) | 20,269 | 22.9% |
| Wagon convoys | 15,338 | 17.3% |
| Medical rail car | 973 | 1.1% |
| Sankra ambulance truck | 340 | 0.3% |
| Total | 88,545 | 100.0% |

a. LKW is the abbreviation for the German word Lastkraftwagen, meaning "truck." The meaning here is presumably motorized trucks.

Galati. With the railroad bridge down, Bessarabian Germans slotted for river transportation out of Galati had to get there via a one-lane pontoon bridge over the Prut that was easily clogged. The roadway approaching the pontoon bridge was further slowed because in crossing from Reni to Galati, the resettlers were leaving the Soviet Union for Romania. As this would be the only time that Soviet border guards might make careful searches of the departing luggage, there were long delays as the guards searched for any valuables that were in excess of the modest limits defined in the agreement. This was not an issue for departures from Reni and Kilija, where border control personnel had far more time to inspect luggage before it was to be loaded onto the ships. Reni and Galati were the most frequently used ports of embarkation, taking together 77.4 percent of the river passengers (table 13–2).[45]

While the logistics issues were complex, they had been well mapped out. In spite of all the difficulties, the resettlement moved with surprising speed. The first group of German resettlers reached Galati on September 24, 1940. The notes taken by German participants in the Joint Commission meeting of October 5 indicate that by then some thirty-three thousand resettlers had left their villages.[46] Less than a week later, as the notes from the October 11, 1940, meeting indicate, the number of evacuees had nearly doubled to approximately sixty thousand German Bessarabians plus another fifteen thousand Germans from Bukovina.[47] By October 22, 1940, just over a month from the arrival of the Joint Commission members in Tarutino, the last group of German resettlers was on the move and would be out of the Bessarabia by October 24.

## How many Bessarabian Germans left in the resettlement?

Ernst Krüger, a Bessarabian German who participated in the resettlement, reports, perhaps from a rumor, that Soviet officials had estimated that no more than 40 percent of the Germans would leave.[48] That was not to be. The counts of the evacuees

45. "Distribution of the Resettlers at the Ports of Departure," #T-81, VOMI 920, Group 1035, Roll 317, Frame 2447168, in Konrad, "Evacuation from Bessarabia and Bukovina."
46. Captain Dobkin, "Minutes #18: Concerning the Discussion on 5 October, 1840 from 7:00 to 9:00 PM," #T-81, VOMI 920, Group 1035, Roll 317, Series 535, Frames 2447382–2447384, in Konrad and Straeuli, "Bessarabian Resettlement Minutes."
47. Mrs. Finkenauer, "Minutes #21: Concerning the Discussion on 11 October, 1940, at 5:00 PM," #T-81, VOMI 920, Group 1035, Roll 317, Series 535, Frames 2447358–2447363, in Konrad and Straeuli, "Bessarabian Resettlement Minutes."
48. Ingeborg Smith, review of *Heimat am Pruth: Erinnerungen an Mariental Bessarabien*, by Ernst Krüger, last modified October 31, 2012, http://library.ndsu.edu/grhc/research/scholarly/book_reviews/heimatampruthreview.html.

TABLE 13-2.  **Distribution of the resettlers at the three Danube ports**

| Port | Number of People | Percent of Total |
|------|------------------|------------------|
| Reni | 39,150 | 44.2% |
| Galati | 29,350 | 33.2% |
| Kilija | 20,045 | 22.6% |
| **Total** | 88,545 | 100.0% |

suggest that the entire German population elected to leave. Resettler counts made at the river ports by German army officials offer the most reliable tabulation of the number who left: between 88,545 and 91,049 Germans made the decision to leave Bessarabia.[49]

Other counts of the numbers of resettlers vary widely. Generally given in round numbers, they vary from a low of 80,000 to a high of 93,000 Germans.[50] These should be considered estimates as most do not refer to specific counts, and are vague about whether or not they include Germans from Bukovina or Germans from Dobrudscha in Romania. Finally, it is interesting to note that the German army's count of the number of Bessarabian Germans transported from the Danube ports is materially below the DAI estimates made as preparations for the resettlement. Allen Konrad has translated three separate DAI estimates. One, the "Estimate of German Resettlers from Bessarabian and Bukovina" from sometime in 1940, broke the Bessarabian German population into four districts with town by town estimates totally 129,257 people.[51] Another, dated July 4, 1940, that also gives town by town estimates within four districts estimates the population to be 128,500,[52] and a third

49. German army documents covering the resettlement provide detailed counts of the number of Bessarabian German resettlers. Several different documents offer the same total: 88,545. In one of them, however, the count of 88,545 is increased by 2,504 to 91,049. The author offers a chart breaking down the number of people, horses, and wagons moved from four districts in Bessarabia. The total number of people resettling is given as 88,545 and then, via an asterisk, With notes below that "to this should be added 2,504 refugees who came from the Galatz Camp: 88,545 + 2,504= 91,049" (With, "Report on Bessarabia"). Although it is clear that With thought this extra number ought to be added to the Bessarabian total, as the Galatz camp also had resettlers from Dobrudscha and possibly from Bukovina, it is not clear that these 2,504 were actually from Bessarabia. There are some arguments that suggest the figure of 88,545 as the correct number. One is that a figure of 88,545 is more in keeping with Kern's total German population in Bessarabia as of the end of 1939 of 87,399 (Kern's data came from parish counts). The second is that the count of 88,545 appears in several places in the German army records and was based on detailed counts of people, wagons, and horses coming from each of the four districts, so while the addition or subtraction of a few people might be expected, the addition of another 2,504 is not. In addition, With's concern here is to match numbers coming out of the Galatz Camp, not necessarily numbers from Bessarabia. Of course, in With's favor is the fact that in the hurried actions of getting the German population quickly out of Bessarabia, it would not be surprising to have groups missed and later added.

50. Schmidt does cite a source when she notes that there were "roughly 93,000 Bessarabian resettlers." She indicates this is based on the card file of the Relief Action Committee of the Evangelical Lutheran Church from Bessarabia (*German Colonists*, 332). As this source sought to register all Germans who had resettled sometime after the collection of data by the German army and by German immigration authorities in the fall of 1940, it is not surprising that it would be higher.

51. Allen Konrad, trans., "Estimate of German Resettlers from Bessarabian and Bukovina," #T-81, Roll 320, Frames 2451408–2451410 (N.p.: Germans from Russia Heritage Society, 2009), http://www.grhs.org/korners/memonly/konrad_doc/estimate_german_resettlers_bess_bukovina.pdf (members-only access).

52. Allen Konrad, trans., "Divisions within Bessarabian Regions and Regional Zones for Resettlement Purposes," #T-81, Roll 317, Group 1035, Item VOMI 922, Frames 2447486–2447487 (N.p.: Germans from Russia Heritage Society, 2011), http://www.grhs.org/korners/memonly/konrad_doc/Divisions%20Within%20Bessarabian%20Districts%20and%20Regional%20Zones%20for%20Resettlement%20Purposes.pdf (members-only access).

from apparently deep in the planning process of the summer of 1940, as it includes the town designation numbers that were to be worn by resettlers, had town by town estimates that totaled 126,759.[53]

There were apparently 3,000 resettlers from Dobrudscha included in the German army's count in Galati.[54] These were citizens of Romania not affected by the Soviet takeover of Bessarabia. The Romanian government, though, was interested in having them leave, and the German government was willing to accept them. It is not clear if Germans in Romanian Dobrudscha wished to leave and resettle in Germany. Germans in Romania were not threatened by Soviet policies of the collectivization of agriculture or the near elimination of private ownership. Some narratives of the 1940 resettlement from Dobrudscha describe the move as "occurring against the will of the people, who were living contently in rustic, peaceful villages."[55]

Did the entire German population of Bessarabia leave as part of the resettlement? Until material in former Soviet archives can be researched, we will never know for sure. However, the German army's count of between 88,545 and 91,049 resettlers certainly suggests that this is or nearly is the entire German population of Bessarabia. The captured DAI materials, however, do include a list of 13 Tarutino residents who seem to elect not to join the resettlement.[56] These include five members of the Gromov family headed by the mother Maria Gromova, age fifty-nine, a German woman who married a Russian or Ukrainian now evidently deceased, who states that she is "staying behind because her four children do not want to join the evacuation,"[57] a thirty-five-year-old Ukrainian woman who married a now-deceased German, three people who state they are too ill to go, two German women married to non-Germans who state their husbands are "not joining the evacuation,"[58] and two men who give no reason for staying.[59] The list is dated October 29, 1940, and

53. Allen Konrad, trans., "Location and Number of Ethnic Germans in Regional Zones for 1940 Resettlement," #T-81, Roll 317, Group 1035, Item VOMI 922, Frames 2447458–2447463 (N.p.: Germans from Russia Heritage Society, 2011), http://www.grhs.org/korners/memonly/konrad_doc/ Locations%20and%20Number%20of%20Ethnic%20Germans%20in%20Regional%20Zones%20 for%201940%20Resettlement.pdf (members-only access).

54. In a brief apparently also done by SS Obersturmführer With, there are 44,656 resettlers counted from Bukovina. To this number is added by asterisk another "3,000 refugees in Romania" (SS Obersturmführer With, "Report on Bukovina: 2 Dec 1940," #T-81, VOMI 920, Group 1035, Roll 317, Serial 535, Frame 2447151, in Konrad, "Evacuation from Bessarabia and Bukovina"). While it might be interpreted that these are other refugees from Bukovina who for some reason were at that moment in Romania, I think it far more likely that these are the Dobrudscha resettlers whom the German army had accepted and who were then waiting for transport in Galati. As the Bukovina resettlers had, like the Bessarabians, come to Romania to be transported to Germany, the reference to additional refugees "in Romania" makes more sense if it is understood that they were *from* Romania.

55. Agatha Tuchscherer, "A Partial History of the Anton Tuchscherer Family," *Heritage Review* 44, no. 4 (2014): 17. Her strong implication is that the Romanian government wanted the Germans to leave and so forced the issue. Without better data it is difficult to estimate how many of the German population left Romanian Dobrudscha, but it would appear that, as in Bessarabia, nearly all of the Dobrudscha Germans left to resettle in Germany at this time.

56. Region A1-6 Authority [presumably in Tarutino], "Ethnic Germans of Tarutino Not Joining the Resettlement of 1940," #T-81, Roll 317, Group 1035, VOMI 922, Frame 2447486, trans. Allen Konrad (N.p.: Germans from Russia Heritage Society, 2011), http://www.grhs.org/korners/ memonly/konrad_doc/Ethnic%20Germans%20of%20Tarutino%20not%20joining%20the%20 Resettlement%20of%201940.pdf (members-only access).

57. Ibid.

58. Ibid. These are "Ida Urbanow nee Mayer," age twenty-five, and "Ida G(??)sa nee Müller," age thirty-six.

59. These were Christian Traut(w)ein, age sixty-four, and Albert (???)ter, age forty-four.

so after the date of October 24, given in another document, on which the last of convoys left for the Danube. This suggests that small numbers of Germans, notably women married to Russians or Ukrainians, may well have remained in Bessarabia and that if such were found in Tarutino, they were likely also to be found in other of the German villages. However, even though the date of this tabulation is late in the evacuation period, one cannot be certain whether some of the persons listed here did in the end elect to leave.

The likelihood that nearly the entire Bessarabian German population elected to resettle is also suggested by the fact that apart from the tabulation of thirteen people in Tarutino, there is no mention of any Germans, either singly or in groups, electing to remain in Bessarabia in the notes taken by the German government's representatives from the period after the all convoys had left for the Danube. Germans remaining in the villages at this time would have been striking to these observers. What did draw attention in the German notes from the Joint Commission were attempts by local Soviet authorities to dissuade, hinder, or block Germans from exercising their rights to leave. The German delegation on the Joint Commission paid close attention to and regularly followed up on reports that Soviet authorities had assessed special taxes, made arrests, or ordered Germans not to sign the affidavit. The German side took care to intervene to have such hurdles removed. For example, one of the final issues settled by the Joint Commission was the issue of Germans held prisoner by the Soviet authorities. This issue, discussed in the minutes of several of the last Joint Commission meetings, was only successfully resolved after the repeated efforts of the German side to have the Soviets release the German prisoners and permit them to join the resettlers. The carefulness exhibited by the German members of the Joint Commission in making sure no one who wished to resettle was prevented from doing so suggests the probability that no one wishing to resettle was left behind.

There is one other source that may suggest some Bessarabian Germans did not resettle and remained in Bessarabia. However, it is more likely that the Germans referred to here are not Bessarabia natives but Germans who were seeking to escape from the Ukraine. Schmidt, who after 1990 reviewed Soviet secret police records, indicates that in the second half of 1945, the NKVD had arrested some seven hundred Germans in the territory of former Bessarabia. At least one of these, as will be noted in the epilogue, was a Bessarabian German resettled in Poland who, as a member of the Volkssturm, had been captured by the Red Army in Poland in January 1945. Later in 1945, he managed to escape from imprisonment in the Ukraine and make his way back to Bessarabia, where he was recaptured. The absence of reports from Bessarabian German families that some of their family members remained in Bessarabia after 1940 would suggest the Germans arrested in Bessarabia in 1945 came from elsewhere. While some of these seven hundred may be the German spouses of Russians and Ukrainians who had remained in Bessarabia, the most likely candidates would be Germans trying to escape from the Soviet Ukraine. Many Germans from the Ukraine, not wishing to return to the prewar conditions there or fearful of exile and punishment, sought to leave the Ukraine as German troops retreated. Not all were successful in remaining ahead of the advancing Red Army. At the close of the war, Stalin ordered that all Germans who had been living in the occupied areas of European Russia were to be exiled to Kazakhstan as punishment for the disloyalty they had allegedly exhibited in giving support to the German army's control of the area in 1941–44.[60]

The resettlement was a dramatic and traumatic period for the German population in Bessarabia. It is astonishing to reflect that, within the space of a month and without clear and detailed advance notice, the entire population heard the terms, and virtually all agreed to resettle, packed clothes and what valuables they could to take with them, and then trekked to the Danube to board river transport for an unknown Germany. During this month there were many other pressures. Soviet authorities made great but only partially successful efforts to harvest crops. Families sought hurriedly to sell animals, furniture, tools, and other possessions to Bulgarians, Ukrainians, and Gaugaz from neighboring villages and even to Soviet officials working in German Bessarabia who also became interested. With departure dates quickly following the agreements to resettle, there was often little time to do more than pack. The Germans had to leave behind everything else: homes, farms and workplaces, animals (including pets), orchards, grain storages, churches, and, of course, the graves of their ancestors. Abandoned were 126 years of settlement that had created prosperity for many and bettered for all the conditions their ancestors had left behind in Prussia and the upper Rhineland.

## There are photographs of the resettlement

In 2004, some eighty photographs covering the resettlement, most in color, came into the public domain. They were taken by Japanese photographer Akira Takiguchi, who was attached to the German delegation of the Joint Commission, and were intended as propaganda to document a positive story. The photographs illustrate the notice and registration process in Bessarabia, the chaotic packing, the travel by horse-drawn wagon trains to the ports on the Danube, the travel by ship to Germany, and finally the processing camps in Germany and the resettlement in new homes in Poland. Most of the photographs are scenes taken in the port of Galati, where the German headquarters were located. Takiguchi's photos show the destroyed Eiffel rail bridge over the Prut River that linked Bessarabia with Galati in Romania and the long line of wagons waiting to cross the one-track pontoon bridge. Takiguchi, though, does not seem to have ventured far into Bessarabia itself. Scenes from the German villages in Bessarabia appear to have been taken in Alexanderfeld and perhaps neighboring villages in the far southwestern corner of Bessarabia, the first German villages one would reach traveling north from Reni by rail. The photographs clearly establish that the German officials were frequently members of the German Army in uniform and included members of the SS.[61]

---

60. Schmidt, *Die Deutschen aus Bessarabien*, 173. Those Germans who remained in their villages in the Ukraine after the German army retreated and abandoned the area in 1944 were arrested and deported to Kazakhstan. Germans who had sought to escape from the Ukraine with the German army and were captured in flight by advancing Soviet troops or were collected by the Soviet authorities in Germany after the close of the war were sent to Siberia.

61. Takiguchi and Hindemith, *Heimkehr der Bessarabiendeutschen*. There are no photos from the larger, older, and more prosperous and even commercial Bessarabian German villages to the northeast.

## Notes taken by the German delegation indicate that the Soviet side successfully held their ground on financial issues

By stubbornly refusing to give ground, particularly on economic issues, Soviet members of the commission correctly bet that the German side cared most about getting the resettlers out. A major sticking point was the valuations that would be assigned to houses. The Soviet members of the Joint Commission were clearly under instructions to minimize these valuations. The German side understood that "houses represented the most important part of the wealth of the resettlers" and as a result did not wish to have housing values reduced to negligible amounts.[62] The German strategy was to try to find an economic standard, such as pre-annexation housing costs, that might form an objective basis for making the valuations. The Soviet side declined to cooperate and began negotiations by asserting that the houses that had belonged to the Germans were "actually a liability to the Soviet government and do not have real value."[63] When German officials sought to use figures from Romanian times, the Soviets would counter with absurdly low numbers. For example, in a discussion about housing values in Alt Posttal where a German assessor, on the basis of pre-annexation values, had come up with a range in value of 70,000–80,000 lei per house, the Soviets countered with assertions that the houses were only worth 10,000 lei.[64] In the end the German side found no way to move the Soviets, and the negotiations ended with no valuations being made. Instead, it was agreed simply to put together an inventory list of the properties without attaching any values to them.

The Soviet members of the Joint Commission also created difficulties in establishing the rules to be used for sales of personal property. The general resettlement agreement adopted in Moscow had acknowledged that such transactions could take place, but the Soviet side on the Joint Commission in Bessarabia wanted transactions limited to sales paid for only with Romanian lei. This was evidently an effort to minimize transactions made with Soviet personnel who would not have had access to foreign currency. The Soviet side may also have had two other goals in mind. By limiting transactions to those paid for with lei, such transactions would help bring out into the open holdings of Romanian lei among non-Germans. As such holdings would soon become illegal, those possessing lei might be identified for later confiscations. As the Moldavians, Bulgarians, Ukrainians, and Gaugaz who were the most likely purchasers of German household items were themselves not generally well-to-do, a second rationale Soviet authorities may have had in mind was to keep sales of German property limited to modest amounts.

In spite of the desire of the Soviet side to limit sales of personal property to transactions conducted in lei, there was mounting pressure to permit sales paid for with Soviet rubles. The German side argued that with the ruble in circulation since early July, some purchasers only had rubles to offer so that restricting transactions to those made in lei unfairly curtailed the number of potential sales. In addition, Soviet civil and military officials wanted to purchase consumer goods from the Germans that

---

62. Mrs. Finkenauer, "Minutes #13: Concerning the Discussion on 27 September, 1940, from 9:00 PM to 2:30 AM," #T-81, VOMI 920, Record Group 1035, Film Roll 317, Series 535, Frames 2447396–2447401, in Konrad and Straeuli, "Bessarabian Resettlement Minutes."

63. Ibid.

64. Mrs. Finkenauer, "Minutes #27: Concerning the Discussion on 22 October, 1940, from 9:00 PM to 11:00 PM," #T-81, VOMI 920, Record Group 1035, Film Roll 317, Series 535, Frames 2447324–2447330, in Konrad and Straeuli, "Bessarabian Resettlement Minutes."

were in short supply or nonexistent in the Soviet Union and they only had Soviet rubles as currency. As the Soviet Union had elected not to make the ruble convertible into international currencies, Soviet rubles would be of little or no reduced value to Germans once they were outside the Soviet Union. While Soviet officials might have seen this as a positive factor in limiting what real funds Germans might take with them, allowing sales in rubles also had major negative connotations for them. The Soviet Union, ever fearful of foreign intrigue and spying, had no wish to allow Germans to take rubles out of the Soviet Union where they might fall into the hands of those wishing to reimport these to bribe Soviet citizens or fund the work of foreign agents. As pressure increased, a rough compromise was worked out under which a limited number of sales of personal property in rubles would be permitted. These transactions, however, could only be for modest amounts in the range of 200–250 rubles. This solution fell in line with the Soviet desire to restrict the sales of personal property in lei. The ultimate goal of the Soviets appears to have been to limit the amount of cash Germans might take out of the country.

If the Hoffnungsfeld chronicle is more widely indicative, the Soviet authorities were notably unsuccessful in efforts to limit the size and frequency of cash transactions. Wernik indicates "droves of people [non-Germans are meant] showed up"[65] once it was clear the villagers were going to leave Bessarabia. "Thanks to the circumstances…there was a lot of Romanian money in Bessarabia, and the people [again non-Germans are the referent] were afraid it would soon be taken out of circulation."[66] In the two-week period between notification and departure, Hoffnungsfeld residents were able to sell everything they "had to sell, except the better furniture and pianos."[67] These latter, as noted below, went to Soviet buyers at much higher prices.

Soviet officials themselves undermined the attempt to limit sales and sale prices for personal goods. The German notes from the September 24th Joint Commission meeting recorded several substantial sales of personal property to Soviet officials. The attention of the German Joint Commission members, though, was not on the size of the transactions but on the fact that Soviet officials had entered into purchase agreements with Germans and then successfully used their authority to alter these to their advantage. Paul Renz of Tarutino sold furniture to a Captain Sneev who later asserted that the articles belonged to the Soviet staff and so could not be sold. Another German sold a pair of horses to a "military authority" for 100,000 lei; the purchaser later came back and said the price was too high and so demanded and got back 20,000 lei.[68] In other cases Soviet officials sought simply to block sales of property, perhaps out of a concern that the Germans were gaining more cash than they had anticipated, or perhaps simply out of the feeling that sales of personal property smacked of capitalistic gain not tolerated elsewhere in the Soviet Union. The German side on the Joint Commission concludes that in general, "a whole number

---

65. Wernik, "Resettlement Chronicle," 7
66. Ibid., 6.
67. Ibid., 7.
68. Mrs. Finkenauer, "Minutes #10: Concerning the Discussion on 24 September, 1940, from 9:00 to 11:30 PM," #T-81, VOMI 920, Record Group 1035, Film Roll 317, Series 535, Frames 2447410–2447414, in Konrad and Straeuli, "Bessarabian Resettlement Minutes." The minutes of this meeting also record confiscations of personal goods: a Soviet policeman forced a German to hand over his motorcycle and then refused to give a receipt.

of cases have come up which show that…the sale of furniture and household items is deliberately obstructed."[69]

The Hoffnungsfeld chronicle, however, offers a different perspective. In it Wernik describes poorly dressed Soviet officials with lots of cash eager to buy good furniture and animals: "It was not uncommon for clothing cupboards [Kleiderschränke] to go for 12,000 to 18,000 lei. Pianos, and there were 12 of them in our small village, brought 40, up to 80 and 90 thousand lei each."[70]

While Soviet army authorities initially were buying cattle at 5,000 to 8,000 lei a head, prices rose to 20,000 lei by the time of departure with exceptionally good cattle going for as high as 50,000 lei. The price for horses started at 15,000 lei and by the time of departure had risen to 60 and 70,000. Wernik describes meetings with a non-German merchant from Kilia whose business had been confiscated and who now wanted to "invest his money…in furnature and home appliances, then, in the upcoming 'black days' sell them…[to] support himself and his family."[71] Without negotiating he bought Wernik's piano for 65,000 lei.

Another topic much discussed during the meetings of the Joint Commission concerned bringing in the harvest. At first, local Soviet authorities ordered Germans to work in their former fields to gather in the harvest. In the short time frames available, this made it difficult for Germans to pack, settle their affairs, and leave. The German commission members seem to have suspected that Soviet actions were directed toward preventing Bessarabian Germans from registering for the resettlement. The commission notes record several instances at the beginning of the resettlement sign-up process of Germans kept away from town meetings by Soviets, who would order them to complete work projects or even arrest them. In one instance, the German side protested that farmers were being required to transport grain to depots 50 or 100 km distant.[72] As the resettlement process engulfed the whole German population, rapidly moving from sign up to evacuation, the Soviet concern passed solely to harvesting as much of the crops in the field as possible and even that proved a task too great. Much of the harvest was apparently left to rot in the fields. The German notes to the October 1 commission meeting, for example, comment that "60% of the harvest was still in the ground."[73] The locksmith Johann Karl Krause of Tarutino gives some flavor of the interplay between Soviets and Germans in a letter written from a resettlement transit camp in Bad Windsheim, Germany, in the winter of 1940–41. He describes Soviet authorities gathering the Tarutino farmers and telling them, probably in September of 1940, that before they would be permitted to leave they would have to pay Soviet taxes, plow their acreage, and sow as much seed as was planted in the previous year. However, as the registrations to resettle began

69. Ibid.
70. Wernik, "Resettlement Chronicle," 7.
71. Ibid., 8.
72. Mrs. Finkenauer, "Minutes #8: Concerning the Discussion of 19 September, 1940 from 4:00 tom 6:15 PM," #T-81, VOMI 920, Record Group 1035, Film Roll 317, Series 535, Frames 2447420–2447424, in Konrad and Straeuli, "Bessarabian Resettlement Minutes."
73. Mrs. Finkenauer, "Minutes # 16: Concerning the Discussion on 1 October, 1940 at 2:00 PM," T 81, VOMI 920, Record Group 1035, Roll 317, Series 535, Frames 2447388-2447391, in Konrad and Straeuli, "Bessarabian Settlement Minutes."

and German trucks arrived to transport the resettlers to the Danube, "one did not ask whether things were paid up or not, it was simply—get up and leave."[74]

The notes from the German side of the Joint Commission report only one instance where Soviet officials actively sought to force Germans to rescind their resettlement elections. The notes from the September 24 meeting report that craftsmen in Arzis were ordered to report to the town's Finance Office, where they were asked the following: "Why do you want to go to Germany? You are needed here and can make a good living. In Germany you will go hungry. You will only get 100 g. of meat a week and 8 kg. of bread a month."[75] The craftsmen were told to hand in their identification papers as well as the information they were given about departing from Arzis and to provide a written statement by October 1 that they would withdraw from the resettlement or face a fine of 500 rubles. When German members of the Joint Commission intervened, the Soviets backed off of this threat and the craftsmen were able to leave Arzis and Bessarabia.

## The resettlement of the citizens of Kulm

Material from Kulm offers an unusually detailed account of a single German Bessarabian village's experience in the resettlement. Treichel's account in the Kulm Heimatbuch reports that four German resettlement officials, led by Dr. Ludwig Pielen, arrived in Kulm on September 15, 1940, the same day other German military and civilian officials first came to Tarutino.[76] A community meeting was held in Kulm the next day in which the German officials went over the terms for resettlement. Registration for resettlement began the next day, September 17. Every German family in Kulm signed the papers and agreed to leave. The first group left Kulm for the Danube ports a week later on September 24. A second group left on October 3, with the remainder of the Kulm villagers departing October 6. The first two groups of Kulm citizens appear to have been transported by trucks in convoys that included German families leaving Romanowka, a multiethnic village north of Leipzig.[77] The third and last group, which also included residents from Romanowka, traveled by horse-drawn wagons. German army planning data for the evacuation of Kulm residents indicate that the convoys were intended to travel in four stages of 30 to 50 kilometers each, stopping at Wittenberg, Neu Dennewitz, and Oancea (in Romania

---

74. Allen Konrad, trans., "Letter of Johann Karl Krause, 1940," #T-81, Roll 599, Serial 816, Group 1035, Item 1266, Frames 5386404-5386405 (N.p.: Germans from Russia Heritage Society, 2009), http://www.grhs.org/korners/memonly/konrad_doc/Letter_Johann_Karl_Krause.PDF (members-only access). Krause goes on to speculate that in villages other than Tarutino, "many had to put up millions and only then could they leave." While this seems rumorous and exaggerated, Wernik confirms it when he notes that some had to pay agricultural taxes of 1,300,000 lei for just 12 hectares of land ("Resettlement Chronicle," 8). To Wernik the high tax was extortion, designed to encourage farmers to be happy to put in with the new collectives. It would seem, however, that in many instances this tax was not collected. The German notes from Joint Commission meetings indicate that tax payments were an ongoing and generally unresolved issue. The result was that this issue was only resolved through the general accounting of the total Bessarabian property values to be repaid by the Soviet Union. As such, the payment made to Germany by the Soviet Union in 1941 was reduced to reflect a figure for taxes.
75. Finkenauer, "Minutes #10," in Konrad and Straeuli, "Bessarabian Resettlement Minutes."
76. This account lists the German officials in Kulm as: Area Deputy Willi Kutter, Dr. Ludwig Pielen, Viktor Moskaliuk, and Paul Kremnitz (Treichel, "Resettlement and Colonization," 35). Dr. Pielen's letter indicates that in 1940 he was a university professor. Pielen survived World War II and was a department head in the West German Federal Ministry of Food, Agriculture, and Forestry in 1969.
77. Ibid. Treichel refers to an "omnibus transport," possibly meaning that the German army had available and was using buses.

on the Prut), and from there going to the Romanian port of Galati, 172 kilometers in all.[78] The resettlers from Kulm remained in a holding camp in Galati, probably at the airport judging from Takiguchi's photographs, until October 19. A large group of Kulm villagers then traveled by ship to Prahova on the Danube just inside the Yugoslav border, where they debarked. Traveling by train from Prahova, they crossed into Germany on October 27 and arrived the next day at a processing center near Schweinfurt in Bavaria where they were to be temporarily housed.

German and Soviet staff members of the Joint Commission remained in Kulm after the villagers departed with the task of completing the valuations of property. Their presence in Kulm until early November suggests that similar teams were stationed in the other large German villages in Bessarabia. The German staff in Kulm report many of the same frustrations as those recorded in the German notes from the meetings of the Joint Commission leadership in Tarutino discussed above. In a letter written December 22, 1940, after he had returned to Germany, Dr. Pielen describes negotiations with the Soviet side. Valuations for the village cattle went "relatively fast, but that was not the case with the buildings. For instance, the Russians bid 40,000 lei for all of [the] buildings—only a twentieth of [his] assessment."[79] In the end, as the Joint Commission notes also indicate, no agreement was reached on the values for houses. An inventory was created where both sides provided their differing estimates of values. Regarding the discussions covering the valuation of houses, Pielen also notes the Soviet side wished to claim some properties had been nationalized and so were not subject to the valuation, a tactic also used by the Soviets in the Joint Commission meetings. Pielen calls this tactic "shabby tricks" and says it precipitated a breakdown in the negotiations. The German side was able to win some points in the Kulm negotiations: After two weeks of haggling on the valuation of grain stores, an actual measurement produced a total that was 20 percent in excess of Pielen's estimate. The Soviet side then responded by arguing that the size of the grain stores should be reduced by 40 percent for contamination, but ultimately yielded to agree to the actual count. Dr. Pielen's letter also tries to comfort the former Kulm residents by saying the now deteriorating village was no longer the place they had built and loved: "It isn't Bessarabia anymore as you remember your home, but…a place where misery, misfortune and hunger prevail." In a sad note, Pielen memorializes this thought by describing the village dogs, which had to be left behind: "Each dog faithfully sat by the door of his respected master, often till he was lean as a skeleton."[80]

## The Bessarabians were taken to processing centers in Germany, where they were counted and interviewed and where it was determined which villages would be resettled together and which would be broken apart

On arrival in Germany, the Bessarabian German refugees were housed in small to medium-sized groups in schools, hospitals, and hotels located throughout Germany.

---

78. "Departure Points and Overnight Points Bessarabia Trek," #T-81, VOMI 920, Group 1035, Roll 317, Series 535, Frames 2447253–2447255 in Konrad, "Evacuation from Bessarabia and Bukovina."
79. Ludwig Pielen, "Letter to Andreas Necker, December 22, 1940" in Treichel, "Resettlement and Colonization," 36–39. Pielen's letter was written to Andreas Necker, a village leader of Kulm. Pielen had been living in the Necker house in Kulm after the villagers had departed.
80. Ibid.

From these first stopping points, they were soon gathered into larger centers where they were processed for resettlement in Germany. The largest of these were in and near Dresden in Saxony and in or near Reichenberg (now Liberec in the Czech Republic) in the Sudetenland.[81] Together these two areas processed 62 percent of the Bessarabians. Table 13–3 provides a list of the regional processing centers used.[82]

One purpose of these processing centers was to bring together all the residents of the same village, which would both give the villagers comfort and allow the German authorities to deal with them more efficiently. Here the refugees were interviewed and processed and here they created the family questionnaires described in the Introduction that provide the best twentieth century census data available on the Bessarabian Germans. The German government, given its fixation on ethnic makeup, appears to have stressed its interest in validating the German background of the resettlers; many took the trouble to note at the bottom of their questionnaires where in the older German states their family's origins lay.

The German government appears to have used this period when the villagers were together in transit camps to address what it considered to be problem issues. During the resettlement sign ups in the Bessarabian villages, the German Joint Commission staff had been tasked with noting any characteristics among the Bessarabian Germans that might be considered troublesome once they were brought to Germany. It is clear that, given its focus on ethnic identity, the German government wished to evaluate to what degree refugees had preserved their Germanness (*Deutschtum*). The Bessarabian Germans had lived outside of Germany for some time, and the German government seemed worried about the degree to which villages, or groups within them, had become assimilated Russians or Romanians. The staff notes also raise issues concerning particular individuals within communities, individuals whose Germanness was questioned or individuals thought to be troublesome because of their religious or political views or lifestyle habits. The staff notes also contain suggestions on what ought to be done with the villages during resettlement. For example, the notes suggest that some villages should be broken up. The issue of Germanness seems raised not just because of worries about cultural assimilation. Other issues that concerned the German staff members were "mixed" marriages with members of other nationalities and the inclusion in the resettlement of some non-German residents of the German villages.

In an effort to minimize any continuing non-German influences, the staff notes recommend merging members of those villages whose Germanness seemed weaker into larger and more clearly native German settlements in Germany. Thus,

---

81. It is likely that the figures quoted here and displayed in table 13–3 do not refer to numbers of refugees processed in a single center but generalize the results from several processing centers located in the same area. Thus, Allen Konrad's translation notes seven different centers in or near Reichenberg in the Sudetenland (trans., "Ethnic German Resettlement Camps in the German Reich from 1940 Onward" [N.p.: Germans from Russia Heritage Society, 2009], http://www.grhs.org/korners/memonly/konrad_doc/Resettlement_Transit_Camps.pdf [members-only access]).

82. The camp locations and numbers of resettlers are from materials found in a DAI file: Allen Konrad, trans., "Regions in the Reich Containing Transit Resettlement Camps," #T-81, VOMI 920, Group 1035, Roll 599, Series 816, Item 1266, Frame 5386396 (N.p.: Germans from Russia Heritage Society, 2009), http://www.grhs.org/korners/memonly/konrad_doc/Regions_Reich_with_Transit_Camps.pdf (members-only access).

concerning the village of Rohrbach,[83] the German staff note the existence of citizens of other ethnic backgrounds and citizens with a weak German "consciousness" and so recommend "not to resettle [the Rohrbach villagers] as one community [by itself] but rather unite [it] with a good community."[84] Religious issues troubled the staff who worked in Beresina. They note that 25–35 percent of the village belonged to a Pentecostal religious sect, the Studen Brüder/Schwestern, which the staff notes refer to as troublesome "grumblers."[85] In resettlement, the German staff suggest separating these people out and not placing them with the rest of the Beresina villagers.

Political issues were also raised in the German staff notes made in Bessarabia, presumably with the intent of identifying people to receive special handling during the processing in Germany. Thus, the staff doing the resettlement for Friedenstal recommend resettling the community "as it was with the same leaders," except for Johannes Lutz and his assistant Gotthilf Bast.[86] Lutz had been put in place as village leader by the Soviets and the German staff felt he had "turned into a traitor against

TABLE 13–3. **Regional locations of the processing centers used for the Bessarabian Germans**

| Resettlement Processing Centers | Number Processed There |
|---|---|
| Dresden (Saxony) | 29,533 |
| Reichenberg (Sudetenland) | 25,833 |
| Linz (Austria) | 9,665 |
| Vienna (Austria) | 8,380 |
| Würzburg (Bavaria) | 7,075 |
| Nuremberg (Bavaria) | 3,612 |
| Thuringia[a] | 1,238 |
| **Total** | **85,336[b]** |

a. Unlike for the other centers, there is no address given in a specific town or city. Konrad's "Ethnic German Resettlement Camps" indicates there were Thuringian centers in and near Gera, Heiligenstadt, Mühlhausen, and Weimar.

b. This is between 3,209 and 5,713 people less than the two counts of Bessarabian resettlers (88,545 and 91,049) made by the German army at the Danube River ports (see footnote 50 above). This source is clearly not aware of the variance. Also noted here are counts some 19,092 resettlers from Dobrudscha placed in four centers and a further group of 14,241 resettlers also noted to be from Dobrudscha who evidently had recently arrived. This would make a total of 33,333 resettlers from Dobrudscha, a figure much too high. Konrad notes this saying, "It is uncertain whether there might be some included from Bukovina" ("Regions of the Reich"). Such a conclusion would seem likely as the apparent German army count of resettlers from Dobrudscha was 3,000 (see footnote 55 above). The 33,333 resettlers designated as from Dobrudscha probably do include some of the 44,656 people coming from Bukovina and possibly some of the missing Bessarabian Germans.

---

83. This was a community founded in 1887 on leased land in central west Bessarabia by settlers coming from Arzis, Alt Elft, and Tarutino. It was not, thus, the large, prosperous (in pre-revolutionary Russia) village of the same name in the Beresan District of Xerson Province that was founded in 1809.

84. "Rohrbach Dorfbericht," in Wise, "Bessarabian Village Reports."

85. "Beresina Dorfbericht," in Wise, "Bessarabian Village Reports." The staff commentary described the "Studen" community as "against [doing any] any social work, for example, the school system, and therefore [such belief] disrupts the village community." Religious and ethnic prejudice of another sort is evident in the refusal of local German staff to sign up for resettlement the Jewish husband of a German woman. When the Soviets brought this up as an example of the Germans not following the treaty agreement, the German delegation head relented but noted "it would be more advantageous for this person to remain in the USSR as he would not be given the opportunity to start a new life in Germany" ("Minutes #13" in Konrad, "Bessarabian Resettlement Minutes").

86. "Friedenstal Dorfbericht," in Wise, "Bessarabian Village Reports."

his own nationals."[87] The German staff who worked in Sarata note that there were several citizens who had been critical of the National Socialist (Nazi) party before 1940 and so formed in the staff's eyes an anti-German element. This group, chastened by the Soviet takeover of Bessarabia, "was glad to be saved by the much-smeared NS."[88] Seeing these Sarata citizens as likely to continue to pose dangers in Germany, the staff notes place them ominously on a "Black List."[89]

In some cases, the staff notes made during the resettlement process suggest breaking up villages altogether as the German staff members felt such villages had lost their positive moral fiber. The staff report for Wittenberg, for example, describes the villagers, though having a strong German consciousness, as "intellectually lazy, politically uninterested…concerned only with [their] own property and family, pronounced misers."[90] The Wittenbergers, moreover, too frequently intermarried and are noted for having a "heavy enjoyment of wine [that created] some drunkard families."[91] The staff, composed perhaps of north Germans, recommend that this village of descendants of South Germans from Württemberg "should be divided and each half settled with North Germans, to bring new blood and good temperament to refresh the slacking community."[92]

Similarly, the staff recommendation for the resettlers from Brienne is to break up the community completely by "distributing the community into different villages [as the heavy] use of wine is unfavorable to the health" of the community.[93] Tartarbunar was given a particularly negative portrait and received the severe recommendation that the community should be "totally scattered."[94] Tartarbunar was a large town with a mixed population of Greeks, Russians, Bulgarians, and Jews. It had a rough reputation; Kern, for example, describes it as "anything but a fairy tale town."[95] The German staff conducting the resettlement found a variety of sins: "They have the highest percentage of mixed marriages and a degenerated tendency in parting from…Germanism. The most raging anti Germans and Russiafied people registered for re-settlement. They had to be taken along as otherwise the re-settlement of the decent Germans would have been endangered."[96]

The materials collected in Kulm's Heimatbuch include details on how the villagers were processed once they reached Germany. The experiences of other Bessarabian

87. Ibid.
88. "Sarata Dorfbericht," in Wise, "Bessarabian Village Reports."
89. The "Black List" is also mentioned with regard to Johann Jesse, who, as noted above in footnote 42, was suspected of wanting to tell the NKVD about German efforts to hide or more likely to bring to Germany by surreptitious means gold bullion from one of the German banks in Bessarabia. The implication is that the Black List identified individuals who were to be carefully watched or even arrested once they arrived in Germany.
90. "Wittenberg Dorfbericht," in Wise, "Bessarabian Village Reports."
91. Ibid.
92. Ibid.
93. "Brienne Dorfbericht," in Wise, "Bessarabian Village Reports."
94. "Tatar Bunar," included in "Sarata Dorfbericht" in Wise, "Bessarabian Village Reports."
95. Kern, Homeland,188. The town's name has been spelled in a variety of ways. I have adopted the single word form used on Berg's map of Bessarabia from the late nineteenth century, the best source of the original Imperial Russian geographic treatment. In many other sources the town's name is spelled in two separate words as Tartar Bunar (such as in the Brockhaus and Efron encyclopedia, edition 1890–1906; Karl Radier's 1901 map of the central Budjak from the "3rd Military Mapping Survey of Austria-Hungary [Sheet 47–46]; and Stumpp's "Karte der deutschen Siedlungen in Bessarabien").
96. "Tatar Bunar," in Wise, "Bessarabian Village Reports."

Germans were likely analogous. When they arrived by train in Germany, the former residents of Kulm, Bessarabia, were first sent to sites near Würzburg in Bavaria and then were reunited in a single resettlement center further upstream along the Main in Werneck about 10 miles southwest of Schweinfurt: "after the resettlement, the whole Kulm community came to Werneck Castle."[97] Formerly the summer residence of the Prince-Bishop of Würzburg, Werneck Castle was in 1940, and still continues to be, a psychiatric hospital.[98] In its report on Kulm made during the sign-up period for resettlement, the German staff recommended that with regard to settlement in Germany, "if possible do [not] settle as a closed unit."[99] As noted below, this recommendation was in fact adopted and the former residents of Kulm were split up and settled in over thirty different places in occupied Poland.

As Germany currently struggles with the unexpected arrival of over a million refugees from war-torn Syria, Afghanistan, Somalia, and North Africa, it is interesting to note how greatly this contrasts with the resettlement of about 150,000 Germans resettling from Bessarabia, Bukovina, and Dobrudscha in 1940–41. In the latter case, as the captured archives reveal, there was some time to prepare estimates of the number of refugees who would need to be helped and so to find and then divide these among schools, hotels, hospitals, and government buildings to register them and provide housing and planning for their ultimate resettlement. The detail shows the significant staff work that was done to make this happen relatively smoothly. It also should be noted that this occurred under a government with dictatorial powers that could order the army to handle the resettlement operations in Bessarabia, could order public and private institutions to temporarily take in the refugees, no matter their other plans, and could, through the conquest of its neighbor and the expropriation of privately held land in that country, settle in a new population without disturbing ongoing life in its home territories.

## The Bessarabian Germans were given land in occupied Poland that had been confiscated from Poles and Jews

The experience of the former citizens of Kulm was typical. In February 1941, many of the families from Kulm were brought to processing centers near Łodz (renamed Litzmannstadt under German occupation) in the new German province of Warthegau. This region, attached to Germany after the defeat of Poland in 1939 and named after the Warthe (Polish Warta) River in its midst, comprised much of what Prussia had absorbed in the Second Partition of Poland of 1793. Prussia renamed

---

97. David Treichel, "Teacher Artur Erdmann" in "Heimatbuch der Gemeinde Kulm," *Heritage Review* 13, no. 4 (1983): 21. Treichel elsewhere indicates that the former Kulm residents went initially to several sites and then were gathered all together at Werneck. This implies that they traveled from Galati to Germany on different boats ("Resettlement and Colonization," 37). The listing of proposed distribution assigns the former residents of Kulm to eight districts in the Main-Franconia region (Allen Konrad, trans., "Proposed Distribution of German Resettlers from Bessarabia and Bukovina," #T-81, Roll 320, Frames 2451411–2451423 [N.p.: Germans from Russia Heritage Society, 2009] http://www.grhs.org/korners/memonly/konrad_doc/Distribution_German_Resettlers.pdf [members-only access]). This appears to be a planning document as the number of Kulm people to be placed in the eight sites, 2,773, far exceeds the 1,814 potential resettlers counted in September 1940 in the German staff report ("Kulm Dorfbericht," in Wise, "Bessarabian Village Reports"). Thus it is not clear whether the sites named here were actually used.
98. The castle was built by Balthasar Neumann in 1733–45 for the then Prince-Bishop of Würzburg, Friedrich Carl von Schönborn. It became a psychiatric clinic in 1855.
99. "Kulm Dorfbericht," in Wise, "Bessarabian Village Reports."

the area South Prussia, lost it to the French in 1807 as the Duchy of Warsaw, then regained much of it in the 1815 Treaty of Paris, and at that time renamed the area the Province of Posen. Farm families from Kulm were taken to a resort in the village of Kolumna (called Waldhorst by the Germans) near Łask, southwest of Łodz. Other families with "technical skills" were sent to directly to Łodz. The Kulm Heimatbuch notes that the farming families from Kulm were then settled in "36 localities and 5 districts."[100] Most were in the districts of Kościan (German Kosten) and Leszno (German Lissa), southwest of the city of Poznan.[101] Daniel Wölfle reports that there were twenty-seven Kulm families, perhaps the largest single group, settled around the village of Donaten (Polish Donatowo) in the Kosten District.[102]

The Kulm resettlers were not assigned empty, uncultivated land; there was little of this even when their ancestors had emigrated from this area 127 years before.[103] The land to which they were assigned had been, until 1941, the property of others, mainly Polish families, but also Jews. These families had been forced out of their houses and farms and moved further east as part of an effort of the German government to make this area, long contested between Germans and Poles, irrecoverably German, a policy now described by the unpleasant euphemism "ethnic cleansing." An estimated 13,700 Germans from Estonia and 50,000 from Latvia had been resettled in the Warthegau in 1940, mainly in towns. In 1941–42, over 150,000 Germans from Bessarabia, Dobrudscha, Northern Bukovina, and Volhynia were settled, mainly in farming villages in the Warthegau. In 1942–43, following the German army's successes in the Ukraine, another estimated 300,000 Germans arrived in the Warthegau from that area.[104] Ironically, some of the Polish families who had been forced to move from the Warthegau were "resettled" in the former German villages in Axis-occupied Bessarabia.

At times, the displacement of Poles from their homes in the Warthegau took place virtually before the eyes of the incoming Bessarabian Germans. Lilli Flato reports that "within one hour the Poles were moved out of their homes and we were moved into their houses."[105] Jews were the victims of this expropriation as well, but suffered far crueler and unspeakably inhumane fates in the death camps created by the German government. Most of the Jews living in this part of Poland were town dwellers, but given their near total displacement from Great Poland, it is likely that some of the German farmers resettled in the Warthegau were placed in Jewish homes within farming villages.

---

100. Treichel, "Resettlement and Colonization," 37.

101. Ibid.

102. Daniel Wölfle, "Our Flight in January 1945," in "Heimatbuch der Gemeinde Kulm," *Heritage Review* 14, no. 4 (1984): 38. Donatowo is about 6 miles west of Śrem (German Schrimm).

103. On the first page of this chapter it was noted that in 1940, when the Germans left Bessarabia, their settlements had been there for 126 years. Here the distance from the original settlements in Bessarabia has grown to 127 years as the comparison is to 1941, when the Bessarabian Germans were given land in occupied Poland.

104. Not all Bessarabian Germans were relocated to the Warthegau, however. Hörst Köhler, president of the Federal Republic of Germany (2004–10), was born to a family of German refugees from northern Bessarabia in 1943 in Skierbieszów, about 12 miles north of Zamość in the General Government region of occupied Poland in what is now the border region of Poland with Belorussia.

105. Lilli Flato, "From Bessarabia to Lodi, California, USA: Germans from Russia, a Life Story of Lilli Flato and her Family," trans. Manfred Trogisch (N.p.: German American Pioneers.org, 2006), 5, http://www.germanamericanpioneers.org/FromBessarabiatoLidaCA. swf?POPUP_ENABLED=true.

Though written well after the end of World War II (and so no longer under the influence of the Nazi government's views), the Kulm Heimatbuch makes little mention of the displacement of people whose farms the Kulmers took over, nor the inheritance by the German incomers of the livestock, stores, tools, furniture, and clothing forcibly left behind. It notes only that the former Kulm residents were fortunate to be given places in May 1941 when other Bessarabian Germans had to stay longer in the processing camps. The Heimatbuch's focus is then directed to the point that the "comfortable and productive laboring in the Wartheland did not last too long."[106] This refers to the fact that in the winter of 1945 the Bessarabian Germans had to abandon the farms in Poland and flee hurriedly west ahead of the advancing Red Army.

## The Bessarabian Germans never received any monetary compensation for the property they were forced to leave behind

In early 1941 the Soviet Union did make payments to the German government for the value of all property that the Bessarabian Germans had been required to leave behind. The payments were made not in cash but in shipments of coal and grain. The amounts of coal and grain were based on a valuation of the German property reached in discussions in Moscow over the winter of 1940–41. This valuation was a compromise that accepted in part the steep reductions the Soviet side wished to make in the estimated worth of the German houses and farmsteads. The Soviet payment also factored in the value of taxes the Soviet government asserted were due from the departed Germans. In accounting for the cash value of the Soviet coal and grain received, the German government credited to itself much of that value as a repayment for the costs incurred in carrying out the resettlement. The remainder was placed as cash in a trust fund, the German Resettlement Trust (Deutsche Umseidlungs-Treuhandgesellschaft m. b. H.), which was put under the control of the SS. Sometime during 1941, the German government adopted the viewpoint that individual Bessarabian Germans were to be considered fully compensated for the property they had left behind by the earnings potential of the land that had been given to them in the conquered parts of Poland. Thus, in a letter dated September 10, 1941, SS General Ulrich Greifelt writes that "the value of the property as left behind in their homeland by the Bessarabian-German resettlers is to be compensated in full by the earning power of the new farms to be established."[107] The funds held by the German Resettlement Trust were instead used by the SS leadership during the period between 1941 and 1945 for operational as well as personal ends. As the use of these funds, particularly for personal ends, was considered a breach of the trust's legal obligations and therefore a criminal act, some of the SS leadership were tried on this score and found guilty at the Nuremberg Trials.[108]

---

106. Treichel, "Resettlement and Colonization," 37.
107. Letter from SS Major General Greifelt to Defendant Schwerin von Krosigk, 10 September 1941, in *Trials of War Criminals Before the Nuernberg Military Tribunals Under Control Council Law*, No. 10, Vol. 13, *United States of America v. Ernst von Weizsaecker, et al.* (Washington, DC: US Government Printing Office, 1952) 608–9, http://forum.axishistory.com/viewtopic.php?t=66094.
108. Ibid. The Nuremberg Court's interest has thus preserved the documents that attest to the ultimate fate of the collective family wealth the Germans left behind in Bessarabia.

## In Poland, the brunt of work in reestablishing the Bessarabian German families fell to women

It must have struck some Bessarabian Germans as ironic or at least strange to find themselves returned to the very region their ancestors had left for Bessarabia 127 years earlier. Some found themselves just miles from the homes of ancestors in Prussian Poland. For example, Emanuel Bohnet, formerly of Nikolajewka, Bessarabia, was resettled with his family on a farm in Lenzhagen (Polish: Łąsko Wielki) roughly 30 miles from Maleschechowo (Polish: Małociechowo), where his great-great-grandfather, Jacob Raugust, was born, and an equal distance from Tscherbin, from which Jacob Raugust had emigrated to Kulm, Bessarabia, in 1814.[109]

In resettling in German Poland, the prosperous and comfortable world the Germans had created in Bessarabia was left behind forever. The agricultural and light manufacturing economy on which that world had been based could not be recreated in Poland. With climate and soil conditions quite different from those in Bessarabia, new farming problems had to be mastered. The problems for farmers were increased by the lack of mechanized equipment and thus the need to rely on physical labor of horses, oxen, and humans alone. This became even more of a problem for farming families, since most of the young men had been drafted into the German army in the resettlement processing camps, and so the labor of building farms fell chiefly to women and men in their mid-thirties and older, and children. For Bessarabian men who relied on craftwork, creating new niches for selling the products of their labor in Polish towns proved quite difficult. Instead of forming virtual monopolies, as they had in the Bessarabian villages, they were in commercially and technically disadvantageous competition with long-established craftworkers in larger towns. Those who had operated manufacturing plants or commercial businesses in Bessarabia had lost everything. Now, without their factories, without their reserves of cash and stock, and without their former markets, they joined their former employees, often near the bottom of the existing labor pool in German Poland.

The process of moving nearly ninety thousand German Bessarabians out of the Soviet Union and into Germany resulted in some family tragedies. Families were living in close quarters at the airport in Galati, Romania, and later in reception centers in Germany under less than sanitary conditions, and disease spread as a result. The most seriously affected were the old and very young. Matilda Grams of Beresina, age sixty-one, died October 19, 1940, soon after arriving at a reception camp in Freiburg, Sudetenland.[110] Her granddaughter, three-year-old Edith Schwandt from Arzis, died December 23, 1940, at a reception camp in Werdau,[111] and the brothers eight-year-old Ewald and two-year-old Hugo Gewinner died in November 1940 at a reception camp in Gablonz, Sudetenland.

Not long after the Bessarabian families were settled in Poland, the German government made a radical shift in the military and political goals it had been

---

109. Bohnet's residence in Lenzhagen may be surmised from the fact that his son Artur and daughter Ilse were born there in April 1942 and January 1944, respectively. Lenzhagen was the German name for this village only in the period from 1942 to 1945. As part of the Imperial German province of Posen before 1918, the German name for Łąsko Wielki was Groß Lonsk.

110. Freiburg had been incorporated into Germany after Czechoslovakia was forced to cede the Sudetenland to Germany in October 1938. After the war it returned to being the Czech town of Příbor 13 miles south of Ostrava.

111. Werdau in Saxony is just west of Zwickau.

pursuing in the war. This shift in policy did not prove successful, and its ultimate consequences brought disaster to both Germany and the Bessarabian Germans. In a massive attack that began in June 1941, Germany's Wehrmacht invaded the Soviet Union. The great shock this created almost caused the military forces and political government of the Soviet Union to collapse. The Soviet Union, however, recovered its balance, and, in three years of warfare noted for unbelievable ferocity, brutality, and cruelty on both sides, the Red Army forced the Wehrmacht out of Russia, out of East Prussia and Poland, and to the ultimate total defeat of the German government in Berlin.

## When the Red Army approached the Bessarabian German settlements in Poland in January 1945, boys and old men were drafted into a fighting force, while women and children fled west on their own

In January 1945, the frontlines approached the villages in the western Warthegau where many of the Bessarabian Germans had been resettled. Boys under age sixteen still living with their families as well as middle-aged and older men were conscripted into the Volkssturm, an ill-trained and poorly armed militia created in a last-ditch attempt to halt the Soviet and Allied advances.[112] The Volkssturm could offer little defense, and their efforts came at the cost of high casualty figures and many prisoners of war. Gotthilf Vogel's experience provides an apt example. In January 1945, he was a forty-five-year-old former Kulm resident settled with his family near Donaten (Polish Donatowo) in the Kosten District, a village in which many Kulm families had been placed. Vogel was drafted into the Volkssturm on January 18, 1945, and on the following day was put into the battle line some 90 miles east near the river crossing of the Warta at Koło (renamed Warthebrücke by the Germans). He was captured a day later on January 19 by forward units of the Red Army and taken ultimately to a prison camp in Stalino (now Donec'k) in the Ukraine.[113] In Kern's listing of Bessarabian German deaths during the war, it is possible to pick out numbers of older men and boys who in January 1945 became war casualty statistics, likely as a result of being conscripted into the Volkssturm. Among these include David Bohnet and Gottlieb Vossler, age fifty-three and fifty-four respectively, both originally from Benkendorf, who were listed as missing in action in January 1945 near Schmückert, Poland, in the Lissa District south of Poznan;[114] Emil Sept of Alt Elft, who had just turned nineteen, was listed as killed in action on January 17, 1945;[115] and

---

112.  The Volkssturm was formed in October 1944 as the Red Army pushed into East Prussia. The name provided a patriotic echo of the irregular Prussian Landsturm that had been established to oppose the invading French in 1812–13. The Volkssturm was made up of German males between the ages of sixteen and sixty not then in the army or employed in producing armaments. British historian Ian Kershaw argues that the creation of the Volkssturm was motivated by a desire to keep the large numbers of men still members of Germany's civilian population under military jurisdiction and under the Nazi Party's control. With the Red Army in the east and the British, Americans, and French in the west within or at the borders of the Reich, party control over the Volkssturm would provide a check against the increasing possibility of internal unrest or calls for the end of the war. Kershaw, *The End: The Defiance and Destruction of Hitler's Germany, 1944-1945* (New York: Penguin Press, 2011), 86–88, 106–8.
113.  Gotthilf Vogel, "An Account of My Captivity and About Kulm" in "Heimatbuch der Gemeinde Kulm," *Heritage Review* 14, no. 4 (1984): 39–40.
114.  Kern, *Homeland Book*, 217. Schmückert, whose Polish name is Bojanowo, was in the Lissa District where numbers of Bessarabian German farmers had been resettled.
115.  Ibid., 207.

seventeen-year-old Otto Kunz, originally from Friedenstal, was listed as having died in battle on January 20, 1945.[116]

Bessarabian German women and children living in the Warthegau were given little or no warning of the impending arrival of the war front. Loading a few possessions and food onto horse-drawn carts or carrying such items on their backs, they scrambled west trying to stay ahead of the fighting. The harsh treatment that had been meted out by the German army to Soviet citizens during the fighting and occupation of the Soviet Union encouraged the Red Army to matching feats of barbarity when they reached Germany. Fleeing ahead of the fighting, Germans were justifiably filled with great fears. Traveling generally in small groups, German refugees suffered in the cold, got lost, ran out of food, were harassed by Poles seeking revenge for years of torment, or sometimes even were helped by Poles who sympathized with their sufferings. Not everyone survived this difficult journey; again, older people and young children were particularly at risk. The Kulm Heimatbuch, in its listing of data on families from that village who made the resettlement, notes, for example, seven adults between the ages of fifty-three and seventy-seven as well as two children under ten who died in early 1945, presumably during or shortly after their flight from Poland.[117] Some families became separated and only with difficulty found each other again months later in Germany.

Ute Schmidt relates many harrowing first-person stories of Bessarabian Germans fleeing Poland for greater safety in Germany.[118] Most of these share the common elements of hurried travel, constant fear, cold and hunger, the frequent unhelpfulness of the German natives once they arrived in Germany, and the bitter state of near helpless degradation to which their flight from Poland had reduced them. On reaching Germany, the Bessarabian Germans became widely scattered: Bessarabian villages that had been kept together in Poland were now finally separated as small groups of refugees and individuals fleeing alone sought to latch on to whatever handholds that could be found. The Kulm Heimatbuch, again the most detailed source for a single Bessarabian German village, reports widespread landing places throughout Germany for the former Kulm residents. There are no large groupings in single villages or towns but clusters in broad areas such as those north of Stuttgart and south of Hamburg in what became West Germany or south of Magdeburg in what became East Germany.

Not all the Bessarabian Germans living in the Warthegau in early 1945 were able to escape. Schmidt reports that some 1,300 Bessarabian Germans, generally women and children, were unable to reach Germany ahead of the Red Army advance. Interned under the Soviet military administration of Poland and Germany, these Bessarabian Germans were lumped together with Germans who had escaped from the Soviet Ukraine and were sent back to the Soviet Union . As the Soviet government considered the presence of such former Soviet citizens in Germany evidence of their disloyalty, upon reentering the Soviet Union, they were sent to labor camps in

---

116.  Ibid., 234.

117.  "Destination of Emigrants from Berssarabia" in "Heimatbuch der Gemeinde Kulm," *Heritage Review* 15, no. 3 (1985): 23–35. Otto Kison, who was six at the time of his death, is described as "Gefallen Juni 1945" (28). Too young to have been "in arms" (the traditional meaning of *gefallen*), this suggests rather that he died as the result of wounds received when his family was inadvertently caught in the fighting.

118.  Schmidt, *Die Deutschen aus Bessarabien.*

Siberia and Kazakhstan.[119] Eager to punish such Soviet Germans, Soviet authorities sought them out even in the western zones of Germany. Again, Soviet authorities made no distinctions between Bessarabian Germans who had resettled and Soviet Germans from the Ukraine who had escaped. The Western allies, focused chiefly on the repatriation of refugees, naively ignored the reasons Germans who had lived in the Soviet Union did not wish to return. As a result, even Bessarabian Germans who had reached the zones in Western Germany administered by the United States, Great Britain, and France were in danger of being handed over to Soviet authorities and sent back to prison camps in the Soviet Union. Bessarabian German men who, as members of the German army were captured by the Red Army, were taken to prisoner-of-war camps in Siberia. Like all such German POWs, they worked in such camps until the 1950s when survivors were repatriated to Germany.

However, near the top of the woes the war inflicted on Bessarabian German families, and German families in general, was the loss of so many men in the fighting. German casualties were significant. Two generations of men had been decimated. Rüdiger Overmans has estimated that over 5,300,000 German soldiers were killed out of a total of 18.5 million men in arms at some time during the war.[120] Deaths among the contingent of Bessarabian Germans who had been conscripted into the German army were commensurate with the high casualty figures experienced by the army as a whole. Nearly every Bessarabian German family suffered losses and the total number of deaths formed a material portion of the total male population of Bessarabian resettlers. Kern has gone to extraordinary lengths to collect the names of Bessarabian Germans who died in World War II fighting as German soldiers. The appendix of Kern's book offers a village-by-village account that lists the names of soldiers killed or presumed killed, and, where available, the date and place of death. Included in this listing are the names of soldiers captured by the Red Army and who later died in Russian prison camps. Adding up Kern's village lists produces a total of 5,971 Bessarabian German men who lost their lives serving in the German army.[121] Where Kern's data indicate a place of death, the great preponderance of deaths, as for those of the German army in general, took place in the east, fighting against the Red Army.

If one presumes that roughly half of the 88,545 Germans who left Bessarabia were male, then the 5,971 deaths represent 13.5% of all the men who resettled from Bessarabia. In comparing Kern's casualty figures for individual villages with the village population figures from 1940 provided in the notes made by German officials as they processed the elections for resettlement,[122] this suggests that while there was a good deal of variance between the experiences of different villages, all villages suffered painful losses (table 13–4).

---

119. Ibid., 255.
120. Rüdiger Overmans, *Deutsche militärische Verluste im Zweiten Weltkreig* (Munich: R. Oldenbourg, 2000).
121. Kern, *Homeland Book*, 203–336. The figure of 5,971 World War II deaths includes data from both Kern's original listing and from the "Supplement from the Second World War" that follows.
122. The village casualty counts come from Kern, *Homeland Book*, 203–336. The data on village populations come from Wise, "Bessarabian Village Reports." In the chart that follows I assume that 50 percent of the total population is male.

Not counted here or elsewhere are the numbers of Bessarabian German men who survived their military experiences but who returned to postwar civilian life physically injured or traumatized.

The story of the Bessarabian Germans ends with the defeat of Germany in 1945. While the resettlement in occupied Poland in 1941 dispersed them throughout the Warthegau, many villages had been able to remain intact or settle together in sufficiently large groups to preserve cohesion. However, when the Bessarabian Germans became refugees, fleeing Poland ahead of the Red Army, they were scattered throughout West and East Germany—sometimes in small groups that were linked by ties of family and friendship, but often just as married couples or individuals. Like their relations in the United States, Canada, Brazil, and Argentina, who were also widely scattered in those countries, their future and their story is not of themselves as a group, but of their participation in the societies and the developing histories of those countries.

TABLE 13–4. **WWII casualty comparisons among Bessarabian German villages**

| Village | Total pop. | Males | WWII deaths | % Males |
|---|---|---|---|---|
| Alt Posttal | 1,513 | 757 | 116 | 15.3% |
| Baimaklia | 188 | 94 | 24 | 25.5% |
| Beresina | 2,763 | 1,382 | 144 | 10.4% |
| Borodino | 2,764 | 1,382 | 154 | 11.1% |
| Kulm | 1,814 | 907 | 182 | 20.1% |
| Leipzig | 2,257 | 1,129 | 212 | 18.8% |
| Lichtental | 2,046 | 1,023 | 195 | 19.1% |
| Neu Annowka | 179 | 90 | 33 | 36.7% |
| Sarata | 2,180 | 1,090 | 137 | 12.6% |
| Tarutino | 6,186 | 3,093 | 228 | 7.4% |
| Teplitz | 2,442 | 1,221 | 166 | 13.6% |
| Wittenberg | 1,366 | 683 | 108 | 15.8% |
| **All Bessarabia** | 88,545 | 44,273 | 5,971 | 13.5% |

# Epilogue

Once the Bessarabian Germans left Bessarabia for Germany in the resettlement of 1940, they broke all connections with their former villages, farms, and homes for a long time. After the Germans left, teams of Soviet officials made searches of the civic buildings, houses, and barns in the former German villages and confiscated items deemed valuable to the state or sometimes to the personal needs of the officials themselves. When the searches were completed, Bulgarians, Gaugaz, and Moldavians from neighboring villages were permitted to move into the vacant houses. Some village names were retained and others were totally changed. In the former German villages, Soviet authorities created new collective farms. When Germany and its allies launched their massive attack on Russia June 22, 1941, Soviet authority in Bessarabia soon collapsed. By late July 1941, the Romanians had pushed the Red Army out of Bessarabia virtually without a fight. Bessarabia then remained under Romanian control again until July 1944.

It would appear that during World War II, the German villages, now stripped of movable and useful items, were only lightly settled. This was the impression gained by Walter Hornbacher who, as a teenager, passed through Tarutino in March 1944. Hornbacher and his family were from a German village in the Beresan District of Soviet Ukraine.[1] In early 1944, they elected to leave the Ukraine ahead of the retreating German army rather than remain and return to the hardships of Soviet collective farm life. His diary mentions passing former German villages above Tarutino with neglected, uninhabited buildings near collapse. Tarutino, though, was in far better shape: "very little was neglected."[2] There is a different picture of Tarutino in the diary of Gertrud Peterreins, whose party of refugees passed through Tarutino two days earlier. She notes being quartered in a "sort of barracks" ("in einer

---

1. Walter Hornbacher, "Removal from the Homeland: A Surviving Eye-Witness Documentary Report on the Evacuation of Ethnic Germans from the Black Sea Region of the Ukraine to Germany in Early 1944," Heritage Review 38, no. 1 (2008): 9–25. Hornbacher does not identify his home village. As he reports that his evacuating party's first day's journey takes them to Michelsfeld, this indicates his home village was on the western edge of the Welfare Committee's Berezan district of the Xerson Province. Michelsfeld is southeast of Hoffnungstal (C-5 on Stumpp's map "Karte der deutschen Siedlungen im Gebiet (Oblast) Odessa"). References in the following day's entry to Neu Berlin, Neu Beresina, and Katarshino confirm this identification.
2. Hornbacher, "Removal from the Homeland," entries for March 25, 1944, through March 29, 1944, 13. Hornbacher does not name the two former German villages that he passes on March 26. The group he was traveling with left Causeni ["Kaushani" to Hornbacher] on the morning of the 26 and arrived in Tarutino on the evening of the 27. His route is likely the road developed in the nineteenth century that ran from Causeni through Manzyr to Tarutino and before reaching Tarutino passed along the edge of Borodino and then went right through Beresina.

Art Kaserne einquartiert"), possibly one of the former school buildings in Tarutino. While it had windows, such spaces were no longer enclosed with glass ("die zwar Fenster, aber leider keine Scheiben hatte").[3]

In September 1946, Gotthilf Vogel made a unique visit to his former home in Kulm. As mentioned in the prior chapter, Vogel was taken prisoner on the second day of his participation in the Volkssturm in January 1945 and was ultimately taken to a prisoner-of-war camp in Stalino (now the city of Donec'k) in the Ukraine. In September 1946 he escaped from the prison camp. Hoping to make his way to Romania and from there to Germany, he managed to get back to Kulm, where he thought he would be able to rest and feed himself until the opportunity came to go further. His family's house in Kulm was now near ruins: "Everything was gone…no pump handle, corn bins, garden fence, corral, pig stall, fodder crib, straw and corn stacks. It was not only that way with my yard, but with all of them."[4]

Most of the houses in Kulm were greatly damaged or even demolished. The impression he formed was that the trees, houses, and barns had been dismembered for building materials or firewood. Vogel reasons that "the people had no firewood and therefore took whatever was around."[5] The former German presence here was not viewed positively. In the cemetery, tombstones had been smashed or taken away for building, the once fine church was now without its steeple, and many windows were broken or boarded. The village was inhabited now by small numbers of Gaugaz whose collective farm worked some of Kulm's fields. Little of the village's agricultural wealth remained. Looking down toward the river valley and the former German village of Leipzig, Vogel "saw no cows or horses or any vehicles moving in the valley. All around it seemed desolate and empty."[6] Vogel spoke with and was given a little food by a Gaugaz woman who was living in his former house. He learned from her that the present inhabitants had not lived there during the war but had moved in after the Soviets retook control. During the war, "only Poles were here."[7] Kulm was thus, ironically, one of the sites used by the Nazi government to "resettle" Poles who had been displaced from central Poland in the German government's effort to make Poland more ethnically German by settling German refugees from Bessarabia, the Baltic countries, and the Ukraine.

When the Soviet Union retook Bessarabia from the Germans in 1944, it reinstated the political boundaries it sought to establish in 1940. The old borders of Imperial Russian Bessarabia were not recreated. Instead, the southern third of what had been pre-revolutionary Russian Bessarabia, where the majority of the German

3.  Gertrud Peterreins, "Unsere Rückkehr nach Deutschland: Tagebuch von Gertrud Peterreins geb. Schlaht" (N.p.: Odessa Digital Library, 2002), http://www.odessa3.org/collections/articles/link/schlaht-g.html. Gertrud Peterreins is also departing from somewhere near Hoffnungstal in the Odessa region, possibly Hoffnungstal itself, as she mentions a party from Neu Berlin arriving before her party set off. Like Hornbacher on leaving Tarutino, she mentions struggling up the hill on the way south. Also like Hornbacher, having lived through the terrible 1930s in Soviet Russia, she is under no illusions about the benefits of communism or a positive future for Germans in the Soviet Union. Both quotes are from the entry for Saturday March 25, 1944.

4.  Vogel, "My Captivity," 40, 41–42. Vogel refers to the new villagers as "Cholchosen" and to the village enterprise as the "Cholchos" or "Colchose," which is a rendering of the Russian word kolxoz, meaning "collective farm," into German. Vogel creates a German plural for the collective farmers, Cholchosen, instead of using the Russian, kolxozniki, which, as a Russian speaker, he apparently knew.

5.  Ibid.

6.  Ibid.

7.  Ibid.

colonies had been located, was attached to the Ukrainian Soviet Socialistic Republic. The northern two-thirds of pre-revolutionary Bessarabia, together with the strip of land on the east side of the Dniester that had been the Moldavian ASSR prior to 1940, became the Moldavian Soviet Socialistic Republic. This was evidently done with several calculations in mind. One was to limit the area of the new Moldavian SSR to the region where the Moldavian-speaking population was the dominant majority. A second factor was to recognize and satisfy the large Ukrainian population in the Budjak, and a third may well have been to make any future claims by Romania more difficult to settle.[8] To further this latter aim, the Soviet government made great efforts to treat Moldavian as a language in its own right and, thus, not a dialect of Romanian. The new border separating the Ukrainian SSR from the Moldavian SSR ran just outside the former German village of Leipzig so that the former Romanowka with the important railroad station, now called Basarabeasca, was in the Moldavian SSR. Following the demise of the Soviet Union in 1990, this border has been maintained; it now forms the national frontier between the countries of the Ukraine and Moldova.

Under the authority of the Ukrainian Soviet government, the names of the former German villages that had a clear Russian or Slavic heritage were retained and those reflecting a German heritage were translated or altered. A detailed Soviet map based on surveys taken in 1948 and 1958 shows names used before the breakup of the Soviet Union and the Google satellite view shows the currently used Ukrainian and Moldavian names that are listed below in table E–1 and table E–2.[9]

The names of former Bessarabian German villages that are now in Moldova have undergone fewer changes. One reason, certainly, is because the German names often had a Moldovian/Romanian linguistic base. Nonetheless, even where the former village name had a Germanic base, this has not proved a barrier to its preservation. Almost all of the former German villages continue to exist, and contemporary conditions in them can be viewed, in some cases with amazing clarity, on the Google satellite view. A few villages, though, have perished. The parallel lines that were once the streets of Katlebug, a village of 403 people in 1940, can clearly be made out in the fields on the western edge of the Alibei Liman. Harder to pick out but still faintly visible are homesites and property lines in Hoffnungstal, a large village of 2,143 inhabitants in 1940, which was leveled to create an area for a Soviet military firing range and training ground.

The Google satellite picture of Kulm offers a detailed view of the once-elegant now ruined church set in a broad, now treeless and deeply eroded common between the two main streets. Former German church buildings are also visible in Alt Elft, Alt Posttal, Borodino, Klöstitz, Krasna, Leipzig, and Paris. In Alt Elft, the monument to veterans mentioned by Kern is also visible in the churchyard.[10] In Eigenfeld, the church's repaired roof and neat yard and walk stand out. In contrast, churches in

---

8.  Markus Schönherr, "Russification and Ethnic Consciousness of Romanians in Bessarabia 1812-1991" [unpublished, undated research paper] (Budapest: International Studies Center, Budapest University of Economics), http://ewwg.vlamynck.eu/cst/cst-mold/bessara.html. Schönherr sees the rationale for placing portions of Imperial Russian Bessarabia in two separate Soviet republics as balancing internal Soviet national politics by following the Roman principle of "divide et impera."

9.  The Soviet names are found in Map L-35-071, "SSSR, Odesskaja oblast,'" in the University of California at Berkeley map collection.

10. Kern, *Homeland Book*, 54.

TABLE E–1.  The names of former German Bessarabian villages now located in the Ukraine

| Former Name | Current Name |
| --- | --- |
| Alt Elft | Sadove (Garden Place) |
| Alt Posttal | Malojaroslavec Vtoroj (Malojaroslavetz II)[a] |
| Arzis | Arciz |
| Beresina | Berezine |
| Borodino | Borodino |
| Brienne | Glinka (Little Clay Place) |
| Friedenstal | Mirnopillja (Peaceful Fields)[b] |
| Dennewitz | Prjamobalka (Straight Ravine) |
| Krasna | Krasne (Beautiful Place) |
| Kulm | Pidgirne (Underhill) |
| Leipzig | Serpneve (Crescent Place) |

a. This was the official Welfare Committee name used for Alt Posttal throughout its history under Imperial Russian rule. Wittenberg, the original Malojaroslavec, became Malojaroslavec I after the colony was divided to create Alt Posttal in 1825. Alt Elft and Neu Elft also had different official names when they were part of Imperial Russia. The official names of Alt and Neu Elft (Fere-Champenoise I and II) were, like Malojaroslavec, derived from the names of battles in which Russian troops helped achieve victories over the French in the Napoleonic Wars.

b. The new names of both Friedental and Lichtental are translations of the German village names.

TABLE E–2.  The names of former German Bessarabian villages now located in Moldova

| Former Name | Current Name |
| --- | --- |
| Unter Albota | Albota de Jus |
| Ober Albota | Albota de Sus |
| Alexanderfeld | Alexanderfeld |
| Baimaklia | Baimaclia |
| Balaban | Balabanu |
| Jargara | Iargara |
| Ketrossy | Chetrosu |
| Alt/Neu Oneschti | Onesti |
| Neu Sarata | Sarata Noua |
| Sofiewka | Sofievca |
| Strymbeni | Strimbeni |

Berezina and Lichtental are roofless shells that lie in now park-like settings. In Neu Posttal, the former church is also a roofless shell and lies across the street from the shell of another large building, likely the remains of the Deutsches Haus completed in 1938 and pictured in Kern. In Wittenberg, the school building continues to stand but the outline of the foundations of the former church are barely visible in what was its yard. In Teplitz, the large German cemetery, neglected and filled with bracken, is visible in front of the regular rows of the cemetery maintained by the current inhabitants. Similar neglected German graveyards can also be picked out in Alt Posttal, Basyrjamka, Brienne, Friedensfeld, Gnadental, Katzbach, Kulm, Leipzig, Lichtental, Neu Posttal, Paris, Sarata, and Wittenberg. Google marks the location of the former Serpneve (Leipzig) railroad station (now a bus stop) on what had been the rail line that ran from Akkerman to Leipzig. The rails, however, have been torn up, and there is no rail station still standing. At the north end of Leipzig, the metal rail bridge still passes over the dry channel of the Skinosa River, but as it now connects rail-less dirt paths, it has a desolate appearance.[11]

The Google satellite views also offer ground-level photos of many of the former German villages. There are pictures of the rebuilt Evangelical Lutheran churches in Arzis, Sarata, and Albota,[12] the former church of Dennewitz that is now reconsecrated as an Orthodox church, and the ruins of the former churches in Berezina, Paris, and Neu Posttal.[13] Attached to the Google view of the former Neu Elft village is a picture of an attractively kept up former German farm house with its orchard and the old stone wall that separates it from the street. Ironically, from a German point of view, the scene is entitled "comfortable Ukrainian houses" ("ujutnye ukrainskie domiki"). Attached to many villages are street scenes that show the rows of farm houses built by the Germans as well as the stone or metal fencing separating them from the street: some houses and fences well repaired, showing the original work, some with new decorative features, some with very hard use and little to show, but all still in use.

Beginning in the early 1980s, small groups of former residents of the German settlements in Bessarabia and their descendants have been making visits to Bessarabia. With the breakup of the Soviet Union in 1990 and the formation of the independent countries of the Ukraine and Moldova, the numbers of such visits have been steadily increasing and have begun to include travelers from North America as well. Such travel, as well as the publication on the Internet of the accounts of the visits and the photographs taken on them, has reopened connections with Bessarabia. The travel accounts tend to repeat themes that emphasize the negative changes that have occurred. Almost all comment on the widespread destruction and the disappearance of houses, barns, and civic buildings. The condition of the former churches has received notably harsh treatment. Also viewed negatively are the vandalized German graveyards with gravestones knocked down or taken away for building projects, the village common areas, farmyards and street fencing that have not been kept up, the missing trees that once lined the village streets, and everywhere the comparatively primitive conditions of roads, services, and infrastructure.[14]

Yet, attractive vestiges remain. Some houses have been kept in particularly good repair, such as the former home of Dr. Leopold Dobler in Sarata, now a children's

---

11. Railroad cars are visible farther east in Arzis. The current rail line from Arzis, though, now goes southwest to Izmail on the Danube instead of northwest to Leipzig.

12. The picture of the rebuilt of Albota church attached to the Google satellite view of Albota de Sus incorrectly guides one to the middle of a wood. The church, with its distinctive red metal roof, is actually at the crossing junction in the middle of the village.

13. The pictures of the remaining walls of the former Neu Postall church are particularly good.

14. Edward Nill and Reinhold Schneider, "The First Approved Visit to Beresina," Germans from Russia Heritage Collection (Fargo: North Dakota State University, 1991), http://library.ndsu.edu/ grhc/history_culture/history/schneider.html; Herb Poppke, "Teplitz and More, 1993" (Bismarck, ND: Germans from Russia Heritage Society, 2002), http://www.grhs.org/data/poppke/poppke3. html; and Duane V. Retzloff, "Journey to the Homeland Tour, Visit to Kulm, Bessarabia, May 1998," Germans from Russia Heritage Collection (Fargo: North Dakota State University, 1998), https://library.ndsu.edu/grhc/outreach/journey/tours/1998memories.html. The *Odessa Book of Mourning* notes that the cemetery in the former German village of Selz across the Dneister River from Bessarabia in South Russia as well as cemeteries in neighboring villages had been "purposely destroyed by the former Soviet regime in 1956" (Weiss, *Odessa Book of Mourning*, 16). Poppke reports with regard to the graveyard in Teplitz that after the time of his visit in 1993 "people from Germany [have] been restoring the cemetery" ("Teplitz and More").

music school. In 2001, Elli Wise photographed a Teplitz house and farmyard from the street, which shows a well-preserved wrought iron gate and passageway seemingly unchanged from the 1930s.[15] In 2004, Alfred Hein photographed Friedrich Hein's former farmstead in Borodino, offering a similar view of a well-kept yard.[16] In 2001, Carolyn Schott photographed the delicate and fanciful wrought iron awning covering the entrance to the former German school in the former Neu Elft.[17] Dan Mueller has a picture of a late-nineteenth or early-twentieth-century brick house in Mannsburg that has preserved much of its delicate exterior decorative work including a pointed second floor window.[18] Another of Mueller's pictures is of a well-preserved gate, house, and wrought iron work in Tepltiz.[19] The surviving wrought iron, wood, and concrete adornments of buildings and fence work attest, in a poignant way, to the continued presence of German peasant artistic culture in Bessarabia.

The visits to Bessarabia have also brought surprises and discoveries. Nill and Schneider, among others, comment on the suspicion they first encountered when they asked permission in Beresina to look into the houses their family members had built and inhabited. Only later did they come to realize that the current occupants were concerned that they might intend to reclaim the houses. Herb Poppke made an even more surprising discovery. In 1993, Poppke was one of the first to go back to visit the former German Bessarabia. He hired a guide, Leonid Dmitrievič Inglik, to help him find places there. During their journey together, Inglik identified himself as Hugo Jüngling, who was born in 1930 in Neu Elft and resettled with his family in Germany in 1940. Jüngling/Inglik ultimately lived with his family in the area near Łodz in the Warthegau. In 1945 when the Red Army arrived, he was either captured or took refuge with the Soviets. Back in Russia, he adopted a Russian name and came back to Neu Elft but settled ultimately in Soviet Volynia. In 1967, he returned to live in the former Alt Elft. Jüngling/Inglik would thus be the only German known to have come back to live permanently in Bessarabia following the resettlement.[20]

The visits to the former German villages in Bessarabia and the accounts and pictures they have produced have led to efforts to commemorate the 126-year German settlement there. Survivors of the resettlement from the villages of Borodino, Hoffnungstal, Kulm, Neu Elft, Plotzk, Scholtoi, Teplitz, and perhaps other villages and their descendants have erected stone monuments in their old villages remembering the German settlement. The monuments note in Russian and German the long German presence in the village and the departure of the inhabitants in 1940. This latter is often noted as being the result of a Soviet-German agreement which appears intended to give oblique emphasis to the fact that this was not the result

15. Elli Wise photographs at "Pictures—Bessarabian Villages," http://www.grhs.org/chapters/bess/memonly/pic/vill/Teplitz%2041.JPG

16. Alfred Hein, Borodino, Summer 2004 [photo collection] (N.p.: Remmick.org, n.d.), http://www.remmick.org/AlfredHeinPhotos/Page2.html.

17. Poppke, "Teplitz and More"; and Carolyn Schott, "The School" [photograph] in Neu Elft, Bessarabia 2008 [album], compiled by Black Sea German Research Community, last modified January 29, 2012, https://www.facebook.com/BlackSeaGermanResearch/photos/a.289215584472132.70149.172727712787587/289216071138750/?type=3&theater..

18. Dan Mueller Photo Gallery, Image 148317, http://www.muellerphoto.exposuremanager.com/p/mannsburg/_mg_148317.

19. Dan Mueller Photo Gallery, Image 119726, http://www.muellerphoto.exposuremanager.com/p/teplitz/_mg_119726.

20. Poppke, "Teplitz and More."

of the German invasion of the Soviet Union. There is a very striking monument on the site of where the settlement of Hoffnungstal once stood. Here, facing the empty fields, a stone tablet noting the existence of the village is set in one of the stone threshing wheels the Germans made and used.

The increasing numbers of tourists visiting these villages have led local inhabitants of the current villages to create their own commemorations of the earlier German settlements, perhaps as a further inducement for tourism. Small museums have been established with collections of photographs, tools, handicrafts, and equipment that the current residents found and preserved. Such museums occupy a room in the village school houses in Kulm, Alt Posttal, and Krasna. In Friedenstal, Edwin Kelm, chairman of the Relief Committee of the Evangelical Church, who has been very active in sponsoring positive connections between German Bessarabians and their former settlements, bought his family's former home, rebuilt it, and made it a museum of German culture and agricultural life in Bessarabia.[21]

Perhaps the most lasting and certainly the most substantial commemorations of the former German settlements in Bessarabia have been the efforts made by former residents and their descendants to improve the current infrastructure in these villages or to restore churches there. Edwin Kelm and the Evangelical Lutheran Church have played a notable role in this. Kelm made several trips to Soviet Bessarabia in the 1980s, leading groups of former residents and establishing connections with the current citizens of the former German settlements. In the 1990s Kelm and the Relief Committee funded the construction of clinics, orphanages, and homes for the aged in Akkerman, Chisinau, Arzis, Schabo, and Tarutino. Other groups of Germans, often those who were once residents of one of the former Bessarabian villages, have also supported repairs made to churches in Bessarabia. In many cases, this has been for the benefit of the local Eastern Orthodox parish. In other cases the work has been in an effort to reestablish an Evangelical Lutheran presence. In Eigenfeld, the church steeple has been restored and the roof and upper story repaired—the restored building is now used by the local Orthodox congregation. In Arzis, the church has undergone significant repairs with the steeple also restored.[22] The façade of the former German church in Neu Elft has been repainted and a new walkway and fountain built in front of it. The restored building has become an Orthodox church.[23] The general features of the former church in Dennewitz are retained in the Orthodox church that now occupies the building. The changes that have been made though suggest the building went through a difficult period before the Orthodox church took it over: the new roof gives the church a higher ceiling but downplays the look of the entry bell tower, the bell tower itself has a larger front door, is missing its former middle section, no longer has its bell, and has a new steeple. Yet in comparing the picture of the church from 1934 in Kern with the contemporary picture attached to the Google satellite view of the village, there is so

21. Attached to the Google satellite view of the former Friedenstal is a picture of the house Edwin Kelm refurbished and the new museum structure next to it.

22. Poppke, "Teplitz and More." If this is the same church that Herb Poppke reports from his 1993 visit ("only a wall of the church remains"), the restoration in Arzis was quite major.

23. Ibid. Poppke has a picture of the Neu Elft church before any restoration has occurred. The restored church appears in several of the Aspenleiter photos of 2008 (Aspenleiter and Aspenleiter, "Trip to Ukraine").

much of the old church preserved that the overall appearance is far more that of a Lutheran house of worship than an Orthodox [24]

The most striking church restorations have occurred in Albota (2008) and Sarata (1994–95), where the interiors of the church buildings have been totally refurbished. These major restorations have also been intended to create Evangelical Lutheran places of worship in Bessarabia. In Sarata, the church is now a joint Evangelical Lutheran and Orthodox house of worship. Former residents of Sarata and their descendants, together with the Relief Committee of the Evangelical Lutheran Church, funded the beautiful reflooring and the rebuilding of the balcony and choir with the work done by local craftsmen.[25]

As a monument, the restored Sarata church makes a hopeful reconciliation with the past. While it preserves the features and functions and maintains the style of the church, it is also a material improvement over the worn appearance that pictures show the church had at the time of resettlement.

24. Kern, *Homeland Book*, 55.

25. Dan Mueller's collection of photographs of his trip to Bessarabia show both the beautiful interior of the refinished church (MG 0748, MG 0751, MG 0752, MG 0753, MG 0756) and pictures of the church's interior in the late 1930s (MG 0736, MG 0739) that were on display during his visit. Dan Mueller Photo Galleries at http://www.muellerphoto.exposuremanager.com/g/sarata. As a contrast to the restored church appearing in Mueller's photos, Herb Poppke's collection includes a photograph from 1993 of the unrestored exterior of the Sarata church (Poppke, "Teplitz and More").

# Bibliography

Adam, Ulrich. *The Political Economy of J. H. G. Justi*. New York: Peter Lang, 2006.

Adauge, M., and A. Furtuna. Basarabia si Basarabenii. Chisinau: Uniunea Scriitorilor din Moldova, 1991. Quoted in Wikipedia, "Sfatul Țării." Last modified June 21, 2015. http://en.wikipedia.org/wiki/Sfatul_%C5%A2%C4%83rii.

Afanas'ev, Ju. N., and V. P. Kozlov, eds. *Istorija stalinskogo Gulaga: Konec 1920-x – pervaja polovina 1950-x godov*. Vol. 4, *Naselenie Gulaga: čislennost' i usloviia soderžanija* [The population of the gulag: the numbers and the conditions maintained], edited by A .B. Bezborodov, V. M. Xrustalev, and I. V. Bezborodova. Moscow: ROSSPĖN, 2004.

Baumann, Arnulf. "Background to Ignaz Lindl's Expulsion from Sarata Bessarabia in the Context of Russia's Political and Religious History." Translated by J. Gessele. *Heritage Review* 36, no. 1 (2006): 32–37.

Baumann, I. "The Reasons for the Emigration of Our Forefathers." *Heritage Review* 14, no. 3 (1984): 46–50.

Baumstark, Heinz, and Ann Justiss. "Little History of Baumstark." Version 26, November 1999. http://heinz-baumstark.homepage.t-online.de/meineHTML/history-e.htm.

Becker, Jakob. *Wie's daheim war: Der Schicksalweg der Bessarabiendeutschen*. Asperg, Ger.: Verlagsdruckerei Wilhelm Altvater, 1950. Exerpt in *Bessarabian Newsletter* 7, no. 2 (2005): 9.

Becker, Ted J. "Krasnaoverhead1" [image]. N.p.: The Krasna Project, c. 2012. http://14ushop.com/krasna/images/krasnaoverhead1.jpg.

———. "Long-houses" [image]. N.p.: The Krasna Project, c. 2012. http://14ushop.com/krasna/images/long-houses.jpg.

———, trans. "Zamosz (Poland) Settlement Contract of 28 February 1785." *Heritage Review* 41, no. 4 (2011): 31–35.

"Bolgrad." Sheet 46-46 in 3rd Military Mapping Survey of Austria-Hungary. http://lazarus.elte.hu/hun/digkonyv/topo/3felmeres.htm.

Benert, Richard. "Land Laws Pertaining to Germans in the Southwest Provinces, Kiev, Podolia, Volhynia 1864–1915." *Journal of the Society for German Genealogy in Eastern Europe* 2, no. 1 (March 2000): 16–21.

Black, Robert E., Simon Cousens, Hope L. Johnson, Joy E. Lawn, Igor Rudan, Diego G. Bassani, Prabhat Jha, et al. "Global, Regional, and National Causes of Child Mortality in 2008: A Systematic Analysis." *The Lancet* 375, no. 9730 (2010): 1969–87. doi: 10.1016/S0140-6736(10)60549-1.

Blejan, A., B. Costache, and A. Iarovici. "International Reserves of the National Bank of Romania 1920–1944." Bucharest: Banca Nationala A Romaniei, December 2006.

Bosch, Anton, Anton Bertsch, and Michael Wanner. *Trauerbuch Odessa: Heimat ist Geschichte – Geschichte ist unser Auftrag: Stalins Staatsterror an den Deutschen in den Gebieten von Odessa und Nikolajew Ukraine, 1928-1953*. Rußland-Deutsche Zeitgeschichte 5. Nürnberg, Ger.: Histor. Forschungsverein der Deutschen aus Russland, 2006.

Boucekkine, Raouf, Bity Diene, and Théophile Azomahou. "A Closer Look at the Relationship between Life Expectancy and Economic Growth." University of Glasgow, last modified August 14, 2007. http://www.gla.ac.uk/media/media_43616_en.pdf.

Brandes, Detlef. "A Success Story: The German Colonists in New Russia and Bessarabia: 1787–1914." *Acta Slavica Iaponica Tomus* 9 (1991). http://library.ndsu.edu/grhc/history_culture/history/brandes.html.

———. *Von den Zaren Adoptiert: Die Deutschen Kolonisten und die Balkansiedler in Neurußland und Bessarabien 1751-1914*. Munich: R. Oldenbourg, 1993.

———. "Wirtschaftliche Entwicklung und soziale Differenzierung in der Deutschen Kolonien Neurußlands und Bessarabiens bis zur Aufhebung der Kolonialstatus." In Meissner, Neubauer, and Eisfeld, *Die Rußlanddeutschen*, 69–78.

Bross, Alexander. "Johann Georg Bross" in "Heimatbuch der Gemeinde Kulm." *Heritage Review* 13, no. 4 (1983): 19.

Buchsweiler, Meir. *Volksdeutsche in der Ukraine am Vorabend und Beginn des Zweiten Weltkriegs—ein Fall doppelter Loyalität*. Gerlingen, Ger.: Bleicher, 1984.

Carlson, Alvar. "German-Russian Houses in Western North Dakota." *Pioneer America* 13, no. 2 (1981): 49–60.

Cașu, Igor. "Stalinist Terror in Soviet Moldavia." In *Stalinist Terror in Eastern Europe*, edited by Kevin McDermott and Matthew Stibbe, 39–56. New York: Manchester University Press, 2010.

Clark, Charles U. "Russia Organizes the Province." Chap. 8 in *Bessarabia: Russia and Romania on the Black Sea*. New York: Dodd, Mead and Co., 1927. http://depts.washington.edu/cartah/text_archive/clark/mobile.html.

Clarkson, Sue. "A History of German Settlements in Southern Hungary." N.p.: The Federation of East European Family History Societies, 2003. http://feefhs.org/links/banat/bhistory.html.

Coleman, David, and John Salt. *The British Population: Patterns, Trends and Processes*. New York: Oxford University Press, 1992.

"The Consequences of Dedovshchina." Human Rights Watch, 2004. https://www.hrw.org/reports/2004/russia1004/6.htm.

Cornish, Nik. *The Russian Army and the First World War.* Stroud, Eng.: Spellmount, 2006.

Crane, Susan A. "Holy Alliances: Creating Religious Communities after the Napoleonic Wars." In *Die Gegenwart Gottes in der modernen Gesellschaft: Transzendenz und religiöse Vergemeinschaftung in Deutschland,* edited by Michael Geyer and Lucian Hölscher, 37–59. Göttingen, Ger.: Wallstein, 2006.

Dabinnus, Georg. *Die ländliche Bevölkerung Pommerellens im Jahre 1772 mit Einschluss des Danziger Gebiets im Jahre 1793.* Marburg, Ger.: N.p., 1953.

Dal', Vladimir I., ed. *Tolkovyj slovar' v 4 tomax.* St. Petersburg: M.O. Vol'f, 1881–82.

Dan Mueller Photo Gallery. Image 119726. http://www.muellerphoto.exposuremanager.com/p/teplitz/_mg_119726.

———. Image 148317. http://www.muellerphoto.exposuremanager.com/p/mannsburg/_mg_148317.

———. MG 0748, MG 0751, MG 0752, MG 0753, MG 0756, MG 0736, MG 0739. http://www.muellerphoto.exposuremanager.com/g/sarata.

Daniels, Emil. "Prussia under Frederick William I." In *Cambridge Modern History,* edited by A. W. Ward, G. W. Prothero, and Stanley Leathes. Vol. 6, *18th Century,* 205–27. Cambridge, UK: Cambridge University Press, 1909.

Davies, R. W., and S. G. Wheatcroft. *The Years of Hunger: Soviet Agriculture 1931-3.* Houndmills, Eng.: Palgrave Macmillan, 2004.

"Destination of [Kulm] Emigrants from Bessarabia" in "Heimatbuch der Gemeinde Kulm." *Heritage Review* 15, no. 3: 23–35.

Dieno, A. "Paris – 1848 Village History." Translated by R. Niessner. N.p.: Odessa Digital Library, 1996. http://www.odessa3.org/collections/history/link/paris.txt.

Dobkin. "Minutes #18: Concerning the Discussion on 5 October, 1840 from 7:00 to 9:00 PM," #T-81, VOMI 920, Group 1035, Roll 317, Series 535, Frames 2447382–2447384. In Konrad and Straeuli, "Bessarabian Resettlement Minutes."

Drefs, Reuben R., trans. "Bessarabian Village Birth Records, 183x–188x." Edited by Marty McMahon. N.p.: Odessa Digital Library, 1997–98. http://odessa3.org/collections/stpete/bess/.

———, trans. "Bessarabian Village Death Records, 183x–188x." Edited by Marty McMahon. N.p.: Odessa Digital Library, 1999. http://odessa3.org/collections/stpete/bess/.

———, trans. "Bessarabian Village Marriage Records, 183x–188x." Edited by Marty McMahon. N.p.: Odessa Digital Library, 1997. http://www.odessa3.org/collections/stpete/bess/.

Dwork, Deborah. "Health Conditions of Immigrant Jews on the Lower East Side of New York: 1880–1914." *Medical History* 25, no. 1 (1981): 1–40.

Dwyer, P. G. "Prussia during the French Revolutionary and Napoleonic Wars, 1786–1815." In Dwyer, *Rise of Prussia*, 239–58.

Dwyer, Philip, ed. *The Rise of Prussia 1700–1830*. New York: Longman, 2000.

Eckert. "Borodino – 1848 Village History." Translated by J. R. Hubert. N.p.: Odessa Digital Library, 1999. http://www.odessa3.org/collections/history/link/borodino. txt.

Eckert, Albert. *Die Mundarten der deutschen Mutterkolonien Bessarabiens und ihre Stammheimat*. Marburg, Ger.: N. G. Elwert, 1941.

Eckert, Jacob. "Friedenstal – 1848 Village History." Translated by Elvire Necker-Eberhardt. N.p.: Odessa Digital Library, 2000. http://www.odessa3. org/collections/history/link/friedtal.txt.

Edwards, W. J. "Marriage Seasonality 1761–1810: An Assessment of Patterns in Seventeen Shropshire Parishes." *Local Population Studies*, no. 19 (1977): 23–27. http://www.localpopulationstudies.org.uk/PDF/LPS19/LPS19_1977_23-27.pdf.

Ehrman, H., and R. Heinle. "Odessa Province Executions 1937 – 1938." N.p.: Odessa Digital Library, 2000. http://www.odessa3.org/collections/war/link/executel.txt.

Fenske, Hans. "International Migration: Germany in the 18th Century." *Central European History* 13 (1980): 332–47.

Figes, Orlando. *The Whisperers: Private Life in Stalin's Russia*. New York: Metropolitan Books, 2007.

Finkenauer. "Minutes #8: Concerning the Discussion of 19 September, 1940 from 4:00 tom 6:15 PM," #T-81, VOMI 920, Record Group 1035, Film Roll 317, Series 535, Frames 2447420–2447424. In Konrad and Straeuli, "Bessarabian Resettlement Minutes."

———. "Minutes #10: Concerning the Discussion on 24 September, 1940, from 9:00 to 11:30 PM," #T-81, VOMI 920, Record Group 1035, Film Roll 317, Series 535, Frames 2447410–2447414. In Konrad and Straeuli, "Bessarabian Resettlement Minutes."

———. "Minutes #13: Concerning the Discussion on 27 September, 1940, from 9:00 PM to 2:30 AM," #T-81, VOMI 920, Record Group 1035, Film Roll 317, Series 535, Frames 2447396–2447401. In Konrad and Straeuli, "Bessarabian Resettlement Minutes."

———. "Minutes #16: Concerning the Discussion on 1 October, 1940 at 2:00 PM," T 81, VOMI 920, Record Group 1035, Roll 317, Series 535, Frames 2447388-2447391. In Konrad and Straeuli, "Bessarabian Settlement Minutes."

———. "Minutes #20: Concerning the Discussion on 7 October, 1940, at 5:00 PM," # T-81, VOMI 920, Group 1035, Roll 317, Series 535, Frames 2447370–2447375. In Konrad and Straeuli, "Bessarabian Resettlement Minutes."

———. "Minutes #21: Concerning the Discussion on 11 October, 1940, at 5:00 PM," #T-81, VOMI 920, Group 1035, Roll 317, Series 535, Frames 2447358–2447363. In Konrad and Straeuli, "Bessarabian Resettlement Minutes."

———. "Minutes #27: Concerning the Discussion on 22 October, 1940, from 9:00 PM to 11:00 PM," #T-81, VOMI 920, Record Group 1035, Film Roll 317, Series 535, Frames 2447324–2447330. In Konrad and Straeuli, "Bessarabian Resettlement Minutes."

Fischer Arends, Shirley. *The Central Dakota Germans: Their History, Language and Culture*. Washington, DC: Georgetown University Press, 1989.

Flato, Lilli. "From Bessarabia to Lodi, California, USA: Germans from Russia, a Life Story of Lilli Flato and her Family." Translated by Manfred Trogisch. N.p.: German American Pioneers.org, 2006. http://www.germanamericanpioneers. org/FromBessarabiatoLidaCA.swf?POPUP_ENABLED=true.

Flegel, Arthur. *Extended Relationships of the Kulm, Leipzig, Tarutino Communities in Bessarabia, Russia*. Germans from Russia Heritage Collection. Fargo: North Dakota State University Libraries, 2005.

Fleischhauer, Ingeborg. "The Case of the Russian Germans." *Journal of Modern History* 53, no. 1 (March 1981): 1065–90.

———. *Die Deutschen im Zarenreich: Zwei Jahrhunderte deutsche-russische Kulturgemeinschaft*. Stuttgart: Deutsche Verlags-Anstalt, 1986.

Flinn, Michael. *The European Demographic System, 1520–1820*. Baltimore: The Johns Hopkins University Press, 1981.

Foerster. "Beresina – 1848 Village History." Translated by E. Necker-Eberhardt. N.p.: Odessa Digital Library, 2000. http://www.odessa3.org/collections/history/link/ beresina.txt.

Frejka, Tomas. "Parity Distribution and Completed Family Size in Europe: Incipient Decline of the Two-Child Family Model." *Demographic Research* 19, article 4 (2008): 47–72.

Friedrich, Karin. *Brandenburg-Prussia, 1466-1806: The Rise of a Composite State*. Basingstoke, Eng.: Palgrave Macmillan, 2012.

———. *The Other Prussia: Royal Prussia, Poland and Liberty, 1569-1772*. New York: Cambridge University Press, 2000.

"From the Financial Statement for 1882." Holy Trinity Cathedral, accessed July 6, 2015. http://www.holy-trinity.org/history/1882/01.01.budget.html.

Geffken, Rolf. *Die große Arbeit: Worpswede in Leben und Werk Rainer Maria Rilkes*. Bremen, Ger.: Falkenberg, 2014.

Gerescher, Konrad. "Das Portal der Ungarndeutschen." Lecture, University of Szeged, College of Teacher Training, Szeged, Hun., September 9, 2002. http:// www.ungarndeutsche.de/de/cms/index.php?page=donauschwaben.

Giesinger, Adam. *From Catherine to Khrushchev: The Story of Russia's Germans*. Battleford, Can.: Marian Press, 1974.

———. "Villages in which Our Forefathers Lived: Early Daughter Colonies near Mariupol." *American Historical Society of Germans from Russia Journal*, 2, no. 3 (1979): 1–4.

Gjonça, Arjan, Cecilia Tomassini, and James W. Vaupel. "Male–Female Differences in Mortality in the Developed World." MPIDR Working Paper WP 1999-009, Max Plank Institute for Demographic Research, Rostock, Germany, 1999. http://www.demogr.mpg.de/Papers/Working/WP-1999-009.pdf.

Goerz, Heinrich. *The Molotschna Settlement*. Translated by Al Reimer and John B. Toews. Winnipeg, Man.: CMBC Publications and Manitoba Mennonite Historical Society, 1993.

Gutsche, Horst. "Bessarabian Village Reports, DAI T81 316." N.p.: Odessa Digital Library, 2002. www.odessa3.org/collections/war/reports/link/supp1.txt.

———. "The Bodamer Family of Kloestitz." *Bessarabian Newsletter* 5, no. 3 (December 2001): 39.

Haas. "Dennewitz – 1848 Village History." Translated by Elvire Necker-Eberhardt. N.p: Odessa Digital Library, 2000. http://www.odessa3.org/collections/history/link/dennew.txt.

Häberlein, Mark. "German Communities in 18th Century Europe and North America." In *European Migrants, Diasporas and Indigenous Ethnic Minorities*, edited by Matjaž Klemenčič and Mary N. Harris, 19–35. Pisa: PLUS-University Press, 2009.

Häfner, Hugo. "125 Jahre Ryschkanowka." Digital copy of original article in *Heimatkalender 1990: Jahrbuch der Deutschen aus Bessarabien*, 187–94. Stuttgart: Landsmannschaft der Deutschen aus Bessarabien, 1990. http://www.bessarabien.de/upload/ryschkanowka_hk1990.pdf.

———. "Wine Growing—An Illustrated Documentation." *Heritage Review* 37, no. 4 (2007): 12.

Hagen, William H. *Germans, Poles, and Jews: The Nationality Conflict in the Prussian East, 1772-1914*. Chicago: University of Chicago Press, 1980.

———. *Ordinary Prussians: Brandenburg Junkers and Villagers, 1500–1840*. New York: Cambridge University Press, 2002.

———. "Village Life in East Elbian Germany and Poland 1400-1800." In *The Peasantries of Europe from the 14th to the 18th Centuries*, edited by Tom Scott, 145–90. Harlow, Eng.: Addison Wesley Longman Higher Education, 1998.

Hahn. "Lichtental – 1848 Village History." Translated by Adam Geisinger. N.p.: Odessa Digital Library, 1996. http://www.odessa3.org/collections/history/link/lichtent.txt.

Haines, Michael. "Fertility and Mortality in the United States." *EH.Net Encyclopedia*, edited by Robert Whaples. Economic History Association. Article published March 19, 2008. http://eh.net/encyclopedia/fertility-and-mortality-in-the-united-states/.

Hajnal, John. "European Marriage Patterns in Perspective." In *Population in History: Essays in Historical Demography*, edited by D. V. Glass and D. E. C. Eversley, 101–43. Chicago: Aldine Publishing Co., 1965.

Handel, Theophil. *Chronik der Gemeinde Teplitz in Bessarabien: Sippenbuch.* Esslingen-Berkheim, Ger.: Self-published, 1994.

Harwood, William Sumner. "A Bit of Europe in Dakota." *Harper's Weekly*, July 11, 1896. http://library.ndsu.edu/grhc/history_culture/history/eureka.html.

Hausleitner, Marianna. "The Development of Interethnic Relations in 19th and 20th Century Bessarabia," translated by James Gessele. *Heritage Review* 42, no. 2 (June 2012): 34–41.

Haxthausen, August von. *The Russian Empire, Its People, Institutions and Resources.* Translated by Robert Faire. 2 vols. Facsimile reprint of 1st ed. London: Cass, 1968.

Hein, Alfred. Borodino, Summer 2004 [photo collection]. N.p.: Remmick.org, n.d. http://www.remmick.org/AlfredHeinPhotos/Page2.html.

Heli, Rick. "Deutsche Genealogie: Donauschwaben im Banat." N.p.: genealogienetz. de, 2000. www.genealogienetz.de/reg/ESE/dsban-d.html.

Hellie, Richard. *The Economy and Material Culture of Russia 1600–1725.* Chicago: University of Chicago Press, 1999.

Hoch, Steven. *Serfdom and Social Control in Russia: Petrovskoe, a Village in Tambov.* Chicago: University of Chicago Press, 1989. Quoted in Melton, "Russian Peasantries," 258–59.

Hofer, Rudolf. "Hoffnungstal, Bessarabia." Germans from Russia Heritage Collection. Fargo: North Dakota State University Libraries, 1983. http://library. ndsu.edu/grhc/history_culture/history/hoffnungstal.html.

Hoffmann, Paul. *Die deutschen Kolonien in Transkaukasien.* Berlin: Verlag von D. Reimer, 1905.

Hornbacher, Walter. "Removal from the Homeland: A Surviving Eye-Witness Documentary Report on the Evacuation of Ethnic Germans from the Black Sea Region of the Ukraine to Germany in Early 1944." *Heritage Review* 38, no. 1 (2008): 9–25.

Janke, Dwayne. "Locusts! Winged Invaders of South Russia's Steppes." Black Sea German Research, updated March 2012. http://www.blackseagr.org/pdfs/ locusts_janke.pdf.

———. "Ups and Downs of Grain Production in the Early Years of Bessarabian Mother Colonies." *Bessarabian Newsletter* 11, no. 2 (2007): 4–6.

Jewsbury, George. *The Russian Annexation of Bessarabia: 1774-1828.* New York: Columbia University Press, 1976.

Kaschuba, Wolfgang. "Peasants and Others: The Historical Contours of Village Class Society." In *The German Peasantry: Conflict and Community in Rural Society from the 18th to the 20th Centuries*, edited by R. Evans and W. Lee, 235–64. New York: St. Martin's Press, 1986.

Kern, Albert. *Homeland Book of the Bessarabian Germans*. Translated by Ilona Richey. Germans from Russia Heritage Collection. Fargo: North Dakota State University, 1998.

Kershaw, Ian. *The End: The Defiance and Destruction of Hitler's Germany, 1944-1945*. New York: Penguin Press, 2011.

Klaus, Aleksandr Avgustovič *Naši kolonii: opyty i materially po istorii i statistike inostrannoj kolonizacii v Rossii*. St. Petersburg: V. V. Nusvalt, 1869.

Kludt, A. "Teplitz – 1848 Village History." Translated by R. Niessner. N.p.: Odessa Digital Library, 1996. http://www.odessa3.org/collections/history/link/teplitz.txt.

Kludt, Wilhelm. "Alt Posttal – 1848 Village History." Translated by E. Necker-Eberhardt. N.p.: Odessa Digital Library, 2000. http://www.odessa3.org/collections/history/link/altpost.txt.

Knowles, Valerie. "The Arrival of the Europeans." Chap. 2 in *Forging Our Legacy: Canadian Citizenship and Immigration, 1900–1977*. Ottowa: Citizenship and Immigration Canada, 2000. http://www.cic.gc.ca/english/resources/publications/legacy/chap-2a.asp.

Koch, Jacob. "Gnadenthal – 1848 Village History." Traslated by E. Wise. N.p.: Odessa Digital Library, 1996. http://www.odessa3.org/collections/history/link/gnadntal.txt.

Koch, Oskar. "Contributions to the Homeland Book" in "Heimatbuch der Gemeinde Kulm." *Heritage Review* 14, no. 2 (1984): 25–27.

Konrad, Allen E. "Bessarabia: Before, During and After the German Settlements." Powerpoint presentation, Germans from Russia Heritage Society Convention, July 22, 2010. http://www.grhs.org/korners/memonly/konrad_doc/Bessarabia-%20Before%20During%20and%20After%20the%20German%20Settlements.ppt (members-only access).

———, trans. "Bessarabian German Population Statistics 1827-1938." N.p.: blackseagr.org, 2011. http://www.blackseagr.org/pdfs/konrad/Bessarabian%20German%20Population%20Statistics%201827-1938.pdf.

———, trans. "Bessarabian Resettlement – Propaganda and Reports, from DAI T81-321." N.p.: Odessa Digital Library, 2004. http://www.odessa3.org/collections/war/dai/link/dai321b.txt.

———, trans. "Divisions within Bessarabian Regions and Regional Zones for Resettlement Purposes," #T-81, Roll 317, Group 1035, Item VOMI 922, Frames 2447486–2447487. N.p.: Germans from Russia Heritage Society, 2011. http://www.grhs.org/korners/memonly/konrad_doc/Divisions%20Within%20Bessarabian%20Districts%20and%20Regional%20Zones%20for%20Resettlement%20Purposes.pdf (members-only access).

————, trans. "Estimate of German Resettlers from Bessarabian and Bukovina," #T-81, Roll 320, Frames 2451408–2451410. N.p.: Germans from Russian Heritage Society, 2009. http://www.grhs.org/korners/memonly/konrad_doc/estimate_german_resettlers_bess_bukovina.pdf (members-only access).

————, trans. "Ethnic German Resettlement Camps in the German Reich from 1940 Onward." N.p.: Germans from Russia Heritage Society, 2009. http://www.grhs.org/korners/memonly/konrad_doc/Resettlement_Transit_Camps.pdf (members-only access).

————, trans. "Evacuation from Bessarabia and Bukovina, 1940." N.p.: Odessa Digital Library, 2002. http://www.odessa3.org/collections/war/link/evac317.txt.

————, trans. "Letter of Johann Karl Krause, 1940." #T-81, Roll 599, Serial 816, Group 1035, Item 1266, Frames 5386404-5386405. N.p.: Germans from Russia Heritage Society, 2009. http://www.grhs.org/korners/memonly/konrad_doc/Letter_Johann_Karl_Krause.PDF (members-only access).

————, trans. "Location and Number of Ethnic Germans in Regional Zones for 1940 Resettlement," #T-81, Roll 317, Group 1035, Item VOMI 922, Frames 2447458–2447463. N.p.: Germans from Russia Heritage Society, 2011. http://www.grhs.org/korners/memonly/konrad_doc/Locations%20and%20Number%20of%20Ethnic%20Germans%20in%20Regional%20Zones%20for%201940%20Resettlement.pdf (members-only access).

————, trans. "Proposed Distribution of German Resettlers from Bessarabia and Bukovina," #T-81, Roll 320, Frames # 2451411–2451423. N.p.: Germans from Russia Heritage Society, 2009. http://www.grhs.org/korners/memonly/konrad_doc/Distribution_German_Resettlers.pdf (members-only access).

————, trans. "Regions in the Reich Containing Transit Resettlement Camps," #T-81, VOMI 920, Group 1035, Roll 599, Series 816, Item 1266, Frame 5386396. N.p.: Germans from Russia Heritage Society, 2009. http://www.grhs.org/korners/memonly/konrad_doc/Regions_Reich_with_Transit_Camps.pdf (members-only access).

Konrad, Allen, and Helmut Straeuli, trans. "DAI Film T81-317 Bessarabian Resettlement Minutes." N.p.: Odessa Digital Library, 2004. http://www.odessa3.org/collections/war/dai/link/dai317e.txt.

Koprince, Ralph. "The International Passport System of Late Imperial Russia." *Heritage Review* 14, no. 4 (November 1984): 16-22.

Kraenbring, Artur. "The Russian Laws of Liquidation of 1915 and the Impact of Their Application in the Bessarabian German Enclave." *Heritage Review* 41, no. 1 (2011): 14–21, 23.

Kuehn, Glenn D. "Hard-Kernelled Red Winter Wheat: A Legacy of Our German-Russian Ancestors on the Great Plains of North America." *Heritage Review* 45, no. 1 (2015): 11–16

Kurtz, L. A. "Hoffnungstal – 1848 Village History." Translated by Irmgard Schlenker. N. p.: Odessa Digital Library, 1996. http://www.odessa3.org/collections/history/link/hoffbess.txt.

Kurz, I. "Neu Elft – 1848 Village History." Translated by R. Niessner. N.p.: Odessa Digital Library, 1996. http://www.odessa3.org/collections/history/link/neuelft. txt.

Kurz, Johann G. "Wittenberg – 1848 Village History." Translated by E. Wise. N.p.: Odessa Digital Library, 1996. http://www.odessa3.org/collections/history/link/ wittenbg.txt.

Laib, Conrad. "Katzbach – 1848 Village History." Translated by Karen Retzlaff. N.p.: Germans from Russia Heritage Society, 1996. http://www.grhs.org/vr/vhistory/ katzbach.htm.

"Lenninskij plan elektrifikacii rossii," Map 29. In *Atlas istorii SSSR, čast' III*, edited by A. M. Pankratovyj, I. A. Golubcov, and A. V. Foxt. Moscow: Glavnoe upravlenie geodezii i kartografii MVD SSSR, 1958.

Letter from SS Major General Greifelt to Defendant Schwerin von Krosigk, 10 September 1941, in *Trials of War Criminals Before the Nuernberg Military Tribunals Under Control Council Law*, No. 10, Vol. 13, *United States of America v. Ernst von Weizsaecker, et al.* Washington, DC: US Government Printing Office, 1952. http://forum.axishistory.com/viewtopic.php?t=66094.

List, Friedrich. *Die Ackerverfassung, die Zwergwirtschaft und de Auswanderung in Schriften, Reden, Briefe*. Berlin: R. Hobbing, 1928.

"List or Manifest of Alien Immigrants for the Commissioner of Immigration" in T 715, Roll 0022, in "Passenger Lists of Vessels Arriving in New York 1897-1957." Washington, DC: National Archives Microfilm Publications, 2010.

Lucchetti, E., M. Manfredini, G. Boetsch, D. Bley, P. Aluja, J. Pena, D. Revello, R. Melleri, and A. Sevin. "Changes in Marriage Seasonality among Some European Rural Populations." *International Journal of Anthropology* 11, no. 2–4 (April 1996): 73–81.

Luebke, Frederick. *Germans in Brazil: A Comparative History of Cultural Conflict during World War I*. Baton Rouge: Louisiana State University Press, 1987.

Mai, Brent. "Ukraine German-Russians." Roll Family website, c. 2014. www.rollintl. com/roll/grsettle.htm.

Malinovskij, Lev V. *Social'naja i xozjajstvennaja istorija nemeckix kolonistov v južnoj Rossii (1762-1917)*. Barnaul, Rus.: IPP Altaj, 2010.

Mammel, Arnold. *Klöstitz: Das Bild der Heimat*. Stuttgart, Ger.: Heimatmuseum der Deutschen aus Bessarabien, 1993.

Map L-35-071, "SSSR, Odesskaja oblast'." University of California at Berkeley Map Collection.

Markstädter, Eduard, Nelly Kossko, Albin Fiebich, Reinhold Kiel, Matthias Hagin, and Herbert Wiens, eds. *Volk auf dem Weg: Deutsche in Rußland und in der GUS: 1763–1997*. 5th ed. Stuttgart: Landsmannschaft der Desutschen aus Rußland, 1997.

Martin, D. "Tarutino – 1848 Village History." Translated by E. Wise. N.p.: Odessa Digital Library, 1996. http://www.odessa3.org/collections/history/link/tarutino. txt.

Mayer, D. "Alt Elft – 1848 Village History." Translated by R. Niessner. N.p.: Odessa Digital Library, 1996. http://www.odessa3.org/collections/history/link/altelft.txt.

Mayr, Florian. "Gundremmingen and the Followers of Lindl." *Heritage Review* 36, no. 1 (2006): 13–24.

"Median Age at First Marriage, 1890–2010." United States Bureau of Census, organized by Infoplease.org, accessed 2011. http://www.infoplease.com/ipa/ A0005061.html.

Meissner, Boris, Helmut Neubauer, and Alfred Eisfeld, eds. *Die Rußlanddeutschen: Gestern und Heute*. Köln, Ger.: Markus Verlag, 1992.

Melton, Edgar. "The Russian Peasantries, 1450–1860." In *The Peasantries of Europe: From the 14th to the 18th Centuries*, edited by Tom Scott, 246–82. Cambridge, Eng.: Longman Pub Group, 1998.

———. "The Transformation of Rural Economy in East Elbian Prussia." In Dwyer, *Rise of Prussia*, 111–28.

Menning, Bruce W. *Bayonets before Bullets: The Imperial Russian Army 1861-1914*. Bloomington: Indiana University Press, 1992.

Microcopy 237, Roll 403 in "Passenger Lists of Vessels Arriving in New York 1820-1897." Washington, DC: National Archives Microfilm Publications, 1957.

Minderlin, C. "Brienne – 1848 Village History." Translated by E. Necker Eberhardt. N.p.: Odessa Digital Library, 2000. http://www.odessa3.org/collections/history/ link/brienne.txt.

Morrison, Elaine, Carolyn Schott, Dale Wahl, and Elli Wise. Sarata, Bessarabia 2001 [photographs; authorship of individual photos not specified], last modified 2008. https://www.facebook.com/media/set/?s et=a.297483176978706.71624.172727712787587&type=1&l=c7e5ccdac7.

Mutschall, Wilhelm. *Geschichte der Gemeinde Tarutino von 1814 bis 1934*. Hannover, Ger.: Hilfskomitee u. Landsmannschaft d. Bessarabiendeutschen, 1966.

———. "History of the Community of Tarutino from 1814 to 1934," translated by Horst Wilhelm Gutsche. *Heritage Review* 42, no. 1 (March 2012): 3–11.

———. "History of the Community of Tarutino from 1814 to 1934," translated by Horst Wilhelm Gutsche. *Heritage Review* 42, no. 2 (2012): 6.

———. "History of the Community of Tarutino from 1814 to 1934," translated by Horst Wilhelm Gutsche. *Heritage Review* 42, no. 4 (December 2012): 5.

———. "History of the Community of Tarutino from 1814 to 1934," translated by Horst Wilhelm Gutsche. *Heritage Review* 43, no. 1 (March 2013): 3–12.

———. "History of the Community of Tarutino from 1814 to 1934," translated by Horst Wilhelm Gutsche. *Heritage Review* 43, no. 2 (June 2013): 4–10.

————. "History of the Community of Tarutino from 1814 to 1934," translated by Horst Wilhelm Gutsche. *Heritage Review* 43, no. 3 (2013): 4–10.

————. "History of the Community of Tarutino from 1814 to 1934," translated by Horst Wilhelm Gutsche. *Heritage Review* 43, no. 4 (December 2013): 4–11.

————. "History of the Community of Tarutino from 1814 to 1934," translated by Horst Wilhelm Gutsche. *Heritage Review* 44, no. 1 (March 2014): 29–34.

————. "History of the Community of Tarutino from 1814 to 1934," translated by Horst Wilhelm Gutsche. *Heritage Review* 44, no. 2 (June 2014): 16–27.

————. "History of the Community of Tarutino from 1814 to 1934," translated by Horst Wilhelm Gutsche. *Heritage Review* 44, no. 3 (September 2014): 16–25.

————. "History of the Community of Tarutino from 1814 to 1934," translated by Horst Wilhelm Gutsche. *Heritage Review* 45, no. 1 (March 2015): 19–27.

————. "History of the Community of Tarutino from 1814 to 1934," translated by Horst Wilhelm Gutsche. *Heritage Review* 45, no. 2 (June 2015): 19–29.

Mutschelknaus, Friedrich. "Migration of the First German Russians to Dakota: Memories of the Years 1872-73." *Dakota Freie Presse*, November 11, 1924. http://library.ndsu.edu/grhc/history_culture/history/migration.html.

Natterer, M. "Sarata – 1848 Village History." Translated by E. Wise. N.p.: Odessa Digital Library, 1996. http://www.odessa3.org/collections/history/link/sarata.txt.

Necker-Eberhardt, Elvire. "The Bessarabian Dialect in Medicine Hat Alberta." PhD diss., University of Alberta, 1973.

————. "Separatists in Bessarabia: A Genealogical Nightmare." N.p.: Germans from Russia Heritage Society, 2011. http://www.grhs.org/korners/memonly/necker_doc/Separatists_in_Bessarabia_sep_10.pdf (members-only access).

Neumann. "Alt-Arcis – 1848 Village History." Translated by E. Necker-Eberhardt. N.p.: Odessa Digital Library, 2000. http://www.odessa3.org/collections/history/link/altarc.txt.

Neutatz, Dietmar. "Die Kolonien des Schwartzmeergebietes im Spannungsfeld nationalstaatlicher Politik 1861-1914." In Meissner, Neubauer, and Eisfeld, *Die Rußlanddeutschen*, 79–99.

Nill, Edward, and Reinhold Schneider. "The First Approved Visit to Beresina." Germans from Russia Heritage Collection. Fargo: North Dakota State University, 1991. http://library.ndsu.edu/grhc/history_culture/history/schneider.html.

Nordhaus, William. "The Health of Nations: The Contribution of Improved Health to Living Standards." Cowles Foundation Discussion Paper No. 1355, Cowles Foundation for Research in Economics, Yale University, New Haven, CT, 2002. http://cowles.yale.edu/sites/default/files/files/pub/d13/d1355.pdf.

Overmans, Rüdiger. *Deutsche militärische Verluste im Zweiten Weltkreig*. Munich: R. Oldenbourg, 2000.

Pantle, Alberta. "Settlement of the Krimmer Mennonite Brethren at Gnadenau, Marion County." *Kansas Historical Quarterly* 13, no. 5 (1945), 259–85.

"Paris." Bessarabiendeutscher Verein. Modified October 10, 2014. http://www. bessarabien.de/upload/paris_1816.pdf.

"Passenger Lists of Vessels Arriving in New York 1897-1957," T 715, Rolls 0022 and 190. Washington, DC: National Archives Microfilm Publications, 1957.

Peterreins, Gertrud. "Unsere Rückkehr nach Deutschland: Tagebuch von Gertrud Peterreins geb. Schlaht." N.p. Odessa Digital Library, 2002. http://www.odessa3. org/collections/articles/link/schlaht-g.html.

Petrescu, Cristina. "Contrasting/Conflicting Identities: Bessarabians, Romanians, Moldovans." In *Nation- Building and Contested Identities: Romanian and Hungarian Case Studies*, edited by Balázs Trencsényi, Dragoș Petrescu, Cristina Petrescu, Constantin Iordachi, and Zoltán Kántor, 153–78. Budapest: Regio Books, 2001.

Pielen, Ludwig. "Letter to Andreas Necker, December 22, 1940." In Treichel, "Resettlement and Colonization," 36–39.

Polovcov, Aleksandr Aleksandrovič, ed. "E. I. Totleben." In *Russkij biografičeskij slovar'*. Vol. 20a, *Tobizen–Todtleben*, 202. St. Petersburg: Tipografija Glavnago Upravlenija Udělov, 1901.

Poppke, Herb. "Teplitz and More, 1993." Bismarck, ND: Germans from Russia Heritage Society, 2002. http://www.grhs.org/data/poppke/poppke3.html.

Rallu, Jean Louis, and Alain Blum, eds. Introduction to *European Population: Demographic Dynamics*. London, Eng.: John Libbey and Company, 1993.

Raugust, Hugo. "The History of Christian Raugust and Wife Carolina Raugust (nee) Gross." Unpublished document in the author's possession.

Reeb, Paul. "Cultural Dynamics in German-Russian Cookery." *Heritage Review* 14, no. 3 (1984): 25–29.

Region A1-6 Authority. "Ethnic Germans of Tarutino Not Joining the Resettlement of 1940," #T-81, Roll 317, Group 1035, VOMI 922, Frame 2447486. Translated by Allen Konrad. N.p.: Germans from Russia Heritage Society, 2011. http:// www.grhs.org/korners/memonly/konrad_doc/Ethnic%20Germans%20of%20 Tarutino%20not%20joining%20the%20Resettlement%20of%201940.pdf (members-only access).

Rempel, Hans. *Deutsche Baurnleistung am Schwarzen Meer, Bevolkerung und Wirtschaft 1825*. Leipzig: S. Hirzel, 1940.

———. *German Farming Achievements in the Black Sea Region, Population and Economy, 1825*. Translated by Roland Wagner. N.p.: Odessa Digital Library, 2002. http://www.odessa3.org/collections/towns/link/bsfarm.txt.

Rempel, Judith. "Dorfberichte – Village Reports." N.p.: Odessa Digital Library, 1997. http://www.odessa3.org/collections/war/reports/link/villrpt.txt.

Retzloff, Duane V. " Journey to the Homeland Tour, Visit to Kulm, Bessarabia, May 1998." Germans from Russia Heritage Collection. Fargo: North Dakota State University, 1998. https://library.ndsu.edu/grhc/outreach/journey/tours/1998memories.html.

Riasanovsky, Nicholas V. *A History of Russia.* 2nd ed. New York: Oxford University Press, 1969.

Riehl, Josef, ed. *History of the Village of Krasna.* Translated by Brigitte Wachter von Budde. Germans from Russia Heritage Collection. Fargo: North Dakota State University Libraries, 1948. http://library.ndsu.edu/grhc/history_culture/history/riehl.html.

"Roll Family Genealogy—Emigration and Travel Experiences." The Roll "Fame" Family, accessed July 6, 2015. http://www.rollintl.com/roll/emigration.htm.

Romaniuc, Anatole, and Liubov Chuiko. "Matrimonial Behavior in Canada and the Ukraine: The Enduring Hold of Culture." *Journal of Comparative Family Studies* 30, no. 3 (1999): 335–61.

Rothstein, Martin. "Centralizing Firms and Spreading Markets: The World of International Grain Traders, 1846–1914." *Business and Economic History*, 2nd ser., 17 (1988): 106–7.

Rüb, Albert. "Things Pertaining to Bessarabian Housekeeping." *Heritage Review* 38, no. 2 (2008): 2-5

Rudnitsky, Jake. "Full Metal Torture." *Vice*, April 1, 2006. http://www.vice.com/read/full-v13n4.

Šmid, A., ed. *Materialy dlja geografii i statistiki Rossii.* Vol. 2, *Xersonskaja gubernija.* St. Petersburg: Tipogr. Tovariščestva "Obščestvennaja Pol´za," 1863. Quoted in and translated by Detlef Brandes, "A Success Story: The German Colonists in New Russia and Bessarabia: 1787–1914." *Acta Slavica Iaponica Tomus* 9 (1991). http://library.ndsu.edu/grhc/history_culture/history/brandes.html.

Sallet, Richard. *Russian-German Settlements in the United States.* Translated by Lavern J. Rippley and Armand Bauer. Fargo: North Dakota Institute for Regional Studies, 1974.

Saul, Norman. "The Migration of Russian-Germans to Kansas." *Kansas Historical Quarterlies* 40, no. 1 (Spring 1974): 38–62. http://www.kancoll.org/khq/1974/74_1_saul.htm.

Schaeff, G. "Kloestitz – 1848 Village History." Translated by E. Wise. N.p.: Odessa Digital Library, 1997. http://www.odessa3.org/collections/history/link/kloes.txt.

Schlecter, Emanuel. "A Letter Written by a Family Who Migrated from Murr, Württemberg, to Bessarabia in 1840." Translated by Oliver Mogck. *Heritage Review* 38, no. 2 (June 2008): 16–20.

Schmaltz, Eric J., and Samuel D. Sinner. "The Nazi Ethnographic Research of Georg Leibbrant and Karl Stumpp in Ukraine, and Its North American Legacy." In *German Scholars and Ethnic Cleansing*, edited by Ingo Haar and Michael Fahlbusch, 51–81. New York: Berghahn Books, 2005.

Schmidt, Ute. *Bessarabia: German Colonists on the Black Sea.* Translated by James T. Gessele. Fargo: GRHC and North Dakota State University Libraries, 2011.

———. *Die Deutschen aus Bessarabien: Eine Minderheit aus Südosteurope (1814 bis heute).* Köln, Ger.: Böhlau, 2004.

Scholz, Harry G. "The German Colonists of Russia: The Repeal of Russia's Law of the Colonists in 1871 and Its Effects on the German Colonist Population." Master's thesis, Chapman College, 1969.

Schönherr, Markus. "Russification and Ethnic Consciousness of Romanians in Bessarabia 1812-1991" [unpublished, undated research paper]. Budapest: International Studies Center, Budapest University of Economics. http://ewwg. vlamynck.eu/cst/cst-mold/bessara.html.

Schott, Carolyn. "The School" [photograph] in Neu Elft, Bessarabia 2008 [album]. Compiled by Black Sea German Research Community, last modified January 29, 2012. https://www.facebook.com/BlackSeaGermanResearch/phot os/a.289215584472132.70149.172727712787587/289216071138750/?type=3&theater.

Scott, H. M. "1763–1786: The Second Reign of Frederick the Great?" In Dwyer, *Rise of Prussia*, 177–200.

———. "Prussia's Emergence as a European Great Power, 1740-1763" in Dwyer, *Rise of Prussia*, 153–76.

Selcho, E. "Craftsmen and Craft Occupations" in "Heimatbuch der Gemeinde Kulm." *Heritage Review* 14, no. 2 (1984): 19–22.

Serbyn, Roman. "The First Man-Made Famine in Soviet Ukraine 1921–23." *Ukrainian Weekly* 56, no. 45 (November 1988). http://www.ukrweekly.com/old/ archive/1988/458814.shtml.

Sinner, S. D. "New Archival Discoveries on Wannsee Conference Participant Georg Leibbrant and 'SS-Mann' Karl Stumpp." Paper presented at the German Studies Association Conference in New Orleans, LA, September 2003. http:// www.samuelzinner.com/uploads/9/1/5/0/9150250/leibrandt2012.pdf.

Smith, Ingeborg. Review of *Heimat am Pruth: Erinnerungen an Mariental Bessarabien*, by Ernst Krüger. Last modified October 21, 2012. http://library.ndsu.edu/grhc/ research/scholarly/book_reviews/heimatampruthreview.htm.

Snyder, Timothy. *Bloodlands: Europe between Hitler and Stalin.* New York: Basic Books, 2010.

Sovič, Silvia. "Families and Households of the Poor: The 19th-Century Slovenian *Gostači.*" *History of the Family* 10, no. 2 (2005): 161–82.

Spurling, Otto. "Pioneer Biography of Daniel Roloff, Kulm, North Dakota." *Heritage Review* 40, no. 1 (2010): 11–14.

Stalin, J. V. *Works.* Vol. 12, *April 1929–June 1930.* Moscow: Foreign Languages Publishing House, 1953.

Stangl, Thomas A. "Bessarabian Village Marriage Records, 183x." N.p.: Odessa Digital Library, 1997. http://www.odessa3.org/collections/stpete/bess/link/bess183m.txt.

Starr, S. Frederick. *Decentralization and Self Government in Russia 1830-70.* Princeton: Princeton University Press, 1972.

Stone, Michelle. "John Jacob Kreischer and Katherine Gilcher: Their Story and Family in Syracuse and Onondaga County, New York." Ancestry.com, accessed July 6, 2015. http://freepages.genealogy.rootsweb.ancestry.com/~mstone/kgbook1.html.

Straub, C. "Kulm – 1848 Village History." Translated by L. R. Ketterling. N.p.: Odessa Digital Library, 1997. http://www.odessa3.org/collections/history/link/kulm.txt.

Stumpp, Karl. "2nd Circular to all Bessarabian Germans in Germany," #T-81, Roll 321, Group 1035, VOMI 947, Frame 2452663-2452665. In Konrad, "Bessarabian Resettlement."

———. "Circular to Bessarabian Germans Present in the Reich," #T-81, Roll 321, Group 1035, VOMI 947, Frame 2452667–2452668. In Konrad, "Bessarabian Resettlement."

———. *Die Rußlanddeutschen: Zweihundert Jahre Unterwegs.* Freilassing, Ger.: Pannonia-Verlag, 1965.

———. *The Emigration from Germany to Russia in the Years 1763 to 1862.* Translated by J. S. Height. Lincoln, NE: American Historical Society of Germans from Russia, 1982.

———. Map Karte der deutschen Siedlungen im Gebiet (Oblast) Odessa (ehem. Westl. Teil des Gouv Cherson), Stand 1940, published 1955. An attachment included with *The Emigration from Germany.*

———.Map Karte der deutschen Siedlungen in Bessarabien, Stand 1940, reworked in 1965. An attachment included with *The Emigration from Germany.*

———. "Letter dated July 16, 1940 to Deutsche Ausland-Institute—Stuttgart," #T-81, Roll 321, Group 1035, VOMI 947, Frame 2452655. In Konrad, "Bessarabian Resettlement."

———. "Lists Concerning [the] Landed Property Situation in Bessarabia." In Konrad, "Bessarabian Resettlement."

———. "Zur 125-Jahr-Feier des Deutschtums in Bessarabien." *Deutsche Post aus dem Osten* no. 12 (1939): 18. Quoted in Sinner, "New Archival Discoveries," 4.

Stumpp, Karl, and Arthur Flegel. Map "Orte, aus denen im Jahre 1814 Auswanderungen nach Rußland, insbesondere nach Bessarabien stattgefunden haben." 1972. An attachment included with *The Emigration from Germany.*

Szreter, Simon. "Debating Mortality Trends in 19th Century Britain." *International Journal of Epidemiology* 33, no. 4 (2004): 705–9.

Takiguchi, Akira, and Axel Hindemith. *Heimkehr der Bessarabiendeutschen: Farbfotos vom Herbst 1940.* Tokyo: Self-published, 2004.

Tolstoy, L. N. *Sobranie sočinenij v dvadcati tomax.* Vol. 4. Moscow: State Publisher of Artistic Literature, 1961.

Trautmann, A. "Leipzig – 1848 Village History." Translated by L. R. Ketterling. N.p.: Odessa Digital Library, 1997. http://www.odessa3.org/collections/history/link/leipzig.txt.

Treichel, David. "Church and School Life in Kulm" in "Heimatbuch der Gemeinde Kulm." *Heritage Review* 13, no. 4 (1983): 10–14.

———. "Resettlement and Colonization" in "Heimatbuch der Gemeinde Kulm." *Heritage Review* 14, no. 4 (1984): 35–38.

———. "Teacher Artur Erdmann" in "Heimatbuch der Gemeinde Kulm." *Heritage Review* 13, no. 4 (1983): 20–22.

Tuchscherer, Agatha. "A Partial History of the Anton Tuchscherer Family." *Heritage Review* 44, no. 4 (2014): 17–20.

Tweton, D. Jerome. "Germans from Russia Now Second Largest Immigrant Group." *GRHS News*, December 2005. http://www.grhs.org/data/grhsnews/Dec2005.pdf.

"Umseidlungsvertrag vom 5 September 1940" [The resettlement agreement]. N.p.: Jethon.de. http://jethon.de/html/umsiedlungsvertrag.html.

UN Inter-agency Group for Childhood Mortality Estimation. "Mortality Rate, Under-5 (per 1,000)." c. 2014. http://data.worldbank.org/indicator/SH.DYN.MORT.

Unknown. "Descendants of Ferdinand Ohlhausen Family History." N.p.: ohlhausen.ca, c. 2011. http://www.ohlhausen.ca/Ferdinand%20Ohlhausen%20Family%20History.pdf.

———. "Gemeinde Katzbach – Teilansicht" [image]. N.p.: bessarabien.de, c. 2015. http://www.bessarabien.de/heimatmuseum/_k8/--20.php.

———. "Leipzig – Blick vom Kirchturm" [image]. N.p.: bessarabien.de, c. 2015. http://www.bessarabien.de/heimatmuseum/_k8/leipzig---blick-vom-kirch-turm--21.php.

———. "Letzes Häuschen aus der Ansiedlerzeit" [image]. N.p.: KloestitzGenealogy.org, 1923. http://www.kloestitzgenealogy.org/bilder/bildergalerie_kloestitz_gestern/b_k_g.htm.

———. "Neu-Posttal – Ansicht vom Kirchturm" [image]. N.p.: bessarabien.de, c. 2015. http://www.bessarabien.de/heimatmuseum/_k8/neu-posttal---ansicht-vom-kirchturm--24.php.

———. "Tarutino Parish Report—1867" in "Heimatbuch der Gemeinde Kulm." *Heritage Review* 13, no. 4 (1983): 17.

Ušakov D. N., ed. *Tolkovyj slovar' russkogo jazyka.* Vols. 1–4. Moskva: Sovetskaja Ènciklopedija, 1935–40.

US Bureau of Labor. "Wages and Hours of Labor 1890–1905. Retail Prices of Food 1890–1905." *Bulletin of the Bureau of Labor* no. 65 (July 1906): 187.

US Department of Health and Human Services, National Center  for Health Statistics. "Life Expectancy by Age, 1850–2011." Organized by Infoplease.org, 2014. www.infoplease.com/ipa/A0005140.

Vasmer, Max. *Etimologičeskij slovar' russkogo jazyka*. Vols. 1–4. Moscow: Progress, 1964–73.

Vogel, Gotthilf. "An Account of My Captivity and about Kulm" in "Heimatbuch der Gemeinde Kulm." *Heritage Review* 14, no. 4 (1984): 39–43.

———. "A Year's Review of Agriculture and Grape Growing" in "Heimatbuch der Gemeinde Kulm." *Heritage Review* 14, no. 2 (1984): 30–32.

Vossler, Günther. "Die Tochterkolonie Hoffnungsfeld." Bessarabiendeutschen. Last modified April 15, 2013. http://www.bessarabien.com/upload/hoffnungsfeld_internet.pdf.

Wagner, Roland. "A Discussion of Local Government in the German Colonies of the Black Sea Region." N.p.: Odessa Digital Library, 2001. http://www.odessa3.org/journal/government.pdf.

———. "Some Reflections on Hans Rempel's German Farming Achievements in the Black Sea Region, Population and Economy, 1825." N.p.: Odessa Digital Library, 2007. http://www.odessa3.org/journal/wagner-forward.pdf.

Wahl, Dale. "Bessarabian Surname Origins Index." N.p.: Odessa Digital Library, 1999. http://www.odessa3.org/collections/refs/link/bessorgn.txt.

———. "Bessarabian Village Names." N.p.: Odessa Digital Library, 1996. http://www.odessa3.org/collections/bess/link/bessvl.txt.

———. "Introduction to the Village History Project." N.p.: Odessa Digital Library, 1996. http://www.odessa3.org/collections/history/link/1848hist.txt.

Wahl, Hans Rudolf. "A Lecture Delivered in Neu Wulmsdorf, Germany, on Saturday, May 31, 2014, on the Occasion of the 200th Anniversary of the Founding of Tarutino." *Heritage Review* 44, no. 4 (2014): 7.

Walker, Mack. *German Home Towns: Community, State, and General Estate, 1648–1871.* Ithaca, NY: Cornell University Press, 1971.

———. *Germany and the Emigration 1816–1885.* Cambridge, MA: Harvard University Press, 1964.

Weise, Erich. *Die Schwabensiedlungen im Posener Kammerdepartement 1799–1804.* Würtzburg, Ger.: Holzner-Verlag, 1961.

Weiss, M. "Excerpt from *Odessa Book of Mourning: Stalin's State Terror against the Germans in the Odessa and Nikolajew Districts of Ukraine 1928-1953.*" *Heritage Review* 37, no. 3 (2007): 11–13.

Weiss, Rudolf. "Wichtige Ereignisse aus der Geschichte der Bessarabiendeutschen." N.p.: Bessarabiendeutscher Verein, 1949. http://www.bessarabien.de/geschichte. php. Originally published in *Kalender 1949*: *Jahrbuch der Deutschen aus Bessarabien und der Dobrudscha*. Hannover, Ger.: Hilfskomitee der ev.-luth. Kirche aus Bessarabien, 1949.

Weiss, Theophil. "Cultivation and Grain Growing" in "Heimatbuch der Gemeinde Kulm." *Heritage Review* 14, no. 2 (1984): 29–30.

———. "District of Kulm and Neighboring Districts" in "Heimatbuch der Gemeinde Kulm." *Heritage Review* 13, no. 4 (1983): 9–10.

———. "Grain Selling and Prices" in "Heimatbuch der Gemeinde Kulm." *Heritage Review* 14, no. 2 (1984): 33.

———. "Oak Forest of Kulm" in "Heimatbuch der Gemeinde Kulm." *Heritage Review* 14, no. 2 (1984): 35–36.

———. "Sheep Breeding" in "Heimatbuch der Gemeinde Kulm." *Heritage Review* 14, no. 2 (1984): 34.

Weiss, Th., E. Widmer, A. Kugele, J. Roloff, and D. Wölfle. "The Wedding" in "Heimatbuch der Gemeinde Kulm." *Heritage Review* 14, no. 3 (1984): 54–56.

Wernick. "Plotzk – 1848 Village History." Translated by Elli Wise. N.p.: Odessa Digital Library, 1996. http://www.odessa3.org/collections/history/link/plotzk. txt.

Wernik, G. "Resettlement Chronicle of Hoffnungsfeld, Bessarabia," #T-81, Roll 599, Serial 816, Group 1035, Item 1266, Frames 5386381–5386389. Translated by Allen Konrad, December 2012. http://www.grhs.org/korners/memonly/konrad_ doc/Resettlement%20Chronicle%20of%20Hoffnungsfeld,%20Bessarabia.pdf (members only access).

Wise, Elli. "Alexanderfeld Bessarabia – A Koblenz Extraction." N.p.: Odessa Digital Library, 2001. http://odessa3.org/collections/bess/koblenz/link/alexfldk.txt.

———, trans. "DAI Film - T81-316 Bessarabian Village Reports." N.p.: Odessa Digital Library, 2000. http://www.odessa3.org/collections/war/reports/link/ dai316.txt.

———. Photographs at "Pictures—Bessarabian Villages." http://www.grhs.org/ chapters/bess/memonly/pic/vill/Teplitz%2041.JPG (members-only access).

———. "Sofiental Bessarabia – A Koblenz Extraction." N.p.: Odessa Digital Library, 2003. http://odessa3.org/collections/bess/koblenz/link/sofiental.txt.

With. "Report on Bessarabia: 2 Dec 1940," #T-81, VOMI 902, Group 1035, Roll 317, Serial 535, Frames 2447147–2447150. In Konrad, "Evacuation from Bessarabia and Bukovina."

———. "Report on Bukovina: 2 Dec 1940," #T-81, VOMI 920, Group 1035, Roll 317, Serial 535, Frame 2447151. In Konrad, "Evacuation from Bessarabia and Bukovina."

Wölfle, Daniel. "The Establishment of the Village of Kulm" in "Heimatbuch der Gemeinde Kulm." *Heritage Review* 13, no. 4 (1983): 3–9.

———. "Johann Roloff" in "Heimatbuch der Gemeinde Kulm." *Heritage Review* 13, no. 4 (1983): 22.

———. "Michael Guse" in "Heimatbuch der Gemeinde Kulm." *Heritage Review* 13, no. 4 (1983): 20.

———. "Our Flight in January 1945" in "Heimatbuch der Gemeinde Kulm." *Heritage Review* 14, no. 4 (1984): 38–39.

"World Population: Major Countries 1810." The Napoleon Series, last modified 2005. http://www.napoleon-series.org/research/abstract/population/population/world/c_world3.html.

Wrigley, E. A. "Family Limitation in Pre-industrial England." *Economic History Review*, 2nd ser., 19, no. 1 (1966): 82–109.

Ziebart, Alfred. *150 Jahre Brienne-Bessarabien.* Ludwigsburg, Ger.: Self-published, 1967.

Ziemann, C. "Neu Arcis – 1848 Village History." Translated by E. Wise. N.p.: Odessa Digital Library, 1996. http://www.odessa3.org/collections/history/link/neuarci.txt.

# Index

62486103R00299

Made in the USA
Charleston, SC
16 October 2016